KDE 2/Qt
Programming Bible

KDE 2/Qt
Programming Bible

Arthur Griffith

IDG Books Worldwide, Inc.
An International Data Group Company

Foster City, CA ✦ Chicago, IL ✦ Indianapolis, IN ✦ New York, NY

KDE 2/Qt Programming Bible

Published by
IDG Books Worldwide, Inc.
An International Data Group Company
919 E. Hillsdale Blvd., Suite 400
Foster City, CA 94404
www.idgbooks.com (IDG Books Worldwide
Web site)

Copyright © 2001 IDG Books Worldwide, Inc. All rights reserved. No part of this book, including interior design, cover design, and icons, may be reproduced or transmitted in any form, by any means (electronic, photocopying, recording, or otherwise) without the prior written permission of the publisher.

ISBN: 0-7645-4682-1

Printed in the United States of America

10 9 8 7 6 5 4 3 2 1

1B/RV/RS/QQ/FC

Distributed in the United States by IDG Books Worldwide, Inc.

Distributed by CDG Books Canada Inc. for Canada; by Transworld Publishers Limited in the United Kingdom; by IDG Norge Books for Norway; by IDG Sweden Books for Sweden; by IDG Books Australia Publishing Corporation Pty. Ltd. for Australia and New Zealand; by TransQuest Publishers Pte Ltd. for Singapore, Malaysia, Thailand, Indonesia, and Hong Kong; by Gotop Information Inc. for Taiwan; by ICG Muse, Inc. for Japan; by Intersoft for South Africa; by Eyrolles for France; by International Thomson Publishing for Germany, Austria, and Switzerland; by Distribuidora Cuspide for Argentina; by LR International for Brazil; by Galileo Libros for Chile; by Ediciones ZETA S.C.R. Ltda. for Peru; by WS Computer Publishing Corporation, Inc., for the Philippines; by Contemporanea de Ediciones for Venezuela; by Express Computer Distributors for the Caribbean and West Indies; by Micronesia Media Distributor, Inc. for Micronesia; by Chips Computadoras S.A. de C.V. for Mexico; by Editorial Norma de Panama S.A. for Panama; by American Bookshops for Finland.

For general information on IDG Books Worldwide's books in the U.S., please call our Consumer Customer Service department at 800-762-2974. For reseller information, including discounts and premium sales, please call our Reseller Customer Service department at 800-434-3422.

For information on where to purchase IDG Books Worldwide's books outside the U.S., please contact our International Sales department at 317-572-3993 or fax 317-572-4002.

For consumer information on foreign language translations, please contact our Customer Service department at 800-434-3422, fax 317-572-4002, or e-mail rights@idgbooks.com.

For information on licensing foreign or domestic rights, please phone +1-650-653-7098.

For sales inquiries and special prices for bulk quantities, please contact our Order Services department at 800-434-3422 or write to the address above.

For information on using IDG Books Worldwide's books in the classroom or for ordering examination copies, please contact our Educational Sales department at 800-434-2086 or fax 317-572-4005.

For press review copies, author interviews, or other publicity information, please contact our Public Relations department at 650-653-7000 or fax 650-653-7500.

For authorization to photocopy items for corporate, personal, or educational use, please contact Copyright Clearance Center, 222 Rosewood Drive, Danvers, MA 01923, or fax 978-750-4470.

Library of Congress Cataloging-in-Publication Data

Griffith, Arthur.
    KDE 2/Qt programming bible / Arthur Griffith.
        p.   cm.
    ISBN 0-7645-4682-1 (alk. paper)
    1. C++ (Computer program language)
2. Graphical user interfaces (Computer systems)
3. Linux   I. Title.
QA76.73.C153.G7426   2001
005.13'3–dc21   00-047247

ABOUT IDG BOOKS WORLDWIDE

Welcome to the world of IDG Books Worldwide.

IDG Books Worldwide, Inc., is a subsidiary of International Data Group, the world's largest publisher of computer-related information and the leading global provider of information services on information technology. IDG was founded more than 30 years ago by Patrick J. McGovern and now employs more than 9,000 people worldwide. IDG publishes more than 290 computer publications in over 75 countries. More than 90 million people read one or more IDG publications each month.

Launched in 1990, IDG Books Worldwide is today the #1 publisher of best-selling computer books in the United States. We are proud to have received eight awards from the Computer Press Association in recognition of editorial excellence and three from Computer Currents' First Annual Readers' Choice Awards. Our best-selling ...For Dummies® series has more than 50 million copies in print with translations in 31 languages. IDG Books Worldwide, through a joint venture with IDG's Hi-Tech Beijing, became the first U.S. publisher to publish a computer book in the People's Republic of China. In record time, IDG Books Worldwide has become the first choice for millions of readers around the world who want to learn how to better manage their businesses.

Our mission is simple: Every one of our books is designed to bring extra value and skill-building instructions to the reader. Our books are written by experts who understand and care about our readers. The knowledge base of our editorial staff comes from years of experience in publishing, education, and journalism — experience we use to produce books to carry us into the new millennium. In short, we care about books, so we attract the best people. We devote special attention to details such as audience, interior design, use of icons, and illustrations. And because we use an efficient process of authoring, editing, and desktop publishing our books electronically, we can spend more time ensuring superior content and less time on the technicalities of making books.

You can count on our commitment to deliver high-quality books at competitive prices on topics you want to read about. At IDG Books Worldwide, we continue in the IDG tradition of delivering quality for more than 30 years. You'll find no better book on a subject than one from IDG Books Worldwide.

John J. Kilcullen

John Kilcullen
Chairman and CEO
IDG Books Worldwide, Inc.

Eighth Annual
Computer Press
Awards ≥ 1992

Ninth Annual
Computer Press
Awards ≥ 1993

Tenth Annual
Computer Press
Awards ≥ 1994

Eleventh Annual
Computer Press
Awards ≥ 1995

Credits

Acquisitions Editors
John Osborn
Debra Williams Cauley

Project Editor
Kathi Duggan

Technical Editor
David Williams

Copy Editor
Luann Rouff

Project Coordinators
Louigene A. Santos
Danette Nurse

Graphics and Production Specialists
Robert Bihlmayer
John Greenough
Jude Levinson
Michael Lewis
Gabriele McCann
Victor Pérez-Varela
Ramses Ramirez

Quality Control Technician
Dina F Quan

Permissions Editors
Laura Carpenter
Laura Moss

Media Development Specialists
Laura Carpenter
Travis Silvers

Media Development Coordinators
Laura Carpenter
Marisa Pearman

Illustrators
Shelley Norris
Rashell Smith

Proofreading and Indexing
York Production Services

Cover Image
Angela F. Hunckler
Joyce Haughey

About the Author

Arthur Griffith has been programming computers for twenty-five years. He has several years of experience in graphics programming, including X11 and motif. His broad background includes oil and gas monitoring, satellite communications, insurance company databases, real-time controls, and hardware diagnostic systems. He specializes in writing computer language interpreters and compilers and has implemented several special-purpose languages. Among the books he has written are *Java Master Reference* and *COBOL For Dummies*. He is also the co-author of *Peter Norton's Complete Guide to Linux*. Arthur now lives in Homer, Alaska, and is a full-time writer and teacher. You can contact him at arthur@belugalake.com.

For Mary

Preface

If you want to write a KDE application, you've come to the right book.

This book is composed of numerous example programs, and each example is accompanied by an explanation. When exploring or learning something new about software, my personal preference is to have a simple example that shows me just what I want and nothing else. Software is complicated enough that it becomes impossible to explain all its nuances without offering examples, and an example can be very confusing unless the key parts of it are clearly visible and explained. Therefore, each example provided here is also a complete running program designed to demonstrate just one thing.

The documentation of a program can be included as comments in the code, or it can be separate text supplied along with the code. The examples in this book have no embedded comments because each one is accompanied by text that explains it. Leaving out comments produces a cleaner format, making it easier for a reader to see the structure of the program. Most of the code is printed in the book with line numbers, so the explanations can refer to specific lines.

What You Will Need

If you know how to program in C++, have access to a Linux computer, and are able to download files from the Internet, this book will supply you with the know-how you need to write KDE applications.

You can find a version of the development software on the CD, which is described in Appendix A. Alternatively, see Appendix B to find out how to get the latest version of everything. Appendix B contains a list of all the software you will need, and where it can be found on the Internet.

Subject to Change

KDE is large and powerful, and it is moving fast. Fortunately, it is also very friendly.

Because KDE is an ongoing project, new things are being added constantly. This will likely be the situation for the foreseeable future. Because of its open source status, this growth will probably continue for the life of Linux and KDE.

From time to time, new methods for getting things done are added to the API, and it is possible that some of the techniques described in this book will become outdated. But KDE is quite stable now, so everything in the book should continue to work even in the event of future changes. In some cases, if you run your applications from the command line, there will be some text output to the console window. This text may describe anything from a severe internal error to a simple piece of pertinent information for the developer of the class you are using. This is typical of open source development software, and symptomatic of software under development. Eventually, in later versions, these messages will go away.

How to Use This Book

The book is divided into three parts. The first part is one continuous tutorial covering the basics of KDE programming. The second part is also composed of tutorials, but the chapters can be consulted in any order on an as-needed basis. The third part was not intended to be read sequentially — it is more of a reference section, as are Appendixes C through G.

Appendix A or B: Installing the Software

If you have a late model Linux on a CD, you will have most of the software and may have it all. If not, you have two options: You can install it from the CD supplied with this book, or you can retrieve it from the Internet. Appendix A discusses the CD, and Appendix B discusses the Internet.

Chapter 20: From Win32 to KDE

If you are a Win32 programmer, start by reading Chapter 20. This chapter is a point-by-point comparison of two simple programs that are identical except that one is written for Win32 and the other is written for KDE. Although there are some basic differences, the underlying concepts behind writing a KDE application are very much like those behind writing a Win32 application. For good measure, a GNOME program is also included so you can compare the relative structure of all three applications.

Part I: Getting Started

Part I starts with the basics and puts the pieces together until you are able to create applications that display buttons, labels, and other widgets, in whatever size, shape, and position you would like them to be. The first chapter explains some of the background information—mostly having to do with the Qt and KDE libraries and how the various classes are used to construct running programs.

Chapter 2 is where the programming starts. This chapter describes the classes available that can be used to create and display the main window for both Qt and KDE applications. Chapter 3 expands on this by demonstrating methods for organizing the contents of windows and dialog boxes. Chapters 4 and 5 both cover the subject of managing pop-up dialogs, both custom-built dialogs and the dialogs that are predefined as part of either Qt or KDE. Chapter 6 explores the construction and management of menus and toolbars. Chapter 7 describes the management of widgets that come in groups—such as collections of buttons that toggle on and off in relation to one another.

Part II: Step by Step

Part II can be studied from beginning to end, or you can skip around from one topic to another as necessary. Although you will find a few cross-references from one chapter to another, for the most part each chapter is independent of the others.

Chapter 8 describes how your program can respond to the mouse and keyboard. Chapter 9 explains how you can manage and display pixel-level graphics—either loaded from a file or compiled right into the program. Chapter 10 explains fonts and the process for displaying strings of characters. Chapter 11 explores the options you have for creating and managing colors. Chapter 12 contains several examples of using the `QPainter` class to perform a wide range of detailed graphics rendering. Chapter 13 delves deeper into graphics by exploring the process of manipulating graphics to fit a specific size or for placement on a printed page. Chapter 13 also includes a special section on animation. Chapter 14 contains examples of dragging and dropping graphic and text objects. Chapter 15 explores the process of communicating data from one application to another. Chapter 16 rounds out the section's presentation of classes with examples of some miscellaneous utilities. Chapter 17 is an exploration of KDE facilities for internationalization.

Part III: Reference and Mechanics

A widget is an object that contains a window of some kind and is capable of being displayed on the screen. Chapter 18 is an alphabetical list of the widgets of Qt, along with some examples of how to use them. Chapter 19 is a list, with examples, of all of the KDE widgets.

Chapter 20 contains simple descriptive examples of the same program written in Win32, KDE, and GNOME.

The Cross-Reference Appendixes

There is a lot of software here, and we all need some way to get a handle on it. The appendixes contain reference information that can be very helpful in finding things.

Appendix	Lists	Contains
C	Methods	Each method name is listed, along with the classes in which it can be found.
D	Returned By	The Qt and KDE classes have constructors, but you can also acquire some of them from other classes by calling methods that produce them. The methods are listed here.
E	Enumerated Types	Enumerated types are listed alphabetically, showing the classes in which they are defined and the names of their values.
F	Signals	Signals are listed alphabetically with their argument types and the classes from which they are emitted.
G	Slots	Slots are listed alphabetically with their argument types and the classes that contain them.

Example Code

Most things described in this book are described by actual code samples. As much as possible, these examples are complete running programs. I find that a simple example—an example that demonstrates just one thing—is most useful to me when I need to figure out (or be reminded) how to do something. Each example is intended to demonstrate one, or possibly two, specific things.

The examples are not meant to demonstrate some kind of "correct" coding practice, or even the "correct" way to do a particular task. There is no correct way because, in KDE as in all other software systems, there is usually more than one way to get any particular job done. And the overall style and design of a program are up to the programmer.

All of the example code, along with the makefiles for each, can be found here:

```
http://www.belugalake.com/book/kdebible
```

Acknowledgments

I want to thank all of the KDE developers. This group has created an excellent graphical user interface, and they have a right to be proud of what they've done. I am grateful to the many members of the KDE developer's group that took the time to answer my questions and help keep me on the right track.

John Osborn came up with the original concept for this book. He defined the original scope of the project and helped keep me in line when I tended to wander. I also want to thank Laura Lewin, Andy Marinkovich, and Debra Williams Cauley for putting things together in such a way that the book became a reality.

Kathi Duggan, while repairing things I wrote that no human being could otherwise read, kept track of every chapter and graphic as it moved from one stage of production to another. I feel more secure in putting my name on the book because David Williams checked everything to make certain that the book was technically accurate. Luann Rouff showed me how to convert my strange sentences into something that could be read and understood.

And, as always, a special thank you to that special lady who makes everything happen: Margot Maley at Waterside.

Contents at a Glance

Contents

Part II: Step by Step   173

Getting Started

What Is This Thing Called KDE?

T he name of the software is the K Desktop Environment,
called KDE for short. This chapter is an introduction to the
application development environment of KDE. It is a graphical
user interface that is popular on Linux and other flavors of the
UNIX family of operating systems. Virtually all graphical interfaces in the UNIX family are built on top of the X Windowing
System. The X Windowing System gives the graphics its portability across many systems; the Qt library of graphics objects
provides the basic building blocks of an application; and the
KDE library provides a standard look and feel.

The Structure of a KDE Application

When you write a KDE application, you are writing code that
will rest on top of a lot of other code. Most of the detailed work
of getting your application written has already been done, and
that work resides in the libraries of code that will link to your
application to do the things you would like for it to do. The
diagram in Figure 1-1 should give you some idea of the levels
of software that make up a KDE application.

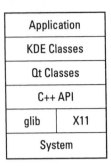

Figure 1-1: The levels of software for a KDE application in Linux

The way the diagram is drawn makes it appear that the levels are completely separate, but that's not the case. For example, perfectly valid calls are made from KDE classes to glib functions, and there is nothing to prevent your application from making calls directly to, say, glib or the system calls. An application typically uses classes from both KDE and Qt. However, the calls are only downward — for example, no part of the Qt API makes use of anything in KDE.

This book is all about using the material at the second and third levels (KDE and Qt) to create things that go at the top level (applications). There is little or no information about using the things at the other levels. Actually, that is one of the main purposes of KDE and Qt — they simplify the process of developing applications by insulating the programmer from the minute details handled at the lower levels.

The Software Levels

The following sections describe each of the software levels shown in Figure 1-1.

System

This is the lowest layer of software available to every Linux application. A set of low-level system calls provides direct access into the operation system, and its drivers, to do things like open files and create directories. Because the Linux kernel is written in C, these are all C function calls.

glib

This is a set of C functions, macros, and structures that are used by all the layers above it; and, quite often, it is also used by applications. The glib library contains functions for memory allocation, string formatting, date and time, I/O, and timers. It also has utility functions for linked lists, arrays, hash tables, trees, quarks, and caches. One of the crucial functions handled by glib is the main loop, which enables KDE to handle multiple resources while it simultaneously executes the code of an application.

X11

This is the graphics layer that handles the low-level functions used to control the display. All the fundamental windowing functions are included—these are the functions that display windows and respond to the mouse and keyboard. This library has become very stable over the years and the version numbers have rarely changed. Currently, it is version 11 (as indicated by its name). And, because version 11 is in release 6, it is also known as X11R6. Its original name was without the version number, so it is often simply called X.

C++ API

Everything above this layer is written using C++, so the C++ run-time system is called on for things such as creating new objects and handling I/O streams.

Qt Classes

This set of C++ classes implements the various widgets (buttons, window frames, and so on) that can be used to create an application. It has the capability of combing windows to together to create complicated graphics dialogs. At the same time that it displays these widgets, it can respond to the mouse and keyboard for more input, and dispatch information from the input window to the correct part of the program.

KDE Classes

These classes modify and add functionality to the Qt classes. There is a large number of KDE classes, but the majority of them extend directly from one or more of the Qt classes. This layer is what gives KDE its unique appearance, and standardizes the way the window, mouse, and keyboard all interact with one another.

Applications

There are two basic flavors of applications. You can create either a Qt application or a KDE application. A Qt application is one that creates a `QApplication` object to initialize itself, while a KDE application initializes itself by creating a `KApplication` object. The `KApplication` class extends the `QApplication` class by adding the things that are necessary for the standard appearance and capabilities of a KDE application.

About Qt

Qt is a library of C++ GUI application development software. Its purpose is to provide everything needed to develop the user interface portion of applications. It does this primarily in the form of a collection of C++ classes.

The Norwegian company Troll Tech (http://www.trolltech.com) first introduced Qt as a commercial product in 1995.

The set of Qt classes is quite robust. There is nothing to stop you from writing complete applications using Qt. In fact, to demonstrate the basic form of an application, the first few examples in this book use only Qt. The Qt classes include everything from basic window controls, drag and drop, and internationalization to network programming.

In the past there has been some concern over the use of Qt in some open source development areas because of limitations in software licensing. But licensing is no longer a concern. Trolltech has recently released a version of Qt that is entirely free, and it is licensed under the GPL (GNU General Public License). The same software can also be used under the QPL (Q Public License), depending on the particular licensing requirements. This dual licensing approach allows for the development of both open source software and proprietary software.

With release Qt 2.2.1, there are three different version of the software:

✦ The Qt Free Edition is licensed under the GPL and can be downloaded and freely used for any open source project.

✦ The Qt Professional Edition is intended for use by commercial and proprietary software development. The license and the software must be purchased.

✦ The Qt Enterprise Edition is licensed the same as the Qt Professional Edition, but contains additional software modules. These extensions include OpenGL, networking, XML, spreadsheets, and a special optimized 2D graphics package.

The QObject Class

All but about a dozen of the Qt classes inherit from the base class QObject. This means that virtually every class in the Qt library contains the same basic set of methods. The constructor for this class can optionally accept the address of a parent object, and a character string that assigns the object a name:

```
QObject(QObject *parent = 0, const char *name = 0);
```

The following methods are defined in QObject. Most of these methods are used in one example or another in this book.

```
void blockSignals(bool b);
QObject *child(const char *name, const char *type = 0);
```

```
    const QObjectList *children() const;
    virtual const char *className() const;
    static bool connect(const QObject *sender, const char *signal,
        const QObject *receiver, const char *member);
    bool connect(const QObject *sender, const char *signal,
        const char *member) const;
    static bool disconnect(const QObject *sender,
        const char *signal, const QObject *receiver,
        const char *member);
    bool disconnect(const char *signal = 0,
        const QObject *receiver = 0, const char *member = 0);
    bool disconnect(const QObject *receiver,
        const char *member = 0);
    void dumpObjectInfo();
    void dumpObjectTree();
    virtual bool event(QEvent *);
    virtual bool eventFilter(QObject *, QEvent *);
    bool highPriority() const;
    bool inherits(const char *) const;
    virtual void insertChild(QObject *);
    void installEventFilter(const QObject *);
    bool isA(const char *) const;
    bool isWidgetType() const;
    void killTimer(int id);
    void killTimers();
    virtual QMetaObject *metaObject() const;
    const char *name() const;
    const char *name(const char *defaultName) const;
    static const QObjectList *objectTrees();
    QObject *parent() const;
    QVariant property(const char *name) const;
    QObjectList *queryList(const char *inheritsClass = 0,
        const char *objName = 0, bool regexpMatch = TRUE,
        bool recursiveSearch = TRUE);
    virtual void removeChild(QObject *);
    void removeEventFilter(const QObject *);
    virtual void setName(const char *name);
    bool setProperty(const char *name, const QVariant &value);
    bool signalsBlocked() const;
    int startTimer(int interval);
    QStringList superClasses(bool includeThis = FALSE) const;
    static QString tr(const char *);
```

Some Qt objects have the ability to emit signals that can be received by other objects
inside your program. A QObject object emits a signal whenever its destructor
is called:

```
    void destroyed();
```

Signals, and the slots that receive them, are briefly described in the next section,
and many examples are included in the book.

The MOC Compiler

One feature used by developers is the Meta Object Compiler (also called the MOC compiler). The MOC compiler reads your source code and generates special C++ source files for you to compile and link along with your application. These special files contain the code necessary for one object to emit a "signal" that is received by a "slot" in one or more other objects. This is the method used to asynchronously transmit information from one object to another within an application.

The MOC compiler is triggered by the presence of the Q_OBJECT macro within a class definition to determine whether to generate code, and what code is generated. The resulting source code can be either compiled separately and linked, or simply included in your code with the #include directive.

Using the MOC compiler not only activates the signals and slots, but also generates code that enables some special methods that are defined in every Qt class (and thus, by inheritance, in every object in your program). These special methods, listed in Table 1-1, are defined in the QtObject class.

<table>
<tr><th colspan="2">Table 1-1
The MOC Methods of QObject</th></tr>
<tr><th>Method</th><th>Description</th></tr>
<tr><td>className()</td><td>Returns, as a character string, the name of the class. This does not require RTTI (Run Time Type Identification) support.</td></tr>
<tr><td>inherits()</td><td>Returns a Boolean value that specifies whether or not this class inherits from some other named class.</td></tr>
<tr><td>tr()</td><td>Performs the translation of a string for internationalization</td></tr>
<tr><td>setProperty()</td><td>Sets an object property by name</td></tr>
<tr><td>property()</td><td>Returns a named object property</td></tr>
<tr><td>metaObject()</td><td>Returns a QMetaObject object for the class. A meta object contains detailed descriptive information for a class.</td></tr>
</table>

About KDE

KDE is an open source development project of a graphical desktop environment. Other than being the first letter of the acronym, the K doesn't stand for anything. It is just a name.

The KDE software is constructed using Qt. The project began in 1996, the year after the first version of Qt was released. Since then, the project has grown to become a very complete desktop environment with a large collection of applications. To learn more about the status and content of KDE, visit the http://www.kde.org Web site.

From the software developer's point of view, KDE is quite simple. While most of the software written as part of the KDE project is used as an integral part of the desktop environment, a large number of classes have also been developed; and they are included as part of a core KDE API. These classes are meant to help give KDE applications a standard look and feel. Most of these classes inherit from one or more classes of the Qt library, and some of the KDE classes add capabilities beyond that of Qt, but most of them are simply for the sake of maintaining the standard appearance of KDE. It would be easy enough to write your entire application using only the classes of Qt, but if you use the KDE classes, your application is more likely to appear integrated with the rest of the desktop.

Events Happen

An application that runs in the K Desktop Environment is an event-driven program. This means that when a program starts running, it displays its window (or windows) and waits for input from the mouse or keyboard. This input comes wrapped inside objects called *events*. An event can also tell the program that a window has been closed, or that the window has been exposed after being hidden behind another window. The application's entire purpose is to respond intelligently to the keyboard and mouse.

An application has one main top-level window. It can also have other windows. These windows can exist for the entire life of the application, or they can appear and disappear as the application responds to events.

Each window is encapsulated in a *widget*. The top-level window of an application is a widget. Each pop-up window is also a widget. In fact, the entire display is made up of widgets. Because one widget is capable of containing and displaying other widgets, every button, label, and menu item is its own individual widget. Programming the graphical display portion of your application is a matter of creating and combining widgets, and then writing the code that activates the widgets and responds to the events received by the widgets.

A widget is any class that inherits from the Qt class named QWidget. A QWidget object contains and manages its own displayable window. It can also be set to respond to events issued by the mouse and keyboard (and whatever else you have for input) that are sent to the window inside the widget. It knows things about its current visibility, its size, its background color, its foreground color, its position on the display, and so on. You can use the widgets defined in either Qt or KDE, or you can create your own by using QWidget as a base class.

The Names of Things

The Qt class names begin with the letter Q and the KDE class names begin with the letter K. That way, when you read the source code of a program, you can determine where a class is defined. If you find two classes that have the same name except for the first letter, it means that one is an extension of the other. For example, the KDE class KPixmap uses the Qt class QPixmap as its base class.

Every class in Qt and KDE is defined in a header file. In every case (well, almost every case), the header file derives its name from the name of the class. For example, the header file for the QPopupMenu class is named qpopupmenu.h, and the class KFontDialog is defined in kfontdialog.h. However, this naming convention is not universally true because more than one class can be defined in a header. For example, the class KFontChooser is also defined in kfontdialog.h. Also, some source filenames are abbreviated. For example, the header for KColorDialog is named kcolordlg.h.

Summary

This chapter provided a short, and very general, introduction to the programming environment of KDE. The concepts introduced in this chapter included:

✦ Several layers of software support the KDE software library.

✦ The X Windowing System controls the low-level GUI interface. The KDE library is a thin layer of software that is very dependent on the Qt software immediately below it.

✦ All applications are event driven. The application displays at least one window, and then waits for input from the mouse or keyboard.

If you are a Windows programmer but are unfamiliar with KDE, you may want to read Chapter 20, which compares a Windows program with a KDE program. Otherwise, proceed to Chapter 2, which starts with examples of very simple KDE applications.

✦   ✦   ✦

Creating and Displaying a Window

T his chapter discusses the fundamental form of a Qt or KDE application program. If you are new to KDE, you are going to be pleasantly surprised. A good deal of effort has gone into making the basics as simple as possible. The creation of a basic application is so simple it would be hard to get it wrong.

The examples in this chapter are designed to explain the basic format of the source and the process necessary to convert that source into an executable program. To keep things as simple as possible, and so you can see the relationship between the various parts of a program, these examples all use simple hand-written makefiles. The first example is a minimal Qt application, and the second is a minimal KDE application. Other examples show how you can respond to a pushbutton and create a display widget containing other widgets.

Hello Qt

The following example program creates and displays a simple window. It doesn't do anything other than display a line of text, but it gives you an idea of the fundamental requirements of a Qt program. The window is shown in Figure 2-1.

```
1 /* helloworld.cpp */
2 #include <qapplication.h>
3 #include <qlabel.h>
4 #include <qstring.h>
5
6 int main(int argc,char **argv)
7 {
```

```
 8        QApplication app(argc,argv);
 9        QLabel *label = new QLabel(NULL);
10        QString string("Hello, world");
11        label->setText(string);
12        label->setAlignment(
13                Qt::AlignVCenter | Qt::AlignHCenter);
14        label->setGeometry(0,0,180,75);
15        label->show();
16        app.setMainWidget(label);
17        return(app.exec());
18 }
```

Figure 2-1: A simple Qt program displaying text

The file qapplication.h included on line 2 is almost always included in the same source file that contains the main() function. This example uses a QLabel widget to display text, so it is necessary to also include qlabel.h. And a QString object is required to specify the text displayed by the QLabel object, so qstring.h is included on line 4.

Line 8 creates a QApplication object named app. The QApplication object is a container that will hold the *top-level* window (or set of windows) of an application. A top-level window is unique in that it never has a parent window in the application. Because the QApplication object takes over things and manages your application, there can only be one of these per program. Also, the creation of a QApplication object initializes the Qt system, so it must exist before any of the other Qt facilities are available.

A Qt program is a C++ program. This means that in order to start the program, a function named main() will be called by the operating system. And, like all C++ programs, command-line options may or may not be passed to the main() function. The command-line options are passed on to the Qt software as part of the initialization process, as shown on line 8.

The two command-line arguments, argc and argv, are used in the construction of app because some special flags and settings can be specified. For example, starting a Qt program with -geometry will specify the size and location of the window it displays. By altering the profile information that starts a program, a user can personalize a program's appearance.

A QLabel widget is created on line 9. A QLabel widget is simply a window that is capable of displaying a string of characters. The label is created with its specified parent widget as NULL because this label is to be the top-level window, and top-level windows have no parents. As it is created, the label contains no text, but it is provided text by being passed the QString object created on line 10. The QString object is inserted into the QLabel with the call to setText() on line 11.

The default action for a QLabel is to display the character string centered vertically and justified to the left, so the call to setAlignment() is made on line 12 to center the text both vertically and horizontally.

The call to setGeometry() on line 14 determines the location, height, and width of the label widget inside the QApplication window. For this example, the label is positioned at location (0,0), which is the upper-left corner of the main window. It is also instructed to be 180 pixels wide by 75 pixels high. Before anything is displayed, the main window will query the label to find out its size, and then the main window will set its own size to contain the label.

The call to show() on line 16 is necessary in order for the label to actually appear on the window. The show() function does not immediately display the widget, it only configures it so that it will be displayed when the time comes. The parent window—in this case, the QApplication window—assumes the task of displaying the label, but will only do so if there has been a call to the label's show() method. Another function, named hide(), can be used to cause a widget to disappear from the display.

The call to setMainWidget() on line 11 inserts the label into the main window. To keep this example simple, the QLabel object is used, but normally the widget will be some sort of compound widget that contains the collection of widgets, text, and other elements of the main window of an application.

Finally, a call is made to exec() on line 17. This function does not return until it is time for the program to cease execution. It returns an int value representing its completion status; and because we are not processing status codes, the value is simply returned to the system.

Because the program is simple and consists of only one source file, the makefile that compiles it is quite simple:

```
INCL= -I$(QTDIR)/include -I$(KDEDIR)/include
CFLAGS= -pipe -O2 -fno-strength-reduce
LFLAGS= -L$(QTDIR)/lib -L$(KDEDIR)/lib -L/usr/X11R6/lib
LIBS= -lqt -lX11 -lXext
CC=g++

helloworld: helloworld.o
    $(CC) $(LFLAGS) -o helloworld helloworld.o $(LIBS)

helloworld.o: helloworld.cpp
```

```
clean:
    rm -f helloworld
    rm -f helloworld.o

.SUFFIXES: .cpp

.cpp.o:
    $(CC) -c $(CFLAGS) $(INCL) -o $@ $<
```

The makefile assumes that the environment variables QTDIR and KDEDIR are defined as the name of the installation directory of the Qt and KDE development systems. Normally, these two environment variables have their definitions configured when you install the software. Five names are defined inside the makefile, as shown in Table 2-1.

Table 2-1
Variables Defined in the Makefile

Name	Contents
INCL	This is the path name of the location of the header files. This is passed to the compiler to tell it where to look for header files. The compiler always looks in /usr/include for the standard headers.
CFLAGS	This is the list of options passed to the compiler. The -pipe option instructs the compiler to use pipes, instead of temporary files, when passing data between two stages of compilation. The -02 option specifies a fairly high level of optimization. The -fno-strength-reduce option prevents the optimization from reducing or eliminating iteration variables.
LFLAGS	This is a list of options passed to the linker. Each of the -L options specifies a directory that is expected to contain one or more libraries.
LIBS	This is the list of library namesthat will be needed by this program. The named libraries will be sought in the directories named by LFLAGS. The name of each will be expanded to name the library file. For example, -lqt is changed to libqt.so, and -lX11 becomes libX11.so.
CC	This is the name of the compiler.

The last two lines of the makefile are used to instruct make on how to form a command that will convert a .cpp file into a .o file. There is only one source file in this example, but if there were more, using the conversion rule allows the compile command to be defined once and be applied to the entire makefile.

There are an infinite number of ways to write a makefile. This example was made relatively simple so it would be easy to read. As you develop an application, you will probably discover other things need to be added to your makefiles.

Hello KDE

This example, shown in Figure 2-2, is the same as the previous one except it is based on a KApplication object, rather than a QApplication object. Because the KApplication class is based on QApplication, there are no fundamental differences other than the addition of KDE facilities such as styles and themes, the capability to use KDE widgets, access to the standard KDE configuration, access to session management information, and the capability to launch the user's Web browser and e-mail client.

```
1  /* hellokde.cpp */
2  #include <kapp.h>
3  #include <qlabel.h>
4  #include <qstring.h>
5
6  int main(int argc,char **argv)
7  {
8      KApplication app(argc,argv,"hellokde");
9      QLabel *label = new QLabel(NULL);
10     QString string("Hello, KDE");
11     label->setText(string);
12     label->setAlignment(
13             Qt::AlignVCenter | Qt::AlignHCenter);
14     label->setGeometry(0,0,180,75);
15     label->show();
16     app.setMainWidget(label);
17     return(app.exec());
18 }
```

Figure 2-2: A simple KDE program displaying text

The KApplication object is defined in the header file kapp.h included on line 2. The kapp.h file includes the qapplication.h file, so every facility available to a Qt program is also available to a KDE program. The header files included on lines 3 and 4 hold the definitions of the QLabel and QString classes.

The KApplication object is created on line 8 by being passed the command-line arguments and a name for the application. This name can be used for such application-specific tasks as locating icons, receiving messages, and reading configuration information.

Because a KDE object is being used in this program, it is necessary to include the KDE library that holds the object. There are some specialized KDE libraries, but the main two libraries are libkdecore and libkdeui.

```
INCL= -I$(QTDIR)/include -I$(KDEDIR)/include
CFLAGS= -O2 -fno-strength-reduce
LFLAGS= -L$(QTDIR)/lib -L$(KDEDIR)/lib -L/usr/X11R6/lib
LIBS= -lkdecore -lkdeui -lqt -lX11 -lXext -ldl
CC=g++

hellokde: hellokde.o
        $(CC) $(LFLAGS) -o hellokde hellokde.o $(LIBS)

hellokde.o: hellokde.cpp

clean:
        rm -f hellokde
        rm -f hellokde.o

.SUFFIXES: .cpp

.cpp.o:
        $(CC) -c $(CFLAGS) $(INCL) -o $@ $<
```

The LIBS definition shows the inclusion of the libraries libkdecore.a, which contains the core functionality of KDE; and libkdeui.a, which contains all of the KDE widgets. KDE internally implements ODBC (Open Database Connectivity) by dynamically loading ODBC drivers, so it is also necessary to include the library libdl.a. The installation of KDE places these libraries in the default directory, so there is no need to add a new search path to LFLAGS.

A Simple Window Class

The following example demonstrates the basic form used to create a widget of your own. This program creates a MyLabel widget and displays it in the main window, as shown in Figure 2-3. The MyLabel widget is quite simple—it inherits everything from QLabel and doesn't add any capabilities. The class definition is in the header file mylabel.h.

```
1 /* mylabel.h */
2 #ifndef MYLABEL_H
```

```
 3 #define MYLABEL_H
 4
 5 #include <qlabel.h>
 6 #include <qstring.h>
 7
 8 class MyLabel: public QLabel
 9 {
10 public:
11     MyLabel(QWidget *parent);
12     ~MyLabel();
13 };
14
15 #endif
```

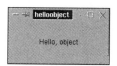

Figure 2-3: Creating and displaying a widget

The preprocessor commands on lines 2, 3, and 15 are not required, but they are a very good idea. As a growing application begins to get more complicated, the same header file is likely to be included more than once in a single source file because it is common to include header files inside other header files. By creating the definition of MYLABEL_H, this header can be included any number of times, but will be compiled only once.

On line 8, the definition of the MyLabel class uses QLabel as its base class. This necessitates the use of the include statement on line 5 to make the definition of QLabel available. The header file qstring.h is included on line 6 as a convenience, because the definition of QString is needed in the MyLabel constructor.

The MyLabel class is implemented in its own source file. It doesn't do anything other than pass the address of the parent widget from the constructor of MyLabel to the constructor of the QLabel base class:

```
1 /* mylabel.cpp */
2 #include "mylabel.h"
3
4 MyLabel::MyLabel(QWidget *parent) : QLabel(parent)
5 {
6 }
7 MyLabel::~MyLabel()
8 {
9 }
```

The following example creates and displays a MyLabel widget. Except for the object used, the main() function of this program is very much the same as the one for the previous example.

```
1  /* helloobject.cpp */
2  #include "mylabel.h"
3  #include <qapplication.h>
4
5  int main(int argc,char **argv)
6  {
7      QApplication app(argc,argv);
8      MyLabel *mylabel = new MyLabel(NULL);
9      QString string("Hello, object");
10     mylabel->setText(string);
11     mylabel->setAlignment(
12             Qt::AlignVCenter | Qt::AlignHCenter);
13     mylabel->setGeometry(0,0,180,75);
14     mylabel->show();
15     app.setMainWidget(mylabel);
16     return(app.exec());
17 }
```

The MyLabel object is created, manipulated, and displayed in exactly the same way as the QLabel object in the previous example. The setAlignment() function is inherited directly from QLabel, while setGeometry() and show() are inherited from QWidget.

Note   Object-oriented programming has numerous advantages, but the most well known are probably the advantages found in handling graphical user interfaces (GUIs). Qt takes full advantage of this fact. Every displayable object inherits its basic capabilities from the base class QWidget, which means that every displayable window—label, button, top-level window, or whatever—all have the same set of basic functions that control things such as size, color, cursor appearance, mouse detection, and scrolling. This not only makes it easy to create your own widgets, it automatically applies a default uniform behavior and appearance to everything on the screen.

The makefile is very much like the previous one, except that it must take into account the two separate .cpp files by compiling them both and linking them together:

```
INCL= -I$(QTDIR)/include -I$(KDEDIR)/include
CFLAGS= -pipe -O2 -fno-strength-reduce
LFLAGS= -L$(QTDIR)/lib -L$(KDEDIR)/lib -L/usr/X11R6/lib
LIBS= -lqt -lX11 -lXext
CC=g++

helloobject: helloobject.o mylabel.o
    $(CC) $(LFLAGS) -o helloobject helloobject.o \
        mylabel.o $(LIBS)

helloobject.o: helloobject.cpp mylabel.h

mylabel.o: mylabel.cpp mylabel.h
```

```
clean:
    rm -f helloobject
    rm -f mylabel.o
    rm -f helloobject.o

.SUFFIXES: .cpp

.cpp.o:
    $(CC) -c $(CFLAGS) $(INCL) -o $@ $<
```

Compound Widgets

The QApplication object displays, as the main window of the application, the widget you assign to it with the call to the method assignMainWidget(). To display a main window that contains more than a single item, you need to create your own widget and use it as the one displayed as the main window. The following example combines two buttons and a label into a single widget:

```
 1 /* threewidget.h */
 2 #ifndef THREEWIDGET_H
 3 #define THREEWIDGET_H
 4
 5 #include <qpushbutton.h>
 6 #include <qlabel.h>
 7
 8 class ThreeWidget: public QWidget
 9 {
10 public:
11     ThreeWidget(QWidget *parent=0,const char *name=0);
12 private:
13     QPushButton *topButton;
14     QPushButton *bottomButton;
15     QLabel *label;
16 };
17
18 #endif
```

Lines 5 and 6 include the header files defining the widgets that are to be included as part of the compound widget. There are to be two buttons and a label, and the locations to store their addresses are defined as private data on lines 13 through 15 of threewidget.h.

```
 1 /* threewidget.cpp */
 2 #include "threewidget.h"
 3
 4 ThreeWidget::ThreeWidget(QWidget *parent,const char *name):
 5                 QWidget(parent,name )
 6 {
 7     setMinimumSize(120,180);
 8     setMaximumSize(120,180);
 9
```

```
10      topButton = new QPushButton("Top Button",this);
11      topButton->setGeometry(15,15,90,40);
12      label = new QLabel("Middle Label",this);
13      label->setGeometry(15,70,90,40);
14      label->setAlignment(AlignVCenter | AlignHCenter);
15      bottomButton = new QPushButton("Bottom Button",this);
16      bottomButton->setGeometry(15,125,90,40);
17 }
```

Because it needs to be a displayable widget, the ThreeWidget class uses QWidget as its base class.

Lines 7 and 8 set the minimum and maximum sizes of this widget. The parent window will query this widget to determine its size. In this example, the minimum and maximum settings are the same, which means that the window cannot be resized. The displayed window, shown in Figure 2-4, cannot have its width or height changed with the mouse.

Figure 2-4: Positioning and sizing buttons and labels

The button at the top is created on line 10. The second argument to the constructor is the widget that is to be the parent of the button. In this example, the parent is the new widget being constructed. The same parent/child relationship is established for the label and the other button on lines 12 and 15.

The newly created widget has a displayable area that is 120 pixels wide and 180 pixels high. The widgets are positioned on this window by calls to setGeometry(). On line 11, a call to setGeometry() positions the top button 15 pixels from the top and 15 pixels from the left side. The same call sets the button width to 80 pixels, and the height to 40 pixels. Similarly, the calls to setGeometry() on lines 13 and 16 position the other widgets. The first two arguments to setGeometry() are left and top; the second two are width and height.

The main() function of this program treats the new compound widget just as it would any other widget.

```
1 /* compound.cpp */
2 #include <qapplication.h>
```

```
 3 #include "threewidget.h"
 4
 5 int main(int argc,char **argv)
 6 {
 7     QApplication app(argc,argv);
 8     ThreeWidget threeWidget;
 9     threeWidget.setGeometry(10,10,100,100);
10     app.setMainWidget(&threeWidget);
11     threeWidget.show();
12     return(app.exec());
13 }
```

The `threeWidget` object is created on line 8. A widget cannot be forced to fit a size that is not valid for it, so the call to `setGeometry()` on line 9 has no effect because of the minimum and maximum size settings in the widget. The call to `show()` on line 11 instructs the widget, and all of the widgets it contains, to be visible.

Listening to a Button

A button is a widget, so it can be displayed just like any other widget. However, your program will need to know when the user clicks on the button. The following example displays the window shown in Figure 2-5 and responds to the button by halting:

```
 1 /* exitbutton.cpp */
 2 #include <qapplication.h>
 3 #include <qpushbutton.h>
 4 #include <qstring.h>
 5
 6 int main(int argc,char **argv)
 7 {
 8     QApplication app(argc,argv);
 9     QString string("Exit");
10     QPushButton *button = new QPushButton(string,NULL);
11     QObject::connect(button,
12             SIGNAL(clicked()),&app,SLOT(quit()));
13     button->setGeometry(0,0,80,50);
14     button->show();
15     app.setMainWidget(button);
16     return(app.exec());
17 }
```

Figure 2-5: A button to exit the program

The button is prepared to respond to the mouse, but the response will go unnoticed unless the button is instructed to send a message to some part of your program. A message of this type is called a *signal*, and a method capable of receiving a signal is called a *slot*. The call to QObject::connect() on lines 10 and 11 causes a copy of the signal to be directed from clicked() in the button to the quit() method in the application.

Note

> If you have worked with other event-driven systems, you are probably familiar with the concept of *callback functions*. A slot is similar to a callback, but there are some differences. The most important difference is that slots are type safe — if the argument types don't match, the program won't compile.

In the call to QObject::connect(), the first two arguments specify the source of the signal as being the method named clicked() in the button. The signal is broadcast. That is, the signal is sent whether or not there are slot functions set to receive it. On the other hand, if several slots are set to receive the signal, they each will receive a copy.

The second pair of arguments on the call to QObject::connect() specify that the receiving slot is to be the quit() method in the QApplication.

Defining a Slot for a Signal

In order to have a widget receive a signal, it must define a slot and connect it to the signal. The following example, shown in Figure 2-6, displays a button and a counter, and whenever the button is pressed, the counter is incremented. Several things need to be done to make this happen, but the Qt system handles most of the details. In particular, there are some special macros and the Meta Object Compiler (MOC) to handle most of the detail work automatically. The main() function in this example simply creates and displays the widget:

```
 1 /* count.cpp */
 2 #include <qapplication.h>
 3 #include "clickcount.h"
 4
 5 int main(int argc,char **argv)
 6 {
 7     QApplication app(argc,argv);
 8     ClickCount clickcount;
 9     app.setMainWidget(&clickcount);
10     clickcount.show();
11     return(app.exec());
12 }
```

Figure 2-6: The slot of the counter receives the signal of the button.

The `ClickCount` widget contains a button and a label. The label is used to display the current counter value:

```
 1 /* clickcount.h */
 2 #ifndef CLICKCOUNT_H
 3 #define CLICKCOUNT_H
 4
 5 #include <qpushbutton.h>
 6 #include <qlabel.h>
 7
 8 class ClickCount: public QWidget
 9 {
10     Q_OBJECT
11 public:
12     ClickCount(QWidget *parent=0,const char *name=0);
13 public slots:
14     void incrementCounter();
15 private:
16     int counter;
17     QLabel *label;
18     QPushButton *button;
19 };
20
21 #endif
```

The macro `Q_OBJECT` on line 10 must be present in any class that has a slot. (It also must be present for a class that broadcasts a signal, as you'll see in Chapter 5.) The `Q_OBJECT` macro defines some of the standard methods that must be present in order for signals and slots to work.

The method, named `incrementCounter()` on line 14, is categorized as a `public slot` by the declaration on line 13. Other than being declared as a slot, `incrementCounter()` is the same as any other method in the class; and it can be called directly as well as being called by a signal.

The constructor of the `ClickCount` class creates the layout containing the button and the label, and makes the connection that will send a signal from the button to the slot named `incrementCounter()`:

```
 1 /* clickcount.cpp */
 2 #include <stdio.h>
```

```
 3 #include "clickcount.h"
 4
 5 ClickCount::ClickCount(QWidget *parent,const char *name):
 6                   QWidget(parent,name )
 7 {
 8     setMinimumSize(120,125);
 9     setMaximumSize(120,125);
10
11     counter = 0;
12     button = new QPushButton("Add 1",this);
13     button->setGeometry(15,15,90,40);
14     label = new QLabel("0",this);
15     label->setGeometry(15,70,90,40);
16     label->setAlignment(AlignVCenter | AlignHCenter);
17
18     QObject::connect(
19             button,SIGNAL(clicked()),
20             this,SLOT(incrementCounter()));
21 }
22 void ClickCount::incrementCounter()
23 {
24     char str[30];
25     sprintf(str,"%d",++counter);
26     label->setText(str);
27 }
```

The calls to setMinimumSize() and setMaximumSize() on lines 8 and 9 fix the
size of the window at 120×125 pixels. The counter value is initialized on line 11,
and the button and the label are created and configured on lines 12 through 16.

The call to QObject::connect() on line 18 attaches a slot to a signal. The first two
arguments, on line 19, specify that the source of the signal is to be a method named
clicked(). The clicked() signal is a member of the button's class, along with the
signals named pressed(), released(), and toggled().

Cross-Reference   You can find examples of creating signal methods in Chapter 5.

The second pair of QObject::connect() arguments, on line 20, specify the object
and method that are to receive the signal. The object is this (the current instance
of ClickCount) and the method is incrementCounter().

Every time the clicked() signal is sent by the button, it is received by the
incrementCounter() method, which adds 1 to the value being displayed and
updates the text of the button.

Note   There is no real connection between the signal and the slot. A signal is broadcast whether or not any slots are listening—and there can be any number of slots listening for the signal. Also, a slot can be set to listen for any number of signals.

The makefile for this example shows how the Meta Object Compiler) takes its input as the source code of the header file defining the class, and produces a new source file to be compiled and linked with the program:

```
1 INCL= -I$(QTDIR)/include -I$(KDEDIR)/include
2 CFLAGS= -O2 -fno-strength-reduce
3 LFLAGS= -L$(QTDIR)/lib -L$(KDEDIR)/include -L/usr/X11R6/lib
4 LIBS= -lqt -lX11 -lXext
5 CC=g++
6
7 count: count.o clickcount.o moc_clickcount.o
8     $(CC) $(LFLAGS) -o count count.o clickcount.o \
9         moc_clickcount.o $(LIBS)
10
11 count.o: count.cpp clickcount.h
12 clickcount.o: clickcount.cpp clickcount.h
13 moc_clickcount.cpp: clickcount.h
14     $(QTDIR)/bin/moc clickcount.h -o moc_clickcount.cpp
15
16 clean:
17     rm -f count
18     rm -f count.o
19     rm -f clickcount.o
20     rm -f moc_*
21
22 .SUFFIXES: .cpp
23
24 .cpp.o:
25     $(CC) -c $(CFLAGS) $(INCL) -o $@ $<
```

The dependencies on line 7 show that the program is not only dependent on count.o and clickount.o, but also depends on something called moc_clickcount.o. The file moc_clickcount.cpp is created by the MOC compiler from clickcount.h. The Q_OBJECT macro adds some method prototypes to the ClickCount class definition, and the MOC compiler generates bodies for the new methods. The result is that the repetitive (and thus error-prone) coding required for signals and slots is almost completely automated.

Cross-Reference   There is more about how and why this is done—Chapter 5 examines the entire process.

Summary

It takes very few lines of code to create a working Qt or KDE application. The details of writing code to create the windows, and the low-level mechanics of listening for user input, are all handled inside the API.

✦ A Qt program is created by having the mainline of the program create a `QApplication` object and use it to control the windows. A KDE program is formed the same way, using a `KApplication` object.

✦ The main window of an application is a single widget. This widget normally contains a collection of other widgets that display information and supply the user interface.

✦ An object can be written to broadcast one or more signals. An object can also contain one or more slots designed to receive broadcast signals. The implementation details of slots and signals are automated through the use of macros and the MOC compiler.

This chapter described how to create and display the main window of an application. The next chapter deals with displaying pop-up windows and dialog boxes. There are some pre-defined KDE and Qt dialog boxes, but you can also create your own.

✦   ✦   ✦

Laying Out Widgets in a Window

This chapter is all about controlling the size and position of a collection of widgets inside a window. Before an application can be programmed to respond to a button or read some text typed by the user, it is necessary to present the button and the text entry widgets in some sort of reasonable arrangement. This chapter explains not only how to place a widget where you want it, but also how to specify its size and the action that will be taken when the window is resized.

Widgets can be positioned and sized by coordinate values or by using a layout. The coordinate values are hard-coded pixel locations that cannot be adjusted by the user. On the other hand, a layout object positions and sizes the widgets (within maximum and minimum limits) relative to one another and relative to the overall size of the containing window.

Geometric Widget Placement

You can specify the exact placement and size of each widget by specifying four values: horizontal offset, vertical offset, width, and height. The coordinate system is that of the parent window—that is, the window that contains the widgets. The following example places three pushbuttons on an application window.

Main

```
1 /* main.cpp */
2 #include <kapp.h>
```

```
 3 #include "setxy.h"
 4
 5 int main(int argc,char **argv)
 6 {
 7     KApplication app(argc,argv,"setxy");
 8     SetXY setxy;
 9     setxy.show();
10     app.setMainWidget(&setxy);
11     return(app.exec());
12 }
```

The mainline is quite simple. The header file is included on line 3. The widget with the buttons is created on line 8, and is specified as the widget to be displayed as the main application window by the call to setMainWidget() on line 10.

SetXY Header

```
 1 /* setxy.h */
 2 #ifndef SETXY_H
 3 #define SETXY_H
 4
 5 #include <qpushbutton.h>
 6
 7 class SetXY: public QWidget
 8 {
 9 public:
10     SetXY(QWidget *parent=0,const char *name=0);
11     ~SetXY();
12 private:
13     QPushButton *button1;
14     QPushButton *button2;
15     QPushButton *button3;
16 };
17
18 #endif
```

The class SetXY is defined using QWidget as its base class. Its only data are the three QPushButton pointers defined on lines 13 through 15. Normally, there would be methods designated as slots to respond to the buttons, but this is a simple placement demonstration so there will be no responses to the buttons.

Note

Because the header file qpushbutton.h is included on line 5 of setxy.h, it will be automatically included by both setxy.cpp and main.cpp. If another widget were being used, and if that other widget also included qpushbutton.h, the same header file would be included twice. That is why it is very important that the precompiler directives on lines 2, 3, and 18 be used to prevent a header file from being compiled more than once.

SetXY

```
 1 /* setxy.cpp */
 2 #include "setxy.h"
 3
 4 SetXY::SetXY(QWidget *parent,const char *name)
 5           : QWidget(parent,name)
 6 {
 7      setMinimumSize(90,40);
 8      setMaximumSize(190,220);
 9      resize(190,220);
10
11      button1 = new QPushButton("Upper Left",this);
12      button1->setGeometry(0,0,90,40);
13
14      button2 = new QPushButton("Middle Right",this);
15      button2->setGeometry(90,70,100,50);
16
17      button3 = new QPushButton("Bottom",this);
18      button3->setGeometry(45,140,50,80);
19 }
20 SetXY::~SetXY() { }
```

All of the work done by SetXY is done in the constructor. Three buttons are defined and displayed, as shown in Figure 3-1.

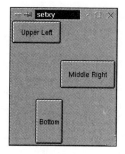

Figure 3-1: Three buttons positioned by coordinates

The button in the upper left corner is created on line 11 and its size and position are set on line 12. The order of the four integers passed to the setGeometry() method is as follows:

```
x,y,width,height
```

The distances are measured in pixels. The x value is the number of pixels from the left of the application window to the left of the contained widget. The y value is the number of pixels from the top of the window to the top of the widget. That is, the upper-left corner is the origin of the coordinate system. Each button is created and then assigned a size and position by a call to setGeometry().

Note   If two widgets are placed so that they occupy the same space, the newer one will obscure the older one; therefore, if you find you are missing a widget, it could be simply hidden.

The calls on lines 7, 8, and 9 define the rules for displaying this widget. The call to setMinimumSize() on line 7 specifies that this widget must be displayed at least 90 pixels wide and 40 pixels high. The minimum setting is important because the widget is to be displayed in a window that can be resized by the user. The widget cannot be reduced beyond the size shown in Figure 3-2. The call to setMaximum Size() on line 8 places an upper limit on the height and width of the widget. Finally, the call to resize() on line 9 sets the initial size of the widget to the maximum allowable size.

Figure 3-2: The minimum size setting obscures two of the three buttons.

There is nothing to be done in the ~SetXY() destructor on line 20 because when this application exits — and this widget is destroyed — it will also destroy the three buttons because this widget is the parent of the buttons.

The Size of a Widget

You need to consider two important factors when laying out widgets on a window. Each widget has a location and a size. In the previous example, location and size are completely controlled by the application program. This is fine if your application needs that detailed a level of control, but most widgets have an opinion about how big they should be.

A number of methods in QWidget give you control over the size of the widget. Some of these methods use height and width values, and some use QSize objects, but they both do the same thing. The QSize class is simply a wrapper for height and width, but it also contains some methods and operators that make life a bit easier when the size manipulation gets complicated. For example, you can use operators to change the size while maintaining the ratio and to combine two QSize objects into one:

```
void setMaximumSize(const QSize &qsize);
void setMaximumSize(int width,int height);
void setMaximumWidth(int width);
```

```
void setMaximumHeight(int height);
void setMinimumSize(const QSize &qsize);
void setMinimumSize(int width,int height);
void setMinimumWidth(int width);
void setMinimumHeight(int height);
```

If a widget is to have a fixed size, you can either make two function calls to set the minimum and maximum to the same values, or you can call one of the following functions:

```
void setFixedSize(const QSize &qsize);
void setFixedSize(int width,int height);
void setFixedWidth(int width);
void setFixedHeight(int height);
```

The following functions retrieve the maximum and minimum sizes:

```
QSize maximumSize();
QSize minimumSize();
```

Fixed Grid Widget Placement

Using a QGridLayout object enables you to define a grid of invisible horizontal and vertical lines and then insert widgets into the cells created by the lines. The following example creates a grid that is five cells wide by five cells high and inserts a button into four of the cells.

Main

```
 1  /* main.cpp */
 2  #include <kapp.h>
 3  #include "fivebyfive.h"
 4
 5  int main(int argc,char **argv)
 6  {
 7      KApplication app(argc,argv,"fivebyfive");
 8      FiveByFive *fivebyfive = new FiveByFive();
 9      fivebyfive->show();
10      app.setMainWidget(fivebyfive);
11      return(app.exec());
12  }
```

The mainline creates an instance of the FiveByFive widget and uses it as the widget to be displayed in the KApplication window. The result is the window displayed in Figure 3-3.

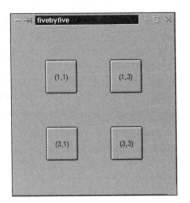

Figure 3-3: Four pushbuttons positioned by a grid layout

FiveByFive Header

```
 1 /* fivebyfive.h */
 2 #ifndef FIVEBYFIVE_H
 3 #define FIVEBYFIVE_H
 4
 5 #include <qwidget.h>
 6 #include <qpushbutton.h>
 7
 8 class FiveByFive: public QWidget
 9 {
10 public:
11     FiveByFive(QWidget *parent=0,const char *name=0);
12     ~FiveByFive();
13 private:
14     QPushButton *b11;
15     QPushButton *b31;
16     QPushButton *b13;
17     QPushButton *b33;
18 };
19
20 #endif
```

The header file defines the FiveByFive class to be a QWidget and to contain the four buttons to be placed on the grid.

FiveByFive

```
 1 /* fivebyfive.cpp */
 2 #include <qlayout.h>
 3 #include "fivebyfive.h"
 4
 5 FiveByFive::FiveByFive(QWidget *parent,const char *name)
 6     : QWidget(parent,name)
 7 {
 8     QGridLayout *layout = new QGridLayout(this,5,5);
```

```
 9
10        b11 = new QPushButton("(1,1)",this);
11        b11->setMaximumSize(100,100);
12        layout->addWidget(b11,1,1);
13        b13 = new QPushButton("(1,3)",this);
14        b13->setMaximumSize(100,100);
15        layout->addWidget(b13,1,3);
16        b31 = new QPushButton("(3,1)",this);
17        b31->setMaximumSize(100,100);
18        layout >addWidget(b31,3,1);
19        b33 = new QPushButton("(3,3)",this);
20        b33->setMaximumSize(100,100);
21        layout->addWidget(b33,3,3);
22
23        for(int i=0; i<5; i++) {
24            layout->addRowSpacing(i,60);
25            layout->addColSpacing(i,60);
26        }
27        resize(10,10);
28
29        layout->activate();
30 }
31
32 FiveByFive::~FiveByFive() { }
```

The file `qlayout.h` is included on line 2. This same header file is also used to define `QVBoxLayout` and `QHBoxLayout`, described later in this chapter.

On line 8, the `QGridLayout` object created is five cells wide and five cells high. The cell in the upper-left corner is numbered (0,0), the one to its right is (0,1), the next one over is (0,2), and so on. To position a widget in a grid so that it is one position over from the left and one down from the top, it is inserted into grid cell (1,1).

Lines 10 and 11 create a button and set both its minimum height and width to 100 pixels. This will allow the button to expand to fill its assigned cell, as long as the cell is less than 100 by 100 pixels. Normally, a button cannot be stretched because of its internal maximum settings.

Lines 10, 11, and 12 create a button with the label "(1,1)" and place it on the grid square at location (1,1). The call to `setMaximumSize()` on line 11 allows the button to expand to fill its containing cell. The `sizeHint()` method is valid for many, but not all, widgets. In this case, it is correctly assumed that the `QPushButton` widget returns a valid size hint, so no validity test is made before it is used. A more generalized form of the code would look like this:

```
QSize *qsize = b11.sizeHint();
if(qsize.isValid())
    b11.setMinimumSize(qsize);
else
    b11.setMinimumSize(30,30);
```

This way, if the widget being tested does not return a valid size setting, something reasonable will be used. The default setting is pretty good, but it is almost never exactly what you want.

> **Note**   As you write your own widgets, you may find it useful to implement sizeHint().
> It is defined in QWidget as a virtual function and will always return an invalid
> QSize unless you override it.

The loop on lines 27 through 30 calls addRowSpacing() for each of the rows and columns in the grid. This sets the minimum width of each column, and the minimum height of each row, to 60 pixels. No maximum is set, so each row and column can be increased to any size, and if you resize this window, you will notice the buttons being resized also. There is more about this stretching in the next example.

The call to resize() on line 31 is a request to make the entire widget shrink to 10 by 10 pixels. The widget is unable to comply with the request because of the minimum size of the rows and columns. Whenever a widget is instructed to resize itself and the new height or width is outside the bounds of its maximum or minimum, the requested value is ignored and the closest valid value is used — that is, either the maximum or the minimum. In this example, the widget is simply reduced to its minimum size.

Stretched Grid Widget Placement

The following example uses a QGridLayout object to position four buttons, and sets some row and column stretching values that control resizing of the buttons when the parent window is resized.

Main

```
 1 /* main.cpp */
 2 #include <kapp.h>
 3 #include "fourbyfour.h"
 4
 5 int main(int argc,char **argv)
 6 {
 7     KApplication app(argc,argv,"fourbyfour");
 8     FourByFour *fourbyfour = new FourByFour();
 9     fourbyfour->show();
10     app.setMainWidget(fourbyfour);
11     return(app.exec());
12 }
```

The mainline creates an instance of the FourByFour widget and uses it as the widget to be displayed in the KApplication window.

FourByFour Header

```
 1 /* fourbyfour.h */
 2 #ifndef FOURBYFOUR_H
 3 #define FOURBYFOUR_H
 4
 5 #include <qwidget.h>
 6 #include <qpushbutton.h>
 7
 8 class FourByFour: public QWidget
 9 {
10 public:
11     FourByFour(QWidget *parent=0,const char *name=0);
12     ~FourByFour();
13 private:
14     QPushButton *b11;
15     QPushButton *b21;
16     QPushButton *b12;
17     QPushButton *b22;
18 };
19
20
21 #endif
```

The header file defines the FourByFour class to be a QWidget that contains, as private data, the four buttons to be placed in the cells for resizing.

FourByFour

```
 1 /* fourbyfour.cpp */
 2 #include <qlayout.h>
 3 #include "fourbyfour.h"
 4
 5 FourByFour::FourByFour(QWidget *parent,const char *name)
 6     : QWidget(parent,name)
 7 {
 8     QGridLayout *layout = new QGridLayout(this,4,4);
 9     QSize buttonMax(400,400);
10
11     b11 = new QPushButton(this);
12     b11->setText("(1,1)");
13     b11->setMinimumSize(b11->sizeHint());
14     b11->setMaximumSize(buttonMax);
15     layout->addWidget(b11,1,1);
16     b12 = new QPushButton(this);
17     b12->setText("(1,2)");
18     b12->setMinimumSize(b12->sizeHint());
19     b12->setMaximumSize(buttonMax);
20     layout->addWidget(b12,1,2);
21     b21 = new QPushButton(this);
22     b21->setText("(2,1)");
23     b21->setMinimumSize(b21->sizeHint());
24     b21->setMaximumSize(buttonMax);
25     layout->addWidget(b21,2,1);
```

```
26      b22 = new QPushButton(this);
27      b22->setText("(2,2)");
28      b22->setMinimumSize(b22->sizeHint());
29      b22->setMaximumSize(buttonMax);
30      layout->addWidget(b22,2,2);
31
32      layout->addRowSpacing(0,20);
33      layout->addRowSpacing(3,20);
34      layout->addColSpacing(0,20);
35      layout->addColSpacing(3,20);
36      resize(10,10);
37
38      layout->setRowStretch(2,100);
39      layout->setColStretch(2,100);
40
41      layout->activate();
42 }
43
44 FourByFour::~FourByFour() { }
```

A QGridLayout object is created, on line 8, to be four cells wide and four cells high. Lines 11 through 30 create four QPushButton objects and add them to the four center cells of the layout grid. The minimum size of each button is set to a value that will guarantee that the text is always visible. The maximum size of each button is set to an arbitrarily large number to allow the QGridLayout to stretch the buttons as necessary to fill its cells.

The calls to addRowSpacing() and addColSpacing() on lines 32 through 35 set the width of the left and right columns, and the height of the top and bottom rows, to 20 pixels each. The result is a 20-pixel margin between the edge of the application window and the four cells in the center that contain the buttons. The call to resize() on line 36 attempts to reduce the widget to a size smaller than its minimum allowed; therefore, the widget is first displayed at its minimum size. The result is shown in Figure 3-4.

Figure 3-4: The minimum size of the four by four widget

The call to setRowStretch() on line 38 sets the *stretch factor* of the third row (the second row of buttons) to 100. The call to setColStretch() on line 34 sets the stretch factor of the third column (the second column of buttons) to 100. Whenever the size of the window is changed in either the vertical or horizontal direction, the rows and columns with larger stretch factors are changed more than those with smaller stretch factors.

The default stretch value is 0 for each row and column. If all rows (or columns) are set to 0, all rows (or columns) may or may not change size. This default is almost never what you want. When the grid is resized, only those rows and columns with a non-zero value are resized with it. The amount that a row or column is resized is determined by the ratio of its stretch factor to the sum of the stretch factors of all cells being resized.

In this example, enlarging the window causes it to be displayed looking like the one shown in Figure 3-5. The stretch factors of column 1 and row 1 are left at zero, so the button in the upper left corner is left unchanged. On the other hand, column 2 and row 2 both have a non-zero value, so the button in the cell at the lower right changes size in both directions.

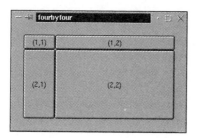

Figure 3-5: Uneven resizing caused by the stretch factor

The amount that a cell actually stretches is determined by the ratio of the stretch factor to the sum of all the stretch factors in the direction being stretched. For example, a change to the stretch factors of FourByFour can cause all the buttons to change size, but some will change more rapidly than others. For example, replace lines 33 and 34 with the following:

```
layout->setRowStretch(1,50);
layout->setRowStretch(2,100);
layout->setColStretch(1,9);
layout->setColStretch(2,1);
```

With these settings, stretching the window vertically will increase the height of row 1 twice as much as row 2. Stretching the window horizontally will cause column 1 to increase nine times as much as column 2. The result of expanding the window is shown in Figure 3-6.

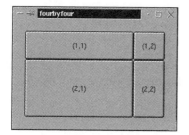

Figure 3-6: Each row and column with its own stretch factor

Widgets in Multiple Grid Cells

While a `QGridLayout` can easily be used to position widgets in a rectangular array — sort of like a checkerboard — it is also possible to have a single widget cover two or more grid squares, allowing for more flexibility. The following example uses this technique to have a label positioned across the top of the window, and a list box cover six cell positions.

Main

```
1 /* main.cpp */
2 #include <kapp.h>
3 #include "multicell.h"
4
5 int main(int argc,char **argv)
6 {
7     KApplication app(argc,argv,"multicell");
8     MultiCell *multicell = new MultiCell();
9     multicell->show();
10    app.setMainWidget(multicell);
11    return(app.exec());
12 }
```

MultiCell Header

```
1 /* multicell.h */
2 #ifndef MULTICELL_H
3 #define MULTICELL_H
4
5 #include <qwidget.h>
6 #include <qpushbutton.h>
7 #include <qlabel.h>
8 #include <qlistbox.h>
9
10 class MultiCell: public QWidget
11 {
12 public:
13     MultiCell(QWidget *parent=0,const char *name=0);
14     ~MultiCell();
15 private:
16     QLabel *label;
17     QListBox *listbox;
18     QPushButton *addButton;
19     QPushButton *deleteButton;
20     QPushButton *cancelButton;
21 };
22
23 #endif
```

Storage for all the different widgets is defined as part of the `MultiCell` class on lines 16 through 20. This means that there must be an include file, on lines 6 through 8, for each one of them.

Note

Although it is quite normal to include pointers for all of the widgets in the class definition, it is not always necessary. Once a widget has been configured for display, there is no need for your program to retain the pointer unless you are going to need it for some special situation. For example, if your program were to change the text of the label or add members to the list box, it would need access to their pointers. Personally, I like to include the widgets in the class as a form of documentation.

MultiCell

```
 1 /* multicell.cpp */
 2 #include <qlayout.h>
 3 #include <stdio.h>
 4 #include "multicell.h"
 5
 6 MultiCell::MultiCell(QWidget *parent,const char *name)
 7      : QWidget(parent,name)
 8 {
 9     QGridLayout *layout = new QGridLayout(this,4,2,20);
10
11     label = new QLabel("A list box with three buttons",
12             this);
13     label->setMinimumSize(label->sizeHint());
14     label->setAlignment(AlignHCenter);
15     layout->addMultiCellWidget(label,0,0,0,1);
16
17     listbox = new QListBox(this);
18     for(int i=0; i<20; i++) {
19         char str[40];
20         sprintf(str,"Selection %d\n",i);
21         listbox->insertItem(str);
22     }
23     listbox->setMinimumWidth(120);
24     layout->addMultiCellWidget(listbox,1,3,0,0);
25
26     addButton = new QPushButton(this);
27     addButton->setText("Add");
28     addButton->setMinimumSize(addButton->sizeHint());
29     layout->addWidget(addButton,1,1);
30
31     deleteButton = new QPushButton(this);
32     deleteButton->setText("Delete");
33     deleteButton->setMinimumSize(deleteButton->sizeHint());
34     layout->addWidget(deleteButton,2,1);
35
36     cancelButton = new QPushButton(this);
37     cancelButton->setText("Cancel");
38     cancelButton->setMinimumSize(cancelButton->sizeHint());
39     layout->addWidget(cancelButton,3,1);
40
41     resize(10,10);
```

```
42      layout->activate();
43 }
44
45 MultiCell::~MultiCell() { }
```

On line 9, the `QGridLayout` is constructed to be 4 cells tall and 2 cells wide. Also, a border value of 20 is used to insert spacing between all cells. The displayed window is shown in Figure 3-7.

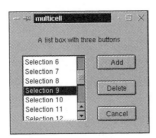

Figure 3-7: Widgets expand to fill multiple grid cells.

Lines 11 through 14 define a label with its text, set its minimum size, and set the alignment so the text will be horizontally centered. On line 15, the label is assigned to two cells of the grid layout with a call to `addMultiCellWidget()`. The first two numbers specify the range of the rows, and the second two numbers specify the range of the columns, like this:

```
startRow,endRow,startCol,endCol
```

Lines 17 through 24 create a list box with 20 entries, and set its minimum width to 120 pixels. The call to `addMultiCellWidget()` on line 24 specifies that the list box is to cover six cells — two cells wide by three cells high.

Lines 26 through 29 create the three buttons on the right, assigning each one to a single cell. The result shown in Figure 3-7 displays the buttons separated by the 20-pixel spacing that as specified for all cells on line 9.

Vertical Box Layout

You can position a group of widgets in a vertical column by inserting them into a `QVBoxLayout` object. The first one inserted will appear at the top of the box, the second one will go underneath it, and each one added after that is positioned at the bottom of the list. The following example inserts five buttons — along with some space and stretch controls — into a vertical box.

Main

```
1 /* main.cpp */
2 #include <kapp.h>
3 #include "verticalbox.h"
4
5 int main(int argc,char **argv)
6 {
7     KApplication app(argc,argv,"verticalbox");
8     VerticalBox *verticalbox = new VerticalBox();
9     verticalbox->show();
10    app.setMainWidget(verticalbox);
11    return(app.exec());
12 }
```

A VerticalBox **object is used as the display widget of the application window.**

VerticalBox Header

```
1 /* verticalbox.h */
2 #ifndef VERTICALBOX_H
3 #define VERTICALBOX_H
4
5 #include <qwidget.h>
6 #include <qlayout.h>
7 #include <qpushbutton.h>
8
9 class VerticalBox: public QWidget
10 {
11 public:
12     VerticalBox(QWidget *parent=0,const char *name=0);
13     ~VerticalBox();
14 private:
15     QPushButton *buttonOne;
16     QPushButton *buttonTwo;
17     QPushButton *buttonThree;
18     QPushButton *buttonFour;
19     QPushButton *buttonFive;
20 };
21
22 #endif
```

VerticalBox

```
1 /* verticalbox.cpp */
2 #include "verticalbox.h"
3
4 VerticalBox::VerticalBox(QWidget *parent,const char *name)
5     : QWidget(parent,name)
6 {
7     QVBoxLayout *layout = new QVBoxLayout(this,5);
```

```
 8        QSize buttonMaximum(400,400);
 9
10        buttonOne = new QPushButton(this);
11        buttonOne->setText("BUTTON ONE");
12        buttonOne->setMinimumSize(buttonOne->sizeHint());
13        buttonOne->setMaximumSize(buttonMaximum);
14        layout->addWidget(buttonOne);
15
16        buttonTwo = new QPushButton(this);
17        buttonTwo->setText("BUTTON TWO");
18        buttonTwo->setMinimumSize(buttonTwo->sizeHint());
19        buttonTwo->setMaximumSize(buttonMaximum);
20        layout->addWidget(buttonTwo,30);
21
22        layout->addSpacing(20);
23
24        buttonThree = new QPushButton(this);
25        buttonThree->setText("BUTTON THREE");
26        buttonThree->setMinimumSize(buttonThree->sizeHint());
27        buttonThree->setMaximumSize(buttonMaximum);
28        layout->addWidget(buttonThree);
29
30        layout->addStretch(30);
31
32        buttonFour = new QPushButton(this);
33        buttonFour->setText("BUTTON FOUR");
34        buttonFour->setMinimumSize(buttonFour->sizeHint());
35        buttonFour->setMaximumSize(buttonMaximum);
36        layout->addWidget(buttonFour);
37
38        layout->addSpacing(5);
39        layout->addStretch(10);
40
41        buttonFive = new QPushButton(this);
42        buttonFive->setText("BUTTON FIVE");
43        buttonFive->setMinimumSize(buttonFive->sizeHint());
44        buttonFive->setMaximumSize(buttonMaximum);
45        layout->addWidget(buttonFive);
46
47        resize(10,10);
48        layout->activate();
49 }
50 VerticalBox::~VerticalBox() { }
```

This class is a widget based on the QVBoxLayout object created on line 7. The second argument on the constructor specifies that a five-pixel border is to be inserted around all the items it contains. If this border is set to zero (the default), the contained items are placed adjacent to one another and flush against the sides.

Lines 10 through 14 create a button, set its text and minimum size, and add it to the layout. Its maximum size is set to an arbitrarily large value to allow the QVBoxLayout object to stretch it to fit. It is the first button added to the layout, so it will appear at the top.

Lines 16 through 20 create the second button and add it to the layout. As shown in Figure 3-8, the distance between the first and second buttons is 10 pixels (a border of 5 on button one plus a border of 5 on button two). The distance between them does not vary even when the layout is stretched. On line 20, a stretch factor of 20 is specified as the button is added to the box, which causes the button itself to participate in stretching as the layout changes size.

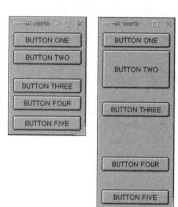

Figure 3-8: A vertical box before and after being stretched vertically

Line 22 inserts a 20-pixel space below button two. Then, on lines 24 through 28, button three is created and added to the layout. This means that there will always be 30 pixels between button two and button three (the two 5-pixel borders plus the 20-pixel space).

Line 30 adds a stretch point with a stretch factor of 30 below button three, and lines 32 through 36 insert button four below that. As shown in Figure 3-8, when the layout is at its minimum size, no space is added by the stretch factor between buttons three and four. However, when the window is stretched vertically, some space appears between the two buttons.

Below button four, line 38 inserts a 5-pixel space and a stretch factor of 10. Then lines 41 through 45 create and insert button five below that. This means that the minimum space between the two buttons is 15 pixels (the two 5-pixel borders plus the 5-pixel space).

Recall that the amount of the stretch is the ratio of the total of all stretch factors to each individual stretch factor. This example specifies stretch factors of 30 (on line 20), 30 (on line 30), and 10 (on line 39). The total of the stretch factors is 70; therefore, as the size of the window is changed, button two will absorb 3/7 of the change, the space between buttons two and three will absorb 3/7, and the space between buttons four and five will absorb 1/7.

Line 47 reduces the initial size of the layout to its minimum. The layout determines its minimum size by summing the minimum size of all the widgets and spaces it contains. Line 48 activates the layout so it will be displayed whenever its parent window is displayed.

Horizontal Box Layout

A horizontal box is the same as a vertical box, except the contained widgets are placed side-by-side from left to right instead of one below the other from top to bottom. The windows shown in Figure 3-9 are generated by a HorizontalBox widget that is identical to the VerticalBox widget in the previous section except for a couple of changes. The constructor of the horizontal box is on line 7.

```
7       QHBoxLayout *layout = new QHBoxLayout(this,5);
```

The names of the buttons were shortened so the window would not be so wide. As you can see by comparing Figure 3-8 to Figure 3-9, the spacing and stretching works the same for both of them.

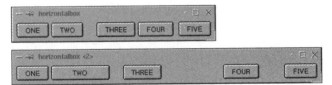

Figure 3-9: A horizontal box before and after being stretched horizontally

Boxes with Alignment

If the widget inserted into a vertical box cannot be resized horizontally, and if the widget is not as wide as the box containing it, you have three choices. The widget can be positioned on the left, on the right, or in the center. The following example produces the window displayed in Figure 3-10 by inserting a wide button at the top of the box and inserting four other fixed-size buttons.

Figure 3-10: A fixed-size widget aligns left, right, or center.

Main

```
 1 /* main.cpp */
 2 #include <kapp.h>
 3 #include "vboxalign.h"
 4
 5 int main(int argc,char **argv)
 6 {
 7     KApplication app(argc,argv,"vboxalign");
 8     VBoxAlign *vboxalign = new VBoxAlign();
 9     vboxalign->show();
10     app.setMainWidget(vboxalign);
11     return(app.exec());
12 }
```

VBoxAlign Header

```
 1 /* vboxalign.h */
 2 #ifndef VBOXALIGN_H
 3 #define VBOXALIGN_H
 4
 5 #include <qwidget.h>
 6 #include <qlayout.h>
 7 #include <qpushbutton.h>
 8
 9 class VBoxAlign: public QWidget
10 {
11 public:
12     VBoxAlign(QWidget *parent=0,const char *name=0);
13     ~VBoxAlign();
14 private:
15     QPushButton *acrossButton;
16     QPushButton *leftButton;
17     QPushButton *centerButton;
18     QPushButton *rightButton;
19     QPushButton *defaultButton;
20 };
21
22 #endif
```

The header file declares the class to contain, as private members, the variable-size button that goes all the way across the box, and the four fixed-size buttons that only go part of the way across.

VBoxAlign

```
 1 /* vboxalign.cpp */
 2 #include "vboxalign.h"
 3
 4 VBoxAlign::VBoxAlign(QWidget *parent,const char *name)
 5     : QWidget(parent,name)
```

```
 6 {
 7     QVBoxLayout *layout = new QVBoxLayout(this);
 8
 9     acrossButton = new QPushButton(this);
10     acrossButton->setText("All the way across");
11     acrossButton->setMinimumSize(acrossButton->sizeHint());
12     layout->addWidget(acrossButton);
13
14     leftButton = new QPushButton(this);
15     leftButton->setText("Left");
16     leftButton->setFixedSize(leftButton->sizeHint());
17     layout->addWidget(leftButton,0,AlignLeft);
18
19     centerButton = new QPushButton(this);
20     centerButton->setText("Center");
21     centerButton->setFixedSize(centerButton->sizeHint());
22     layout->addWidget(centerButton,0,AlignCenter);
23
24     rightButton = new QPushButton(this);
25     rightButton->setText("Right");
26     rightButton->setFixedSize(rightButton->sizeHint());
27     layout->addWidget(rightButton,0,AlignRight);
28
29     defaultButton = new QPushButton(this);
30     defaultButton->setText("Default");
31     defaultButton->setFixedSize(defaultButton->sizeHint());
32     layout->addWidget(defaultButton);
33
34     resize(10,10);
35     layout->activate();
36 }
37 VBoxAlign::~VBoxAlign() { }
```

Lines 9 through 12 create and install a button that has only its minimum size specified. Also, because this button's label is longer than that of the others, its minimum
width will be greater than any other buttons in the box, so this button will determine the minimum width of the box itself.

Lines 14 through 17 create and install the button that is always positioned at the
left side of the box. The call to setFixedSize() on line 16 determines the required
size of the button and sets both the minimum and maximum limits to that size. The
call to addWidget() on line 17 sets the spacing to zero (the default) and specifies
the alignment to be AlignLeft. Another fixed-size button is created on lines 19
through 22 and added to the box with the AlignCenter option. The button created
on lines 24 through 27 is set to AlignRight. The last button, defined on lines 29
through 32, is not given a specific alignment setting, but it turns out that the default
is AlignCenter.

A horizontal box works the same way as a vertical box, but with slightly different alignment mode names. The three names for horizontally aligning widgets in a vertical box are as follows:

```
AlignLeft
AlignCenter
AlignRight
```

Similarly, following are the three names for vertically aligning widgets in a horizontal box:

```
AlignTop
AlignCenter
ALignBottom
```

A Layout Within a Layout

The following example demonstrates how one layout can be contained inside another, producing the window displayed in Figure 3-11. The parent layout is a 2×2 QGridLayout. It contains a QLCDNumber widget in its upper-left corner, and a QSlider widget spanning its two bottom cells. The cell at the upper-right contains a QVBoxLayout, which, in turn, contains a column of four buttons.

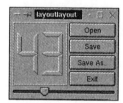

Figure 3-11: A QVBoxLayout inside a QGridLayout

Note   While it is possible to achieve almost any layout by placing all the widgets on a QGridLayout, there are times when it is more convenient to subdivide the layout work this way. Dealing with the widgets in small groups can simplify the task of programming a complicated window.

Main

```
1  /* main.cpp */
2  #include <kapp.h>
3  #include "layoutlayout.h"
4
5  int main(int argc,char **argv)
6  {
7      KApplication app(argc,argv,"layoutlayout");
```

```
 8      LayoutLayout *layoutlayout = new LayoutLayout();
 9      layoutlayout->show();
10      app.setMainWidget(layoutlayout);
11      return(app.exec());
12 }
```

LayoutLayout Header

```
 1 /* layoutlayout.h */
 2 #ifndef LAYOUTLAYOUT_H
 3 #define LAYOUTLAYOUT_H
 4
 5 #include <qwidget.h>
 6 #include <qlayout.h>
 7 #include <qlcdnumber.h>
 8 #include <qpushbutton.h>
 9 #include <qslider.h>
10
11 class LayoutLayout: public QWidget
12 {
13 public:
14     LayoutLayout(QWidget *parent=0,const char *name=0);
15     ~LayoutLayout() { };
16 private:
17     QLCDNumber *lcd;
18     QPushButton *openButton;
19     QPushButton *saveButton;
20     QPushButton *saveasButton;
21     QPushButton *exitButton;
22     QSlider *slider;
23 };
24
25 #endif
```

The class definition includes the six widgets that are to be displayed. They are all members of the LayoutLayout widget class even though they will be placed and sized by different layout managers. Two hierarchies are involved here, but the layout hierarchy is not related to the widget hierarchy. The layout hierarchy does nothing but geographically position and size the widgets; but in order to be of any use, each widget (except the top-level widget used for a main window) must have a parent in the widget tree.

LayoutLayout

```
 1 /* layoutlayout.cpp */
 2 #include "layoutlayout.h"
 3
 4 LayoutLayout::LayoutLayout(QWidget *parent,const char *name)
 5     : QWidget(parent,name)
 6 {
```

```
 7        QGridLayout *layout = new QGridLayout(this,2,2,3);
 8
 9        lcd = new QLCDNumber(this);
10        lcd->setNumDigits(2);
11        lcd->display(43);
12        lcd->setMinimumSize(100,100);
13        layout->addWidget(lcd,0,0);
14
15        QVBoxLayout *vertButtonLayout = new QVBoxLayout(3);
16        layout->addLayout(vertButtonLayout,0,1);
17
18        openButton = new QPushButton("Open",this);
19        openButton->setMinimumSize(openButton->sizeHint());
20        vertButtonLayout->addWidget(openButton);
21
22        saveButton = new QPushButton("Save",this);
23        saveButton->setMinimumSize(saveButton->sizeHint());
24        vertButtonLayout->addWidget(saveButton);
25
26        saveasButton = new QPushButton("Save As..",this);
27        saveasButton->setMinimumSize(saveasButton->sizeHint());
28        vertButtonLayout->addWidget(saveasButton);
29
30        exitButton = new QPushButton("Exit",this);
31        exitButton->setMinimumSize(exitButton->sizeHint());
32        vertButtonLayout->addWidget(exitButton);
33
34        slider = new QSlider(QSlider::Horizontal,this);
35        slider->setMinimumSize(slider->sizeHint());
36        layout->addMultiCellWidget(slider,1,1,0,1);
37
38        resize(10,10);
39        layout->activate();
40 }
```

The main layout grid is created as a 2×2 grid on line 7. The `this` argument specifies that this is to be the main layout object for the `LayoutLayout` object. The grid
layout is also created so it will insert a 3-pixel border around all of its contained
items. Every item to be displayed by this widget must be positioned by this grid
layout. (While it is possible to display child widgets without including them in
a layout, their position in the window will be unpredictable.)

Lines 9 through 13 create a `QLCDNumber` object, to display the 2-digit number 43,
and install it at the upper left corner of the grid.

A vertical layout box is created on line 15. The vertical box has no parent specified
because it is going to be included as a child of the main layout. In fact, the very next
line of code, line 16, calls the method `addLayout()` to insert the vertical box as the
item in the upper right corner of the grid layout. This establishes the layout hierarchy

with the `LayoutLayout` object being the top; the `QGridLayout` created on line 7 at the next level; and the `QVBoxLayout` created on line 15 as the third level. Note that the argument `this` was used to create the grid, thus establishing it as the top-level container. The `this` argument is not used to create the vertical box, so the call must be made to `addLayout()` to establish its hierarchy.

> **Note**   A `QLayout` object must have a parent before it can have child widgets or layouts added to it. The main layout must be the child of the enclosing widget, and all other layouts must be children (or grandchildren) of it.

Lines 18 through 20 create a `QPushButton` and add it to the vertical box. A minimum size is set for the buttons, but there is no maximum, so the button will expand as needed to fill the box. Lines 22 through 32 create and add three more buttons to the box. This results in the column of buttons shown earlier in the upper right corner of Figure 3-11.

Lines 34 through 36 create a `QSlider` and attach it to the grid layout so it covers the two bottoms cells. Like the buttons, it is assigned a minimum size, but is allowed to expand to fill the cells of the grid layout.

The call to `resize()` on line 38 guarantees that the initial size of the produced widget is at its minimum. The minimum size is determined by the `LayoutLayout` widget asking the `QGridLayout` for its minimum size. The `QGridLayout` asks the `QLCDNumber`, the `QSlider`, and the `QVBoxLayout` for their minimum sizes and then sums the result — taking into account the border spacing — to find its own minimum size. The `QVBoxLayout` determines its minimum size by requesting the minimum size of each of the buttons, and then uses the largest horizontal value and the sum of the vertical values for its minimum width and height.

A Layout That Is Also a Widget

The `KContainerLayout` widget can be used to position and size other widgets. It is something like a combination of the `QVBoxLayout` and the `QHBoxLayout`, but it also has some special properties. The following example demonstrates using the `KContainerLayout` widget to size and position a group of buttons as shown in Figure 3-12.

Figure 3-12: A KContainerLayout organizing widgets vertically

Main

```
 1 /* main.cpp */
 2 #include <kapp.h>
 3 #include "container.h"
 4
 5 int main(int argc,char **argv)
 6 {
 7     KApplication app(argc,argv,"container");
 8     Container *container = new Container();
 9     container->show();
10     app.setMainWidget(container);
11     return(app.exec());
12 }
```

Container Header

```
 1 /* container.h */
 2 #ifndef CONTAINER_H
 3 #define CONTAINER_H
 4
 5 #include <qwidget.h>
 6 #include <kcontainer.h>
 7 #include <qpushbutton.h>
 8
 9 class Container: public QWidget
10 {
11 public:
12     Container(QWidget *parent=0,const char *name=0);
13     ~Container();
14 private:
15     QPushButton *sbOne;
16     QPushButton *sbTwo;
17     QPushButton *sbThree;
18     QPushButton *ebOne;
19     QPushButton *ebTwo;
20     QPushButton *ebThree;
21 };
22
23 #endif
```

Lines 15 through 20 declare pointers to the six buttons to be displayed.

Container

```
 1 /* container.cpp */
 2 #include "container.h"
 3
 4 Container::Container(QWidget *parent,const char *name)
 5     : QWidget(parent,name)
 6 {
```

```
 7      KContainerLayout *layout = new KContainerLayout(this);
 8      layout->setOrientation(KContainerLayout::Vertical);
 9
10      sbOne = new QPushButton(this);
11      sbOne->setText("startONE");
12      sbOne->setMinimumSize(sbOne->sizeHint());
13      layout->packStart(sbOne);
14
15      sbTwo = new QPushButton(this);
16      sbTwo->setText("startTWO");
17      sbTwo->setMinimumSize(sbTwo->sizeHint());
18      layout->packStart(sbTwo);
19
20      sbThree = new QPushButton(this);
21      sbThree->setText("startTHREE");
22      sbThree->setMinimumSize(sbThree->sizeHint());
23      layout->packStart(sbThree);
24
25      ebOne = new QPushButton(this);
26      ebOne->setText("endONE");
27      ebOne->setMinimumSize(ebOne->sizeHint());
28      layout->packEnd(ebOne);
29
30      ebTwo = new QPushButton(this);
31      ebTwo->setText("endTWO");
32      ebTwo->setMinimumSize(ebTwo->sizeHint());
33      layout->packEnd(ebTwo);
34
35      ebThree = new QPushButton(this);
36      ebThree->setText("endTHREE");
37      ebThree->setMinimumSize(ebThree->sizeHint());
38      layout->packEnd(ebThree);
39
40      resize(10,10);
41  }
42  Container::~Container() { }
```

On line 7, the KContainerLayout widget is created, with the Container object as its parent widget. On line 8, the orientation is specified as vertical, which means that all widgets added to the layout will be positioned one above the other, as they appeared in Figure 3-12.

The first button is created on lines 10 through 12. The button is added to the layout by the call to packStart() on line 13. Because this button was added first, and because it was added by packStart(), it will always appear at the very top. A second button is created on lines 20 through 22, and is also added to the layout using packStart(), so it will take the position directly beneath the first button. A third button is created and added to the layout on lines 20 through 23, and again packStart() is used to add the button, so it will always appear immediately beneath the first two.

Packing widgets from the end has the same effect as packing them from the start, except each widget is placed in the next available location starting at the bottom. The first button added to the bottom is the one created on lines 25 through 27, and added by the call to `packEnd()` on line 28. The button created and added on lines 30 through 33 takes the position directly on top of the other button packed from the bottom, and the one on lines 35 through 38 takes up a position directly above the other two at the bottom.

Note   The actions taken when a `KContainerLayout` widget is resized depends on how the widgets were added. Those added at the start will remain against the start edge (top or left), and those added at the end will stay against the end edge (bottom or right).

To orient the packed layout horizontally, either remove the statement on line 8 (because horizontal is the default), or replace it with the following:

```
layout->setOrientation(KContainerLayout::Horizontal);
```

When the layout orientation is horizontal, the `packStart()` method inserts widgets on the left and the `packEnd()` method inserts them on the right. The result is shown in Figure 3-13.

Figure 3-13: A KContainerLayout organizing widgets horizontally

ISa Instead of HASa

All of the previous examples in this chapter were widgets that internally created a layout manager of some sort. However, because `KContainerLayout` is also a widget, it can be extended instead of simply used. That is, the widget no longer *has* a layout object, it *is* a layout object. The following is an example of creating a widget that is capable of containing other widgets.

Main

```
1 /* main.cpp */
2 #include <kapp.h>
3 #include "iscontainer.h"
4
5 int main(int argc,char **argv)
6 {
7     KApplication app(argc,argv,"iscontainer");
8     IsContainer *iscontainer = new IsContainer();
```

```
 9      iscontainer->show();
10      app.setMainWidget(iscontainer);
11      return(app.exec());
12 }
```

This widget is treated just as any other widget would be. It is created on line 8 and set as the main-window widget on line 10. It doesn't matter whether it *has* a layout component or *is* a layout component, as long as it is a widget.

IsContainer Header

```
 1 /* iscontainer.h */
 2 #ifndef ISCONTAINER_H
 3 #define ISCONTAINER_H
 4
 5 #include <qwidget.h>
 6 #include <kcontainer.h>
 7 #include <qpushbutton.h>
 8
 9 class IsContainer: public KContainerLayout
10 {
11 public:
12     IsContainer(QWidget *parent=0,const char *name=0);
13     ~IsContainer();
14 private:
15     QPushButton *One;
16     QPushButton *Two;
17     QPushButton *Three;
18 };
19
20 #endif
```

The main difference between this class definition and the ones in the previous examples is that, on line 8, IsContainer inherits from KContainerLayout instead of inheriting directly from QWidget. The IsContainer class is still a widget because KContainerLayout inherits from QWidget.

IsContainer

```
 1 /* iscontainer.cpp */
 2 #include "iscontainer.h"
 3
 4 IsContainer::IsContainer(QWidget *parent,const char *name)
 5     : KContainerLayout(parent,name)
 6 {
 7     setOrientation(KContainerLayout::Vertical);
 8
 9     One = new QPushButton(this);
10     One->setText("BUTTON ONE");
11     One->setMinimumSize(One->sizeHint());
12     packStart(One);
```

```
13
14        Two = new QPushButton(this);
15        Two->setText("BUTTON TWO");
16        Two->setMinimumSize(Two->sizeHint());
17        packStart(Two);
18
19        Three = new QPushButton(this);
20        Three->setText("BUTTON THREE");
21        Three->setMinimumSize(Three->sizeHint());
22        packStart(Three);
23
24        resize(10,10);
25 }
26 IsContainer::~IsContainer() { }
```

The super classes (including the QWidget class) are initialized by the code on line 5. Line 7 sets the orientation to vertical. Lines 9 through 22 create and add three buttons to the container by calling packStart(). The resulting display is shown in Figure 3-14.

Figure 3-14: A widget container layout with three child widgets

Widgets Inside Widgets (Horizontal)

Because KContainerLayout is a widget, and has the ability to contain other widgets, it can contain other KContainerLayout widgets. The following example is a collection of horizontal KContainerLayout widgets contained inside a vertical KContainerLayout widget. This example also displays the effect of using different combinations of options when creating the container and adding child widgets to it.

Main

```
1 /* main.cpp */
2 #include <kapp.h>
3 #include "horizlayout.h"
4
5 int main(int argc,char **argv)
6 {
7      KApplication app(argc,argv,"horizlayout");
8      HorizLayout *horizlayout = new HorizLayout();
9      horizlayout->show();
10     app.setMainWidget(horizlayout);
11     return(app.exec());
12 }
```

HorizLayout Header

```
1  /* horizlayout.h */
2  #ifndef HORIZLAYOUT_H
3  #define HORIZLAYOUT_H
4
5  #include <qwidget.h>
6  #include <kcontainer.h>
7  #include <qpushbutton.h>
8
9  class HorizLayout: public QWidget
10 {
11 public:
12     HorizLayout(QWidget *parent=0,const char *name=0);
13     ~HorizLayout();
14 private:
15     void add(KContainerLayout *layout,int count,
16             bool homogeneous,bool expand,bool fill);
17 };
18
19 #endif
```

HorizLayout

```
1  /* horizlayout.cpp */
2  #include "horizlayout.h"
3  #include <qlabel.h>
4
5  HorizLayout::HorizLayout(QWidget *parent,const char *name)
6      : QWidget(parent,name)
7  {
8      KContainerLayout *layout = new KContainerLayout(this,
9          NULL,
10         KContainerLayout::Vertical,
11         FALSE,
12         5,
13         0,
14         TRUE);
15
16     int count = 1;
17     add(layout,count++,FALSE,TRUE,TRUE);
18     add(layout,count++,TRUE,TRUE,TRUE);
19     add(layout,count++,FALSE,FALSE,TRUE);
20     add(layout,count++,TRUE,FALSE,TRUE);
21     add(layout,count++,FALSE,TRUE,FALSE);
22     add(layout,count++,TRUE,TRUE,FALSE);
23     add(layout,count++,FALSE,FALSE,FALSE);
24     add(layout,count++,TRUE,FALSE,FALSE);
25
26     layout->sizeToFit();
27 }
```

```
28 void HorizLayout::add(KContainerLayout *outer,int count,
29        bool homogeneous,bool expand,bool fill)
30 {
31     QPushButton *button;
32
33     QString str(tr("%1. ").arg(count));
34     if(homogeneous)
35         str.append("Homogeneous");
36     else
37         str.append("Non-homogeneous");
38     if(expand)
39         str.append(", expand");
40     else
41         str.append(", no-expand");
42     if(fill)
43         str.append(", fill");
44     else
45         str.append(", no-fill");
46
47     QLabel *label  = new QLabel(str,outer);
48     label->setMinimumSize(label->sizeHint());
49     outer->packStart(label);
50
51     KContainerLayout *inner = new KContainerLayout(outer,
52         NULL,
53         KContainerLayout::Horizontal,
54         homogeneous,
55         5,
56         0,
57         TRUE);
58
59     button = new QPushButton(inner);
60     button->setText("ONE");
61     button->setMinimumSize(button->sizeHint());
62     inner->packStart(button,expand,fill);
63
64     button = new QPushButton(inner);
65     button->setText("BUTTON TWO");
66     button->setMinimumSize(button->sizeHint());
67     inner->packStart(button,expand,fill);
68
69     button = new QPushButton(inner);
70     button->setText("THREE");
71     button->setMinimumSize(button->sizeHint());
72     inner->packStart(button,expand,fill);
73
74     inner->sizeToFit();
75     outer->packStart(inner);
76 }
77 HorizLayout::~HorizLayout() { }
```

The vertically oriented KContainerLayout that acts as the container for the top-level window is created on line 8. Each of the calls to add(), on lines 17 through 24, adds a new label and a horizontal KContainerLayout widget to the top-level KContainerLayout. To set positioning for the widgets within the horizontal container, there are three basic mode toggles, so the add() method is called once for each of the eight possible combinations. The first argument to add() is the address of the container widget, the second is a number to be assigned to the displayed data, and the other three arguments are the mode switch settings that will control widget placement. The result is shown in Figure 3-15.

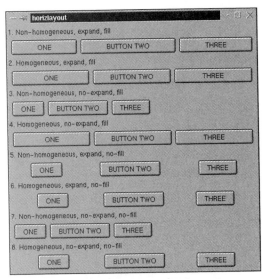

Figure 3-15: The eight KContainerLayout horizontal configuration settings

The method add(), starting on line 28, creates a descriptive label and a horizontal KContainerLayout widget, and then adds them to the KContainerLayout widget passed in as the first argument. The method begins by creating a QString that describes the option settings. The string construction begins on line 33 with the conversion of the number into a string. Lines 34 through 45 test each of the three Boolean settings and append text accordingly. The string is used to construct a QLabel on line 47; and on line 49, the label is packed into the top of the KContainer Layout of the main window.

The horizontal container is created on lines 51 through 57. Note that the KContainerLayout that is going to contain it is named as the parent widget on line 51. It is not assigned a name, but is set to horizontal orientation on line 53. Whether or not the sizing and placement is to be homogeneous is set on line 54 according to the argument passed in to this method. Lines 59 through 72 create three buttons and add them to the horizontal `KContainerLayout` widget. The other two configuration settings, expand and fill, are used on the calls to `packStart()`, which adds the buttons to the container.

Each of the buttons is created with its container as its parent, but still must be packed into the container to be displayed. For example, the first button is created on line 59 using the inner `KContainerLayout` widget as its parent. This is necessary because messages propagate up and down the widget hierarchy, and there must be communications between the button and its container. Then, on line 67, the button is packed into the start of the container, thus being assigned its specific position within the container. With these two relationships, the container can read size information from the button, calculate the exact size and position the button is to fill, and write any necessary information back to the button.

The three settings — homogeneous, expand, and fill — all deal with the size and position of the widgets in a container, and they all have slightly different meanings. In Figure 3-15, you could see the effects of each. Table 3-1 briefly describes the effects of each setting.

Table 3-1	
The Widget Positional Options in a KContainerLayout	
Option	**Description**
homogeneous	If TRUE, all the widgets in the container will be assigned the same amount of space. This assignment is made regardless of the actual size of the widget. If FALSE, each widget will determine its own space requirements, and the widgets could possibly be different sizes. Whether TRUE or FALSE, expansion and contraction of the window will expand and contract the widgets according to their allocated space.
expand	If TRUE, the widget should make use of the entire space allocated to it by the container.
fill	If expand is TRUE, setting fill to TRUE will instruct the widget to size itself to fill the entire space allocated to it by the container.

Widgets Inside Widgets (Vertical)

This example is the same as the previous one, except for the orientation. This program organizes button widgets in columns. The top-level widget is a horizontally oriented `KContainerLayout` widget that has been filled with a collection of vertically oriented `KContainerLayout` widgets.

Each column in this example is configured the same way as its corresponding row in the previous example. As shown in Figure 3-16, each vertical KContainerLayout is numbered. You can use these numbers to compare the appearance of the vertical layout shown in Figure 3-16 to its horizontal counterpart, shown in Figure 3-15.

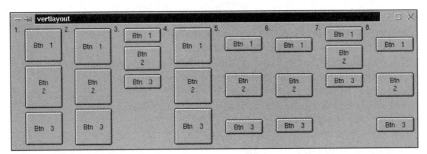

Figure 3-16: The eight KContainerLayout vertical configuration settings

Main

```
1 /* main.cpp */
2 #include <kapp.h>
3 #include "vertlayout.h"
4
5 int main(int argc,char **argv)
6 {
7     KApplication app(argc,argv,"vertlayout");
8     VertLayout *vertlayout = new VertLayout();
9     vertlayout->show();
10     app.setMainWidget(vertlayout);
11     return(app.exec());
12 }
```

VertLayout Header

```
1 /* vertlayout.h */
2 #ifndef VERTLAYOUT_H
3 #define VERTLAYOUT_H
4
5 #include <qwidget.h>
6 #include <kcontainer.h>
7 #include <qpushbutton.h>
8
9 class VertLayout: public QWidget
10 {
11 public:
12     VertLayout(QWidget *parent=0,const char *name=0);
13     ~VertLayout();
14 private:
```

```
15        void add(KContainerLayout *layout,int count,
16             bool homogeneous,bool expand,bool fill);
17 };
18
19 #endif
```

VertLayout

```
 1 /* vertlayout.cpp */
 2 #include "vertlayout.h"
 3 #include <qlabel.h>
 4
 5 VertLayout::VertLayout(QWidget *parent,const char *name)
 6     : QWidget(parent,name)
 7 {
 8     KContainerLayout *layout = new KContainerLayout(this,
 9         NULL,
10         KContainerLayout::Horizontal,
11         FALSE,
12         3,
13         0,
14         TRUE);
15
16     int count = 1;
17     add(layout,count++,FALSE,TRUE,TRUE);
18     add(layout,count++,TRUE,TRUE,TRUE);
19     add(layout,count++,FALSE,FALSE,TRUE);
20     add(layout,count++,TRUE,FALSE,TRUE);
21     add(layout,count++,FALSE,TRUE,FALSE);
22     add(layout,count++,TRUE,TRUE,FALSE);
23     add(layout,count++,FALSE,FALSE,FALSE);
24     add(layout,count++,TRUE,FALSE,FALSE);
25
26     layout->sizeToFit();
27 }
28 void VertLayout::add(KContainerLayout *outer,int count,
29         bool homogeneous,bool expand,bool fill)
30 {
31     QPushButton *button;
32
33     KContainerLayout *inner = new KContainerLayout(outer,
34         NULL,
35         KContainerLayout::Vertical,
36         homogeneous,
37         5,
38         0,
39         TRUE);
40
41     QString str(tr("%1. ").arg(count));
42     QLabel *label  = new QLabel(str,outer);
43     label->setMinimumSize(label->sizeHint());
```

```
44      label->setMaximumSize(label->sizeHint());
45      outer->packStart(label,FALSE,FALSE);
46
47      button = new QPushButton(inner);
48      button->setText("Btn   1");
49      button->setMinimumSize(button->sizeHint());
50      inner->packStart(button,expand,fill);
51
52      button = new QPushButton(inner);
53      button->setText("Btn\n2");
54      button->setMinimumSize(button->sizeHint());
55      inner->packStart(button,expand,fill);
56
57      button = new QPushButton(inner);
58      button->setText("Btn   3");
59      button->setMinimumSize(button->sizeHint());
60      inner->packStart(button,expand,fill);
61
62      inner->sizeToFit();
63      outer->packStart(inner,TRUE);
64 }
65 VertLayout::~VertLayout() { }
```

The VertLayout class is very much like the HorizLayout class shown in the previous example. The only real difference is the orientation. In this example, the top-level window is a horizontal KContainerLayout object filled with labels and vertical KContainerLayout objects. The descriptive labels were reduced to numbers to save space.

The KContainerLayout widget used as the top-level widget is created, with horizontal orientation, on line 8. Lines 16 through 24 repeatedly call the add() method to create the set of labeled vertical KContainerLayout widgets and add them to the top-level KContainerLayout widget.

The add() method starting on line 28 creates a label and a vertically oriented KContainerLayout widget and adds them (label first) to the KContainerLayout widget passed in as the first argument. The second button, created on lines 52 through 55, contains a newline character in its text so the text will be displayed as two lines — this makes the second button larger than the others to demonstrate how the shifting and sizing works with non-uniform widgets.

Summary

There is a variety of ways in which widgets can be configured for size and position. Some of these will automatically resize widgets, while some will not. Similarly, some techniques allow you to overlap widgets, while others do not. You should be familiar with all the options so you can apply the one that fits best with your application.

✦ Specific x and y coordinates, along with height and width, can be used to hard-code the position and size of a widget.

✦ An imaginary grid can be installed as the main window, and widgets can be hung on it like pictures on a wall.

✦ A widget can be instructed to change its size and shape to fit its place in a window. These changes are limited by the maximum and minimum size settings of the widget.

✦ Horizontal and vertical boxes display linear rows and columns of widgets. Spacing and positioning controls can be specified between each pair of widgets.

✦ Horizontal and vertical layouts display linear rows and columns of widgets. Moreover, because a layout is itself a widget, it can be contained in another layout, box, or grid; or even placed by specific x and y coordinates.

This chapter covered the creation of top-level windows. The next chapter describes the construction of pop-up windows. Every tool and technique that positions widgets for top-level windows can also be used for positioning widgets in a pop-up window. The basic difference is that a dialog (also called a popup) is a temporary window used to display information to the user, and to return some kind of response.

✦   ✦   ✦

Displaying a Pop-Up Dialog

A dialog is a window, usually temporary, that displays some specific piece of information to the user, requests some specific information from the user, or both. Many dialogs are very simple and only require a yes or no answer, but it is not uncommon for a dialog to be quite complicated and contain several pages of widgets that display and accept information.

A dialog is parented to a window in your application, but it always appears on the display as a standalone window. It looks very much the same as a top-level window except that some of the window controls and menus are missing.

There are a number of ways your program can create a dialog because there are a number of extendable dialog base classes. Furthermore, the base classes themselves can be used to create relatively simple dialogs. This chapter describes and contains examples of the various ways to create a dialog from the base classes, each of which has its own set of advantages.

A Simple Dialog

The `QDialog` widget is a base class that you can use to create dialogs, but it can also be used directly to handle the layout of simple widgets. `QDialog` is a simple widget that doesn't display anything other than its blank window, but it can be used as a container for your widgets and it has the capability to display itself in a standalone window. There are also some built-in facilities to respond to buttons that you may decide to add to the window.

The following example demonstrates the basics of creating and displaying a dialog. It shows how a QDialog object is capable of being displayed as a dialog. Figure 4-1 shows the top-level window on the left. It contains a single button that is used to pop up the dialog shown on the right. The dialog has a button that can be used to close the dialog.

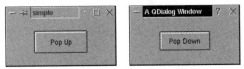

Figure 4-1: A top-level window and the dialog it pops up

Main

```
1 /* simple.cpp */
2 #include <kapp.h>
3 #include "toplevel.h"
4
5 int main(int argc,char **argv)
6 {
7     KApplication app(argc,argv,"simple");
8     TopLevel toplevel;
9     toplevel.show();
10    app.setMainWidget(&toplevel);
11    return(app.exec());
12 }
```

The mainline of the program creates a KApplication object and then creates and installs a TopLevel widget as its top-level window.

TopLevel Header

```
1 /* toplevel.h */
2 #ifndef TOPLEVEL_H
3 #define TOPLEVEL_H
4
5 #include <qwidget.h>
6
7 class TopLevel: public QWidget
8 {
9     Q_OBJECT
10 public:
11     TopLevel(QWidget *parent=0,const char *name=0);
12 private slots:
13     void popupDialog();
14 };
15
16 #endif
```

The `TopLevel` window is a widget, because it inherits from `QWidget`, and it is designed for use as the top-level window of the program. The class definition only contains a constructor and the minimum amount of information required in order for there to be a response to a button. The `Q_OBJECT` macro on line 12 must be present in order for there to be a slot, as declared on lines 12 and 13. The slot method `popupDialog()` will be called whenever the button is clicked.

 Note   The concept of signals and slots was introduced in Chapter 2, and is covered in detail later in this chapter.

TopLevel

```
 1 /* toplevel.cpp */
 2 #include "toplevel.h"
 3 #include <qdialog.h>
 4 #include <qpushbutton.h>
 5
 6 TopLevel::TopLevel(QWidget *parent,const char *name)
 7          : QWidget(parent,name)
 8 {
 9     setMinimumSize(200,80);
10     setMaximumSize(200,80);
11
12     QPushButton *button = new QPushButton("Pop Up",this);
13     button->setGeometry(50,20,100,40);
14     connect(button,SIGNAL(clicked()),
15             this,SLOT(popupDialog()));
16 }
17 void TopLevel::popupDialog()
18 {
19     QDialog *dialog = new QDialog(0,"popup",FALSE);
20     dialog->setCaption("A QDialog Window");
21     dialog->setMinimumSize(200,80);
22     dialog->setMaximumSize(200,80);
23
24     QPushButton *button =
25             new QPushButton("Pop Down",dialog);
26     button->setGeometry(50,20,100,40);
27     connect(button,SIGNAL(clicked()),
28             dialog,SLOT(accept()));
29
30     dialog->show();
31 }
```

This code contains the definition of the `TopLevel` widget, including the method that creates and displays the dialog.

The `TopLevel` widget is the main window of the program. In its constructor, on lines 9 and 10, the size of the window is set so it cannot be changed—the maximum and minimum size limits are set to the same values. On line 12, a button is created. The geometry settings on line 13 specify the height and width of the button, and the position of its upper-left corner. The call to connect() on line 14 requests that signals originating from the clicked() signal in the button be passed to the popup Dialog() slot in the TopLevel widget.

The method popupDialog() on line 17 will be called every time the user clicks on the button in the TopLevel window. Lines 19 through 22 instantiate a QDialog widget and specify its size and caption. The button it is to hold is created and sized on lines 24 through 26. The call to connect() on line 27 requests that signals originating from clicked() in this button be passed to the accept() method inside the QDialog widget. Because the QDialog widget is capable of appearing in its own window, the call to show() on line 30 causes it to appear.

The QDialog widget is flexible enough that you could use it almost exclusively to create all of your dialogs. You can close the dialog with the slot method accept(), as in this example, and you can also call reject() to close it. The only difference between the two methods is that one of them sets the result to TRUE and the other sets it to FALSE. These settings correspond to the Cancel and OK buttons that commonly appear on dialogs.

When the dialog is closed with a call to either accept() or reject(), the dialog is not destroyed. Its window is closed by a call to the hide() method. This has the advantage that your program can read the setting, but you will have to get rid of the dialog yourself. If, however, you are going to be using the same dialog over and over, you can create it once and then hide() and show() it as you desire.

This simple example has two problems. First, you can pop up as many of the dialogs you want. Every time you click the Pop Up button, a new dialog is spawned and left to run on its own. Second, when you close the dialog with the Pop Down button, it is not deleted. It is closed with the call to accept(), but it still exists and the program has no pointer to it.

Note   There is a KDialog widget that is nearly identical to the QDialog widget, except that it adds some methods to set the window caption and alter the sizes and margins. Anywhere you can use a QDialog you can use a KDialog.

Using Signals and Slots

This example uses QDialog as a base class to construct a dialog that accepts a string of characters; and, if the OK or Apply button is selected, a string is sent to the program's main window, which installs it as the new caption for the title bar. The window on the left in Figure 4-2 shows the main window and its single button. On the right is the dialog that is popped up to accept a new caption string.

Figure 4-2: A button and the dialog it pops up

Mainline

```
1 /* responder.cpp */
2 #include <kapp.h>
3 #include "mainwidget.h"
4
5 int main(int argc,char **argv)
6 {
7     KApplication app(argc,argv,"responder");
8     MainWidget mainwidget;
9     mainwidget.show();
10    app.setMainWidget(&mainwidget);
11    return(app.exec());
12 }
```

The mainline of the program is quite simple. On lines 8 and 9 a `MainWidget` object is created, and line 10 installs it as the main window.

MainWidget Header

```
1 /* mainwidget.h */
2 #ifndef MAINWIDGET_H
3 #define MAINWIDGET_H
4
5 #include <qwidget.h>
6 #include <qstring.h>
7
8 class MainWidget: public QWidget
9 {
10    Q_OBJECT
11 public:
12    MainWidget(QWidget *parent=0,const char *name=0);
13 private slots:
14    void popupEnterName();
15    void changeCaption(QString &);
16 };
17
18 #endif
```

This is the header file of the widget that is to act as the main window for this example. Other than the constructor, defined on line 12, this class only contains a pair of slots. The slot named `popupEnterName()` causes the dialog to pop up, and the slot named `changeCaption()` will change the text of the caption of this widget (which is the caption of the main window).

Because there are slots in this class, it is necessary to use the `Q_OBJECT` macro as the first member of the class. The definitions in `Q_OBJECT` allow this header file to compile normally as standard C++ code, and it inserts some special information used by the Meta Object Compiler (MOC) to generate the code necessary to handle slots and signals.

MainWidget

```
1 /* mainwidget.cpp */
2 #include "mainwidget.h"
3 #include "entername.h"
4 #include <qpushbutton.h>
5
6 MainWidget::MainWidget(QWidget *parent,const char *name)
7            : QWidget(parent,name)
8 {
9     setMinimumSize(200,80);
10    setMaximumSize(200,80);
11
12    QPushButton *button =
13            new QPushButton("Update Name",this);
14    button->setGeometry(50,20,100,40);
15    connect(button,SIGNAL(clicked()),
16            this,SLOT(popupEnterName()));
17 }
18 void MainWidget::popupEnterName()
19 {
20    EnterName *dialog = new EnterName(0,"entername");
21    connect(dialog,SIGNAL(captionString(QString &)),
22            this,SLOT(changeCaption(QString &)));
23    dialog->exec();
24    delete dialog;
25 }
26 void MainWidget::changeCaption(QString &caption)
27 {
28    setCaption(caption);
29 }
```

This class is used as the main window of the application. It appears in Figure 4-2, shown at the beginning of this section, as the window on the left.

This class is a widget because it inherits from `QWidget` on line 7. Lines 9 and 10 set the maximum and minimum sizes to the same values, making this a fixed-size widget.

The `QPushButton` is created on lines 12 and 13, and it is positioned at the center of the window on line 14. The button has a signal named `clicked()` that is emitted whenever the button is clicked by the mouse. The call to connect() on line 15 specifies that whenever the clicked() signal is emitted, the local slot method popupEnterName() will be called.

Note Using a method as a slot does not prevent it from being called directly. In this example, the method popupEnterName() is being called by a signal, but it could just as easily be called from inside another method of this class, or even from some other class. A slot is a normal method with the added feature that it can be used to catch signals.

The method popupEnterName() on line 18 creates an EnterName dialog to prompt the user for a new caption. The call to connect() on line 21 establishes a connection so that the captionString() signal in the dialog will make a call to the changeCaption() local slot.

The call to exec() on line 23 pops up the dialog and in such a way that the dialog has exclusive access to the input queue. This method does not return until after the user has responded by selecting either the OK or Cancel button. Until the user responds, no other window owned by this application will receive mouse or keyboard signals. On line 23, after the selection has been made, the dialog is deleted.

The slot method on line 26 is called only when the user selects the OK button on the dialog, so the new caption string is set for the main window.

EnterName Header

```
 1 /* entername.h */
 2 #ifndef ENTERNAME_H
 3 #define ENTERNAME_H
 4
 5 #include <qdialog.h>
 6 #include <qlineedit.h>
 7 #include <qpushbutton.h>
 8
 9 class EnterName: public QDialog
10 {
11     Q_OBJECT
12 private:
13     QLineEdit *lineedit;
14     QPushButton *okButton;
15     QPushButton *applyButton;
16     QPushButton *cancelButton;
17 public:
18     EnterName(QWidget *parent=0,const char *name=0);
19 private slots:
20     void okButtonSlot();
21     void applyButtonSlot();
22     void cancelButtonSlot();
```

```
23 signals:
24     void captionString(QString &);
25 };
26
27 #endif
```

This header file defines the class of the pop-up dialog used to prompt for a new caption string. It has slots to receive button clicks, and a signal that is sent with the new caption text.

This class is the definition of a dialog because, on line 9, it uses QDialog as a super class. Any class that contains either a slot or a signal must include the Q_OBJECT macro as its first member. Lines 13 through 16 declare storage space for the four widgets to be used to construct the members of the dialog.

Lines 19 through 22 specify the names of the slots. The okButtonSlot(), applyButtonSlot(), and cancelButtonSlot() methods are local slots to receive button clicks. The signal captionString() on line 24 is the signal that will be emitted whenever the user issues a new caption string.

EnterName

```
1 /* entername.cpp */
2 #include "entername.h"
3 #include <qdialog.h>
4 #include <qlayout.h>
5
6 EnterName::EnterName(QWidget *parent,const char *name)
7          : QDialog(parent,name,TRUE)
8 {
9     QString caption("Enter Name");
10    setCaption(caption);
11
12    QVBoxLayout *vLayout = new QVBoxLayout(this,10);
13
14    lineedit = new QLineEdit(this);
15    vLayout->addWidget(lineedit);
16
17    QHBoxLayout *hLayout = new QHBoxLayout(vLayout,10);
18
19    okButton = new QPushButton("OK",this);
20    connect(okButton,SIGNAL(clicked()),
21            this,SLOT(okButtonSlot()));
22    hLayout->addWidget(okButton);
23
24    applyButton = new QPushButton("Apply",this);
25    connect(applyButton,SIGNAL(clicked()),
26            this,SLOT(applyButtonSlot()));
27    hLayout->addWidget(applyButton);
```

```
28
29     cancelButton = new QPushButton("Cancel",this);
30     connect(cancelButton,SIGNAL(clicked()),
31             this,SLOT(cancelButtonSlot()));
32     hLayout->addWidget(cancelButton);
33 }
34 void EnterName::okButtonSlot()
35 {
36     QString str = lineedit->text();
37     emit captionString(str);
38     accept();
39 }
40 void EnterName::applyButtonSlot()
41 {
42     QString str = lineedit->text();
43     emit captionString(str);
44 }
45 void EnterName::cancelButtonSlot()
46 {
47     reject();
48 }
```

This class is a dialog that enables the user to enter text and, by selecting an appropriate button, have that text installed as the caption of the main window:

The arguments to the EnterName constructor on line 6 are passed on to the QDialog super class on line 7. The third argument to QDialog is TRUE, specifying that this is to be a modal dialog.

The vertical box created on line 12 is used as the main container for the window. The QLineEdit object created on line 14 is inserted into the top of the vertical box. A horizontal box is created as a child of the vertical box, which causes the horizontal box to become the next member of the vertical box (just below the QLineEdit widget). Inserting the three buttons into the horizontal box (on lines 22, 27, and 32) completes the layout previously shown on the right in Figure 4-2.

The calls to the connect() methods on lines 20, 25, and 30 associate the clicked() signals of the buttons to their respective slots.

The slot method okButtonSlot() on line 34 is called whenever the OK button is clicked. The call to the text() method of the QLineEdit object retrieves the string that was entered by the user. Line 37 emits the signal named captionString(). The signal is emitted with nearly the same syntax you would use to call a method, but with the keyword *emit* in front to signify that it is not a method call—it is a signal being sent. The slot method concludes by calling accept() on line 38. This call sets an internal flag to TRUE, indicating that there was a positive response from the user, and then calls hide() to make the widget invisible.

Whenever the Apply button is clicked, the `applyButtonSlot()` method on line 40 is called. Just as is done with the OK button slot, the string is retrieved and emitted to using the signal method `captionString()`. The `accept()` method is not called because the dialog is to remain visible.

Whenever the Cancel button is clicked, the `cancelButtonSlot()` method on line 45 is called. The user has cancelled the action of changing the caption name, so no signal is sent. A call is made to `reject()` to set the internal flag to `FALSE` and to close the dialog's window.

Makefile

```
 1 INCL= -I$(QTDIR)/include -I$(KDEDIR)/include
 2 CFLAGS= -O2 -fno-strength-reduce
 3 LFLAGS= -L$(QTDIR)/lib -L$(KDEDIR)/lib -L/usr/X11R6/lib
 4 LIBS= -lkdecore -lkdeui -lqt -lX11 -lXext -ldl
 5 CC=g++
 6
 7 recaption: recaption.o mainwidget.o moc_mainwidget.o \
 8         entername.o moc_entername.o
 9    $(CC) $(LFLAGS) -o recaption recaption.o \
10         mainwidget.o moc_mainwidget.o \
11         entername.o moc_entername.o $(LIBS)
12
13 recaption.o: recaption.cpp mainwidget.h
14 mainwidget.o: mainwidget.cpp mainwidget.h
15 moc_mainwidget.cpp: mainwidget.h
16    $(QTDIR)/bin/moc mainwidget.h -o moc_mainwidget.cpp
17 entername.o: entername.cpp entername.h
18 moc_entername.cpp: entername.h
19    $(QTDIR)/bin/moc entername.h -o moc_entername.cpp
20
21 clean:
22    rm -f recaption
23    rm -f *.o
24    rm -f moc_*
25
26 .SUFFIXES: .cpp
27
28 .cpp.o:
29    $(CC) -c $(CFLAGS) $(INCL) -o $@ $<
```

As this code illustrates, special entries need to be included in the makefile when either slots or signals are included in the source. The code is not only compiled directly, it is also translated by the MOC compiler into a separate source file that needs to be compiled.

Line 7 has the list of dependencies for linking `recaption`. Not only are there the `.o` files with names matching those of the `.cpp` files, there are some other `.o` files that begin with the four characters moc_. Any class that includes Q_OBJECT as its first member — any class that has slots and/or signals — must have its header file processed by the MOC compiler. The dependency on line 15 specifies that the source file moc_mainwidget.cpp is dependent on the source file mainwidget.h. The command on line 16 uses mainwidget.h as input to create moc_mainwidget.cpp. Then moc_mainwidget.cpp is compiled into moc_mainwidget.o and included in the link on line 9.

A Signals and Slots Checklist

The creation of signals and slots is really quite simple. Most of the work is automated in the form of macros and the MOC compiler. The process of emitting a signal is completely separate from that of the slots that receive the signals. An object can issue any number of signals without knowing how many, if any, slots are receiving them. The following steps include everything that needs to be done in order to create a signal and send it to the slots:

1. Add the Q_OBJECT macro as the first line of the class definition. While the other items in the class require a semicolon terminator, the Q_OBJECT macro does not, but you can include one if you prefer (because the compiler simply throws semicolons away). For example, the definition of a class named Receiver would start this way:

```
class Sender {
    Q_OBJECT
        . . .
```

Any number of slots and signals can be defined in an object, but the Q_OBJECT macro only needs to appear once.

2. Add the prototype of the signal to the class definition. For example, if the signal is to send a string object as an argument, the prototype would look like this:

```
        . . .
signals:
    void newName(QString &name);
        . . .
```

There is no public or private specification because there will not be an actual method — this is only a definition of the prototype that will be used to call the receiving slot.

3. Use an emit statement to call all of the slot methods listening for a signal. This is done with the same syntax you would use for calling a local method, except the call follows an emit keyword:

```
    QString name;
    emit newName(name);
```

Note that there is no actual definition of the body of the signal method. The emit command does not look for a local method; instead, it calls every slot method in the list of those that have been connected to this signal.

The following steps are necessary to create a slot and connect it to a signal:

1. The same as for a signal, a slot requires that the Q_OBJECT macro appear at the top of the class definition:

```
class Receiver {
    Q_OBJECT
    . . .
```

2. Add the prototypes of the slot methods to the class definitions. The prototype must be the same (that is, have the same set of arguments) as the signal it is to receive. Because slots are methods, and can be called directly as well as being used as a slot, the slot method can be made publicly available:

```
    . . .
public slots:
    void nameChange(QString &name);
    . . .
```

The more usual case of the slot being used only for the purpose of receiving signals allows you to declare it as private:

```
    . . .
private slots:
    void nameChange(QString &name);
    . . .
```

3. Include the header file that defines the class that will be emitting the signal.

4. Write the code that will create an instance of the class that is to emit the signal. It must exist in order for you to attach the slot to the signal.

5. Connect the slot to the signal. This is often done in the constructor, but it can be done later if the object is to be constructed later. A call to the connect() method will add your slot to the list of methods that will be called whenever a specific signal is emitted. A call to connect() looks like this:

```
connect(sender,SIGNAL(newName(QString &),
    this,SLOT(nameChange(QString &)));
```

The first two arguments specify the source of the signal, and the second two specify the destination slot. The macros SIGNAL() and SLOT() both require a complete method prototype, and the prototypes must be such that the set of arguments used to call one of the methods is the same as can be used for the other.

Whenever an emit statement is used to send a signal, it is exactly as if your program called each one of the slot methods directly. That is, your program cannot continue until the slot method returns. Therefore, you should normally keep the processing inside the slot method as simple as possible so that it will not cause the signal emitter to pause. The emitter of the signal could be a user-interface process and result in the appearance of slow or sluggish operation.

You must be very careful not to create a circular situation. If a slot method emits a signal that, directly or indirectly, executes a method that emits a signal received by the original slot, the signals will continuously call the slots and your program will crash. For example, if the method named first() emits signal A, signal A is received by slot second(), the slot second() emits signal B, and the slot named first() receives signal B, a circular situation exists and the loop will continue until the program crashes (or the user gets tired of waiting).

You also need to be aware that if your slot and signal methods on a connect statement don't have matching arguments, you will not get an error message until an attempt is made to resolve the references when the program is running. To avoid this, make certain that you test every addition or change that you make to the slots and signals. The only error message is a string written to the console (standard out) when the connect() method fails to find a pairing—after that, the program silently ignores the signals. And you can only see the console output when running the application from the command line.

KDialogBase

The widget KDialogBase is sort of a dialog kit. Most dialogs take the same basic form: a collection of data-entry widgets with a row of buttons across the bottom. With that in mind, the KDialogBase widget was designed with a built-in row of buttons. The following example program displays the default configuration of a KDialogBase, as shown in Figure 4-3.

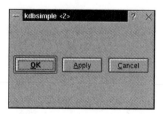

Figure 4-3: The default buttons of a KDialogBase window

Mainline

```
1 /* kdbsimple.cpp */
2 #include <kapp.h>
3 #include "mainwidget.h"
```

```
 4
 5 int main(int argc,char **argv)
 6 {
 7     KApplication app(argc,argv,"kdbsimple");
 8     MainWidget mainwidget;
 9     mainwidget.show();
10     app.setMainWidget(&mainwidget);
11     return(app.exec());
12 }
```

The `mainwidget` created on line 8 is assigned the task of being the main window for the application on line 10.

MainWidget Header

```
 1 /* mainwidget.h */
 2 #ifndef MAINWIDGET_H
 3 #define MAINWIDGET_H
 4
 5 #include <qwidget.h>
 6
 7 class MainWidget: public QWidget
 8 {
 9     Q_OBJECT
10 public:
11     MainWidget(QWidget *parent=0,const char *name=0);
12 private slots:
13     void  popupKdb();
14 };
15
16 #endif
```

The main window only has two methods. One is the constructor and the other is the slot that will be connected to the pushbutton. The purpose of `popupKdb()` is to display the `KDialogBase` window.

MainWidget

```
 1 /* mainwidget.cpp */
 2 #include "mainwidget.h"
 3 #include <qpushbutton.h>
 4 #include <kdialogbase.h>
 5
 6 MainWidget::MainWidget(QWidget *parent,const char *name)
 7           : QWidget(parent,name)
 8 {
 9     setMinimumSize(200,80);
10     setMaximumSize(200,80);
11
12     QPushButton *button =
```

```
13              new QPushButton("Popup",this);
14      button->setGeometry(50,20,100,40);
15      connect(button,SIGNAL(clicked()),
16              this,SLOT(popupKdb()));
17 }
18
19 void MainWidget::popupKdb()
20 {
21      KDialogBase *dialog = new KDialogBase(this,
22              "kdbwidget",TRUE);
23      dialog->exec();
24      delete dialog;
25 }
```

This widget is used as the main window of the example. It contains only a "Popup" button and the slot that will execute whenever the button is clicked.

Whenever the button is clicked, the KDialogBase widget is constructed (on line 21). A call to exec() on line 23 causes the dialog to appear as shown previously in Figure 4-3. When the window first appears, the OK button is selected, so simply pressing the Return or Enter key is the same as clicking OK. Also, as you can see from the figure, each of the buttons has a designated accelerator character — for example, typing Alt-C is the same as selecting the Cancel button.

Unless you connect a slot to the Apply button, it does nothing. The Cancel and OK buttons both close the dialog. To use the buttons as intended, it is simply a matter of connecting the OK and Apply buttons to the slot that will accept and process the data from the dialog.

KDialogBase Buttons

The previous example showed that the three default buttons are OK, Apply, and Cancel. There are, however, some other buttons included, and you can add up to three buttons of your own. The following example will display the window shown in Figure 4-4, showing all eight buttons.

Figure 4-4: The button order of the KDialogBase class

The header file and the mainline of the program are identical to those in the previous example. The only difference between the programs is the set of arguments passed to the constructor of KDialogBase.

MainWidget

```
 1  /* mainwidget.cpp */
 2  #include "mainwidget.h"
 3  #include <qpushbutton.h>
 4  #include <kdialogbase.h>
 5
 6  MainWidget::MainWidget(QWidget *parent,const char *name)
 7          : QWidget(parent,name)
 8  {
 9      setMinimumSize(200,80);
10      setMaximumSize(200,80);
11
12      QPushButton *button =
13              new QPushButton("Popup",this);
14      button->setGeometry(50,20,100,40);
15      connect(button,SIGNAL(clicked()),
16              this,SLOT(popupKdb()));
17  }
18
19  void MainWidget::popupKdb()
20  {
21      QString caption("All Buttons");
22      QString button1("User1");
23      QString button2("User2");
24      QString button3("User3");
25
26      int buttons = KDialogBase::Ok
27                  | KDialogBase::Apply
28                  | KDialogBase::Cancel
29                  | KDialogBase::Help
30                  | KDialogBase::Default
31                  | KDialogBase::User1
32                  | KDialogBase::User2
33                  | KDialogBase::User3;
34
35      KDialogBase *dialog = new KDialogBase(
36          this,     // parent
37          "kdbwidget", // name
38          TRUE, // modal
39          caption, // caption
40          buttons, // buttonmask
41          KDialogBase::Cancel, // default button
42          FALSE,    // separator
43          button1, // button caption
44          button2, // button caption
```

```
45          button3); // button caption
46      dialog->exec();
47      delete dialog;
48 }
```

This widget is used as the main window of the application. It contains a button that, when clicked, displays the KDialogBase window.

The slot method popupKdb() is executed whenever the main window button (the one created on line 12) is clicked. The KDialogBase widget is created by the constructor on line 35. As is indicated by the previous example, all of the arguments have default values defined for them, but this example specifies a value for each of them. The named values are described in Table 4-1.

Table 4-1
Parameters Accepted by the Constructor of KDialogBase

Parameter	Description
parent	The parent widget. This is normally the widget that causes the KDialogBase to pop up. The default is NULL.
name	The internal name of the widget. Used for internal purposes and for generating error messages. The default is NULL.
modal	If set to TRUE, this widget displays as modal. If set to FALSE, nonmodal. The default is TRUE.
caption	The text of the caption in the title bar at the top of the window. The default is the name of the application.
button mask	A set of one-bit flags specifying which buttons are to be activated for this dialog. The default is the three-button set Ok, Apply, and Cancel.
default button	The button that is to be selected (and thus responsive to the Return or Enter key) when the dialog first appears. The default is the Ok button.
separator	If TRUE, there is a separator line drawn above the buttons. If FALSE, there is no separator line. The default is FALSE.
button caption	This is the text that will appear on the face of the user-defined button. The default is NULL, which causes the user button to be blank.

The order of the buttons, as shown previously in Figure 4-4, is determined internally by the KDialogBase widget. You can determine which buttons are to be included, but the order of their appearance will always be in the order shown.

Table 4-2 lists all the buttons that are available in the `KDialogBase` widget. Receiving the information from any of these buttons is simply a matter of connecting your slot method to the appropriate `KDialogBase` signal method. The buttons that cause the dialog to close also set a status code indicating the result. To retrieve the result code, insert a line between lines 46 and 47 of the preceding example, as shown here:

```
dialog->exec();
int resultCode = dialog->result();
delete dialog;
```

Table 4-2
Buttons and Signals of KDialogBase

Button	Signal	Notes
Apply	`applyClicked()`	If both the Apply button and the Try button are specified, the Try button will not appear.
Cancel	`closeClicked()`	This button can be used in place of the Close button.
Close	`closeClicked()`	If both Close and Cancel are specified, only Close will appear. The result code is set to FALSE and the dialog is closed.
Default	`defaultClicked()`	
Help	`helpClicked()`	This button also calls the method `invokeHTML Help()` to display the help text defined by the call to `setHelp()`.
No	`noClicked()`	This button appears in place of the User1 button when the dialog is in message-box mode. The result code is set to FALSE and the dialog is closed.
OK	`okClicked()`	The result code is set to TRUE and the dialog is closed.
Try	`tryClicked()`	This button can be used in place of the Apply button.
User1	`user1Clicked()`	An argument on the constructor specifies the label. This button is replaced by the No button in message-box mode.
User2	`user2Clicked()`	An argument on the constructor specifies the label. This button is replaced by the Yes button in message-box mode.
User3	`user3Clicked()`	
Yes	None	This button appears in the place of the User2 button when the dialog is in message-box mode. The result code is set to TRUE and the dialog is closed.

Using KDialogBase to Build a Dialog

The following example program uses `KDialogBase` as the base class of a dialog that enables the user to specify a line of text and two integer values. In this example, the information entered into the dialog is used to change the text displayed by a label and to resize the main window. Figure 4-5 shows the main window (on the left) after it has been reconfigured by the values shown in the dialog (on the right).

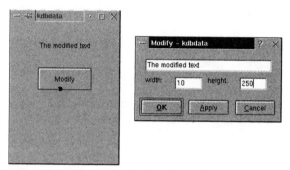

Figure 4-5: The main window is modified from a dialog.

Mainline

```
 1 /* kdbdata.cpp */
 2 #include <kapp.h>
 3 #include <kcmdlineargs.h>
 4 #include "mainwidget.h"
 5
 6 int main(int argc,char **argv)
 7 {
 8     KCmdLineArgs::init(argc,argv,"kdbdata",
 9         "KDialogBase demo","0.0");
10     KApplication app;
11     MainWidget mainwidget;
12     mainwidget.show();
13     app.setMainWidget(&mainwidget);
14     return(app.exec());
15 }
```

The mainline of the program creates a `MainWidget` on line 11 and sets it as the main window of the application on line 13.

The `KApplication` object is created on line 10 without arguments. This can be done because the static `init()` method of the `KCmdLineArgs` class is called on line 8. The `KCmdLineArgs` class stores command-line arguments, along with other information, and makes it available to other parts of your application.

Cross-Reference Chapter 15 provides more detail about the capabilities of KCmdLineArgs.

MainWidget Header

```
1 /* mainwidget.h */
2 #ifndef MAINWIDGET_H
3 #define MAINWIDGET_H
4
5 #include <qwidget.h>
6 #include <qpushbutton.h>
7 #include <qlabel.h>
8
9 class MainWidget: public QWidget
10 {
11     Q_OBJECT
12 public:
13     MainWidget(QWidget *parent=0,const char *name=0);
14 private:
15     QLabel *label;
16     QPushButton *button;
17 private slots:
18     void popupKdb();
19     void slotSettings(QString &,int,int);
20 };
21
22 #endif
```

This widget is the main window of the program. It contains only one button and one label. The slot named popupKdb() is used to pop up the dialog. The slot slotSettings() receives the values returned by the dialog.

MainWidget

```
1 /* mainwidget.cpp */
2 #include "mainwidget.h"
3 #include "modify.h"
4 #include <qpushbutton.h>
5 #include <kdialogbase.h>
6
7 MainWidget::MainWidget(QWidget *parent,const char *name)
8         : QWidget(parent,name)
9 {
10     setMinimumSize(200,140);
11
12     QString str("Modify Me");
13     label = new QLabel(str,this);
14     label->setAlignment(Qt::AlignCenter);
15     label->setGeometry(50,20,100,40);
16
```

```
17        button = new QPushButton("Modify",this);
18        button->setGeometry(50,80,100,40);
19        connect(button,SIGNAL(clicked()),
20                  this,SLOT(popupKdb()));
21        resize(10,10);
22 }
23 void MainWidget::popupKdb()
24 {
25        Modify *modify = new Modify(this,"modify");
26        connect(
27            modify,SIGNAL(signalSettings(QString &,int,int)),
28            this,SLOT(slotSettings(QString &,int,int)));
29        modify->exec();
30        delete modify;
31 }
32 void MainWidget::slotSettings(QString &str,
33            int height,int width)
34 {
35        resize(width,height);
36        label->setText(str);
37 }
```

This widget is used as the main window of the program. It contains only a label and a button. The button is used to pop up a dialog.

Lines 18 through 20 create a button, place it in the window, and attach its clicked() signal to the local slot popupKbd(). The popupKbd() slot, beginning on line 23, creates a Modify dialog and connects its signal, named signalSettings(), to the local slot named slotSettings(). A call is made to exec(), which displays the dialog and waits until it is closed.

The slot name slotSettings() beginning on line 32 accepts three values as arguments, and uses these values to specify the size of the main window, and the text that is to be displayed in the label of the main window. The call to resize() on line 35 cannot reduce the size below that specified as the minimum on line 10, but it can adjust either dimension to a larger size.

Modify Header

```
 1 /* modify.h */
 2 #ifndef MODIFY_H
 3 #define MODIFY_H
 4
 5 #include <kdialogbase.h>
 6 #include <qlineedit.h>
 7 #include <qpushbutton.h>
 8
 9 class Modify: public KDialogBase
10 {
```

```
11      Q_OBJECT
12 public:
13      Modify(QWidget *parent=0,const char *name=0);
14 private:
15      QLineEdit *lineedit;
16      QLineEdit *width;
17      QLineEdit *height;
18 private slots:
19      void slotSendValues();
20 signals:
21      void signalSettings(QString &,int,int);
22 };
23
24 #endif
```

This is the header file for the dialog. It inherits directly from the `KDialogBase` class, and defines its own slot and signal.

This design declares the slot named `slotSendValues()` to receive responses from the buttons on the dialog. Whenever `slotSendValues()` executes, it will send the signal named `signalSettings()` with the new text and dimensions.

The dialog itself inherits directly from `KdialogBase`, so most of the work has already been done. It is only necessary to add the prompts, the data-entry widgets, and a signal to be transmitted whenever the user specifies a new set of values, as is done in the following code.

Modify

```
 1 /* modify.cpp */
 2 #include "modify.h"
 3 #include <qlayout.h>
 4 #include <qlabel.h>
 5
 6 Modify::Modify(QWidget *parent,const char *name)
 7          : KDialogBase(parent,name,TRUE,"Modify")
 8 {
 9      QWidget *mainWidget = new QWidget(this,"modifymain");
10
11      QVBoxLayout *vLayout = new QVBoxLayout(mainWidget,10);
12
13      lineedit = new QLineEdit(mainWidget);
14      vLayout->addWidget(lineedit);
15
16      QHBoxLayout *hLayout = new QHBoxLayout();
17      vLayout->addLayout(hLayout);
18
19      QLabel *wLabel = new QLabel("width:",this);
20      wLabel->setAlignment(Qt::AlignCenter);
21      hLayout->addWidget(wLabel);
22      width = new QLineEdit(mainWidget);
```

```
23      width->setMaximumWidth(50);
24      hLayout->addWidget(width);
25      QLabel *hLabel = new QLabel("height:",this);
26      hLabel->setAlignment(Qt::AlignCenter);
27      hLayout->addWidget(hLabel);
28      height = new QLineEdit(mainWidget);
29      height->setMaximumWidth(50);
30      hLayout->addWidget(height);
31
32      connect(this,SIGNAL(okClicked(void)),
33          this,SLOT(slotSendValues(void)));
34      connect(this,SIGNAL(applyClicked(void)),
35          this,SLOT(slotSendValues(void)));
36
37      setMainWidget(mainWidget);
38 }
39 void Modify::slotSendValues()
40 {
41      QString text = lineedit->text();
42      int w = (width->text()).toInt();
43      int h = (height->text()).toInt();
44      emit signalSettings(text,h,w);
45 }
```

The constructor, beginning on line 6, passes its arguments through to the base class. Two arguments are added to the call on the base class to specify a modal dialog and assign a caption to the window.

An empty widget is created on line 9. This widget is filled by the vertical box layout created on line 11. A QLineEdit widget is inserted into the top of the vertical box on lines 13 and 14. A horizontal box is created on line 16 and is used to position the widgets that go into the second box of the vertical widget. This horizontal box is filled with QLabel and QLineEdit widgets on lines 20 through 30. On line 37 the filled widget is added to the dialog as its main window.

The button selection is allowed to default, so the buttons appearing on the dialog are the OK, Cancel, and Apply buttons included in the dialog. Whenever the Cancel button is selected the dialog will close. In this example, there is no action to be taken in response to the Cancel button; its signal is ignored. The two connect() method calls on lines 32 and 34 will cause the slot named slotSendValues() to be executed. The connections are from this and back to this because slots and the signals are all in the same object — the signals are inherited and the slot is defined locally.

The slot method beginning on line 39 gathers the information that was entered by the user and uses the data to emit a signal. The text retrieved from the lineedit is to be used to modify the caption of a label, so it can stay in the same form. The width and height QLineEdit objects also return QString objects, but these are converted to int values with the call to toInt().

An Alternate Approach To KDialogBase Data

The following example program is a modification of the previous one. Sometimes it is more convenient to have your program retrieve values from a dialog instead of hooking them together with slots and signals. This technique applies only to situations in which you never need to retrieve data from the dialog until after it closes.

In the previous example, the Apply button causes data to be supplied to the application without the window closing. This example removes the Apply button, creating the window shown in Figure 4-6, and eliminates all the slots and signals (except the one in the mainline that pops up the dialog).

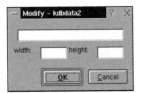

Figure 4-6: Data can be entered without the use of slots.

Because the Apply button cannot be used, it is necessary to remove it. To do this, change lines 6 and 7 of modify.cpp to the following:

```
Modify::Modify(QWidget *parent,const char*name)
     : KDialogBase(parent,name,TRUE,"Modify,Ok | Cancel)
```

The next step is to remove lines 23 through 37 of mainwidget.cpp and replace them with the following method:

```
void MainWidget::popupKdb()
{
    Modify *modify = new Modify(this,"modify");
    modify->exec();
    if(modify->result() == TRUE) {
        QString text = modify->getText();
        int height = modify->getHeight();
        int width = modify->getWidth();
        resize(width,height);
        label->setText(text);
    }
    delete modify;
}
```

When the dialog is closed, the exec() method returns. If the OK button was used to close it, the return value from result() is TRUE; otherwise, it is FALSE. If the result is TRUE, the user-entered data is extracted from the widgets and used on calls to resize() and setText() to modify the display. Because the exec() method does not return until the dialog closes, there is no way, other than a slot, to determine the selecting of a button that does not close the window—that's why the Apply button is not present.

To be able to retrieve the values, the following methods are added to the Modify class:

```
QString Modify::getText()
{
    return(lineedit->text());
}
int Modify::getWidth()
{
    return((width->text()).toInt());
}
int Modify::getHeight()
{
    return((height->text()).toInt());
}
```

Note There are many ways to get information back from a dialog. The method you use depends on your application. For example, you can pass the address of a struct to the dialog and have it fill in the data. Or you can use a combination of slots, signals, and directly reading the values. You can even have a dialog write its output to a configuration file that will be used by your program later.

KMesageBox Derives From KDialogBase

A very common type of dialog is one that displays a line or two of text, and the user responds to the dialog with a simple yes or no answer, or simply presses the button that closes the dialog. The KDialogBase class has a constructor that is specially suited to write message box dialogs, and the KMessageBox class uses this special constructor to implement a group of commonly used message box dialogs.

These message boxes are all modal, which requires the user to respond before moving on. Moreover, each one is popped up with a simple function call that blocks (does not return to the caller) until the user responds and closes the message box. This simplifies programming because it is simply a matter of inserting a call to a static function at any point in your code.

The following example demonstrates one of each of the nine message boxes. The main window, shown in Figure 4-7, has a button for each of the nine dialogs. At the bottom of the window is a label whose text is updated whenever there is a response from the dialog. The figure shows that the last selection was a Yes button.

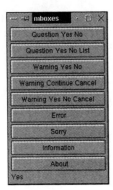

Figure 4-7: Select a button to display a message box.

Mainline

```
1 /* main.cpp */
2 #include <kapp.h>
3 #include <kcmdlineargs.h>
4 #include "mboxes.h"
5
6 int main(int argc,char **argv)
7 {
8     KCmdLineArgs::init(argc,argv,"mboxes",
9         "Message Boxes","0.0");
10    KApplication app;
11    Mboxes mboxes;
12    mboxes.show();
13    app.setMainWidget(&mboxes);
14    return(app.exec());
15 }
```

The mainline creates an Mboxes object and installs it as the main window of the application.

Mboxes Header

```
1 /* mboxes.h */
2 #ifndef MBOXES_H
3 #define MBOXES_H
4
5 #include <qwidget.h>
6 #include <qlabel.h>
7
8 class Mboxes: public QWidget
9 {
10    Q_OBJECT
11 public:
12    Mboxes(QWidget *parent=0,const char *name=0);
```

```
13 private:
14     QLabel *label;
15 private slots:
16     void button1();
17     void button2();
18     void button3();
19     void button4();
20     void button5();
21     void button6();
22     void button7();
23     void button8();
24     void button9();
25 };
26
27 #endif
```

The definition of the class includes one slot for each of the nine buttons, and it includes the label that will be placed at the bottom of the display.

Mboxes

```
 1 /* mboxes.cpp */
 2 #include "mboxes.h"
 3 #include <qpushbutton.h>
 4 #include <kmessagebox.h>
 5 #include <qlayout.h>
 6
 7 Mboxes::Mboxes(QWidget *parent,const char *name)
 8         : QWidget(parent,name)
 9 {
10     QPushButton *button;
11     QVBoxLayout *layout = new QVBoxLayout(this,3);
12
13     button = new QPushButton("Question Yes No",this);
14     layout->addWidget(button);
15     connect(button,SIGNAL(clicked()),this,SLOT(button1()));
16
17     button = new QPushButton("Question Yes No List",this);
18     layout->addWidget(button);
19     connect(button,SIGNAL(clicked()),this,SLOT(button2()));
20
21     button = new QPushButton("Warning Yes No",this);
22     layout->addWidget(button);
23     connect(button,SIGNAL(clicked()),this,SLOT(button3()));
24
25     button =
26         new QPushButton("Warning Continue Cancel",this);
27     layout->addWidget(button);
28     connect(button,SIGNAL(clicked()),this,SLOT(button4()));
29
```

```
30      button = new QPushButton("Warning Yes No Cancel",this);
31      layout->addWidget(button);
32      connect(button,SIGNAL(clicked()),this,SLOT(button5()));
33
34      button = new QPushButton("Error",this);
35      layout->addWidget(button);
36      connect(button,SIGNAL(clicked()),this,SLOT(button6()));
37
38      button = new QPushButton("Sorry",this);
39      layout->addWidget(button);
40      connect(button,SIGNAL(clicked()),this,SLOT(button7()));
41
42      button = new QPushButton("Information",this);
43      layout->addWidget(button);
44      connect(button,SIGNAL(clicked()),this,SLOT(button8()));
45
46      button = new QPushButton("About",this);
47      layout->addWidget(button);
48      connect(button,SIGNAL(clicked()),this,SLOT(button9()));
49
50      label = new QLabel("-",this);
51      layout->addWidget(label);
52      resize(10,10);
53 }
54 void Mboxes::button1()
55 {
56      int result = KMessageBox::questionYesNo(this,
57          "Are you sure you want to delete\nall "
58          "the files in this directory?",
59          "questionYesNo");
60      switch(result) {
61      case KMessageBox::Yes:
62          label->setText(QString("Yes"));
63          break;
64      case KMessageBox::No:
65          label->setText(QString("No"));
66          break;
67      }
68 }
69 void Mboxes::button2()
70 {
71      QStringList list;
72      list.append("fork");
73      list.append("spoon");
74      list.append("knife");
75      int result = KMessageBox::questionYesNoList(this,
76          "Are you sure you want to delete\nall "
77          "the items shown in the list?",
78          list,
79          "questionYesNoList");
80      switch(result) {
```

```
 81       case KMessageBox::Yes:
 82           label->setText(QString("Yes"));
 83           break;
 84       case KMessageBox::No:
 85           label->setText(QString("No"));
 86           break;
 87       }
 88 }
 89 void Mboxes::button3()
 90 {
 91     int result = KMessageBox::warningYesNo(this,
 92         "Reset all status codes?",
 93         "warningYesNo");
 94     switch(result) {
 95     case KMessageBox::Yes:
 96         label->setText(QString("Yes"));
 97         break;
 98     case KMessageBox::No:
 99         label->setText(QString("No"));
100         break;
101     }
102 }
103 void Mboxes::button4()
104 {
105     int result = KMessageBox::warningContinueCancel(this,
106         "Overwrite the existing file?",
107         "warningContinueCancel",
108         QString("Overwrite"));
109     switch(result) {
110     case KMessageBox::Continue:
111         label->setText(QString("Continue"));
112         break;
113     case KMessageBox::Cancel:
114         label->setText(QString("Cancel"));
115         break;
116     }
117 }
118 void Mboxes::button5()
119 {
120     int result = KMessageBox::warningYesNoCancel(this,
121         "Quitting without saving the file could result\n"
122         "in loss of data. Save before quitting?",
123         "warningYesNoCancel");
124     switch(result) {
125     case KMessageBox::Yes:
126         label->setText(QString("Yes"));
127         break;
128     case KMessageBox::No:
129         label->setText(QString("No"));
130         break;
131     case KMessageBox::Cancel:
```

```
132            label->setText(QString("Cancel"));
133            break;
134      }
135  }
136  void Mboxes::button6()
137  {
138      KMessageBox::error(this,
139          "Unable to save configuration data.");
140  }
141  void Mboxes::button7()
142  {
143      KMessageBox::sorry(this,
144          "The file you specified contains no data.");
145  }
146  void Mboxes::button8()
147  {
148      KMessageBox::information(this,
149          "Pressing Esc will clear the window.");
150  }
151  void Mboxes::button9()
152  {
153      KMessageBox::about(this,
154          "This is a simple about-box that can\n"
155          "contain several lines of text");
156  }
```

The widget used as the main window creates nine buttons and a label and packs them all into a vertical box. Each button has its clicked() signal connected to a local slot that will create and display one of the message boxes.

A vertical box is created on line 11. Lines 13 through 51 create the nine buttons and the label that make up the main window.

Lines 13 through 15 create a button and connect it to the slot button1() on line 54. The call to the method questionYesNo() on line 56 pops up the message box shown in Figure 4-8 and waits for the user to respond. The string parameter on line 59 is the caption of the message box window. The value returned from the function is determined by which button is selected. All of the return values from all of the message boxes are defined in the KMessageBox class.

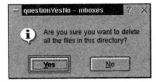

Figure 4-8: A Yes/No question message box

Note   The return values from the message boxes are *not* Boolean. They cannot be used in an expression that tests for TRUE or FALSE.

The switch statement on line 61 determines whether the return value from question YesNo() is Yes or No. The label at the bottom of the main window is updated with a string that represents the result.

For all message boxes, the size and shape of the display is under your control because you determine the length of the lines of text, and the number of lines displayed. The text for the questionYesNo() message box is declared on lines 57 and 58. The text is defined as a single string with '\n' characters inserted wherever the line is to be broken. Fortunately, the C++ concatenates strings on separate lines into one large string, so the text can be more easily written in the code.

Lines 17 through 19 create a button and connect it to the slot button2() beginning on line 69. This message box, created on line 75 and displayed in Figure 4-9, asks a yes or no question as in the previous example, and also contains a window displaying a list of items. Use this message box when you need to ask a question that involves a group of items. There is no way the user can add or delete items — it is a blanket approval or rejection of the entire list.

Figure 4-9: A Yes/No list question message box

The list displayed is a QStringList object created on line 71, and filled with three strings on lines 72 through 74. This string list is used as an argument on line 78, and the string on line 79 specifies the window caption.

Lines 21 through 23 create a button and connect it to the slot button3() beginning on line 89. The call to warningYesNo() on line 91 is much the same as the call to questionYesNo() on line 56, except for the difference in the graphic displayed with the text. The warning message box is shown in Figure 4-10.

Figure 4-10: A Yes/No warning message box

Lines 25 through 28 create a button and connect it to the slot button4(), which begins on line 103. The warningContinueCancel() message box was designed to let the user know that some action is about to begin, enabling the user to determine whether it should proceed or stop. This example, shown in Figure 4-11, warns the user that continuing will overwrite an existing file.

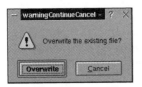

Figure 4-11: A Continue/Cancel warning message box

Some of the message boxes allow the user to override the button labels. In this example, the QString used as an argument on line 108 changed the button label to Overwrite from the default Continue. Changing the caption on the button does not change the returned value—the case statement on line 110 matches the value named Continue, which is issued by the button labeled Overwrite.

There are times when a simple yes or no answer won't suffice. Lines 30 through 32 create a button and connect it to the slot button5(), which begins on line 118. This situation comes up quite often. For example, consider the message "Preparing to delete files. Do you wish to delete subdirectories also?" The user needs to be able to specify that the directories be deleted along with the files, that the directories be retained, or to forget the whole thing. The message box created by the call to warningYesNoCancel() on line 120 is shown in Figure 4-12.

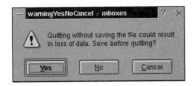

Figure 4-12: A Yes/No/Cancel warning message box

Lines 34 through 36 create a button and connect it to the slot button6(), which begins on line 136. The call to error() on line 138 creates the message box shown in Figure 4-13. This message box has no return value because it is intended for use only when your program is unable to do something it normally should be able to do.

Figure 4-13: An Error message box

Lines 38 through 40 create a button and connect it to the slot `button7()`, which begins on line 141. The function `sorry()` is called on line 143 and displays the window shown in Figure 4-14. This is intended for situations in which the program cannot continue, but the cause is outside the control of the program (such as a missing file).

Figure 4-14: A Sorry message box

Lines 42 through 44 create a button and connect it to the slot `button8()`, which begins on line 146. The function `information()` is called on line 148 and displays the window shown in Figure 4-15. This is intended to contain information that doesn't affect processing, but may be something the user needs to know.

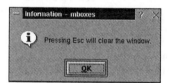

Figure 4-15: An Information message box

Lines 46 through 48 create a button and connect it to the slot `button9()` beginning on line 151. This is the simplest message box of all. It has no graphic decoration and it returns no value. Figure 4-16 shows the message box created by the call to `about()` on line 153. The function being named `about()` implies that it could be (or once was) used as a very simple About box. (A much more elaborate About box is described in the next chapter.)

Figure 4-16: A simple message box

Summary

You can create a dialog in a number of ways. The main window of a dialog is always a single widget, and it can be any widget. This way, the mechanics of displaying a dialog, retrieving the user input, and laying out the window can all be addressed separately. The main points covered in this chapter include the following:

✦ If you have a special requirement for a dialog, it is possible to create your dialog by using `QDialog` or `KDialog` as the basis of the construction.

✦ The `KDialogBase` facilitates the construction of a dialog by supplying a set of standard buttons and a layout manager that you can use to insert your widget.

✦ A dialog can send a signal containing the user input data, and your program can receive the data using a slot.

✦ The `KMessageBox` class is a collection of static functions, each of which uses `KDialogBase` to construct a standard dialog.

Every program, except the very simplest, uses dialogs. They can be popped up from buttons (as described in this chapter), they can be popped up from an event inside the program (such as an error writing to a file), or they can be popped up when the user makes a menu or toolbar selection. One way to standardize the look and feel of a program is to make use of the set of built-in dialogs. This chapter described some of the simple built-in dialogs, and the next chapter discusses some of the more complicated ones.

✦   ✦   ✦

The Predefined Dialogs

Quite a few dialogs are defined in both KDE and Qt. This chapter demonstrates some of the more general-purpose dialogs. While you can use the dialog classes as base classes to create your own customized version, more often than not, all you will need to do is instantiate the dialog in the mode and with the options you need. This chapter doesn't include all of the dialogs. Some special-purpose dialogs are also covered in other chapters. For example, the KFontDialog is described in Chapter 10, "Fonts," and KColorDialog is described in Chapter 11, "Colors."

The About Dialog

Every completed application has an About box, a window that displays pertinent information about the heritage of the software. This is where the programmers can get their names up in pixels. The About box can be popped up from a button, but it is more often available as a menu selection.

The KAboutDialog class is very flexible. It has a collection of optional parts that you can include or exclude. It also has two separate constructors that give it two different basic looks. Just about the only thing that appears by default is the OK button used to close it. For even more flexibility, it inherits from the KDialogBase class, which also supplies a number of options.

Cross-Reference The KDialogBase class is described in Chapter 4.

The KAboutDialog class has two constructors. Beyond having different sets of arguments, they each place the dialog into a different mode, and each mode has its own set of options. Constructor I is in the standard Qt format, with the three normal arguments of parent widget, the internal name, and whether or not the window is to be modal:

```
KAboutDialog(QWidget *parent,const char *name=0,
    bool modal=true)
```

Constructor II has a number of parameters (most of which have defaults), including some flags that can be used to configure the dialog to display itself in one of a variety of configurations:

```
KAboutDialog(int dialogLayout,const QString &caption,
    int buttonMask,int defaultButton,QWidget *parent=0,
    const char *name=0,bool modal=false,bool separator=false,
    const QString &user1=QString::null,
    const QString &user2=QString::null,
    const QString &user3=QString::null)
```

The following example uses both Constructor I and Constructor II to create and display some of the possible configurations. There are many more possible combinations other than the ones demonstrated here, but they are all variations on these basic themes. The main window of the program is shown in Figure 5-1 and consists of the buttons that can be used to pop up four versions of the About dialog.

Figure 5-1: The buttons used to select four About dialogs

ShowAbout Header

```
 1 /* showabout.h */
 2 #ifndef SHOWABOUT_H
 3 #define SHOWABOUT_H
 4
 5 #include <qwidget.h>
 6
 7 class ShowAbout: public QWidget
 8 {
 9     Q_OBJECT
10 public:
11     ShowAbout(QWidget *parent=0,const char *name=0);
12 private slots:
13     void emptyAbout();
```

```
14      void simpleAbout();
15      void kdeStandardAbout();
16      void appStandardAbout();
17  };
18
19  #endif
```

The only purpose of this class is to pop up the requested dialog, so there is only a constructor and the slot that will be used by the four buttons. Each slot pops up a different version of the About dialog.

ShowAbout

```
 1  /* showabout.cpp */
 2  #include <kapp.h>
 3  #include <qpushbutton.h>
 4  #include <qlayout.h>
 5  #include <kaboutdialog.h>
 6  #include <kcmdlineargs.h>
 7  #include "showabout.h"
 8
 9  int main(int argc,char **argv)
10  {
11      KCmdLineArgs::init(argc,argv,"showabout",
12          "About Boxes","0.0");
13      KApplication app;
14      ShowAbout showabout;
15      showabout.show();
16      app.setMainWidget(&showabout);
17      return(app.exec());
18  }
19
20  ShowAbout::ShowAbout(QWidget *parent,const char *name)
21          : QWidget(parent,name)
22  {
23      QPushButton *button;
24      QVBoxLayout *box = new QVBoxLayout(this);
25
26      button = new QPushButton("Empty",this);
27      box->addWidget(button);
28      connect(button,SIGNAL(clicked()),
29              this,SLOT(emptyAbout()));
30
31      button = new QPushButton("Simple",this);
32      box->addWidget(button);
33      connect(button,SIGNAL(clicked()),
34              this,SLOT(simpleAbout()));
35
36      button = new QPushButton("KDE Standard",this);
37      box->addWidget(button);
```

```
38      connect(button,SIGNAL(clicked()),
39              this,SLOT(kdeStandardAbout()));
40
41      button = new QPushButton("App Standard",this);
42      box->addWidget(button);
43      connect(button,SIGNAL(clicked()),
44              this,SLOT(appStandardAbout()));
45
46      resize(10,10);
47      box->activate();
48 }
49 void ShowAbout::emptyAbout()
50 {
51      KAboutDialog *about = new KAboutDialog(0,"about");
52      about->exec();
53 }
54 void ShowAbout::simpleAbout()
55 {
56      KAboutDialog *about = new KAboutDialog(0,"about");
57
58      about->setCaption("Simple About Configuration");
59      about->setVersion("Version 0.0.1");
60
61      QPixmap logo;
62      if(logo.load("tinylogo.png"))
63          about->setLogo(logo);
64
65      about->setAuthor("Bertha D Blues",
66          "bertha@belugalake.com",
67          "http://www.belugalake.com",
68          "Mallet Operator");
69
70      about->setMaintainer("Tony Stryovie",
71          "stryovie@belugalake.com",
72          "http://www.belugalake.com",
73          "Finder of Lost Code");
74
75      about->addContributor("Walter Heater",
76          "heat@belugalake.com",
77          "http://www.belugalake.com",
78          "Asker of Questions");
79
80      about->exec();
81 }
82 void ShowAbout::kdeStandardAbout()
83 {
84      KAboutDialog *about = new KAboutDialog(
85          KAboutDialog::AbtKDEStandard,
86          "KDE Standard Configuration",
87          KDialogBase::Ok | KDialogBase::Help,
88          KDialogBase::Ok,
```

```
 89             this,
 90             "about",
 91             TRUE);
 92
 93     about->setTitle("The example that is all about About");
 94     about->setCaption("KDE Standard About");
 95     about->setImage("penguin1.png");
 96     about->setImageBackgroundColor(QColor("red"));
 97     about->setImageFrame(TRUE);
 98
 99     about->addTextPage("Purpose",
100         "This program is intended to provide an "
101         "example that\ndemonstrates how to use "
102         "the KAboutDialog.");
103     about->addTextPage("Version",
104         "Version 0.0.1 pre-alpha experimental.\n"
105         "Saturday, April 1, 2000");
106
107     about->exec();
108 }
109 void ShowAbout::appStandardAbout()
110 {
111     KAboutDialog *about = new KAboutDialog(
112         KAboutDialog::AbtAppStandard,
113         "App Configuration",
114         KDialogBase::Ok,
115         KDialogBase::Ok,
116         this,
117         "about",
118         TRUE);
119
120     about->setTitle("The example that is about About");
121     about->setProduct("ShowAbout",
122         "0.0.1 Pre-Alpha",
123         "Bertha D Blues",
124         "Saturday, April 1, 2000");
125
126     about->addTextPage("Purpose",
127         "This program is intended to provide an "
128         "example that\ndemonstrates how to use "
129         "the KAboutDialog.");
130     about->addTextPage("Version",
131         "Version 0.0.1 pre-alpha experimental.\n"
132         "Saturday, April 1, 2000");
133
134     about->exec();
135 }
```

Lines 9 through 18 are the mainline of the program, which creates an instance of the ShowAbout class, inserts it as the widget to be used in the main window, and waits for it to exit.

The ShowAbout constructor beginning on line 16 organizes pushbuttons into a vertical box. Each of the four buttons is connected to one of the slots that displays a version of KAboutDialog.

The slot emptyAbout() on line 49 displays the empty KAboutDialog shown in Figure 5-2. The only things that show up in this default version are the OK button that closes the dialog, and a place that would normally hold a graphic of the logo for the application. The dialog created on line 51 is modal, so the method exec() called on line 52 does not return until the user closes the window.

Figure 5-2: An empty KAboutDialog

The slot simpleAbout() beginning on line 54 uses the same constructor, on line 52, that was used to create the empty KAboutDialog shown in Figure 5-3. KAboutDialog methods are called to insert displayable information. Table 5-1 lists the methods that are specifically designated for use by Constructor I dialogs. The call to setCaption() on line 58 defines the caption for the title bar of the window, and the call to setVersion() specifies a version number to be inserted at the top of the window.

Figure 5-3: A KAboutDialog can feature the developers' names.

Table 5-1
KAboutDialog Methods for Constructor I

Method	Purpose
setLogo()	Specifies the pixmap image that is to be displayed as the logo
setAuthor()	Specifies the name, e-mail address, URL, and job performed by the author of the software
setContributor ()	Specifies the name, e-mail address, URL, and job performed by an individual contributor to the software
setMaintainer()	Specifies the name, e-mail address, URL, and job performed by the individual currently supporting the software
setVersion()	Specifies the current software version

The QPixmap created on line 61 loads its image information from the file named tinylogo.png on line 62. The call to setLogo() on line 63 sets the image as the logo to be displayed in the upper left corner of the window.

Lines 65 through 78 add names and addresses by calling setAuthor(), set Maintainer(), and addContributor(). There can only be one author and one maintainer, but there can be any number of contributors. While there are different methods to insert each of these names, all the methods have the same set of parameters. The first string is the name, the second is the person's URL, the third is the e-mail address, and the last one is a description of the job the person performs on the development team. Once displayed, both the URL and the e-mail address are active — that is, you can click on them to either send e-mail or load the Web page.

The slot kdeStandardAbout() beginning on line 82 uses Constructor II to create the customized dialog shown in Figure 5-4. The flag set named AbtKDEStandard on line 85 specifies which elements are to be used to make up the display. Table 5-2 lists the flags and the element that each includes. The arguments on line 87 are used to tell the super class KDialogBase which buttons are to appear. In this example, there is an OK button, which will automatically close the window; and a Help button. The button specified on line 88 is the one that will be selected when the dialog first opens.

Cross-Reference The description of KDialogBase in Chapter 4 explains how to make the OK and Help buttons do what they're meant to do.

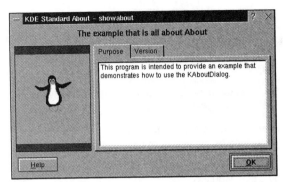

Figure 5-4: A KAboutDialog with an image and text pages

Table 5-2	
KAboutDialog Flags That Configure the Display	
Flag Name	***Description***
AbtAppStandard	Enables a combination of AbtTabbed, AbtTitle, and AbtProduct.
AbtImageAndTitle	Enables a combination of AbtPlain and AbtImageOnly.
AbtImageLeft	Displays the image on the left side of the window.
AbtImageOnly	Displays the image in the center because no other item will be beside it.
AbtImageRight	Displays the image on the right side of the window.
AbtKDEStandard	Enables a combination of AbtTabbed, AbtTitle, and AbtImageLeft.
AbtPlain	None of the default KAboutDialog components will be displayed. This can be used in combination with other flags to customize the dialog.
AbtProduce	Displays the application name, the version, the author, and the date.
AbtTabbed	Displays a collection of one or more windows with tabs that enable the user to switch from one to the other.
AbtTitle	Displays the title immediately beneath the title bar.

After the flags are set telling the dialog which of its elements it should display, it is still necessary for you to supply the elements. Table 5-3 lists the methods that are available when using Constructor II.

Table 5-3
KAboutDialog Methods for Constructor II

Method	Purpose
addContainer()	Adds a KAboutContainer that you can use to display text and images
addContainerPage()	Adds a KAboutContainer as a tabbed page. You can use it to display text and images.
addPage()	Adds an empty page to the collection of tabbed pages. You can use it to contain any widget you would like to display.
addTextPage()	Adds a page of text to the collection of tabbed pages
setImage()	Specifies the image that is to be displayed as the logo
setImageBackground()	Specifies the color to be used as background and fill when displaying the image
setImageFrame()	Enables or disables the frame around the image. The default is enabled.
setProduct()	Sets the four strings defining the name of the application, the version, the author, and the date
setTitle()	Inserts the title at the top of the window (just under the title bar)

The call to setTitle() on line 93 is necessary because the flag setting included AbtTitle, and it is necessary to supply the title to be displayed. The call to set Caption() on line 94 is a pass-through call to the super class to set the caption text of the title bar at the top.

The method calls on lines 95 through 97 specify the name of the file containing the image to be used as a logo; the background color to be used behind the image; and whether the image is to have a border drawn around it. The background color will fill any areas not filled by the window, as previously shown in Figure 5-4, and will also be the fill color for any transparent portion of the image. The default is to have the border drawn, but the method setImageFram() can be used to turn it off.

The method `addTextPage()` can be used a number of times — once for each page you wish to add to the tabbed window. As you can see by the examples on lines 99 and 103, the only arguments are the string that is to become the label for the tab, and the text that is to become the body of the text. It is necessary to insert the newline character '`\n`' to format the text in multiple lines.

The slot named `appStandardAbout()` beginning on line 109 produces the dialog shown in Figure 5-5.

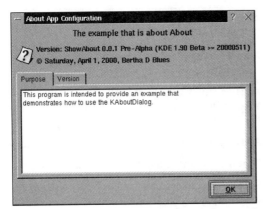

Figure 5-5: A KAboutDialog with headings and tabbed pages

The text at the top of the window is set by two method calls. The call to `setTitle()` on line 116 sets the text of the title that is centered at the top. The call to `set Product()` on line 121 sets the rest of the text. The two tabbed pages are added by the calls to `addTextPage()` on lines 126 and 130.

QFileDialog

The `QFileDialog` allows you to prompt the user for the name of a file or a directory. You can specify that the selection be limited to files that already exist, or enable the user to enter a new filename. Also, using filters, you can limit the available filenames to only those that match specific criteria.

ShowFile Header

```
1 /* showfile.h */
2 #ifndef SHOWFILE_H
3 #define SHOWFILE_H
4
```

```
 5 #include <qwidget.h>
 6 #include <qlabel.h>
 7 #include <qstring.h>
 8
 9 class ShowFile: public QWidget
10 {
11     Q_OBJECT
12 public:
13     ShowFile(QWidget *parent=0,const char *name=0);
14 private:
15     QLabel *filelabel;
16     QString filename;
17 private slots:
18     void popupOpen();
19     void popupSave();
20     void popupDirectory();
21     void popupFilter();
22 };
23
24 #endif
```

The header file defines the ShowFile class. The class contains the name of the current file or directory and the QLabel widget used to display it. Each of the four slot methods is connected to a button that will pop up a QFileDialog in a different mode. The main window, with the labels and the buttons, is shown in Figure 5-6.

Figure 5-6: A full path name and four ways to select it

ShowFile

```
 1 /* showfile.cpp */
 2 #include <kapp.h>
 3 #include <qpushbutton.h>
 4 #include <qlayout.h>
 5 #include <qfiledialog.h>
 6 #include "showfile.h"
 7
 8 int main(int argc,char **argv)
 9 {
10     KApplication app(argc,argv,"showfile");
11     ShowFile showfile;
12     showfile.show();
13     app.setMainWidget(&showfile);
```

```
14        return(app.exec());
15  }
16  ShowFile::ShowFile(QWidget *parent,const char *name)
17          : QWidget(parent,name)
18  {
19      QPushButton *button;
20      QVBoxLayout *box = new QVBoxLayout(this,0,3);
21
22      filelabel = new QLabel("",this);
23      filelabel->setAlignment(Qt::AlignHCenter);
24      box->addWidget(filelabel);
25
26      button = new QPushButton("Select File to Open",this);
27      box->addWidget(button);
28      connect(button,SIGNAL(clicked()),
29              this,SLOT(popupOpen()));
30
31      button = new QPushButton("Select Save File",this);
32      box->addWidget(button);
33      connect(button,SIGNAL(clicked()),
34              this,SLOT(popupSave()));
35
36      button = new QPushButton("Select Directory",this);
37      box->addWidget(button);
38      connect(button,SIGNAL(clicked()),
39              this,SLOT(popupDirectory()));
40
41      button = new QPushButton("Filter Selection",this);
42      box->addWidget(button);
43      connect(button,SIGNAL(clicked()),
44              this,SLOT(popupFilter()));
45
46      resize(10,10);
47      box->activate();
48  }
49  void ShowFile::popupOpen()
50  {
51      QString name = QFileDialog::getOpenFileName("",
52              NULL,this);
53      if(!name.isEmpty()) {
54          filename = name;
55          filelabel->setText(filename);
56      }
57  }
58  void ShowFile::popupSave()
59  {
60      QString name = QFileDialog::getSaveFileName(filename,
61              NULL,this);
62      if(!name.isEmpty()) {
63          filename = name;
64          filelabel->setText(filename);
```

```
65         }
66  }
67  void ShowFile::popupDirectory()
68  {
69      QString name = QFileDialog::getExistingDirectory();
70      if(!name.isEmpty()) {
71          filename = name;
72          filelabel->setText(filename);
73      }
74  }
75  void ShowFile::popupFilter()
76  {
77      QString filter =
78              "All (*)\n"
79              "C Source (*.c *.cc *.cpp *.cxx)\n"
80              "C Header (*.h)\n"
81              "Text (*.txt)\n"
82              "HTML (*.html *.shtml *.HTML *.htm)";
83      QString name = QFileDialog::getOpenFileName("",
84              filter,this);
85      if(!name.isEmpty()) {
86          filename = name;
87          filelabel->setText(filename);
88      }
89  }
```

Lines 8 through 15 are the mainline of the program, which initializes the application, and then creates and displays the ShowFile window shown in Figure 5-6. The constructor, beginning on line 16, is a widget that contains a label and four buttons inside a vertical box. The label is used to display the latest file or directory selection. The buttons are each connected to a slot that will create a QFileDialog object and retrieve the result of the user's input. Each of the four modes of operation uses the same display format, but the title bar caption and button operations vary a bit. Figure 5-7 shows the layout of the QFileDialog window.

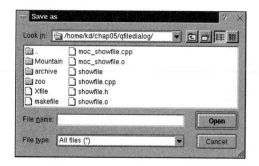

Figure 5-7: A QFileDialog, listing files and directories

The slot named popupOpen() beginning on line 49 opens a QFileDialog window that enables the user to select the name of an existing file. The call to the static function getOpenFileName() on line 51 creates the dialog. The first argument (in this example, a zero-length string) can be the complete path name of a file to suggest to the user. If no filename is specified, the dialog opens on the last directory accessed by this application; or, by default, the current directory. Whenever a file is selected in the window, the button changes its text to OK, and allows the user to select the file.

The slot named popupSave() beginning on line 58 opens a QFileDialog that allows the user to select an existing file or enter the name of a nonexistent file. The call to getSaveFileName() on line 60 creates the dialog. The first argument passed to the constructor is the name of the last file retrieved, and this becomes the current file displayed in the window for selection.

The slot named popupDirectory() on line 67 uses a QFileDialog to select a directory. In this mode, the dialog will only return the name of a selected directory. If a filename is selected by the user, the filename is stripped off and only the directory path is returned.

The slot named popupFilter() on line 75 specifies the group of filename filters shown in Figure 5-8. The filters are a collection of filename suffixes that are used to select which filenames are to appear in the window. The filters are all defined as a single QString beginning on line 77. The file suffixes are organized into categories, and shown by the "C Source" category shown in Figure 5-8. To define a category, the category name is followed by the valid file suffixes enclosed in parentheses. Inside the parentheses, the suffixes are separated by spaces. The different categories are separated by newline characters "\n"; or, if you prefer, a pair of semi-colons (";;").

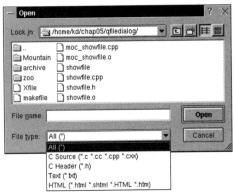

Figure 5-8: Filtering specifies which files are listed.

Note   In almost every case, and in this example, the filters are used to select files with specific suffixes. But the filter is actually a regular expression and can be used in other forms. For example, the filter sh* would limit the list to only files that being with sh.

Figures 5-7 and 5-8 show the ordering of file and directory names. The directories are tagged with tan rectangles and are always listed before the files. In both groups, because they are sorted by their ASCII values, uppercase letters come before lowercase letters. If a listed directory is a symbolic link, its icon has a small mark in its lower right corner.

 Cross-Reference   You can customize the appearance of the QFileDialog window by providing your own icons, as described in Chapter 13, which discusses the manipulation of graphic files.

QTabDialog

The QTabDialog packs two or more dialogs into one by stacking them on top of one another and supplying tabs that can be used to switch from one to the other. The following program creates the simple QTabDialog shown in Figure 5-9.

Figure 5-9: A QTabDialog with the second widget showing

ShowTabs Header

```
 1 /* showtabs.h */
 2 #ifndef SHOWTABS_H
 3 #define SHOWTABS_H
 4
 5 #include <qwidget.h>
 6
 7 class ShowTabs: public QWidget
 8 {
 9     Q_OBJECT
10 public:
11     ShowTabs(QWidget *parent=0,const char *name=0);
12 private slots:
13     void slotTab();
14 };
15
16 #endif
```

ShowTabs

```
 1 /* showtabs.cpp */
 2 #include <kapp.h>
 3 #include <qpushbutton.h>
 4 #include <qtabdialog.h>
 5 #include <qlayout.h>
 6 #include <kfontdialog.h>
 7 #include <kdatepik.h>
 8 #include <kselect.h>
 9 #include "showtabs.h"
10
11 int main(int argc,char **argv)
12 {
13     KApplication app(argc,argv,"showtabs");
14     ShowTabs showtabs;
15     showtabs.show();
16     app.setMainWidget(&showtabs);
17     return(app.exec());
18 }
19
20 ShowTabs::ShowTabs(QWidget *parent,const char *name)
21         : QWidget(parent,name)
22 {
23     QPushButton *button;
24     QVBoxLayout *box = new QVBoxLayout(this,12);
25
26     button = new QPushButton("Show Tab Dialog",this);
27     box->addWidget(button);
28     connect(button,SIGNAL(clicked()),
29             this,SLOT(slotTab()));
30
31     resize(10,10);
32     box->activate();
33 }
34 void ShowTabs::slotTab()
```

```
35 {
36      QTabDialog *tab = new QTabDialog(this,"tabdial",TRUE);
37      tab->setCaption("The QTabDialog Widget");
38      tab->setCancelButton();
39
40      QWidget *fonts = new KFontChooser(this,"fonts");
41      tab->addTab(fonts,"Fonts");
42
43      QWidget *date = new KDatePicker(this);
44      tab->addTab(date,"Date");
45
46      QWidget *hgradient = new KGradientSelector(
47              KSelector::Horizontal,this);
48      tab->addTab(hgradient,"H Gradient");
49
50      QWidget *vgradient = new KGradientSelector(
51              KSelector::Vertical,this);
52      tab->addTab(vgradient,"V Gradient");
53
54      tab->show();
55 }
```

The ShowTabs class is used only to pop up the QtabDialog, so all that its definition contains, other than the constructor, is a slot method that will pop up the dialog.

The mainline of the program, beginning on line 11, creates a ShowTabs widget and installs it as the widget displayed as the main window.

The ShowTabs constructor, beginning on line 20, uses a container to hold a single pushbutton. On line 28, the button has its clicked() signal attached to the slot method named slotTab().

The slot method slotTab(), beginning on line 34, creates and displays the QTabDialog. The dialog is created on line 36. The first argument is to be the dialog's parent widget; the second is the name assigned to it; and the third specifies that the QTabDialog be modal. The default is for a nonmodal dialog.

The call to setCaption() on line 37 specifies the caption to be displayed in the title bar of the dialog window. The call setCancelButton() specifies that a Cancel button be included as part of the dialog.

The dialog can have as many as four buttons. By default, there is always an OK button present, but you will need to specify any other buttons that you would like. Other buttons could have been included with calls to setDefaultButton(), setHelpButton(), and setApplyButton(). The methods that include buttons can be called with no arguments, as on line 38, or with a string that specifies the text of the button (including setOkButton()). To receive signals from the button, you need to connect slots to applyButtonPressed(), cancelButtonPressed(), defaultButtonPressed(), and helpButtonPressed().

Lines 40 through 52 create the four pages (sometimes called *tabs* or *tab pages*) that inhabit the QTabDialog. To keep the code simple, four of the standard KDE widgets were used, and none of them have the software required to extract the data that was entered by the user. You can certainly construct your own widgets. Normally, there would be a slot connected to the OK and Apply buttons that would read the information from the four widgets.

The size of the dialog is determined by the size of the widgets it contains. It will appear as tall and wide as it needs to be for the largest widgets; and the smaller widgets are centered, both vertically and horizontally. Popping up dialogs that use tabs to switch from one widget to another is becoming increasingly popular. It shows the user all the available options without also displaying a confusing page filled with data entry options.

QProgressDialog

Sometimes your program needs to do something that will take a few seconds, or a few minutes. If the time delay is short, changing the cursor to the image of a watch is a way of saying, "The program is busy. One moment please." If the delay is long (for example, 15 seconds or more), it is only polite to give the user a bit more information about what's going on. The QProgressDialog can be used to display the percentage of task completion, and it can be set so that it only pops up when the duration becomes long enough to warrant it.

The following program demonstrates two ways of using a QProgressDialog. Figure 5-10 shows the main window of the application with its two buttons, which are used to pop up the QProgressDialog windows. While this dialog is normally used to present the progress transmitting data, sorting a large file, or something else that takes time, the examples in this program simply operate based on the progress of timers.

Figure 5-10: Start one of two QProgressDialog windows

Progress Header

```
1 /* progress.h */
2 #ifndef PROGRESS_H
3 #define PROGRESS_H
4
5 #include <qprogressdialog.h>
```

```
 6 #include <qwidget.h>
 7 #include <qtimer.h>
 8
 9 class Progress: public QWidget
10 {
11     Q_OBJECT
12 public:
13   . Progress(QWidget *parent=0,const char *name=0);
14 private:
15     QProgressDialog *progressDialog;
16     QTimer *timer;
17 private slots:
18     void slot15();
19     void slot60();
20     void timerStep();
21 };
22
23 #endif
```

The Progress class has three slots and a timer. The slot methods slot15()
and slot60() are called to start progress dialogs that last for 15 and 60 seconds,
respectively. The timer, and the timerStep() slot, are used internally to track
the elapsed time.

Progress

```
 1 /* progress.cpp */
 2 #include <unistd.h>
 3 #include <kapp.h>
 4 #include <qpushbutton.h>
 5 #include <qlayout.h>
 6 #include "progress.h"
 7
 8 int main(int argc,char **argv)
 9 {
10     KApplication app(argc,argv,"progress");
11     Progress progress;
12     progress.show();
13     app.setMainWidget(&progress);
14     return(app.exec());
15 }
16
17 Progress::Progress(QWidget *parent,const char *name)
18         : QWidget(parent,name)
19 {
20     QPushButton *button;
21     QVBoxLayout *box = new QVBoxLayout(this,12);
22
23     button = new QPushButton("15 Seconds",this);
24     box->addWidget(button);
```

```
25      connect(button,SIGNAL(clicked()),
26              this,SLOT(slot15()));
27
28      button = new QPushButton("60 Seconds",this);
29      box->addWidget(button);
30      connect(button,SIGNAL(clicked()),
31              this,SLOT(slot60()));
32
33      resize(10,10);
34      box->activate();
35 }
36 void Progress::slot15()
37 {
38      int currentStep = 0;
39      int steps = 15;
40
41      progressDialog = new QProgressDialog(
42          "Fifteen seconds..","Cancel",
43          steps,this,"pgrs",TRUE);
44      progressDialog->setCaption("Progress");
45      while(currentStep < steps) {
46          progressDialog->setProgress(currentStep++);
47          if(progressDialog->wasCancelled())
48              break;
49          sleep(1);
50      }
51      progressDialog->setProgress(steps);
52      delete progressDialog;
53      progressDialog = NULL;
54 }
55 void Progress::slot60()
56 {
57      int currentStep = 0;
58      int steps = 20;
59
60      progressDialog = new QProgressDialog(this,"prgs",TRUE);
61      progressDialog->setCaption("Progress");
62      progressDialog->setLabelText("Sixty seconds...");
63      progressDialog->setCancelButtonText("Quit");
64      progressDialog->setTotalSteps(steps);
65      progressDialog->setMinimumDuration(3000);
66
67      timer = new QTimer(this);
68      connect(timer,SIGNAL(timeout()),
69              this,SLOT(timerStep()));
70      timer->start(3000,FALSE);
71 }
72 void Progress::timerStep()
73 {
74      int currentStep;
75      int steps = 20;
```

```
76
77        if(progressDialog == NULL)
78            return;
79
80        if(progressDialog->wasCancelled()) {
81            delete timer;
82            delete progressDialog;
83            progressDialog = NULL;
84            return;
85        }
86        currentStep = progressDialog->progress();
87        if(currentStep >= steps) {
88            delete timer;
89            delete progressDialog;
90            progressDialog = NULL;
91        } else {
92            progressDialog->setProgress(currentStep + 1);
93        }
94  }
```

The mainline of the program, beginning on line 8, creates a Progress object and installs it as the top-level window. The top-level widget is a Progress widget created by the constructor on line 17. A vertical box is used to contain two pushbuttons. The buttons are connected to the slots slot15() and slot60(). The result is the window shown in Figure 5-15.

The slot method slot15(), beginning on line 36, demonstrates how you can use a progress bar inside a loop. The progress percentage is determined by the ratio of the current step number to the total number of steps. Line 38 specifies the current step (the starting step) to be 0, and line 39 defines the total number of steps to be 15. The constructor on line 41 creates the QProgressDialog and sets the total number of steps. It also sets the text of the captions and the name of the widget; and specifies TRUE, that the dialog is to be modal. The call to setCaption() on line 44 specifies the text for the dialog title bar.

Note   The examples included here are both modal dialogs, but it is common to have nonmodal progress dialogs. For example, when a Web browser is downloading a file or two, each download has its standalone progress dialog, and you are still able to access other functions of the browser.

The loop beginning on line 45 is there to simulate an activity to be reported by the progress bar. All this loop does is increment the current step count and sleep for a second. In a real-world application, you could compute the value of the next step and call setProgress() with the value. The call to wasCancelled() on line 47 will return TRUE if the user has selected the Cancel button, so the loop will exit early. The result is the progress window shown in Figure 5-11. Normally, with the selection of the Cancel button, you would have code inside the loop that would put a stop to whatever was being timed, but there is nothing to do here so it just jumps out of the loop.

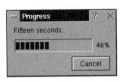

Figure 5-11: A QProgressDialog with fifteen steps

The call to setProgress() on line 51 guarantees that the dialog closes properly. When a modal QProgressDialog starts running, it first changes the cursor to a watch symbol. It then waits for a short period of time before it pops up. The display is updated each time the current value is increased. Once the last step is reached, it restores the original cursor and pops itself down. The call to setProgress() on line 51 is necessary because the loop can exit without reaching the maximum step value.

The slot method named slot60() beginning on line 55 uses an entirely different method to create and update a QprogressDialog, as shown in Figure 5-12. Lines 57 and 58 set the starting value to 0 and the number of steps to 20. The dialog is created on line 60, using a simpler constructor than the one in the previous example. The method calls on lines 61 through 65 set the window caption text, specify the text of the label that appears in the dialog, change the text of the Cancel button, and set the total number of steps to completion.

Figure 5-12: A QProgressDialog using a signal

The call to setMinimumDuration() on line 65 sets the pop-up delay time to 3,000 milliseconds (3 seconds). This is the amount of time the dialog will wait before popping itself up. Setting it to 3,000 milliseconds causes the cursor to change to a watch and do nothing else until the 3 seconds pass. This way, the dialog will never appear for tasks that take less than three seconds.

Lines 67 through 70 create a timer and start it running. The timeout() signal of the timer is connected to the timerStep() slot of this class. The call to start() on line 70 initiates the timer to expire at 3 seconds. The second parameter being set to FALSE means that this is not a one-shot timer — it will run continuously, triggering every 3 seconds, until it is stopped. If this second parameter were set to TRUE, the timer would trigger only once. Actually, to have a continuously running timer, one mode is about as good as another. If it is running continuously, you will have to kill it at the end. If it is a one-shot timer, you can restart it each time it triggers.

The slot named `timerStep()` on line 72 executes each time the timer triggers. If the user selects the Cancel button to halt the operation, the call to `wasCancelled()` on line 80 will be `TRUE`. The call to `progress()` on line 86 retrieves the current step value and, if line 87 finds that it has reached the end, the timer and the dialog are both deleted. If it is still in progress, the call to `setProgress()` on line 92 increments the current step number.

The pointer named `progressDialog` is set to `NULL` whenever the dialog is deleted, and there is a test for whether it is `NULL` on line 77. This test is necessary because of the way `QTimer` works. To achieve timing, `QTimer` inserts special events into the incoming event queue; and because the event queue is asynchronous from the application, `QTimer` could have a time event still in the input queue when the `QProgressDialog` is deleted. This means the slot `timerStep()` would be executed one more time.

Summary

This chapter demonstrated some ways to use a few of the many KDE and Qt dialogs. There are many more predefined dialogs, and all of these dialogs have a number of options. This chapter explored dialogs that can be used in the following ways:

✦ Create an About window that is standard enough that your application can be recognized as being part of the KDE system.

✦ Present a selection of files and directories, and allow the user to pick one.

✦ Stack widgets on top of one another and supply the user with a set of tabs to switch from one widget to another.

✦ Display a progress bar to reassure the user that your program is doing what it should be doing.

The dialogs not covered in this chapter are covered in chapters where they are relevant. But dialogs are not the only things that pop up. The next chapter begins examining the process of creating and displaying menus and toolbars.

✦   ✦   ✦

Menus and Toolbars

This chapter is all about decorating the main window of your application with widgets that can be used to access parts of your program and keep the user informed about what is going on inside the application. Because this is mostly done using the main window of an application, there is a special top-level window class named KTMainWindow. It contains everything that is needed to manage the menu bar, the toolbars, and/or the status bar. At your request, the KTMainWindow will construct these items for you, supply you with a place to insert the widget that is to be used as the main window of your application, and then manage the user's interaction with the various pieces it contains. You could, if you wish, create all of these widgets and manage them yourself, but it is much simpler to let KTMainWindow do it.

KTMainWindow

The KTMainWindow class is a widget that is a combination of facilities designed to make it ideal for the top-level window of an application. Not only is it a container that holds the main widget (also called the *view widget*), it also handles the basic mechanics of creating and managing a menu bar, a status bar, and one or more toolbars.

Note

The KTMainWindow must always be created with the new command because, when the KTMainWindow closes, it frees itself along with its internally allocated memory. If it is either defined as a global object or on the stack, the program will crash in the attempt to free the memory.

The following example program uses a KTMainWindow to create a top-level window that has a simple menu, a toolbar, and a status bar surrounding a top-level widget, as shown in Figure 6-1.

Figure 6-1: Using a KTMainWindow to create and control the main window of an application

SimpleMain Header

```
 1 /* simplemain.h */
 2 #ifndef SIMPLEMAIN_H
 3 #define SIMPLEMAIN_H
 4
 5 #include <ktmainwindow.h>
 6 #include <kmenubar.h>
 7 #include <ktoolbar.h>
 8 #include <kstatusbar.h>
 9
10 class SimpleMain: public KTMainWindow
11 {
12     Q_OBJECT
13 public:
14     SimpleMain();
15 private slots:
16     void slotExit();
17     bool queryClose();
18 private:
19     void createMainWidget();
20     void createMenu();
21     void createStatusBar();
22     void createToolBar();
23 };
24
25 #endif
```

Lines 5 through 8 include the header files that define the KTMainWindow class and the three classes that will be included as part of the main window. On line 10, the SimpleMain class definition specifies KTMainWindow as its base class. While it is possible to instantiate a KTMainWindow directly, using it as a base class provides much more flexibility.

SimpleMain

```
 1 /* simplemain.cpp */
 2 #include <kapp.h>
 3 #include <kcmdlineargs.h>
 4 #include <qpushbutton.h>
 5 #include "simplemain.h"
 6
 7 int main(int argc,char **argv)
 8 {
 9     KCmdLineArgs::init(argc,argv,"simplemain",
10         "Simple Main","0.0");
11     KApplication app;
12     SimpleMain *simplemain = new SimpleMain();
13     simplemain->show();
14     return(app.exec());
15 }
16 SimpleMain::SimpleMain() : KTMainWindow()
17 {
18     createMainWidget();
19     createMenu();
20     createStatusBar();
21     createToolBar();
22 }
23 void SimpleMain::createMainWidget()
24 {
25     QPushButton *button =
26             new QPushButton("Top Level\nWidget",this);
27     setView(button);
28 }
29 void SimpleMain::createMenu()
30 {
31     KMenuBar *menubar =  menuBar();
32     QPopupMenu *popup = new QPopupMenu();
33     popup->insertItem("E&xit",this,SLOT(slotExit()));
34     menubar->insertItem("&File",popup);
35 }
36 void SimpleMain::createStatusBar()
37 {
38     KStatusBar *status = statusBar();
39     status->insertItem("Status Bar",1);
40 }
41 void SimpleMain::createToolBar()
42 {
43     KToolBar *toolbar = toolBar(0);
44     QPixmap pixmap("flag.png");
45     toolbar->insertButton(pixmap,5);
46 }
47 void SimpleMain::slotExit()
48 {
49     kapp->exit(0);
```

```
50 }
51 bool SimpleMain::queryClose()
52 {
53     return(TRUE);
54 }
```

The mainline of the program is declared on lines 7 through 15. Line 11 initializes KDE by creating a KApplication object. The main window of the application is created on line 12. Notice that it is not necessary to connect the app object with the SimpleMain object (that is, the KTMainWindow object) because the relationships are established internally. That is part of the reason why there can only be one KTMainWindow object in an application. The call to show() on line 13 causes the main window to display, so the program proceeds immediately into the command loop by calling exec() on line 14.

The constructor is defined on line 16. All it does is call four methods to create the four parts of the main window's display. The method createMainWidget() on line 23 creates the widget that becomes the main window of the application. In this example, the main window is simply the QPushButton created on line 25. The call to setView() on line 27 inserts the widget as the main window—that is, as the *view*.

The menu bar is configured in the method createMenu() beginning on line 29. The menu bar is created by the call to the method menuBar() on line 31. This method can be called any number of times and it will always return the same KMenuBar pointer because there can only be one menu bar in a KTMainWindow. The first call to menuBar() will create a new menu only if one does not already exist. If you prefer, you can create your own menu and insert it into the KTMainWindow as follows:

```
KMenuBar *myMenuBar = new KMenuBar();
setMenu(myMenuBar);
```

To flesh out the menu bar, a QPopupMenu object is created on line 32. This object can be inserted into the KMenuBar to act as the pop-up container of a column of buttons. This example inserts only a single button with the call to insertItem() on line 33. The button is labeled "E&xit" and will call the slot method slotExit(). The call to insertItem() on line 34 inserts the pop-up menu into the menu bar.

As shown in Figure 6-2, the user can drag the toolbar to the side of the window, converting the toolbar to a vertical orientation. It is also possible to place the toolbar on the right or at the bottom of the window.

Figure 6-2: Alternate locations for the menu bar and toolbar

The method createStatusBar() on line 36 calls statusBar() to create and install a widget capable of displaying a single line of text. Your program has access to the text of the status bar, so it can keep it constantly updated. Unlike the toolbar and the menu bar, the status bar cannot be moved to another location.

The method createToolBar() on line 41 creates a toolbar by calling toolBar() on line 43. An ID number is required as an argument because your application can have as many toolbars as you would like. You supply the ID number and, if there is no toolbar with that ID, one is created and returned. Using the same ID number will always return the same toolbar. For this example, a pixmap is used to create a single toolbar button.

The toolbar can be moved outside of its parent window. Figure 6-3 shows the result of using the handle at the left end of the toolbar to "tear off" the menu from its parent window and establish it as its own stand-alone window.

Figure 6-3: Tear-off menus and toolbars

The method named slotExit() on line 47 is called whenever the user selects Exit from the menu. You may need to do some kind of cleanup here and save currently unsaved data, but this example simply calls the exit() method in the application. The global variable named kapp always contains a pointer to the KApplication object.

The slot method named queryClose() on line 51 is called when the figure X in the upper right corner of the application's frame is selected. If this slot returns TRUE, the application is immediately closed. If it returns FALSE, no action will be taken (the signal from the X button will be ignored).

This is the skeleton of an application. Allowing KTMainWindow to do most of the work, your top-level window can be very sophisticated with only a few lines of code. The rest of this chapter describes the details of configuring the menu bar and toolbars, and displaying information via the status bar.

The Menu Bar

Basically, a menu is a collection of buttons with a slot attached to each one. The dynamics of a menu simplifies access to the buttons by making a specific subset of them available at any one time. There are different ways of organizing and decorating the buttons. The following example creates the window shown in Figure 6-4. This menu bar was contrived to demonstrate the different things you can use in the construction of a menu.

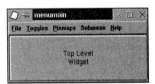

Figure 6-4: An application with a menu bar at the top

The header file mostly contains declarations of slots that will be called whenever a menu button is selected, but there is also some private data that is needed to track the status of menu buttons that are toggled from one state to another. The MenuMain class inherits from the KTMainWindow class, so it already has the capability to display and manage a menu.

MenuMain Header

```
 1 /* menumain.h */
 2 #ifndef MENUMAIN_H
 3 #define MENUMAIN_H
 4
 5 #include <ktmainwindow.h>
 6 #include <kmenubar.h>
 7 #include <ktoolbar.h>
 8 #include <kstatusbar.h>
 9
10 class MenuMain: public KTMainWindow
11 {
12     Q_OBJECT
13 public:
14     MenuMain();
15 private:
16     QPopupMenu *checkPopup;
17     int enableColorsID;
18     int enableGraphicsID;
19 private slots:
20     void slotExit();
21     bool queryClose();
22     void slotNew();
23     void slotSave();
```

```
24      void slotSaveAs();
25      void slotClose();
26      void slotLogo();
27      void slotSub();
28      void slotEnableColors();
29      void slotEnableGraphics();
30 private:
31      void createMainWidget();
32      void createMenu();
33 };
34
35 #endif
```

MenuMain

```
 1 /* menumain.cpp */
 2 #include <kapp.h>
 3 #include <khelpmenu.h>
 4 #include <kcmdlineargs.h>
 5 #include <qpushbutton.h>
 6 #include <qwhatsthis.h>
 7 #include "menumain.h"
 8
 9 int main(int argc,char **argv)
10 {
11     KCmdLineArgs::init(argc,argv,"menumain",
12         "Menu Main","0.0");
13     KApplication app;
14     MenuMain *menumain = new MenuMain();
15     menumain->show();
16     return(app.exec());
17 }
18 MenuMain::MenuMain() : KTMainWindow()
19 {
20     createMainWidget();
21     createMenu();
22 }
23 void MenuMain::createMainWidget()
24 {
25     QPushButton *button =
26             new QPushButton("Top Level\nWidget",this);
27     QWhatsThis::add(button,
28         "Button\n\n"
29         "This button is used as the top\n"
30         "level widget for this example. It\n"
31         "is very safe to click the button\n"
32         "because it doesn't do anything.\n");
33     setView(button);
34 }
35 void MenuMain::createMenu()
36 {
```

```
37    QPopupMenu *popup;
38    QPopupMenu *popup2;
39    QPixmap pixmap;
40    KMenuBar *menubar =  menuBar();
41
42    popup = new QPopupMenu();
43    popup->insertItem("&New",this,
44            SLOT(slotNew()),ALT+Key_N);
45    popup->insertItem("&Save",this,
46            SLOT(slotSave()),CTRL+Key_S);
47    popup->insertItem("Save As",this,
48            SLOT(slotSaveAs()),CTRL+SHIFT+Key_S);
49    pixmap.load("flag.png");
50    QIconSet iconset(pixmap);
51    popup->insertItem(iconset,"Close",this,
52            SLOT(slotClose()));
53    popup->insertSeparator();
54    popup->insertItem("Exit",this,
55            SLOT(slotExit()),ALT+Key_X);
56    menubar->insertItem("&File",popup);
57
58    checkPopup = new QPopupMenu();
59    checkPopup->setCheckable(TRUE);
60    enableColorsID = checkPopup->insertItem(
61            "Enable Colors",this,SLOT(slotEnableColors()));
62    checkPopup->setItemChecked(enableColorsID,TRUE);
63    enableGraphicsID = checkPopup->insertItem(
64            "Enable Graphics",this,
65            SLOT(slotEnableGraphics()));
66    checkPopup->setItemChecked(enableGraphicsID,FALSE);
67    menubar->insertItem("&Toggles",checkPopup);
68
69    popup = new QPopupMenu();
70    pixmap.load("tinylogo.png");
71    popup->insertItem(pixmap,this,SLOT(slotLogo()));
72    pixmap.load("qtlogo.png");
73    popup->insertItem(pixmap,this,SLOT(slotLogo()));
74    menubar->insertItem("&Pixmaps",popup);
75
76    popup = new QPopupMenu();
77    popup2 = new QPopupMenu();
78    popup2->insertItem("Horizontal",this,SLOT(slotSub()));
79    popup2->insertItem("Vertical",this,SLOT(slotSub()));
80    popup->insertItem("Orientation...",popup2);
81    menubar->insertItem("Submenu",popup);
82
83    KHelpMenu *help = new KHelpMenu(this,
84        "Text that will appear in\n"
85        "a very simple About box");
86    popup = help->menu();
```

```
87        menubar->insertItem("&Help",popup);
88  }
89  void MenuMain::slotExit()
90  {
91        kapp->exit(0);
92  }
93  bool MenuMain::queryClose()
94  {
95        return(TRUE);
96  }
97  void MenuMain::slotEnableColors()
98  {
99        if(checkPopup->isItemChecked(enableColorsID))
100           checkPopup->setItemChecked(enableColorsID,FALSE);
101       else
102           checkPopup->setItemChecked(enableColorsID,TRUE);
103 }
104 void MenuMain::slotEnableGraphics()
105 {
106       if(checkPopup->isItemChecked(enableGraphicsID))
107           checkPopup->setItemChecked(enableGraphicsID,FALSE);
108       else
109           checkPopup->setItemChecked(enableGraphicsID,TRUE);
110 }
111 void MenuMain::slotNew() {}
112 void MenuMain::slotSave() {}
113 void MenuMain::slotSaveAs() {}
114 void MenuMain::slotClose() {}
115 void MenuMain::slotLogo() {}
116 void MenuMain::slotSub() {}
```

The mainline of the program, beginning on line 10, creates a MenuMain object, displays it, and calls exec() to wait for input. The constructor of MenuMain, beginning on line 15, calls createMainWidget() to provide a widget to act as the main window, and then calls createMenu() to add the menu bar to the top of the window.

The method createMainWidget(), beginning on line 23, creates a pushbutton and installs it as the main window of the application. The button is installed by the call to setView() on line 33. The call to QWhatsThis::add() on line 27 is called to relate some descriptive text with the button—the user can display the text from the Help menu.

The method createMenu() beginning on line 35 creates the menu bar and all of its members. There is one menu bar inside the KTMainWindow widget, and its address is retrieved and stored in the menubar pointer on line 37. Actually, the menu bar does not exist until the menuBar() method is called, but subsequent menuBar() calls return the same menu bar pointer.

Each button appearing on the menu bar represents one QPopupMenu object. The first one is created on line 42 and added to the menu bar on line 56. Between lines 42 and 56 a number of items are inserted in the pop-up menu, resulting in a menu that looks like the one shown in Figure 6-5.

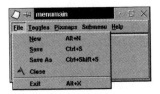

Figure 6-5: A menu with icons and accelerators

The call to insertItem() on line 56 specifies that the name of the menu be "File," and the accelerator key be Alt-F. That is, writing the label as "&File" instead of simply "File" results in the letter being underlined when it is displayed; and pressing the Alt-F key combination will cause the menu to appear, just as if you had selected it with the mouse. The up and down arrow keys can be used to locate a member of the menu; and the Return or Enter key will select it, just as if you had clicked it with the mouse.

The item labeled "New" is created with the call to insertItem() on line 43. The accelerator key is specified by the constant value ALT+Key_N. This is a shortcut for selecting the menu item; whenever the application has the keyboard focus, typing ALT-N produces the same result as selecting the New entry with the mouse. The accelerator key appears on the right, as you can see in Figure 6-5. Notice that the ampersand preceding the letter *N* causes it to be underlined; however, unlike the menu bar, this does not automatically assign an accelerator key. You can underline, or not underline, as you choose. The "Save As" selection has an accelerator key, but does not have a letter underlined.

The accelerator keys are specified by special values that specify the key and its modifiers. Three modifiers are available: ALT, CTRL, and SHIFT. You can use none, one, two, or all three of them in combination with a key. For example, the "Save As" entry defined on line 47 uses both the CTRL and SHIFT modifiers. Many keys can be used for accelerators. The following list contains some of the more commonly used keys.

There are more keys defined than will appear on any one keyboard, but most of the ones in this list are common enough that they should be useful, although I have never seen a keyboard with 35 function keys. If you have some special keys that you would like to use, look in the source of the Qt header file named qnamespace.h, where you will find more than 230 keys listed.

Key_0 through Key_9	Key_Down	Key_Period
Key_Apostrophe	Key_End	Key_Plus
Key_Asterisk	Key_Enter	Key_Print
Key_A through Key_Z	Key_Equal	Key_QuoteDbl
Key_Backslash	Key_Escape	Key_Return
Key_BackSpace	Key_F1 through Key_F35	Key_Right
Key_Backspace	Key_Home	Key_ScrollLock
Key_BraceLeft	Key_Insert	Key_Semicolon
Key_BraceRight	Key_Left	Key_Slash
Key_BracketLeft	Key_Minus	Key_Space
Key_BracketRight	Key_Next	Key_SysReq
Key_CapsLock	Key_NumLock	Key_Tab
Key_Colon	Key_PageDown	Key_Underscore
Key_Comma	Key_PageUp	Key_Up
Key_Delete		

The Close menu item defined on lines 49 through 52 is shown in Figure 6-5 with an icon displayed on its left. To do this, the first step is to create a pixmap containing the graphics. This is done on line 49 by loading the data from the local disk file named flag.png. The second step is to create a QIconSet object from the pixmap, as is done on line 50. The menu item itself is created by the call to insertItem() on line 48, with the QIconSet inserted as the first argument; otherwise, the arguments are the same as before.

 Cross-Reference Chapter 13, "Graphic Manipulation," describes other ways to create pixmaps.

To complete the File menu, line 53 inserts the horizontal separator line that appears between Close and Exit. Lines 54 and 55 create the Exit menu member.

Figure 6-6 shows a menu with a pair of checkable buttons that can be toggled on and off. The checkmark appears only when the button has been toggled on. In the figure, the Enable Colors button is on and the Enable Graphics button is off.

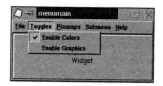

Figure 6-6: A menu with toggle buttons

The Toggles menu is created on line 58 and inserted into the menu bar on line 74. The call to setCheckable() on line 59 configures the pop-up menu so that all of its items can be toggled on and off. This way, you can turn any item on the pop-up menu into a toggled item simply by toggling it on and off.

The actual toggling is not automatic. The two slots for the toggle buttons — on lines 97 through 110 — check the current state of the toggle by calling isItemCheck(), and then call setItemChecked() to toggle it to the other state. Because of the arguments required to toggle buttons in the slot methods, it was necessary to store a pointer to the pop-up menu, along with the ID numbers of the two buttons, on lines 16 through 18 of the header file. The ID numbers are the return values from itemInsert(), on lines 60 and 63, and are the only way you can address a specific item inside a pop-up menu.

Instead of text, you can decorate your menus with pixmaps. Figure 6-7 shows a menu using pixmaps for buttons. They work just like the text menu buttons, so they can have accelerator keys and be toggle buttons. In the figure, you can see that one pixmap is larger than the other — it is up to you to size your pixmaps, because each menu item will expand to accommodate whatever you give to it.

Figure 6-7: A menu using pixmaps for buttons

The pop-up menu with the pixmaps is created on lines 70 through 74. Notice that the same QPixmap object is used for both of the buttons — this works because the insertItem() method makes its own local copy. The only difference between a pixmap and a text button is the type of the first argument — on lines 71 and 73, a QPixmap object reference is the first argument.

A submenu can be created by inserting one pop-up menu into another as one of its items. Lines 76 through 81 create a second pop-up menu, named popup2, and insert it into its parent menu with the label "Orientation..." The resulting menu, when selected, looks like the one shown in Figure 6-8.

Figure 6-8: A menu with a submenu

The `KHelpMenu` object is created on line 80 and installed as the rightmost member of the menu bar on lines 86 and 87. The resulting menu is shown in Figure 6-9.

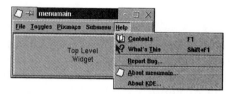

Figure 6-9: The layout of the standard help menu

The "Contents" item, with the accelerator key F1, will display help text. The text itself is provided by you as an HTML file. The name of the file depends on the name of the application. For this example, named `menumain`, the index file of the help tree for the English version is as follows:

```
/usr/doc/kde/HTML/en/menumain/index.html
```

The "What's This" menu item will switch your application into a mode in which every widget on display can be selected to display explanatory text about itself. In this example, the call to the static method `QWhatsThis` on line 24 inserts the explanatory text into the button used as the main window. Making the selection from the menu changes the cursor to a question mark that, when used to select an item, will display the text. The text is displayed in a window with a simple border and a yellow background, as shown in Figure 6-10.

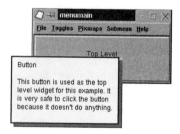

Figure 6-10: Text displayed as a response to "What's this?"

The two bottom buttons on the menu are the About boxes. The default About box for the application is a simple block of text with an OK button, and there is a standard About box with information about the current version of KDE.

You can use `KHelpMenu` and replace the built-in About box with one of your own. To do this, extend the `KHelpMenu` class and include a slot named `aboutApplication()`. Instead of popping up the default About box, this slot will be executed—and you can create your own About box and display it.

You can find some examples of creating About boxes in Chapter 5.

Pop-up Menus

A QPopupMenu object does not need to be connected to a QMenuBar. A menu can be popped up in the middle of a widget. All your application has to do is specify the location and call the show() method. The following example responds to the right mouse button by displaying a pop-up menu, as shown in Figure 6-11.

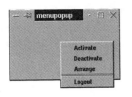

Figure 6-11: A menu pops up from the middle of a widget

MenuPopup Header

```
 1 /* menupopup.h */
 2 #ifndef MENUPOPUP_H
 3 #define MENUPOPUP_H
 4
 5 #include <qpopupmenu.h>
 6
 7 class MenuPopup: public QWidget
 8 {
 9     Q_OBJECT
10 public:
11     MenuPopup(QWidget *parent=0,const char *name=0);
12 protected:
13     virtual void mousePressEvent(QMouseEvent *event);
14 private:
15     QPopupMenu *popup;
16 private slots:
17     void slotStub();
18 };
19
20 #endif
```

On line 7, the class MenuPopup uses QWidget as its base class. And, because it is a widget, it inherits the virtual protected method mousePressEvent(), which is called whenever the mouse pointer is within the widget and a mouse button is pressed.

MenuPopup

```
1 /* menupopup.cpp */
2 #include <kapp.h>
3 #include "menupopup.h"
4
5 int main(int argc,char **argv)
6 {
7     KApplication app(argc,argv,"setxy");
8     MenuPopup menupopup;
9     menupopup.show();
10     app.setMainWidget(&menupopup);
11     return(app.exec());
12 }
13
14 MenuPopup::MenuPopup(QWidget *parent,const char *name)
15         : QWidget(parent,name)
16 {
17     setMinimumSize(90,40);
18     resize(200,100);
19
20     popup = new QPopupMenu(this);
21     popup->insertItem("Activate",this,SLOT(slotStub()));
22     popup->insertItem("Deactivate",this,SLOT(slotStub()));
23     popup->insertItem("Arrange",this,SLOT(slotStub()));
24     popup->insertSeparator();
25     popup->insertSeparator();
26     popup->insertItem("Logout",this,SLOT(slotStub()));
27 }
28
29 void MenuPopup::mousePressEvent(QMouseEvent *event)
30 {
31     if(event->button() == RightButton) {
32         popup->move(x() + event->x(),y() + event->y());
33         popup->exec();
34     }
35 }
36 void MenuPopup::slotStub() {}
```

The constructor of MenuPopup, beginning on line 14, creates a QPopupMenu object and stores its address in popup, found on line 15 in the class definition. It isn't required, but the parent widget of the QPopupMenu is normally the widget that pops up the menu. Lines 21 through 26 insert the items into the menu.

The virtual method mousePressedEvent() on line 29 overrides the one in the parent QWidget class. The method is called whenever a mouse button is clicked. The test on line 31 determines whether the right mouse button is the one selected; if so, the call to move() positions the menu and the call to exec() pops it up. The coordinate position, supplied to the call to move() on line 32, is the sum of the x and y coordinates of the parent widget and those of the mouse pointer. The resulting coordinate is the location of the mouse on the screen, causing the menu to appear directly beneath the mouse.

The Toolbar

KTMainWindow will manage as many toolbars as you care to insert into it. By default, they will appear at the top of the window in the order that you insert them. If there is also a menu, the toolbars will appear beneath it. And you can have more things in a toolbar than just button icons. The following example, shown in Figure 6-12, installs two toolbars containing buttons, separators, a combo box, and even a label widget.

Figure 6-12: A pair of toolbars containing several items

ToolbarMain Header

```
 1 /* toolbarmain.h */
 2 #ifndef TOOLBARMAIN_H
 3 #define TOOLBARMAIN_H
 4
 5 #include <ktmainwindow.h>
 6 #include <ktoolbar.h>
 7
 8 class ToolbarMain: public KTMainWindow
 9 {
10     Q_OBJECT
11 public:
12     ToolbarMain();
13 private slots:
14     void slotExit();
15     void slotStub();
16     void slotFont(int index);
17     bool queryClose();
18 private:
19     void createMainWidget();
20     void createToolBarOne();
21     void createToolBarTwo();
22 };
23
24 #endif
```

Because it is KTMainWindow that manages the toolbars, the class ToolbarMain is defined as a subclass of KTMainWindow on line 8. The slots defined on lines 14 through 16 receive calls when toolbar items are selected. The slot queryClose() on line 17 is used by the system to ask your application for permission to close it.

ToolbarMain

```
 1 /* toolbarmain.cpp */
 2 #include <kapp.h>
 3 #include <qpushbutton.h>
 4 #include <qstrlist.h>
 5 #include <qcstring.h>
 6 #include "toolbarmain.h"
 7
 8 int main(int argc,char **argv)
 9 {
10     KApplication app(argc,argv,"toolbarmain");
11     ToolbarMain *toolbarmain = new ToolbarMain();
12     toolbarmain->show();
13     return(app.exec());
14 }
15 ToolbarMain::ToolbarMain() : KTMainWindow()
16 {
17     createMainWidget();
18     createToolBarOne();
19     createToolBarTwo();
20 }
21 void ToolbarMain::createMainWidget()
22 {
23     QPushButton *button =
24             new QPushButton("Top Level\nWidget",this);
25     setView(button);
26 }
27 void ToolbarMain::createToolBarOne()
28 {
29     QPixmap fpix("flag.png");
30     QPixmap rpix("redo.png");
31     QPixmap upix("undo.png");
32     QPixmap spix("stop.png");
33     QPixmap epix("exit.png");
34
35     KToolBar *toolbar = toolBar(1);
36     toolbar->insertButton(fpix,5,SIGNAL(clicked()),
37             this,SLOT(slotStub()),TRUE,"Flag As Used");
38     toolbar->insertButton(rpix,6,SIGNAL(clicked()),
39             this,SLOT(slotStub()),TRUE,"Redo");
40     toolbar->insertButton(upix,7,SIGNAL(clicked()),
41             this,SLOT(slotStub()),TRUE,"Undo");
42     toolbar->insertSeparator();
43     toolbar->insertButton(spix,7,SIGNAL(clicked()),
44             this,SLOT(slotStub()),TRUE,"Stop");
45     toolbar->insertButton(epix,8,SIGNAL(clicked()),
46             this,SLOT(slotExit()),TRUE,"Exit Program");
47 }
48 void ToolbarMain::createToolBarTwo()
49 {
```

```
50        QPixmap fpix("bottom.png");
51        KToolBar *toolbar = toolBar(2);
52        toolbar->insertButton(fpix,10,SIGNAL(clicked()),
53                this,SLOT(slotStub()),TRUE,"Go To Bottom");
54
55        toolbar->insertLineSeparator();
56
57        QStrList *list = new QStrList();
58        list->insert(0,"Courier");
59        list->insert(1,"Times Roman");
60        list->insert(2,"Arial");
61        toolbar->insertCombo(list,11,FALSE,
62                SIGNAL(activated(int)),
63                this,SLOT(slotFont(int)),
64                TRUE,"Select Font",110);
65
66        toolbar->insertSeparator();
67
68        QLabel *label = new QLabel("Any Widget",toolbar);
69        toolbar->insertWidget(12,90,label);
70 }
71 void ToolbarMain::slotExit()
72 {
73        kapp->exit(0);
74 }
75 bool ToolbarMain::queryClose()
76 {
77        return(TRUE);
78 }
79 void ToolbarMain::slotStub() {}
80 void ToolbarMain::slotFont(int index) {}
```

The ToolbarMain constructor, beginning on line 15, calls methods to create a widget for the main window and a pair of toolbars. The main widget created in the method createMainWidget() found on line 21 is simply a pushbutton.

Toolbar number one (the top toolbar) is created in the method createToolBar One() on line 27. As shown previously in Figure 6-12, each member of this toolbar has its own pixmap. The pixmaps are loaded from files on lines 29 through 33. The KToolBar is created by calling the method toolBar() that this class inherited from KTMainWindow. Unlike the menu creation method described earlier, the toolBar() method creates and returns a new toolbar every time you call it. And the toolbar it returns to you has already been inserted into KTMainWindow as part of the display.

There is a small space between the third and fourth members of the top toolbar. This space is inserted by the call to insertSeparator() on line 42. If you want a wider space, you can insert more separators.

The second toolbar, created by the method `createToolBarTwo()` on line 48, contains more than simple toolbar buttons. A normal toolbar button is added by the call to `insertButton()` on line 52; and just to its right, a vertical line separator is inserted with the call to `insertLineSeparator()` on line 55.

An array of strings is inserted into a `QStrList` object with calls to `insert()` on lines 58 through 60, and the array is used to install a combo box in the toolbar by calling `insertCombo()` on line 61. Internally, `KToolBar` creates a standard `QComboBox` to manage the list, so most of the information passed to `insertCombo()` is passed on to the `QComboBox`. The `insert()` methods on lines 58 through 60 define the combo box text, and assign an ID number to each one. The call to `insertCombo()` on line 61 specifies that the list be used to create the `QComboBox`, that it has an ID number of 11, and that it is not writeable by the user. The signal is `activated()` and the slot is `slotFont()`, and they both have an `int` argument so that the ID number of the selection can be passed to the slot method. The `TRUE` argument specifies that the `QComboBox` is to be enabled. The string "Select Font" specifies the text of the tooltip, and the number 110 specifies the width in pixels.

Note   The combo box in this example calls the slot with the ID number, but it is possible to use the character string instead. To do this, use the method `activated (String &)` as the signal, and `slotFont(String &)` as the slot.

You can install any widget into a toolbar. If, for example, you want to have more control over the `QComboBox` than you would have by calling `insertCombo()`, you can create your own combo box and install it by calling `insertWidget()`. The code on lines 68 and 69 creates and installs a label. Notice that the label doesn't respond to the mouse the way the other items do. When you are installing a widget, the toolbar assumes you have set up all of the signals and slots you will need to get your responses.

The Status Bar

There is an optional `KStatusBar` widget included as part of `KTMainWindow`. It is normally displayed at the bottom of the window, and it can be used by your application to display, and continuously update, a line of text. The following example, shown in Figure 6-13, uses a status bar to display the current value of an internal counter that is incremented and decremented by a pair of buttons.

Figure 6-13: A status bar tracking a value

StatusBarMain Header

```
 1 /* statusbarmain.h */
 2 #ifndef STATUSBARMAIN_H
 3 #define STATUSBARMAIN_H
 4
 5 #include <ktmainwindow.h>
 6 #include <kstatusbar.h>
 7
 8 class StatusBarMain: public KTMainWindow
 9 {
10     Q_OBJECT
11 public:
12     StatusBarMain();
13 private:
14     int counter;
15     KStatusBar *status;
16 private slots:
17     bool queryClose();
18     void slotAddOne();
19     void slotSubtractOne();
20 private:
21     void createMainWidget();
22     void createStatusBar();
23 };
24
25 #endif
```

The class StatusBarMain, defined beginning on line 8, inherits from the KTMain
Window class, which means it inherits a KStatusBar. The value to be tracked is
defined as counter on line 14; and, for convenient access, the KStatusBar pointer
will be stored in status, defined on line 15.

StatusBarMain

```
 1 /* statusbarmain.cpp */
 2 #include <kapp.h>
 3 #include <qpushbutton.h>
 4 #include <kcontainer.h>
 5 #include "statusbarmain.h"
 6
 7 int main(int argc,char **argv)
 8 {
 9     KApplication app(argc,argv,"statusbarmain");
10     StatusBarMain *statusbarmain = new StatusBarMain();
11     statusbarmain->show();
12     return(app.exec());
13 }
14 StatusBarMain::StatusBarMain() : KTMainWindow()
15 {
16     counter = 0;
```

```
17        createMainWidget();
18        createStatusBar();
19 }
20 void StatusBarMain::createMainWidget()
21 {
22        KContainerLayout *layout =
23                new KContainerLayout(this,"layout");
24        layout->setOrientation(KContainerLayout::Vertical);
25
26        QPushButton *button;
27        button = new QPushButton("Add One",this);
28        connect(button,SIGNAL(clicked()),
29                this,SLOT(slotAddOne()));
30        layout->packStart(button);
31        button = new QPushButton("Subtract One",this);
32        connect(button,SIGNAL(clicked()),
33                this,SLOT(slotSubtractOne()));
34        layout->packStart(button);
35
36        layout->sizeToFit();
37        setView(layout);
38 }
39 void StatusBarMain::createStatusBar()
40 {
41        status = statusBar();
42        status->insertItem(QString(">>"),1);
43        status->insertItem(QString("Add or Subtract"),2);
44 }
45 void StatusBarMain::slotAddOne()
46 {
47        status->changeItem(
48                QString("Plus 1 = %1").arg(++counter),2);
49 }
50 void StatusBarMain::slotSubtractOne()
51 {
52        status->changeItem(
53                QString("Minus 1 = %1").arg(--counter),2);
54 }
55 bool StatusBarMain::queryClose()
56 {
57        return(TRUE);
58 }
```

The mainline of the program creates a StatusBarMain object, which, because it inherits from KTMainWindow, automatically becomes the top-level window of the application. The StatusBarMain constructor, beginning on line 14, initializes the internal counter value to zero, and then creates the main widget and installs the initial text of the status bar.

The method `createMainWidget()` beginning on line 20 uses a `KContainerLayout` widget to hold the two buttons, as shown previously in Figure 6-13. One button is connected to the slot method `slotAddOne()` and the other is connected to `slotSubtractOne()`.

The status bar itself is initialized in the method `createStatusBar()` on line 39. The call to `statusBar()` instantiates the status bar and returns a pointer to it. Because there can only be one `KStatusBar` in a `KTMainWindow`, subsequent calls to `statusBar()` will return the address of the same status bar object. In fact, if you are only going to need access to the status bar from inside this class, there is no need to save the pointer yourself because it can always be retrieved.

Lines 42 and 43 call the `insertItem()` method of the status bar to insert the displayed string. The string is inserted in two parts (there can be more), and each one is assigned an ID number. The strings will each be displayed in the order in which you add them, and the ID numbers are needed if you wish to change them. This way, you can change part of the string without the necessity of changing all of it. For example, the slot method `slotAddOne()` on line 45 is called whenever the "Add" button is selected, causing the counter to be incremented; and the status bar text with ID number 2 is replaced by the call to `changeItem()`. The text with the ID number 1 is not changed. Similarly, the "Subtract" button executes `slotSubtractOne()` on line 50, which decrements the counter and changes only the text of ID number 2.

Note   The `arg()` methods of the `QString` class are used to format various data types into strings. Examples of all the data types, and the formatting options, are described in Chapter 16, which discusses some of the utility classes.

You can break the displayed string into as many text segments (or, if you prefer, text items) as you wish, and work with each one individually. You can also call the `KStatusBar` method `clear()` to remove the text from all the ID numbers.

Summary

The `KTMainWindow` class is a special top-level window containing code that can be used to supply the user with access to the facilities of the application, and to keep the user informed of the application's current status.

✦ A menu bar can be displayed at either the top or bottom of the top-level window. At the user's discretion, it can be torn off the top-level window and appear as a separate entity on the screen.

✦ Any window can have a menu pop up under control of the mouse or keyboard. Making a selection from this menu, or clicking the mouse on another location, will remove the menu from the display.

✦ A number of toolbars can be individually positioned on any of the four sides of the top-level window, or each one can be torn off to appear as an independent item on the screen.

✦ A status bar, with constantly updated text, can be made to appear at the bottom of the top-level window.

Chapter 7 describes widgets that can be used to create and display related collections, such as a group of radio buttons that can all interact with one another so that only one of them can be selected at any one time, or a combo box that allows the user to select one or more items from a list.

✦   ✦   ✦

Grouping Widgets

This chapter examines several of the widgets and containers that can be used to solve some of the problems that often arise when windows are being laid out. For example, it is possible to create a single widget that holds a set of buttons, and to have all these buttons attached to the same slot. There is a need to relate radio buttons to one another because selecting one of them causes the others in the group to become deselected. Sometimes groups of widgets are related by the function they perform, and there is a way to draw a frame around them so you can indicate this to the user.

KButtonBox

It is very common to have a row of buttons across the bottom of a dialog window. The class KButtonBox is a container widget that simplifies the task of positioning the row of buttons. The following example uses a KButtonBox to manage three buttons arranged horizontally:

```
1 /* hbuttonbox.cpp */
2 #include <kapp.h>
3 #include <kbuttonbox.h>
4
5 int main(int argc,char **argv)
6 {
7     QPushButton *button1;
8     QPushButton *button2;
9     QPushButton *button3;
10     KApplication
app(argc,argv,"vbuttonbox");
11
12     KButtonBox *box =
13             new
KButtonBox(0,KButtonBox::HORIZONTAL,25,15);
```

```
14      button1 = box->addButton("First Button");
15      button2 = box->addButton("Second Button");
16      button3 = box->addButton("Third Button");
17      box->layout();
18      box->show();
19      box->resize(10,10);
20
21      app.setMainWidget(box);
22      return(app.exec());
23  }
```

The button box is created on lines 12 and 13. The first argument is normally the address of the parent widget, but because this example is using it as a top-level window, it has no parent. The second argument specifies the orientation of the buttons — HORIZONTAL or VERTICAL. The two last arguments specify the minimum spacing to be inserted around the buttons. The first number specifies the minimum distance in pixels between each button and the edge of the KButtonBox. The second number specifies the distance in pixels between the buttons. The result is the row of buttons shown in Figure 7-1.

Figure 7-1: Three buttons contained in a KButtonBox

The calls to addButton() on lines 14 through 16 create the buttons — that is, the KButtonBox creates each button and returns a pointer to it. To keep the example simple, the buttons are not connected to slots. The call to layout() on line 17 is necessary because it tells the KButtonBox that you are not going to be adding anything else and that it should go ahead and configure itself. Lines 18 and 19 are the same as for any other widget — the KButtonBox is instructed to display itself (and, thus, all its contents); and it is sized in such a way that it assumes its minimum height and width.

The buttons in Figure 7-1 are all the same size. If you would rather have the width of the buttons vary according to the length of the text they contain, you can specify this as the second argument to the addButton() method. For example, the following code causes the buttons to vary in width according to the text they contain:

```
button1 = box->addButton("First Button",TRUE);
button2 = box->addButton("Second Button",TRUE);
button3 = box->addButton("Third Button",TRUE);
```

Making this second argument FALSE (the default) will cause KButtonBox to determine the size of the widest button and resize the others to match it.

Rarely does the width of the `KButtonBox` match exactly the width of the dialog that contains it, so you may want to specify how and where it stretches itself to fit. The layout at the top of Figure 7-2 shows the default stretch, with all the buttons on the left. The layout at the bottom of the figure shows what happens if you specify a stretch point.

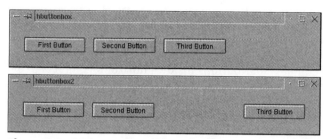

Figure 7-2: A KButtonBox with and without stretch defined

To do this, insert the stretch point between two buttons as follows:

```
button1 = box->addButton("First Button");
button2 = box->addButton("Second Button");
box->addStretch(1)
button3 = box->addButton("Third Button");
```

The stretching is done the same as it is for the containers discussed in Chapter 3. That is, you can add as many stretch points as you like; and each one will stretch in proportion to the others — the proportions are determined by the value of the argument in `addStretch()`.

With a single change, the previous example can be converted to a vertical orientation. Change the second argument on the constructor to `VERTICAL`:

```
KButtonBox *box =
        new KButtonBox(0,KButtonBox::VERTICAL,25,15);
```

The resulting window is shown in Figure 7-3. The space separating the buttons from the edges and from one another are specified in the same way. When the window is stretched vertically, the `KButtonBox` will simply insert space at the bottom, or at whatever locations you specify for stretching.

Figure 7-3: A KButtonBox with vertical orientation

Grouping Buttons with a Single Slot

A QButtonGroup object can be used to organize a group of buttons either horizontally or vertically. Each button added to the group is assigned an ID number and you can, if you wish, use a single slot method for all of the buttons. While you can create a QButtonGroup directly, it is simpler to use either a QHButtonGroup or a QVButtonGroup, depending on whether you want the buttons to be arranged horizontally or vertically. A QButtonGroup is also a QFrame, so you can use the QFrame method calls to change the appearance of the grouping.

The following example contains four buttons inside a horizontal QButtonGroup. Beneath the row of buttons, as shown in Figure 7-4, is a label that has its text updated as each button is pushed.

Figure 7-4: The QHButtonGroup widget organizes buttons horizontally.

HorizPush Header

```
 1 /* horizpush.h */
 2 #ifndef HORIZPUSH_H
 3 #define HORIZPUSH_H
 4
 5 #include <qwidget.h>
 6 #include <qlabel.h>
 7
 8 class HorizPush: public QWidget
 9 {
10     Q_OBJECT
11 public:
12     HorizPush(QWidget *parent=0,const char *name=0);
13 private:
14     QLabel *label;
15     enum ButtonChoice { SetColor, Configure, Clear, Exit };
16 private slots:
17     void slotButton(int ID);
18 };
19
20 #endif
```

The label declared on line 14 is the one that displays the text at the bottom of the window. The enumerated list on line 15 is used as the ID numbers attached to each of the buttons so the slot method can determine which button was clicked.

HorizPush

```
 1  /* horizpush.cpp */
 2  #include <kapp.h>
 3  #include <qlayout.h>
 4  #include <qhbuttongroup.h>
 5  #include <qpushbutton.h>
 6  #include "horizpush.h"
 7
 8  int main(int argc,char **argv)
 9  {
10      KApplication app(argc,argv,"horizpush");
11      HorizPush *horizpush = new HorizPush();
12      horizpush->show();
13      app.setMainWidget(horizpush);
14      return(app.exec());
15  }
16
17  HorizPush::HorizPush(QWidget *parent,const char *name)
18      : QWidget(parent,name)
19  {
20      QPushButton *button;
21      QVBoxLayout *layout = new QVBoxLayout(this,5);
22
23      QHButtonGroup *group = new QHButtonGroup(this,"hg1");
24      button = new QPushButton("Set Color",group);
25      group->insert(button,SetColor);
26      button = new QPushButton("Configure",group);
27      group->insert(button,Configure);
28      button = new QPushButton("Clear",group);
29      group->insert(button,Clear);
30      button = new QPushButton("Exit",group);
31      group->insert(button,Exit);
32      connect(group,SIGNAL(clicked(int)),
33              this,SLOT(slotButton(int)));
34      layout->addWidget(group);
35
36      label = new QLabel(" ",this);
37      layout->addWidget(label);
38
39      resize(10,10);
40      layout->activate();
41  }
42  void HorizPush::slotButton(int ID)
43  {
44      switch(ID) {
45      case SetColor:
46          label->setText("Set Color button pressed");
47          break;
48      case Configure:
49          label->setText("Configure button pressed");
50          break;
```

```
51      case Clear:
52          label->setText(" ");
53          break;
54      case Exit:
55          kapp->exit(0);
56      }
57 }
```

The constructor, beginning on line 17, creates the window layout. The principal layout manager is a vertical box, created on line 21, that contains two widgets—QHButtonGroup on the top and QLabel on the bottom.

The QHButtonGroup is created on line 23 using the HorizPush object as its parent widget, because although the QVBoxLayout object acts as a container, it is not a widget. The HorizPush object inherits QWidget, so it can act as the parent of another widget.

Lines 24 through 31 create the four pushbuttons and insert them into the QHButtonGroup. Because a QHButtonGroup is also a widget, it can act as the parent of the pushbutton widgets. The calls to insert() assign an ID number to each button as it inserts it into the group. If you do not specify ID numbers, the first button will default to 0, the second to 1, and so on. However, because these ID numbers are the only way you will have to identify the buttons, it is a good idea to specify them yourself. In this example, the values are declared as values in an enumerated type, which should make it a simple matter to add or remove buttons.

On line 32, a call to connect() attaches the checked() signal of the QHButtonGroup to the local slot named slotButton(). On line 34, the QHButtonGroup is inserted into the top of the vertical box. On lines 36 and 37, a label is created and stored in the bottom of the vertical box.

Internally, the QHButtonGroup has a slot that receives the clicked() signals from each of the buttons. It then issues its own clicked() signal, which carries the ID number assigned to the button. The slot named slotButton() on line 42 receives the signal and uses the ID number to determine what action is to be taken. If the ID is equal to SetColor or Configure, the text is set accordingly. If the ID is equal to Clear, the text is cleared. An Exit value will cause the program to exit.

Whereas a QHButtonGroup widget can be used to display buttons horizontally, a QVButtonGroup can be used to display them vertically. The process required is exactly the same as the one used to create the horizontal grouping. To change the previous example so it displays the window shown in Figure 7-5, change line 4 to include the vertical button group instead of the horizontal button group:

```
#include <qhbuttongroup.h>
```

Then change line 23 so it creates a vertical instead of horizontal button group, like this:

```
QVButtonGroup *group = new QVButtonGroup(this,"vg1");
```

Figure 7-5: The QVButtonGroup widget organizes buttons vertically.

Grouping Radio Buttons

A QVButtonGroup can be used to handle the relationship among a vertical set of radio buttons, and a QHButtonGroup can be used to control a horizontal set. Whenever a QRadioButton is inserted into a QButtonGroup, it becomes related to the other buttons in such a way that only one can be selected. The window shown in Figure 7-6 is produced by the following example.

Figure 7-6: The QVButtonGroup widget controls a set of radio buttons.

VertRadio Header

```
 1 /* vertradio.h */
 2 #ifndef VERTRADIO_H
 3 #define VERTRADIO_H
 4
 5 #include <qwidget.h>
 6 #include <qlabel.h>
 7
 8 class VertRadio: public QWidget
 9 {
10     Q_OBJECT
11 public:
12     VertRadio(QWidget *parent=0,const char *name=0);
13 private:
14     QLabel *label;
15     enum ButtonChoice { Total, Average,
16             Maximum, Minimum, Exit };
17 private slots:
18     void slotButton(int ID);
19 };
20
21 #endif
```

Each button has a unique ID number, and the values in the enumeration `Button Choice` defined on line 15 enable your program to refer to each number by a name.

VertRadio

```
 1 /* vertradio.cpp */
 2 #include <kapp.h>
 3 #include <qlayout.h>
 4 #include <qvbuttongroup.h>
 5 #include <qradiobutton.h>
 6 #include <qpushbutton.h>
 7 #include "vertradio.h"
 8
 9 int main(int argc,char **argv)
10 {
11     KApplication app(argc,argv,"vertradio");
12     VertRadio *vertradio = new VertRadio();
13     vertradio->show();
14     app.setMainWidget(vertradio);
15     return(app.exec());
16 }
17
18 VertRadio::VertRadio(QWidget *parent,const char *name)
19     : QWidget(parent,name)
20 {
21     QRadioButton *button;
22     QVBoxLayout *layout = new QVBoxLayout(this,5);
23
24     QVButtonGroup *group = new QVButtonGroup(this,"vg1");
25     button = new QRadioButton("Total",group);
26     group->insert(button,Total);
27     button = new QRadioButton("Average",group);
28     group->insert(button,Average);
29     button = new QRadioButton("Maximum",group);
30     group->insert(button,Maximum);
31     button = new QRadioButton("Minimum",group);
32     group->insert(button,Minimum);
33     QPushButton *pButton = new QPushButton("Exit",group);
34     group->insert(pButton,Exit);
35     connect(group,SIGNAL(clicked(int)),
36             this,SLOT(slotButton(int)));
37     layout->addWidget(group);
38
39     label = new QLabel(" ",this);
40     layout->addWidget(label);
41
42     resize(10,10);
43     layout->activate();
44 }
45 void VertRadio::slotButton(int ID)
46 {
47     switch(ID) {
48     case Total:
49         label->setText("Total");
```

```
50              break;
51         case Average:
52              label->setText("Average");
53              break;
54         case Maximum:
55              label->setText("Maximum");
56              break;
57         case Minimum:
58              label->setText("Minimum");
59              break;
60         case Exit:
61              kapp->exit(0);
62         }
63 }
```

This example creates a VertRadio object and uses it as the top-level window's widget. The constructor, beginning on line 18, uses a QVBoxLayout to contain the list of buttons with a label beneath it. The label is used to indicate which button is active.

Lines 24 through 32 create four radio buttons and insert them into the QVButton Group. A normal QPushButton is created on line 33 and installed in the same QVButtonGroup widget on line 34. To create the buttons, the QVButtonGroup is used as the parent widget. All radio buttons in QButtonGroup automatically become related so that only one at a time will be selected. You can mix the types of buttons in the group because the QVButtonGroup relates radio buttons only — any other kinds of buttons will remain independent entities.

The slot method slotButton() defined on line 45 is called for all of the buttons, no matter what their type. Examining the value of the button ID, the slot method sets the text of the label to indicate which radio button is currently on. The nonradio button can be used to exit the program.

While it usually makes more sense to organize radio buttons vertically, if you find yourself in a situation in which you need to arrange them horizontally, it can be done very easily. The result of converting the previous example to a horizontal orientation is shown in Figure 7-7. To make the conversion, change line 5 to the following:

```
#include <qhbuttongroup.h>
```

And change line 24 to the creation of a horizontal group box:

```
QHButtonGroup *group = new QHButtonGroup(this,"hg1");
```

Figure 7-7: A group of radio buttons organized horizontally

Grouping Check Buttons

A QCheckBox is a button that can be toggled between *off* and *on* states. The state is maintained inside the QCheckBox itself. A check button is sometimes referred to as a *toggle button*. The following example creates the collection of check buttons shown in Figure 7-8. The checkmark only appears if a check button is in the *on* state.

Figure 7-8: A group of QCheckBox buttons organized vertically

VertCheck Header

```
 1 /* vertcheck.h */
 2 #ifndef VERTCHECK_H
 3 #define VERTCHECK_H
 4
 5 #include <qwidget.h>
 6 #include <qlabel.h>
 7 #include <qvbuttongroup.h>
 8
 9 class VertCheck: public QWidget
10 {
11     Q_OBJECT
12 public:
13     VertCheck(QWidget *parent=0,const char *name=0);
14 private:
15     QVButtonGroup *group;
16     QLabel *label;
17     enum ButtonChoice { Total, Average,
18             Maximum, Minimum, Exit };
19     bool totalFlag;
20     bool averageFlag;
21     bool minimumFlag;
22     bool maximumFlag;
23 private slots:
24     void slotButton(int ID);
25 };
26
27 #endif
```

The `QVButtonGroup` is included as part of the class data, on line 15, because the slot that receives button information only supplies the button ID number, making it necessary to query the `group` for the check button status. The current `QCheckButton` status settings are stored in the Boolean variables defined on lines 19 through 22.

VertCheck

```
 1 /* vertcheck.cpp */
 2 #include <kapp.h>
 3 #include <qlayout.h>
 4 #include <qcheckbox.h>
 5 #include <qpushbutton.h>
 6 #include "vertcheck.h"
 7
 8 int main(int argc,char **argv)
 9 {
10     KApplication app(argc,argv,"vertcheck");
11     VertCheck *vertcheck = new VertCheck();
12     vertcheck->show();
13     app.setMainWidget(vertcheck);
14     return(app.exec());
15 }
16
17 VertCheck::VertCheck(QWidget *parent,const char *name)
18     : QWidget(parent,name)
19 {
20     QCheckBox *button;
21     QVBoxLayout *layout = new QVBoxLayout(this,5);
22
23     group = new QVButtonGroup(this,"vg1");
24     button = new QCheckBox("Total",group);
25     group->insert(button,Total);
26     button = new QCheckBox("Average",group);
27     group->insert(button,Average);
28     button = new QCheckBox("Maximum",group);
29     group->insert(button,Maximum);
30     button = new QCheckBox("Minimum",group);
31     group->insert(button,Minimum);
32     QPushButton *pButton = new QPushButton("Exit",group);
33     group->insert(pButton,Exit);
34     connect(group,SIGNAL(clicked(int)),
35             this,SLOT(slotButton(int)));
36     layout->addWidget(group);
37
38     label = new QLabel(" ",this);
39     layout->addWidget(label);
40
41     totalFlag = FALSE;
42     averageFlag = FALSE;
43     minimumFlag = FALSE;
44     maximumFlag = FALSE;
```

```
45
46       resize(10,10);
47       layout->activate();
48  }
49  void VertCheck::slotButton(int ID)
50  {
51       QButton *button = group->find(ID);
52       switch(ID) {
53       case Total:
54           totalFlag = ((QCheckBox *)button)->isChecked();
55           break;
56       case Average:
57           averageFlag = ((QCheckBox *)button)->isChecked();
58           break;
59       case Maximum:
60           maximumFlag = ((QCheckBox *)button)->isChecked();
61           break;
62       case Minimum:
63           minimumFlag = ((QCheckBox *)button)->isChecked();
64           break;
65       case Exit:
66           kapp->exit(0);
67       }
68       QString string;
69       if(totalFlag)
70           string += QString("Tot ");
71       if(averageFlag)
72           string += QString("Avg ");
73       if(maximumFlag)
74           string += QString("Max ");
75       if(minimumFlag)
76           string += QString("Min ");
77       label->setText(string);
78  }
```

The VertCheck constructor, beginning on line 17, creates a vertical box container; and installs a QVButtonGroup for its top widget and a QLabel for its bottom widget. The address of the QVButtonGroup is stored as group in the class. The call to addWidget() makes the QVButtonGroup the top widget of the QVBoxLayout layout manager.

Lines 24 through 31 create the four QCheckBox objects and insert them into the QVButtonGroup. A fifth button — a standard pushbutton — is created and inserted into group on lines 32 through 35. On lines 38 and 39, a label used to display the text at the bottom of the window is created and installed into the layout.

The default condition of a QCheckBox is *off*, which is represented as FALSE, so lines 41 through 44 are used to set the four internal flags to the same values as the check boxes. If you wish to preset one or more of the check boxes to being initially *on*, it could be done like this:

```
button->setChecked(TRUE);
```

You would then set its corresponding Boolean value to TRUE. In fact, more than two states are possible in the check box, as explained in the next section.

The slot method slotButton() on line 49 is called each time any one of the check buttons is toggled. The ID value of the activated button is supplied as the argument and, because this method will need to determine the check button's internal state, the call to find() on line 51 is used to retrieve the address of the check box itself. The switch statement on line 52 is used to determine which button has been selected. If the button is a check box, a call to isChecked() returns TRUE if the button is *on* and FALSE if it is *off*. Storing the check box state in a local Boolean variable gives the program quick access to the state of all the buttons.

If the value of ID indicates that it is the Exit button, the case statement on line 65 executes, causing a call to exit() to halt the application.

Lines 68 through 77 create a string specifying which of the toggles are currently *on*, and set the string as the text of the label displayed at the bottom of the window shown earlier in Figure 7-8.

Usually, groups of toggle buttons are arranged vertically, but there may be situations where you would like to arrange them horizontally. The previous example can be reorganized to configure itself horizontally, as shown in Figure 7-9, by changing line7 of vertcheck.h to the following:

```
#include <qhbuttongroup.h>
```

Also change line 15 of vertcheck.h to the following:

```
QHButtonGroup *group;
```

Also change line 23 of vertcheck.cpp to the following:

```
group = QHButtonGroup(this,"hg1");
```

Figure 7-9: A group of QCheckBox buttons organized horizontally

Some Widgets Are Also Frames

If you need to enclose a collection of widgets in a frame or box to indicate that the widgets are somehow related, act as a unit, or should otherwise be set apart from other widgets in the same window, a QFrame widget can be used to enclose them in a box. Even when no widgets are left outside the QFrame enclosure, the decorative look of the frame can improve the overall appearance of a window.

In the inheritance tree, the immediate base class of QFrame is QWidget. This means that any widget you construct can be decorated by simply using QFrame instead of QWidget as the base class. And many of the existing widgets are already constructed this way. For example, the QLabel widget uses QFrame as its base class but defaults to having the decorations turned off—adding a frame to a label is simply a matter of specifying the type and size. The following example displays the window shown in Figure 7-10, which shows four labels with their frames enabled.

Figure 7-10: Four labels with their frames enabled

LabelFrame

```
 1 /* labelframe.cpp */
 2 #include <qlayout.h>
 3 #include <qframe.h>
 4 #include <kapp.h>
 5 #include <qlabel.h>
 6 #include "labelframe.h"
 7
 8 int main(int argc,char **argv)
 9 {
10     KApplication app(argc,argv,"labelframe");
11     LabelFrame *labelframe = new LabelFrame();
12     labelframe->show();
13     app.setMainWidget(labelframe);
14     return(app.exec());
15 }
16
17 LabelFrame::LabelFrame(QWidget *parent,const char *name)
18     : QWidget(parent,name)
19 {
20     QLabel *lab;
```

```
21        QVBoxLayout *layout = new QVBoxLayout(this,8);
22
23        lab = new QLabel("QFrame::Box",this);
24        lab->setFrameStyle(QFrame::Box | QFrame::Sunken);
25        lab->setLineWidth(2);
26        lab->setMidLineWidth(1);
27        lab->setAlignment(AlignVCenter | AlignHCenter);
28        lab->setMargin(8);
29        layout->addWidget(lab);
30
31        lab = new QLabel("QFrame::Box",this);
32        lab->setFrameStyle(QFrame::Box | QFrame::Raised);
33        lab->setLineWidth(1);
34        lab->setMidLineWidth(1);
35        lab->setAlignment(AlignVCenter | AlignHCenter);
36        lab->setMargin(8);
37        layout->addWidget(lab);
38
39        lab = new QLabel("QFrame::WinPanel",this);
40        lab->setFrameStyle(QFrame::WinPanel | QFrame::Raised);
41        lab->setAlignment(AlignVCenter | AlignHCenter);
42        lab->setMargin(8);
43        layout->addWidget(lab);
44
45        lab = new QLabel("QFrame::Panel",this);
46        lab->setFrameStyle(QFrame::Panel | QFrame::Sunken);
47        lab->setAlignment(AlignVCenter | AlignHCenter);
48        lab->setLineWidth(4);
49        lab->setMargin(8);
50        layout->addWidget(lab);
51
52        resize(10,10);
53        layout->activate();
54 }
```

The constructor beginning on line 17 creates a vertical box layout manager and populates it with four labels.

Lines 23 through 29 create a label that uses a combination of the Box shape with the shadowing set to Sunken. The resulting shadow pattern makes the box look as if it were engraved into the surface. The lineWidth() method on line 25 specifies the pixel width of each of the two lines that make up the edges of the trough in the center. The setMidLine() method on line 26 specifies the width of the trough in the center of the line. The calls to setAlignment() and setMargin() on lines 27 and 28 center the text and put an eight-pixel boundary between the text and the frame.

Lines 31 through 37 create another label with the Box shape, but this time it uses the Raised shadowing. This causes the box to appear as if it were a ridge sticking out of the surface. The lines drawn for this frame are narrower than those drawn for the previous one because the call to setLineWidth() on line 33 specifies that the edges of the ridge be only one pixel wide.

Lines 39 through 43 create a label with the style `WinPanel`, which is to be shadowed such that it appears to be raised. The width is allowed to default, and there is no midline width because there is no trough or ridge.

Lines 45 through 50 create a label with the style `Panel`, which is shadowed to make the entire label appear to be sunken into the surface. Each line drawn around the edge is four pixels wide, because of the call to `setLineWidth()` on line 48.

Many of the Qt and KDE widgets use `QFrame` as a base class. Some of them display a frame by default, but they are all capable of displaying a frame. With any of the following widgets, a call to the method `setFrameStyle()` causes a frame to appear:

KAboutContainer	KMenuBar	QHButtonGroup
KAboutContributor	KMultiLineEdit	QHGroupBox
KAccelMenu	KMultiWallpaperList	QIconView
KApplicationTree	KPopupMenu	QIconView
KBackgroundDockWidget	KProgress	QLCDNumber
KCharSelect	KRuler	QLabel
KCharSelectTable	KSeparator	QListBox
KColorCells	KSplitList	QListView
KColorPatch	KStatusBar	QMenuBar
KContainerLayout	KStatusBarLabel	QMultiLineEdit
KDMView	KTabListBoxTable	QPopupFrame
KDatePicker	KTextBrowser	QPopupMenu
KDateTable	KThemeListBox	QProgressBar
KDesktop	KToolBar	QScrollView
KDockWindow	KURLLabel	QSpinBox
KEdit	KfindWindow	QSplitter
KEyesWidget	KiKbdButton	QTableView
KFileSimpleView	KiKbdMapInfoWidget	QTextBrowser
KFormulaToolBar	KickerClientMenu	QTextEdit
KGroupBox	QButtonGroup	QTextView
KHTMLWidget	QCanvasView	QVBox
KIOListView	QfileListBox	QVButtonGroup
KIconLoaderCanvas	QfileListView	QVGroupBox

KIconStyle	QGrid	QWellArray
KImageTrackLabel	QGroupBox	QWidgetStack
KIntSpinBox	QHBox	

Framing Options

You can use a number of settings to specify the appearance of a frame: Box, Panel, WinPanel, Hline, or Vline. Moreover, each of these styles can be set to appear raised, sunken, or plain. And the widths of the lines can be specified. The following examples demonstrate the different ways in which a frame can be configured.

The Box QFrame

The program named boxframe displays the different appearances of a Box type of frame. The three possible adjustments are the line width, the midline width, and whether the appearance should be sunken, plain, or raised. Figure 7-11 shows the appearance of the frames with line widths varying from 1 to 3, and midline widths varying from 0 to 2.

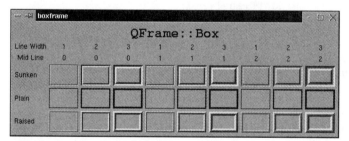

Figure 7-11: Twenty-seven different appearances of the Box QFrame type

The following program is used to generate the set of frames shown in Figure 7-11. It uses a grid layout to position all the frames and labels, and has a loop that creates and inserts the frames with different settings.

```
1 /* boxframe.cpp */
2 #include <qlayout.h>
3 #include <qframe.h>
4 #include <qlabel.h>
5 #include <kapp.h>
6 #include "boxframe.h"
7
8 int main(int argc,char **argv)
```

```
 9  {
10      KApplication app(argc,argv,"boxframe");
11      BoxFrame *boxframe = new BoxFrame();
12      boxframe->show();
13      app.setMainWidget(boxframe);
14      return(app.exec());
15  }
16
17  BoxFrame::BoxFrame(QWidget *parent,const char *name)
18      : QWidget(parent,name)
19  {
20      QLabel *label;
21      QFrame *frame;
22      QGridLayout *layout = new QGridLayout(this,6,10,5);
23
24      label = new QLabel("QFrame::Box",this);
25      label->setFont(QFont("Courier",24,QFont::Bold));
26      label->setAlignment(Qt::AlignHCenter);
27      layout->addMultiCellWidget(label,0,0,0,9);
28
29      label = new QLabel("Line Width",this);
30      label->setAlignment(Qt::AlignHCenter);
31      layout->addWidget(label,1,0);
32      label = new QLabel("Mid Line",this);
33      label->setAlignment(Qt::AlignHCenter);
34      layout->addWidget(label,2,0);
35      label = new QLabel("Sunken",this);
36      layout->addWidget(label,3,0);
37      layout->setRowStretch(3,1);
38      label = new QLabel("Plain",this);
39      layout->addWidget(label,4,0);
40      layout->setRowStretch(4,1);
41      label = new QLabel("Raised",this);
42      layout->addWidget(label,5,0);
43      layout->setRowStretch(5,1);
44
45      for(int i=0; i<9; i++) {
46          int lineWidth = (i % 3) + 1;
47          int midLineWidth = i / 3;
48          label = new QLabel(
49                  QString("%1").arg(lineWidth),this);
50          label->setAlignment(Qt::AlignHCenter);
51          layout->addWidget(label,1,i+1);
52          label = new QLabel(
53                  QString("%1").arg(midLineWidth),this);
54          label->setAlignment(Qt::AlignHCenter);
55          layout->addWidget(label,2,i+1);
56
57          frame = new QFrame(this);
58          frame->setFrameStyle(QFrame::Box | QFrame::Sunken);
59          frame->setLineWidth(lineWidth);
60          frame->setMidLineWidth(midLineWidth);
61          layout->addWidget(frame,3,i+1);
62
```

```
63          frame = new QFrame(this);
64          frame->setFrameStyle(QFrame::Box | QFrame::Plain);
65          frame->setLineWidth(lineWidth);
66          frame->setMidLineWidth(midLineWidth);
67          layout->addWidget(frame,4,i+1);
68
69          frame = new QFrame(this);
70          frame->setFrameStyle(QFrame::Box | QFrame::Raised);
71          frame->setLineWidth(lineWidth);
72          frame->setMidLineWidth(midLineWidth);
73          layout->addWidget(frame,5,i+1);
74      }
75
76      resize(600,200);
77      layout->activate();
78 }
```

The label at the top of the window and the labels on the left are all created, and stored in the grid layout, on lines 24 through 27.

The loop beginning on line 45 iterates nine times because nine columns of frames are to be displayed. Lines 46 and 47 compute the values of lineWidth and midLineWidth by using the value of the loop counter. For the current column, labels to display the two width values are created on lines 48 through 55. The three frames in the column are created on lines 57 through 73. All three of the calls to setFrameStyle() use the QFrame::Box style, but are given different shadowing patterns. For each frame, the line widths are set to the calculated values.

The rest of the examples in this section use the same basic code to display the options of the other styles. However, as you will see in the figures, the options available to any one style vary.

The Panel QFrame

The program named panelframe displays the window shown in Figure 7-12, demonstrating the appearance of a Panel style of frame. The frame is made from a single line that can be shaded to cause the enclosed area of the frame to appear raised above the surface or sunken below it. The midline value used in the previous example has no effect here because the frame is constructed from a single line.

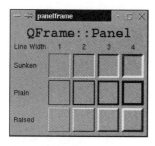

Figure 7-12: The three forms of a Panel frame, with varying line thickness

The WinPanel QFrame

The program `winpanelframe` displays the window shown in Figure 7-13. The appearance of the `WinPanel` frame is the same as a `Panel` frame with the line width set to two pixels. In a `WinPanel`, the line thickness cannot be varied. In this style of frame was originally designed to mimic the appearance of the Windows operating system.

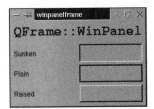

Figure 7-13: The three forms of a WinPanel frame

Using QFrame to Draw Lines

Two `QFrame` styles are not frames at all — they are lines. You can use the `HLine` style to instruct `QFrame` to draw itself as a horizontal line, as shown in Figure 7-14. All of the modifications that can be applied to the appearance of a `Box` can also be applied to an `HLine`. That is, each line is drawn as three lines, with the midline value specifying the width of middle line, and the line width value specifying the width of the other two lines. The shading is set so that the line appears to be raised above or sunken into the surface.

				QFrame::HLine				
Line Width	1	2	3	1	2	3	1	2	3
Mid Line	0	0	0	1	1	1	2	2	2
Sunken									
Plain									
Raised									

Figure 7-14: A QFrame drawn as a horizontal line

It is also possible to draw a vertical line, as shown in Figure 7-15. It can be configured using the same set of options as the horizontal line.

Figure 7-15: A QFrame drawn
as a vertical line

Sharing Window Real Estate

Using a QSplitter widget, it is possible to display more than one widget in a window and make it simple for the user to change the size of the individual widgets so they don't overlap. Figure 7-16 shows a splitter being used to contain a pair of text edit windows.

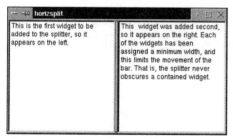

Figure 7-16: A QSplitter containing two
edit windows

The bar between the two edit panes can be moved from side to side, increasing the width of one widget as it increases the size of the other. In this example, the edit widgets are set to automatically wrap the text they are displaying, so moving the bar to the left (as shown in Figure 7-17) resizes both edit widgets, which causes the text to rearrange itself.

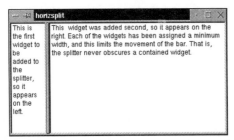

Figure 7-17: A QSplitter showing the result
of resizing two edit windows

The following program creates the windows displayed in Figures 7-16 and 7-17.

HorizSplit Header

```
1 /* horizsplit.h */
2 #ifndef HORIZSPLIT_H
3 #define HORIZSPLIT_H
4
5 #include <qsplitter.h>
6
7 class HorizSplit: public QSplitter
8 {
9     Q_OBJECT
10 public:
11     HorizSplit(QWidget *parent=0,const char *name=0);
12 };
13
14 #endif
```

This header file defines the class HorizSplit, which inherits the behaviors from
QSplitter.

HorizSplit

```
1 /* horizsplit.cpp */
2 #include <kapp.h>
3 #include <qmultilineedit.h>
4 #include "horizsplit.h"
5
6 int main(int argc,char **argv)
7 {
8     KApplication app(argc,argv,"horizsplit");
9     HorizSplit *horizsplit = new HorizSplit();
10     horizsplit->show();
11     app.setMainWidget(horizsplit);
12     return(app.exec());
```

```
13 }
14
15 HorizSplit::HorizSplit(QWidget *parent,const char *name)
16     : QSplitter(parent,name)
17 {
18     QMultiLineEdit *leftEdit = new QMultiLineEdit(this);
19     leftEdit->setMinimumWidth(50);
20     leftEdit->setWordWrap(QMultiLineEdit::WidgetWidth);
21
22     QMultiLineEdit *rightEdit = new QMultiLineEdit(this);
23     rightEdit->setMinimumWidth(50);
24     rightEdit->setWordWrap(QMultiLineEdit::WidgetWidth);
25
26     resize(400,200);
27 }
```

The process of setting up a split window is simply a matter of inserting a widget for each of the panes in the splitter. The constructor, beginning on line 15, creates a pair of QMultiLineEdit objects using this as the parent class. (Recall that this is a reference to the current object.) Because the HorizSplit class is also a QSplitter class, and a QSplitter manages all of its child widgets in separate panes, nothing else is necessary. The minimum allowable width of the text edit windows is set to 50 to give a lower limit to the movement of the splitter bar — if you have no lower limit, the bar can be moved to completely obscure a window.

The QSplitter default is to arrange the widgets horizontally. The following example arranges the widget vertically:

VertSplit

```
1 /* vertsplit.cpp */
2 #include <kapp.h>
3 #include <qmultilineedit.h>
4 #include "vertsplit.h"
5
6 int main(int argc,char **argv)
7 {
8     KApplication app(argc,argv,"vertsplit");
9     VertSplit *vertsplit = new VertSplit();
10     vertsplit->show();
11     app.setMainWidget(vertsplit);
12     return(app.exec());
13 }
14
15 VertSplit::VertSplit(QWidget *parent,const char *name)
16     : QSplitter(parent,name)
17 {
18     setOrientation(Vertical);
19
20     QMultiLineEdit *topEdit = new QMultiLineEdit(this);
```

```
21      topEdit->setMinimumHeight(50);
22      topEdit->setWordWrap(QMultiLineEdit::WidgetWidth);
23
24      QMultiLineEdit *middleEdit = new QMultiLineEdit(this);
25      middleEdit->setMinimumHeight(50);
26      middleEdit->setWordWrap(QMultiLineEdit::WidgetWidth);
27
28      QMultiLineEdit *bottomEdit = new QMultiLineEdit(this);
29      bottomEdit->setMinimumHeight(50);
30      bottomEdit->setWordWrap(QMultiLineEdit::WidgetWidth);
31
32      resize(200,400);
33 }
```

The call to setOrientation() on line 16 instructs this QSplitter to arrange its widgets one above the other. The first one added is at the top. It is possible to add a number of widgets to the splitter — this example contains three widgets, so it has two bars to separate them. The result is shown in Figure 7-18.

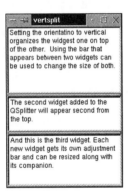

Figure 7-18: A vertical QSplitter containing three edit windows

Summary

This chapter demonstrated some of the basic techniques you can use to organize widgets in such a way that they mean something to your application, and to the user viewing the window. This chapter covered the following:

✦ Using some special widgets, it is possible to organize the display of a group of buttons and, at the same time, have all the buttons use the same slot to report a mouse click.

✦ A group of radio buttons must relate to one another physically in order to limit the selection to only one button at a time.

✦ While check buttons (also called toggle buttons) don't relate to one another physically, they often relate to one another logically, and should be considered as a group.

✦ Decorative frames can be drawn around widgets. More than decoration, frames can be used to clarify widget relationships on an otherwise confusing display.

✦ A collection of widgets can share the same space by enabling the user to slide a bar back and forth between them.

This chapter completes Part I of the book. The chapters in Part II are less broad, detailing some subjects that have been only briefly touched on in Part I. For example, the next chapter explores the mouse and all the things you can do with it. While basic mouse operations are demonstrated in every chapter in Part I, there is much more that you can do with a mouse.

✦   ✦   ✦

Step by Step

The Mouse and the Keyboard

A normal KDE/Qt application does nothing until it hears from the user. When an application is first executed, it performs any necessary initializations, displays its window, and then goes to sleep, waiting for the user to do something. In the majority of cases, it is waiting for input from the mouse or keyboard, but the input can be from a light pen, a mouse wheel, a graphics tablet, a trackball, or some other input device. Most applications can be written using the predefined set of signals and slots that are included as part of the widgets, but it is sometimes necessary to attach your program directly to the incoming stream of events. Also, if you are going to create a widget of your own, you need to know how to translate the incoming events into signals.

From a Port to a Slot

The following is a brief, simple description of the life cycle of an event.

An event starts with the hardware. The mouse is moved to a new location, a keyboard key is released, a mouse button is pressed, or a keyboard button is held down long enough for the auto-repeat mechanism to kick in. The device issuing the event is physically connected to the computer, so the event will cause an interrupt, and a small program — known as a *device driver* — reads the information from the port. The primary job of the device driver is to translate the hardware event into a software event.

The device driver must be instructed to wait for events on a specific port. This is done from inside a program when it opens a port, in much the same way that an application would open a file. The ports are all found in the /dev directory, and a port can be addressed by a program just as if it were a file. When a program opens a port (that is, a name in the /dev directory), the Linux kernel selects a device driver and gives it the job of passing information back and forth between the port and the application.

For Qt and KDE, the application retrieving events from the driver is the X Windowing System. Each event from the device driver is formatted into a special internal format known as an XEvent. The window manager inspects the XEvent to determine its destination window. If, for example, the event is a keyboard click, the event is to be sent to the window that currently has the focus. If it is a mouse click, the *x* and *y* coordinates of the mouse pointer usually determines which window. By knowing which window is to receive the event, the window manager can determine which application is to receive the event.

For an X Window program to process events, it sets up a loop to continuously call the low-level queue reading function XNextEvent(). Each time this function returns, it has retrieved an event from the queue. The events are dispatched to your application by calling a method assigned to handle events of its type.

When your program calls QApplication::exec() or KApplication::exec() in its mainline, it executes a continuous loop, calling XNextEvent(), which reads an XEvent, translates it into one of the Qt events, and calls the appropriate method to deal with it. These event-receiving methods are defined as part of the QWidget class, and are declared as being both virtual and private. The actions performed by these methods are minimal, so it is necessary to create subclasses of QWidget that override the methods to receive the events. For example, the QButton class overrides the QWidget method named mouseReleaseEvent() so QButton can emit a clicked() signal. This enables your application to set up a slot to receive the clicked() signal whenever the mouse is used to activate the button.

The Mouse Events

A mouse event contains the current location of the mouse pointer and indicators of which, if any, buttons are currently being pressed. A method in the QWidget class is called whenever a mouse event arrives. If you wish to write your own detailed mouse event processing, you can override the event handling methods defined in QWidget.

The following program tracks the mouse and displays the buttons, keys, and position of the mouse pointer. As shown in Figure 8-1, the blank widget on the right is the one being monitored for mouse movement, while each mouse action is listed on the left. This example demonstrates how an incoming event is translated into a signal. Whenever a mouse event arrives, the data from it is used to create a descriptive string. This string is emitted as a signal and is received by a slot of another class.

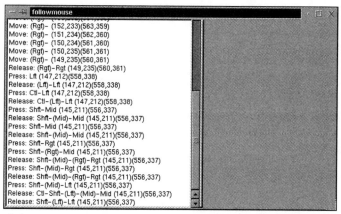

Figure 8-1: A program to track and display mouse activity

MouseSensor Header

```
 1 /* mousesensor.h */
 2 #ifndef MOUSESENSOR_H
 3 #define MOUSESENSOR_H
 4
 5 #include <qwidget.h>
 6 #include <qevent.h>
 7 #include <qstring.h>
 8
 9 class MouseSensor: public QWidget
10 {
11     Q_OBJECT
12 public:
13     MouseSensor(QWidget *parent=0,const char *name=0);
14 private:
15     void emitDescription(const QString &,QMouseEvent *);
16     virtual void mousePressEvent(QMouseEvent *event);
17     virtual void mouseReleaseEvent(QMouseEvent *event);
18     virtual void mouseDoubleClickEvent(QMouseEvent *event);
19     virtual void mouseMoveEvent(QMouseEvent *event);
20 signals:
21     void description(QString &);
22 };
23
24 #endif
```

The MouseSensor class is a widget that tracks mouse activities. It appears as the blank panel on the right in Figure 8-1. The virtual methods on lines 16 through 19 override the methods in the base class QWidget, so all the mouse events will arrive here instead of in the base class.

MouseSensor

```
1 /* mousesensor.cpp */
2 #include <qstring.h>
3 #include "mousesensor.h"
4
5 MouseSensor::MouseSensor(QWidget *parent,const char *name)
6     : QWidget(parent,name)
7 {
8     setMinimumSize(300,300);
9 }
10 void MouseSensor::mousePressEvent(QMouseEvent *event)
11 {
12     emitDescription(QString("Press: "),event);
13 }
14 void MouseSensor::mouseReleaseEvent(QMouseEvent *event)
15 {
16     emitDescription(QString("Release: "),event);
17 }
18 void MouseSensor::mouseDoubleClickEvent(QMouseEvent *event)
19 {
20     emitDescription(QString("DoubleClick: "),event);
21 }
22 void MouseSensor::mouseMoveEvent(QMouseEvent *event)
23 {
24     emitDescription(QString("Move: "),event);
25 }
26 void MouseSensor::emitDescription(const QString &typeStr,
27         QMouseEvent *event)
28 {
29     QString btnStr(typeStr);
30     ButtonState state = event->state();
31     if(state & ControlButton)
32         btnStr+= "Ctl-";
33     if(state & AltButton)
34         btnStr+= "Alt-";
35     if(state & ShiftButton)
36         btnStr+= "Shft-";
37     if(state & LeftButton)
38         btnStr += "(Lft)-";
39     if(state & MidButton)
40         btnStr += "(Mid)-";
41     if(state & RightButton)
42         btnStr += "(Rgt)-";
43     ButtonState button = event->button();
44     if(button & LeftButton)
45         btnStr += "Lft";
46     if(button & MidButton)
47         btnStr += "Mid";
48     if(button & RightButton)
49         btnStr += "Rgt";
```

```
50
51     QString str = QString("%1 (%2,%3)(%4,%5)")
52          .arg(btnStr)
53          .arg(event->x()).arg(event->y())
54          .arg(event->globalX()).arg(event->globalY());
55
56     emit description(str);
57 }
```

The MouseSensor class is a widget because it uses QWidget as its base class. The four methods in this class that receive mouse events override four virtual methods in the base class. The method mousePressEvent() is called every time one of the mouse buttons is pressed, and the method mouseReleaseEvent() is called every time one of the mouse buttons is released. The method mouseDoubleClick() is called whenever a mouse button is pressed and released twice within a certain time span. This means that a double-click action will generate five events — two button press events, two button release events, and one double-click event. This may seem like overkill, but because the events can easily be separated by type, you can write your application to only receive the ones you need to deal with.

The method mouseMoveEvent() on line 22 is called whenever the mouse is moved to a new location within the window. There are two modes of operation: The method can be called for every mouse movement, or it can be called for only those movements that occur while a mouse button is being held down. The default requires one of the buttons to be held down, but a call to the method setMouseTracking(TRUE) causes the mouse position to always be reported.

The method emitDescription() beginning on line 26 is used by all of the event-receiving methods to create a descriptive string and send a signal containing the string. The information is all inside the QMouseEvent object.

A ButtonState value is retrieved by calling the state() method of the event on line 30. This variable contains flags representing the buttons (if any) that were being held down at the time of the mouse event. Six possible buttons can be set: the three mouse buttons along with Alt, Ctrl, and Shift. The ButtonState value retrieved by the call to button() on line 43 is the button (if any) that caused the event. For example, if you are holding down the Ctrl key and the right mouse button, pressing the left mouse button will cause the Ctrl key and the right mouse button indicator to be returned from the call to state(), and the left mouse button indicator to be returned from button().

Note
While the Alt key can be represented by a flag value in ButtonState, the Alt key is actually never reported in the mouse events. This is because KDE intercepts the Alt key when it is used with the mouse. Alt-left mouse button can be used to move a window; Alt-middle button will rotate focus the next window, and Alt-right button will resize the current window. If you are using a two-button mouse, you can usually emulate the middle button by pressing both buttons simultaneously, and keyboards without an Alt key generally have a Meta key that works the same way.

There are two mouse locations in the QMouseEvent object. One represents the x and y coordinates relative to the top, left corner of the entire screen, and the other represents the x and y values relative to the top, left corner of the current window. On line 51, a QString object is created to hold a description of the event. Lines 53 and 54 format both of the coordinates as part of the string describing the event. Usually, the local coordinates are the ones you want, but sometimes you may need to know the global location of the mouse.

The emit statement on line 56 is the final step in converting the incoming event into an outgoing signal. This same sort of process occurs in, for example, a QPush Button that converts mouse button events into a signal named click(). In this example, a signal is emitted that carries with it a QString containing a description of the event:

FollowMouse Header

```
 1 /* followmouse.h */
 2 #ifndef FOLLOWMOUSE_H
 3 #define FOLLOWMOUSE_H
 4
 5 #include <qsplitter.h>
 6 #include <qstring.h>
 7 #include <qmultilineedit.h>
 8
 9 class FollowMouse: public QSplitter
10 {
11     Q_OBJECT
12 public:
13     FollowMouse(QWidget *parent=0,const char *name=0);
14 public slots:
15     void newline(QString &);
16 private:
17     QMultiLineEdit *edit;
18 };
19
20 #endif
```

The FollowMouse class is the top-level window shown previously in Figure 8-1. It is based on a QSplitter, which enables it to manage both the QMultiLineEdit object on the left and the MouseSensor object on the right.

FollowMouse

```
 1 /* followmouse.cpp */
 2 #include <kapp.h>
 3 #include <qstring.h>
 4 #include "mousesensor.h"
 5 #include "followmouse.h"
 6
```

```
 7 int main(int argc,char **argv)
 8 {
 9     KApplication app(argc,argv,"followmouse");
10     FollowMouse *followmouse = new FollowMouse();
11     followmouse->show();
12     app.setMainWidget(followmouse);
13     return(app.exec());
14 }
15
16 FollowMouse::FollowMouse(QWidget *parent,const char *name)
17     : QSplitter(parent,name)
18 {
19     edit = new QMultiLineEdit(this);
20     edit->setMinimumWidth(80);
21     edit->setReadOnly(TRUE);
22
23     MouseSensor *sensor = new MouseSensor(this);
24     sensor->setMinimumWidth(80);
25
26     connect(sensor,SIGNAL(description(QString &)),
27             this,SLOT(newline(QString &)));
28
29     resize(10,10);
30 }
31 void FollowMouse::newline(QString &str)
32 {
33     edit->insertLine(str);
34     edit->setCursorPosition(5000,0);
35 }
```

The FollowMouse constructor, beginning on line 16, creates a QMultiLineEdit
widget on lines 19 through 21. The call to setReadOnly() disables the editing facilities and makes the editor a display-only text window. Because the editor widget is
created first, it appears on the left. The MouseSensor, created on line 23, appears
on the right.

In order for this class to receive mouse event descriptions, a call to connect()
is made on line 26, establishing a connection from the description() signal of
MouseSensor to the slot newLine() of FollowMouse.

The slot method on line 31 is called with a descriptive string of every mouse event.
The call to insertLine() on line 33 appends the string to the bottom of the text
being displayed by the QMultiLineEdit widget. The call to setCursorPos()
ensures that the newest string (the one at the bottom) is visible. Specifying an index
greater than the actual number of members of the list causes QMultiLineEdit to
choose the last one.

Mouse Grabbing and Releasing

A single widget in your application can take control of the mouse. It doesn't restrict the movement of the mouse pointer, but it does prevent all other widgets (in this or any other application) from receiving any events from the mouse.

Caution If you grab the mouse, you must also make sure there is a release mechanism. If your program grabs the mouse and doesn't release it, the terminal is effectively locked. The keyboard works, but the mouse is disabled until your program is killed.

The following program displays a window like the one shown in Figure 8-2. The top button grabs the mouse and changes the cursor appearance to cross hairs. The lower button releases the mouse.

Figure 8-2: A grabbed mouse cannot move outside its window.

GrabMouse Header

```
 1 /* grabmouse.h */
 2 #ifndef GRABMOUSE_H
 3 #define GRABMOUSE_H
 4
 5 #include <qwidget.h>
 6 #include <qlayout.h>
 7 #include <qpushbutton.h>
 8
 9 class GrabMouse: public QWidget
10 {
11     Q_OBJECT
12 public:
13     GrabMouse(QWidget *parent=0,const char *name=0);
14 private:
15     QPushButton *grabButton;
16     QPushButton *relButton;
17 public slots:
18     void mouse_grab();
19     void mouse_release();
20 };
21
22 #endif
```

GrabMouse

```
 1 /* grabmouse.cpp */
 2 #include <kapp.h>
 3 #include <qcursor.h>
 4 #include "grabmouse.h"
 5
 6 int main(int argc,char **argv)
 7 {
 8     KApplication app(argc,argv,"grabmouse");
 9     GrabMouse *grabmouse = new GrabMouse();
10     grabmouse->show();
11     app.setMainWidget(grabmouse);
12     return(app.exec());
13 }
14
15 GrabMouse::GrabMouse(QWidget *parent,const char *name)
16     : QWidget(parent,name)
17 {
18     QVBoxLayout *layout = new QVBoxLayout(this,20);
19
20     grabButton = new QPushButton("Grab Mouse",this);
21     grabButton->setMinimumSize(grabButton->sizeHint());
22     layout->addWidget(grabButton);
23     connect(grabButton,SIGNAL(clicked()),
24             this,SLOT(mouse_grab()));
25
26     relButton = new QPushButton("Release Mouse",this);
27     relButton->setMinimumSize(relButton->sizeHint());
28     layout->addWidget(relButton);
29     connect(relButton,SIGNAL(clicked()),
30             this,SLOT(mouse_release()));
31
32     resize(10,10);
33     layout->activate();
34 }
35 void GrabMouse::mouse_grab()
36 {
37     relButton->grabMouse(QCursor(CrossCursor));
38 }
39 void GrabMouse::mouse_release()
40 {
41     relButton->releaseMouse();
42 }
```

The GrabMouse class is a widget that uses a vertical box, created on line 18, to hold a pair of buttons. The top button, named grabButton, has its clicked() signal connected to the slot method mouse_grab() defined on line 35. Similarly, relButton is connected to the slot method mouse_released(), defined on line 39.

Whenever the top button is selected, the `grabMouse()` method of `relButton` is called, causing `relButton` to grab the mouse. Passing a cursor definition to `grabMouse()` causes the appearance of the cursor to be modified for the duration of the grab. Because it was the `relButton` that executed the grab, it is the only widget that will respond to the mouse, and it does so by calling `releaseMouse()` to return mouse control to the system.

Changing the Cursor's Appearance

You can use a standard set of built-in cursors to notify the user of the program's current status. The method that changes the cursor is found in `QWidget`, so any displayable object can have its cursor changed.

When you change the cursor's appearance, the change applies only to the region you specify. For example, if you change the cursor for the top-level window of your application, it will not be changed for the title bar, but it will be changed for every widget that is a child or grandchild of your top-level window. However, if one of the child widgets has its own cursor setting, it (and all of its descendents) will have its own cursor.

The following example allows you to dynamically choose among all of the standard cursors. You can apply one cursor to the entire window and another to a single button inside the window. As shown in Figure 8-3, the names of the cursors are listed on the left. Whenever the name of a cursor is selected, it becomes the default cursor for the entire window. Using the Select button on the right causes the currently selected cursor to be assigned as its own private cursor — that is, its cursor is no longer inherited from its parent.

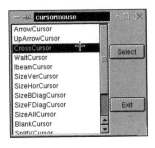

Figure 8-3: A cursor selection list

CursorMouse Header

```
1 /* cursormouse.h */
2 #ifndef CURSORMOUSE_H
3 #define CURSORMOUSE_H
```

```
 4
 5 #include <qlayout.h>
 6 #include <qpushbutton.h>
 7
 8 class CursorMouse: public QWidget
 9 {
10     Q_OBJECT
11 public:
12     CursorMouse(QWidget *parent=0,const char *name=0);
13 private:
14     QPushButton *selectButton;
15     QPushButton *exitButton;
16     int cursorID;
17 public slots:
18     void changeCursor(int);
19     void selectCursor();
20     void shutdown();
21 };
22
23 #endif
```

The CursorMouse class includes three slots. Two of them are used to change the cursor; the third exits the program. The cursorID, defined on line 16, holds the ID number of the currently selected cursor.

CursorMouse

```
 1 /* cursormouse.cpp */
 2 #include <kapp.h>
 3 #include <qcursor.h>
 4 #include <qlistbox.h>
 5 #include "cursormouse.h"
 6
 7 struct cursStruct {
 8     QString name;
 9     int number;
10 } curs[] = {
11     { "ArrowCursor",ArrowCursor },
12     { "UpArrowCursor",UpArrowCursor },
13     { "CrossCursor",CrossCursor },
14     { "WaitCursor",WaitCursor },
15     { "IbeamCursor",IbeamCursor },
16     { "SizeVerCursor",SizeVerCursor },
17     { "SizeHorCursor",SizeHorCursor },
18     { "SizeBDiagCursor",SizeBDiagCursor },
19     { "SizeFDiagCursor",SizeFDiagCursor },
20     { "SizeAllCursor",SizeAllCursor },
21     { "BlankCursor",BlankCursor },
22     { "SplitVCursor",SplitVCursor },
23     { "SplitHCursor",SplitHCursor },
```

```
24      { "PointingHandCursor",PointingHandCursor },
25      { "BitmapCursor",BitmapCursor }
26 };
27
28 int main(int argc,char **argv)
29 {
30     KApplication app(argc,argv,"cursormouse");
31     CursorMouse *cursormouse = new CursorMouse();
32     cursormouse->show();
33     app.setMainWidget(cursormouse);
34     return(app.exec());
35 }
36
37 CursorMouse::CursorMouse(QWidget *parent,const char *name)
38     : QWidget(parent,name)
39 {
40     QHBoxLayout *horlayout = new QHBoxLayout(this);
41
42     QListBox *list = new QListBox(this);
43     for(int i=0; i<sizeof(curs)/sizeof(cursStruct); i++)
44         list->insertItem(curs[i].name);
45     horlayout->addWidget(list);
46     connect(list,SIGNAL(highlighted(int)),
47             this,SLOT(changeCursor(int)));
48
49     QVBoxLayout *verlayout = new QVBoxLayout(30);
50
51     selectButton = new QPushButton("Select",this);
52     selectButton->setMinimumSize(selectButton->sizeHint());
53     verlayout->addWidget(selectButton);
54     connect(selectButton,SIGNAL(clicked()),
55             this,SLOT(selectCursor()));
56
57     exitButton = new QPushButton("Exit",this);
58     exitButton->setMinimumSize(exitButton->sizeHint());
59     verlayout->addWidget(exitButton);
60     connect(exitButton,SIGNAL(clicked()),
61             this,SLOT(shutdown()));
62
63     horlayout->addLayout(verlayout);
64
65     resize(250,200);
66     horlayout->activate();
67 }
68 void CursorMouse::changeCursor(int index)
69 {
70     cursorID = curs[index].number;
71     setCursor(QCursor(cursorID));
72 }
73 void CursorMouse::selectCursor()
74 {
```

```
75        selectButton->setCursor(QCursor(cursorID));
76   }
77   void CursorMouse::shutdown()
78   {
79        kapp->exit(0);
80   }
```

The array on lines 7 through 26 holds the names and ID numbers of the predefined cursors. The names are used as the selection text in a list box, and the ID values are used as arguments on the constructor of QCursor.

The CursorMouse class, defined beginning on line 37, is the top-level widget of the application. It uses a horizontal box to hold a QListBox on the left, and a vertical box with two buttons on the right, as shown previously in Figure 8-3.

The list box is created on line 43. The loop on lines 43 and 44 populate the list box with the cursor names. The call to connect() on line 46 connects the list box signal named highlighted() to the local slot named changeCursor(). The change Cursor() slot will be executed whenever a list box member is highlighted. It isn't used here, but there is also a selected() signal from the list box that requires a double-click on a list box member. Both of these list box signals supply the index number of the list box item.

The selectButton is created on line 51, and it has its clicked() signal connected to the local slot selectCursor(). The exitButton is created on line 57, with its clicked() signal connected to the local slot shutdown().

The slot method changeCursor() on line 68 is passed the index of each newly selected list box item. The text of the list box was loaded from the array names, so the index from the list box is also an index into the array. Line 70 extracts the cursor ID from the array and makes it the current cursor ID number by storing it in cursorID. The call to setCursor() on line 71 sets the cursor to the one supplied as the argument. The QCursor constructor accepts the cursor ID of one of the predefined cursors, as selected from the list box.

The slot method selectCursor() on line 73 sets the cursor of the selectButton to whatever is the currently selected cursor. If no cursor is ever set for this button, it will use the same one as its parent window (that is, the cursor defined on line 71). Once the call to setCursor() on line 75 has been made, the selectButton will use its own cursor.

All of this means that three cursors are being used in this one application. The default cursor (the one named ArrowCursor) will continue to be used for the title bar of the main window. Whichever cursor is currently highlighted in the list box will be used for everything else inside the main window. The only exception is that the Select button will have its own cursor — it will be the one that was highlighted when the button was selected.

There are a couple of special cursors in the list. The cursor named `BlankCursor` has no graphic — the cursor simply disappears. It is a valid cursor in that you can still move it around and try to find things to click on, but you can't see it. The other special cursor is the one named `BitmapCursor`. For this to work, you must supply a cursor of your own making, which is the subject of the next section.

Designing Your Own Cursor

A cursor is a rectangle of pixels. Each pixel can be black, white, or transparent. For example, the KDE default arrow cursor is a black arrow with a white outline. All the other pixels are transparent. Filling with one color and outlining with another makes the cursor visible no matter what background color the cursor passes over.

To create a cursor, you need to create a pair of bitmaps. Both bitmaps must be the same height and width because one of them is a mask that overlays the other. The masking is necessary because there is only one bit per pixel, but there are three ways to display a pixel: black, white, or transparent.

Figure 8-4 shows the shape of a 16×16 cursor. The pixel at the top — the one with the diamond in it — is the hot spot for this cursor. The hot spot is usually at the end of a pointer or at the center of cross hairs — it determines the exact cursor position that is reported to your application. Figure 8-5 shows another bitmap that acts as the mask for the cursor. The two bitmaps are combined using the rules in Table 8-1.

Table 8-1		
Cursor Bitmap Display Rules		
Cursor Bit Setting	**Cursor Mask Bit Setting**	**Result**
1	1	Black
0	1	White
0	0	Transparent

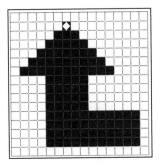

Figure 8-4: The definition of the shape of a cursor

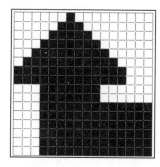

Figure 8-5: The definition of a cursor mask

There are several utility programs that you can use to create the bitmaps describing the cursor. One is supplied as part of the X11 system. Normally found as /usr/ X11R6/bin/bitmap, it is quite easy to use to create 16×16 cursor images — just start the program running and select the pixels with the mouse. You can learn more about this utility, and about bitmaps in general, in Chapter 9.

The following example uses the cursor bitmaps shown in Figures 8-4 and 8-5 to create a cursor.

MyCursor Header

```
 1 /* mycursor.h */
 2 #ifndef GRABMOUSE_H
 3 #define GRABMOUSE_H
 4
 5 #include <qwidget.h>
 6
 7 class MyCursor: public QWidget
 8 {
 9 public:
10     MyCursor(QWidget *parent=0,const char *name=0);
11 };
12
13 #endif
```

MyCursor

```
 1 /* mycursor.cpp */
 2 #include <kapp.h>
 3 #include <qcursor.h>
 4 #include <qbitmap.h>
 5 #include "mycursor.h"
 6
 7 #define upleft_width 16
 8 #define upleft_height 16
 9 #define upleft_x_hot 6
```

```
10 #define upleft_y_hot 1
11 static unsigned char upleft_bits[] = {
12     0x00, 0x00, 0x40, 0x00, 0xe0, 0x00, 0xf0, 0x01, 0xf8,
13     0x03, 0xfc, 0x07, 0xfe, 0x0f, 0xf0, 0x01, 0xf0, 0x01,
14     0xf0, 0x01, 0xf0, 0x01, 0xf0, 0x7f, 0xf0, 0x7f, 0xf0,
15     0x7f, 0xf0, 0x7f, 0x00, 0x00};

17 #define upleftmask_width 16
18 #define upleftmask_height 16
19 static unsigned char upleftmask_bits[] = {
20     0x40, 0x00, 0xe0, 0x00, 0xf0, 0x01, 0xf8, 0x03, 0xfc,
21     0x07, 0xfe, 0x0f, 0xff, 0x1f, 0xff, 0x1f, 0xf8, 0x03,
22     0xf8, 0x03, 0xf8, 0xff, 0xf8, 0xff, 0xf8, 0xff, 0xf8,
23     0xff, 0xf8, 0xff, 0xf8, 0xff};

25 int main(int argc,char **argv)
26 {
27     KApplication app(argc,argv,"mycursor");
28     MyCursor *mycursor = new MyCursor();
29     mycursor->show();
30     app.setMainWidget(mycursor);
31     return(app.exec());
32 }

34 MyCursor::MyCursor(QWidget *parent,const char *name)
35     : QWidget(parent,name)
36 {
37     QBitmap upleft(upleft_width,upleft_height,
38             upleft_bits,TRUE);
39     QBitmap upleftmask(upleftmask_width,upleftmask_height,
40             upleftmask_bits,TRUE);
41     QCursor upleftCursor(upleft,upleftmask,
42             upleft_x_hot,upleft_y_hot);
43     setCursor(upleftCursor);
44     resize(100,100);
45 }
```

The cursor body is defined on lines 7 through 15. This format of the data is the actual output from the bitmap utility — it was simply inserted into the source code of the program. The height and width of the cursor, and the location of the hot spot, all appear as defined constants. You can make a cursor of just about any size you would like, but most cursors are either 16×16 or 32×32 pixels. The bitmap used for the cursor mask is defined on lines 17 through 23.

The procedure for turning bitmap data into a cursor occurs in the constructor, which begins on line 34. On line 37, the cursor bitmap data is used to create a QBitmap object. In the same way, the mask is used to create a QBitmap on line 39. Notice that the defined constants are required so that the QBitmap constructor can determine the height and width that is to be applied to the array of bits. Finally, using the two bitmaps and the location of the hot spot, the cursor is created on line 41. The call to setCursor() on line 43 installs the cursor image to the current window. The result is shown in Figure 8-6.

Figure 8-6: A custom cursor

Keyboard Events

Two events are issued from the keyboard. One is issued when a key is pressed; the other is issued when the key is released. This makes it possible for the software to determine which key combinations are being pressed. For example, if the Shift key has been pressed and not released, a letter key should result in uppercase instead of lowercase. Fortunately, the Qt library keeps track of the keys for you.

The following program displays the two-pane window shown in Figure 8-7. The panel on the right is set to receive keystroke information, and each keystroke is listed in the panel on the left. Each line begins with a P or R, indicating whether this was a Press or Release event. The number following the colon is the unique ID number of the key. This is followed by a description of the key (for this example, however, they do not all have descriptions). If the keyboard event was generated because a key was being held down, the word "repeat" appears on the right.

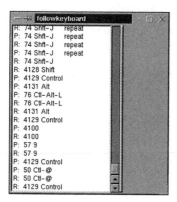

Figure 8-7: Displaying information from each keystroke

Note

Qt recognizes about 240 unique keys. When you Include the Control, Alt, and Shift modifier key combinations, the total comes to almost 2,000 because many specialized keyboards have special keys and special characters. If you are going to be working with the special keys, look in the file qnamespace.h for the complete list.

FollowKeyboard Header

```
 1 /* followkeyboard.h */
 2 #ifndef FOLLOWKEYBOARD_H
 3 #define FOLLOWKEYBOARD_H
 4
 5 #include <qsplitter.h>
 6 #include <qstring.h>
 7 #include <qmultilineedit.h>
 8
 9 class FollowKeyboard: public QSplitter
10 {
11     Q_OBJECT
12 public:
13     FollowKeyboard(QWidget *parent=0,const char *name=0);
14 public slots:
15     void newline(QString &);
16 private:
17     QMultiLineEdit *edit;
18 };
19
20 #endif
```

FollowKeyboard

```
 1 /* followkeyboard.cpp */
 2 #include <kapp.h>
 3 #include <qstring.h>
 4 #include "keyboardsensor.h"
 5 #include "followkeyboard.h"
 6
 7 int main(int argc,char **argv)
 8 {
 9     KApplication app(argc,argv,"followkeyboard");
10     FollowKeyboard *followkeyboard = new FollowKeyboard();
11     followkeyboard->show();
12     app.setMainWidget(followkeyboard);
13     return(app.exec());
14 }
15
16 FollowKeyboard::FollowKeyboard(QWidget *parent,
17     const char *name) : QSplitter(parent,name)
18 {
19     edit = new QMultiLineEdit(this);
20     edit->setMinimumWidth(80);
21     edit->setReadOnly(TRUE);
22     edit->setMinimumWidth(200);
23
24     KeyboardSensor *sensor = new KeyboardSensor(this);
25     sensor->setMinimumWidth(80);
26
```

```
27      connect(sensor,SIGNAL(description(QString &)),
28              this,SLOT(newline(QString &)));
29
30      resize(10,10);
31 }
32 void FollowKeyboard::newline(QString &str)
33 {
34      edit->insertLine(str);
35      edit->setCursorPosition(5000,0);
36 }
```

The FollowKeyboard constructor, beginning on line 16, is a horizontal QSplitter widget that contains two widgets. On the left is a QMultiLineEdit object that is used to display the text, and on the right is a KeyboardSensor widget that is used to receive keystroke information. The slot method newline() on line 32 appends a string to the bottom of the text in the QMultiLineEdit object. The call to setCursor Position() on line 35 makes the bottom line of the text window visible.

KeyboardSensor Header

```
 1 /* keyboardsensor.h */
 2 #ifndef KEYBOARDSENSOR_H
 3 #define KEYBOARDSENSOR_H
 4
 5 #include <qwidget.h>
 6 #include <qevent.h>
 7 #include <qstring.h>
 8
 9 class KeyboardSensor: public QWidget
10 {
11      Q_OBJECT
12 public:
13      KeyboardSensor(QWidget *parent=0,const char *name=0);
14 private:
15      void emitDescription(const QString &,QKeyEvent *);
16      virtual void keyPressEvent(QKeyEvent *event);
17      virtual void keyReleaseEvent(QKeyEvent *event);
18 signals:
19      void description(QString &);
20 };
21
22 #endif
```

This header file defines the class KeyboardSensor to be a QWidget. The declarations of keyPressEvent() and keyReleaseEvent() on lines 16 and 17 override those in the QWidget base class, and they will be called once for each keystroke. The signal description() on line 19 emits descriptions of each keystroke.

KeyboardSensor

```
1  /* keyboardsensor.cpp */
2  #include <qstring.h>
3  #include <ctype.h>
4  #include "keyboardsensor.h"
5
6  KeyboardSensor::KeyboardSensor(QWidget *parent,
7      const char *name) : QWidget(parent,name)
8  {
9      setFocusPolicy(QWidget::StrongFocus);
10      setMinimumSize(300,300);
11  }
12  void KeyboardSensor::keyPressEvent(QKeyEvent *event)
13  {
14      emitDescription(QString("P: "),event);
15  }
16  void KeyboardSensor::keyReleaseEvent(QKeyEvent *event)
17  {
18      emitDescription(QString("R: "),event);
19  }
20  void KeyboardSensor::emitDescription(
21          const QString &typeStr,QKeyEvent *event)
22  {
23      int key = event->key();
24      int ascii = event->ascii();
25      ButtonState state = event->state();
26
27      QString keyStr = QString("%1").arg(key);
28
29      QString charStr = QString("");
30      if(key == Key_Control) {
31          charStr += QString("Control");
32      } else if(key == Key_Alt) {
33          charStr += QString("Alt");
34      } else if(key == Key_Shift) {
35          charStr += QString("Shift");
36      } else {
37          if(state & ControlButton)
38              charStr += "Ctl-";
39          if(state & AltButton)
40              charStr += "Alt-";
41          if(state & ShiftButton)
42              charStr += "Shft-";
43          if(isgraph(ascii))
44              charStr += ascii + QString(" ");
45          else if(state & ControlButton)
46              charStr += (ascii + 64) + QString(" ");
47      }
48
49      if(event->isAutoRepeat())
```

```
50              charStr += "     repeat";
51
52        QString str = QString("%1 %2 %3")
53              .arg(typeStr).arg(keyStr).arg(charStr);
54
55        emit description(str);
56 }
```

Only one window on the display has the keyboard focus at any one time — any keystroke entered will go *only* to that one window. Some windows are capable of receiving the focus and others are not. The constructor, on line 6, calls set FocusPolicy() to specify the way in which this widget is to receive the keyboard focus. By default, your widget will not receive the keyboard focus. Table 8-2 contains a description of the possible focus settings.

Table 8-2
Settings to Control Focus Policy

Name	Description
ClickFocus	The focus moves to this widget only if selected by the mouse.
NoFocus	This widget does not accept focus.
StrongFocus	This policy is a combination of TabFocus and ClickFocus.
TabFocus	Only the Tab key can be used to move the focus from one widget to another. This is normally used with a collection of widgets in a dialog.
WheelFocus	The focus can be changed to this widget using TabFocus, ClickFocus, or the movement of the mouse wheel.

The method keyPressEvent() and keyReleaseEvent() on lines 12 through 19 override virtual methods in the base class, and are called with each keystroke. Both methods are passed a QKeyEvent object, and they pass it on to the method emit Description() to format it as a string.

The method emitDescription() beginning on line 20 extracts the data from the QKeyEvent and emits a description() signal with a descriptive string.

Each key has a unique number. This number is retrieved from the QKeyEvent by the call to key() on line 27. If the key is a displayable ASCII character, the key value is the same as its ASCII value. Nondisplayable keys are assigned larger numbers. For example, as shown previously in Figure 8-7, the Shift key's value is 4128; the Alt key is 4131; and the Return key is 4100.

The conditional code (on lines 30 through 35) determines whether the key is one of the three modifier keys. If it is not, the code on lines 27 through 46 lists any modifiers that are being held down, and then displays the character itself (if it is displayable). The test on line 43 will be true if the character is displayable. However, if the Control key is being held down, the character value itself is modified (adding 64 to any Control character reveals the original displayable character).

Line 49 checks the Boolean method `isAutoRepeat()` to determine whether the key is being held down, causing the events to be automatically generated.

Summary

The Qt library simplifies the processing of data coming from the mouse and the keyboard. Events are formatted into a descriptive object and are directed to the correct widget. This chapter explained the following:

✦ There can be a direct relationship between an event in the hardware and a method call in your application.

✦ Any widget can monitor the mouse for both movement and mouse button clicks.

✦ Changing the appearance of the mouse cursor will change it only for that one window and all of its child windows, unless a child window makes its own change.

✦ Keyboard events are issued for every key press and every key release.

This chapter touched briefly on the graphic process required to create a custom cursor. The following chapter explores graphic processing further, and uses graphic files to decorate window backgrounds, buttons, menus, and other parts of an application.

✦   ✦   ✦

Graphics File Formats

This chapter primarily concerns itself with loading graphic data from disk files and displaying it. KDE is capable of recognizing and reading a number of formats of graphic files. Everything that appears on the display has a window because it inherits the one from QWidget. Also, every class that has a window is capable of displaying a pixmap (a full-color graphic) in its window.

Your program can get its graphic data from one of two locations. It can be stored in a file on disk, in one of several formats, and your program can then read the file and convert the data into an internal pixmap. Also, if you prefer, there is a way to convert the contents of the graphic file into C source code so it can be compiled directly into your program. The two methods result in the same thing—a QPixmap object that can be used to paint a window.

Two Kinds of Graphics

The two basic kinds of graphics are *bitmaps* and *pixmaps*:

♦ A ***pixmap*** is a rectangular array of pixel values. Each value in the array represents a color for one pixel. A pixmap can contain as many colors as you can load into your palette at any one time.

♦ A ***bitmap*** is a rectangular array of bits in which each bit corresponds to one pixel. A bitmap has only two colors—that is, each pixel is either "on" or "off." Normally, this is displayed as black and white, but KDE enables you to display a bitmap using any two colors. A bitmap is really just a special case of a pixmap, but it is used often enough that it has its own special file format.

There seems to be no end to graphics file formats. Thanks to a "universal" conversion utility, almost any graphics file format can be used inside a KDE application. The `convert` utility (described in more detail later in this chapter) can convert a graphics file from some external format into a format that can be displayed. For example, the following command shows how to convert a JPEG file into a pixmap—a form that can be compiled directly into your program:

```
convert rickrack.jpeg rickrack.xpm
```

If you want to include a bitmap (no color) in your program, you can make the conversion as follows:

```
convert rickrack.jpeg rickrack.xbm
```

The `convert` utility looks at the contents of the input file to determine what kind of file it is (it doesn't trust the file suffix on input), and looks at the suffix of the output filename to determine what kind of graphics file to produce.

The XPM Format

The *XPM (XPixMap)* graphics format is a standard in X11 for storing graphics as ASCII text. This format enables you to use your text editor to create or modify simple color graphics. Not only is an XPM definition ASCII, but its format is C source code that you can compile directly into your program.

The following is an example of an XPM graphic with four colors:

```
 1 /* XPM */
 2 /** essPixmap.xpm **/
 3 static const char *essPixmap[] = {
 4 "12 14 4 1",
 5 "  c None",
 6 "X c #FFFFFF",
 7 "R c Red",
 8 "B c #0000FF",
 9 "    RRBB    ",
10 "XXXXXXXXXXXX",
11 "XXXXXXXXXXXX",
12 "XX   RRBB   ",
13 "XX   RRBB   ",
14 "XX   RRBB   ",
15 "XXXXXXXXXXXX",
16 "XXXXXXXXXXXX",
17 "    RRBB  XX",
18 "    RRBB  XX",
19 "    RRBB  XX",
20 "XXXXXXXXXXXX",
21 "XXXXXXXXXXXX",
22 "    RRBB    ",
23 };
```

The syntax of this XPM file is defined as an array of character strings. The comment on the first line must be present because it is used by utilities to determine the file type.

Line 4 contains four numbers that are used to describe the data that follow. The first number specifies that the pixmap is 12 pixels wide, and the second number specifies that it is 14 pixels high. The next number specifies that four colors are used in drawing the graphic. The last digit specifies that one letter is used as the tag for each of the colors.

Lines 5 through 9 are the color definitions. Each string begins with a character that is to be used as the tag that will identify the color. Any ASCII character can be used. Line 5 defines the space character as the color named None. This specifies that no pixel is to be painted, which produces transparency because the background is not overwritten. Line 6 assigns the value of white to the letter X. The hexadecimal value FFFFFF is the red-green-blue value for white (in base 10, the values are 255 255 255). Line 8 uses the hexadecimal value 0000FF to assign the color blue to the letter B. Line 7 uses a name to define a color for the letter R—the name must be one of the RGB names found in the file /usr/X11R6/lib/X11/rgb.txt.

The graphic itself begins on line 9 and concludes with line 22. Each string is 12 characters long because the graphic is 12 pixels wide and only 1 character is used to represent a pixel. There are 14 of these strings because the graphic is 14 pixels high. Every pixel is assigned a value by containing one of the 4 color characters defined earlier.

An XPM file can be used to contain large, high-resolution images with a large number of colors. For example, the Linux distribution includes a file named logo.gif that contains the Linux penguin. You can convert the GIF file to an XPM file with the following command:

```
convert logo.gif logo.xpm
```

In the resulting XPM file, more than 24 bits of color information are included, which means there are more colors than can be represented by single characters. The entire XPM file is 560 lines long. Here is an excerpt:

```
/* XPM */
static const char *magick[] = {
"257 303 251 2",
"   c Gray0",
".  c #080800000404",
"X  c #080808080000",
"o  c Gray3",
"0  c #101004040404",
"+  c #101010100404",
      . . .
"{. c #f0f0b8b80808",
"}. c #f8f8b0b00808",
"|. c #f8f8b8b80808",
```

```
" X  c #f0f0b0b01010",
".X  c #f0f0b8b81010",
"XX  c #f8f8b8b81010",
"BX  c #d8d8d8d8e8e8",
"VX  c #e0e0e0e0d8d8",
"CX  c #f0f0e8e8d8d8",
"ZX  c Gray88",
"AX  c Gray91",
"SX  c #e8e8e8e8f0f0",
"DX  c #f0f0e8e8ecec",
"FX  c #f0f0f0f0e8e8",
"GX  c Gray94",
"HX  c #f8f8f8f8f8f8",
"JX  c None",
        . . .
```

This XPM graphic is 257 pixels wide and 303 pixels tall. It contains a total of 251 colors and uses 2 characters to represent each color. The first few characters may appear to be defined by a single character, but, in fact, 2 characters are used because the blank serves as the second character. As you can see later in the file, the period and X characters are used. Because 2 characters are required to specify a color, each string defining a row of pixel values has to be 514 characters long (twice 257).

Also, notice that the hexadecimal numbers for the colors have 12 digits instead of 6. This is still an RGB format, but each color is 16 bits (4 hexadecimal digits). Either length is valid for an XPM file — the software that reads it counts the digits to determine the format. The colors in the file /usr/X11R6/lib/X11/rgb.txt, and many colors found in other places, are defined as three 8-bit values. The following simple program converts three 8-bit values into both the long and short hexadecimal strings required by XPM:

```c
/* hexcolor */
#include <stdio.h>
#include <stdlib.h>
char *usage[] = {
"        Usage: hexcolor r g b",
" Enter the three RBG color values in the",
" range of 0 to 256. The output is both a",
" 24-bit and 48-bit hexadecimal number of the",
" color that can be used in an XPM file."
};
int main(int argc,char *argv[])
{
    int i;
    int r,g,b;

    if(argc < 4) {
        for(i=0; i<5; i++)
            printf("%s\n",usage[i]);
        exit(1);
    }
```

```
        r = atoi(argv[1]);
        g = atoi(argv[2]);
        b = atoi(argv[3]);
        printf("#%02X%02X%02X\n",r,g,b);
        printf("#%02X00%02X00%02X00\n",r,g,b);
        exit(0);
    }
```

Showing XPM from Data

Because the `convert` utility can convert virtually any graphics file into an XPM file, and because the XPM format is C source code, almost any graphic can be compiled directly into your program. This is mostly used for icons, button labels, list bullets, and other small decorative items.

Note   The `convert` utility converts image data into C, not C++. Before you can actually use an XPM file to create a `QPixmap` inside your program, you need to edit the top line to insert the `const` modifier to the name declaration. Without the `const`, the declaration compiles okay, but the `QPixmap` constructor complains about it not being `const`. And if you are going to use more than one XPM file in your program, you need to rename the array, because `convert` always names it `magick`.

The following program is an example of compiling an XPM file directly into the code and displaying it:

```
 1 /* showxpm.cpp */
 2 #include <kapp.h>
 3 #include <qwidget.h>
 4 #include <qpixmap.h>
 5
 6 #include "logo.xpm"
 7
 8 int main(int argc,char **argv)
 9 {
10      KApplication app(argc,argv,"showxpm");
11      QPixmap pixmap(magick);
12      QWidget *widget = new QWidget();
13      widget->setFixedSize(pixmap.width(),pixmap.height());
14      widget->setBackgroundPixmap(pixmap);
15      widget->show();
16      app.setMainWidget(widget);
17      return(app.exec());
18 }
```

The `#include` statement on line 6 causes the XPM data to be compiled directly into the program. Line 11 creates a `QPixmap` from the XPM data.

Any widget can be used to display a pixmap as its background; therefore, for this example, a generic widget is created on line 12. The call to setFixedSize() on line 13 causes the widget to be exactly the same size as the pixmap. The call to setBackgroundPixmap() on line 14 inserts the pixmap into the widget. The result is shown in Figure 9-1.

Figure 9-1: Displaying compiled XPM data

If you set your window to a fixed size, and you have a pixmap of that exact size, the pixmap is shown in its entirety. If the widget's window is smaller than the pixmap, the image is trimmed on the bottom and on the right. If the window is larger than the pixmap, the pixmap is tiled until it fills the window. The following example uses the smaller pixmap (defined earlier in this chapter as essPixmap) to tile the background of a widget:

```
1 /* showxpmtile.cpp */
2 #include <kapp.h>
3 #include <qwidget.h>
4 #include <qpixmap.h>
5
6 #include "essPixmap.xpm"
7
8 int main(int argc,char **argv)
9 {
10     KApplication app(argc,argv,"showxpmtile");
11     QPixmap pixmap(essPixmap);
12     QWidget *widget = new QWidget();
13     widget->setBackgroundPixmap(pixmap);
14     widget->resize(200,100);
15     widget->show();
16     app.setMainWidget(widget);
17     return(app.exec());
18 }
```

This example creates a small pixmap from the XPM data included in the source on line 6. The actual size of the pixmap is ignored, and it is set as the background pixmap on line 13; the size of the widget is set on line 14. The result is the window shown in Figure 9-2.

Figure 9-2: Displaying compiled XPM data as a tiled background

Loading a Pixmap from a File

You can load a graphic from a file, instead of compiling it as part of the program, by making a slight change to the previous example. All that is needed is a different method to create the pixmap. The following program loads and displays the logo pixmap previously shown in Figure 9-1:

```
 1 /* showfilexpm.cpp */
 2 #include <kapp.h>
 3 #include <qwidget.h>
 4 #include <qpixmap.h>
 5
 6 int main(int argc,char **argv)
 7 {
 8     KApplication app(argc,argv,"showfilexpm");
 9     QPixmap pixmap("logo.xpm");
10     QWidget *widget = new QWidget();
11     widget->setFixedSize(pixmap.width(),pixmap.height());
12     widget->setBackgroundPixmap(pixmap);
13     widget->show();
14     app.setMainWidget(widget);
15     return(app.exec());
16 }
```

The QPixmap constructor on line 9 uses a file to locate the graphic data. You can use file types other than XPM. For example, to load a different type of file, change the filename on line 9 as follows:

```
    QPixmap pixmap("logo.gif");
```

The software does not look at the suffix of the filename to determine the file type. Instead, it loads a block of data from the beginning of the file and inspects it to determine the file type. This is why the commented string containing the characters XPM must remain at the top of an XPM file.

If the software complains about an invalid XPM file, it may be in an older format. The file must be in version 3 in order for you to use it. Make the conversion with a command like the following:

```
sxpm -nod oldform.xpm -o newform.xpm
```

In order to load from a graphic file, the software must understand the file format. The Qt software supports the file types PNG, BMP, GIF, JPEG, XBM, XPM, and PNM. The Qt software was designed in such a way that it may be extended later to include other formats. Also, because of patent issues, it is probably not a good idea to count on the GIF format being available in all countries.

Nothing special is required to read from the various file formats. The following example program loads and displays a JPEG version of the graphic shown previously in Figure 9-1:

```cpp
/* showfilejpeg.cpp */
#include <kapp.h>
#include <qwidget.h>
#include <qpixmap.h>

int main(int argc,char **argv)
{
    KApplication app(argc,argv,"showfilejpeg");
    QPixmap pixmap("logo.jpeg");
    QWidget *widget = new QWidget();
    widget->setFixedSize(pixmap.width(),pixmap.height());
    widget->setBackgroundPixmap(pixmap);
    widget->show();
    app.setMainWidget(widget);
    return(app.exec());
}
```

Using a Pixmap to Decorate a Button

A button contains a window just like any other widget, so it can display a picture as well as text. In fact, the QPushButton class has some special enhancements that cause the pixmap to represent the current state of the button. The following program uses a PNG file to paint the face of the button shown in Figure 9-3:

```cpp
1 /* decobutton.cpp */
2 #include <kapp.h>
3 #include <kpixmap.h>
4 #include "decobutton.h"
5
6 int main(int argc,char **argv)
7 {
8     KApplication app(argc,argv,"decobutton");
```

```
 9        DecoButton decobutton;
10        decobutton.show();
11        app.setMainWidget(&decobutton);
12        return(app.exec());
13  }
14
15  DecoButton::DecoButton(QWidget *parent,const char *name)
16          : QWidget(parent,name)
17  {
18        setFixedSize(200,150);
19
20        QPixmap pixmap("hil-app-go.png");
21        button = new QPushButton(this);
22        button->setPixmap(pixmap);
23        button->setGeometry(50,50,100,50);
24  }
```

Figure 9-3: A button with a graphic instead of text

The widget used for the top-level window is DecoButton. Its constructor begins on line 15. Line 18 sets the widget to a fixed size of 200 pixels wide and 150 high.

The pixmap is created from a file named hil-app-go.png on line 20. A button is created and the pixmap is inserted into it with the call to setPixmap() on line 22. On line 23, the button is sized to fit properly with this pixmap.

The QPushButton class does something special when the button is pressed. To make the button appear depressed, the background is changed to a darker color and the graphic itself is shifted one pixel down and one to the right. The result is shown in Figure 9-4.

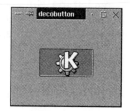

Figure 9-4: An activated button with a graphic instead of text

When the button is activated, the area not covered by the graphic icon is darkened. The icon is actually square, so to darken some of the pixels within the graphic itself it is necessary for them to be transparent. The transparent pixels changing color gives the user the expected feedback from selecting a button. But the graphic of the icon itself is also modified, as you can see by comparing Figures 9-3 and 9-4. This modification is made with the QIconSet class described later in this chapter.

The XBM Format

If there are only two colors (usually black and white), it is more efficient to store a picture with a single bit for each pixel, as is done in *XBM (XBitMap)* format. The XBM format is most often used to define mouse and keyboard cursors, but it also has other purposes. Like the XPM format, an XBM file is an ASCII file that can be compiled directly into a C program. The following is an example of an XBM file:

```
#define arrow_width 16
#define arrow_height 16
#define arrow_x_hot 15
#define arrow_y_hot 7
static unsigned char arrow_bits[] = {
    0x00, 0x00, 0x00, 0x00, 0xc0, 0x07, 0x80, 0x0f, 0x80,
    0x1f, 0xfc, 0x3f, 0xfc, 0x7f, 0xfc, 0xff, 0xfc, 0x7f,
    0xfc, 0x3f, 0x80, 0x1f, 0x80, 0x0f, 0xc0, 0x07, 0x00,
    0x00, 0x00, 0x00, 0x00, 0x00, 0x00};
```

The first two lines determine the width and height in pixels. The next two lines specify the coordinates of the hot spot. The *hot spot* is the exact *x* and *y* pixel location inside the bitmap that is considered to be the mouse location whenever the bitmap is used as a mouse cursor. The specification of the hot spot is optional, so the two lines can be omitted. Figure 9-5 shows the appearance of this bitmap. The hot spot is at the tip of the arrow point on the right.

 Figure 9-5: A bitmap defines graphics in black and white.

In the file, the bit settings are written as byte values, and each number specifies the on or off status of eight pixels. The pixels are first mapped from left to right, and then from top to bottom. They are all held in a single array, so the software that uses it must have the height and width information to know where the lines break.

The Bitmap Utility

There is a utility that you can use to create bitmap files and to modify them once they are created. To create a new bitmap with the default size of 16×16, just enter the command name with no arguments. If you want to create a new bitmap that is 24 pixels wide and 32 pixels high, enter the command as follows:

```
bitmap -size 24x32
```

Once a bitmap is created and written to disk, it can be loaded again for editing by being named on the command line as follows:

```
bitmap arrow.xbm
```

The window used to edit the arrow is shown in Figure 9-6. As you can see from the array of controlling buttons, you can edit the figure in a number of ways. The figure layout is displayed in the grid on the right, enabling you to use the left mouse button to set pixel values to 0, and the right mouse button to set them to 1. The diamond-shaped pixel on the right indicates the hot spot—and there can be only one hot spot. To set the hot spot, select the Set Hot Spot button and then select a pixel.

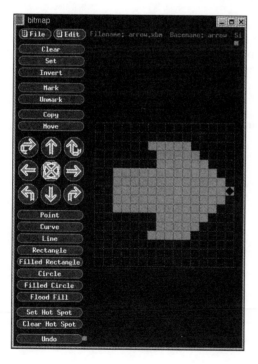

Figure 9-6: The bitmap editor with arrow.xbm loaded

The bitmap utility can be used to create cursors. A cursor requires two bitmaps—one for the cursor and one for the mask. The process of creating a cursor is described in Chapter 8.

Note This program is part of the standard X11 distribution. Its buttons and menu labels look very different from the ones in KDE because this program was developed using a completely different set of widgets and utilities. Fortunately, the underlying X11 standards and protocols allow programs based on completely different software to all execute simultaneously on the same display.

Customizing Graphics for Menus and Toolbars

The graphic icon indicator on a toolbar button can be modified to indicate that the selection is either not available or that the toolbar button widget is currently being selected by the user with the mouse button. To indicate the conditions, it is necessary to make modifications to the appearance of the pixmap. To do this, the QIconSet class accepts a single QPixmap as input and generates three pixmaps in two different sizes. These six different versions of the pixmap can be used in toolbars and menus, as described in Chapter 6.

The following example program allows you to browse through a selection of graphics files and display the six different forms of the one you select, as shown in Figure 9-7. A QFileDialog, described in Chapter 5, is used to select and load a QPixmap from a graphic file. A QIconSet object is then used to create the six versions of the pixmap displayed in the figure.

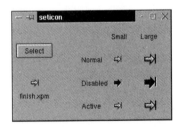

Figure 9-7: An icon shown in six different forms

SetIcon Header

```
 1 /* seticon.h */
 2 #ifndef SETICON_H
 3 #define SETICON_H
 4
 5 #include <qwidget.h>
 6 #include <qlayout.h>
 7 #include <qlabel.h>
 8 #include <qpixmap.h>
 9 #include <qpushbutton.h>
10
11 class SetIcon: public QWidget
12 {
13     Q_OBJECT
14 public:
```

```
15      SetIcon(QWidget *parent=0,const char *name=0);
16 private:
17      QVBoxLayout *makeVerticalBox();
18      QGridLayout *makeGrid();
19      void insertNewPixmap();
20 private:
21      QPixmap pixmap;
22      QString pixmapName;
23      QPushButton *button;
24      QLabel *picLabel;
25      QLabel *nameLabel;
26      QLabel *normal;
27      QLabel *disabled;
28      QLabel *active;
29      QLabel *small;
30      QLabel *large;
31      QLabel *normalSmall;
32      QLabel *normalLarge;
33      QLabel *disabledSmall;
34      QLabel *disabledLarge;
35      QLabel *activeSmall;
36      QLabel *activeLarge;
37 public slots:
38      void newPixmap();
39 };
40
41 #endif
```

Three internal methods are defined on lines 17 through 19. The methods make
VerticalBox() and makeGrid() are used by the constructor to help in the layout
of the top-level window. The method insertNewPixmap() is called whenever a
new QPixmap has been created and needs to be displayed.

The QPixmap and QString on lines 21 and 22 hold the current pixmap and its name.

The pushbutton and the labels declared on lines 23 through 36 are the ones that
appear on the display. The labels named picLabel and nameLabel display the
unmodified pixmap and the name of the file from which it was loaded. The labels
on lines 26 through 30 are used to annotate the table shown in Figure 9-7, and
the labels on lines 31 through 36 are used to display each of the six versions
of the pixmap.

SetIcon

```
1 /* seticon.cpp */
2 #include <kapp.h>
3 #include <qfiledialog.h>
4 #include "seticon.h"
5
6 int main(int argc,char **argv)
7 {
8      KApplication app(argc,argv,"seticon");
```

```
 9      SetIcon seticon;
10      seticon.show();
11      app.setMainWidget(&seticon);
12      return(app.exec());
13 }
14
15 SetIcon::SetIcon(QWidget *parent,const char *name)
16          : QWidget(parent,name)
17 {
18      pixmapName = "hil-app-go.png";
19      pixmap = QPixmap(pixmapName);
20
21      QHBoxLayout *hbox = new QHBoxLayout(this,5);
22      QVBoxLayout *vbox = makeVerticalBox();
23      hbox->addLayout(vbox);
24      hbox->addSpacing(50);
25      QGridLayout *grid = makeGrid();
26      hbox->addLayout(grid);
27      hbox->activate();
28
29      insertNewPixmap();
30
31      connect(button,SIGNAL(clicked()),
32              this,SLOT(newPixmap()));
33 }
34
35 QVBoxLayout *SetIcon::makeVerticalBox()
36 {
37      QVBoxLayout *vbox = new QVBoxLayout(5);
38
39      vbox->addStretch(1);
40
41      button = new QPushButton("Select",this);
42      button->setFixedSize(button->sizeHint());
43      vbox->addWidget(button);
44
45      vbox->addStretch(1);
46
47      picLabel = new QLabel("",this);
48      picLabel->setAutoResize(TRUE);
49      picLabel->setAlignment(AlignHCenter | AlignVCenter);
50      vbox->addWidget(picLabel);
51
52      nameLabel = new QLabel("",this);
53      nameLabel->setAutoResize(TRUE);
54      nameLabel->setAlignment(AlignHCenter | AlignVCenter);
55      vbox->addWidget(nameLabel);
56
57      vbox->addStretch(1);
58
59      return(vbox);
60 }
61 QGridLayout *SetIcon::makeGrid()
62 {
```

```
 63        QGridLayout *grid = new QGridLayout(4,3);
 64
 65        normal = new QLabel("Normal",this);
 66        grid->addWidget(normal,1,0);
 67        disabled = new QLabel("Disabled",this);
 68        grid->addWidget(disabled,2,0);
 69        active = new QLabel("Active",this);
 70        grid->addWidget(active,3,0);
 71        small = new QLabel("Small",this);
 72        grid->addWidget(small,0,1);
 73        large = new QLabel("Large",this);
 74        grid->addWidget(large,0,2);
 75
 76        normalSmall = new QLabel("",this);
 77        grid->addWidget(normalSmall,1,1);
 78        normalLarge = new QLabel("",this);
 79        grid->addWidget(normalLarge,1,2);
 80        disabledSmall = new QLabel("",this);
 81        grid->addWidget(disabledSmall,2,1);
 82        disabledLarge = new QLabel("",this);
 83        grid->addWidget(disabledLarge,2,2);
 84        activeSmall = new QLabel("",this);
 85        grid->addWidget(activeSmall,3,1);
 86        activeLarge = new QLabel("",this);
 87        grid->addWidget(activeLarge,3,2);
 88
 89        return(grid);
 90 }
 91 void SetIcon::insertNewPixmap()
 92 {
 93        picLabel->setPixmap(pixmap);
 94        nameLabel->setText(pixmapName);
 95
 96        QIconSet iconset(pixmap);
 97
 98        QPixmap p;
 99        p = iconset.pixmap(QIconSet::Small,QIconSet::Normal);
100        normalSmall->setPixmap(p);
101        p = iconset.pixmap(QIconSet::Large,QIconSet::Normal);
102        normalLarge->setPixmap(p);
103
104        p = iconset.pixmap(QIconSet::Small,QIconSet::Disabled);
105        disabledSmall->setPixmap(p);
106        p = iconset.pixmap(QIconSet::Large,QIconSet::Disabled);
107        disabledLarge->setPixmap(p);
108
109        p = iconset.pixmap(QIconSet::Small,QIconSet::Active);
110        activeSmall->setPixmap(p);
111        p = iconset.pixmap(QIconSet::Large,QIconSet::Active);
112        activeLarge->setPixmap(p);
113 }
114 void SetIcon::newPixmap()
115 {
116        QString filter = "Icon (*.png *.xpm *.xbm)";
```

```
117     QString name = QFileDialog::getOpenFileName("",
118                  filter,this);
119     if(!name.isEmpty()) {
120         int length = name.length() - name.findRev('/');
121         pixmapName = name.right(length - 1);
122         pixmap = QPixmap(name);
123         insertNewPixmap();
124     }
125 }
```

The `SetIcon` widget, with its constructor beginning on line 15, is used as the top-level window of the application on line 11. Lines 18 and 19 specify the name and value of the initial pixmap. The window is laid out as the horizontal box `hbox`, which contains a `QVBoxLayout` named `vbox` on the left and a `QGridLayout` named `grid` on the right. The call to `makeVerticalBox()` and `makeGrid()` on lines 22 and 25 create the two sub-layouts included in the horizontal box.

The call to `insertNewPixmap()` on line 29 installs the initial pixmap as the one currently displayed. The call to `connect()` on line 31 establishes the slot method `newPixmap()` as the one to be executed whenever the button is clicked.

The method `makeVerticalBox()` on line 35 creates the Select button, the display label to display the unmodified graphic, and the label holding the name of the graphic file. These are all inserted into a vertical box. The button is created and inserted on lines 41 through 43. The two labels are created and added to the vertical box on lines 47 through 55. The labels are left empty for now because the pixmap and its filename will be installed in them later.

The method `makeGrid()` beginning on line 61 uses a `QGridLayout` to create a table of `QLabel` objects that are used to display the various incarnations of the current pixmap. The grid is 3 cells wide and 4 cells high. The first row and the first column are used for annotation labels, as you can see on the right side of the window in Figure 9-7. The labels created on lines 65 through 74 are the annotations, so they are all created with the text included. The labels created on lines 76 through 87 are intended to display pixmap graphics, so they are created without text.

The method `insertNewPixmap()` on line 91 uses the current pixmap information to fill out the display. This method is called once when the program first starts running, to install the default pixmap; and once again whenever a new pixmap is selected.

The `QIconSet` object `iconset` is created on line 96 using the pixmap that was stored in the `pixmap` field of the object. All that is needed now is for each of the six modified pixmaps to be retrieved and inserted into the label widgets for display. The method `pixmap()` is used to retrieve each version of the graphic. The arguments passed to the method determine which of the six is returned. The first argument specifies that the returned pixmap be either `Small` or `Large`. The second argument requests that it be `Normal`, `Disabled`, or `Active`. The argument values are defined as `enums` in the `QIconSet` class.

If the pixmap you select is the correct size for a small icon, then the original is unchanged for Small and an expanded version is created for Large. If, on the other hand, the pixmap is already the size of a Large icon, a Small icon will be produced from it. The sizes are not adjusted to absolute dimensions—they are relative to the original size of the graphic. For example, if you select a very large graphic, its size will not be changed for the Large icon, and will only be slightly reduced for the Small icon.

The slot method `newPixmap()` on line 114 is called whenever the Select button is clicked. It pops up a `QFileDialog` with the call to `getOpenFileName()` on line 117 to select a graphics file. The filter, defined on line 116, limits the files to those with the `.png`, `.xpm`, and `.xbm` suffixes, but you could include other graphic files if you wish. If a filename is selected, its full path name is returned. The `QString` methods `findRev()` and `length()` on line 120 are used to determine the length of the filename without its path, and the call to `right()` on line 121 extracts the name of the file to be displayed. The new pixmap is created on line 122, and the new display is constructed by the call to `insertNewPixmap()` on line 123.

Summary

There is a lot more to graphics, but this chapter presents enough of an introduction that you can create graphic buttons for menus and toolbars. This chapter explained the following:

✦ The two basic types of graphics are the bitmap and the pixmap. A bitmap contains no color information—it just specifies either 1 or 0 for each pixel. A pixmap can be any number of colors. And both the pixmap (known as the XPM format) and the bitmap (known as the XBM format) can be compiled directly into your program or dynamically loaded at run time.

✦ Any object that inherits from `QWidget` has the capability of displaying a pixmap instead of solid colors for its background.

✦ KDE recognizes a number of graphic file formats, and the software is designed so that others can be added later. In fact, they can be added to a shared library and used by your program without recompiling.

The pixmaps introduced in this chapter are often used as identifiers so the user can tell which button does what. But sometimes only text will work. The next chapter explores the various fonts and font-rendering techniques that are available to your application.

✦ ✦ ✦

Fonts

The way that fonts are used by X11 (and thus by Qt and KDE) may confuse you at first. But once you see what is going on, it becomes quite simple. A method was devised that keeps font handling very flexible and, at the same time, quite straightforward. In your application, you can be specific and use exactly the font you like, or you can leave some leeway in your font selection and allow each system to pick a font that fits with the selection criteria. There is also a pair of widgets that enable a user to choose the font.

Fonts vary in size and shape in different ways. There is a special set of metrics applied to fonts. By using the standard values to position characters on the display, you can treat all fonts (no matter how radical) the same way. This chapter deals with acquiring, positioning, and rendering fonts of different types and sizes.

The Anatomy of a Font

A number of different measurements can be made on a character, or a string of characters, in a font. Complicating the issue is the fact that some characters are taller than others, some descend lower than others, and some characters are wider than others. It also is possible to have one character overlap another when they are adjacent to each other in a string — this is quite common in an italic font, where the top of a tall character extends above the bottom of the character to its right.

Figure 10-1 shows the measurements that can be made on each character. The origin is the x and y coordinate point that is used to draw the character. In other words, when you draw the letter t at a specific coordinate point, it actually appears above and to the right of that point. On the other hand, the letter p appears to the right of the point, but both above and below it. The pixel rendering, or graphic design, of a character is called a *glyph*. Every glyph is designed relative to an origin point in such a way that it is only necessary for you to line up the origin points of the characters to line up the characters themselves. This string of origin points is called the *baseline*. The *ascent* and *descent* values are the measurements from the baseline to the top and bottom of the character — the sum of the ascent and the descent is the height of the character. The width of the character is measured from the origin point to the right side of the character. The *lbearing* (left bearing) is the distance from the origin to the character, and the *rbearing* (right bearing) is the width of the graphic part of the character.

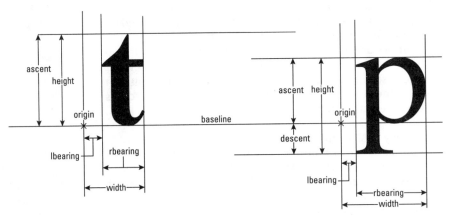

Figure 10-1: Font measurements on single characters

You can see from the ascent, descent, and height measurements in Figure 10-1 that the value of the descent can be zero. It also is possible for the lbearing value to be zero. In fact, it can even be negative in the case of the character's glyph being drawn to the left of the origin. (For example, this can happen with the bottom portion of an italic font.)

Figure 10-2 shows the set of measurements that can be made on a string of characters. The ascent, descent, and height can include a leading area that extends outside the maximum extent upward, downward, or both. The same is true of width. The border around the string allows your program to easily place pieces of text, even text in different fonts, next to one another and have the spacing be correct. The origin of the string — the *x* and *y* coordinates used to draw the string — is the origin of the leftmost letter in the string. The origins of the other letters are used internally to place each letter next to one another when the string is drawn.

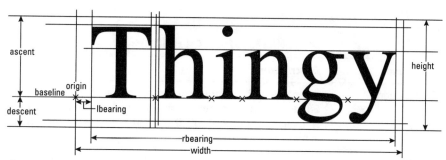

Figure 10-2: Font measurements on a string of characters

Names of the Fonts

The fonts are stored in disk files. The font files are part of the standard X distribution. When an application requests a font, it is loaded from the file into the X server, not into the application. Because the fonts are in the server, there is no overhead of passing detailed font information from the application to the server for display. This reduction in traffic can save you a lot of time because it is common to open a local X window (with its local server) controlled by an application in another computer. Besides, if more than one application is using the same font, only one copy has to be loaded.

The font files usually are stored in subdirectories of /usr/lib/X11/fonts. In each subdirectory, the font files have the suffix .pcf or .pcf.gz. In the same directory as the fonts, there is a file named fonts.dir that maps alias names to the actual font filenames. There is also a fonts.alias file that you can use to assign alternate names to the fonts defined in fonts.dir. For example, you can use the font file named 10x20.pcf.gz by specifying its name like this:

```
10x20
```

Or you can use the alias name assigned to it:

```
-misc-fixed-medium-r-normal--20-200-75-75-c-100-iso8859-1
```

The short form has the advantage of being easy to remember, but the long form has the advantage of being descriptive. And the software enables you to make selections using wildcards for the various parts of the name. Each part of the name has a specific meaning. Table 10-1 describes each of the parts of the name shown in Figure 10-3.

```
   font foundry    font family          slant            pixels  points    verticle dpi  pixel width
-adobe-courier-bold-r-normal--11-80-100-100-m-60-iso8859-2
              weight     proportional width          horizontal dpi   spacing      character set
```

Figure 10-3: The parts of a font name

Table 10-1
Parts of a Font Name

Part Name	Description
font foundry	The name of the company or organization that created the font. Some of the more common names are adobe, b&h, bitstream, dec, schumacher, sony, and sun. If no foundry claims the font, the name is misc.
font family	The name of a set of related fonts, of which this font is a member. Possible names are lucida, times, courier, helvetica, and so on.
weight	This is the stroke weight. It is usually either medium or bold, but it also can be black, book, demibold, light, or regular.
slant	The angle of each letter can be italic, oblique, or r (short for roman, meaning upright).
proportional width	The relationship between height and width is usually normal, but it can be condensed, semi-condensed, narrow, or double.
pixels	The size of the font in pixels. Normally, font sizes are measured in points (a point is 1/72 of an inch). To arrive at the pixel-size value, the point size is translated into the pixel size, which means that the point size may have to be rounded up or down to come out on a pixel boundary.
points	The point size of the font in tenths of a point. In the example, the value 80 indicates that this is an 8-point font. The relationship between the point size and the pixel size is determined by the vertical and horizontal *dpi (dots per inch) values*. In this example, at 100 dpi, an 8-point font has a pixel size of 11. At the same dpi, a 12-point font has a pixel size of 17.
horizontal dpi	The number of horizontal pixels per inch of resolution. This value is used to compute the pixel and point sizes. It also is used as a ratio with vertical dpi to determine the horizontal vertical dpi that will cause the font to display properly.
vertical dpi	The number of vertical pixels per inch of resolution.
spacing	This can be m (for monospace), p (for proportional), or c (for character cell). A monospace font is one in which all characters are the same width. A proportional font has characters of various widths (for example, the letter w is wider than the letter i). A character-cell font is a fixed-width font based on the way typewriter fonts are spaced.
pixel width	The average width, in tenths of a pixel, of all the characters in the font.
character set	This is the version of the standard used to define the character set. The *International Organization for Standardization (ISO)* has established standards for the sets of characters that are included in the alphabet of various languages.

Not only are the long-font names descriptive, they are in a form that enables you to use wildcard characters in searching for a font. This way, you only need to specify the things you care about, and let the rest of it default. For example:

```
-*-bookman-light-r-normal--14-*-*-*-p-*-iso8859-1
```

The parts specified in the name must be an exact match with an actual font, while the asterisks can match any value. Of course, several fonts may match, but the first match encountered is the one returned. The preceding example could select this font:

```
-adobe-bookman-light-r-normal--14-135-75-75-p-82-iso8859-1
```

When specifying a font name, you should be specific only with the parts you need. This way, you have a better chance of matching an actual font name. If your specifi-cations do not match the name of a font, the default font named fixed is used, and it is almost never the one you want.

Setting the Font of a Widget

A QFont object can be created and used to specify the font used by a widget. The following example displays three labels, each of which uses a different font, as shown in Figure 10-4:

```
1 /* fontset.cpp */
2 #include <kapp.h>
3 #include <qlabel.h>
4 #include <qlayout.h>
5 #include <qfont.h>
6 #include "fontset.h"
7
8 int main(int argc,char **argv)
9 {
10     KApplication app(argc,argv,"fontset");
11     FontSet fontset;
12     fontset.show();
13     app.setMainWidget(&fontset);
14     return(app.exec());
15 }
16 FontSet::FontSet(QWidget *parent,const char *name)
17         : QWidget(parent,name)
18 {
19     QVBoxLayout *vbox = new QVBoxLayout(this,10);
20
21     QLabel *label1 = new QLabel(
22             "Bold 14-point Courier",this);
23     QFont font1("Courier",14,QFont::Bold,FALSE);
24     label1->setFont(font1);
25     vbox->addWidget(label1);
26
```

```
27      QLabel *label2 = new QLabel(
28              "20-point Fixed",this);
29      QFont font2("Fixed",20,QFont::Normal,FALSE);
30      label2->setFont(font2);
31      vbox->addWidget(label2);
32
33      QLabel *label3 = new QLabel(
34              "Bold Italic 18-point Charter",this);
35      QFont font3("Charter",18,QFont::Bold,TRUE);
36      label3->setFont(font3);
37      vbox->addWidget(label3);
38 }
```

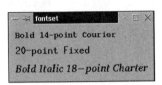

Figure 10-4: Setting the fonts for labels

Once the QFont object is created, the call to setFont() installs it in the label. The setFont() method is a virtual method inherited from the QWidget class, so the same method should work for any widget that displays text.

The QFont constructor accepts a list of arguments that specify the name of the font. These arguments contain the same information as the font filenames specified earlier, but they are in an easier to use format. To create a QFont, you need to specify the font family name, the point size, the weight of the characters, and whether or not the font is to be italic. The weight numbers, each defined as an enum in the QFont class, are Light, Normal, DemiBold, Bold, and Black.

Using the arguments on the constructor, it is possible to describe a font that doesn't really exist — for example, a 12-point fixed italic — but the constructor will succeed in finding a font because the font naming convention is used to find the closest match to the one requested. Before hard-coding a QFont constructor, you may want to use one of the programs in the chapter to browse the available fonts.

If you wish to specify the exact name of a font, you can do so using the method setRawName() on a QFont object. For example, the following code creates a QFont object that is italic, of the Utopia family, and produced by Adobe:

```
QFont font;
font.setRawName(
   "-adobe-utopia-regular-i-normal--15-140-75-75-p-79-iso8859-1");
```

Selecting a Font with QFontDialog

The following program presents on its main window a button that can be used to pop up a QFontDialog. A font selection made in the dialog will cause both the text and the font of the button to be changed — each font description is presented in its own font. Figure 10-5 shows three different appearances of the main window and its button.

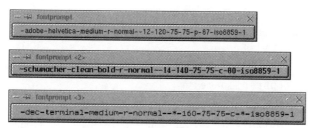

Figure 10-5: Three fonts displayed by a button

FontPrompt Header

```
 1 /* fontprompt.h */
 2 #ifndef FONTPROMPT_H
 3 #define FONTPROMPT_H
 4
 5 #include <qwidget.h>
 6 #include <qpushbutton.h>
 7
 8 class FontPrompt: public QWidget
 9 {
10     Q_OBJECT
11 public:
12     FontPrompt(QWidget *parent=0,const char *name=0);
13 private:
14     QPushButton *button;
15 private slots:
16     void popupDialog();
17 };
18
19 #endif
```

The FontPrompt class is quite simple. It only contains the button to be clicked and the slot to be executed to pop up the dialog.

FontPrompt

```
 1  /* fontprompt.cpp */
 2  #include <kapp.h>
 3  #include <qfontdialog.h>
 4  #include "fontprompt.h"
 5
 6  int main(int argc,char **argv)
 7  {
 8      KApplication app(argc,argv,"fontprompt");
 9      FontPrompt fontprompt;
10      fontprompt.show();
11      app.setMainWidget(&fontprompt);
12      return(app.exec());
13  }
14  FontPrompt::FontPrompt(QWidget *parent,const char *name)
15          : QWidget(parent,name)
16  {
17      button = new QPushButton("",this);
18      QFont font = button->font();
19      button->setText(font.rawName());
20      button->setFixedSize(button->sizeHint());
21      setFixedSize(button->sizeHint());
22
23      connect(button,SIGNAL(clicked()),
24              this,SLOT(popupDialog()));
25  }
26  void FontPrompt::popupDialog()
27  {
28      bool okay;
29
30      QFont oldFont = button->font();
31      QFont newFont =
32              QFontDialog::getFont(&okay,oldFont,this);
33      if(okay) {
34          button->setFont(newFont);
35          button->setText(newFont.rawName());
36          button->setFixedSize(button->sizeHint());
37          setFixedSize(button->sizeHint());
38      }
39  }
```

The FontPrompt constructor, starting on line 14, creates and installs the button in the main window. The call to font() on line 18 retrieves the current (default) font of the button. The call rawName() on line 19 retrieves the full name of the font, and then calls setText() to specify that the font name be used as the button text. Line 20 calls setFixedSize() so that the size of the button is exactly the same as the size of the text. The call to setFixedSize() on line 21 sizes the main window to just fit the button. The button is connected to the slot method on line 26. The resulting window, showing the default text, looks like the one shown earlier at the top of Figure 10-5.

The `popupDialog()` slot method on line 26 does all of the work of retrieving and installing a new font. The call to `font()` on line 30 retrieves the existing font from the button. The call to `getFont()` on line 32 passes the existing font to the dialog, which uses it as the default. The initial window, displaying the default font, looks like the one shown in Figure 10-6.

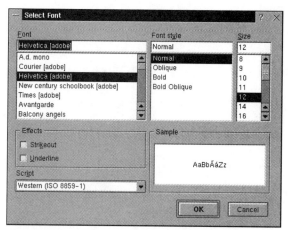

Figure 10-6: A font selection dialog showing the default font

> **Note**   A couple of options on the dialog are not included as part of the standard font definition. Toggle buttons for Strikeout and Underline are part of the dialog because these are two font options added by the `QFont` class.

If the OK button is selected, the new font is returned as `newFont` on line 31. Also, the Boolean variable `okay` will be set to `TRUE`. To update the display, there is a call to `setFont()` on line 34. The `setFont()` method is defined as part of the `QWidget` class, which means the same method can be used to set the text of any widget displaying text. Line 35 calls `rawName()` and `setText()` to insert the full description of the new font into the button. Lines 36 and 37 are necessary to resize the button and the window because changing the font almost always changes the size of the window.

Selecting a Font with KFontDialog

The following font selection program is very much like the previous one, except that it uses a `KFontDialog` to do the selection. The pop-up dialog is shown in Figure 10-7.

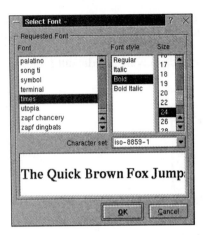

Figure 10-7: A font selection dialog showing a large font

FontPrompt2 Header

```
1 /* fontprompt2.h */
2 #ifndef FONTPROMPT2_H
3 #define FONTPROMPT2_H
4
5 #include <qwidget.h>
6 #include <qpushbutton.h>
7
8 class FontPrompt2: public QWidget
9 {
10     Q_OBJECT
11 public:
12     FontPrompt2(QWidget *parent=0,const char *name=0);
13 private:
14     QPushButton *button;
15 private slots:
16     void popupDialog();
17 };
18
19 #endif
```

FontPrompt2

```
1 /* fontprompt2.cpp */
2 #include <kapp.h>
3 #include <kfontdialog.h>
4 #include "fontprompt2.h"
5
6 int main(int argc,char **argv)
7 {
8     KApplication app(argc,argv,"fontprompt2");
9     FontPrompt2 fontprompt2;
10    fontprompt2.show();
11    app.setMainWidget(&fontprompt2);
12    return(app.exec());
```

```
13 }
14 FontPrompt2::FontPrompt2(QWidget *parent,const char *name)
15          : QWidget(parent,name)
16 {
17     button = new QPushButton("",this);
18     QFont font = button->font();
19     button->setText(font.rawName());
20     button->setFixedSize(button->sizeHint());
21     setFixedSize(button->sizeHint());
22
23     connect(button,SIGNAL(clicked()),
24             this,SLOT(popupDialog()));
25 }
26 void FontPrompt2::popupDialog()
27 {
28     QFont font = button->font();
29     int result = KFontDialog::getFont(font);
30     if(result == QDialog::Accepted) {
31         button->setFont(font);
32         button->setText(font.rawName());
33         button->setFixedSize(button->sizeHint());
34         setFixedSize(button->sizeHint());
35     }
36 }
```

The FontPrompt2 constructor, beginning on line 14, creates a window with a button. The appearance of the button is initialized on lines 18 and 19 so it will show the name of its own font. Lines 20 and 21 size the top-level window and the button to the size of the text.

The slot method popupDialog() on line 26 is called whenever the button is clicked. The call to the static method getFont() on line 29 pops up the dialog and returns the value QDialog::Accepted if a selection was made, or QDialog:: Rejected if a selection was not made. Lines 31 and 32 update the button to use the chosen font and specify the text of the button to be the descriptive name of the font. Lines 32 and 33 resize the button and window to fit the text.

The dialogs KFontDialog and QFontDialog are very much alike, except QFont Dialog has a couple of extra options (Underline and Strikethrough), while the KFontDialog allows you to work with the sample text at the bottom of the window. Both of them allow you to edit the string of characters — so you can see what the font looks like for the text you are going to be using — but only the KFontDialog allows you to both initialize it and return it to your program. To do this, create the dialog as follows:

```
int result = KfontDialog::getFontAndText(font,btext);
```

The btext argument is a QString object that will receive the text displayed at the bottom of the dialog window whenever the OK button is clicked.

Font Placement by Metrics

There are metric values available that you can use to position the fonts in a window. The following application allows you to choose from any font and have it displayed in positions calculated from the font's metrics.

Figure 10-8 shows the top-level window of the program, with the buttons that can be used to select the font and position the text. The three buttons at the top position the text vertically inside the black rectangle, and the three buttons at the bottom position the text horizontally. The large button at the bottom pops up a dialog like the one shown earlier in Figure 10-6, which can be used to change the font.

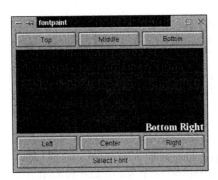

Figure 10-8: Positioning text in a window

FontPaint Header

```
 1 /* fontpaint.h */
 2 #ifndef FONTPAINT_H
 3 #define FONTPAINT_H
 4
 5 #include <qwidget.h>
 6 #include <qframe.h>
 7 #include <qpushbutton.h>
 8
 9 class FontPaint: public QWidget
10 {
11     Q_OBJECT
12 public:
13     FontPaint(QWidget *parent=0,const char *name=0);
14 private:
15     void updateDisplay();
16 protected:
17     void paintEvent(QPaintEvent *);
18 private:
19     enum { Hleft, Hcenter, Hright };
20     enum { Vtop, Vmiddle, Vbottom };
21     int Hposition;
22     int Vposition;
23     QPushButton *topButton;
24     QPushButton *middleButton;
```

```
25      QPushButton *bottomButton;
26      QPushButton *leftButton;
27      QPushButton *centerButton;
28      QPushButton *rightButton;
29      QPushButton *selectFontButton;
30      QWidget *frame;
31      QFont font;
32 private slots:
33      void popupDialog();
34      void setTop() { Vposition = Vtop;
35                       updateDisplay(); }
36      void setMiddle() { Vposition = Vmiddle;
37                         updateDisplay(); }
38      void setBottom() { Vposition = Vbottom;
39                         updateDisplay(); }
40      void setLeft() { Hposition = Hleft;
41                       updateDisplay(); }
42      void setCenter() { Hposition = Hcenter;
43                         updateDisplay(); }
44      void setRight() { Hposition = Hright;
45                        updateDisplay(); }
46 };
47
48 #endif
```

The FontPaint class is the widget used as the top-level window. The enumerated types on lines 19 and 20 are used to specify the vertical and horizontal positions of the text, with the current positions stored in Hposition and Vposition on lines 21 and 22. The pushbuttons defined on lines 23 through 28 are each used to store values in Vposition and Hposition. Each of the slot methods on lines 34 through 45 is connected to a button; and when the method is called, it updates the position of the text and calls updateDisplay() to paint the window.

FontPaint

```
1 /* fontpaint.cpp */
2 #include <kapp.h>
3 #include <qfontdialog.h>
4 #include <qpainter.h>
5 #include <qlayout.h>
6 #include "fontpaint.h"
7
8 int main(int argc,char **argv)
9 {
10     KApplication app(argc,argv,"fontpaint");
11     FontPaint fontpaint;
12     fontpaint.show();
13     app.setMainWidget(&fontpaint);
14     return(app.exec());
15 }
16 FontPaint::FontPaint(QWidget *parent,const char *name)
17         : QWidget(parent,name)
18 {
```

```
19        QHBoxLayout *hbox;
20        QVBoxLayout *vbox = new QVBoxLayout(this,5);
21
22        hbox = new QHBoxLayout(5);
23        topButton = new QPushButton("Top",this);
24        hbox->addWidget(topButton);
25        connect(topButton,SIGNAL(clicked()),
26                this,SLOT(setTop()));
27        middleButton = new QPushButton("Middle",this);
28        hbox->addWidget(middleButton);
29        connect(middleButton,SIGNAL(clicked()),
30                this,SLOT(setMiddle()));
31        bottomButton = new QPushButton("Bottom",this);
32        hbox->addWidget(bottomButton);
33        connect(bottomButton,SIGNAL(clicked()),
34                this,SLOT(setBottom()));
35        vbox->addLayout(hbox);
36
37        frame = new QWidget(this);
38        frame->setMinimumSize(150,150);
39        vbox->addWidget(frame);
40
41        hbox = new QHBoxLayout(5);
42        leftButton = new QPushButton("Left",this);
43        hbox->addWidget(leftButton);
44        connect(leftButton,SIGNAL(clicked()),
45                this,SLOT(setLeft()));
46        centerButton = new QPushButton("Center",this);
47        hbox->addWidget(centerButton);
48        connect(centerButton,SIGNAL(clicked()),
49                this,SLOT(setCenter()));
50        rightButton = new QPushButton("Right",this);
51        hbox->addWidget(rightButton);
52        connect(rightButton,SIGNAL(clicked()),
53                this,SLOT(setRight()));
54        vbox->addLayout(hbox);
55
56        selectFontButton = new QPushButton("Select Font",this);
57        vbox->addWidget(selectFontButton);
58        connect(selectFontButton,SIGNAL(clicked()),
59                this,SLOT(popupDialog()));
60
61        Hposition = Hcenter;
62        Vposition = Vmiddle;
63        font = frame->font();
64        updateDisplay();
65 }
66 void FontPaint::popupDialog()
67 {
68        bool okay;
69
70        QFont newFont = QFontDialog::getFont(&okay,font,this);
71        if(okay) {
72            font = newFont;
```

```
 73              updateDisplay();
 74          }
 75 }
 76 void FontPaint::updateDisplay()
 77 {
 78      int x;
 79      int y;
 80      QString text;
 81      QPainter painter(frame);
 82      painter.setFont(font);
 83      QFontMetrics fm = painter.fontMetrics();
 84
 85      painter.setBackgroundColor(QColor("black"));
 86      painter.setPen(QColor("white"));
 87
 88      QRect rect = painter.window();
 89      painter.eraseRect(rect);
 90
 91      switch(Vposition) {
 92      case Vtop:
 93          y = fm.ascent();
 94          text = "Top ";
 95          break;
 96      case Vmiddle:
 97          y = rect.height() / 2;
 98          y += (fm.ascent() - fm.descent()) / 2;
 99          text = "Middle ";
100          break;
101      case Vbottom:
102          y = rect.height() - fm.descent();
103          text = "Bottom ";
104          break;
105      }
106      switch(Hposition) {
107      case Hleft:
108          x = 0;
109          text += "Left";
110          break;
111      case Hcenter:
112          text += "Center";
113          x = (rect.width() - fm.width(text)) / 2;
114          break;
115      case Hright:
116          text += "Right";
117          x = rect.width() - fm.width(text);
118          break;
119      }
120      painter.drawText(x,y,text);
121 }
122 void FontPaint::paintEvent(QPaintEvent *)
123 {
124      updateDisplay();
125 }
```

The FontPaint constructor, beginning on line 16, uses a vertical box as the primary layout, and fills it with widgets on lines 19 through 59. The two rows of three buttons are each contained in horizontal boxes. Each of the six position buttons is connected to one of the slot methods defined in fontpaint.h. The frame widget created on line 37 is the black rectangle used to display the text as shown in Figure 10-8. The button at the very bottom, created on lines 56 through 59, is connected to the slot method named popupDialog().

The popupDialog() slot defined on line 66 uses the static method getFont() in the QFontDialog class to retrieve a new font. If a new font is selected, it becomes the current font on line 72 and a call is made to updateDisplay() to display a new frame window.

The work of displaying the text is done in the method updateDisplay() starting on line 76. To display the text it is necessary to create a QPainter object, as is done on line 81. A QPainter object contains one font, and uses it to paint all of its text. On line 82, the selected font is assigned to the Qpainter object. On line 83, the QFontMetrics object containing information about this font is retrieved from the QPainter object.

Note   The QPainter class can be used for a large number of fundamental graphics functions, as described in Chapter 12. In this example, the QPainter constructor uses frame as its target widget, but it is also possible to create a QPainter object that is independent of a widget and can be attached to one only when painting needs to be done.

Line 85 sets the background color to black and the foreground to white. This means that when the widget is cleared, it appears black; and the text painted on it appears white.

There are three options each for the vertical and horizontal positions of the text, and these are selected by the switch statements on lines 91 and 106. To draw a string of characters, it is necessary to specify the vertical position of the baseline and the horizontal position of the left side of the left character. Using the font metric information, it is possible to determine the location required in order to place a string exactly where you want it.

On line 93, the text is placed at the top by setting y to the value of the ascent of the font. That is, the vertical placement of the baseline is such that the top of the tallest characters will just touch the top of the window.

On lines 97 and 98, the vertical position is set so the text appears in the center. The expression on line 97 determines the vertical center of the window, but because the ascent and descent are almost certain to have different values, it is necessary to adjust the center so that the text (not the baseline) is centered. Line 98 determines the difference between the ascent and descent, and adds that difference to the center. Although it is not as intuitive as breaking it into two statements, the same expression can be written as follows:

```
y = (height + ascent - descent) / 2;
```

Line 102 calculates the vertical position such that the lowest font descender will just rest on the bottom of the window, as previously shown in Figure 10-8. To do this, it is necessary to use the entire height of the window and subtract just the descent.

Line 108 starts the text at the left of the window. Because a string is always drawn immediately to the right of its x coordinate, it is only necessary to set x to zero.

Line 112 determines the x coordinate for the text to be horizontally centered. Half of the width of the window is the center of the window. Adjusting the location to the left by half the length of the character string results in the correct position for the string to be centered. Notice that the call to the width method uses the text as an argument — this is because the width is calculated not just from the number of characters in the string, but from the sum of each actual character width. Fixed width fonts, such as Courier, can calculate the width from simple character counts, but variable width fonts need to be measured one character at a time.

Line 117 calculates the starting point of the text so that its last character ends flush with the right side of the window, as shown previously in Figure 10-8. To get the value, the width of the entire window has the width of the string subtracted from it.

Once the text string has been constructed, and the x and y coordinates have been calculated, the call to `drawText()` on line 120 is used to paint the text on the window.

The method `paintEvent()` on line 122 is called whenever the window becomes exposed — for any reason — and needs to be repainted. If this method were not defined here, the window would only be painted when a new font or new position is selected.

Font Placement by Rectangles

The previous example used a `QFontMetric` object to calculate various font positions within a rectangle. Replacing the `updateDisplay()` method with the following code will result in exactly the same display:

```
    . . .
76 void FontPaint2::updateDisplay()
77 {
78      int align;
79      QString text;
```

```
80      QPainter painter(frame);
81      painter.setFont(font);
82
83      painter.setBackgroundColor(QColor("black"));
84      painter.setPen(QColor("white"));
85
86      QRect rect = painter.window();
87      painter.eraseRect(rect);
88
89      switch(Vposition) {
90      case Vtop:
91          align = AlignTop;
92          text = "Top ";
93          break;
94      case Vmiddle:
95          align = AlignVCenter;
96          text = "Middle ";
97          break;
98      case Vbottom:
99          align = AlignBottom;
100         text = "Bottom ";
101         break;
102     }
103     switch(Hposition) {
104     case Hleft:
105         align |= AlignLeft;
106         text += "Left";
107         break;
108     case Hcenter:
109         align |= AlignHCenter;
110         text += "Center";
111         break;
112     case Hright:
113         align |= AlignRight;
114         text += "Right";
115         break;
116     }
117     painter.drawText(rect,align,text);
118 }
        . . .
```

In this example, the align variable is used as a set of flags. The call to drawText() on line 117 uses the QRect object that defines the size of the entire window, along with the flags that specify the location of the text within the rectangle. All of the flags are described in Table 10-2. Actual pixel values to position the text, as used in the previous example, are not required. Also, the rectangle doesn't necessarily have to include the entire window — you can specify a smaller rectangle somewhere inside the window.

Table 10-2
Flags for Painting Text in a Rectangle

Flag Name	Action
`AlignBottom`	The text is positioned so that the bottom of the lowest descender in the font is flush against the bottom of the rectangle. Cannot be used with `AlignTop` or `AlignVCenter`.
`AlignHCenter`	The text is positioned so that it is centered horizontally between the two sides of the rectangle. Cannot be used with `AlignLeft` or `AlignRight`.
`AlignLeft`	The leftmost character of the text is flush with the left side of the rectangle. Cannot be used with `AlignRight` or `AlignHCenter`.
`AlignRight`	The rightmost character of the text is flush with the right side of the rectangle. Cannot be used with `AlignLeft` or `AlignHCenter`.
`AlignTop`	The text is positioned so that the top of the tallest character in the font is flush against the top of the rectangle. Cannot be used with `AlignBottom` or `AlignVCenter`.
`AlignVCenter`	The text is positioned so that it is centered vertically between the top and bottom of the rectangle. Cannot be used with `AlignTop` or `AlignBottom`.
`DontClip`	By default, if the rectangle is smaller than the window, and is also smaller than the text, the string will be trimmed to fit the rectangle. With this flag set, the text is not trimmed to fit the rectangle.
`ExpandTabs`	By default, each tab character `'\t'` is converted to a single space. With this flag set, sufficient spaces are inserted so that the next character appears on an 8-character boundary counting from the beginning of the string.
`ShowPrefix`	By default, an ampersand character in the text appears normally. With this flag set, the ampersand character is removed and the character to its right appears underlined. For example, the text `"Mi&ddle &Center"` will appear as Mi<u>d</u>dle <u>C</u>enter with this flag set, and as Mi&ddle &Center if it is not set.
`SingleLine`	By default, each newline `'\n'` character will break the text and cause it to be displayed on more than one line. With this flag set, each newline character is converted to a single space.
`WordBreak`	If the text does not fit the rectangle, this flag will allow newline characters to be inserted in place of spaces to attempt to make it fit.

The text can be broken into more than one line and the resulting block will be positioned according to the alignment flags. In the previous examples, the two words of the text were separated with a single space so they appeared as one line. Figure 10-9 shows the alignment resulting from using the '\n' character to insert a new-line character between the words by changing the code in the previous example to this:

```
 .  .  .
  89      switch(Vposition) {
  90      case Vtop:
  91          align = AlignTop;
  92          text = "Top\n";
  93          break;
  94      case Vmiddle:
  95          align = AlignVCenter;
  96          text = "Middle\n";
  97          break;
  98      case Vbottom:
  99          align = AlignBottom;
 100          text = "Bottom\n";
 101          break;
 102      }
 .  .  .
```

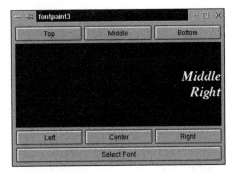

Figure 10-9: Positioning multi-line text in a window

Summary

Of all the elements displayed as part of a graphical user interface, the eye is most critical of letters, numbers, and punctuation. We have been reading and writing all of our lives, so our brain instantly recognizes single characters and patterns of groups of characters. Some character fonts appear to be nice and friendly, even attractive; while others appear to be klunky or stiff. The actual difference between the one we like and the one we don't can be very small. Although characters normally are displayed as very small graphic objects in a window, it is easy for us to instantly recognize the details of their shape. This preconceived notion of the appearance of characters is why a font can seem so dramatic to us.

In this chapter, the fundamentals of font manipulation were described:

✦ Each font is stored in its own file, so it is easy to add new fonts or delete old ones.

✦ Your application can refer to a specific font by its exact name; or it can select a font by using descriptive terms, such as the font family and point size.

✦ You can use a standard set of metrics to position text in the window, and to determine the size of the displayed text.

✦ A `QFontDialog` or `KFontDialog` widget can be included in your program to enable the user to pick a font.

This chapter discussed painting text on a widget's window. The next chapter explains how to create and assign colors to the text and its background. It also describes how colors are constructed, and how your program can create and use them.

✦   ✦   ✦

Colors

This chapter explains how to control the color of the various widgets that make up your application's interface. You can use broad coloring techniques to standardize all the colors in all of the widgets you use; you can set specify unique colors for each individual part of each individual widget; or you can use a combination of these two approaches. KDE and Qt allow you to set and reset the widget colors any way you like.

An X11 color is defined as a single numeric value that can be broken into its fundamental primary color parts. A `QColor` object is a wrapper for a single X11 color. A `QColorGroup` object contains a suite of `QColor` objects used to color the various parts of a widget's window. A `QPalette` object contains a trio of `QcolorGroups`, which are used to contain colors for each of the states of a widget. All of these are under the control of your application.

At the lowest level, a color is a numeric value applied to a displayed pixel. The fundamental principles are always the same, but different graphics cards take slightly different approaches. This chapter briefly describes these approaches and some of the things you can do in your program to detect which approach is being taken on your system—and some of the things you can do to take advantage of the situation.

The Architecture of Color

The X Window System's color system uses each of the three primary colors, represented by a binary value. The intensity of each color is the ratio of the color value to the maximum value possible. For example, to get 50 percent red on a system with 8 bits per color, the value would be 127. To get 50 percent on a system with 16 bits per color, the value would be 32,767. Colors can also be represented by floating-point values, usually in the range of 0.0 to 1.0, so a 50 percent color level would be 0.5.

There are a number of different kinds of display architectures. The X11 has devised a method of dealing with them in a standard way. The KDE/Qt software is built on top of this generalized system, so you probably will never need to know all the low-level details (unless you need to do something very special). However, some of the operations your program needs to perform make a lot more sense if you have some idea of what's going on in the basement.

A physical display has a hardware storage location for each pixel it places on the screen. Each of the values in storage determines the color and brightness of its associated pixel—to change a pixel, simply change the contents of its storage location. Hardware uses different methods of converting the stored value into a color—some use the numeric value and directly convert it into a color, and others use the stored value as an index into a table of colors. The table of colors is known as a *color map*. Different hardware requires different kinds of color maps. Table 11-1 lists the various types.

Table 11-1
The Classes of Physical Displays

Name	Description
Pseudo Color	The pixel value indexes a color map containing RGB values. The color map can be modified dynamically.
Direct Color	The pixel value is split into three values and used to index three separate color maps: one for the red component, one for the blue, and one for the green. The color maps can be modified dynamically.
Gray Scale	The pixel value indexes a color map containing displayable gray-scale values. The color map can be modified dynamically.
Static Color	The pixel value indexes a color map containing RGB values. The color map is static in the hardware and cannot be changed.
True Color	The pixel value is split into three values and used to index three separate color maps: one for the red component, one for the blue, and one for the green. Each of the color maps is an even (or near-even) gradient from no color to full saturation and cannot be altered.
Static Gray	The pixel value indexes a color map containing displayable gray-scale values. The color map is static and cannot be modified.

The color map is used by the display hardware to paint all pixels in all windows, so changing the color map changes the appearance of everything. Some color maps allow this sort of change, and some don't. You seldom need to make a color map change, but if your application does change the color map, it is polite to put the original one back when you lose focus to another application.

The following program tells you what kind of display you have, the number of bits per pixel, the size of the color map, and some other related information:

```cpp
1  /* showvisual.cpp */
2  #include <kapp.h>
3  #include <qlabel.h>
4  #include <qlayout.h>
5  #include <X11/Xlib.h>
6  #include "showvisual.h"
7
8  int main(int argc,char **argv)
9  {
10     KApplication app(argc,argv,"showvisual");
11     ShowVisual showvisual;
12     showvisual.show();
13     app.setMainWidget(&showvisual);
14     return(app.exec());
15 }
16 ShowVisual::ShowVisual(QWidget *parent,const char *name)
17         : QWidget(parent,name)
18 {
19     QString str;
20     QLabel *label;
21
22     QVBoxLayout *vbox = new QVBoxLayout(this,10);
23
24     str.sprintf("%4d   Screen number",x11Screen());
25     label = new QLabel(str,this);
26     vbox->addWidget(label);
27
28     str.sprintf("%4d   Bits per pixel",x11Depth());
29     label = new QLabel(str,this);
30     vbox->addWidget(label);
31
32     str.sprintf("%4d   X dots per inch",x11AppDpiX());
33     label = new QLabel(str,this);
34     vbox->addWidget(label);
35
36     str.sprintf("%4d   Y dots per inch",x11AppDpiY());
37     label = new QLabel(str,this);
38     vbox->addWidget(label);
39
40     Visual *visual = (Visual *)x11Visual();
41
42     str.sprintf("%4d   Bits per RGB",
43             visual->bits_per_rgb);
44     label = new QLabel(str,this);
45     vbox->addWidget(label);
46
47     str.sprintf("%4d   Colormap entries",
```

```
48                     visual->map_entries);
49      label = new QLabel(str,this);
50      vbox->addWidget(label);
51
52      switch(visual->c_class) {
53      case StaticGray:
54          str.sprintf("%4d   StaticGray class",
55              visual->c_class);
56          break;
57      case GrayScale:
58          str.sprintf("%4d   GrayScale class",
59              visual->c_class);
60          break;
61      case StaticColor:
62          str.sprintf("%4d   StaticColor class",
63              visual->c_class);
64          break;
65      case PseudoColor:
66          str.sprintf("%4d   PseudoColor class",
67              visual->c_class);
68          break;
69      case TrueColor:
70          str.sprintf("%4d   TrueColor class",
71              visual->c_class);
72          break;
73      case DirectColor:
74          str.sprintf("%4d   DirectColor class",
75              visual->c_class);
76          break;
77      }
78      label = new QLabel(str,this);
79      vbox->addWidget(label);
80
81      str.sprintf("0x%08X  Red Mask",
82              visual->red_mask);
83      label = new QLabel(str,this);
84      vbox->addWidget(label);
85
86      str.sprintf("0x%08X  Green Mask",
87              visual->green_mask);
88      label = new QLabel(str,this);
89      vbox->addWidget(label);
90
91      str.sprintf("0x%08X  Blue Mask",
92              visual->blue_mask);
93      label = new QLabel(str,this);
94      vbox->addWidget(label);
95
96      resize(10,10);
97  }
```

All of the information displayed by this program is actually supplied by the low-level X11 system. The `QWidget` object inherits these methods from the `QPaintDevice` base class, so the same information can be retrieved from any widget. Figure 11-1 shows the display produced by a system that can display 256 colors simultaneously.

Figure 11-1: The color characteristics of a display

Lines 24 through 26 create a label that displays the screen number. This number is almost always zero, but because X11 is designed to simultaneously handle any number of screens, there will be a different number for each one. Also, because X11 was designed for networking, the screens can be on another computer. In fact, it is possible for the same application to simultaneously have screens displayed on multiple computers.

Lines 28 through 30 create a label that displays the number of hardware bits assigned to each pixel. Two pixels that have the same numeric value will have exactly the same color, so the total number of simultaneous colors is limited to 256.

Lines 32 through 38 create a pair of labels that specify the number of dots per inch in both the horizontal and vertical directions. You should be aware that these values are only approximations because there is no way for the software to know about the configuration of the terminal. A CRT has adjustable width and height, and the display area is seldom straight on all edges.

The call to `x11Visual()` on line 40 retrieves a `Visual` struct, which is a low-level X11 struct containing some fundamental information about the display. These values are used to create the rest of the displayed window. This struct is part of the X software, so it is necessary to include the file `Xlib.h`, as is done on line 5.

Lines 42 through 45 create a label stating that there are 6 bits per RGB value. That is, 18 bits (6 for each primary color) represent a complete color value. There is often another 6-bit value (the alpha value) that specifies the level of transparency of the color; thus, 6 pixels per RGB is often referred to as a 24-bit color system.

Because each of the 6-bit integers can contain values from 0 to 63, and because 64 to the third power is 262,144, that it is the total number of colors that this system can store. However, it can only display 256 of the colors simultaneously. Lines 47 through 50 create a label that shows the total number of entries in the color map. The number 256 is indicated by the fact that there are 8 bits per pixel. Each member of the color map array is 24 bits wide, so each can hold the four values (red, green, blue, and alpha) of a color.

Lines 52 through 76 create a label that specifies the class of the display. The classes are the lines listed earlier in Table 11.1. The type names are defined in the X header files, which are included on line 5. In this example, the display uses Pseudo Color, which means that the value stored in the 8-bit pixel is used as an index into the color map array, and the values in the color map can be modified by the application.

Lines 81 through 94 create labels that display the values of the three color masks. They are zero in this example because they apply only to True Color and Direct Color. Both of these display classes use a separate color map for each of the primary colors, and the masks are used to extract, from the pixel value, the index values into each of the arrays. In fact, because each color map contains only one color, and there is even shading from no color (black) to full brightness of color, there is often no actual color map. Instead, the size of the mask — which can be a different size for each color — is used to determine where the color is to fall between these two extremes.

There is more information about windows and screens from the lower level X11 system, but you probably won't need to bother with them. One of the advantages of avoiding the X11 routines is that your code is simpler. Moreover, the application you produce will be portable from one system to another. The rest of this chapter deals with high-level color controls and leaves the details to KDE and Qt.

Constructing a QColor Object

A QColor object contains the definition of a color. There are a number of ways to create QColor objects. The following program demonstrates different ways to create a QColor object by creating the set of colored labels shown in Figure 11-2, using a different set of QColor constructor arguments for each one.

```
1 /* colormaker.cpp */
2 #include <kapp.h>
3 #include <qlabel.h>
4 #include <qlayout.h>
5 #include "colormaker.h"
6
```

```
 7 int main(int argc,char **argv)
 8 {
 9     KApplication app(argc,argv,"colormaker");
10     ColorMaker colormaker;
11     colormaker.show();
12     app.setMainWidget(&colormaker);
13     return(app.exec());
14 }
15 ColorMaker::ColorMaker(QWidget *parent,const char *name)
16         : QWidget(parent,name)
17 {
18     QString str;
19     QLabel *label;
20
21     QVBoxLayout *vbox = new QVBoxLayout(this,3);
22
23     label = new QLabel("Defined by RGB numbers",this);
24     label->setBackgroundColor(QColor(250,150,100));
25     vbox->addWidget(label);
26
27     label = new QLabel("Defined by RGB numbers",this);
28     label->setBackgroundColor(QColor(150,250,100,
29             QColor::Rgb));
30     vbox->addWidget(label);
31
32     label = new QLabel("Defined by HSV numbers",this);
33     label->setBackgroundColor(QColor(310,150,250,
34             QColor::Hsv));
35     vbox->addWidget(label);
36
37     label = new QLabel("Defined by QRgb value",this);
38     QRgb rgb = 0x00F0E000;
39     label->setBackgroundColor(QColor(rgb));
40     vbox->addWidget(label);
41
42     label = new QLabel("Defined by colormap index",this);
43     label->setBackgroundColor(QColor(rgb,86));
44     vbox->addWidget(label);
45
46     label = new QLabel("Defined by RGB name",this);
47     label->setBackgroundColor(QColor("#F58F95"));
48     vbox->addWidget(label);
49
50     label = new QLabel("Defined by file name",this);
51     label->setBackgroundColor(QColor("green"));
52     vbox->addWidget(label);
53
54     resize(10,10);
55 }
```

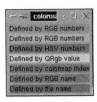

Figure 11-2: A few basic ways to create color

Every widget has a background color. This example uses QColor objects to set the background colors of a collection of QLabel widgets. The background color is used to paint all the pixels of a widget that are not otherwise painted or drawn. In a Qlabel, the background color is used to fill the entire widget; then the text is written on top of it. Whenever you create a QColor object, it may be necessary for the constructor to insert a new member into the current color map. If the color is already in the color map, no action is necessary. However, if a color must be added, and there is no room in the color map, the QColor object simply attaches itself to the closest thing it can find in the color map. Because of this, an application with a lot of colors may look a little different under different circumstances.

Lines 23 through 25 create a label with the color specified as RGB values. Each value is in the range of 0 to 255, with 0 being none of the color and 255 being the maximum amount. The RGB values 0,0,0 are black; and the values 255,255,255 are white.

Lines 27 through 30 create a color using the RGB values, just as in the previous example, except for the extra argument that tells the constructor that the three values are to be interpreted as RGB values.

Lines 32 through 35 use the same QColor constructor as on line 28, but it creates a QColor object using HSV (hue, saturation, value) instead of RGB. An HSV color is defined by three numbers, as is an RGB color, but the numbers have very different meaning. You will also see HSV referred to as HSB (hue, saturation, brightness). The H value is the hue (also called tint), which specifies the frequency of the light within the color spectrum. The S value is the saturation (also called shade), which specifies the amount of black or white that is mixed with the base color to make it lighter or darker. The B or V value (also called brightness or luminosity) specifies the intensity at which the color is displayed.

When creating an HSV color, the H value passed to the constructor can be in the range of 0 to 360 to select the color, or it can be -1 to specify that the color is to be without hue (gray, black, or white). The S value ranges from 0 (maximum black mixed in) to 255 (maximum white mixed in). To get a pure color, use 127 for the saturation. The V or B value ranges from 0 (minimum brightness) to 255 (maximum brightness).

Lines 37 through 40 specify the colors with RGB values, but the three values are all stored in the single integer. For convenience, the value itself is declared as a hexadecimal value on line 38. The first byte of the value is ignored—the red color value is 0xF0, the green is 0xE0, and the blue is 0x00.

Lines 42 through 44 specify the color by using an index into the color map. The second argument to the constructor (the number 86) is the index into the color map, while the first argument is an integer containing an RGB value. The index value is an unsigned number, but if you were to specify it as 0xFFFFFFFF, the index will be ignored and the RGB value will be used instead.

Lines 46 through 48 use the hexadecimal character form of an RGB value to specify the color. The form of the number string used in the example is "#RRGGBB", but it could also have been "#RGB", "#RRRGGGBBB", or even "#RRRRGGGGBBBB". The color-defining software detects the leading # character and divides the remaining string into equal parts before extracting the values.

Lines 50 through 52 use a QColor object created from an entry in the file /usr/lib/X11/rgb.txt. This is a plain text file, and each entry contains a name and the RGB values for a color. For example:

```
 60 179 113  MediumSeaGreen
 32 178 170  LightSeaGreen
152 251 152  PaleGreen
  0 255   0  green
  0 250 154  MediumSpringGreen
```

There are over 750 entries in this file, and the file is distributed with X11, so you can feel safe using the names you find there. There are less than 750 unique colors in the file because almost all the colors have more than one name. Also, if you wish, you can add your own names and your program will find them, but your application won't be as portable.

The KColorDialog

You can take several approaches to setting the colors in your application. You can simply ignore the colors and use the defaults, you can set specific color values to each widget, or you can enable the user to select the colors. The KColorDialog is a pop-up dialog that prompts the user to make a color selection. The following example demonstrates how you can pop up a KColorDialog and retrieve the color information chosen by the user.

The main window of the application, shown in Figure 11-3, contains a button at the bottom that will pop up the dialog. At the top of the window are the hexadecimal RGB (Red, Green, Blue) values of the currently selected color. In the center of the window is a block that displays the color.

Figure 11-3: Clicking the button to change the color

ShowColor Header

```
1 /* showcolor.h */
2 #ifndef SHOWCOLOR_H
3 #define SHOWCOLOR_H
4
5 #include <qwidget.h>
6 #include <qlabel.h>
7 #include <qstring.h>
8
9 class ShowColor: public QWidget
10 {
11     Q_OBJECT
12 public:
13     ShowColor(QWidget *parent=0,const char *name=0);
14 private:
15     QLabel *label;
16     QWidget *widget;
17     QColor color;
18     QString colorName;
19 private slots:
20     void popup();
21 };
22
23 #endif
```

The ShowColor class is the widget that displays the main window in Figure 11-3. It contains the label that appears at the top with the RGB values, and the widget that appears in the middle to display the color. It also stores the current color, as a QColor object; and the name of the color, as a QString object. The name of the color is the hexadecimal representation of the RGB value. The slot named popup() is used to display the KColorDialog whenever the button is clicked.

ShowColor

```
1 /* showcolor.cpp */
2 #include <kapp.h>
3 #include <qpushbutton.h>
4 #include <qlayout.h>
5 #include <kcmdlineargs.h>
6 #include <kcolordlg.h>
7 #include "showcolor.h"
8
9 int main(int argc,char **argv)
10 {
11     KCmdLineArgs::init(argc,argv,"showcolor",
12         "Show Color","0.0");
13     KApplication app;
14     ShowColor showcolor;
15     showcolor.show();
16     app.setMainWidget(&showcolor);
```

```
17        return(app.exec());
18 }
19 ShowColor::ShowColor(QWidget *parent,const char *name)
20            : QWidget(parent,name)
21 {
22     QVBoxLayout *box = new QVBoxLayout(this,0,3);
23
24     colorName = "#FF0000";
25     color.setNamedColor(colorName);
26     label = new QLabel(colorName,this);
27     label->setFont(QFont("Courier",16));
28     label->setAlignment(Qt::AlignHCenter);
29     box->addWidget(label);
30
31     widget = new QWidget(this);
32     widget->setFixedHeight(40);
33     widget->setBackgroundColor(color);
34     box->addWidget(widget);
35
36     QPushButton *button = new QPushButton("Select Color",
37                this);
38     box->addWidget(button);
39     connect(button,SIGNAL(clicked()),
40                this,SLOT(popup()));
41
42     resize(10,10);
43     box->activate();
44 }
45 void ShowColor::popup()
46 {
47     int cond = KColorDialog::getColor(color,this);
48     if(cond == KColorDialog::Accepted) {
49         colorName = color.name();
50         label->setText(colorName);
51         widget->setBackgroundColor(color);
52     }
53 }
```

For convenience, this source file includes both the main() function and the executable code for the ShowColor class. The main() function, starting on line 7, simply creates a top-level window and inserts a ShowColor widget into it.

The ShowColor constructor, beginning on line 15, creates a vertical box and inserts three widgets into it. Lines 24 and 25 set the initial color, which is red. The label that displays the name is created on line 26. Line 27 calls the method setFont() so the hexadecimal digits will be displayed in a fixed font. The call to setAlignment() positions the text in the center, and the call to addWidget() on line 29 inserts the label into the box.

The block of color displayed in the center of the window is a simple widget with only its background color set. It is created on line 31, and has its height fixed to 40 pixels on line 28. It is not necessary to set its width because the vertical box will control that. On line 33, a call is made to setBackgroundColor() to paint the otherwise blank widget.

Lines 36 through 40 create a button, insert it into the box, and connect it to the popup() slot.

The popup() slot beginning on line 45 is executed whenever the button is clicked. It begins by calling the static method getColor(), which displays the KColorDialog window shown in Figure 11-4. This method does not return until the user has made a selection or closes the dialog without making a selection. If a color selection is made, the value of cond will be equal to the constant value KColorDialog::Accepted, indicating that a color has been selected. If no color has been selected, there is nothing to do. If a color has been selected, it will have been placed into the QColor object that was passed to getColor() as its first argument. On line 49, the name of the new color is extracted and, on line 50, the name is inserted into the label. Line 51 calls setBackgroundColor() to update the color being displayed by the widget in the center.

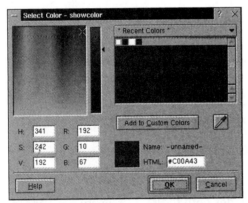

Figure 11-4: The KColorDialog window

The call to getColor() on line 47 uses the QColor object as its first argument. The color passed in is the default color value, and it initializes the display of the KColorDialog window. Because this example always passes in the color being displayed, the default color of the dialog is always the current color.

The KColorDialog widget can be used in more than one way to select the color. The grouping in the upper left corner presents a collection of system colors — colors that are defined as part of the KDE system and used by many of its components. These colors have the advantage of being "pure" in the sense that they look very much the same on different computers. A color can also be selected by using the mouse on the two shaded boxes at the upper right. As you drag a cross-hair pointer around the large box you will see the RGB and HSV values change at the lower right. The third way to select a color is to use one of the custom colors you have stored in the collection at the lower left.

Note The custom colors, which are persistent for each user, are stored in the file ~/. kde/share/config/kdeglobals and are retrieved whenever a KColorDialog is popped up.

To add a custom color, first select one of the boxes in the collection of custom colors. Next, using the mouse, select a color from either the system colors on the left or by using the color pad on the right. Once selected, clicking the button labeled Add to Custom Colors will insert it.

QColors in a QColorGroup

Several colors can be involved in the drawing of a widget. For example, a pushbutton has a background color, a top-shading color, a bottom-shading color, and a color for the text. There must be a QColor object that the button can use to paint all these colors. Other widgets have different requirements for sets of colors. And the requirements can change from one moment to the next as a button is pressed or the mouse passes over a sensitive widget.

The QColorGroup class is designed to encapsulate all of the colors a widget will need into a single unit. With all of the different kinds of widgets, and the different forms they can take, the QColorGroup needs to contain a wide color selection. Table 11-2 lists the fourteen colors that are included in each QColorGroup.

Table 11-2
Colors Contained in a QColorGroup Object

Name	Description
Background	This color is used for the background of almost all widgets.
Base	This is a background color for widgets that you would like to be a lighter color than the one defined as Background. This is often white, but it's always a light color.
BrightText	This color can be used to make text show up when Dark is used as the background.

Continued

Table 11-2 *(continued)*

Name	Description
Button	This is the background color for a button. The widget is filled with this color before the rest of it is drawn.
ButtonText	This color can be used to make text show up when Button is used as the background.
Dark	This color is darker than the Button color and is used with Light for shading to give the button its 3-D appearance.
Foreground	This color is used for any lettering or drawing on the face of the widget.
Highlight	This is the background color used to paint a highlighted or selected item.
HighlightedText	This is a color that contrasts with Highlight as the background in such a way that it is suitable for displaying text.
Light	This color is lighter than the Button color and is used with Dark for shading to give a widget the 3-D appearance.
Mid	This color is between Button and Dark for widgets that require more sophisticated shading.
Midlight	This color is between Button and Light for widgets that require more sophisticated shading.
Shadow	This color is very dark and is used for pronounced shadowing. It is often black.
Text	This is the color used to paint text onto the face of the widget. It is usually, but not always, the same as Foreground.

The following program retrieves the current QColorGroup of a widget and displays all of the colors contained in it. Because this application makes no changes to the colors in the group, the default colors and values are displayed. As shown in Figure 11-5, the program displays all fourteen colors, the color names, and the hexadecimal representation of each.

```
1 /* showgroup.cpp */
2 #include <kapp.h>
3 #include <qlabel.h>
4 #include <qpalette.h>
5 #include "showgroup.h"
6
7 struct namelistStruct {
8     QString name;
9     QColorGroup::ColorRole value;
```

```
10  } namelist[] = {
11      { "Background", QColorGroup::Background },
12      { "Base", QColorGroup::Base },
13      { "BrightText", QColorGroup::BrightText },
14      { "Button", QColorGroup::Button },
15      { "ButtonText", QColorGroup::ButtonText },
16      { "Dark", QColorGroup::Dark },
17      { "Foreground", QColorGroup::Foreground },
18      { "Highlight", QColorGroup::Highlight },
19      { "HighlightedText", QColorGroup::HighlightedText },
20      { "Light", QColorGroup::Light },
21      { "Mid", QColorGroup::Mid },
22      { "Midlight", QColorGroup::Midlight },
23      { "Shadow", QColorGroup::Shadow },
24      { "Text", QColorGroup::Text }
25  };
26
27  int main(int argc,char **argv)
28  {
29      KApplication app(argc,argv,"showgroup");
30      ShowGroup showgroup;
31      showgroup.show();
32      app.setMainWidget(&showgroup);
33      return(app.exec());
34  }
35  ShowGroup::ShowGroup(QWidget *parent,const char *name)
36          : QWidget(parent,name)
37  {
38      QHBoxLayout *hbox;
39      QVBoxLayout *vbox = new QVBoxLayout(this,0,3);
40      int size = sizeof(namelist)/sizeof(namelistStruct);
41      for(int i=0; i<size; i++) {
42          hbox = newColorLine(i);
43          vbox->addLayout(hbox);
44      }
45      resize(10,10);
46  }
47  QHBoxLayout *ShowGroup::newColorLine(int i)
48  {
49      QLabel *label;
50      QHBoxLayout *hbox = new QHBoxLayout();
51      QColorGroup group = colorGroup();
52      QColor color = group.color(namelist[i].value);
53
54      label = new QLabel("",this);
55      label->setBackgroundColor(color);
56      label->setMinimumWidth(100);
57      hbox->addWidget(label);
58
59      label = new QLabel(color.name(),this);
60      label->setFixedWidth(60);
61      label->setFont(QFont("Courier"));
```

```
62      hbox->addWidget(label);
63
64      label = new QLabel(namelist[i].name,this);
65      hbox->addWidget(label);
66
67      return(hbox);
68 }
```

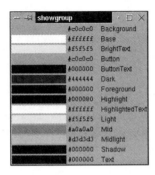

Figure 11-5: The KColorDialog window

Lines 7 through 25 declare the `namelist` array that contains the name of each color, and the `ColorRole` value that is used to retrieve it from its `QColorGroup`. The array was defined to simplify the code by allowing the processing to be done in a loop.

The constructor begins on line 35. The top-level container is a vertical box. The loop, beginning on line 41, constructs one horizontal box for each member of the `namelist` array. Storing each horizontal box in the vertical box, with the call to `addLayout()` on line 43, creates the display shown in Figure 11-5.

The method `newColorLine()` beginning on line 47 is called once for each color. The argument passed to it is used as an index into the `namelist` array. This method creates a horizontal box and stores three labels in it. The first label displays the color itself, the second displays the hexadecimal value of the color, and the third displays the `QColorGroup` name of the color.

Line 52 retrieves the `QColor` object from the `QColorGroup` by using an enumerated value from the table in the call to the `color()` method. An alternative way to retrieve a color would be to call one of the methods dedicated to a color. For example, the following lines of code could have been used to retrieve the `Button` and `Midlight` colors:

```
QColor bcolor = group.button();
QColor mcolor = group.midlight();
```

Lines 54 through 57 create a label without text, but with its background set to the currently indexed color in the `namelist` array. The color is inserted into the label by the call to `setBackgroundColor()` on line 55.

Lines 59 through 62 create the label that holds the hexadecimal name of the color. The name is retrieved from the QColor object by the call to name() on line 59. In order for the numbers to be displayed properly, the font had to be changed to Courier, which is a fixed-width font.

Lines 64 and 65 create the third label containing the QColorGroup name of the color.

QColorGroups in a QPalette

A QPalette object is nothing more than a container holding three QColorGroups. Every widget has one. Each widget uses its assigned QPalette object to draw itself. Whenever a widget draws itself, it uses the QColorGroup that matches the current state of the widget. The three widget states are described in Table 11-3.

Table 11-3		
Three States of a Widget		
Name	**Description**	
Normal	This is the default state. The Normal state is assumed when the widget is in neither of the other two states.	
Active	The widget that currently has the focus is in the Active state. The colors for this state are usually the same as for the Normal state.	
Disabled	The widget is disabled. The QColorGroup for this state is normally grayed, or otherwise subdued, to indicate the widget's dormant state.	

In the previous example program, a call was made to the QWidget method color Group() on line 51 to retrieve the current QColorGroup. The actual QColorGroup object returned could be any one of the three because it is determined by the current state of the widget. The advantage of using the colorGroup() method is that you don't need to be concerned about which QColorGroup to use — just get the color you want out of the current QColorGroup.

All three QColorGroup objects are available to a widget. The following code can be used by a widget to retrieve a copy of all three:

```
QPalette myPalette = palette();
QColorGroup normalGroup = myPalette.normal();
QColorGroup activeGroup = myPalette.active();
QColorGroup disabledGroup = myPalette.disabled();
```

Setting Colors for a Few Widgets

There is a way to define colors for widgets that not only gives you complete control over the colors of the widgets you write yourself, but also allows you to control all of the colors used by each widget in your program. You can do this selectively by setting the colors for a single widget, or for the widgets in a single widget tree, or even for a selected set of widgets within a tree. And it's relatively easy to do.

The key to this is writing your widgets so they use the colors in a QPalette. If you write your widget so it always gets its colors from the QColorGroup returned from the colorGroup() method, your program will be able to exercise complete control over the colors and can change them at will. Virtually all of the widgets supplied with KDE and Qt use the colors supplied in the QWidget's QPalette for coloring its various parts.

Which widgets are affected depends on how you set up your program to propagate the palette settings through your widgets. The options, which, by the way, affect font settings as well as color settings, are listed in Table 11-4.

Table 11-4
How Palette and Font Changes Affect Child Widgets

Name	Description
NoChildren	Changing this widget's palette or font will have no effect on its child widgets.
AllChildren	Changing this widget's palette or font will cause the same change to apply to all child widgets.
SamePalette	Changing this widget's palette or font will cause the same change to apply to all child widgets for which no font or palette has been set.
SameFont	Same as SamePalette.

If you have one widget that is going to need some special coloring, but you want to apply the colors to that single widget, you can create a special version of a QPalette for it to use. You can create the whole thing from scratch by specifying all 42 colors — the 14 colors for each of the three QColorGroups — but more than likely you will want to just create a modified version of the existing QPalette. The following example demonstrates how this can be done:

```
1 /* colorone.cpp */
2 #include <kapp.h>
3 #include <qlabel.h>
4 #include <qpushbutton.h>
5 #include <qcolor.h>
6 #include <qlayout.h>
```

```
 7  #include "colorone.h"
 8
 9  int main(int argc,char **argv)
10  {
11      KApplication app(argc,argv,"colorone");
12      ColorOne colorone;
13      colorone.show();
14      app.setMainWidget(&colorone);
15      return(app.exec());
16  }
17  ColorOne::ColorOne(QWidget *parent,const char *name)
18          : QWidget(parent,name)
19  {
20      QString str;
21      QLabel *label;
22      QPushButton *button;
23
24      QPalette newPalette = palette().copy();
25
26      QColorGroup normalGroup = newPalette.normal();
27      normalGroup.setColor(QColorGroup::ButtonText,
28              QColor("white"));
29      normalGroup.setColor(QColorGroup::Button,
30              QColor("blue"));
31      normalGroup.setColor(QColorGroup::Foreground,
32              QColor("red"));
33      newPalette.setNormal(normalGroup);
34
35      setPalettePropagation(AllChildren);
36      setPalette(newPalette,TRUE);
37
38      QVBoxLayout *vbox = new QVBoxLayout(this,15);
39
40      button = new QPushButton("The Top Button",this);
41      vbox->addWidget(button);
42
43      label = new QLabel("The Label in the Middle",this);
44      vbox->addWidget(label);
45
46      button = new QPushButton("The Bottom Button",this);
47      vbox->addWidget(button);
48
49      resize(10,10);
50  }
```

The call to copy() on line 24 duplicates the currently active QPalette. This new
QPalette contains all of the color values of the original and can be modified without having any effect on the original. The call to copy() creates a duplicate of the
palette. Because QPalette objects tend to be large, each widget retains a reference
to the palette it uses, instead of making its own private copy. Therefore, because
the palette() method returns the reference to a QPalette object (which could be
the one used in a number of widgets), and you want to limit your changes to only
those widgets you know about, it is best to make a copy of it using the copy()

method. This is a deep enough copy that you can consider it to be your own private instance of QPalette.

The normal QColorGroup is retrieved from the new QPalette on line 26. Lines 27 through 32 call setColor() to replace three of the existing color definitions in the color group. Two of these colors are specifically for buttons, while the other is set to modify the foreground color for all widgets. The call to setNormal() on line 33 stores the modified color group as the normal color group in the new QPalette.

The call to setPalettePropagation() on line 35 configures the widget so that all the child widgets will use the newly modified QPalette. The call to setPalette() on line 36 establishes the new palette as the one to be used by this widget and all its child widgets.

Lines 38 through 47 create the widget layout shown in Figure 11-6. The label uses the normal foreground color for its text, so it becomes red. The pushbutton's text is painted in white, and the background of the button is blue. These colors remain for the button until its state changes from normal (by the mouse entering the button).

Figure 11-6: Changing the color of only the parent widget

If you specify the propagation to be SamePalette, which is the default, then all child widgets with the exact same palette as this one will have their palettes changed to the updated one. This enables you to apply the new palette to some of the child widgets, but leave others unaltered. To do this, create a new palette and assign it to all the widgets you wish to be able to modify, and to a parent widget. From then on, assigning a new palette to the parent widget using the SamePalette setting will cause only those specified widgets to have their palettes changed.

Using the QPalette for Your Own Coloring

Whenever you create a widget of your own that performs some form of low-level graphics, you will need to select the colors. If you wish, you can specify the exact colors to be used, or you can extract the ones that are stored in the QPalette. Using the predefined QPalette colors has the advantage that, as the colors are changed in your application, the colors for you widget will change with them.

The following example demonstrates how a widget can use the colors stored in the QPalette:

```
1  /* usepalette.cpp */
2  #include <kapp.h>
3  #include <qpainter.h>
4  #include "usepalette.h"
5
6  int main(int argc,char **argv)
7  {
8      KApplication app(argc,argv,"usepalette");
9      UsePalette usepalette;
10     usepalette.show();
11     app.setMainWidget(&usepalette);
12     return(app.exec());
13 }
14 UsePalette::UsePalette(QWidget *parent,const
15          char *name) : QWidget(parent,name)
16 {
17     setFixedSize(375,250);
18 }
19 void UsePalette::paintEvent(QPaintEvent *)
20 {
21     QColorGroup group = colorGroup();
22     QColor midColor = group.color(QColorGroup::Mid);
23     QColor lightColor = group.color(QColorGroup::Light);
24     QBrush midBrush(midColor);
25     QBrush lightBrush(lightColor);
26     QPainter p;
27     p.begin(this);
28     p.fillRect(75,50,150,100,midBrush);
29     p.fillRect(150,100,150,100,lightBrush);
30     p.end();
31 }
```

Whenever the UsePalette widget needs to be painted, there is a call to paintEvent() on line 19.

The call to the QWidget method colorGroup() on line 21 returns the current QColorGroup. The actual color group returned will vary according to the state of the widget, so if you use the colors from the group, the colors of your widget will change to reflect its current state.

Lines 22 and 23 call the color() method of the QColorGroup to return the two color objects that will be used to do the painting. The colors are then used on lines 24 and 25 to create a pair of QBrush objects (one for each color), which are used on lines 28 and 29 to paint the rectangles shown in Figure 11-7. You can find more information about this paintEvent() method, and using QPainter, in Chapter 12.

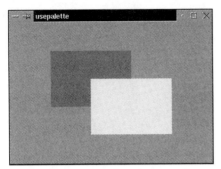

Figure 11-7: Examples of externally modifiable colors

Summary

By taking advantage of the special color classes defined in KDE and Qt, it can be quite straightforward to control, set, and modify the colorful appearance of a complete application. This chapter explained the following:

✦ The number of colors available depends on the hardware capabilities of a given system. Not only is a finite number of total colors available, but there is usually only a subset of them available at any one time.

✦ The QColor object contains fundamental color information for a color in such a way that it is hardware-independent. A QColor object's appearance will vary from one system to another, but the colors are close enough that the difference usually doesn't matter.

✦ Colors are collected into groups, and the groups are collected into palettes, all of which are configured to allow each widget in an application to easily select the right color for drawing or painting each of its parts.

✦ The colors used in your application can be obtained from the set of defaults, explicitly defined by red-green-blue numbers, extracted from the list of prede-fined color names, or entered as part of the configuration by the user of your application.

The next chapter expands on the topic of color by using colors in primitive graphic operations. It demonstrates a special QPainter object that supplies methods that can be used to draw lines and outlines, fill shapes, draw curves and circles, and much more.

✦   ✦   ✦

Drawing and Painting with QPainter

This is the first of two chapters discussing the mechanics involved with creating graphics. This chapter contains examples of the fundamental functions necessary to draw pixels, lines, curves, text, and filled regions.

The underlying graphics technology is, of course, the X11 graphics library. The Qt software wraps the X11 functions inside a collection of C++ classes, so if you are familiar with X11, all of this may seem a bit odd at first. No graphics contexts are used to draw to a window, but there is a QPainter that can be used to draw directly to a QWidget.

Painting Pixels to a QPaintDevice

It is possible to use a QPainter object to draw and paint pixels into a QPaintDevice. The QPaintDevice is a base class that is inherited by the classes described in Table 12-1.

A QPainter object does all the drawing and painting. The QPainter object contains a QPen object and a QBrush object. The QPen object is used for all pixel drawing, line drawing, and to paint text. The QBrush object is used for area fills. Although your program can change them from time to time, only one QPen and one QBrush are contained inside a QPainter object at any one time.

Table 12-1
Classes That Accept QPainter Graphic Commands

Class	Description
QPicture	A QPicture object accepts graphics command from the QPainter and records them. The commands can subsequently be drawn on another QPaintDevice object, and they can also be written to a file for later recovery. You can find examples in Chapter 13.
QPixmap	A QPainter can be used to draw and paint directly to a QPixmap object. This can be done if you wish to modify an existing pixmap graphic or if the graphic you need to draw is so complicated that you only want to do it once.
QPrinter	Graphics drawn to a QPrinter object will be converted to postscript and sent to the print spooler (lp, lpr, or whatever). Qprinter has some methods for pagination — setting the page size, sending the current page to the printer, setting the orientation, and so on.
QWidget	Every displayable object is a QWidget, so it is possible to paint and draw directly to any displayed object. Empty widgets work best because if the widget already has some graphics of its own (such as the text on a button), the widget's graphics could conflict with yours.

This chapter uses a QWidget object to demonstrate the graphics resulting from calling the QPainter methods. The drawing itself is done inside a method named paintEvent(), which is called whenever the widget needs to be painted (or repainted). The method is called whenever the program starting to run exposes or resizes the window, or removes an obscuring window. Whenever this method is called, the window has already been cleared to the background color, so no erasing is required. All your program has to do is render the drawing. Internally, the drawing you make is buffered and copied to the display in such a way that there is no flicker as the screen updates.

Some Rectangle Tricks

A number of shapes can be drawn using QPainter, and there are dozens of ways to draw them. This section demonstrates the basics of Qt graphics by using examples of some basic ways to draw and fill a simple rectangle. The following example program creates a blank widget and draws a rectangle onto its window.

DrawRectangle Header

```
1 /* drawrectangle.h */
2 #ifndef DRAWRECTANGLE_H
3 #define DRAWRECTANGLE_H
4
5 #include <qwidget.h>
6
7 class DrawRectangle: public QWidget
8 {
9 public:
10     DrawRectangle(QWidget *parent=0,const char *name=0);
11 protected:
12     virtual void paintEvent(QPaintEvent *);
13 };
14
15 #endif
```

The DrawRectangle class is a widget that is used as the top-level widget of the application. The virtual method paintEvent() overrides the one in the QWidget class, and is called whenever there is a need to paint (or to repaint) the face of the widget.

DrawRectangle

```
1 /* drawrectangle.cpp */
2 #include <kapp.h>
3 #include <qpainter.h>
4 #include "drawrectangle.h"
5
6 int main(int argc,char **argv)
7 {
8     KApplication app(argc,argv,"drawrectangle");
9     DrawRectangle drawrectangle;
10     drawrectangle.show();
11     app.setMainWidget(&drawrectangle);
12     return(app.exec());
13 }
14 DrawRectangle::DrawRectangle(QWidget *parent,const
15         char *name) : QWidget(parent,name)
16 {
17     setFixedSize(400,200);
18 }
19 void DrawRectangle::paintEvent(QPaintEvent *)
20 {
21     QPainter p;
22     p.begin(this);
23     p.drawRect(50,50,300,100);
24     p.end();
25 }
```

The constructor, beginning on line 14, creates a widget with a fixed-size window. There is no drawing done by the constructor because graphics can only be put on display after a window has been realized (that is, it actually has a place to store pixel values).

The paintEvent() method is called any time the display needs to be refreshed. That is, the window does not memorize what you have drawn and automatically replace it. Your program must be prepared to draw the window again and again — it should draw it from scratch every time this method is called. Normally, there is no real cost to drawing the whole thing even if only part of the widget is exposed, but if the graphics get complicated and require some time to produce, it is possible to limit your drawing to only the effected area. This kind of limitation is called *clipping*.

Internally, a QPainter object uses a QPen object to draw pixels and lines. The default QPen is black and draws a line that is one pixel wide.

The method paintEvent() on line 19 draws the rectangle shown in Figure 12-1. A Qpainter object is created on line 21. This QPainter object cannot be used for painting because it has no window. The call to begin() on line 22 connects the QPainter, and the drawing of the rectangle occurs on line 23 with the call to drawRect(). The arguments passed to drawRect() are the *x* and *y* coordinates of the upper left corner of the rectangle, followed by its width and height. When the image has been completely rendered (in this case, a simple rectangle), a call is made to the end() method, which disassociates the Qpainter and the QWidget.

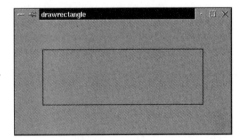

Figure 12-1: A rectangle drawn in the center of a window

While both the begin() and end() methods must be called, you can let the constructor and destructor do it by specifying the target for the drawing as a constructor argument. The following method works exactly the same as the previous one — which one you use is a matter of personal preference.

```
void DrawRectangle2::paintEvent(QPaintEvent *)
{
    QPainter p(this);
    p.drawRect(50,50,300,100);
}
```

In this example, the call to begin() is made inside the constructor; and the call to end() is made in the destructor (which is called automatically when QPainter goes out of scope at the end of the method).

Note   Every time the begin() method is called, the QPainter object is completely initialized, so there is no way to preset QPainter with pens and brushes and then use it to draw multiple widgets.

Filling a rectangle is a little different than drawing one. The following example uses the same basic dimensions as those of the previous examples, but produces the filled rectangle shown in Figure 12-2.

```
1  /* fillrectangle.cpp */
2  #include <kapp.h>
3  #include <qpainter.h>
4  #include "fillrectangle.h"
5
6  int main(int argc,char **argv)
7  {
8      KApplication app(argc,argv,"fillrectangle");
9      DrawRectangle fillrectangle;
10     fillrectangle.show();
11     app.setMainWidget(&fillrectangle);
12     return(app.exec());
13 }
14 DrawRectangle::DrawRectangle(QWidget *parent,const
15         char *name) : QWidget(parent,name)
16 {
17     setFixedSize(400,200);
18 }
19 void DrawRectangle::paintEvent(QPaintEvent *)
20 {
21     QBrush brush(QColor("black"));
22     QPainter p;
23     p.begin(this);
24     p.fillRect(50,50,300,100,brush);
25     p.end();
26 }
```

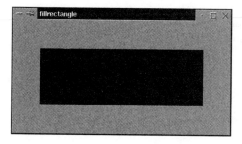

Figure 12-2: A filled rectangle in the center of a window

The drawing is executed in the paintEvent() method beginning on line 19. Whereas drawing is done with a QPen object, and the default is a black pen, filling is done with a brush, and the default brush does no painting. Therefore, line 21 of the paintEvent() method creates a QBrush object that can be used to fill all of an area with black pixels.

The QPainter object is created on line 22 and attached to the widget on line 23. The call to fillRect() on line 24, as drawRect() earlier, requires the *x* and *y* coordinates of the upper left corner of the rectangle, along with the rectangle's width and height. It also requires the brush that it uses to fill the rectangle.

It is possible to both draw and fill a rectangle. The following example first fills the rectangle by painting with a white brush, and then outlines the white area with the default black pen:

```
void FillRectangle2::paintEvent(QPaintEvent *)
{
    QBrush brush(QColor("white"));
    QPainter p;
    p.begin(this);
    p.fillRect(50,50,300,100,brush);
    p.drawRect(50,50,300,100);
    p.end();
}
```

The result is shown in Figure 12-3. The rectangle must be filled before it is drawn because the outer edge of the drawn rectangle matches exactly with the outer edge of the filled rectangle, and the act of filling the rectangle erases anything that may be already there.

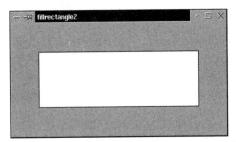

Figure 12-3: Filling and outlining a rectangle

There is another approach. All of the draw methods can be used to both outline and fill a shape. For the outline, the pen is used; for the fill, the brush is used. The rectangle shown in Figure 12-3 can also be produced by the following paint Event() method:

```
void FillRectangle3::paintEvent(QPaintEvent *)
{
```

```
QBrush brush(QColor("white"));
QPainter p;
p.begin(this);
p.setBrush(brush);
p.drawRect(50,50,300,100);
p.end();
}
```

In this example, the default QPen (which is a black, thin line) is used to draw the outline, but there is no default QBrush, so one must be created and assigned to the QPainter before a figure can be filled. The call to drawRect() first fills the rectangular area with the brush color and then outlines it with the pen.

Pens

In order for a QPen to draw a line, it must have three attributes: color, width, and a dot/dash pattern. The default pen has a width of zero, which draws a hairline (a line that is one pixel wide). This is almost, but not quite, the same as setting the line width to 1. A line drawn with a pixel width of zero will always remain exactly one pixel wide no matter how the drawing is scaled, whereas a line drawn one or more pixels in width will have its thickness scaled to wider or narrower as the drawing zooms in or out.

The following example displays the window shown in Figure 12-4. It draws a black, two-pixel-wide line in each of the six available styles. The first style, the NoPen style, does not draw anything. If you want to use a brush to, for example, fill a rectangle, but you don't want to draw the rectangle's outline, you can use the NoPen style.

Figure 12-4: The six QPen line styles

This example shows the different line styles using drawLine(), but the line styles apply to all the draw methods, including drawArc(), drawRect(), and drawPolyline().

PenStyles Header

```
 1 /* penstyles.h */
 2 #ifndef PENSTYLES_H
 3 #define PENSTYLES_H
 4
 5 #include <qwidget.h>
 6 #include <qlabel.h>
 7
 8 class PenStyles: public QWidget
 9 {
10 public:
11     PenStyles(QWidget *parent=0,const char *name=0);
12 private:
13     QLabel *label[6];
14     QWidget *widget[6];
15 protected:
16     virtual void paintEvent(QPaintEvent *);
17 };
18
19 #endif
```

The PenStyles class contains arrays of labels and widgets that are used in the display. It is necessary to include the array of widgets as part of the class because the paintEvent() callback method needs access to them.

PenStyles

```
 1 /* penstyles.cpp */
 2 #include <kapp.h>
 3 #include <qpainter.h>
 4 #include <qlayout.h>
 5 #include "penstyles.h"
 6
 7 struct pstyleStruct {
 8     QString name;
 9     Qt::PenStyle style;
10 } pstyle[6] = {
11     { "NoPen", Qt::NoPen },
12     { "SolidLine", Qt::SolidLine },
13     { "DashLine", Qt::DashLine },
14     { "DotLine", Qt::DotLine },
15     { "DashDotLine", Qt::DashDotLine },
16     { "DashDotDotLine", Qt::DashDotDotLine }
17 };
18
19 int main(int argc,char **argv)
20 {
21     KApplication app(argc,argv,"penstyles");
22     PenStyles penstyles;
23     penstyles.show();
```

```
24      app.setMainWidget(&penstyles);
25      return(app.exec());
26 }
27 PenStyles::PenStyles(QWidget *parent,const
28          char *name) : QWidget(parent,name)
29 {
30      QVBoxLayout *vbox = new QVBoxLayout(this,0,3);
31
32      for(int i=0; i<6; i++) {
33          label[i] = new QLabel(pstyle[i].name,this);
34          vbox->addWidget(label[i]);
35          widget[i] = new QWidget(this);
36          widget[i]->setFixedHeight(20);
37          widget[i]->setFixedWidth(200);
38          vbox->addWidget(widget[i]);
39      }
40      resize(10,10);
41 }
42 void PenStyles::paintEvent(QPaintEvent *)
43 {
44      QColor black("black");
45      QPainter p;
46      for(int i=0; i<6; i++) {
47          p.begin(widget[i]);
48          QPen pen(black,2,pstyle[i].style);
49          p.setPen(pen);
50          p.drawLine(10,5,190,5);
51          p.end();
52      }
53 }
```

The array of structures on lines 7 through 17 is simply a convenience for holding the names and values of the different line styles. The names of the styles are defined in qnamespace.h, which defines the Qt class. There is almost never a need to explicitly include this file because QObject and a few other fundamental classes inherit it.

The constructor, beginning on line 27, uses a vertical box to contain a column of 12 widgets. There are 6 QLabel widgets and 6 plain QWidget widgets. The labels are used to display the name of the line style, and the QWidget is used to display the line. The loop beginning on line 32 creates both the labels and the widgets, sizes them, adds them to the vertical box, and stores a reference to them in the arrays in the class.

The actual drawing of the lines is done in the paintEvent() method on line 42, which is called whenever it is necessary to draw the window. The labels take care of themselves, so all that is left to do is draw the lines. The loop beginning on line 46 draws a single line on the window of the six widgets. To enable drawing, a call is made to begin() on line 47, which assigns the QPainter object to the widget that is to receive the line. Line 48 creates a QPen of the appropriate style, and line 49 calls setPen() to establish the new pen as the one to be used to do all drawing. The line is drawn with the call to drawLine() on line 50. At the bottom of the loop, the end() method is called to disassociate the QPainter with this widget so it can be used for the next widget in the array at the top of the loop.

> **Note**   The text for the QLabel widgets is inserted in the constructor, but none of the lines are drawn. This is because nothing is drawn until the method paint Event() is called. In fact, even though the program inserts text into the label, it does not actually draw itself until there is a callback to its paintEvent().

Standard Brushes

In order for a QBrush to fill a region, it must have two attributes: color and fill pattern. The default color is black and the default pattern is SolidPattern. A total of 15 predefined patterns are available, but you can also create your own. The following program displays the predefined patterns, as shown in Figure 12-5.

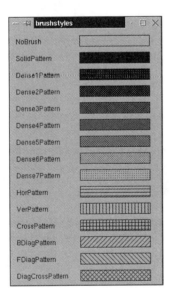

Figure 12-5: The 15 pre-defined brush styles

BrushStyles Header

```
1 /* brushstyles.h */
2 #ifndef BRUSHSTYLES_H
3 #define BRUSHSTYLES_H
4
5 #include <qwidget.h>
```

```
 6
 7 class BrushStyles: public QWidget
 8 {
 9 public:
10     BrushStyles(QWidget *parent=0,const char *name=0);
11 protected:
12     virtual void paintEvent(QPaintEvent *);
13 };
14
15 #endif
```

The `BrushStyles` class is a blank widget, so it is possible to draw both text and filled rectangles on its window.

BrushStyles

```
 1 /* brushstyles.cpp */
 2 #include <kapp.h>
 3 #include <qpainter.h>
 4 #include <qlayout.h>
 5 #include "brushstyles.h"
 6
 7 struct bstyleStruct {
 8     QString name;
 9     Qt::BrushStyle style;
10 } bstyle[15] = {
11     { "NoBrush", Qt::NoBrush },
12     { "SolidPattern", Qt::SolidPattern },
13     { "Dense1Pattern", Qt::Dense1Pattern },
14     { "Dense2Pattern", Qt::Dense2Pattern },
15     { "Dense3Pattern", Qt::Dense3Pattern },
16     { "Dense4Pattern", Qt::Dense4Pattern },
17     { "Dense5Pattern", Qt::Dense5Pattern },
18     { "Dense6Pattern", Qt::Dense6Pattern },
19     { "Dense7Pattern", Qt::Dense7Pattern },
20     { "HorPattern", Qt::HorPattern },
21     { "VerPattern", Qt::VerPattern },
22     { "CrossPattern", Qt::CrossPattern },
23     { "BDiagPattern", Qt::BDiagPattern },
24     { "FDiagPattern", Qt::FDiagPattern },
25     { "DiagCrossPattern", Qt::DiagCrossPattern }
26 };
27
28 int main(int argc,char **argv)
29 {
30     KApplication app(argc,argv,"brushstyles");
31     BrushStyles brushstyles;
32     brushstyles.show();
33     app.setMainWidget(&brushstyles);
34     return(app.exec());
```

```
35 }
36 BrushStyles::BrushStyles(QWidget *parent,const
37         char *name) : QWidget(parent,name)
38 {
39     setFixedSize(280,455);
40 }
41 void BrushStyles::paintEvent(QPaintEvent *)
42 {
43     int xText = 10;
44     int xFill = 130;
45     int yText = 25;
46     int yFill = 10;
47     QColor black("black");
48     QPainter p(this);
49     for(int i=0; i<15; i++) {
50         QBrush brush(black,bstyle[i].style);
51         p.setBrush(brush);
52         p.drawText(xText,yText,bstyle[i].name);
53         p.drawRect(xFill,yFill,130,20);
54         yText += 30;
55         yFill += 30;
56     }
57 }
```

The array of structures defined on lines 7 through 26 is a convenience for holding the names and values of each of the 15 predefined styles. The style names are defined in qnamespace.h.

The constructor, beginning on line 36, does nothing other than set the window to a fixed size that will contain all the text and rectangles drawn to it.

The paintEvent() method on lines 41 through 57 is called whenever the window needs to be painted. The values xText and yText specify the starting point of the line of text, while xFill and yFill determine the upper left corner of the rectangle to be filled. The loop, beginning on line 49, executes once for each fill style. Line 50 creates a QBrush object based on one of the predefined styles, and line 51 installs it into the QPainter. The name of the style is written as text by the call to drawText() on line 52. The rectangular area is filled by the call to drawRect() on line 53. The rectangle is both filled and outlined because the default black QPen is still in force, and the new patterned QBrush has been added.

Creating Custom Brushes

To fill a region, the QBrush creates a small pixmap and tiles it into the window. Therefore, it is a simple matter for you to specify your own fill pattern in the form of a QPixmap. The following program uses a pixmap to fill a rectangular region of a window.

BrushCustom

```
 1 /* brushcustom.cpp */
 2 #include <kapp.h>
 3 #include <qpainter.h>
 4 #include <qlayout.h>
 5 #include "brushcustom.h"
 6
 7 static const char *mypattern[] = {
 8 "16 16 4 1",
 9 "  c blue",
10 ". c white",
11 "x c red",
12 "y c green",
13 "yy....    ....yy",
14 "yy....    ....yy",
15 "......    ......",
16 "......    ......",
17 "......    ......",
18 "......    ......",
19 " .....     x    ",
20 " ....    xxx    ",
21 " ...   xxxxx   ",
22 " ..  xxxxxxx  ",
23 ".   ..xxxxxxxxx",
24 "..    ..........",
25 "...    .........",
26 "....    ........",
27 "yy...    .....yy",
28 "yy....    ....yy"
29 };
30
31 int main(int argc,char **argv)
32 {
33     KApplication app(argc,argv,"brushcustom");
34     BrushCustom brushcustom;
35     brushcustom.show();
36     app.setMainWidget(&brushcustom);
37     return(app.exec());
38 }
39 BrushCustom::BrushCustom(QWidget *parent,const
40         char *name) : QWidget(parent,name)
41 {
42     setFixedSize(220,120);
43 }
44 void BrushCustom::paintEvent(QPaintEvent *)
45 {
46     QBrush brush;
47     QPixmap pixmap(mypattern);
48     brush.setPixmap(pixmap);
49
```

```
50      QPainter p(this);
51      p.setBrush(brush);
52      p.drawRect(20,20,180,80);
53 }
```

The pixmap to be used as a filler is in the XPM format on lines 7 through 29.

Cross-Reference Chapter 9 explains the XPM format and how to use it.

The constructor, beginning on line 39, does nothing more than set the widget's window to a fixed size of 220 pixels wide by 120 pixels high.

The drawing occurs in `paintEvent()` on line 44. Line 47 uses the pixmap data to create a `QPixmap` object, and line 48 calls `setPixmap()` to install the pixmap into the `QBrush`. Installing the pixmap sets the brush style to `CustomPattern`, a value that was not included in the previous example because it is only used with a pixmap. That's all there is to it. The window this example produces is shown in Figure 12-6. Once the brush is defined and installed in the `Qpainter`, it will be used for fill until you change it to something else.

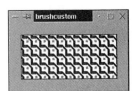

Figure 12-6: Using a custom brush to fill a rectangle

The tiling is done without regard to the location of the actual figure you are drawing. The origin can be moved, as you will see later in this chapter, but the default origin on the upper left corner is where the first tile is laid, and all the others are tiled adjacent to it. It is not necessary for the origin tile to be visible, but, visible or not, the position of all the other tiles are measured from it. If you look closely at Figure 12-6 and compare it with the XPM data in the program, you can see that the upper-left portion of the upper-left tile is clipped.

Every QPaintDevice Has Metrics

It often happens that graphics drawn into a window need to be resized or reoriented as the window changes size. The class `QPaintDeviceMetrics` can be used to determine the current size (and some other information) of the `QPaintDevice`. The following example program uses the information in a `QPaintDeviceMetrics` object to vary the positions and sizes of things painted on the window. As shown in Figures 12-7 and 12-8, the text spaces itself vertically at even intervals in the window, and the white rectangle in the background reshapes itself to fit the window.

Figure 12-7: Text moves closer together to fit the window

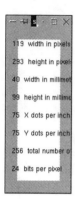

Figure 12-8: Text moves further apart to fill the window

ShowMetrics Header

```
1 /* showmetrics.h */
2 #ifndef SHOWMETRICS_H
3 #define SHOWMETRICS_H
4
5 #include <qwidget.h>
6
7 class ShowMetrics: public QWidget
8 {
9 public:
10     ShowMetrics(QWidget *parent=0,const char *name=0);
11 protected:
12     virtual void paintEvent(QPaintEvent *);
13 };
14
15 #endif
```

ShowMetrics

```
1 /* showmetrics.cpp */
2 #include <kapp.h>
3 #include <qpainter.h>
4 #include <qpaintdevicemetrics.h>
5 #include "showmetrics.h"
6
7 int main(int argc,char **argv)
8 {
9     KApplication app(argc,argv,"showmetrics");
10     ShowMetrics showmetrics;
```

```
11      showmetrics.show();
12      app.setMainWidget(&showmetrics);
13      return(app.exec());
14  }
15  ShowMetrics::ShowMetrics(QWidget *parent,const
16          char *name) : QWidget(parent,name)
17  {
18      resize(400,300);
19  }
20  void ShowMetrics::paintEvent(QPaintEvent *)
21  {
22      QString str;
23      QPaintDeviceMetrics metrics(this);
24      QBrush brush(QColor("white"));
25      int yincr = metrics.height() / 9;
26      int y = yincr;
27      int x = 10;
28
29      QPainter p(this);
30      if((metrics.width() > 40) && (metrics.height() > 40)) {
31          p.setPen(Qt::NoPen);
32          p.setBrush(brush);
33          p.drawRect(20,20,
34              metrics.width() - 40,metrics.height() - 40);
35          p.setPen(Qt::SolidLine);
36          p.setBrush(Qt::NoBrush);
37      }
38      str.sprintf("%d  width in pixels",
39              metrics.width());
40      p.drawText(x,y,str);
41      y += yincr;
42      str.sprintf("%d  height in pixels",
43              metrics.height());
44      p.drawText(x,y,str);
45      y += yincr;
46      str.sprintf("%d  width in millimeters",
47              metrics.widthMM());
48      p.drawText(x,y,str);
49      y += yincr;
50      str.sprintf("%d  height in millimeters",
51              metrics.heightMM());
52      p.drawText(x,y,str);
53      y += yincr;
54      str.sprintf("%d  X dots per inch",
55              metrics.logicalDpiX());
56      p.drawText(x,y,str);
57      y += yincr;
58      str.sprintf("%d  Y dots per inch",
59              metrics.logicalDpiY());
60      p.drawText(x,y,str);
61      y += yincr;
```

```
62        str.sprintf("%d  total number of colors",
63              metrics.numColors());
64        p.drawText(x,y,str);
65        y += yincr;
66        str.sprintf("%d  bits per pixel",
67              metrics.depth());
68        p.drawText(x,y,str);
69 }
```

The `paintEvent()` method on line 20 is called whenever the window needs to be painted. This will happen whenever the window first appears, whenever it is exposed by having a window removed from in front of it, and, most important to this application, whenever the size of the window changes.

The `QPaintDeviceMetrics` object is created on line 23, and it contains all of the information we need to scale the graphics. There are two height and width values — one is measured in pixels and the other is in millimeters. The one you should use depends on the characteristics of the device being painted. For example, if you are painting to a printer, the precise millimeter information can be very handy. Drawings made to a displayed window, however, can vary widely in size (even at the same pixel resolution), so it is best to work with pixel measurements. The same sort of situation applies to the vertical and horizontal dots-per-inch values.

Lines 25 through 27 set up the x and y coordinates of the first string to be displayed, and calculate the increment by which the y value will change for spacing the strings down the window. Eight strings are to be displayed, so, counting the top and bottom, there are 9 vertical spaces — the overall height of the window is divided by 9 to determine the distance between them.

The code on lines 30 through 37 draws a white rectangle that is sized to fit the window. The rectangle is drawn so that it is exactly 20 pixels from all four edges of the window. The `if` statement on line 30 will skip the rectangle if there is not enough room to draw one. To suppress rectangle outlining, the call to `setPen()` on line 31 removes the current pen. The call to `setBrush()` on line 32 installs the white brush that will fill the rectangle, and the call to `drawRect()` on line 33 draws the rectangle. The rectangle has its upper-left corner positioned 20 pixels from the edges of the window, and its width and height are calculated so that the rectangle ends 20 pixels before reaching the opposite edges of the window. Lines 35 and 36 restore the default pen and remove the white brush.

Lines 38 through 68 print the numbers and text on the window. The value of x does not vary, which causes every string to begin at the same distance from the left side of the window. After each line is printed, the value stored in `yincr` is added to y so that each string will appear one-ninth of the total window height below the one above it.

Pixel Drawing

The following program demonstrates drawing one pixel at a time by creating a grid and drawing an amplified sine wave on it, as shown in Figure 12-9.

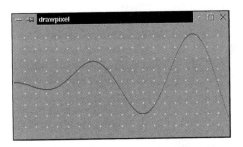

Figure 12-9: A curve and a grid drawn one pixel at a time

DrawPixel Header

```
1 /* drawpixel.h */
2 #ifndef DRAWPIXEL_H
3 #define DRAWPIXEL_H
4
5 #include <qwidget.h>
6
7 class DrawPixel: public QWidget
8 {
9 public:
10     DrawPixel(QWidget *parent=0,const char *name=0);
11 protected:
12     virtual void paintEvent(QPaintEvent *);
13 };
14
15 #endif
```

DrawPixel

```
1 /* drawpixel.cpp */
2 #include <kapp.h>
3 #include <qpainter.h>
4 #include "drawpixel.h"
5
6 int main(int argc,char **argv)
7 {
8     KApplication app(argc,argv,"drawpixel");
9     DrawPixel drawpixel;
10     drawpixel.show();
11     app.setMainWidget(&drawpixel);
12     return(app.exec());
```

```
13 }
14 DrawPixel::DrawPixel(QWidget *parent,const
15          char *name) : QWidget(parent,name)
16 {
17     setFixedSize(400,200);
18 }
19 void DrawPixel::paintEvent(QPaintEvent *)
20 {
21     QPainter p(this);
22     p.setPen(QColor("white"));
23     for(int x=20; x<400; x += 20) {
24         for(int y=20; y<200; y += 20) {
25             p.drawPoint(x-1,y);
26             p.drawPoint(x+1,y);
27             p.drawPoint(x,y-1);
28             p.drawPoint(x,y+1);
29         }
30     }
31     p.setPen(QColor("red"));
32     for(double x=0; x<400; x++) {
33         double y = sin(x / 30);
34         y *= x / 4;
35         y += 100;
36         p.drawPoint((int)x,(int)y);
37     }
38 }
```

The paintEvent() method beginning on line 19 draws the grid points and the curve. Points, by the way, are drawn with the QPen, normally used to draw lines. You can think of a pixel as the shortest of all possible lines. Line 22 calls setPen() to establish a white pen for drawing the points, and line 31 calls setPen() to establish the red pen for drawing the dots making up the curve.

The loop on lines 23 through 30 draws the collection of white points shown in Figure 12-9. The points are drawn at 20-pixel intervals both vertically and horizontally. Each point is drawn as four pixels — one above and one to each side of the center point.

The loop on lines 32 through 37 draws a sine wave that increases in amplitude from left to right. The variables x and y are declared as double to simplify the calculations. The window is fixed at 400 pixels wide, so the value of x varies from 0 to 400, resulting in one painted pixel in each of the 400 "pixel columns." Line 33 calculates the sine, treating the value of x as a number of radians (using a divisor other than 30 here will change the number of cycles that appear in the window). Line 34 multiplies the y value such that its magnitude becomes larger as x becomes larger. Line 35 adds 100 to the y value so it will be vertically centered in the window. The call to drawPoint() on line 36 paints the pixel.

Drawing Arrays of Pixels

In the previous example, all of the points were calculated each time the window was painted. Sometimes it is more convenient to calculate the points only once, or load them from a file and store them in an array. The following example displays the same window as the previous example, shown in Figure 12-9, but it calculates the pixel locations only once and stores them in an array.

DrawPixel2 Header

```
 1 /* drawpixel2.h */
 2 #ifndef DRAWPIXEL_H
 3 #define DRAWPIXEL_H
 4
 5 #include <qwidget.h>
 6 #include <qpointarray.h>
 7
 8 class DrawPixel2: public QWidget
 9 {
10 public:
11     DrawPixel2(QWidget *parent=0,const char *name=0);
12 private:
13     QPointArray *grid;
14     QPointArray *curve;
15 protected:
16     virtual void paintEvent(QPaintEvent *);
17 };
18
19 #endif
```

Lines 13 and 14 declare pointers to a pair of QPointArray objects. The one named curve is used to contain the points defining the trace, and the one named grid will contain the locations of the white points in the background.

DrawPixel2

```
 1 /* drawpixel2.cpp */
 2 #include <kapp.h>
 3 #include <qpainter.h>
 4 #include "drawpixel2.h"
 5
 6 int main(int argc,char **argv)
 7 {
 8     KApplication app(argc,argv,"drawpixel2");
 9     DrawPixel2 drawpixel2;
10     drawpixel2.show();
11     app.setMainWidget(&drawpixel2);
12     return(app.exec());
13 }
```

```
14 DrawPixel2::DrawPixel2(QWidget *parent,const
15        char *name) : QWidget(parent,name)
16 {
17     int index;
18     setFixedSize(400,200);
19
20     grid = new QPointArray(4 * 20 * 10);
21     index = 0;
22     for(int x=20; x<400; x += 20) {
23         for(int y=20; y<200; y += 20) {
24             grid->setPoint(index++,x-1,y);
25             grid->setPoint(index++,x+1,y);
26             grid->setPoint(index++,x,y-1);
27             grid->setPoint(index++,x,y+1);
28         }
29     }
30     curve = new QPointArray(400);
31     index = 0;
32     for(double x=0; x<400; x++) {
33         double y = sin(x / 30);
34         y *= x / 4;
35         y += 100;
36         curve->setPoint(index++,(int)x,(int)y);
37     }
38 }
39 void DrawPixel2::paintEvent(QPaintEvent *)
40 {
41     QPainter p(this);
42     p.setPen(QColor("white"));
43     p.drawPoints(*grid);
44     p.setPen(QColor("red"));
45     p.drawPoints(*curve);
46 }
```

The constructor, beginning on line 14, does all of the calculation work and stores the result in the arrays. The call to setFixedSize() on line 18 prohibits the window from being resized.

The QPointArray object to contain the grid points is created on line 20. There is one entry in the array for each of the points, so the total size of the array is the product of 4 (the number of pixels in each grid point), 20 (the number of grid points that will appear along the *x* axis), and 10 (the number of grid points that will appear along the *y* axis). The loop on lines 22 through 29 inserts four pixel locations for each of the grid points.

The QPointArray object to contain the trace of the curve is created on line 30. The calculations, and the number of points, are the same as they were in the previous example. There are 400 points calculated, and all 400 are stored in the array by the call to setPoint() on line 36.

The `paintEvent()` method starting on line 39 has much less to do than in the previous example. A `QPainter` object is created, a white pen is used to draw the points defined in `grid`, and a red pen is used to draw the points in `curve`.

Sometimes you need to recalculate the values under some circumstances, but not under others. For example, if you wish to recalculate the values only when the window changes size, the top of your `paintEvent()` method — using the values in `QPaintDeviceMetrics` — determines whether the window size has changed and, if so, calls the method that does the calculation.

Vector Line Drawing

Two methods can be used to implement vector drawing. They don't do anything that can't be done with `drawLine()`, but they can be very convenient in the creation of certain kinds of drawings. The methods `moveTo()` and `lineTo()` are really left over from the days when graphics were done using a pen plotter. Both methods move the pen from one location to another, but only one of them holds the pen down, causing a line to be drawn. The pen always has a position, so in order to draw a line, it is only necessary to specify the other end of the line. Once the line has been drawn, the pen assumes the new position.

The following example reads the drawing instructions from a file and uses them to display the graphic shown in Figure 12-10. Each line of the input text file contains an opcode (m for move and d for draw) and the coordinate point for the action to take place. The file used in this example starts like this:

```
m 60 110
d 60 10
d 160 10
d 160 60
m 160 80
d 160 180
     . . .
```

The first line is an instruction to move to the point (60,110). The second command will draw a line from the pen's position at (60,110) to a new location at (60,10).

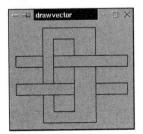

Figure 12-10: A line drawing defined in a file

```
1  /* drawvector.cpp */
2  #include <kapp.h>
3  #include <qpainter.h>
4  #include <stdio.h>
5  #include "drawvector.h"
6
7  int main(int argc,char **argv)
8  {
9      KApplication app(argc,argv,"drawvector");
10     DrawVector drawvector;
11     drawvector.show();
12     app.setMainWidget(&drawvector);
13     return(app.exec());
14 }
15 DrawVector::DrawVector(QWidget *parent,const
16         char *name) : QWidget(parent,name)
17 {
18     setFixedSize(230,190);
19 }
20 void DrawVector::paintEvent(QPaintEvent *)
21 {
22     FILE *fd;
23     char code[20];
24     int x;
25     int y;
26
27     if((fd = fopen("points.dat","r")) !=  NULL) {
28         QPainter p(this);
29         while(fscanf(fd,"%s %d %d",code,&x,&y) == 3) {
30             if(code[0] == 'm')
31                 p.moveTo(x,y);
32             else if(code[0] == 'd')
33                 p.lineTo(x,y);
34         }
35         fclose(fd);
36     }
37 }
```

All of the drawing is done in the loop on lines 28 through 34. Line 28 initializes
graphic operations by creating a QPainter object for this widget. The call to
fscanf() on line 29 reads a line of input data — the command, the *x* coordinate,
and the *y* coordinate. If the command is to move the current cursor, the method
moveTo() is called on line 31. If the command is to draw a line from the current
cursor to this new location, a call is made to lineTo() on line 33.

Line Segments and Polygons

Some QPainter methods allow you to store a set of points in a QPointArray object and then use the points to draw polygons. The following program demonstrates some of the different ways a collection of line segments can be drawn:

```
1  /* drawpoly.cpp */
2  #include <kapp.h>
3  #include <qpainter.h>
4  #include "drawpoly.h"
5
6  int main(int argc,char **argv)
7  {
8      KApplication app(argc,argv,"drawpoly");
9      DrawPoly drawpoly;
10     drawpoly.show();
11     app.setMainWidget(&drawpoly);
12     return(app.exec());
13 }
14 DrawPoly::DrawPoly(QWidget *parent,const
15         char *name) : QWidget(parent,name)
16 {
17     setFixedSize(500,100);
18 }
19 void DrawPoly::paintEvent(QPaintEvent *)
20 {
21     int offset = 0;
22     QPointArray parray(10);
23     QPainter p(this);
24
25     setPoints(parray,offset);
26     p.drawLineSegments(parray);
27
28     setPoints(parray,offset += 100);
29     p.drawPolyline(parray);
30
31     setPoints(parray,offset += 100);
32     p.drawPolygon(parray);
33
34     p.setBrush(QColor("white"));
35     setPoints(parray,offset += 100);
36     p.drawPolygon(parray,TRUE);
37
38     setPoints(parray,offset += 100);
39     p.drawPolygon(parray,FALSE);
40 }
41 void DrawPoly::setPoints(QPointArray &parray,int offset)
42 {
43     parray.setPoint(0,10+offset,50);
44     parray.setPoint(1,70+offset,50);
45     parray.setPoint(2,70+offset,30);
```

```
46        parray.setPoint(3,50+offset,30);
47        parray.setPoint(4,50+offset,90);
48        parray.setPoint(5,30+offset,90);
49        parray.setPoint(6,30+offset,10);
50        parray.setPoint(7,90+offset,10);
51        parray.setPoint(8,90+offset,70);
52        parray.setPoint(9,10+offset,70);
53  }
```

The setPoints() method on line 41 inserts the points into the array. The same set of points is used for each drawing, as shown in Figure 12-11, except the horizontal position is shifted to the right by the amount of the offset.

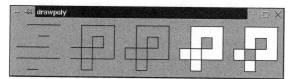

Figure 12-11: Five ways to draw a polygon

The call to drawLineSegments() on line 26 draws the version of the polygon shown on the far left of Figure 12-11. The lines are not joined together because only line segments are drawn. That is, the first line is drawn between point[0] and point[1], the second is drawn between point[2] and point[3], and so on. For every line drawn, there must be two members in the array of points. Of course, you can force the lines to join into a polygon by using the ending point of a line as the starting point of the next.

The call to drawPolyLine() on line 32 uses the same input information as draw LineSegments(), but it draws all the line segments by starting each new line segment at the point where the previous line segment left off. That is, the first line is drawn between point[0] and point[1], the second is drawn between point[1] and point[2], and so on. In the array of point data, the last point does not coincide with the first point, so the polygon is not closed.

The call to drawPolygon() on line 32 draws the figure in the same way as drawLine Sgemetns(), but it also draws a line from the end point back to the beginning, resulting in a closed shape.

The call to drawPolygon() on line 36 draws the shape after a QBrush has been stored in the QPainter object, and this results in the polygon being filled. Just as with any of the other shapes, the area is filled before it is outlined, causing the outlining to appear on top of the fill. The second argument to the method call sets the winding rule to TRUE, which means that all areas of the polygon will be filled without regard to overlaps of itself.

The call to drawPolygon() on line 39 is the same as the previous one, except the winding rule is set to FALSE. This setting means that the only regions of the polygons that are filled are those covered with an odd number of layers. The rightmost drawing in Figure 12-11 shows that the area where the shape overlaps itself is not filled — that is, there are two layers of the shape at the overlap point. If the shape were to overlap the same point with a third layer, it would be filled again.

Ellipses and Circles

The method drawEllipse() is used to render both circles and ellipses because a circle is simply an ellipse with equal height and width. The following program displays the window shown in Figure 12-12, containing two ellipses and a circle:

```
1 /* drawellipse.cpp */
2 #include <kapp.h>
3 #include <qpainter.h>
4 #include "drawellipse.h"
5
6 int main(int argc,char **argv)
7 {
8     KApplication app(argc,argv,"drawellipse");
9     DrawEllipse drawellipse;
10    drawellipse.show();
11    app.setMainWidget(&drawellipse);
12    return(app.exec());
13 }
14 DrawEllipse::DrawEllipse(QWidget *parent,const
15         char *name) : QWidget(parent,name)
16 {
17    setFixedSize(260,140);
18 }
19 void DrawEllipse::paintEvent(QPaintEvent *)
20 {
21    QPainter p(this);
22
23    p.drawEllipse(10,50,110,40);
24    p.setBrush(QColor("white"));
25    p.drawEllipse(130,25,90,90);
26    p.setPen(NoPen);
27    p.drawEllipse(230,10,20,120);
28 }
```

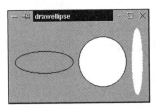

Figure 12-12: Two ellipses and a circle

The drawEllipse() method requires that you define a bounding box to specify the four sides of the ellipse. The bounding box is defined by the x and y coordinates of its upper-left corner, and the width and height of the box. For example, the ellipse on the left in Figure 12-12 is drawn by the call to drawEllipse() on line 23, with its upper-left corner 10 pixels from the left edge and 50 pixels from the top. The width of the ellipse is 110 pixels and its height is 40 pixels.

A QBrush object is added to QPainter by the call to setBrush() on line 24, so the rest of the ellipses are filled with the brush color. Line 26 calls setPen() to remove the pen from QPainter, so the ellipse on the right has no outline.

It may happen that you need to draw a circle or an ellipse around a center point instead of the upper left corner. To do this, simply subtract the radius from the center point (in each direction) to locate the upper-left corner:

```
p.drawEllipse(x - (w / 2),y - (h / 2),w,h);
```

Drawing Parts of Circles and Ellipses

There are three ways you can draw part of a circle or an ellipse. The process is the same as drawing a circle or ellipse, as in the previous example, except you must also specify a starting and ending angle.

To specify which part of the circle or ellipse is to be drawn, it is necessary to specify the starting and ending angles. The angles are measured in units of one-sixteenth of a degree. If you are going to be entering hard-coded angles, Table 12-2 lists some of the more commonly used values.

Table 12-2 Comparison of Angle Measurement Units		
Qt Units	**Degrees**	**Radians**
0	0	0
720	45	0.7854
1440	90	1.5708
2160	135	2.3562
2880	180	3.1416
3600	225	3.9270
4320	270	4.7124
5040	315	5.4978
5760	360	6.2832

If you are going to be calculating the angles, most math software utilities use either degrees or radians; you will need to convert back and forth. The following statements will convert degrees and radians to the Qt scale:

```
angle = degree * 16;
angle = (radian * 180) / PI;
```

And these statements will convert Qt scale values to degrees and radians:

```
degree = angle / 16;
radian = (angle * PI) / 180;
```

Positive rotation is counterclockwise. The zero-degree point is on the right. The starting and ending angles are expressed in relative terms. That is, the starting angle specifies the distance from the zero point that the drawing is to begin, and the ending angle specifies the distance from the starting angle to the end of the drawing. Both numbers can be either positive or negative. If the starting angle is less than the ending angle, the drawing occurs in the positive (counterclockwise) direction. If the starting angle is less than the ending angle, the drawing occurs in the negative (clockwise) direction.

The following example demonstrates three different approaches to drawing an arc:

```
 1 /* arcpiechord.cpp */
 2 #include <kapp.h>
 3 #include <qpainter.h>
 4 #include "arcpiechord.h"
 5
 6 int main(int argc,char **argv)
 7 {
 8     KApplication app(argc,argv,"arcpiechord");
 9     ArcPieChord arcpiechord;
10     arcpiechord.show();
11     app.setMainWidget(&arcpiechord);
12     return(app.exec());
13 }
14 ArcPieChord::ArcPieChord(QWidget *parent,const
15         char *name) : QWidget(parent,name)
16 {
17     setFixedSize(260,420);
18 }
19 void ArcPieChord::paintEvent(QPaintEvent *)
20 {
21     QPainter p(this);
22
23     p.drawArc(10,50,110,40,0,4000);
24     p.drawChord(10,190,110,40,0,4000);
25     p.drawPie(10,330,110,40,0,4000);
26     p.setBrush(QColor("white"));
```

```
27        p.drawArc(130,25,90,90,0,2000);
28        p.drawChord(130,165,90,90,0,2000);
29        p.drawPie(130,305,90,90,0,2000);
30        p.setPen(NoPen);
31        p.drawArc(230,10,20,120,720,4320);
32        p.drawChord(230,150,20,120,720,4320);
33        p.drawPie(230,290,20,120,720,4320);
34  }
```

The call to drawArc() on line 23 creates the shape in the upper-left corner of Figure
12-13. This shape is drawn using the default QPainter with a black pen and no
brush. The same bounding rectangle approach is used as is used with the ellipse.
That is, you choose the *x* and *y* coordinates of the upper-left corner of the bounding
box of the entire ellipse, even though you are only going to be drawing a portion of
it. The starting angle is 0 and the ending angle is 4000, which is almost 270 degrees.

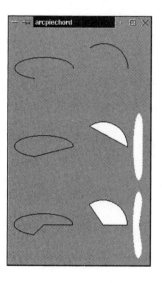

Figure 12-13: Some ways to draw arcs,
pies, and chords

The call to drawArc() on line 27 creates the shape in the center of the first row of
Figure 12-13. Even though this figure is drawn with a QPainter that has a brush,
there is no filling because an arc is not a closed figure. The call to drawArc() on
line 31 does not appear because the pen has been disabled and drawArc() does
not use the brush.

The call to drawChord() on line 24 draws the leftmost shape in the center row of
Figure 12-13. A chord is like an arc, except that it always draws a line between the
end points of the arc to create a closed figure. Because a chord is a closed figure,
the calls to drawChord() on lines 28 and 32 both fill the enclosed area with the
brush color.

The call to `drawPie()` on line 25 draws the leftmost shape of the bottom row of Figure 12-13. A pie is like an arc, except that it always draws two lines between the center and the two end points to create a closed figure. Because a pie is a closed figure, the calls to `drawPie()` on lines 29 and 33 both fill the enclosed area with the brush color.

Rectangles with Rounded Corners

The `QPainter` method `drawRoundRect()` can be used to draw rectangles with varying degrees of rounding on the corners. The following example demonstrates the flexibility of `drawRoundRect()`, which can be used to draw squares, rectangles, circles, and ellipses as well as rounded-corner rectangles. The program draws a number of shapes, as shown in Figure 12-14.

```
 1 /* roundrectangle.cpp */
 2 #include <kapp.h>
 3 #include <qpainter.h>
 4 #include "roundrectangle.h"
 5
 6 int main(int argc,char **argv)
 7 {
 8      KApplication app(argc,argv,"roundrectangle");
 9      RoundRectangle roundrectangle;
10      roundrectangle.show();
11      app.setMainWidget(&roundrectangle);
12      return(app.exec());
13 }
14 RoundRectangle::RoundRectangle(QWidget *parent,const
15          char *name) : QWidget(parent,name)
16 {
17      setFixedSize(190,370);
18 }
19 void RoundRectangle::paintEvent(QPaintEvent *)
20 {
21      QPainter p(this);
22      p.setBrush(QColor("white"));
23
24      p.drawRoundRect(10,10,50,50);
25      p.drawText(30,35,"1");
26
27      p.drawRoundRect(70,10,50,50,50,50);
28      p.drawText(90,35,"2");
29
30      p.drawRoundRect(130,10,50,50,100,100);
31      p.drawText(150,35,"3");
32
33      p.drawRoundRect(10,70,170,50);
```

```
34        p.drawText(90,95,"4");
35
36        p.drawRoundRect(10,130,170,50,0,50);
37        p.drawText(90,155,"5");
38
39        p.drawRoundRect(10,190,170,50,50,80);
40        p.drawText(90,215,"6");
41
42        p.drawRoundRect(10,250,170,50,100,100);
43        p.drawText(90,275,"7");
44
45        p.drawRoundRect(10,310,170,50,9,30);
46        p.drawText(90,335,"8");
47 }
```

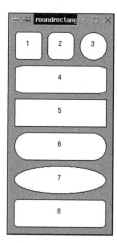

Figure 12-14: Some of the many forms of rounded rectangles

Calling one of the following two methods draws a rounded rectangle:

```
drawRoundRect(int x,int y,int w,int h)
drawRoundRect(int x,int y,int w,int h,
    int xround,int yround)
```

The first four arguments define a rectangle. The last two arguments (which both default to 25) specify the roundedness of the corners in both the vertical and horizontal directions.

Rectangle 1 in Figure 12-14 is drawn by the call to drawRoundeRect() on line 24. The first two arguments specify the *x* and *y* location of the upper left corner of where the rectangle would be if it were not clipped off by being rounded. The figure is a square that is 50 pixels on a side, and the roundedness of the corners was allowed to default at 25 in both the *x* and *y* directions. This means that 25 percent of the vertical distance and 25 percent of the horizontal distance will be used to create the rounded corners.

Rectangle 2 is drawn by the call to `drawRoundedRect()` on line 27. Like rectangle 1, this call also produces a square, but the horizontal and vertical roundedness amounts have been set to 50 percent each instead of being allowed to default to 25 percent.

Rectangle 3 demonstrates that setting the height and width to the same values, and setting the roundedness to 100 percent, causes the entire length of the sides to be included in the curved portion; the result is a circle.

Rectangle 4 is drawn on line 33. The vertical and horizontal roundedness are both allowed to default to 25 percent, but because the rectangle is wider than it is tall, more pixels are involved in the horizontal direction than in the vertical direction, resulting in a curve that is not symmetrical.

Rectangle 5 is drawn on line 36 to demonstrate the fact that setting one (or both) of the roundedness values to 0 percent will cause the corner to be square. In this example, the vertical roundedness is set to 50 percent, but it cannot be used to make a curve because the horizontal setting is 0 percent, which forces the horizontal line to go all the way to the corner.

Rectangle 6 is created on line 39 by setting the vertical roundedness to 100 percent and the horizontal roundedness to 30 percent.

Rectangle 7 is drawn on line 42 with both the horizontal and vertical roundedness being set to 100 percent. The result is an ellipse.

Rectangle 8, drawn on line 45, is designed to have symmetrical roundedness — that is, the same number of pixels are involved in the curve in both the vertical and horizontal directions. Because roundedness is expressed as a percentage, it is necessary to select a pixel value and then use it to determine the percent in each direction:

```
xround = (100 * pixels) / height;
yround = (100 * pixels) / width;
```

Drawing Pixmaps and Text

You can draw all or part of a pixmap and define the font to be used to draw any text. The following example draws an entire pixmap, then part of a pixmap, and then writes text on top of the drawing, as shown in Figure 12-15.

Figure 12-15: Pixmap with text

DrawPixmap Header

```
1 /* drawpixmap.h */
2 #ifndef DRAWPIXMAP_H
3 #define DRAWPIXMAP_H
4
5 #include <qwidget.h>
6
7 class DrawPixmap: public QWidget
8 {
9 public:
10     DrawPixmap(QWidget *parent=0,const char *name=0);
11 private:
12     QPixmap logo;
13 protected:
14     virtual void paintEvent(QPaintEvent *);
15 };
16
17 #endif
```

The QPixmap to be drawn is created from data, so it is only created once. It is stored as logo on line 12, so it will be available for display later.

DrawPixmap

```
1 /* drawpixmap.cpp */
2 #include <kapp.h>
3 #include <qpainter.h>
4 #include <qfont.h>
5 #include "drawpixmap.h"
6
7 #include "logo.xpm"
```

```
 8
 9 int main(int argc,char **argv)
10 {
11     KApplication app(argc,argv,"drawpixmap");
12     DrawPixmap drawpixmap;
13     drawpixmap.show();
14     app.setMainWidget(&drawpixmap);
15     return(app.exec());
16 }
17 DrawPixmap::DrawPixmap(QWidget *parent,const
18         char *name) : QWidget(parent,name)
19 {
20     logo = QPixmap(magick);
21     setFixedSize(360,330);
22 }
23 void DrawPixmap::paintEvent(QPaintEvent *)
24 {
25     QPainter p(this);
26
27     p.drawPixmap(10,10,logo);
28     p.drawPixmap(250,80,logo,50,50,100,100);
29
30     QFont font = p.font();
31     font.setPointSize(18);
32     p.setFont(font);
33
34     p.setPen(QColor("white"));
35     p.drawText(200,250,"Penguin");
36 }
```

The constructor, beginning on line 17, creates the logo pixmap from the data file logo.xpm included on line 7. It then sets the display window to a fixed size.

The call to drawPixmap() on line 27 paints the entire logo pixmap. The upper-left corner of the pixmap is located 10 pixels over and 10 pixels down from the upper-left corner of the widgets. Because no other arguments were specified, the entire pixmap is copied to the target location.

The call to drawPixmap() on line 28 paints only a portion of the logo pixmap. This method first extracts a rectangular area from the pixmap and then paints the extraction to the target window. The last four method arguments determine the extracted area by specifying the upper left corner and the height and width. The area to be extracted is 60 pixels from the left and 50 pixels from the top of the pixmap, its width is 100 pixels, and its height is 80 pixels. The first two arguments specify where the pixmap is to be drawn—its upper left corner is placed 250 pixels from the left and 80 pixels from the top.

Every QPainter object contains a QFont object that it uses to draw text. You can use this default font, create a new font, or, as in this example, modify the existing font. The call to font() on line 30 retrieves the QFont object from the QPainter object. In this example, a call is made to setPointSize() on line 31 to make the text a bit larger. The call to setFont() establishes the new font as the one that will be used to paint all of QPainter text.

Cross-Reference   See Chapter 10 for more information about creating and modifying fonts.

Line 34 calls setPen() to make the text appear as white (instead of the default black), and the call to drawText() on line 35 paints the text on the window, with the left end of the text baseline 200 pixels from the left and 250 pixels from the top of the window.

Summary

The QPainter methods described in this chapter should supply you with over 90 percent of the graphics you will ever need. With only two objects that render graphics, a QPen and a QBrush, you can create anything you want. If you need extreme flexibility, you can use the pixel-by-pixel approach to get exactly what you want.

This chapter explored QPainter methods that can be used to accomplish the following:

✦ Draw one pixel at a time to the window, or define objects to hold arrays of pixels and draw them all at once.

✦ Draw lines, in multiple colors and various widths, from any point to any other point. Also, multisegmented lines can be drawn either one at a time or all at once.

✦ Draw ellipses and circles in their entirety, or draw only a portion of the curve. You can use different styles to fill and slice the circles and ellipses.

✦ Draw pixmaps — in their entirety or select a rectangular area.

The following chapter builds on the information in this chapter. Some methods in the QPainter object can be used to manipulate graphics to change their shape, angle, and colors. You can also use some very specialized graphics objects to do things like record a sequence of graphics commands for later playback.

✦   ✦   ✦

Graphics Manipulation

The previous chapter demonstrated some of the fundamentals of drawing and painting graphics to windows, and this chapter demonstrates some of the special capabilities in KDE and Qt for manipulating graphics.

Because everything displayed in a widget is graphic, many of the techniques described in this chapter can be used to modify any graphic content. Probably the most useful information pertains to the processes for rotating and positioning images, but there is quite a bit more. For one thing, depending on the capabilities of your printer, it is a very simple process to print a graphic image in color or in black and white. It is possible to reshape graphics scaling and shearing, or even to modify images by making changes to bit values of each pixel. And animation can be performed by drawing one frame after another and displaying the frames in a controlled, timed sequence.

Using a QPicture to Store Graphics

Anything that can be drawn to the window of a widget can also be drawn to a `QPicture` object. The `QPicture` object can then save the drawing instructions to a disk file, and another `QPicture` object can read the file and execute the drawing instructions. There are a number of uses for this, including the capability to store complicated drawings and transmit graphics from one system to another. The following program creates a simple drawing and saves it to a disk file:

Record

```
1 /* record.cpp */
2 #include <iostream.h>
3 #include <kapp.h>
4 #include <qpainter.h>
```

```
 5 #include <qpicture.h>
 6 #include <qwidget.h>
 7
 8 int main(int argc,char **argv)
 9 {
10      KApplication app(argc,argv,"record");
11      QPainter paint;
12      QPicture pic;
13
14      paint.begin(&pic);
15      paint.setBrush(QColor("black"));
16      paint.drawRect(50,75,350,100);
17      paint.setBrush(QColor("white"));
18      paint.drawEllipse(150,50,150,150);
19      paint.setPen(QWidget::NoPen);
20      paint.drawRect(100,100,250,50);
21      paint.end();
22      if(!pic.save("recplay.qpic"))
23          cout << "Unable to create recplay.qpic" << endl;
24 }
```

This program creates graphics, but does not display a window. Instead, it uses a
QPicture object as the target of the drawing, and the QPicture object records all
of the instructions and then writes them to a disk file.

On line 10, the KAapplication object app is created to define this as a KDE application because a QPainter object can only be used inside a KDE application. Lines
11 and 12 create the QPainter object that is used to do the drawing, and the
QPicture object that records the QPainter instructions.

Line 14 begins the graphics session by calling begin(). The object of the drawing
is the QPicture object, rather than a widget. Lines 15 through 20 set the QPainter
pen and brush values, and call the methods to do the actual drawing. The QPicture
object records each of these method calls. The drawing session is halted by the call
to end() on line 21. The call to save() on line 22 creates the file named recplay.
qpic that contains all of the drawing instructions.

Playback Header

```
 1 /* playback.h */
 2 #ifndef PLAYBACK_H
 3 #define PLAYBACK_H
 4
 5 #include <qwidget.h>
 6
 7 class Playback: public QWidget
 8 {
 9 public:
10      Playback(QWidget *parent=0,const char *name=0);
11 protected:
12      virtual void paintEvent(QPaintEvent *);
13 };
```

```
14
15 #endif
```

Playback

```
 1  /* playback.cpp */
 2  #include <kapp.h>
 3  #include <qpainter.h>
 4  #include <qpicture.h>
 5  #include "playback.h"
 6
 7  int main(int argc,char **argv)
 8  {
 9      KApplication app(argc,argv,"playback");
10      Playback playback;
11      playback.show();
12      app.setMainWidget(&playback);
13      return(app.exec());
14  }
15  Playback::Playback(QWidget *parent,const
16          char *name) : QWidget(parent,name)
17  {
18      setFixedSize(450,250);
19  }
20  void Playback::paintEvent(QPaintEvent *)
21  {
22      QPainter p(this);
23      QPicture picture;
24
25      if(picture.load("recplay.qpic"))
26          p.drawPicture(picture);
27  }
```

The `paintEvent()` method on line 20 creates a `QPicture` object to retrieve the previously stored instructions. The call to `load()` on line 25 retrieves the list of instructions and, if the call to `load()` is successful, the call to `drawPicture()` on line 26 executes all of the instructions stored in the file. The result is the window shown in Figure 13-1.

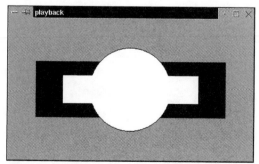

Figure 13-1: The playback of previously recorded graphics commands

The previously recorded graphic instructions are painted using a `QPainter` object, so there is nothing to prevent your program from embellishing the recorded instructions with some of your own. For example, the image shown in Figure 13-2 results from changing the paint commands in the `paintEvent()` method to the following:

```
if(picture.load("recplay.qpic"))
    p.drawPicture(picture);
p.setBrush(QColor("black"));
p.drawRect(110,110,230,30);
```

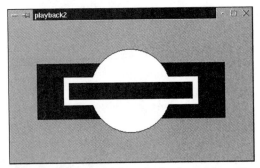

Figure 13-2: Combining playback and current graphics commands

Painting Graphics to a Printer

It is just as easy to paint pages on the printer as it is to paint windows on the display. The following example program displays the same graphics window as the one previously shown in Figure 13-1, except for the addition of a Print button in the lower right corner. Selecting the button will cause the dialog shown in Figure 13-3 to appear, allowing the user to make decisions about the print. If the user selects the OK button, the graphic is printed.

PrintGraphic Header

```
 1 /* printgraphic.h */
 2 #ifndef PRINTGRAPHIC_H
 3 #define PRINTGRAPHIC_H
 4
 5 #include <qwidget.h>
 6 #include <qpushbutton.h>
 7
 8 class PrintGraphic: public QWidget
 9 {
10     Q_OBJECT
```

```
11 public:
12     PrintGraphic(QWidget *parent=0,const char *name=0);
13 private:
14     QPushButton *printButton;
15 private slots:
16     void printSlot();
17 protected:
18     virtual void paintEvent(QPaintEvent *);
19 };
20
21 #endif
```

PrintGraphic

```
1 /* printgraphic.cpp */
2 #include <kapp.h>
3 #include <qpainter.h>
4 #include <qprinter.h>
5 #include "printgraphic.h"
6
7 int main(int argc,char **argv)
8 {
9     KApplication app(argc,argv,"printgraphic");
10    PrintGraphic printgraphic;
11    printgraphic.show();
12    app.setMainWidget(&printgraphic);
13    return(app.exec());
14 }
15 PrintGraphic::PrintGraphic(QWidget *parent,const
16         char *name) : QWidget(parent,name)
17 {
18    setFixedSize(450,250);
19    printButton = new QPushButton("Print",this);
20    printButton->setGeometry(370,200,70,40);
21    connect(printButton,SIGNAL(clicked()),
22            this,SLOT(printSlot()));
23 }
24 void PrintGraphic::paintEvent(QPaintEvent *)
25 {
26    QPainter paint;
27
28    paint.begin(this);
29    paint.setBrush(QColor("black"));
30    paint.drawRect(50,75,350,100);
31    paint.setBrush(QColor("white"));
32    paint.drawEllipse(150,50,150,150);
33    paint.setPen(QWidget::NoPen);
34    paint.drawRect(100,100,250,50);
35    paint.end();
36 }
37 void PrintGraphic::printSlot()
38 {
```

```
39      QPainter paint;
40      QPrinter printer;
41
42      if(printer.setup(this)) {
43          paint.begin(&printer);
44          paint.setBrush(QColor("black"));
45          paint.drawRect(50,75,350,100);
46          paint.setBrush(QColor("white"));
47          paint.drawEllipse(150,50,150,150);
48          paint.setPen(QWidget::NoPen);
49          paint.drawRect(100,100,250,50);
50          paint.end();
51      }
52 }
```

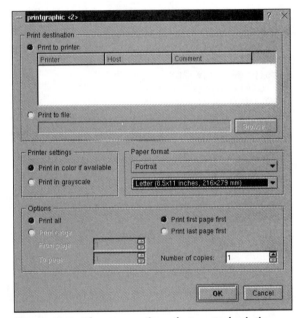

Figure 13-3: The user options that control printing

The constructor, on line 15, sets the size of the window and installs a button in the lower right corner. The slot method printSlot() is attached to the button.

The paintEvent() method on line 24 draws graphics on the window of the widget.

The slot method printSlot() on line 37 prompts the user for printer settings, and if the user selects the OK button in the dialog shown in Figure 13-3, it draws the graphics on a page of the printer. The call to setup() on line 42 pops up the dialog, and a return value of TRUE indicates that the print should proceed. Line 43 calls begin() to attach the QPainter object to the printer. The graphics are then drawn just as they would be if they were being drawn to the screen.

The call to end() on line 50 ends the drawing and sends the graphics instructions on to the printer. This call also closes the output to the printer and sends the page (or pages) to the spooler for printing. If, in the middle of your printing, you wish to eject the current page and start with a new one, you can do so with the following method call:

```
print.newPage();
```

At any point during the printing process, you can delete all the pages before they are sent to the spooler as follows:

```
print.abort();
```

Printer Information and Control

While it is just as easy to draw to a printer as it is to a window, you need to be able to find out information about things like the size of the page and the number of dots per inch. The following example program displays some of the basic printer information in the window shown in Figure 13-4. You can run this program and use the pop-up dialog to modify the printer settings and see the values change.

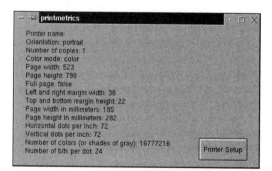

Figure 13-4: Some of the values describing a printer

PrintMetrics Header

```
1 /* printmetrics.h */
2 #ifndef PRINTMETRICS_H
3 #define PRINTMETRICS_H
4
```

```
 5 #include <qwidget.h>
 6 #include <qpushbutton.h>
 7 #include <qprinter.h>
 8
 9 class PrintMetrics: public QWidget
10 {
11     Q_OBJECT
12 public:
13     PrintMetrics(QWidget *parent=0,const char *name=0);
14 private:
15     QPrinter printer;
16     QPushButton *printButton;
17 private slots:
18     void printSetupSlot();
19 protected:
20     virtual void paintEvent(QPaintEvent *);
21 };
22
23 #endif
```

A QPrinter object is included as part of the class. Because it is a class member, any configuration changes made by the user will remain intact for the life of the PrintMetrics object.

PrintMetrics

```
 1 /* printmetrics.cpp */
 2 #include <kapp.h>
 3 #include <qpainter.h>
 4 #include <qpaintdevicemetrics.h>
 5 #include "printmetrics.h"
 6
 7 int main(int argc,char **argv)
 8 {
 9     KApplication app(argc,argv,"printmetrics");
10     PrintMetrics printmetrics;
11     printmetrics.show();
12     app.setMainWidget(&printmetrics);
13     return(app.exec());
14 }
15 PrintMetrics::PrintMetrics(QWidget *parent,const
16         char *name) : QWidget(parent,name)
17 {
18     setFixedSize(450,250);
19     printButton = new QPushButton("Printer Setup",this);
20     printButton->setGeometry(340,200,90,40);
21     connect(printButton,SIGNAL(clicked()),
22             this,SLOT(printSetupSlot()));
23 }
24 void PrintMetrics::printSetupSlot()
```

```
25 {
26      printer.setup(this);
27 }
28 void PrintMetrics::paintEvent(QPaintEvent *)
29 {
30      QPainter paint;
31      QPaintDeviceMetrics metrics(&printer);
32      QString string;
33
34      paint.begin(this);
35
36      QFontMetrics fm = paint.fontMetrics();
37      int x = 20;
38      int y = 20;
39
40      string = "Printer name: " + printer.printerName();
41      paint.drawText(x,y,string);
42      y += fm.height();
43
44      if(printer.outputToFile()) {
45          string = "Output to file: "
46                    + printer.outputFileName();
47          paint.drawText(x,y,string);
48          y += fm.height();
49      }
50
51      if(printer.orientation() == QPrinter::Portrait)
52          string = "Orientation: portrait";
53      else
54          string = "Orientation: landscape";
55      paint.drawText(x,y,string);
56      y += fm.height();
57
58      string = "Number of copies: ";
59      string += QString::number(printer.numCopies());
60      paint.drawText(x,y,string);
61      y += fm.height();
62
63      if(printer.colorMode() == QPrinter::GrayScale)
64          string = "Color mode: gray scale";
65      else
66          string = "Color mode: color";
67      paint.drawText(x,y,string);
68      y += fm.height();
69
70      string = "Page width: ";
71      string += QString::number(metrics.width());
72      paint.drawText(x,y,string);
73      y += fm.height();
74
75      string = "Page height: ";
```

```
 76        string += QString::number(metrics.height());
 77        paint.drawText(x,y,string);
 78        y += fm.height();
 79
 80        if(printer.fullPage())
 81            string = "Full page: true";
 82        else
 83            string = "Full page: false";
 84        paint.drawText(x,y,string);
 85        y += fm.height();
 86
 87        string = "Left and right margin width: ";
 88        string += QString::number(printer.margins().width());
 89        paint.drawText(x,y,string);
 90        y += fm.height();
 91
 92        string = "Top and bottom margin height: ";
 93        string += QString::number(printer.margins().height());
 94        paint.drawText(x,y,string);
 95        y += fm.height();
 96
 97        string = "Page width in millimeters: ";
 98        string += QString::number(metrics.widthMM());
 99        paint.drawText(x,y,string);
100        y += fm.height();
101
102        string = "Page height in millimeters: ";
103        string += QString::number(metrics.heightMM());
104        paint.drawText(x,y,string);
105        y += fm.height();
106
107        string = "Horizontal dots per inch: ";
108        string += QString::number(metrics.logicalDpiX());
109        paint.drawText(x,y,string);
110        y += fm.height();
111
112        string = "Vertical dots per inch: ";
113        string += QString::number(metrics.logicalDpiY());
114        paint.drawText(x,y,string);
115        y += fm.height();
116
117        string = "Number of colors (or shades of gray): ";
118        string += QString::number(metrics.numColors());
119        paint.drawText(x,y,string);
120        y += fm.height();
121
122        string = "Number of bits per dot: ";
123        string += QString::number(metrics.depth());
124        paint.drawText(x,y,string);
125        y += fm.height();
126
127        paint.end();
128 }
```

The slot method `printSetupSlot()` on line 24 pops up a printer-configuration dialog, like the one shown previously in Figure 13-3, that can be used to modify the user-configurable settings for the printer.

The `paintEvent()` method on line 24 creates a window that displays a list of the current printer descriptive information and settings. Some of the information is retrieved from a `QPaintDeviceMetrics` object, and some is retrieved directly from the `QPrinter` object itself.

The printer name, on line 36, is the name the user selected from the list of available printers. If the user has not selected a printer, a zero-length string is returned from `printerName()` and any printed output will be directed to the default printer. If the output has been directed to a file instead of a printer, the call to `outputToFile()` on line 44 returns `TRUE` and a call to `outputFileName()` will return the name of the file. When directed to a file, the printed data is sent to the file in postscript format.

The call to `orientation()` on line 51 indicates whether the output will be printed in portrait or landscape mode. If portrait, the output is taller than it is wide. If landscape, it is wider than it is tall. The default is portrait.

The call to `numCopies()` on line 63 returns a count of the number of copies to be printed. The default is 1.

The call to `colorMode()` on line 63 indicates whether the printing is to be done in color or grayscale. This may not always be accurate, because many printers are capable of accepting color print data, but will convert it to shades of gray for printing. In any case, it is always safe to print color data because, if necessary, it will be converted to shades of gray either by the printing software or by the printer itself.

The page width and height on lines 71 and 76 are a measure of the printable area. If you need a height and width value to render graphics, as you would if painting graphics to a window, you can use these numbers in conjunction with the margin values and the full-page indicator. If the call to `fullPage()` on line 80 returns `TRUE`, the height and width extend to the edges of the paper. If the `fullPage()` method returns `FALSE`, the height and width are the measurements inside the margins. You can set the printer to full-page mode by calling `printer.setFullPage(TRUE)`, or you can set the page size to adjust for margins (the default) by calling `printer.setFullPage(FALSE)`.

The margin values, retrieved by calls to `margins()` on lines 88 and 93, are either the actual margin values when not in full-page mode, or the suggested margins when in full-page mode.

Unlike a window, which has no exact fixed width and height, a printer has a fixed physical width and a fixed number of dots per inch, so these values can be determined. However, the numbers are not entirely trustworthy because your printer may not report the values to your computer, or your printer configuration could be in error, or the user could have chosen to print to a file. In any case, the width and height of the page are reported in millimeters, on lines 98 and 103; and the number of dots per inch is reported on lines 108 and 113.

The total number of colors (or number of shades of gray) per dot is returned from the call to numColors() on line 118. The same information is also reported as the number of bits per dot with the call to depth() on line 123.

Fitting a Drawing to a Window

You can establish your own coordinate system, use it to draw graphics in a window, and have your coordinate system automatically translated to that of the actual window. The following example shows how this can be done:

FitWindow Header

```
1 /* fitwindow.h */
2 #ifndef FITWINDOW_H
3 #define FITWINDOW_H
4
5 #include <qwidget.h>
6
7 class FitWindow: public QWidget
8 {
9 protected:
10     virtual void paintEvent(QPaintEvent *);
11 };
12
13 #endif
```

FitWindow

```
1 /* fitwindow.cpp */
2 #include <kapp.h>
3 #include <qpainter.h>
4 #include "fitwindow.h"
5
6 int main(int argc,char **argv)
7 {
8     KApplication app(argc,argv,"fitwindow");
9     FitWindow fitwindow;
10     fitwindow.show();
11     app.setMainWidget(&fitwindow);
12     return(app.exec());
13 }
14 void FitWindow::paintEvent(QPaintEvent *)
15 {
16     QPainter p(this);
17
18     p.setWindow(0,0,300,300);
19
20     p.drawRoundRect(50,50,200,200,30,30);
21     p.setBrush(QColor("black"));
22     p.drawEllipse(100,100,100,100);
```

```
23      p.setBrush(QColor("white"));
24      p.drawPie(50,50,100,100,270*16,90*16);
25      p.drawPie(150,150,100,100,90*16,90*16);
26 }
```

The call to setWindow() on line 18 establishes the upper left corner as the origin of the coordinate system. It also establishes both the height and width of the window as being 300. Whenever something is drawn to the window, the 300×300 size is assumed for the sake of the drawing dimensions, but when the actual pixels are drawn, they are mapped to the actual window size. Figure 13-5 shows the window displayed from this program after being resized two different ways.

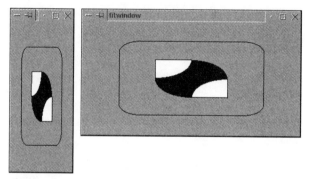

Figure 13-5: Resizing the window resizes the graphics.

Fitting a Drawing to a Subwindow

The setWindow() method of the previous example can be used in conjunction with the setViewport() method to scale drawing and painting to subwindows within a window. The following example maps the same drawing to four subwindows within a window and results in the display shown in Figure 13-6.

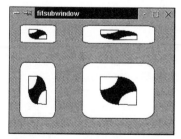

Figure 13-6: The same graphic appearing four times in the same window

FitSubWindow Header

```
 1 /* fitsubwindow.h */
 2 #ifndef FITSUBWINDOW_H
 3 #define FITSUBWINDOW_H
 4
 5 #include <qwidget.h>
 6 #include <qpainter.h>
 7
 8 class FitSubWindow: public QWidget
 9 {
10 public:
11     FitSubWindow(QWidget *parent=0,const char *name=0);
12 private:
13     void paintFigure(QPainter &);
14 protected:
15     virtual void paintEvent(QPaintEvent *);
16 };
17
18 #endif
```

FitSubWindow

```
 1 /* fitsubwindow.cpp */
 2 #include <kapp.h>
 3 #include "fitsubwindow.h"
 4
 5 int main(int argc,char **argv)
 6 {
 7     KApplication app(argc,argv,"fitsubwindow");
 8     FitSubWindow fitsubwindow;
 9     fitsubwindow.show();
10     app.setMainWidget(&fitsubwindow);
11     return(app.exec());
12 }
13 FitSubWindow::FitSubWindow(QWidget *parent,
14         const char *name) : QWidget(parent,name)
15 {
16     setFixedSize(300,200);
17 }
18 void FitSubWindow::paintEvent(QPaintEvent *)
19 {
20     QPainter p(this);
21
22     p.setViewport(0,0,100,50);
23     paintFigure(p);
24     p.setViewport(100,0,200,50);
25     paintFigure(p);
26     p.setViewport(0,50,100,150);
27     paintFigure(p);
28     p.setViewport(100,50,200,150);
29     paintFigure(p);
```

```
30 }
31 void FitSubWindow::paintFigure(QPainter &p)
32 {
33     p.setWindow(0,0,300,300);
34     p.setBrush(QColor("white"));
35     p.drawRoundRect(50,50,200,200,30,30);
36     p.setBrush(QColor("black"));
37     p.drawEllipse(100,100,100,100);
38     p.setBrush(QColor("white"));
39     p.drawPie(50,50,100,100,270*16,90*16);
40     p.drawPie(150,150,100,100,90*16,90*16);
41 }
```

The constructor fixes the size of the window at 300 pixels wide and 200 pixels high with the call to setFixedSize() on line 16. The paintEvent() method on line 18 is called whenever the window is to be painted, and makes four calls to setViewport() and paintFigure() to paint the window shown previously in Figure 13-6.

The call to setViewport() on line 22 specifies that all drawing is to be done in the upper left corner, at location (0,0) in the window, and that the drawing is to be limited to an area 100 pixels wide by 50 pixels high. The call to paintFigure() on line 23 does the actual painting of the pixels. In the same fashion, three other shapes are drawn to view ports (subwindows) by first calling setViewport() to specify a subwindow and then calling paintFigure() to draw the graphics.

The method paintFigure() beginning on line 31 draws the graphic. It starts out by calling setWindow() on line 33 to specify that the window is to be drawn to a square area with a scale of 300×300 pixels, with its origin at the upper-left corner. The graphic is then built up in the 300×300 square by calling the primitive drawing methods drawRoundRect(), drawEllipse(), and drawPie(). The physical location of the pixels, and the aspect ratio of the resulting picture, was set by the call to setViewport() before the call to paintFigure(). This allows the paintFigure() method to calculate and render graphics independently of the actual pixel positions.

Clipping

It is possible to limit a drawing to a specific region. That is, everything drawn outside the region is clipped off and not drawn. The following example draws the same ellipse using three different brushes, but the second and third ellipses are clipped so that the original ellipse is still partially visible:

ClipArea

```
1 /* cliparea.cpp */
2 #include <kapp.h>
3 #include <qpainter.h>
```

```
 4 #include <qbrush.h>
 5 #include <qpointarray.h>
 6 #include "cliparea.h"
 7
 8 int main(int argc,char **argv)
 9 {
10     KApplication app(argc,argv,"cliparea");
11     ClipArea cliparea;
12     cliparea.show();
13     app.setMainWidget(&cliparea);
14     return(app.exec());
15 }
16 ClipArea::ClipArea(QWidget *parent,
17         const char *name) : QWidget(parent,name)
18 {
19     setFixedSize(300,200);
20 }
21 void ClipArea::paintEvent(QPaintEvent *)
22 {
23     QPainter p(this);
24
25     p.setBrush(QColor("white"));
26     p.drawEllipse(25,25,250,150);
27
28     p.setBrush(QBrush(QColor("black"),Qt::VerPattern));
29     p.setClipRect(30,30,70,70);
30     p.drawEllipse(25,25,250,150);
31
32     p.setBrush(QBrush(QColor("black"),Qt::Dense5Pattern));
33     QPointArray pa;
34     pa.setPoints(3,100,140,200,50,220,180);
35     QRegion region(pa);
36     p.setClipRegion(region);
37     p.drawEllipse(25,25,250,150);
38 }
```

The call to setBrush() on line 25 and the call to drawEllipse() on line 26 draw the white ellipse with the black outline shown in Figure 13-7.

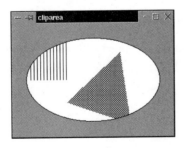

Figure 13-7: An ellipse drawn with clipping and different brushes

Lines 28 through 30 draw the area of vertical lines in the upper-left corner of the ellipse. The brush is set to a black VerPattern, resulting in the vertical lines; and the call to setClipRect() on line 29 limits the drawing to only the rectangular area that is 70 pixels wide by 70 pixels tall, and has its left corner at the location (30,30). Although the call to drawEllipse() on line 30 attempts to draw the entire figure, the actual drawing is restricted to the clipped area. Also, because the brush pattern allows the background to show through, a portion of the original ellipse is also visible.

The same technique is used to paint the triangular area on the right side of the ellipse. In this case, the clipping region is defined by the call to setClipRegion() on line 36. The QPointArray named pa contains only the three points of a triangle, but it could contain as complex a polygon as you would like to define.

Also, because you can define only one clipping region, defining a new clipping region deletes the previous one. If you wish to disable the clipping region, you can call the setClipping() method as follows:

```
p.setClipping(FALSE);
```

Scale

A drawing can be scaled to larger and smaller sizes by changing the coordinates in QPainter prior to drawing the picture. The following example shows the result of changing the scale and drawing a pixmap:

ScaleShape Header

```
 1 /* scaleshape.h */
 2 #ifndef SCALESHAPE_H
 3 #define SCALESHAPE_H
 4
 5 #include <qwidget.h>
 6
 7 class ScaleShape: public QWidget
 8 {
 9 public:
10     ScaleShape(QWidget *parent=0,const char *name=0);
11 private:
12     QPixmap marble;
13 protected:
14     virtual void paintEvent(QPaintEvent *);
15 };
16
17 #endif
```

ScaleShape

```
 1 /* scaleshape.cpp */
 2 #include <kapp.h>
 3 #include <qpainter.h>
 4 #include "scaleshape.h"
 5
 6 #include "bluemarble.xpm"
 7
 8 int main(int argc,char **argv)
 9 {
10     KApplication app(argc,argv,"scaleshape");
11     ScaleShape scaleshape;
12     scaleshape.show();
13     app.setMainWidget(&scaleshape);
14     return(app.exec());
15 }
16 ScaleShape::ScaleShape(QWidget *parent,const
17         char *name) : QWidget(parent,name)
18 {
19     marble = QPixmap(magick);
20     setFixedSize(360,288);
21 }
22 void ScaleShape::paintEvent(QPaintEvent *)
23 {
24     QPainter p(this);
25
26     p.drawPixmap(0,0,marble);
27     p.scale(2.0,2.0);
28     p.drawPixmap(36,0,marble);
29     p.scale(1.0,2.0);
30     p.drawPixmap(108,0,marble);
31 }
```

The XPM file included on line 6 is converted to a QPixmap on line 19. The pixmap is
72×72 pixels. The call to drawPixmap() on line 26 draws the pixmap in its normal
size in the upper-left corner of the window, as shown in Figure 13-8.

The default scale values are 1.0 along both the x and y axes. To change the value,
the scale() method is called with multipliers of both of the values. The call to
scale() on line 27 doubles the scale in both the x and y directions, so the call to
drawPixmap() on line 28 draws a pixmap twice as large as the first one. Notice
that, on the call to drawPixmap(), in order to offset the drawing 72 pixels to the
right, a coordinate value of 36 is needed because it is also being scaled to twice its
normal size. The call to scale() on line 29 makes no change to the scale along the
x axis because it multiplies the current scale setting by 1.0, leaving it at 2.0, but
doubles the scale along the y axis, causing the vertical scale factor to become 4.0.
The call to drawPixmap() on line 30 draws the pixmap twice as wide and four times
as high as the default.

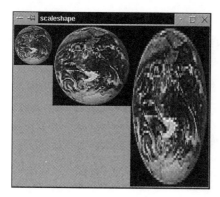

Figure 13-8: A pixmap drawn to three different scales

Shear

To *shear* a figure is to skew it so that the x axis no longer lies along the horizontal plane, or the y axis is no longer vertical, or both. Increasing the shear value of the y axis moves the bottom of the y axis to the right, while increasing the shear value of the x axis moves its right end downward. The amount of the movement is determined by the size of the window. Negative shear factors move the axes in the opposite directions. For example, if a window is 100 pixels wide, an x axis shear value of 0.5 will move the right side of any drawn figure 50 pixels down; a shear value of 1.0 will move the right side 100 pixels down; and a shear value of -1.0 will move the right side up 100 pixels.

The following example shows the result of shearing in both the x and y directions. Figure 13-9 shows the same figure drawn with (from left to right) an x shear factor of 1.0, no shearing, and a y shear factor of 1.0.

Figure 13-9: Vertical shear, no shear, and horizontal shear

ShearShape Header

```
1 /* shearshape.h */
2 #ifndef SHEARSHAPE_H
3 #define SHEARSHAPE_H
4
```

```
 5 #include <qwidget.h>
 6
 7 class ShearShape: public QWidget
 8 {
 9 public:
10     ShearShape(QWidget *parent=0,const char *name=0);
11 private:
12     QPixmap marble;
13 protected:
14     virtual void paintEvent(QPaintEvent *);
15 };
16
17 #endif
```

ShearShape

```
 1 /* shearshape.cpp */
 2 #include <kapp.h>
 3 #include <qpainter.h>
 4 #include "shearshape.h"
 5
 6 #include "bluemarble.xpm"
 7
 8 int main(int argc,char **argv)
 9 {
10     KApplication app(argc,argv,"shearshape");
11     ShearShape shearshape;
12     shearshape.show();
13     app.setMainWidget(&shearshape);
14     return(app.exec());
15 }
16 ShearShape::ShearShape(QWidget *parent,const
17         char *name) : QWidget(parent,name)
18 {
19     marble = QPixmap(magick);
20     setFixedSize(288,144);
21 }
22 void ShearShape::paintEvent(QPaintEvent *)
23 {
24     QPainter p(this);
25
26     p.shear(1.0,0.0);
27     p.drawPixmap(0,0,marble);
28     p.shear(-1.0,0.0);
29     p.drawPixmap(72,0,marble);
30     p.shear(0.0,1.0);
31     p.drawPixmap(144,0,marble);
32 }
```

The XPM file included on line 6 is converted to a QPixmap on line 19. The call to shear() on line 26 lowers the right end of the *x* axis so that all horizontal lines are drawn pointing down to the right by 45 degrees. The result of the call to drawPixmap() on line 27 is the skewed pixmap at the left of Figure 13-9.

The call to shear() on line 28 reverses the action of the previous call to shear() and allows the figure to be drawn unsheared by the call to drawPixmap() on line 29. The call to shear() on line 30 adjusts the shear value of the *y* axis and causes the call to drawPixmap() on line 31 to result in the pixmap shown at the right of Figure 13-9.

Translate

The origin of drawing is normally at the upper-left corner of the window, but it can be moved to any other location. Once moved, locations are still specified with larger *y* values extending downward from the origin and larger *x* values extending to the right, while locations above and to the left of the origin can be addressed with negative coordinate values. The following example translates the origin to the center of the window and displays pixmaps around it:

TranslateShape Header

```
 1 /* translateshape.h */
 2 #ifndef TRANSLATESHAPE_H
 3 #define TRANSLATESHAPE_H
 4
 5 #include <qwidget.h>
 6
 7 class TranslateShape: public QWidget
 8 {
 9 public:
10     TranslateShape(QWidget *parent=0,const char *name=0);
11 private:
12     QPixmap marble;
13 protected:
14     virtual void paintEvent(QPaintEvent *);
15 };
16
17 #endif
```

TranslateShape

```
 1 /* translateshape.cpp */
 2 #include <kapp.h>
 3 #include <qpainter.h>
 4 #include "translateshape.h"
 5
 6 #include "bluemarble.xpm"
 7
 8 int main(int argc,char **argv)
 9 {
10     KApplication app(argc,argv,"translateshape");
11     TranslateShape translateshape;
12     translateshape.show();
13     app.setMainWidget(&translateshape);
14     return(app.exec());
```

```
15 }
16 TranslateShape::TranslateShape(QWidget *parent,const
17          char *name) : QWidget(parent,name)
18 {
19     marble = QPixmap(magick);
20     setFixedSize(180,180);
21 }
22 void TranslateShape::paintEvent(QPaintEvent *)
23 {
24     QPainter p(this);
25
26     p.translate(90,90);
27     p.drawPixmap(-72,-72,marble);
28     p.drawPixmap(0,0,marble);
29 }
```

The XPM file included on line 6 is converted to a QPixmap on line 19. The call to translate() on line 26 moves the origin of all drawing to the location (90,90) in the window. With the origin translated, the call to drawPixmap() on line 27 places the upper-left corner of the pixmap at what would normally be the location (18,18) in the window. The call to drawPixmap() on line 28 places the upper-left corner of a pixmap at the new origin — the point that would normally be (90,90). The resulting window is shown in Figure 13-10.

Figure 13-10: Positioning pixmaps from a new origin

Rotate

The entire coordinate system can be rotated around the origin. The default origin is at the upper-left corner, and this is seldom a useful location for the center of rotation. The following example uses origin translation to place the center of rotation in the center of a pixmap:

RotateShape Header

```
1 /* rotateshape.h */
2 #ifndef ROTATESHAPE_H
3 #define ROTATESHAPE_H
4
```

```
 5 #include <qwidget.h>
 6
 7 class RotateShape: public QWidget
 8 {
 9 public:
10     RotateShape(QWidget *parent=0,const char *name=0);
11 private:
12     QPixmap marble;
13 protected:
14     virtual void paintEvent(QPaintEvent *);
15 };
16
17 #endif
```

RotateShape

```
 1 /* rotateshape.cpp */
 2 #include <kapp.h>
 3 #include <qpainter.h>
 4 #include "rotateshape.h"
 5
 6 #include "bluemarble.xpm"
 7
 8 int main(int argc,char **argv)
 9 {
10     KApplication app(argc,argv,"rotateshape");
11     RotateShape rotateshape;
12     rotateshape.show();
13     app.setMainWidget(&rotateshape);
14     return(app.exec());
15 }
16 RotateShape::RotateShape(QWidget *parent,const
17         char *name) : QWidget(parent,name)
18 {
19     marble = QPixmap(magick);
20     setFixedSize(320,160);
21 }
22 void RotateShape::paintEvent(QPaintEvent *)
23 {
24     QPainter p(this);
25
26     p.translate(80,80);
27     p.rotate(20.0);
28     p.drawPixmap(-36,-36,marble);
29     p.rotate(-20.0);
30     p.translate(80,0);
31     p.rotate(40.0);
32     p.drawPixmap(-36,-36,marble);
33     p.rotate(-40.0);
34     p.translate(80,0);
35     p.rotate(60.0);
36     p.drawPixmap(-36,-36,marble);
37 }
```

The XPM file included on line 6 is converted to a QPixmap on line 19. The call to translate() on line 26 moves the origin to location (80,80) in the window. The call to rotate() on line 27 rotates the coordinate system around the origin by 20 degrees. The call to drawPixmap() on line 28 draws the pixmap with its center at the origin (because the pixmap is 72 pixel high and 72 pixels wide).

As shown in Figure 13-11, the second pixmap is centered directly to the right of the first one. If the previous rotation setting were left in place, the translation call on line 30 would move the origin to the right and downward at an angle of 20 degrees. To prevent this, the call to rotate() on line 29 reverses the previous rotation by setting the rotation value back to zero, causing the call to translate() on line 30 to move the origin directly to the right. After the origin has been moved, the call to rotate() on line 31 sets the rotation to 40 degrees, which is the amount of rotation of the second pixmap, drawn by the call to drawPixmap() on line 32. In the same way, the rotation is removed on line 33 to allow the call to translate() on line 34 to move the origin to the right once more; then the rotation is set to 60 degrees on line 35 for the final call to drawPixmap().

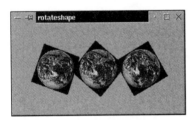

Figure 13-11: Rotating pixmaps around three origins

A Quadratic Bezier Curve

The QPointArray class has a method that can be used to produce a Bezier curve from four points. Figure 13-12 shows the original points and the curve produced from the following example.

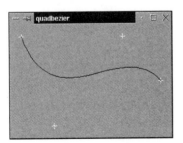

Figure 13-12: A Bezier curve produced from four points

QuadBezier

```
1 /* quadbezier.cpp */
2 #include <kapp.h>
3 #include <qpen.h>
4 #include "quadbezier.h"
5
6 int main(int argc,char **argv)
7 {
8     KApplication app(argc,argv,"quadbezier");
9     QuadBezier quadbezier;
10    quadbezier.show();
11    app.setMainWidget(&quadbezier);
12    return(app.exec());
13 }
14 QuadBezier::QuadBezier(QWidget *parent,
15        const char *name) : QWidget(parent,name)
16 {
17    setFixedSize(300,200);
18 }
19 void QuadBezier::paintEvent(QPaintEvent *)
20 {
21    static QCOORD points[] =
22        { 20,20, 80,180, 210,20, 280,100 };
23    QPointArray pa(4,points);
24    QPainter p(this);
25
26    p.setPen(QColor("white"));
27    paintPoints(p,pa);
28    QPointArray bpa = pa.quadBezier();
29    p.setPen(QColor("black"));
30    p.drawPolyline(bpa);
31 }
32 void QuadBezier::paintPoints(QPainter &p,QPointArray &pa)
33 {
34    int x;
35    int y;
36
37    for(int i=0; i<pa.size(); i++) {
38        pa.point(i,&x,&y);
39        p.drawLine(x-5,y,x+5,y);
40        p.drawLine(x,y-5,x,y+5);
41    }
42 }
```

On line 23, the QPointArray object named "pa" is created to contain four points. Line 26 specifies a white pen, so the call to paintPoints() on line 27 will indicate the point positions in white. The call to quadBezier() on line 28 uses the original four points to create a new QPointArray object that contains a collection of points representing the trace of a quadratic Bezier curve between the first and fourth points, being shaped by the two middle points. The calls to setPen() and drawPolyline() on lines 29 and 30 draw the curve in black.

The paintPoints() method on line 32 places a small cross, 10 pixels high by 10 pixels wide, at the location of each point in the QPointArray. In the loop, a call is made to point() to return the *x* and *y* values for a point, and then drawLine() is called twice — once to draw a vertical line and again to draw a horizontal line — to mark the point.

Animation with Pixmap Sequences

Performing animation is a matter of displaying one frame after another. These frames can be a sequence of images loaded from files (sort of like a movie), or they can be drawn using the normal graphics functions. The following example uses a pixmap to draw and animate the collection of bouncing balls shown in Figure 13-13.

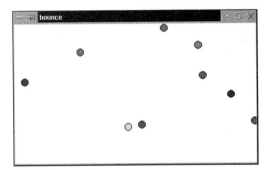

Figure 13-13: Animated bouncing balls

Ball Header

```
1 /* ball.h */
2 #ifndef BALL_H
3 #define BALL_H
4
5 #include <qcolor.h>
6
7 #define RADIUS 7
8
9 class Ball
10 {
11 public:
12      Ball(int width,int height);
13 private:
14      double x;
15      double y;
```

```
16        double xVelocity;
17        double yVelocity;
18        QColor *color;
19 public:
20        double getDiameter() { return(RADIUS * 2.0); }
21        double getX() { return(x); }
22        double getY() { return(y); }
23        double getXVelocity() { return(xVelocity); }
24        double getYVelocity() { return(yVelocity); }
25        QColor &getColor() { return(*color); }
26        void setXVelocity(double value) { xVelocity = value; }
27        void setYVelocity(double value) { yVelocity = value; }
28        void nextPosition();
29 };
30
31 #endif
```

Each ball has the same radius, as defined on line 7. At any given moment, the location of the ball in the window is specified the values x and y on lines 14 and 15. The horizontal velocity of the ball is specified by xVelocity, with movement to the right being positive and movement to the left being negative. The vertical velocity value of yVelocity is positive if the ball is moving down, and negative if it is moving up. Each ball has its own color, as defined on line 18.

The methods defined on lines 20 through 25 provide access to the values stored in the Ball class. The methods setXVelocity() and setYVelocity() on lines 26 and 27 can be used to set the velocity of the ball.

Ball

```
 1 /* ball.cpp */
 2 #include <stdlib.h>
 3 #include "ball.h"
 4
 5 Ball::Ball(int width,int height)
 6 {
 7     x = (((double)rand()*width)/RAND_MAX);
 8     y = (((double)rand()*height)/RAND_MAX) - height;
 9     yVelocity = 0.0;
10     do {
11         xVelocity = (((double)rand()*4)/RAND_MAX) - 2;
12     } while(fabs(xVelocity) < 0.5);
13     color = new QColor(rand() % 255,
14                        rand() % 255,
15                        rand() % 255);
16 }
17 void Ball::nextPosition()
18 {
19     x += xVelocity;
20     y += yVelocity;
21 }
```

The constructor on line 5 initializes the position, velocity, and color of the ball to random settings. The ball is positioned horizontally between the two edges of the window and vertically at some location above the window, but no higher than twice the height of the visible window space. The vertical velocity is set to zero because gravity will accelerate it downward. The loop on line 10 makes certain that the horizontal velocity is sufficient to ensure that the ball will not bounce vertically long enough to come to rest within the window. The color is set to a random RGB value.

The nextPosition() method on line 17 is called to move the ball from its current position to its next position. This is done by simply adding the velocity amount to the current position. The magnitude of the velocity determines how far the ball will travel, and the sign of the velocity determines its direction.

Bounce Header

```
 1 /* bounce.h */
 2 #ifndef BOUNCE_H
 3 #define BOUNCE_H
 4
 5 #include <qwidget.h>
 6 #include <qtimer.h>
 7 #include <qpixmap.h>
 8 #include "ball.h"
 9
10 #define BOUNCE_HEIGHT 250
11 #define BOUNCE_WIDTH 450
12 #define BALL_COUNT 10
13 #define GRAVITY 0.2
14
15 class Bounce: public QWidget
16 {
17     Q_OBJECT
18 public:
19     Bounce(QWidget *parent=0,const char *name=0);
20 private:
21     QTimer *timer;
22     QPixmap *pixmap;
23     Ball *ball[BALL_COUNT];
24 private slots:
25     void frameSlot();
26 protected:
27     virtual void paintEvent(QPaintEvent *);
28 };
29
30 #endif
```

The Bounce class is the widget that contains that window used to display the balls. The constant values defined on lines 10 through 13 determine the height and width of the window, the number of balls, and the force of gravity to accelerate the balls downward.

The QTimer defined on line 21 is used to specify the amount of time between frames. The QPixmap on line 22 is used to paint each frame before displaying it in the window. Line 23 declares an array of pointers — one for each ball that is bouncing in the window.

Bounce

```
1 /* bounce.cpp */
2 #include <kapp.h>
3 #include <qpainter.h>
4 #include "bounce.h"
5
6 int main(int argc,char **argv)
7 {
8     KApplication app(argc,argv,"bounce");
9     Bounce bounce;
10     bounce.show();
11     app.setMainWidget(&bounce);
12     return(app.exec());
13 }
14 Bounce::Bounce(QWidget *parent,const
15         char *name) : QWidget(parent,name)
16 {
17     setFixedSize(BOUNCE_WIDTH,BOUNCE_HEIGHT);
18     timer = new QTimer(this,"clock");
19     connect(timer,SIGNAL(timeout()),
20             this,SLOT(frameSlot()));
21     timer->start(20);
22     for(int i=0; i<BALL_COUNT; i++)
23         ball[i] = new Ball(BOUNCE_WIDTH,BOUNCE_HEIGHT);
24     pixmap = new QPixmap(BOUNCE_WIDTH,BOUNCE_HEIGHT);
25 }
26 void Bounce::paintEvent(QPaintEvent *)
27 {
28     QPainter paint;
29     Ball *b;
30
31     paint.begin(pixmap);
32     paint.eraseRect(0,0,BOUNCE_WIDTH,BOUNCE_HEIGHT);
33     for(int i=0; i<BALL_COUNT; i++) {
34         b = ball[i];
35         paint.setBrush(b->getColor());
36         paint.drawEllipse(b->getX(),b->getY(),
37             b->getDiameter(),b->getDiameter());
38     }
39     paint.end();
40     bitBlt(this,0,0,pixmap,0,0,
41             BOUNCE_WIDTH,BOUNCE_HEIGHT,CopyROP);
42 }
43 void Bounce::frameSlot()
```

```
44 {
45     Ball *b;
46
47     for(int i=0; i<BALL_COUNT; i++) {
48         b = ball[i];
49         if((b->getX() >= BOUNCE_WIDTH) ||
50                 (b->getX() < -b->getDiameter())) {
51             delete b;
52             ball[i] = new Ball(BOUNCE_WIDTH,BOUNCE_HEIGHT);
53             continue;
54         }
55         if(b->getY() + b->getDiameter() >= BOUNCE_HEIGHT) {
56             if(b->getYVelocity() > 0)
57                 b->setYVelocity(-b->getYVelocity() * 0.9);
58         } else {
59             b->setYVelocity(b->getYVelocity() + GRAVITY);
60         }
61         b->nextPosition();
62     }
63     repaint(0,0,BOUNCE_WIDTH,BOUNCE_HEIGHT,FALSE);
64 }
```

The Bounce constructor, beginning on line 14, creates all of the objects that will be used for the animation. The QTimer that will control the rate of speed of animation—the amount of time that is to elapse between frames—is created on line 18. The call to connect() on line 19 connects the timer to the slot method frameSlot() so it will be called each time the timer expires. The call to start() on line 20 starts the timer running so that it will call the slot method once every 20 milliseconds (0.20 seconds). The loop on line 22 creates the balls used in the animation, and a working pixmap is created on line 24.

The call to paintEvent() draws each of the balls on the window in its current position. The drawing is done to the pixmap, not directly to the widget's window. A call is made to eraseRect() on line 32 to clear the pixmap. The detailed drawing of each ball is done in the loop beginning on line 32. The setBrush() call on line 35 sets the current brush to the color of the ball, and the call to drawEllipse() uses the information in the ball object to draw a filled circle at the appropriate location.

The call to a function with the unlikely name bitBlt() on line 40 copies the entire pixmap directly to the window of the widget. The detailed painting could have been done directly onto the widget window but clearing and repainting the window would cause it to flicker. Clearing a pixmap and copying the pixels as a block eliminates the flicker. The first three arguments passed to bitBlt() specify the source, the next three the destination, and the next two the size of the rectangle to be copied. The last argument specifies the method of transferring the pixel data—the CopyROP option specifies that each destination pixel be simply overwritten by its corresponding source pixel. There are many other options, as listed in Table 13-1.

Table 13-1
Raster Operations Available for Copying Pixels with bitBlt()

Name	Destination Becomes...
AndNotROP	Source AND (NOT Destination)
AndROP	Source AND Destination
ClearROP	0
CopyROP	Source
NandROP	NOT (Source AND Destination)
NopROP	Destination
NorROP	NOT (Source OR Destination)
NotAndROP	(NOT Source) AND Destination
NotCopyROP	NOT Source
NotOrROP	(NOT Source) AND Destination
NotROP	NOT Destination
NotXorROP	(NOT Source) XOR Destination
OrNotROP	Source OR (NOT Destination)
OrROP	Source OR Destination
SetROP	1
XorROP	Source XOR Destination

The slot method frameSlot() is called whenever the timer expires. This method does not actually draw a new window, but it does calculate the next position of each of the balls and then schedules a call to paintEvent() by calling repaint() on line 63. The call to repaint() specifies the rectangle to be painted (this information is passed to the paintEvent() method inside the QPaintEvent argument), and also specifies whether the window is to be erased first. For animation, the window clearing option is set to FALSE because doing so would reintroduce the flickering we are trying to avoid.

The loop beginning on line 47 determines the next position of each ball. If the conditional on line 49 is TRUE, the ball has moved outside of the window to either the right or left, so it is deleted and replaced with a new one. The test on line 55 determines whether the ball is at the bottom of the window and if it is moving downward (that is, its vertical velocity is positive); if so, the velocity is reversed so the ball will start back up. The velocity is reduced by 10 percent (friction loss of energy) so the ball will bounce a bit lower each time. If the ball is in flight within the window, the expression on line 59 adjusts the velocity downward by the amount of the force of gravity. Finally, the call to nextPosition() on line 61 adjusts the x and y location of the ball according to its current velocity.

Accessing Pixel Values with QImage

A QImage object can be used to hold image information and provide low-level access to individual pixel information. The following example creates a QPixmap, converts it to a QImage to modify the pixel color values, and converts it back to a QPixmap for display. There are three forms of a QImage—it can contain 1 bit per pixel, 8 bits per pixel, or 32 bits per pixel.

If a QImage object contains only 1 bit per pixel, then the QImage contains only black and white graphic information. Actually, the one-bit value is used as an index into a color map that normally contains the colors black and white, but it can contain any two colors. Although you can apply the color methods and flags to a QImage object of this type, they will have no effect.

Depending on the color model being used, a QImage object may store the actual color data in a color map, or directly in each pixel location, as described in Chapter 11. Your program is capable of modifying the colors in either case. If a color map is used, you can modify the index into the color map, or the contents of the color map itself. If a color map is not used, you can modify each individual pixel.

ImageModify Header

```
 1 /* imagemodify.h */
 2 #ifndef IMAGEMODIFY_H
 3 #define IMAGEMODIFY_H
 4
 5 #include <qwidget.h>
 6
 7 class ImageModify: public QWidget
 8 {
 9 public:
10     ImageModify(QWidget *parent=0,const char *name=0);
11 private:
12     QPixmap logo;
13     QPixmap modlogo;
14     QRgb rgbModify(QRgb rgb);
15 protected:
16     virtual void paintEvent(QPaintEvent *);
17 };
18
19 #endif
```

The `logo` pixmap on line 12 is used to hold the original pixmap, and `modlogo` on line 13 is used to hold the modified pixmap.

ImageModify

```
 1 /* imagemodify.cpp */
 2 #include <kapp.h>
 3 #include <qpainter.h>
 4 #include <qimage.h>
 5 #include <qcolor.h>
 6 #include "imagemodify.h"
 7
 8 #include "logo.xpm"
 9
10 int main(int argc,char **argv)
11 {
12     KApplication app(argc,argv,"imagemodify");
13     ImageModify imagemodify;
14     imagemodify.show();
15     app.setMainWidget(&imagemodify);
16     return(app.exec());
17 }
18 ImageModify::ImageModify(QWidget *parent,const
19         char *name) : QWidget(parent,name)
20 {
21     logo = QPixmap(magick);
22     QImage image = logo.convertToImage();
23     if(image.numColors() > 0) {
24         for(int i=0; i<image.numColors(); i++) {
25             QRgb rgbOrig = image.color(i);
26             QRgb rgbMod = rgbModify(rgbOrig);
27             image.setColor(i,rgbMod);
28         }
29     } else {
30         for(int x=0; x<image.width(); x++) {
31             for(int y=0; y<image.height(); y++) {
32                 QRgb rgbOrig = image.pixel(x,y);
33                 QRgb rgbMod = rgbModify(rgbOrig);
34                 image.setPixel(x,y,rgbMod);
35             }
36         }
37     }
38     modlogo.convertFromImage(image,ThresholdDither);
39     setFixedSize(514,303);
40 }
41 QRgb ImageModify::rgbModify(QRgb rgb) {
42     int alpha = rgb & 0xFF000000;
43     QRgb rgbMod = qRgb(qGreen(rgb) & 0xC0,
44             qRed(rgb) & 0xC0,
45             qBlue(rgb) & 0xC0);
46     rgbMod |= alpha;
```

```
47      return(rgbMod);
48 }
49 void ImageModify::paintEvent(QPaintEvent *)
50 {
51      QPainter p(this);
52
53      p.drawPixmap(0,0,logo);
54      p.drawPixmap(257,0,modlogo);
55 }
```

The constructor, beginning on line 18, creates two pixmaps. The pixmap named logo is created on line 21 from the XPM data included on line 8. The call to convertToImage() on line 22 uses the contents of the QPixmap object to create a QImage object.

The test on line 23 determines the color model. The value returned from the method numColors() is a count of the number of colors stored in the color map. If the number is zero, there is no color map and the pixel colors are to be modified directly.

The loop beginning on line 24 executes once for each entry in the color map. The method color() on line 25 retrieves the color pixel value as a QRgb value. The QRgb data type is an unsigned integer that contains the pixel information (described in detail in Chapter 11). That is, the leftmost byte holds the alpha (transparency) value, and each of the other three bytes holds one of the three color values. The call to rgbModify() on line 26 uses the QRgb value from the image to create, and return, a new QRgb value. The call to setColor() on line 27 stores a modified version of color values at the same index location in the color table. Because you have direct access to the color values stored in the color map, your program can make any changes you like.

If there is no color map, the colors are stored directly in each pixel of the QImage. The nest loop on lines 30 and 31 uses the height and width values of the QImage to loop through all the pixels. The actual conversion is done using the rgbModify() method — the same method is used to convert the members of both color models. The color values are read from the QImage object by the call to pixel() on line 32, and the modified QRgb values are written to the QImage object by the call to setPixel() on line 34.

The call to convertFromImage() on line 38 converts the modified image data back into a pixmap so it can be displayed later. The first argument to the method is the QImage object, and the second method is a set of flags that control the conversion process. The flags can be a combination of one each from tables 13-2, 13-3, 13-4, and 13-5.

Table 13-2
Color Preference Flags for Creating a QPixmap

Flag Name	Description
AutoColor	This is the default. If there is 1 bit per pixel, the resulting QPixmap is black and white; otherwise, it is dithered and converted to the native color depth.
ColorOnly	The QPixmap will be dithered and converted to the native color depth.
MonoOnly	The resulting QPixmap is black and white.

Table 13-3
Dithering Preference Flags for Creating a QPixmap

Flag Name	Description
DiffuseDither	This is the default. This is a dithering algorithm designed to produce a high-quality result.
OrderedDither	This is a dithering algorithm designed for speed and efficiency.
ThresholdDither	This algorithm has no dithering. The closest color is used.

Table 13-4
Alpha Channel Dithering Mode Preference Flags for Creating a QPixmap

Flag Name	Description
DiffuseAlphaDither	This is a dithering algorithm designed to produce a high-quality result.
OrderedAlphaDither	This is a dithering algorithm designed for speed and efficiency.
ThresholdAlphaDither	This is the default, which is no dithering.

Table 13-5
Color Production Preference Flags for Creating a QPixmap

Flag Name	Description
PreferDither	This is the default. Always dither 32-bit images when they are being converted to 8-bit images.
AvoidDither	Only dither 32-bit images that contain more than 256 colors that are being converted to 8-bit images.

The method rgbModify() on line 41 performs the actual color conversion. The alpha value is stored in the first byte of a color value, and this conversion method saves the value in the variable alpha so it can restore the value to the modified color later. This is necessary only if you wish to retain existing transparency information. The three macros qGreen, qRed, and qBlue are convenient for extracting each of the three color values. Each of the colors is modified (by a bitwise ANDing with the value 0xC0), and the macro qRgb() packs the three separate color values back into a single QRgb data type named rgbMod. The original alpha value is added back in. This example simply clears all but the first two bits from each color value, effectively reducing the total color resolution to six bits (two for each color). Also, the values of red and green are swapped. Figure 13-14 shows the window displaying the original pixmap on the left and the modified pixmap on the right.

Figure 13-14: Individual pixels can be modified using a QImage

There is no limit to the variation that can be applied to an image. For example, to remove all the color information and have the figure appear in shades of gray, it is simply a matter of creating each shade of gray by averaging the red, green, and blue values. The following `rgbModify()` method retains any alpha transparency, and produces an image in shades of gray:

```
QRgb ImageModify2::rgbModify(QRgb rgb) {
    int alpha = rgb & 0xFF000000;
    int average = qGreen(rgb) + qRed(rgb) + qBlue(rgb);
    average /= 3;
    QRgb rgbMod = qRgb(average,average,average);
    rgbMod |= alpha;
    return(rgbMod);
}
```

Using an Icon Provider in a QFileDialog

There is a facility built into `QFileDialog` that you can use to customize the icons for each of the file types. To do this, create a `QFileIconProvider` to supply the icons, and attach it to the dialog. The following example demonstrates defining custom icons for files with certain suffixes attached to their names. Figure 13-15 shows the icons chosen for files that end with `.png`, `.o`, and `.cpp`.

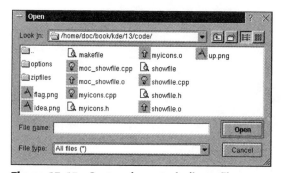

Figure 13-15: Custom icons to indicate file types

MyIcons Header

```
 1 /* myicons.h */
 2 #ifndef MYICONS_H
 3 #define MYICONS_H
 4
 5 #include <qfiledialog.h>
 6
 7 class MyIcons: public QFileIconProvider
 8 {
 9 public:
10     MyIcons(QWidget *parent=0,const char *name=0);
11     ~MyIcons();
```

```
12      const QPixmap *pixmap(const QFileInfo &);
13      const QPixmap *pixmap(const QUrlInfo &);
14 private:
15      const QPixmap *selectPixmap(QString &);
16 private:
17      QPixmap *cppPixmap;
18      QPixmap *oPixmap;
19      QPixmap *pngPixmap;
20      QPixmap *filePixmap;
21      QPixmap *directoryPixmap;
22 };
23
24 #endif
```

The MyIcons class, which inherits from the QFileIconProvider base class, contains all of the pixmaps that will be used to indicate the different file types. The two methods named pixmap(), declared on lines 12 and 13, override virtual methods in the base class. These two methods are used by QFileDialog to retrieve an appropriate pixmap for each file.

MyIcons

```
 1 /* myicons.cpp */
 2 #include <qfiledialog.h>
 3 #include "myicons.h"
 4
 5 static const char *file_xpm[]={
 6 "22 22 6 1",
 7 "   c Gray0",
 8 ". c Gray51",
 9 "X c Gray65",
10 "o c #dfdfdf",
11 "0 c Gray100",
12 "+ c None",
13 "++++++++++++++++++++++",
14 "++++++++++++++++++++++",
15 "++++++++++++++++++++++",
16 "+++          +++++++++++",
17 "+++ 0000000o +++++++++++",
18 "+++ 000000+o +++++++++",
19 "+++ 000000+0o +++++++++",
20 "+++ 000000+    +++++++",
21 "+++ 000000000+ +++++++",
22 "+++ 0000000    +++++++",
23 "+++ 000000 .++. ++++++",
24 "+++ 00000 .XX+.. +++++",
25 "+++ 00000 +X++.+ +++++",
26 "+++ 00000 ++++.+ +++++",
27 "+++ 00000 .++X.. +++++",
28 "+++ 000000 .++. .+++++",
```

```
29      "+++ 0000000     .   ++++",
30      "+++ 0000000000 +    +++",
31      "+++             ++   +++",
32      "+++++++++++++++++++++++",
33      "+++++++++++++++++++++++",
34      "+++++++++++++++++++++++"
35      };
36
37      static const char *directory_xpm[]={
38          "15 15 6 1",
39          ". c None",
40          "b c #ffff00",
41          "d c #000000",
42          "* c #999999",
43          "a c #cccccc",
44          "c c #ffffff",
45          "...............",
46          "..*****........",
47          ".*ababa*.......",
48          "*abababa*****.",
49          "*cccccccccccc*d",
50          "*cbababababab*d",
51          "*cabababababa*d",
52          "*cbababababab*d",
53          "*cabababababa*d",
54          "*cbababababab*d",
55          "*cabababababa*d",
56          "*cbababababab*d",
57          "*************d",
58          ".ddddddddddddd",
59          "..............."};
60
61      MyIcons::MyIcons(QWidget *parent,const char *name)
62              : QFileIconProvider(parent,name)
63      {
64          cppPixmap = new QPixmap("idea.png");
65          oPixmap = new QPixmap("up.png");
66          pngPixmap = new QPixmap("flag.png");
67          filePixmap = new QPixmap(file_xpm);
68          directoryPixmap = new QPixmap(directory_xpm);
69      }
70      MyIcons::~MyIcons()
71      {
72          delete cppPixmap;
73          delete oPixmap;
74          delete pngPixmap;
75          delete filePixmap;
76          delete directoryPixmap;
77      }
78      const QPixmap *MyIcons::pixmap(const QFileInfo &inf)
79      {
```

```
 80      QString name = inf.fileName();
 81      const QPixmap *qpixmap = selectPixmap(name);
 82      if(qpixmap == NULL) {
 83          if(inf.isDir())
 84              return(directoryPixmap);
 85          else
 86              return(filePixmap);
 87      }
 88      return(qpixmap);
 89  }
 90  const QPixmap *MyIcons::pixmap(const QUrlInfo &inf)
 91  {
 92      QString name = inf.name();
 93      const QPixmap *qpixmap = selectPixmap(name);
 94      if(qpixmap == NULL) {
 95          if(inf.isDir())
 96              return(directoryPixmap);
 97          else
 98              return(filePixmap);
 99      }
100      return(qpixmap);
101  }
102  const QPixmap *MyIcons::selectPixmap(QString &name)
103  {
104      if(name.right(4) == ".cpp")
105          return(cppPixmap);
106      if(name.right(2) == ".o")
107          return(oPixmap);
108      if(name.right(4) == ".png")
109          return(pngPixmap);
110      return(NULL);
111  }
```

The constructor, beginning on line 61, uses the XPM data to create the set of pixmaps to be associated with the filenames. Two pixmaps are defined as XPM data on lines 5 and 37. These are the default pixmaps—the ones that are used whenever no specific pixmap is assigned to a file.

The two methods named pixmap(), declared on lines 78 and 90, are called with the description of a file to determine the pixmap that should be displayed in association with the file. The two methods do exactly the same thing, but accept slightly different arguments. The call to selectPixmap() on lines 81 and 93 is used to choose a pixmap for the file, but if a pixmap is not returned from selectPixmap(), one of the two default pixmaps is selected.

The method selectPixmap() on line 102 examines the filenames and determines whether a pixmap has been assigned to them. This example simply looks at the filename, but the examination could go as far as to check the magic number contained in the file to determine its type. For more information on magic numbers, see the man page for file.

ShowFile Header

```
1  /* showfile.h */
2  #ifndef SHOWFILE_H
3  #define SHOWFILE_H
4
5  #include <qwidget.h>
6  #include <qlabel.h>
7  #include <qstring.h>
8
9  class ShowFile: public QWidget
10 {
11     Q_OBJECT
12 public:
13     ShowFile(QWidget *parent=0,const char *name=0);
14 private:
15     QLabel *filelabel;
16     QString filename;
17 private slots:
18     void popupOpen();
19 };
20
21 #endif
```

ShowFile

```
1  /* showfile.cpp */
2  #include <kapp.h>
3  #include <qpushbutton.h>
4  #include <qlayout.h>
5  #include <qfiledialog.h>
6  #include "showfile.h"
7  #include "myicons.h"
8
9  int main(int argc,char **argv)
10 {
11     KApplication app(argc,argv,"showfile");
12     QFileIconProvider *provider = new MyIcons();
13     QFileDialog::setIconProvider(provider);
14     ShowFile showfile;
15     showfile.show();
16     app.setMainWidget(&showfile);
17     return(app.exec());
18 }
19 ShowFile::ShowFile(QWidget *parent,const char *name)
20         : QWidget(parent,name)
21 {
22     QPushButton *button;
23     QVBoxLayout *box = new QVBoxLayout(this,0,3);
24
25     filelabel = new QLabel("",this);
26     filelabel->setAlignment(Qt::AlignHCenter);
```

```
27        box->addWidget(filelabel);
28
29        button = new QPushButton("Select File to Open",this);
30        box->addWidget(button);
31        connect(button,SIGNAL(clicked()),
32                this,SLOT(popupOpen()));
33
34        resize(10,10);
35        box->activate();
36 }
37 void ShowFile::popupOpen()
38 {
39        QString name = QFileDialog::getOpenFileName("",
40                NULL,this);
41        if(!name.isEmpty()) {
42            filename = name;
43            filelabel->setText(filename);
44        }
45 }
```

This program associates the icon provider with the file dialog, and provides a button that can be used to pop up the dialog.

The icon provider is created on line 12. The call to the static method setIcon Provider() on line 13 assigns the MyIcon object as the icon provider for all QFileDialog objects. This mechanism replaces the default icon provider with a new one. You could have a number of icon providers and, using this technique, change them as often as you like.

Whenever the button is pressed, the slot method popupOpen() on line 17 is called. A QFileDialog window is popped up with the call to getOpenFilename() on line 39. The test on line 41 determines whether a filename has been selected and, if so, the name of the file is displayed.

Summary

This chapter covered some very special graphics operations. The facilities included as part of the KDE and Qt API make it possible for you to do just about anything you would like to do with a graphic image:

✦ The same API that is used to draw pixels on a window can be used to paint pixels to a printed page.

✦ The step-by-step instructions required to create a graphic image, or part of a graphic image, can be recorded and played back any number of times.

✦ A graphic object can be scaled to fit a window either larger or smaller than the one for which it was originally intended.

✦ A number of operations can be performed on a graphic object, including scaling, clipping, shearing, translating, and rotating.

✦ Animation can be achieved by using a sequence of graphic frames and a timer.

The next chapter covers a very specialized area of a graphical user interface—drag and drop. It is a fairly simply matter to drag and drop objects within an application, but when things from one program are dropped onto the window of another, the receiving application needs to also be supplied with information about the object being dropped.

✦   ✦   ✦

Drag and Drop

◆   ◆   ◆   ◆

In This Chapter

Dragging and
dropping text within
an application

Dragging and
dropping text and
graphics among
applications

Cutting and pasting
graphics using the
system clipboard

◆   ◆   ◆   ◆

Standard data transfer capabilities can enable applications
that have no awareness of one another to interact in such
a way that they seem, to the user, to be fully integrated. This
interaction is commonly achieved in two ways. Using the
mouse to drag a graphic object from one window to another
can cause data to be transferred from one application to
another. Another approach is to enable the user to copy data
to a system clipboard and have another application read the
data from the clipboard.

While dragging and dropping are very useful for communicating among applications, they can also be quite useful for operations limited to a single application. The user can move
things from one form to another within an application, or
change the position of things within a single window.

This chapter is all about the sequence of events that must
occur in a drag-and-drop operation: the application recognizes
that a drag operation has been requested, the data must be
packaged for dragging, the drop target must recognize that a
drop has occurred, and the package of data must be opened
and dealt with.

A Simple Text Drag and Drop

The following program implements dragging and dropping
of text from one label to another. Any widget can act as the
source of a drag operation, the target of a drop operation, or
both. The mainline of the program is not involved — all drag
and drop operations are controlled directly by the source and
target widgets themselves.

DragDrop Header

```
1 /* dragdrop.h */
2 #ifndef DRAGDROP_H
3 #define DRAGDROP_H
```

```
 4
 5 #include <qwidget.h>
 6 #include <qstring.h>
 7 #include "dragfrom.h"
 8 #include "dropto.h"
 9
10 class DragDrop: public QWidget
11 {
12 public:
13     DragDrop(QWidget *parent=0,const char *name=0);
14 private:
15     DragFrom *apples;
16     DragFrom *oranges;
17     DropTo *target;
18 };
19
20 #endif
```

The two widgets, apples, and oranges on lines 15 and 16, act as sources for text drag operations, and the widget target can be used as the target of a text drop operation.

DragDrop

```
 1 /* dragdrop.cpp */
 2 #include <kapp.h>
 3 #include <qlayout.h>
 4 #include <qlabel.h>
 5 #include "dragdrop.h"
 6
 7 int main(int argc,char **argv)
 8 {
 9     KApplication app(argc,argv,"dragdrop");
10     DragDrop dragdrop;
11     dragdrop.show();
12     app.setMainWidget(&dragdrop);
13     return(app.exec());
14 }
15
16 DragDrop::DragDrop(QWidget *parent,const char *name)
17         : QWidget(parent,name)
18 {
19     QVBoxLayout *box = new QVBoxLayout(this,30);
20     box->addSpacing(30);
21
22     target = new DropTo("target",this);
23     box->addWidget(target);
24
25     apples = new DragFrom("apples",this);
26     box->addWidget(apples);
```

```
27
28      oranges = new DragFrom("oranges",this);
29      box->addWidget(oranges);
30
31      box->activate();
32 }
```

The DragDrop window is the host of three widgets that are drag-and-drop enabled. The target of the drop operation is added to the vertical box layout on lines 22 and 23. The two text drag source widgets are added to the main window on lines 25 through 29. Figure 14-1 shows the window after text from the apples widget has been dragged and dropped on the target.

Figure 14-1: Text can be dragged from the bottom and dropped at the top.

DragFrom Header

```
 1 /* dragfrom.h */
 2 #ifndef DRAGFROM_H
 3 #define DRAGFROM_H
 4
 5 #include <qlabel.h>
 6 #include <qstring.h>
 7
 8 class DragFrom: public QLabel
 9 {
10 public:
11     DragFrom(const char *text,QWidget *parent=0);
12 private:
13     QString string;
14 protected:
15     virtual void mousePressEvent(QMouseEvent *);
16 };
17
18 #endif
```

DragFrom

```
1  /* dragfrom.cpp */
2  #include <qlabel.h>
3  #include <qfont.h>
4  #include <qdragobject.h>
5  #include "dragfrom.h"
6
7  DragFrom::DragFrom(const char *text,QWidget *parent)
8          : QLabel(parent)
9  {
10     string = text;
11     QString label("Source for ");
12     label.append(text);
13     setText(label);
14     setAlignment(Qt::AlignHCenter);
15     QFont font("Courier",18,QFont::Bold,FALSE);
16     setFont(font);
17 }
18 void DragFrom::mousePressEvent(QMouseEvent *)
19 {
20     QDragObject *textdrag = new QTextDrag(string,this);
21     textdrag->dragCopy();
22 }
```

The `DragFrom` widget uses the `QLabel` widget as its base class. The text supplied to the constructor on line 7 is the text that can be dragged from this widget, by being stored into `string` on line 10, while the displayed text is preceded by "Source for" on lines 11 through 13. Lines 14 through 16 center the text and specify its font.

The method `mousePressEvent()` is called whenever a mouse button is pressed, and a `QTextDrag` object is created on line 20. The call to `dragCopy()` causes the `QTextDrag` object to follow the mouse. The object will be deleted by the drag-and-drop operation (when the mouse button is released, whether or not it reaches its destination), so you should not delete it in your program. This program can create and send any number of `QTextDrag` objects, but it will never be notified of the final disposition of any of them.

DropTo Header

```
1  /* dropto.h */
2  #ifndef DROPTO_H
3  #define DROPTO_H
4
5  #include <qlabel.h>
6  #include <qevent.h>
7  #include <qstring.h>
8
9  class DropTo: public QLabel
10 {
```

```
11 public:
12     DropTo(const char *text,QWidget *parent=0);
13 protected:
14     void dragEnterEvent(QDragEnterEvent *e);
15     void dropEvent(QDropEvent *e);
16 };
17
18 #endif
```

The methods dragEnterEvent() and dropEvent() override the method declarations in the QWidget base class. These methods are called during the drag-and-drop operations when the mouse is searching for a place to make the drop.

DropTo

```
 1 /* dropto.cpp */
 2 #include <qlabel.h>
 3 #include <qfont.h>
 4 #include <qdragobject.h>
 5 #include "dropto.h"
 6
 7 DropTo::DropTo(const char *text,QWidget *parent)
 8          : QLabel(text,parent)
 9 {
10     setAlignment(Qt::AlignHCenter);
11     QFont font("Courier",18,QFont::Bold,FALSE);
12     setFont(font);
13     setAcceptDrops(TRUE);
14 }
15 void DropTo::dragEnterEvent(QDragEnterEvent *e)
16 {
17     e->accept(QTextDrag::canDecode(e));
18 }
19 void DropTo::dropEvent(QDropEvent *e)
20 {
21     QString text;
22
23     if(QTextDrag::decode(e,text))
24         setText(text);
25 }
```

The base class of the DropTo class is QLabel, making it capable of displaying the text that is dropped on it. Lines 10 through 12 of the constructor specify the alignment and the font of the displayed text.

The call to setAcceptDrops() on line 13 activates this widget as the target of mouse drag-and-drop operations. Whenever the mouse is performing a drag operation and the mouse pointer enters this widget, the method dragEnterEvent() will be called with information about the data being dragged. Also, the dropEvent() method will be called if the data is dropped within this widget.

The `dragEnterEvent()` on line 15 is called whenever a mouse drag enters the boundary of this widget. The purpose of this method is to determine whether or not this widget is willing to accept the drop. You can perform any test you would like, but this example simply calls the static `canDecode()` method of the `QTextDrag` class to determine whether the dragged data can be converted into text. If it can, the call `accept()` is made with a `TRUE` argument; otherwise, it is made with `FALSE`.

The method `dropEvent()` on line 19 is called only if a certain sequence of events have occurred. Only if the mouse is in a drag-and-drop operation, and it has entered this widget, and the `dragEnterEvent()` method called the `accept()` method of the event with `TRUE`, will this method be called. This example only accepts text — line 23 makes a call to the static `decode()` method of the `QTextDrag` class, and the resulting decoded text is used to set the text of the label. The drag-and-drop operation has completed successfully.

Drag and Drop of Both Text and Image Data

The following pair of programs demonstrates dragging and dropping objects from one application to another, and the capability of the receiving program to determine the type of data that is being dropped. There are two drag sources — one for text and one for images — but there is only one drop target. The drop target determines the incoming data type and acts accordingly.

DateImage Header

```
1 /* dateimage.h */
2 #ifndef DATEIMAGE_H
3 #define DATEIMAGE_H
4
5 #include <qwidget.h>
6 #include <qlabel.h>
7 #include <qdragobject.h>
8
9 class DateImage: public QWidget
10 {
11 public:
12     DateImage(QWidget *parent=0,const char *name=0);
13 };
14
15 class DateSource: public QLabel
16 {
17 public:
18     DateSource(QWidget *parent=0);
19 protected:
20     virtual void mousePressEvent(QMouseEvent *);
21 };
```

```
22
23 class ImageSource: public QLabel
24 {
25 public:
26     ImageSource(QWidget *parent=0);
27 protected:
28     virtual void mousePressEvent(QMouseEvent *);
29 };
30
31 #endif
```

This header file contains the definition of the classes that are the source of dragged data. The DateImage class is a top-level window that, when displayed, contains both a DateSource object and an ImageSource object. Both the DateSource and the ImageSource classes are subclasses of QLabel, so they both display text and can be used as the source of a drag-and-drop operation. The data dragged from DateSource is a text string, and data dragged from ImageSource is a QImage object.

DateImage

```
1 /* dateimage.cpp */
2 #include <kapp.h>
3 #include <qlayout.h>
4 #include <qlabel.h>
5 #include <qfont.h>
6 #include <time.h>
7 #include "dateimage.h"
8
9 #include "bluemarble.xpm"
10
11 int main(int argc,char **argv)
12 {
13     KApplication app(argc,argv,"dateimage");
14     DateImage dateimage;
15     dateimage.show();
16     app.setMainWidget(&dateimage);
17     return(app.exec());
18 }
19
20 DateImage::DateImage(QWidget *parent,const char *name)
21         : QWidget(parent,name)
22 {
23     QVBoxLayout *box = new QVBoxLayout(this,30);
24
25     DateSource *ds = new DateSource(this);
26     box->addWidget(ds);
27
28     ImageSource *is = new ImageSource(this);
29     box->addWidget(is);
30
```

```
31      box->activate();
32 }
33
34 DateSource::DateSource(QWidget *parent)
35          : QLabel("Date",parent)
36 {
37      setAlignment(Qt::AlignHCenter);
38      QFont font("Courier",18,QFont::Bold,FALSE);
39      setFont(font);
40 }
41 void DateSource::mousePressEvent(QMouseEvent *)
42 {
43      time_t t;
44      char *ct;
45
46      t = time((time_t *)0);
47      ct = ctime(&t);
48      QString string(ct);
49      QDragObject *textdrag = new QTextDrag(string,this);
50      textdrag->dragCopy();
51 }
52
53
54 ImageSource::ImageSource(QWidget *parent)
55          : QLabel("Image",parent)
56 {
57      setAlignment(Qt::AlignHCenter);
58      QFont font("Courier",18,QFont::Bold,FALSE);
59      setFont(font);
60 }
61 void ImageSource::mousePressEvent(QMouseEvent *)
62 {
63      QImage image(magick);
64      QDragObject *imagedrag = new QImageDrag(image,this);
65      imagedrag->dragCopy();
66 }
```

The DateImage constructor on line 20 uses a vertical box to contain a DateSource object and an ImageSource object. Both DateSource and ImageSource use QLabel as their base classes, resulting in a window that looks like the one shown in Figure 14-2.

Figure 14-2: Sources of text and image drag operations

The `DateSource` constructor on line 34 sets its own font and text alignment. The initialization of the `QLabel` base class on line 35 specifies "Date" as the displayed text. The `mousePressEvent()` on line 41 creates a character string containing the current system time and uses it to construct a `QTextDrag` object on line 49. The call to `dragCopy()` on line 50 attaches the `QTextDrag` object to the mouse and sends it on its way.

The `ImageSource` constructor on line 54 sets its own font and text alignment. The initialization of the `QLabel` base class on line 55 specifies "Image" as the displayed text. The `mousePressEvent()` on line 61 creates a `QImage` object from the XPM data included on line 9. The `QImage` object is used in the creation of a `QImageDrag` object on line 64. The call to `dragCopy()` on line 65 attaches the `QImageDrag` object to the mouse so it can be dragged away.

Target Header

```
 1 /* target.h */
 2 #ifndef TARGET_H
 3 #define TARGET_H
 4
 5 #include <qwidget.h>
 6 #include "target.h"
 7
 8 class Target: public QWidget
 9 {
10 public:
11     Target(QWidget *parent=0,const char *name=0);
12 protected:
13     void dragEnterEvent(QDragEnterEvent *e);
14     void dropEvent(QDropEvent *e);
15 };
16
17 #endif
```

The target of the drop is the top-level window of a widget. To accomplish this, it is necessary to override the `QWidget` virtual methods `dragEnterEvent()` and `dropEvent()`.

Target

```
 1 /* target.cpp */
 2 #include <kapp.h>
 3 #include <qpainter.h>
 4 #include <qdragobject.h>
 5 #include "target.h"
 6
 7 int main(int argc,char **argv)
 8 {
 9     KApplication app(argc,argv,"target");
```

```
10      Target target;
11      target.show();
12      app.setMainWidget(&target);
13      return(app.exec());
14 }
15
16 Target::Target(QWidget *parent,const char *name)
17          : QWidget(parent,name)
18 {
19      setFixedSize(400,300);
20      setAcceptDrops(TRUE);
21 }
22 void Target::dragEnterEvent(QDragEnterEvent *e)
23 {
24      e->accept(QTextDrag::canDecode(e) ||
25              QImageDrag::canDecode(e));
26 }
27 void Target::dropEvent(QDropEvent *e)
28 {
29      QString text;
30      QImage image;
31
32      if(QTextDrag::decode(e,text)) {
33          drawText(e->pos(),text);
34      }
35      if(QImageDrag::decode(e,image)) {
36          QPainter *p = new QPainter(this);
37          p->drawImage(e->pos(),image);
38      }
39 }
```

The constructor, on line 16, fixes the size of the main window and calls setAccept Drops() to enable this window as a drop target.

The dragEnterEvent() on line 22 is called whenever a dragging mouse enters the boundaries of this window. A call is made to the accept() method of the QDragEnterEvent object with TRUE if this window can accept the data type being dragged, or FALSE if it cannot. This window can accept both text and image data, so the ability to decode either of these will result in TRUE.

If the mouse drops the data on this widget, a call is made to dropEvent() on line 27. On line 32, a call to decode() of QTextDrag is made to attempt to retrieve the data. If the decoding succeeds, the data is stored in text, and the call to drawText() on line 33 paints the text on the window. The exact location of the text on the local window is determined by the location of the dropping mouse pointer, which is retrieved as a QPoint object from the call to pos() of the QDropEvent object. The decoding procedure is repeated by calling the decode() method of the QImageDrag class. If an image is successfully decoded, a QPainter object is used to paint the image on the window at the location of the drop. Figure 14-3 shows the target window after several text and image drops have been made.

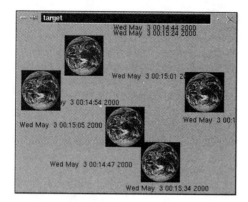

Figure 14-3: Both text and image data can be dropped onto the same window.

Two other methods can optionally be used by the drop target widget in case you want to display some special graphics. The following method would be called whenever a dragging mouse leaves the window without having dropped anything:

```
void Target::dragExitEvent(QDragExitEvent *e)
```

You can use this method to supply more feedback to the user. For example, this method, in combination with dragEnterEvent(),highlights the target widget whenever a dragging mouse is hovering over the window. This can be useful when several small target windows are next to one another. You could also track the potential location of a drop with this next method, which is called whenever the mouse changes positions inside the target window:

```
void Target::dragMoveEvent(QDragMoveEvent *e)
```

One example of using this method would be to place crosshairs, or some other indicator, at the location of the potential drop.

Cut and Paste

The same underlying mechanism used for dragging and dropping is used for cutting and pasting. Dragging an object from one application to another is the same as copying it to or from the clipboard, so the only real difference is in the user interface.

The following program is capable of using cut, copy, and paste operations to move image data between itself and the clipboard. Figure 14-4 shows the program's window and the buttons it uses to transfer a pixmap to and from the KDE clipboard.

Figure 14-4: An image can be copied to and from the KDE clipboard.

CutPaste Header

```
 1 /* cutpaste.h */
 2 #ifndef CUTPASTE_H
 3 #define CUTPASTE_H
 4
 5 #include <qwidget.h>
 6 #include <qpixmap.h>
 7
 8 class CutPaste: public QWidget
 9 {
10     Q_OBJECT
11 public:
12     CutPaste(QWidget *parent=0,const char *name=0);
13 private:
14     QWidget *widget;
15     QPixmap *pixmap;
16 private slots:
17     void loadButton();
18     void copyButton();
19     void cutButton();
20     void pasteButton();
21 };
22
23 #endif
```

The QWidget on line 14 is used to display a QPixmap. The QPixmap on line 15 is the one currently being displayed. The four slot methods are the ones that respond to the pushbuttons.

CutPaste

```
 1 /* cutpaste.cpp */
 2 #include <kapp.h>
 3 #include <qlayout.h>
 4 #include <qimage.h>
```

```
 5 #include <qdragobject.h>
 6 #include <qclipboard.h>
 7 #include <qpushbutton.h>
 8 #include "cutpaste.h"
 9
10 int main(int argc,char **argv)
11 {
12     KApplication app(argc,argv,"cutpaste");
13     CutPaste *cutpaste = new CutPaste();
14     cutpaste->show();
15     app.setMainWidget(cutpaste);
16     return(app.exec());
17 }
18
19 CutPaste::CutPaste(QWidget *parent,const char *name)
20     : QWidget(parent,name)
21 {
22     QPushButton *button;
23     QHBoxLayout *hlayout = new QHBoxLayout(this,5);
24     QVBoxLayout *vlayout = new QVBoxLayout();
25
26     pixmap = NULL;
27
28     button = new QPushButton("Load",this);
29     connect(button,SIGNAL(clicked()),
30             this,SLOT(loadButton()));
31     vlayout->addWidget(button);
32
33     button = new QPushButton("Copy",this);
34     connect(button,SIGNAL(clicked()),
35             this,SLOT(copyButton()));
36     vlayout->addWidget(button);
37
38     button = new QPushButton("Cut",this);
39     connect(button,SIGNAL(clicked()),
40             this,SLOT(cutButton()));
41     vlayout->addWidget(button);
42
43     button = new QPushButton("Paste",this);
44     connect(button,SIGNAL(clicked()),
45             this,SLOT(pasteButton()));
46     vlayout->addWidget(button);
47
48     widget = new QWidget(this);
49     widget->setFixedSize(257,303);
50     widget->setBackgroundColor(QColor("white"));
51
52     hlayout->addWidget(widget);
53     hlayout->addLayout(vlayout);
54
55     resize(10,10);
56     hlayout->activate();
57 }
```

```
58 void CutPaste::loadButton()
59 {
60     if(pixmap != NULL)
61         delete pixmap;
62     pixmap = new QPixmap("logo.xpm");
63     widget->setBackgroundPixmap(*pixmap);
64 }
65 void CutPaste::copyButton()
66 {
67     if(pixmap != NULL) {
68         QImage image = pixmap->convertToImage();
69         QDragObject *drag = new QImageDrag(image,this);
70         QClipboard *clipboard = QApplication::clipboard();
71         clipboard->setData(drag);
72     }
73 }
74 void CutPaste::cutButton()
75 {
76     if(pixmap != NULL) {
77         copyButton();
78         widget->setBackgroundColor(QColor("white"));
79         delete pixmap;
80         pixmap = NULL;
81     }
82 }
83 void CutPaste::pasteButton()
84 {
85     QClipboard *clipboard = QApplication::clipboard();
86     QMimeSource *mime = clipboard->data();
87     QImage image;
88     if(QImageDrag::decode(mime,image)) {
89         QPixmap *newPixmap = new QPixmap();
90         if(newPixmap->convertFromImage(image)) {
91             if(pixmap != NULL)
92                 delete pixmap;
93             pixmap = newPixmap;
94             widget->setBackgroundPixmap(*pixmap);
95         }
96     }
97 }
```

The constructor, beginning on line 19, initializes the data and creates the display by inserting a set of buttons into a vertical box, and then inserts the vertical box and a widget into a horizontal box. No initial pixmap is being displayed, so it is initialized to NULL on line 26. The graphic display widget is created on line 48, and it is initialized with a solid white background.

The slot method loadButton() on line 58 loads a new pixmap from a file. Lines 60 and 61 delete any previously existing pixmap, and the call to setBackground Pixmap() on line 63 displays the newly loaded pixmap.

The slot method `copyButton()` on line 65 tests whether a pixmap exists and, if so, copies it to the clipboard. The call to `convertToImage()` on line 68 converts the pixmap to a `QImage`, because that is the form of the graphic required by `QImageDrag`. The address of the `QClipboard` object is returned from the call to the `clipboard()` method on line 70, and the data is stored in the clipboard with the call to `setData()` on line 71.

The slot method `cutButton()` on line 74 tests whether a pixmap exists and, if so, copies it to the clipboard and deletes it locally. The call to `copyButton()` copies the pixmap to the clipboard. The call to `setBackgroundColor()` clears the pixmap from the window, and lines 79 and 80 remove the pixmap from memory.

The slot method `pasteButton()` on line 83 reads a pixmap from the clipboard to this application. The call to the static method `clipboard()` on line 85 retrieves the address of the system clipboard. The clipboard holds data as a `QMineSource` object, which is retrieved by the call to `data()` on line 86. Several different types of data can be stored on the clipboard, so the Boolean return value from the call to `decode()` on line 88 must be checked to ensure that the data was successfully converted to a `QImage` object. If the conversion succeeded, the call to `convertFromImage()` on line 90 creates a pixmap from the data, and lines 91 through 94 replace the existing pixmap with the new one, and store it in the widget as the new display background.

Summary

Dragging data from one location to another, or cutting data from one location and pasting it into another, requires that both the sender and the receiver agree on the type of the data and how it is packaged. From the application's point of view, transmitting and receiving data is not much more than simply making a function call. This chapter described the fundamentals of dragging and dropping data, including:

✦ To drag data to another location, it first must be encapsulated in a `QDrag Object`. For a window to receive a dropped object, it must be prepared to decode the data in the `QDragObject`.

✦ A call to `setAcceptDrops()` must be made before a widget will accept dropped data.

✦ The cut and paste operations are fundamentally the same as drag and drop, except that the system `QClipboard` object is used as an intermediary to store the data.

The next chapter discusses *applets* — the small icon-like windows that appear on the panel at the bottom (or some other edge) of the main window in the KDE environment. The chapter also discusses some other methods of passing data from one application to another.

✦   ✦   ✦

Interprocess Communications and Applets

There are two basic ways that data are passed from one program to another. At startup, arguments can be supplied on the command line, and during execution, blocks of data can be generated by one application and passed to another process that is expecting it. KDE has made some special provisions for both of these communications methods.

There is a command-line class that analyzes and stores information from the command line. More than that, it provides access to the KDE option flags that, to some extent, standardize the settings available to the applications. That is, by using this object, different applications can be programmed to respond in a standard way to a standard set of flags.

The interprocess communications model requires a server running in the background to handle messages. This server is sort of like a post office. Each application gets a P.O. box that is identified by a name, and other applications can store messages in it.

An applet is a special application that displays its window as an icon in the KDE panel (sometimes call the KDE *kicker*) that is present at one edge of the main KDE window. An applet has the disadvantage of having a very small window as its top-level window, but it has the advantage of always being visible to the user.

This chapter explains the various ways that your program can take advantage of these data-exchange methods and applets.

The DCOP Communications Model

The DCOP (Desktop Communications Protocol) software was developed to provide a very simple method of establishing interprocess communications among a group of processes. All communications pass through a daemon process called dcop server. A process wishing to send or receive messages first registers its name with dcopserver, and other processes can then address messages to it by sending them to that name in care of the dcopserver.

DCOP is actually a simple form of an RPC (Remote Procedure Call) mechanism. A message is sent in the form of a function call that may or may not require arguments, and may or may not return a value.

The following example consists of three programs. The program named wilbur registers itself with dcopserver and waits for a message to arrive. The program tellwilbur sends a message to wilbur and does not wait for a response, while askwilbur sends a message and waits for the response.

Wilbur Header

```
 1 /* wilbur.h */
 2 #ifndef WILBUR_H
 3 #define WILBUR_H
 4
 5 #include <qmultilineedit.h>
 6 #include <dcopobject.h>
 7
 8 class WilReceiver: public QMultiLineEdit, public DCOPObject
 9 {
10 public:
11     WilReceiver(const char *name=0);
12     bool process(const QCString &function,
13         const QByteArray &data,QCString &replyType,
14         QByteArray &replyData);
15     double cubeRoot(double value);
16 private:
17 };
18
19 #endif
```

The WilReceiver is a DCOPObject, so it is capable of receiving messages, executing a local procedure, and returning the result to the originator of the message. WilReceiver is also a widget because it inherits from the QMultiLineEdit widget.

The method process(), declared on line 12, is required because it is a pure virtual method in the DCOPObject class. It is the method that is called whenever a message is received from another process. The method cubeRoot() declared on line 15 is the one that can be called from other processes.

Wilbur

```cpp
 1  /* wilbur.cpp */
 2  #include <kapp.h>
 3  #include <qcstring.h>
 4  #include <qmultilineedit.h>
 5  #include <dcopclient.h>
 6  #include <math.h>
 7  #include "wilbur.h"
 8
 9  int main(int argc,char **argv)
10  {
11      QString str;
12      KApplication app(argc,argv,"wilbur");
13
14      DCOPClient *client = app.dcopClient();
15      QCString dcopID = client->registerAs(app.name(),FALSE);
16
17      WilReceiver *wilbur = new WilReceiver("wilreceiver");
18      app.setMainWidget(wilbur);
19
20      str.sprintf("wilbur registered as \"%s\"",
21              dcopID.data());
22      wilbur->insertLine(str);
23
24      int returnValue = app.exec();
25      client->detach();
26      return(returnValue);
27  }
28  WilReceiver::WilReceiver(const char *name)
29          : DCOPObject(name)
30  {
31      setReadOnly(TRUE);
32      show();
33  }
34  bool WilReceiver::process(const QCString &function,
35          const QByteArray &data,
36          QCString &replyType,
37          QByteArray &replyData)
38  {
39      if(function == "cubeRoot(double)") {
40          double inValue;
41          double outValue;
42          QDataStream inStream(data,IO_ReadOnly);
43          inStream >> inValue;
44          outValue = cubeRoot(inValue);
45          QDataStream outStream(replyData,IO_WriteOnly);
46          outStream << outValue;
47          replyType = "double";
48          return(TRUE);
49      } else {
```

```
50              QString string;
51              string.sprintf("call to unknown function %s",
52                      function.data());
53              insertLine(string);
54              return(FALSE);
55          }
56 }
57 double WilReceiver::cubeRoot(double value)
58 {
59      QString string;
60      double root = cbrt(value);
61      string.sprintf("Cube root of %g is %g",value,root);
62      insertLine(string);
63      return(root);
64 }
```

This program uses a WilReceiver object as its top-level widget. This gives it the ability to both display text and respond to incoming messages.

Every process that is to communicate through the dcopserver must register itself as a client. The call to dcopClient() on line 14 creates a local DCOPClient object and returns its address. The call to registerAs() on line 15 registers the name of this client with the dcopserver daemon. The name of this application — specified on line 12 — is "wilbur", so from now on, any message sent to "wilbur" will come to this application. The actual registration name is the return value stored as a string in dcopID on line 15.

No two processes can be registered by the same name, so the dcopserver detects collisions and modifies the registration name The first collision will result in the registration name being "wilbur-2," the next will be "wilbur-3," and so on. Alternatively, you can choose to generate unique registration names by using TRUE as the second argument to registerAs(), causing the process ID number to be appended as part of the name. For example, if the process ID of an instance wilbur is 34212, the registration name would be "wilbur-34212." This is guaranteed to always produce a unique registration name.

The top-level widget is established on lines 17 and 18. The name assigned to the widget is "wilreceiver." It is perfectly valid for a single process to contain more than one DCOPObject, and each one of them can be used to receive messages, so it is necessary to supply a name for each one.

Lines 20 through 22 display the registered name of this DCOPClient.

The main loop of the GUI application is executed by the call to exec() on line 24. The call to detach() on line 25 is made to remove the registration from dcopserver. This is not strictly necessary because the registration is removed automatically whenever a process ceases execution.

The constructor of `WilReceiver` on line 28 sets the `QMultiLineEdit` window to read-only, which means that the text displayed there cannot be edited.

The `process()` method on line 34 is called whenever a message arrives from the `dcopserver`. There are four arguments to the method:

`const QCString function`	The name and argument types of the procedure to be called
`const QByteArray &data`	The arguments to be passed to the called procedure
`QCString &replyType`	The data type of the value returned from the procedure
`QByteArray &replyData`	The returned value

The `if` statement on line 39 verifies that the function and data type match the one that is available. A number of local procedures can be available — it is only necessary to add a test for each one to determine which is to be called.

Note

The terminology tends to get a bit confusing with remote procedure calls. The remote process requests a call to a procedure named `cubeRoot(double)`, which could be either a function or a method. Or it could be simply an inline execution, or even implemented in an entirely different language. As long as the interface is consistent, and the results are achieved, the details of the actual process don't matter.

The argument (or arguments) to be passed to the procedure arrive packed into a `QByteArray`, so it is necessary to use the `QDataStream` created on line 42 to extract the actual values. In this example, there is only one argument, and it is extracted into `inValue` on line 43. The method `cubeRoot()` is called on line 44, with the results stored in `outValue`. The return value is packed into `replyData` on line 46 using the output stream created on line 45. The data type of the return value is stored in `replyType` on line 47. The return value of `TRUE` is used to indicate success.

Note

If the code required to respond to a message seems a bit clumsy, that is because it has been designed for automatic generation. This entire process should all be simplified in the near future because there is a project underway to have the contents of the `process()` method automatically generated by a compiler, much like the MOC compiler generates the code for signals and slots.

The `cubeRoot()` method on line 57 accepts a double value as an argument and returns its cube root. It also displays the incoming number, and its root, as a line of text in the window. This method is called remotely, but it is a normal method and could be called locally as well.

TellWilbur

```
1 /* tellwilbur.cpp */
2 #include <kapp.h>
3 #include <qcstring.h>
4 #include <dcopclient.h>
5
6 int main(int argc,char **argv)
7 {
8     KApplication app(argc,argv,"tellwilbur");
9
10    DCOPClient *client = app.dcopClient();
11    QCString dcopID = client->registerAs(app.name());
12
13    QByteArray params;
14    QDataStream stream(params,IO_WriteOnly);
15    stream << (double)999.0;
16    if(!client->send("wilbur","wilreceiver",
17            "cubeRoot(double)",params)) {
18        qDebug("Well, that didn't work!");
19    }
20
21    client->detach();
22    return(0);
23 }
```

This program sends a message to wilbur, but does not wait for the response.

To be able to communicate using DCOP, it is necessary to register with dcopserver. This means that it is necessary to create a KApplication object, use it to retrieve the address of the local DCOPClient, and then call registerAs() with the name of this application.

Because the arguments to the remote procedure are sent packed into a QByteArray, it is necessary to create a QDataStream object on line 14 and store a double argument value in it on line 15. The call to send() on line 16 sends the message, but does not wait for an answer. The first argument is "wilbur", which is the registered name of the application to receive the message. The second argument is "wilreceiver", which is the name of a DCOPObject inside the application. The procedure to be called is named "cubeRoot(double)". The final argument, params, contains the argument values to be passed to the procedure.

Note   As described earlier, the registration name may have a number appended to it, such as "wilbur-29003." To discover what the actual name is, your application may need to call registeredApplications() of the DCOPClient class. This method returns a QCStringList object containing all of the registered names, and your application can search it to find the name (or names) you need.

The send() method does not wait for the answer, so there is no provision for a return value. All that is left to do is the call to detach() on line 21 that removes the registration from dcopserver.

AskWilbur

```
 1 /* askwilbur.cpp */
 2 #include <kapp.h>
 3 #include <qcstring.h>
 4 #include <dcopclient.h>
 5
 6 int main(int argc,char **argv)
 7 {
 8     KApplication app(argc,argv,"askwilbur");
 9
10     DCOPClient *client = app.dcopClient();
11     QCString dcopID = client->registerAs(app.name());
12
13     QByteArray params;
14     QByteArray reply;
15     QCString replyType;
16     QDataStream stream(params,IO_WriteOnly);
17     stream << (double)888.0;
18     if(!client->call("wilbur","wilreceiver",
19             "cubeRoot(double)",params,
20             replyType,reply)) {
21         qDebug("Well, that didn't work!");
22     } else {
23         QDataStream inStream(reply,IO_ReadOnly);
24         if(replyType == "double") {
25             double root;
26             inStream >> root;
27             QString str;
28             str.sprintf("The return value is %g",root);
29             qDebug(str);
30         }
31     }
32
33     client->detach();
34     return(0);
35 }
```

This example does the same thing the previous one does, except this one waits for and displays a result.

The call to call() on line 18 sends the message and waits for the result. The call is the same as send() in the previous example, except for the two return-value arguments on line 20. The replyType argument returns with the data type of the return value, and the reply argument contains the actual return value.

If the call to call() succeeds, the QDataStream on line 23 is created to read the values from the returned QByteArray. The data type of the returned value is verified on line 24, and is extracted into the local variable root on line 26. It is used to build the string named str, and then displayed. The output looks like this:

```
The return value is 9.61179
```

Figure 15-1 shows the window displayed by wilbur after one message has been received from tellwilbur and another from askwilbur.

Figure 15-1: Wilbur after receiving two messages

Command-Line Arguments

The KCmdLineArgs class not only handles most of the work of validating and parsing the command-line arguments, it also does it in such a way that the command-line arguments for all KDE applications will be consistent. The following simple program demonstrates the basics of using KCmdLineArgs.

CommandLine

```
 1 /* commandline.cpp */
 2 #include <kcmdlineargs.h>
 3 #include <iostream.h>
 4
 5 static KCmdLineOptions options[] = {
 6     {"x","A binary option",0},
 7     {"o <name>","An option with data","/dev/null"},
 8     {"longbin","A binary option",0},
 9     {"longdata <name>","An option with data","/dev/null"},
10     {"t",0,0},
11     {"twoforms","Two forms of a binary option",0},
12     {0,0,0}
13 };
14
15 int main(int argc,char **argv)
16 {
17     QCString option;
18     KCmdLineArgs::init(argc,argv,
19             "commandline",
```

```
20                    "Example of command line parsing",
21                    "Version 0.0");
22        KCmdLineArgs::addCmdLineOptions(options);
23        KCmdLineArgs *pargs = KCmdLineArgs::parsedArgs();
24
25        if(pargs->isSet("x"))
26            cout << "   -x is set" << endl;
27        else
28            cout << "   -x is not set" << endl;
29        option = pargs->getOption("o");
30        cout << "   -o is set to " << option << endl;
31        if(pargs->isSet("longbin"))
32            cout << "   --longbin is set" << endl;
33        else
34            cout << "   --longbin is not set" << endl;
35        option = pargs->getOption("longdata");
36        cout << "   --longdata is set to " << option << endl;
37
38        pargs->clear();
39        return(0);
40 }
```

The available command-line arguments are defined as an array of KCmdLineOptions objects on line 5. Each option definition consists of three strings. The first string is the letter (or letters) that appear on the command line, the second is a brief description of the option, and the third is an optional initial value string. The array of options is terminated by an entry containing three null strings on line 12.

The call to the static method init() on line 18 initializes the static data of the KCmdLineArgs class. The first two arguments are the standard argc and argv variables from the C++ command line. These are followed by the name of the program, a brief description of the program, and the program's current version number.

The call to addCmdLineOptions() on line 22 stores the KCmdLineOptions table information inside the KCmdLineArgs class. This list of options, along with the predefined ones inside the KCmdLineArgs class, is all the information needed to determine the value for all the possible option settings.

The call to the static method parseArgs() on line 23 validates the command line against the defined options. If there are no errors, this method returns a pointer to a KCmdLineArgs object with the argument values prepared for retrieval by your program. If an invalid argument is found on the command line, the program displays an error message and halts the program.

The -x option, defined on line 6, is a binary flag. That is, it carries no information other than whether or not it appeared on the command line. The call to isSet() on line 25 will return TRUE if the value appeared on the line, and return FALSE if not.

The -o option, defined on line 7, is an option requiring that a value follow it on the command line. The definition supplies the default value string that will be used if one is not supplied on the command line. The call to getOption() on line 29 retrieves the argument value, whether or not it is the default.

If the name of an option is more than one character in length, it requires a double dash on the command line. The --longbin option defined on line 8 is a binary flag that is tested by the call to isSet() on line 31. The --longdata option requires that data accompany it, and its value is returned by the call to getOption() on line 35.

Lines 10 and 11 are an example of defining two flags that mean the same thing. By leaving both the second and third arguments as null pointers, the -t option becomes a synonym for the --twoforms option. You can use either one on the command line, and inside the program.

The call to clear() on line 38 is not really necessary in this example because the program is about to exit, but you may find this method useful to free allocated memory in cases where the argument data is very large.

With this example, the following command line specifies two of the flags:

```
commandline -x --longdata /mnt/fred
```

The text displayed by the program looks like this:

```
-x is set
-o is set to /dev/null
--longbin is not set
--longdata is set to /mnt/fred
```

If there is an error, the call to parseArgs() on line 23 halts the program and displays a message. For example, the following command line specifies an unknown flag:

```
commandline -x -j
```

The output includes the name of the program and specifies the unknown option like this:

```
commandline: Unknown option '-j'.
commandline: Use --help to get a list of available
        command line options.
```

Using the --help option results in a complete list of the available options:

```
Usage: commandline [Qt-options] [KDE-options] [options]

Example of command line parsing
```

```
Generic options:
  --help                    Show help about options
  --help-qt                 Show Qt specific options
  --help-kde                Show KDE specific options
  --help-all                Show all options
  --author                  Show author information
  -V, --version             Show version information
  --                        End of options

Options:
  -x                        A binary option
  -o <name>                 An option with data [/dev/null]
  --longbin                 A binary option
  --longdata <name>         An option with data [/dev/null]
  -t, --twoforms            Two forms of a binary option
```

A Unique Application

Certain applications need to guard against having more than one copy of themselves being executed at any one time. This is achieved by having an application attempt to register with the DCOP server and, if it finds itself already registered, assume that another copy of itself is already running. The following example uses KUniqueApplication instead of KApplication to guarantee that there will never be more than one instance of the program:

Unique

```
1  /* unique.cpp */
2
3  #include <kuniqueapp.h>
4  #include <kaboutdata.h>
5  #include <kcmdlineargs.h>
6  #include <qlabel.h>
7  #include <iostream.h>
8
9  static KCmdLineOptions options[] = {
10     {"x","A Binary option",0},
11     {0,0,0}
12 };
13
14 int main(int argc,char **argv)
15 {
16     KAboutData about("unique",
17         "Example of unique application",
18         "0.1");
19     KCmdLineArgs::init(argc,argv,&about);
20     KCmdLineArgs::addCmdLineOptions(options);
21     KUniqueApplication::addCmdLineOptions();
22
23     if(!KUniqueApplication::start()) {
24         cout << "Unique is already running" << endl;
```

```
25          exit(0);
26      }
27
28      KUniqueApplication kuapp;
29      QLabel *label = new QLabel("Unique",0);
30      label->setAlignment(Qt::AlignVCenter
31              | Qt::AlignHCenter);
32      label->show();
33      kuapp.setMainWidget(label);
34      return(kuapp.exec());
35  }
```

The call to the `init()` method of `KCmdLineArgs` on line 19 parses and stores any command-line arguments. The `KAboutData` object contains the basic application definition strings — the program name, a brief descriptive name, and the version number. The call to `addCmdLineOptions()` on line 20 is used to define the options declared in the table declared on line 9, and the call to `addCmdLineOptions()` on line 21 includes any options that are specified to the `KUniqueApplication` class.

The call to `start()` on line 23 is only necessary if you need to know whether this instance of the program is going to run, or if it is going to be terminated because it is not unique. If you don't make the call to `start()`, and a copy of the program is already running, this program will silently halt when the attempt is made to create the `KUniqueApplication` object on line 28.

The `KUniqueApplication` class uses `KApplication` as a base class, so the `kuapp` object created on line 28 can be treated as if it were a `KApplication` object. A `QLabel` widget is created and installed as the main window widget on lines 29 through 33, and the application's execution loop is invoked on line 34.

An Example Applet

An applet is a program that displays a single small window; and the window is in the KDE panel, or kicker, that normally appears at the bottom of the display. Other that this windowing limitation, an applet can be as large and as complicated as any other program.

The follow example applet displays a panel window containing some text, and it responds to a mouse button by starting the `kmail` application. This is a very simple applet. To be useful, it would be necessary to add safeguards to prevent the application from being accidentally started several times, and supply some sort of feedback so the user will know that the applet is responding to the mouse.

Because the panel can be configured to show itself either vertically or horizontally, and because the window sizing rules are slightly different between the two orientations, it is necessary for the applet to tell the panel what its size is for each of the orientations.

MailApplet Header

```
 1 /* mailapplet.h */
 2 #ifndef MAILAPPLET_H
 3 #define MAILAPPLET_H
 4
 5 #include <qfontmetrics.h>
 6 #include <kpanelapplet.h>
 7
 8 class MailApplet: public KPanelApplet
 9 {
10     Q_OBJECT
11 public:
12     MailApplet(QWidget *parent=0,const char *name=0);
13     int widthForHeight(int height);
14     int heightForWidth(int width);
15     void about();
16     void help();
17     void preferences();
18 protected:
19     void paintEvent(QPaintEvent *e);
20     void mousePressEvent(QMouseEvent *e);
21 };
22
23 #endif
```

The base class of an applet is KPanelApplet. Because KPanelApplet uses QWidget as one of its base classes, your code will have direct access to the window. The macro Q_OBJECT on line 10 is used by the MOC compiler, just as with any other KDE windowing application, so you can use the standard form of slots and signals. The methods widthForHeight() and heightForWidth() are declared as virtual methods in the base class, so they must be implemented by the applet.

MailApplet

```
 1 /* mailapplet.cpp */
 2 #include <kapp.h>
 3 #include <kcmdlineargs.h>
 4 #include <kmessagebox.h>
 5 #include <kaboutdialog.h>
 6 #include <qpainter.h>
 7 #include <stdlib.h>
 8 #include "mailapplet.h"
 9
10 #define vText "VERT"
11 #define hText "HORIZ"
12
13 int main(int argc,char **argv)
14 {
15     KCmdLineArgs::init(argc,argv,
16         "mailapplet",
```

```
17              "Mail Applet Example",
18              "Version 0.0");
19      KApplication app;
20      MailApplet *applet = new MailApplet(0,"mailapplet");
21      app.setMainWidget(applet);
22      applet->init(argc,argv);
23      return(app.exec());
24 }
25 MailApplet::MailApplet(QWidget *parent,const char *name)
26              : KPanelApplet(parent,name)
27 {
28      setActions(About | Help | Preferences);
29      setFont(QFont("Courier",16,QFont::Bold));
30 }
31 void MailApplet::about()
32 {
33      KAboutDialog *about = new KAboutDialog(0,"mailapplet");
34      about->exec();
35 }
36 void MailApplet::help()
37 {
38      KMessageBox::information(0,
39              "The MailApplet Help Dialog");
40 }
41 void MailApplet::preferences()
42 {
43      KMessageBox::information(0,
44              "The MailApplet Preferences Dialog");
45 }
46 int MailApplet::heightForWidth(int width)
47 {
48      QFontMetrics fm = fontMetrics();
49      return(fm.height());
50 }
51 int MailApplet::widthForHeight(int height)
52 {
53      QFontMetrics fm = fontMetrics();
54      return(fm.width(hText));
55 }
56 void MailApplet::paintEvent(QPaintEvent *e)
57 {
58      QPainter p(this);
59      QFontMetrics fm = fontMetrics();
60      if(orientation() == Vertical) {
61          int y = height() / 2;
62          y += (fm.ascent() - fm.descent()) / 2;
63          int x = (width() - fm.width(vText)) / 2;
64          p.drawText(x,y,vText);
65      } else {
66          int y = height() / 2;
67          y += (fm.ascent() - fm.descent()) / 2;
```

```
68              int x = (width() - fm.width(hText)) / 2;
69              p.drawText(x,y,hText);
70         }
71 }
72 void MailApplet::mousePressEvent(QMouseEvent *e)
73 {
74      system("kmail &");
75 }
```

An applet is very much like any other application. The main difference is that the main widget uses the KPanelApplet class for its base class (which, in turn, uses QWidget as its base class).

The mainline of the applet, beginning on line 13, uses KCmdLineArgs to read any command-line information and to initialize the descriptive text information. On line 19, a KApplication object is created without arguments because it uses the global information stored by the init() method of KCmdLineArgs. The main widget of this application is created on lines 20 and 21. On line 22, the call to the init() method of the KPanelApplet base class of the MailApplet passes any command-line arguments to the applet.

The MailApplet constructor on line 25 passes the parent widget and the applet name to the KPanelApplet constructor. The call to setActions() on line 28 specifies which of the three optional menu items are to be included on the applet menu. (To make this menu appear, use the right mouse button on the bar that moves an applet.) In this example, all three of the optional menu items will appear. The call to setFont() on line 29 sets the default font of the widget.

Because the About option was specified by setActions() on line 28, the about() method on line 31 is called whenever the user selects "About" from the menu. This example simply displays an empty About box. In the same way, the "Help" and "Preferences" menu items cause the help() and preference() methods, on lines 36 and 41, to be called because both Help and Preference were specified in the call to setActions().

When the panel is oriented horizontally, all of the applets have a fixed height, but can vary in width. To determine the width, a call is made to the method widthFor Height() on line 51. In case your applet needs it to make size determinations, the value of the height is supplied and this method must calculate and return the width. In this example, the width is simply the horizontal extent of the text, as shown in Figure 15-2.

Figure 15-2: An applet with the panel oriented horizontally

When the panel is oriented vertically, the applets all have a fixed width, but each one can specify its own height. To do this, the method `heightForWidth()` on line 46 is called. In this example, the height is that of the text being displayed, as shown in Figure 15-3.

Figure 15-3: An applet with the panel oriented vertically

The `paintEvent()` method, on line 56, is called whenever the widget needs to be drawn. The `orientation()` method on line 60 returns either `Vertical` or `Horizontal` depending on the orientation of the panel. In this example, text is chosen that describes the orientation, and the position of the text is calculated so it will appear in the center of the applet window.

This example implements the `mousePressEvent()` method on line 72 and responds to any mouse click by starting the `kmail` application.

Summary

Ease of communications among applications can be very important in systems that are complex enough to require more than one running program. Furthermore, using a standard method enables communication with applications written as part of other projects. This chapter explored the following:

✦ KDE sends and receives interprocess messages though the intermediate background process named `dcopserver`.

✦ Using the `KCmdLineArgs` class to read and process command-line arguments simplifies the task of programming command-line parsing, and standardizes the argument format for all KDE applications.

✦ Using `KUniqueApplication` in place of `KApplication` ensures that only one copy of your program is running at any one time.

The following chapter describes a few general utility classes that you can employ to handle tasks such as read and writing files, and manipulating date and time information.

✦   ✦   ✦

Some General Utility Classes

◆ ◆ ◆ ◆

In This Chapter

Manipulating strings by using the string classes

Running a timer that notifies your program when it expires

Marking the current time and checking for elapsed time later

Performing date and calendar arithmetic

Reading text from a file

Writing text to a file

◆ ◆ ◆ ◆

Along with the classes used for creating a GUI interface are some utility classes that come in handy for some other tasks. In particular, the ability to quickly and efficiently work with strings of characters can be very important. With so much string manipulation involved in displaying and retrieving data, programming the string handling can be very time-consuming without some facilities to make the job easier.

Another issue that often arises in programming an application is the ability to handle calendar and clock arithmetic. While there is always an operating system call that will return the time in some form or another, the ability to perform sophisticated operations on the time values can take a lot of programming — for example, if you have a pair of dates, how can you determine how many days are between them?

Most large data files are given over to a database package for storage and retrieval, but most programs of any size use small text files to contain special data. Although the C and C++ standard languages supply some very simple ways to read and write these files, there is still the problem of formatting and unformatting the data they contain.

This chapter covers some very handy classes that go a long way toward solving these problems. While it is by no means a complete list of all the classes available in Qt, it covers a collection of some of the core classes — some of the most obviously useful ones.

The String Classes

A lot of programming involves string manipulation. This is true of all programming, but it is particularly true of programming for a user interface. The data is converted into strings to be displayed, and the data entered by the user is converted from strings of characters to some internal data form. Making all of this easier to handle are some special string handling classes.

Examining a QString

The QString class is probably the most fundamental string class, and the one you should probably be using. The QString class has a large number of methods that can be used for string manipulation, and it stores the data internally as Unicode.

There is no incompatibility between Unicode and the ASCII character set, except that Unicode contains a lot more characters. The standard 7-bit ASCII character set is limited to 127 characters, which include the Latin alphabet, digits, punctuation, and a few control characters (such as Carriage Return and Escape). The Unicode standard uses 16-bit characters, so it can contain up to 65,536 unique characters. However, the first 127 characters of the Unicode character set (numeric values 0 through 127) are the same as the ASCII character set, so it is trivial to convert ASCII into Unicode. It is also trivial to convert Latin character Unicode into ASCII.

Cross-Reference   For more information about using Unicode, see Chapter 17.

The following example shows some of the methods available to locate and extract sections of a string:

```
1  /* stringexamine.cpp */
2  #include <qstring.h>
3  #include <iostream.h>
4
5  int main(int argc,char **argv)
6  {
7      QString qstring;
8      QChar qchar;
9
10     qstring =
11       "There is much more to KDE than just a pretty face.";
12
13     cout << qstring << endl;
14     cout << "The string contains "
15             << qstring.length() << " characters." << endl;
16     qchar = qstring[4];
17     cout << "The 5th charater is '"
18             << (char)qchar.unicode() << "'." << endl;
19     cout << "The first 'u' is at "
20             << qstring.find('u') << "." << endl;
21     cout << "The last 'u' is at "
22             << qstring.findRev('u') << "." << endl;
```

```
23        cout << "The first 're' is at "
24                << qstring.find("re") << "." << endl;
25        cout << "The last 're' is at "
26                << qstring.findRev("re") << "." << endl;
27        cout << "There are "
28                << qstring.contains('e') << " 'e's." << endl;
29        cout << "There are "
30                << qstring.contains("re") << " 're's." << endl;
31        cout << "The leading 7 characters are '"
32                << qstring.left(7) << "'." << endl;
33        cout << "The trailing 7 characters are '"
34                << qstring.right(7) << "'." << endl;
35        cout << "The 8 characters at index 22 are '"
36                << qstring.mid(22,8) << "'." << endl;
37
38        return(0);
39 }
```

The output from this program looks like the following:

```
There is much more to KDE than just a pretty face.
The string contains 50 characters.
The 5th charater is 'e'.
The first 'u' is at 10.
The last 'u' is at 32.
The first 're' is at 3.
The last 're' is at 39.
There are 5 'e's.
There are 3 're's.
The leading 7 characters are 'There i'.
The trailing 7 characters are 'y face.'.
The 8 characters at index 22 are 'KDE than'.
```

There are a variety of constructors that can be used to create a QString. A QString can be created from a simple char array, a QByteArray, a QChar, an array of QChar objects, another QString, or by specifying nothing at all (resulting in a string of zero length). A QChar object is a wrapper for a single Unicode character, and is described in more detail in the next chapter.

There are a few overloaded operators that provide string manipulation. On lines 10 and 11 of this example, the assignment operator is used to convert a character string to Unicode and store it in the QString object. There are also assignment operator overloads for QString, QCString, QChar, and char. Similarly, the += operator can be used to append a QString, QChar, or char onto the end of an existing QString.

The find() methods on lines 20 and 23 scan from the beginning of the string to find the first occurrence of a character, or a string of characters, and return the index to the start of the located substring. The findRev() methods on lines 22 and 26 scan from the end of the string to find the last occurrence, and return the index of the start of the substring. The `contains()` methods on lines 28 and 30 scan the entire string and return a count of the number of occurrences of a character or a substring.

The methods `left()` and `right()` on lines 32 and 34 return a QString containing the specified number of characters found at the beginning or end of a string. The `mid()` method on line 36 returns a QString containing the specified number of characters from an index point of the string. (In this example, the index is 22 and the character count is 8.)

Modifying a QString

A number of methods can be used to modify the contents of a QString. The following example demonstrates some of the more useful ones:

```
 1 /* stringmodify.cpp */
 2 #include <qstring.h>
 3 #include <iostream.h>
 4
 5 QString init(QString str)
 6 {
 7     str = "There is more to KDE than a pretty face.";
 8     return(str);
 9 }
10
11 int main(int argc,char **argv)
12 {
13     QString qstring;
14
15     cout << "Unchanged: "
16            << init(qstring) << endl;
17     cout << "Uppper case: "
18            << init(qstring).upper() << endl;
19     cout << "Lower case: "
20            << init(qstring).lower() << endl;
21     cout << "Insert 'X': "
22            << init(qstring).insert(10,'X') << endl;
23     cout << "Insert 'ABC': "
24            << init(qstring).insert(10,"ABC") << endl;
25     cout << "Prepend 'X': "
26            << init(qstring).prepend('X') << endl;
27     cout << "Prepend 'ABC': "
28            << init(qstring).prepend("ABC") << endl;
29     cout << "Append 'X': "
30            << init(qstring).append('X') << endl;
31     cout << "Append 'ABC': "
32            << init(qstring).append("ABC") << endl;
33     cout << "Remove 10: "
34            << init(qstring).remove(15,10) << endl;
```

```
35          cout << "Replace 10: "
36                  << init(qstring).replace(15,10,"ABC") << endl;
37
38          return(0);
39 }
```

The output looks like this:

```
Unchanged: There is more to KDE than a pretty face.
Uppper case: THERE IS MORE TO KDE THAN A PRETTY FACE.
Lower case: there is more to kde than a pretty face.
Insert 'X': There is mXore to KDE than a pretty face.
Insert 'ABC': There is mABCore to KDE than a pretty face.
Prepend 'X': XThere is more to KDE than a pretty face.
Prepend 'ABC': ABCThere is more to KDE than a pretty face.
Append 'X': There is more to KDE than a pretty face.X
Append 'ABC': There is more to KDE than a pretty face.ABC
Remove 10: There is more t a pretty face.
Replace 10: There is more tABC a pretty face.
```

This example uses the init() function on line 5 to initialize the string because each of the QString methods modifies the contents of the QString object.

The upper() and lower() methods on lines 18 and 20 convert every alphabetical character in a string to either uppercase or lowercase. There is no change to any characters other than those that are alphabetical and are the opposite case of the method.

The insert() methods on lines 22 and 24 lengthen the string by shifting a portion of the string to the right by the number of characters to be inserted. The character, or characters, passed as arguments are then inserted into the hole left in the string.

The prepend() methods on lines 26 and 28 lengthen the string by shifting all of the characters of the string to the right by the number of characters to be inserted. The character, or characters, passed as arguments are then inserted into the hole left at the front of the string.

The append() methods on lines 30 and 32 lengthen the string by the number of characters to be inserted, and then store the character in the hole left at the right end of the string.

The remove() method on line 34 shortens the line by shifting the right end of the string left by the number of specified characters. This overwrites a group of characters in the middle, effectively removing them from the string. In this example, the index is 15 and the number of characters removed is 10.

The replace() method on line 36 can be used to lengthen the string, shorten it, or leave it the same length. In any case, some of the characters in the string are replaced. The process is functionally the same as a remove() followed by an insert(). The characters to the right of the index point (in this example, 15) are shifted to the right or left depending on the number of characters to be inserted and removed (in this example, the shift is to the left by 7 characters because 10 are to be removed and 3 inserted). The specified string is then used to overwrite the line at the point of the index.

QString Number Conversion

Included as part of the QString class are some direct conversion methods between numbers and character representations of numeric values. The following example demonstrates how they work:

```
1  /* stringnumber.cpp */
2  #include <qstring.h>
3  #include <iostream.h>
4
5  int main(int argc,char **argv)
6  {
7      QString qstring;
8      bool Ok;
9
10     int inum = 9421;
11     qstring.setNum(inum);
12     cout << "Short string: " << qstring << endl;
13     inum = qstring.toInt(&Ok);
14     cout << "Short value: " << inum << endl;
15
16     double dnum = 2813.8282190;
17     qstring.setNum(dnum);
18     cout << "Double string at 6: " << qstring << endl;
19     dnum = qstring.toDouble(&Ok);
20     cout << "Double value at 6: " << dnum << endl;
21
22     dnum = 2813.8282190;
23     qstring.setNum(dnum,'g',9);
24     cout << "Double string at 9: " << qstring << endl;
25     dnum = qstring.toDouble(&Ok);
26     cout << "Double value at 9: " << dnum << endl;
27
28     ulong ulnum = 0xCFA90B2;
29     qstring.setNum(ulnum,16);
30     cout << "Ulong string: " << qstring << endl;
31     ulnum = qstring.toULong(&Ok,16);
32     cout << "Ulong value: " << ulnum << endl;
33
34     qstring.sprintf("The int is %d and the long is %lu",
35             inum,ulnum);
36     cout << qstring << endl;
```

```
37
38      return(0);
39 }
```

The output from this program looks like the following:

```
Short string: 9421
Short value: 9421
Double string at 6: 2813.83
Double value at 6: 2813.83
Double string at 9: 2813.82822
Double value at 9: 2813.83
Ulong string: cfa90b2
Ulong value: 217747634
The int is 9421 and the long is 217747634
```

This example shows just a few of the data types. Along with the int, double, and ulong data types shown here, the same technique can be used for long, uint, short, ushort, char, and QChar.

The call to setNum() on line 11 converts the value of an int into a string of characters, as displayed by cout on line 12. The call to toInt() on line 13 reads the characters of the QString and converts them to an int value, as displayed on line 14. The bool argument passed to toInt() will result in TRUE if the conversion was successful, or FALSE if it was not (for example, if there were no digits in the string).

The call to setNum() on line 17 converts the double value into a string. The default is for the number to contain six digits, as shown by the cout statement on line 18. Notice that to reduce the number of digits, the value is rounded instead of simply truncated. When converted back from a string to its numeric form by the call to toDouble() on line 19, it only contains the six digits that were stored in the character string.

Lines 22 through 26 use the same double value as before, but this time the number of digits is set to 9, resulting in a longer string and a bit more accuracy. The letter *g* is used to format the string. This is the default, but the standard sprintf() real number options are available; that is, *f*, *F*, *e*, *E*, *g*, or *G*.

As shown by the call to setNum() on line 29, it is possible to convert values in bases other than 10. This example converts a 32-bit hexadecimal number from a ulong type to a string. Calling toULong() on line 31 converts the string of hexadecimal characters back into the binary form. The setNum() method converts the numbers into all lowercase letters, but toULong() will convert back from both lowercase and uppercase.

The traditional sprintf() function is available, as shown on line 34. The format of the arguments is the same as in standard C, and the resulting string is stored inside the QString object.

The QString Translator

The built-in translator can be very convenient for constructing strings that are to be displayed as the text of a dialog, or as the text of a button or label. It is similar to the sprintf() function, but it is somewhat easier to use because it automatically detects different data types. The following example shows how it works with a pair of int values:

```
 1 /* stringargs.cpp */
 2 #include <kapp.h>
 3 #include <qlabel.h>
 4
 5 class StringArgs: public QWidget
 6 {
 7 public:
 8     StringArgs(QWidget *parent=0,const char *name=0);
 9 };
10 int main(int argc,char **argv)
11 {
12     KApplication app(argc,argv,"stringargs");
13     StringArgs stringargs;
14     app.setMainWidget(&stringargs);
15     stringargs.show();
16     return(app.exec());
17 }
18
19 StringArgs::StringArgs(QWidget *parent,const char *name)
20         : QWidget(parent,name)
21 {
22     int y = 60;
23     int x = 210;
24     QString str;
25
26     resize(x,y);
27     str = tr("Width is %1 and height is %2").arg(x).arg(y);
28     QLabel *label = new QLabel(str,this);
29     label->setGeometry(20,20,170,20);
30 }
```

The tr() method on line 27 creates a QString object and uses the two arg() methods to convert data to strings and insert the strings at the positions tagged as %1 and %2. There can be as many of the arg() methods as necessary to convert all the data. The arg() methods are positional, with the first one corresponding to %1, the second to %2, and so on. The window displayed by this program is shown in Figure 16-1.

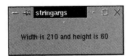

Figure 16-1: Data conversion and formatting

Other than the `int` data types in this example, there are overloaded `arg()` methods for `long`, `ulong`, `uint`, `short`, `ushort`, `char`, `QChar`, `QString`, and `double`. This kind of translation can only be used inside an object that inherits from `QObject` because the translation method is `QObject::tr()`.

The White Space of a QString

In character strings, the whitespace characters are tab (\t), newline (\n), form feed (\f), carriage return (\r), and the space character. There are a couple of handy methods for cleaning up the white space in a character string. The following string is an example:

```
"     This has\t tabs \nand\nnewlines in it    \n    "
```

The white space can be removed from the front and back of the string as follows:

```
str.stripWhiteSpace();
```

The result looks like this:

```
"This has\t tabs \nand\nnewlines in it"
```

The white space from the interior of the line, as well as the front and back, can be cleaned up as follows:

```
str.simplifyWhiteSpace();
```

The front and back are trimmed, and multiple internal whitespace characters are reduced to single spaces. The result looks like this:

```
"This has tabs and newlines in it"
```

QStringList

A `QStringList` object is a variable length array of `QString` objects. You can perform some special operations on it that can make it very useful. The following example demonstrates ways to insert strings into the array, and some ways that the strings can be manipulated:

```
1 /* stringlist.cpp */
2 #include <qstringlist.h>
3 #include <iostream.h>
4
5 int main(int argc,char **argv)
6 {
7     QStringList list;
8
```

```
 9      list.append("First");
10      list += "Second";
11      list << "Third" << "Fourth" << "Fifth";
12      for(int i=0; i<list.count(); i++)
13          cout << list[i] << endl;
14
15      QString joined = list.join("^");
16      cout << endl << joined << endl;
17
18      list << "Apple" << "apple";
19      list.sort();
20      cout << endl;
21      for(int i=0; i<list.count(); i++)
22          cout << list[i] << endl;
23
24      list = list.grep("e");
25      cout << endl;
26      for(int i=0; i<list.count(); i++)
27          cout << list[i] << endl;
28
29      list = QStringList::split("|","Make|a|list|from|this");
30      cout << endl;
31      for(int i=0; i<list.count(); i++)
32          cout << list[i] << endl;
33
34      list[1] = "This replaces the 'a' string";
35      cout << endl;
36      for(int i=0; i<list.count(); i++)
37          cout << list[i] << endl;
38
39      return(0);
40  }
```

The output from this program looks like the following:

```
First
Second
Third
Fourth
Fifth

First^Second^Third^Fourth^Fifth

Apple
Fifth
First
Fourth
Second
Third
apple
```

```
Apple
Second
apple

Make
a
list
from
this

Make
This replaces the 'a' string
list
from
this
```

Lines 9 through 11 show the different ways a string can be appended to the end of the array. The append() method and the += operator can both be used to add a string at the end of the array. The << operator can be used for the same thing; it can also be used to add several strings as a single operation. You can see from the output that the strings are stored in the order they are appended to the code. The [] operator is overloaded to retrieve strings according to their index value.

The join() method on line 15 creates one long string from all the members of the array by inserting the specified separator string between them.

Two more members are appended to the end of the array on line 18. The sort() method on line 19 sorts the array of strings using the numeric values of the characters. This is a very fast sort, and it can be useful in many instances, but there are times when the order may not be what you want. For example, as shown in the output, uppercase letters always come before lowercase letters.

The call to grep() on line 24 creates a new QStringList object that contains only the characters matched by the specified expression on the method call. In this example, only strings containing the letter *e* are stored in the new QStringList object.

A QStringList object can be created from a single string by breaking it up using a specified delimiter string. There is a third argument (not used in the example) that is set to TRUE if two back-to-back delimiters should be considered as one, or set to FALSE if the zero-length strings should be allowed. The default is TRUE.

The use of the [] operator on line 34 shows that it is possible to replace an existing string by using its index. Care must be taken, however, that the subscript value is valid—the size of the array cannot be modified this way.

Running a Timer

The bouncer program in Chapter 13 includes an example of using a QTimer object to implement a one-shot interval timer, but there is another (possibly simpler) way to run a continuous timer, one that uses events instead of signals. The following example shows how you can implement continuous timers by using the methods in the QObject class:

```cpp
1 /* stringlist.cpp */
2 #include <qapplication.h>
3 #include <iostream.h>
4
5 class TwoTimer: public QObject
6 {
7 public:
8     TwoTimer(QObject *parent=0,const char *name=0);
9 private:
10    int ID1;
11    int ID2;
12    bool timer2;
13 protected:
14    void timerEvent(QTimerEvent *event);
15 };
16
17 TwoTimer::TwoTimer(QObject *parent,const char *name)
18         : QObject(parent,name)
19 {
20    ID1 = startTimer(2000);
21 }
22 void TwoTimer::timerEvent(QTimerEvent *event)
23 {
24    if(event->timerId() == ID1) {
25        cout << "Timer 1" << endl;
26        if(timer2) {
27            killTimer(ID2);
28            timer2 = FALSE;
29        } else {
30            ID2 = startTimer(200);
31            timer2 = TRUE;
32        }
33    } else if(event->timerId() == ID2) {
34        cout << "Timer 2" << endl;
35    }
36 }
37
38 int main(int argc,char **argv)
39 {
40    QApplication app(argc,argv);
41    TwoTimer *to = new TwoTimer();
42    return(app.exec());
43 }
```

You can run as many simultaneous timers as you need. Each timer, while it is running, is assigned a unique ID number. The `TwoTimer` class in this example runs two timers and stores the ID numbers in `ID1` and `ID2` on lines 10 and 11.

The constructor, beginning on line 17, starts one of the timers running by calling `startTimer()` on line 20. This timer is set to trigger every 2,000 milliseconds (two seconds), and has its ID number stored as `ID1`.

The method `timerEvent()` is a protected method defined in the `QObject` class, and is overridden on line 22 of this example. Every timer calls this same event method. The `QTimerEvent` object contains the ID number of the timer, so it is relatively simple to determine which timer has expired and caused the method call.

In this example, whenever the first timer expires, the second timer is either started or stopped. On line 26, the Boolean `timer2` is tested. If it is `TRUE`, the second timer is running; and it is stopped by calling `killTimer()`. If it is `FALSE`, the second timer is started with a call to `startTimer()`, with an interval time of 200 milliseconds (2/10 of a second).

The mainline of the program, beginning on line 38, creates a `QApplication` object, which initializes the Qt system that will control the timers. After the timer is created, a call is made to the `exec()` method of `QApplication` object. The timing is all managed inside the `exec()` loop.

There is one other method that deals with timers, but it is not used in this example. A call to the method `killTimers()` will stop all timers.

The QDate Class

The following example demonstrates the `QDate` class, which is capable of containing any date from 1752 to about the year 8000. The reason why 1752 is the lower limit is because that is the year marking the beginning of the Gregorian calendar, with the leap year pattern we use today. (To see how the calendar was adjusted in that year, enter `cal 1752` from the command line and take a look at September.) The year can also be entered into a `QDate` object as a two-digit value (00 to 99), and the century 1900 will be assumed. I suppose there was some solution to the Y2K problem that required that it be this way, but it just means you need to be careful now.

```
1 /* showdate.cpp */
2 #include <qdatetime.h>
3 #include <qstring.h>
4 #include <iostream.h>
5
6 int main(int argc,char **argv)
7 {
```

```
 8      if(argc != 4) {
 9          cout << "Usage: showdate <yy> <mm> <dd>" << endl;
10          return(1);
11      }
12      QString yy = argv[1];
13      QString mm = argv[2];
14      QString dd = argv[3];
15      QDate date(yy.toInt(),mm.toInt(),dd.toInt());
16      if(!date.isValid()) {
17          cout << "Invalid date" << endl;
18          return(2);
19      }
20
21      cout << "Date: " << date.toString() << endl;
22      cout << "yyyy/mm/dd: " << date.year() << "/"
23          << date.month() << "/" << date.day() << endl;
24      cout << "Day of week: " << date.dayOfWeek() << " ("
25          << date.dayName(date.dayOfWeek()) << ")" << endl;
26      cout << "Month name: "
27          << date.monthName(date.month()) << endl;
28      cout << "Day of year: " << date.dayOfYear() << endl;
29      cout << "Days in month: "
30          << date.daysInMonth() << endl;
31      cout << "Days in year: " << date.daysInYear() << endl;
32
33      return(0);
34  }
```

To run this program, enter the year, month, and day on the command line:

```
showdate 1964 3 12
```

The output from the program looks like the following:

```
Date: Thu Mar 12 1964
yyyy/mm/dd: 1964/3/12
Day of week: 4 (Thu)
Month name: Mar
Day of year: 72
Days in month: 31
Days in year: 366
```

There are two ways to store a date into a QDate object. One way is to specify the year, month, and day values on the constructor, as shown in this example. The other way is to specify the year, month, and day values in a call to setYMD(). Care must be taken to ensure that the date is valid before you use the information from a QDate object. As shown on line 16 of this example, a call to isValid() is all that is required. Also, the setYMD() method returns a bool value indicating whether the date is valid.

You can use a static method to create a QDate object containing the current date:

```
QDate qdate = QDate::currentDate();
```

You can also adjust a date by specifying a number of days to move forward or backward. For example, use the following line to move the date 15 days into the future:

```
QDate date2 = date.addDays(15);
```

If the number of days is negative, the new QDate object will contain a date 15 days in the past, instead of the future. This is the only date adjustment needed. It is a simple matter to use the other available values to adjust the date to any specific point. For example, the following will move the date to the first day of the following month:

```
QDate date2 = date.addDays(date.daysInMonth()-date.day()+1);
```

The number of days, positive or negative, from one date to another can be determined as follows:

```
int days = date.daysTo(date2);
```

Finally, the following group of comparison operators can determine the relationship between two dates:

```
if(date1 == date2) . . .
if(date1 != date2) . . .
if(date1 < date2) . . .
if(date1 > date2) . . .
if(date1 <= date2) . . .
if(date1 >= date2) . . .
```

The QTime Class

The QTime class is simpler than the QDate class in the sense that the counting is more regular (unlike months and years, hours and minutes all have the same length). However, the fact that it can be used as an elapsed timer adds some complexity the QTime class. Here's an example:

```
 1 /* showtime.cpp */
 2 #include <qdatetime.h>
 3 #include <iostream.h>
 4 #include <unistd.h>
 5
 6 int main(int argc,char **argv)
 7 {
 8     if(argc != 5) {
```

```
 9              cout << "Usage: showtime <hh> <mm> <ss> <ms>"
10                   << endl;
11              return(1);
12          }
13          QString hh = argv[1];
14          QString mm = argv[2];
15          QString ss = argv[3];
16          QString ms = argv[4];
17          QTime qtime(hh.toInt(),mm.toInt(),
18                  ss.toInt(),ms.toInt());
19          if(!qtime.isValid()) {
20              cout << "Invalid time" << endl;
21              return(2);
22          }
23
24          cout << "Time: " << qtime.toString() << endl;
25          cout << "hh:mm:ss.ms: " << qtime.hour() << ":"
26              << qtime.minute() << ":" << qtime.second() << "."
27              << qtime.msec() << endl;
28
29          qtime.start();
30          cout << "Start time: " << qtime.toString() << endl;
31          sleep(2);
32          int milliseconds = qtime.restart();
33          cout << "Restart time: " << qtime.toString()
34              << " (after " << milliseconds << " milliseconds)"
35              << endl;
36          for(int i=0; i<5; i++) {
37              cout << "Elapsed: " << qtime.elapsed() << endl;
38              sleep(1);
39          }
40
41          return(0);
42  }
```

The output from this program looks like the following:

```
Time: 15:04:22
hh:mm:ss.ms: 15:4:22.431
Start time: 08:42:07
Restart time: 08:42:09 (after 2010 milliseconds)
Elapsed: 1
Elapsed: 1010
Elapsed: 2020
Elapsed: 3030
Elapsed: 4040
```

The QTime constructor has a fourth argument that is the fractional part of a second in milliseconds (from 0 to 999). This fourth argument is optional and defaults to 0. To avoid entering a number that is outside the normal range for hours, minutes, and seconds, you should call the isValid() method to make sure the time is valid before you try to use the QTime object.

The start() method on line 29 does two things: It loads the QTime object with the current time and sets an elapsed timer value to 0. You can also create a new QTime object that contains the current time by calling the static method currentTime():

```
QTime qtime = QTime::currentTime();
```

The call to the restart() method on line 32 also sets the QTime object to the current time and restarts the elapsed timer, but it returns the value of the elapsed timer, which is the count of the number of milliseconds since the last call to start() or restart(). As you can see from the sample output, the elapsed time is 2 seconds (2,000 milliseconds) plus another 10 milliseconds of overhead before the value is displayed.

The loop beginning on line 36 makes repeated elapsed() calls and pauses for 1 second. From the output, you can see that the elapsed time continues to count upward, and there is a 10-millisecond delay to read and display the elapsed timer.

Note
    The elapsed timer is only good for 24 hours, at which time it will automatically reset to 0. Also, the current time of QTime is based on your computer's system clock, so changing the system clock in any way will have an effect on the elapsed timer. This includes the automatic switching to and from daylight saving time.

You can use either of two methods to adjust the time into the future or the past. They both operate by creating a new QTime object that contains the new time value:

```
QTime qtime2 = qtime.addSecs(int seconds);
QTime qtime2 = qtime.addMSecs(int milliseconds);
```

A negative value will adjust the time into the past, and a positive value will adjust it into the future. It is valid to add or subtract values sufficient to cause the time to advance beyond midnight. For example, if the current time is 23:59:45 and you add 30 seconds, the result will be 00:00:15.

The following group of comparison operators can determine the relationship between two times:

```
if(time1 == time2) . . .
if(time1 != time2) . . .
if(time1 <  time2) . . .
if(time1 >  time2) . . .
if(time1 <= time2) . . .
if(time1 >= time2) . . .
```

The QDateTime Class

The QDateTime class is basically a wrapper around a combination of a QDate class and a QTime class. It has some methods that enable you to operate on the two as if they were one. The following example demonstrates the basic operations available in the QDateTime class:

```
 1  /* showtime.cpp */
 2  #include <qdatetime.h>
 3  #include <iostream.h>
 4  #include <time.h>
 5
 6  int main(int argc,char **argv)
 7  {
 8      time_t bintime;
 9
10      QDate qdate(2002,5,12);
11      QTime qtime(04,32,58);
12      QDateTime dt(qdate,qtime);
13      if(!dt.isValid()) {
14          cout << "Invalid QDateTime" << endl;
15          return(2);
16      }
17
18      cout << "Date and Time: " << dt.toString() << endl;
19      QDate d = dt.date();
20      cout << "Date: " << d.toString() << endl;
21      QTime t = dt.time();
22      cout << "Time: " << t.toString() << endl;
23
24      QDateTime current;
25      bintime = time((time_t *)0);
26      current.setTime_t(bintime);
27      cout << "Current date and time: "
28          << current.toString() << endl;
29      cout << "Days between: "
30          << current.daysTo(dt) << endl;
31      cout << "Seconds between: "
32          << current.secsTo(dt) << endl;
33
34      return(0);
35  }
```

The output from this program looks like the following:

```
Date and Time: Sun May 12 04:32:58 2002
Date: Sun May 12 2002
Time: 04:32:58
Current date and time: Wed Jun 28 09:51:26 2000
Days between: 683
Seconds between: 58992092
```

Lines 10 through 12 show the construction of a QDateTime object using both a QDate and QTime object. There is also a constructor that requires only a QDate object — internally it constructs a QTime object set to 00:00:00.

The QDate object can be extracted by the call to date(), as shown on line 19. There is also a setDate() method that can be used to insert a new QDate object. The same is true for the QTime object with the methods time() (as shown on line 21), and setTime().

Both the time and date values can be set from the 32-bit system time number, which is the count of seconds from January 1, 1970. The system call to the time() function on line 25 returns the value, and the call to the setTime_t() method of QDateTime is used on line 26 to set the date and time of the QDateTime object.

The call to daysTo() on line 30 returns a count of the number of days between two dates. In the same way, the call to secsTo() on line 32 returns the count of seconds for the same period of time.

The following comparison operators can determine the relationship between two points in time:

```
if(datetime1 == datetime2) . . .
if(datetime1 != datetime2) . . .
if(datetime1 < datetime2) . . .
if(datetime1 > datetime2) . . .
if(datetime1 <= datetime2) . . .
if(datetime1 >= datetime2) . . .
```

Writing to a File

The following example uses a QFile object to create a new file and write two lines of text to it:

```
 1 /* writefile.cpp */
 2 #include <qfile.h>
 3
 4 int main(int argc,char **argv)
 5 {
 6     char line1[] = "The first line\n";
 7     char line2[] = "The second line\n";
 8
 9     QFile qfile("rwfile.txt");
10     if(qfile.open(IO_WriteOnly)) {
11         for(int i=0; i<strlen(line1); i++)
12             qfile.putch(line1[i]);
13         for(int i=0; i<strlen(line2); i++)
14             qfile.putch(line2[i]);
15         qfile.close();
16     }
```

```
17
18      return(0);
19 }
```

The constructor on line 9 creates the QFile object without making a reference to the disk drive. At this point, the file may or may not exist.

 Note   The QFile class inherits from the QIODevice class, which means that it can be used to stream input and output. For most purposes, using a QDataStream or QTextStream object is simpler than using the QFile object directly.

The open() method on line 10 opens the file for write-only, and returns TRUE if successful or FALSE if opening the file fails. Opening a file for write-only will create the file if it does not exist, or truncate it to zero length if it does. The file opening modes are shown in Table 16-1. These flags can be combined by using the OR operator between them. For example, to write without buffering, a file could be opened as IO_Raw | WriteOnly.

Table 16-1
Modes Available for Opening a File

Mode	Description
IO_Raw	The file is opened without buffering. The default is to use buffering.
IO_ReadOnly	The file is opened for reading. If the file does not exist, it is created.
IO_WriteOnly	The file is opened for writing only. The file is truncated to zero length, or a new zero-length file is created.
IO_ReadWrite	The file is opened for both reading and writing. An existing file will not be truncated. A non-existent file will be created.
IO_Append	The file is opened for writing, with the next write position being the end of the file. An existing file will not be truncated. A non-existent file will be created.
IO_Truncate	Truncates the file to zero length.
IO_Translate	Files will be translated to and from the DOS format. Writing a newline character will cause both a carriage return and line feed to be written to the file. The reading of a carriage return and line feed will be translated to a single newline character.

All writing is done one byte at a time. The putch() method on lines 12 and 14 writes one character at a time to the file. The close() method on line 15 should be called when the writing is done—this flushes the buffers to make sure the data gets written to disk.

from character to numeric format, and you know the format of the file. The following is an example of formatted text in a file:

```
orange 255 127 80 72.81 J
```

The following example reads the line of text while converting each word on the line into an appropriate data type, and then displays data by re-creating the format of the input line:

```
 1  /* streamtextin.cpp */
 2  #include <qfile.h>
 3  #include <qtextstream.h>
 4  #include <iostream.h>
 5
 6  int main(int argc,char **argv)
 7  {
 8      QString name;
 9      int r;
10      int g;
11      int b;
12      double percent;
13      char code;
14
15      QFile qfile("strext.txt");
16      if(qfile.open(IO_ReadOnly)) {
17          QTextStream stream(&qfile);
18          stream >> name;
19          stream >> r >> g >> b;
20          stream >> percent;
21          stream >> code;
22          cout << name << " "
23               << r << " " << g << " " << b << " "
24               << percent << " " << code << endl;
25          qfile.close();
26      }
27
28      return(0);
29  }
```

The file is opened for input as a QFile object on lines 15 and 16. The QTextStream object is created as a wrapper of the QFile object on line 17. The >> operator on line 18 reads all the characters up until the space is encountered, and stores them in the QString object named name. The three int values are read by a single statement on line 19. These values could have been read by using three separate statements. Or, you can have your code read the entire line in one statement simply by chaining the >> operators. After reading the double and char values on lines 20 and 21, the original input line is re-created and written to the standard output on lines 22 through 24.

Summary

The classes described in this chapter are all very useful. Any program of any size will require some facet of almost everything covered in this chapter. While these are not the classes that grab the glory by displaying themselves, the work they do is essential. In this chapter you discovered:

✦ The QString class is very flexible, and is used so much by the other classes that it becomes one of the most fundamental classes in Qt and KDE software development.

✦ Because every class inherits from QObject, there is an interval timer available inside every object. It can be started, stopped, and set to trigger at any specific interval. It notifies your program when it expires by issuing an event.

✦ The classes QDate, QTime, and QDateTime provide a number of methods that can be used for calendar and clock arithmetic.

✦ A QFile object can be used to read and write any kind of data to and from a file.

✦ A QTextStream object can be used to read and write formatted data to and from a file.

Among other things, the next chapter includes a description of Unicode and the QChar class. The QChar class is almost as fundamental as the QString class described in this chapter. Because the strings and string manipulation utilities of Qt and KDE are based on Unicode, supplying multiple translations for an application is a very straightforward process.

✦   ✦   ✦

Internationalization and Configuration

The acronym *i18n* is short for "i-eighteen-letters-n" and represents the term *internationalization*. Built into the KDE development system are some facilities that make programming international versions of KDE applications quite simple. If you follow some basic rules as you write your program, preparing translation tables for your application becomes a straightforward process. Once these tables are created, your program will instantly translate itself when it starts running. You will also find some utilities that not only facilitate the initial translation into other languages, but also facilitate updating the translations that follow any future changes to the software.

This chapter explains how you can also set up configuration files that enable each user to customize an application. These files can be maintained globally, so every user gets the same configuration; or locally, so each user can have individual configuration settings.

A Translatable Application

It is remarkably simple to create a KDE application that can be translated into multiple languages as it runs. By following a few rules in declaring text that is to be displayed and/or printed, and having your application test for the presence of a translation file, your application will be capable of translating itself into almost any language.

The following example demonstrates how you can write an application and create translation files for it.

TriLang Header

```
 1 /* trilang.h */
 2 #ifndef TRILANG_H
 3 #define TRILANG_H
 4
 5 #include <qwidget.h>
 6 #include <qlabel.h>
 7
 8 class TriLang: public QWidget
 9 {
10     Q_OBJECT
11 public:
12     TriLang(QWidget *parent=0,const char *name=0);
13 private:
14     QLabel *label;
15     enum ButtonChoice { Rock, Paper, Scissors,
16             Clear, Exit };
17     QString emptyString;
18 private slots:
19     void slotButton(int ID);
20 };
21
22 #endif
```

This header defines the TriLang widget that is to be displayed as the top-level window. It includes the enum value definitions used to determine which button has been clicked.

Every string to be displayed is declared inside a tr() method call, which does the actual translation. In this example, if a language code is specified on the command line, an attempt is made to read a file by that name. If text is found, it is translated. If it is not found, a message window pops up and the program continues to run without translation.

TriLang

```
 1 /* trilang.cpp */
 2 #include <kapp.h>
 3 #include <qlayout.h>
 4 #include <qhbuttongroup.h>
 5 #include <qpushbutton.h>
 6 #include <qmessagebox.h>
 7 #include <qfileinfo.h>
 8 #include "trilang.h"
 9
10 int main(int argc,char **argv)
11 {
12     KApplication app(argc,argv,"trilang");
13
```

```
14        QString lang = argv[1];
15        QString langFile = "trilang_" + lang + ".qm";
16        QFileInfo finfo(langFile);
17        if(finfo.exists()) {
18            QTranslator *qtranslator = new QTranslator(0);
19            qtranslator->load(langFile,".");
20            app.installTranslator(qtranslator);
21        } else {
22            QMessageBox::warning(0,"Language File",
23                "Unable to open language file " + langFile);
24        }
25
26        TriLang *trilang = new TriLang();
27        trilang->show();
28        app.setMainWidget(trilang);
29        return(app.exec());
30 }
31
32 TriLang::TriLang(QWidget *parent,const char *name)
33     : QWidget(parent,name)
34 {
35        QPushButton *button;
36        QVBoxLayout *layout = new QVBoxLayout(this,5);
37
38        QHButtonGroup *group = new QHButtonGroup(this,"group");
39        button = new QPushButton(tr("Rock"),group);
40        group->insert(button,Rock);
41        button = new QPushButton(tr("Paper"),group);
42        group->insert(button,Paper);
43        button = new QPushButton(tr("Scissors"),group);
44        group->insert(button,Scissors);
45        button = new QPushButton(tr("Clear"),group);
46        group->insert(button,Clear);
47        button = new QPushButton(tr("Exit"),group);
48        group->insert(button,Exit);
49        connect(group,SIGNAL(clicked(int)),
50                this,SLOT(slotButton(int)));
51        layout->addWidget(group);
52
53        emptyString = tr("-0-");
54        label = new QLabel(emptyString,this);
55        label->setAlignment(AlignVCenter | AlignHCenter);
56        layout->addWidget(label);
57
58        resize(10,10);
59        layout->activate();
60 }
61 void TriLang::slotButton(int ID)
62 {
63        switch(ID) {
64        case Rock:
```

```
65              label->setText(tr("Rock breaks scissors"));
66              break;
67         case Paper:
68              label->setText(tr("Paper covers rock"));
69              break;
70         case Scissors:
71              label->setText(tr("Scissors cut paper"));
72              break;
73         case Clear:
74              label->setText(emptyString);
75              break;
76         case Exit:
77              kapp->exit(0);
78         }
79 }
```

Lines 14 through 16 construct the name of a translation file from the code supplied on the command line. This is normally a two-character code, such as de for German and en for English, but there is no inherent requirement. However, many applications follow the naming convention presented here — application name, underscore, two-letter language code, and a suffix of qm — so it would normally be prudent for your application to do the same.

The text on line 17 determines whether the file exists. If it does, a QTranslator object is created on line 18. A QTranslator object is capable of loading and containing translation tables. Once the QTranslator is loaded, the find() method can be used to translate a known set of words and phrases. The load() method on line 19 reads the translation tables stored in the file that was selected by the code on the command line. The call to installTranslator() on line 20 establishes this new QTranslator as the one to be used to translate all the strings for this application.

If there is no translation file, the QMessageBox on line 22 notifies the user, but the program continues with execution. A missing translation file is not an error as far as the program is concerned — it will run normally, but without any translations.

A horizontal button group is created on line 38 of the TriLang constructor. The widget is assigned the internal name "group," and this name will not be translated. You could translate it, but there is no need to translate strings that are for internal use. The only strings that need to be translated are the ones to be displayed.

A QPushButton is created on line 39. The label for the button is declared as "Rock" and, to make the label translatable, the label is declared as an argument to the method tr(). Because it is declared inside tr(), this string is subject to translation. The labels for the other buttons, on lines 41 through 47, are all declared the same way.

On line 53, the QString object named emptyString is assigned its initial value. Again, the quoted literal string is defined as an argument passed to tr(), so it is also subject to translation.

The `slotButton()` method, beginning on line 61, sets the text to one of several values. In each case, the literal string is defined inside a call to `tr()`. The call to `setText()` on line 75 uses `emptyString`, but it doesn't have to be translated because the value that was stored in `emptyString` has already been translated.

If you run this program without translation (by either not specifying a file or specifying a file that doesn't exist), the window looks like the one shown in Figure 17-1.

Figure 17-1: Running TriLang without a translation file

There are two translation files (described in detail in the following sections) that cause the same application to look very different. A translation file doesn't have to change every string displayed. Figure 17-2 shows the appearance of the same window with only two or three of the strings translated.

Figure 17-2: Running TriLang with minimal translation

It is possible to change every string displayed. Figure 17-3 shows a result of translating everything available in the translation file.

Figure 17-3: Running TriLang with full translation

Declaring Translatable Strings

Other than loading the translation file, about all your application will need to do is make sure that the things you want to translate are declared as an argument to the `tr()` method. The `tr()` method is available to every object that inherits `QObject`. This includes all `QWidget` objects, so it should be available almost everywhere you are working with displayable text.

The `tr()` method returns a `QString` object, so anywhere you would normally use `QString`, you can use `tr()`. For example, let's say you have a `QLabel` declaration that looks like the following:

```
QLabel *label = new QLabel("Select",this);
```

To make it translatable, you would change the code to enclose the string as an argument in a `tr()` call:

```
QLabel *label = new QLabel(tr("Select"),this);
```

It is possible that you find yourself without access to a `tr()` method, where you are declaring the string is outside of an object inheriting from `QObject`. There are still some things you can do. The most obvious solution is to borrow `tr()` from another widget. For example, if you are working inside a function and want to create a label to be used later, you can use the `QLabel`'s parent widget as follows:

```
QLabel *label = new QLabel(parent::tr("Select"),parent);
```

If you need to declare a static string, two macros can be used. One is for use inside the method of a class. For example:

```
TriLang::fstr() {
    static char *f = QT_TR_NOOP("String text");
}
```

The `QT_TR_NOOP` macro doesn't contain any executable code, but it does mark the string in the source code for translation. This string will be translated as a member of the `TriLang` class, because it is declared inside a method that is a member of that class. If you need to make a static declaration outside of a class, a slightly different macro is needed:

```
static char *f QT_TRANSLATE_NOOP("TriLang","String text");
```

Because the declaration is outside of a class, the name of a class is also required. This is because the class name is used internally as a key for the translation process, as described later in this chapter. You can use the name of any class. Again, this macro doesn't do anything except mark the text for translation.

Manipulating Translated Strings

If you are going to be formatting strings in any way, always do it using `QString`. Never use an array of `char` or the `QCString` class to manipulate displayable strings. If you are going to be working with individual characters, use `QChar` because it provides all the functionality you need to work with a Unicode character. (There is more information about Unicode and `QChar` later in this chapter.)

If you are going to format data into a string, use the arg() facility of QString. For example, say you want to use an int and a double value to display the following line:

```
Step 3 is 34.6 percent complete.
```

The following is the correct way to format this string:

```
QString report;
report = tr("Step %1 is %2 percent complete.")
        .arg(step).arg(percent);
```

This way, the string presented to the person doing the translation is the following:

```
"Step %1 is %2 percent complete."
```

Translation may require that the values be inserted in a different order. This gives the translator the freedom to re-order the values if necessary. For example, the statement could be simply reworded this way:

```
"Completion now at %2 percent of step %1"
```

Constructing the Translation Files

Once the application has been written and all the character strings have been defined properly for translation, it is time to construct the translation files.

The findtr utility is used to create a file containing all the strings to be translated. In the example we are using in this chapter, there is the untranslated version in English, and two other versions devised just for this example. To create the starter files, the following commands are entered:

```
findtr *.cpp *.h >trilang.po
cp trilang.po trilang_en.po
cp trilang.po trilang_sh.po
cp trilang.po trilang_sl.po
```

All three of the translation files start off with the same contents. The findtr utility creates the file with some header information at the top, but the active portion of the file looks like this:

```
#: trilang.cpp:53
msgid "TriLang::-0-"
msgstr ""

#: trilang.cpp:45
msgid "TriLang::Clear"
msgstr ""
```

```
#: trilang.cpp:47
msgid "TriLang::Exit"
msgstr ""

#: trilang.cpp:68
msgid "TriLang::Paper covers rock"
msgstr ""

#: trilang.cpp:41
msgid "TriLang::Paper"
msgstr ""

#: trilang.cpp:65
msgid "TriLang::Rock breaks scissors"
msgstr ""

#: trilang.cpp:39
msgid "TriLang::Rock"
msgstr ""

#: trilang.cpp:71
msgid "TriLang::Scissors cut paper"
msgstr ""

#: trilang.cpp:43
msgid "TriLang::Scissors"
msgstr ""
```

The msgid string is the key used to search for translations. Each msgid entry is the string as it appears in the original program. Each string is preceded by the name of the class that contains it, and a pair of colons. The msgstr is to contain the translated string. If the translated string is left empty, as in this example, no translation will take place. All of the files start off containing the same thing, and only the msgstr entries need to be changed for each entry. For example, the file trilang_sh.po file contains the following:

```
#: trilang.cpp:53
msgid "TriLang::-0-"
msgstr "***"

#: trilang.cpp:45
msgid "TriLang::Clear"
msgstr "Erase"

#: trilang.cpp:47
msgid "TriLang::Exit"
msgstr ""

#: trilang.cpp:68
msgid "TriLang::Paper covers rock"
```

```
msgstr "Sheet covers rock"

#: trilang.cpp:41
msgid "TriLang::Paper"
msgstr "Sheet"

#: trilang.cpp:65
msgid "TriLang::Rock breaks scissors"
msgstr ""

#: trilang.cpp:39
msgid "TriLang::Rock"
msgstr ""

#: trilang.cpp:71
msgid "TriLang::Scissors cut paper"
msgstr "Scissors cut sheet"

#: trilang.cpp:43
msgid "TriLang::Scissors"
msgstr ""
```

The name of the class is not included as part of the translated string in `msgstr`. It is included as part of the `msgid` only as a key to match the strings with the translations. Also, it is not necessary to do anything at all with entries that are not to be translated.

Once you have created and edited the `.po` files, it is necessary to convert them into the `.qm` files that are used by the application. The utility `msg2qm` is used to convert the three files in this example as follows:

```
msg2qm trilang_en.po trilang_en.qm
msg2qm trilang_sh.po trilang_sh.qm
msg2qm trilang_sl.po trilang_sl.qm
```

That's it. When the program runs, it reads and uses the appropriate `.qm` file. If you need to modify the translation in any way, it is simply a matter of editing the `.po` file and using it to create a new `.qm` file.

If you change your program so that the strings it contains are changed in some way, you don't have to start over. The `mergetr` utility enables you to retain the work you have already done and merge the information into it. You will need to generate a new `.po` file and merge the changes as follows:

```
findtr *.cpp *.h >trilang.po
mergetr trilang_en.po trilang.po
mergetr trilang_sh.po trilang.po
mergetr trilang_sl.po trilang.po
```

This will give you three updated .po files with all of the previous information intact, and with the changes merged in. If one of the entries was changed in the original code, requiring a change to a previously translated string, the previous translation is included as a comment so the translator will have something to start with when updating the files.

Unicode and QChar

The standard character set of KDE and Qt is Unicode. Each character is represented by 16 bits, which means that there can be as many as 65,536 distinct characters. Thus far, this has been enough space to contain every possible character from every language in the world.

Note   Unicode has been able to represent every character handed to it, and will continue to do so in the foreseeable future. It even includes the complete Klingon alphabet. However, there is speculation that, in the not-too-distant future, each Unicode character may need to be expanded to 32 bits to include characters yet to come.

The Unicode values 0 through 127 represent the same characters as the ASCII character set (in which each character is a 7-bit value in the range 0 to 127). This makes mapping a character from ASCII to Unicode trivial, but mapping from Unicode to ASCII will require some translation. In any case, this allows you to write your programs in ASCII and have things automatically converted to Unicode as necessary.

When working with text, it is often necessary to be able to recognize spaces, punctuation, case, and other character attributes. In ASCII, this is easy to do because there are so few characters. Unicode is another matter, and new characters can be added at any time. To handle this, each Unicode character is assigned a set of attributes. Your program can check a character for some specific attribute and determine whether it is, say, an uppercase letter or a digit. Each category is represented by a two-letter code. Table 17-1 lists the *Normative* categories — which are descriptive of the basic nature of the character in its linguistic origin. Table 17-2 lists the *Informative* categories — which are descriptive of things about the character other than its basic linguistic origin.

Table 17-1 Unicode Normative Categories	
Name	*Code*
Mark_Enclosing	**Me**
Mark_NonSpacing	**Mn**
Mark_SpacingCombining	**Mc**

Name	Code
Number_Letter	Nl
Number_Other	No
Other_Control	Cc
Other_Format	Cf
Other_NotAssigned	Cn
Other_PrivateUse	Co
Other_Surrogate	Cs
Separator_Line	Zl
Separator_Paragraph	Zp
Separator_Space	Zs

Table 17-2
Unicode Informative Categories

Name	Code
Letter_Uppercase	Lu
Letter_Lowercase	Ll
Letter_Titlecase	Lt
Letter_Modifier	Lm
Letter_Other	Lo
Punctuation_Connector	Pc
Punctuation_Dash	Pd
Punctuation_Open	Ps
Punctuation_Close	Pe
Punctuation_InitialQuote	Pi
Punctuation_FinalQuote	Pf
Punctuation_Other	Po
Symbol_Math	Sm
Symbol_Currency	Sc
Symbol_Modifier	Sk
Symbol_Other	So

All of this means that, if you are working with internationalization, determining whether a character is a letter, digit, punctuation, or some kind of white space is a bit more difficult than using the traditional isspace() and isupper() macros defined in C for ASCII. To simplify things, the class contains a single Unicode character and provides a number of methods that manipulate it and provide information about its characteristics.

The following constructors can be used to create a QChar object:

```
QChar()
QChar(char c)
QChar(uchar c)
QChar(uchar cell, uchar row)
QChar(const QChar &c)
QChar(ushort rc)
QChar(short rc)
QChar(uint rc)
QChar(int rc)
```

All of these use the numeric value passed in as the 16-bit Unicode character. If no argument is supplied, the Unicode null character 0x0000 is used. The two constructors that accept 8-bit values assume that the value is an ASCII character and set the most significant byte to 0. The constructor expecting two 8-bit values uses the value of cell for the least significant byte, and row as the most significant.

The following Boolean methods can be used to determine basic characteristics of the characters:

```
bool isDigit() const
bool isLetter() const
bool isLetterOrNumber() const
bool isMark() const
bool isNull() const
bool isNumber() const
bool isPrint() const
bool isPunct() const
bool isSpace() const
```

Each method determines its return value by looking at the characteristics of the character. For example, isNumber() will return TRUE if the character is a digit in any language—that is, if it is either a Number_Letter or Number_Other from Table 17-1.

If you need more detailed information, the following method returns an enumerated type that contains an entry for each of the types named in Tables 17-1 and 17-2:

```
Category category() const
```

The most common character conversion is changing its case, which can be done with the following methods:

```
QChar lower() const
QChar upper() const
```

The following methods can be used to return the numeric value of the Unicode character:

```
ushort unicode() const
char latin1() const
uchar &cell()
uchar cell() const
uchar &row()
uchar row() const
int digitValue() const
```

The `unicode()` method returns the 16-bit value of the character. The `latin1()` method returns the 8-bit value of an ASCII character — if the character is not ASCII, the method returns 0. The `cell` value is the least significant byte; the `row` value is the most significant. The `digitValue()` method does not return the character — if the character is a digit, the method returns the numeric value of the digit as an `int`.

Configuration

The `KConfig` class can be used to save environment settings from one invocation of the program to the next. The settings are saved in text files with a special format. Each setting is saved as a keyword andvalue pair, and these pairs can be optionally divided into groups. The following example demonstrates how this works by displaying a window that can be moved and resized, and retains its size and position even when you stop the process and start it over again.

Remember Header

```
 1 /* remember.h */
 2 #ifndef REMEMBER_H
 3 #define REMEMBER_H
 4
 5 #include <qwidget.h>
 6
 7 class Remember: public QWidget
 8 {
 9 public:
10     void configure();
11 private:
```

```
12      QSize windowSize;
13      QPoint windowPosition;
14 protected:
15      virtual void paintEvent(QPaintEvent *);
16      virtual void resizeEvent(QResizeEvent *);
17      virtual void moveEvent(QMoveEvent *);
18      virtual void closeEvent(QCloseEvent *);
19 };
20
21 #endif
```

The Remember **widget is the toplevel window of the application. The** windowSize **and** windowPosition **values on lines 12 and 13 hold the continuously updated geography information for the window.**

Remember

```
 1 /* remember.cpp */
 2 #include <kapp.h>
 3 #include <kconfig.h>
 4 #include <qpainter.h>
 5 #include <qdir.h>
 6 #include "remember.h"
 7
 8 int main(int argc,char **argv)
 9 {
10     KApplication app(argc,argv,"remember");
11     Remember remember;
12     remember.configure();
13     remember.show();
14     app.setMainWidget(&remember);
15     return(app.exec());
16 }
17 void Remember::paintEvent(QPaintEvent *)
18 {
19     QPainter p(this);
20
21     p.setWindow(0,0,300,300);
22     p.drawRoundRect(50,50,200,200,30,30);
23     p.setBrush(QColor("white"));
24     p.drawEllipse(100,100,100,100);
25 }
26 void Remember::resizeEvent(QResizeEvent *event)
27 {
28     windowSize = event->size();
29 }
30 void Remember::moveEvent(QMoveEvent *event)
31 {
32     windowPosition = event->pos();
```

```
33 }
34 void Remember::closeEvent(QCloseEvent *event)
35 {
36     QString str;
37
38     KConfig *config =
39         new KConfig(QDir::homeDirPath() + "/.remember");
40     config->setGroup("Geometry");
41     config->writeEntry("width",
42             str.setNum(windowSize.width()));
43     config->writeEntry("height",
44             str.setNum(windowSize.height()));
45     config->writeEntry("xPosition",
46             str.setNum(windowPosition.x()));
47     config->writeEntry("yPosition",
48             str.setNum(windowPosition.y()));
49     config->sync();
50     delete config;
51
52     event->accept();
53 }
54 void Remember::configure()
55 {
56     int width;
57     int height;
58     int x;
59     int y;
60     QString str;
61
62     KConfig *config =
63         new KConfig(QDir::homeDirPath() + "/.remember");
64     config->setGroup("Geometry");
65     width = config->readNumEntry("width",100);
66     height = config->readNumEntry("height",100);
67     x = config->readNumEntry("xPosition",10);
68     y = config->readNumEntry("yPosition",10);
69
70     windowSize = QSize(width,height);
71     windowPosition = QPoint(x,y);
72
73     resize(windowSize);
74     move(windowPosition);
75 }
```

The main() function of the program begins on line 8. It creates a Remember widget
to be used as the top-level window. On line 12, before the window is displayed,
there is a call to the configure() method to read the configuration data and set
the window size and position.

The `paintEvent()` method on line 17 uses a `QPainter` object that automatically rescales its drawing to fit the actual window size. To do this, you call `setWindow()` to establish the maximum values of the width and height, and use those dimensions to fill the rectangle with graphics. Figure 17-4 shows the Remember window in different sizes.

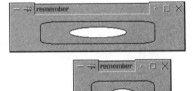

Figure 17-4: The window remembers its size and position.

The `Remember` widget keeps continuous track of its current size and location. The `resizeEvent()` method on line 26 is called whenever the size of the window changes, and the `moveEvent()` on line 30 is called whenever the window is moved. This pair of methods constantly updates the values stored in `windowSize` and `windowPosition`.

The `closeEvent()` method on line 34 is called whenever the application is being closed. To save the current configuration settings, a `KConfig` object is created by opening a file named `.remember` in the user's home directory. The static method `QDir::homeDirPath()` returns the complete path to the current user's home directory, which means that each user will have a separate configuration file for this program.

The call to `setGroup()` on line 40 specifies the group name — inside the file — that will contain the configuration information. There can be any number of groups in a file, and the same key value can appear in any number of the groups. At any one time, the `KConfig` object can only address one group, but you can switch from one group to another by calling `setGroup()`. Each of the calls to `writeEntry()`, on lines 41 through 48, writes a single entry into the configuration. Each entry consists of a value string and the key that is used to find it. The text written to the file by this example looks like the following:

```
[Geometry]
height=170
width=406
xPosition=346
yPosition=130
```

In the file, the group names are included in square brackets, and all the key and value pairs following it are within the group.

The writeEntry() method does not write directly to the file. When the KConfig object was created, it read the file (if any) and loaded all the definitions from it. The calls to writeEntry() on lines 41 through 48 simply update the RAM-resident list of keys and values. That's why it is necessary to call the sync() method on line 49. The sync() method synchronizes the RAM data with the file data by writing everything to the file.

You can actually use the closeEvent() method to prevent the application from closing. In this example, the call to accept() on line 52 indicates that this application accepts the request to close, so the system should go ahead and close the window. If this method were not called, the application would not close, and the default closeEvent() method simply calls accept().

The call to configure() on line 54 reads the previous configuration setting (if any) and uses the data to configure the current application. A KConfig object is created on lines 62 and 63, just is it was in the closeEvent() method, which loads all the configuration information from the file. The call to setGroup() on line 64 specifies that the data be read from the group named "Geometry". The calls to readNumEntry() on lines 65 through 68 are given the keys and return the int values associated with each one. The second argument in the call is the default value returned if the key value is not found. Having a default value in the function call simplifies error handling—if the key is not found, the default value will be used. On lines 70 and 71, these values are stored locally, so they will be saved, changed, or unchanged when the application closes. The calls to resize() and move() on lines 73 and 74 configure the window itself.

Summary

With the advent of the Internet and international distribution of software, it is more important than ever that software be made portable across languages. The facilities built into KDE greatly simplify the process of creating and maintaining software interfaces that can be translated. This chapter discussed portability items such as:

✦ Enclosing literal strings as an argument to the tr() method of QObject will cause the strings to be translated as the program runs.

✦ The translation of statically declared strings that are outside of methods requires that they be enclosed in special macros that cause them to be marked for translation when the program runs.

✦ There are simple utilities to scan the source code of a program and create translation files that can be easily edited by the person doing the actual translations. The content of these files is then read, and substitutions are made for the actual translation process.

✦ Configuration data can be stored in text files in a format that organizes the settings into groups and assigns each one a key with which it can be located.

This chapter completes Part II of the book. The next chapter begins Part III, which primarily consists of reference material, but also includes information needed in some special circumstances. The first chapter of Part III is an alphabetical listing, with brief descriptions, of all the Qt widgets.

✦   ✦   ✦

Reference and Mechanics

The Widgets of Qt

A widget is a class that contains a displayable window. In Qt, all classes that have a displayable window inherit the window capabilities from the QWidget class.

This chapter contains an alphabetical listing of all of the widgets. Each widget is listed with the name of its header file, the names of all the superclasses, the names of all the Qt and KDE subclasses, and the public methods, slots, signals, and enumerated types.

There is at least one example program for each widget, and each example creates a displayable form of the widget. Some of the widgets are demonstrated by being assigned as the top-level widget and displayed as the main window. Some special-purpose widgets, however, are included in a specific environment. In many cases, the widgets are more complicated than can be demonstrated in a simple example, so there are references to locations elsewhere in this book where the widget is used in an example.

QButton

This widget is displayed as a raised rectangle containing text that will respond to the mouse by changing its appearance and issuing a signal.

File
```
#include <qbutton.h>
```
Base Classes
```
QObject QPaintDevice QWidget Qt
```

Inherited By

```
KColorButton KDialogBaseButton KDirectionButton
    KDockButton_Private KIconButton KKeyButton KTabButton
    KToolBarButton QCheckBox QPushButton QRadioButton
    QToolButton
```

Constructors

```
QButton(QWidget *parent = 0, const char *name = 0,
    WFlags f = 0);
```

Methods

```
int accel() const;
bool autoRepeat() const;
bool autoResize() const;
bool focusNextPrevChild(bool next);
QButtonGroup *group() const;
bool isDown() const;
bool isExclusiveToggle() const;
bool isOn() const;
bool isToggleButton() const;
const QPixmap *pixmap() const;
virtual void setAccel(int);
virtual void setAutoRepeat(bool);
virtual void setAutoResize(bool);
virtual void setDown(bool);
virtual void setPixmap(const QPixmap &);
virtual void setText(const QString &);
ToggleState state() const;
QString text() const;
ToggleType toggleType() const;
```

Slots

```
void animateClick();
void toggle();
```

Signals

```
void clicked();
void pressed();
void released();
void stateChanged(int);
void toggled(bool);
```

Enums

```
enum ToggleType { SingleShot, Toggle, Tristate };
enum ToggleState { Off, NoChange, On };
```

Cross-Reference   There is an example of the QButton **widget in Chapter 7.**

QButtonGroup

This widget is a container of a collection of buttons organized either horizontally or vertically.

File

```
#include <qbuttongroup.h>
```

Base Classes

```
QFrame QGroupBox QObject QPaintDevice QWidget Qt
```

Inherited By

```
QHButtonGroup QVButtonGroup
```

Constructors

```
QButtonGroup(QWidget *parent = 0, const char *name = 0);
QButtonGroup(const QString &title, QWidget *parent = 0,
    const char *name = 0);
QButtonGroup(int columns, Orientation o, QWidget *parent = 0,
    const char *name = 0);
QButtonGroup(int columns, Orientation o, const QString &title,
    QWidget *parent = 0, const char *name = 0);
```

Methods

```
int count() const;
QButton *find(int id) const;
int id(QButton *) const;
int insert(QButton *, int id = - 1);
bool isExclusive() const;
bool isRadioButtonExclusive() const;
virtual void moveFocus(int);
void remove(QButton *);
QButton *selected();
virtual void setButton(int id);
virtual void setExclusive(bool);
virtual void setRadioButtonExclusive(bool);
```

Signals

```
void clicked(int id);
void pressed(int id);
void released(int id);
```

This class is not meant to be used directly.

Cross-Reference

You can find examples of QHButtonGroup and QVButtonGroup in Chapter 7.

QCheckBox

This widget is a single check box. A box check can be toggled on and off by the mouse and always displays its current state.

File

```
#include <qcheckbox.h>
```

Base Classes

```
QButton QObject QPaintDevice QWidget Qt
```

Constructors

```
QCheckBox(QWidget *parent, const char *name = 0);
QCheckBox(const QString &text, QWidget *parent,
    const char *name = 0)
```

Methods

```
bool isChecked() const;
void setChecked(bool check);
void setNoChange();
void setTristate(bool y = TRUE);
QSize sizeHint() const;
QSizePolicy sizePolicy() const;
```

 Cross-Reference   Chapter 7 contains a number of examples of the QCheckBox widget being used in vertical and horizontal button groups.

QColorDialog

This class is a collection of static methods that can be used to pop up a dialog prompting the user to select a color.

File

```
#include <qcolordialog.h>
```

Base Classes

```
QDialog QObject QPaintDevice QWidget Qt
```

Methods

```
static QRgb customColor(int);
static int customCount();
static QColor getColor(QColor, QWidget *parent = 0,
    const char *name = 0);
static QRgb getRgba(QRgb, bool *ok = 0, QWidget *parent = 0,
    const char *name = 0);
static void setCustomColor(int, QRgb);
```

The following example uses red as the default selection and prompts the user to either accept that color or select a different one. The dialog is shown in Figure 18-1.

```
/* showcolordialog.cpp */
#include <qapplication.h>
#include <qcolordialog.h>

int main(int argc,char **argv)
{
    QApplication app(argc,argv);
    QColor seedColor("red");
    QColor newColor;
    newColor = QColorDialog::getColor(seedColor);
    return(app.exec());
}
```

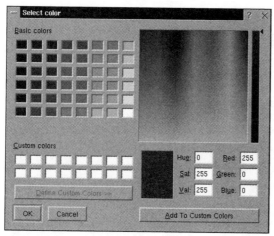

Figure 18-1: A QColorDialog widget

QComboBox

This widget uses a button to enable the user to make a selection from a list. It always displays the current selection.

File

```
#include <qcombobox.h>
```

Base Classes

```
QObject QPaintDevice QWidget Qt
```

Inherited By

KColorCombo KComboBox KFileComboBox KFileFilter KURLComboBox

Constructors

```
QComboBox(QWidget *parent = 0, const char *name = 0);
QComboBox(bool rw, QWidget *parent = 0, const char *name = 0);
```

Methods

```
bool autoCompletion() const;
bool autoResize() const;
void changeItem(const QString &text, int index);
void changeItem(const QPixmap &pixmap, int index);
void changeItem(const QPixmap &pixmap, const QString &text,
    int index);
void clear();
int count() const;
int currentItem() const;
QString currentText() const;
bool duplicatesEnabled() const;
bool eventFilter(QObject *object, QEvent *event);
void insertItem(const QString &text, int index = - 1);
void insertItem(const QPixmap &pixmap, int index = - 1);
void insertItem(const QPixmap &pixmap, const QString &text,
    int index = - 1);
void insertStrList(const QStrList &, int index = - 1);
void insertStrList(const QStrList *, int index = - 1);
void insertStrList(const char **, int numStrings = - 1,
    int index = - 1);
void insertStringList(const QStringList &, int index = - 1);
Policy insertionPolicy() const;
QLineEdit *lineEdit() const;
QListBox *listBox() const;
int maxCount() const;
const QPixmap *pixmap(int index) const;
void removeItem(int index);
virtual void setAutoCompletion(bool);
virtual void setAutoResize(bool);
virtual void setBackgroundColor(const QColor &);
virtual void setCurrentItem(int index);
void setDuplicatesEnabled(bool enable);
virtual void setEnabled(bool);
virtual void setFont(const QFont &);
virtual void setInsertionPolicy(Policy policy);
virtual void setListBox(QListBox *);
virtual void setMaxCount(int);
virtual void setPalette(const QPalette &);
virtual void setSizeLimit(int);
virtual void setValidator(const QValidator *);
QSize sizeHint() const;
int sizeLimit() const;
virtual QSizePolicy sizePolicy() const;
```

```
QString text(int index) const;
const QValidator *validator() const;
```

Slots

```
void clearEdit();
void clearValidator();
virtual void setEditText(const QString &);
```

Signals

```
void activated(int index);
void activated(const QString &);
void highlighted(int index);
void highlighted(const QString &);
void textChanged(const QString &);
```

Enums

```
enum Policy { NoInsertion, AtTop, AtCurrent, AtBottom,
    AfterCurrent, BeforeCurrent };
```

The following example creates a QComboBox with four selections. Figure 18-2 shows the widget after the mouse has been used to pop up the list, and with the second selection as the default.

```
/* showcombobox.cpp */
#include <qapplication.h>
#include <qcombobox.h>

const char *list[] = {
    "First Selection",
    "Second Selection",
    "Third Selection",
    "Fourth Selection"
};

int main(int argc,char **argv)
{
    QApplication app(argc,argv);
    QComboBox *combobox = new QComboBox();
    combobox->insertStrList(list,4);
    combobox->show();
    app.setMainWidget(combobox);
    return(app.exec());
}
```

Figure 18-2: A QComboBox widget with four selections

QDialog

This widget is the base class for dialogs. It can be used as a base class, or it can be instantiated and populated with widgets to dynamically construct a dialog.

File

```
#include <qdialog.h>
```

Base Classes

```
QObject QPaintDevice QWidget Qt
```

Inherited By

```
KAboutDialog KAboutKDE KBugReport KColorDialog KCookieWin
    KDialog KDialogBase KEdFind KEdGotoLine KEdReplace
    KEditToolbar KFileDialog KFileDialogConfigureDlg
    KFontDialog KIconDialog KKeyDialog KLineEditDlg
    KOpenWithDlg KPasswordDialog KTextPrintDialog
    KURLRequesterDlg KWizard KabAPI QColorDialog QFileDialog
    QFontDialog QInputDialog QMessageBox QPrintDialog
    QTabDialog QWizard
```

Constructors

```
QDialog(QWidget *parent = 0, const char *name = 0,
    bool modal = FALSE, WFlags f = 0);
```

Methods

```
int exec();
void hide();
void move(int x, int y);
void move(const QPoint &p);
void resize(int w, int h);
void resize(const QSize &);
int result() const;
void setGeometry(int x, int y, int w, int h);
void setGeometry(const QRect &);
void show();
```

Enums

```
enum DialogCode { Rejected, Accepted };
```

Cross-Reference There are examples of using a QDialog widget to construct dialog windows in Chapter 4.

QFileDialog

This dialog pops up to prompt the user for the name and location of a file.

File

```
#include <qfiledialog.h>
```

Base Classes

```
QDialog QObject QPaintDevice QWidget Qt
```

Constructors

```
QFileDialog(const QString &dirName,
    const QString &filter = QString::null, QWidget *parent = 0,
    const char *name = 0, bool modal = FALSE);
QFileDialog(QWidget *parent = 0, const char *name = 0,
    bool modal = FALSE);
```

Methods

```
const QDir *dir() const;
QString dirPath() const;
bool eventFilter(QObject *, QEvent *);
static QString getExistingDirectory(
    const QString &dir = QString::null, QWidget *parent = 0,
    const char *name = 0);
static QString getExistingDirectory(const QString &dir,
    QWidget *parent, const char *name, const QString &caption);
static QString getOpenFileName(
    const QString &initially = QString::null,
    const QString &filter = QString::null, QWidget *parent = 0,
    const char *name = 0);
static QString getOpenFileName(const QString &initially,
    const QString &filter, QWidget *parent, const char *name,
    const QString &caption);
static QStringList getOpenFileNames(
    const QString &filter = QString::null,
    const QString &dir = QString::null, QWidget *parent = 0,
    const char *name = 0);
static QStringList getOpenFileNames(const QString &filter,
    const QString &dir, QWidget *parent, const char *name,
    const QString &caption);
static QString getSaveFileName(
    const QString &initially = QString::null,
    const QString &filter = QString::null, QWidget *parent = 0,
    const char *name = 0);
static QString getSaveFileName(const QString &initially,
    const QString &filter, QWidget *parent, const char *name,
    const QString &caption);
static QFileIconProvider *iconProvider();
bool isContentsPreviewEnabled() const;
bool isInfoPreviewEnabled() const;
Mode mode() const;
PreviewMode previewMode() const;
void rereadDir();
void resortDir();
void selectAll(bool b);
```

```
QString selectedFile() const;
QStringList selectedFiles() const;
QString selectedFilter() const;
void setContentsPreview(QWidget *w, QFilePreview *preview);
void setContentsPreviewEnabled(bool);
void setDir(const QDir &);
static void setIconProvider(QFileIconProvider *);
void setInfoPreview(QWidget *w, QFilePreview *preview);
void setInfoPreviewEnabled(bool);
void setMode(Mode);
void setPreviewMode(PreviewMode m);
void setSelection(const QString &);
void setShowHiddenFiles(bool s);
void setViewMode(ViewMode m);
bool showHiddenFiles() const;
QUrl url() const;
ViewMode viewMode() const;
```

Slots

```
void setDir(const QString &);
void setFilter(const QString &);
void setFilters(const QString &);
void setFilters(const char **);
void setFilters(const QStringList &);
void setUrl(const QUrlOperator &url);
```

Signals

```
void dirEntered(const QString &);
void fileHighlighted(const QString &);
void fileSelected(const QString &);
```

Enums

```
enum Mode { AnyFile, ExistingFile, Directory, ExistingFiles };
enum ViewMode { Detail, List };
enum PreviewMode { NoPreview, Contents, Info };
```

 Cross-Reference   You can find several examples of QFileDialog in Chapter 5.

QFontDialog

This class consists of static methods that pop up a dialog prompting the user for a font.

File

```
#include <qfontdialog.h>
```

Base Classes

```
QDialog QObject QPaintDevice QWidget Qt
```

Methods

```
static QFont getFont(bool *ok, const QFont &def,
    QWidget *parent = 0, const char *name = 0);
static QFont getFont(bool *ok, QWidget *parent = 0,
    const char *name = 0);
```

Signals

```
void fontHighlighted(const QFont &font);
void fontSelected(const QFont &font);
```

Cross-
Reference

There are a number of examples of QFontDialog in Chapter 10.

QFrame

This is a base class of widgets that are surrounded by a frame. Also, because it is an empty widget, it can be instantiated and populated with other widgets.

File

```
#include <qframe.h>
```

Base Classes

```
QObject QPaintDevice QWidget Qt
```

Inherited By

```
KAboutContainer KAboutContributor KAccelMenu KAnimWidget
    KApplicationTree KCharSelect KCharSelectTable
    KColorCells KColorPatch KCombiView KContainerLayout
    KDateInternalMonthPicker KDatePicker KDateTable
    KDockWidgetAbstractHeader KDockWidgetAbstractHeaderDrag
    KDockWidgetHeader KDockWidgetHeaderDrag KDockWindow
    KEdit KFileDetailView KFileIconView KFilePreview
    KFormulaToolBar KHTMLView KIconCanvas KIconView
    KImageTrackLabel KIntSpinBox KListBox KListView KMenuBar
    KPopupMenu KPopupMenu KProgress KRuler KSeparator
    KSplitList KStatusBarLabel KTextBrowser KToolBar
    KURLLabel KURLRequester QButtonGroup QCanvasView QGrid
    QGroupBox QHBox QHButtonGroup QHGroupBox QIconView
    QLCDNumber QLabel QListBox QListView QMenuBar
    QMultiLineEdit QPopupFrame QPopupMenu QProgressBar
    QScrollView QSpinBox QSplitter QTableView QTextBrowser
    QTextView QVBox QVButtonGroup QVGroupBox QWellArray
    QWidgetStack
```

Constructors

```
QFrame(QWidget *parent = 0, const char *name = 0, WFlags f = 0,
    bool = TRUE);
```

Methods
```
QRect contentsRect() const;
QRect frameRect() const;
Shadow frameShadow() const;
Shape frameShape() const;
int frameStyle() const;
int frameWidth() const;
bool lineShapesOk() const;
int lineWidth() const;
int margin() const;
int midLineWidth() const;
virtual void setFrameRect(const QRect &);
void setFrameShadow(Shadow);
void setFrameShape(Shape);
virtual void setFrameStyle(int);
virtual void setLineWidth(int);
virtual void setMargin(int);
virtual void setMidLineWidth(int);
QSize sizeHint() const;
QSizePolicy sizePolicy() const;
```

Enums
```
enum Shape { NoFrame=0, Box=0x0001, Panel=0x0002,
      WinPanel=0x0003, HLine=0x0004, VLine=0x0005,
      StyledPanel=0x0006, PopupPanel=0x0007, MShape=0x000f };
enum Shadow { Plain=0x0010, Raised=0x0020, Sunken=0x0030,
      MShadow=0x00f0 };
```

Cross-Reference

There are a number of examples that use the QFrame widget in Chapter 7.

QGrid

This layout manager sizes and positions its child widgets according to coordinate positions on an internally maintained grid.

File
```
#include <qgrid.h>
```

Base Classes
```
QFrame QObject QPaintDevice QWidget Qt
```

Constructors
```
QGrid(int n, QWidget *parent = 0, const char *name = 0,
    WFlags f = 0);
QGrid(int n, Direction, QWidget *parent = 0,
    const char *name = 0, WFlags f = 0);
```

Methods
```
void setSpacing(int);
QSize sizeHint() const;
```

Enums

```
enum Direction { Horizontal, Vertical };
```

Cross-Reference There are a number of examples of QGrid in Chapter 3.

QGroupBox

This widget is capable of containing other widgets and providing them with a border and a title.

File

```
#include <qgroupbox.h>
```

Base Classes

```
QFrame QObject QPaintDevice QWidget Qt
```

Inherited By

```
QButtonGroup QHButtonGroup QHGroupBox QVButtonGroup
    QVGroupBox
```

Constructors

```
QGroupBox(QWidget *parent = 0, const char *name = 0);
QGroupBox(const QString &title, QWidget *parent = 0,
    const char *name = 0);
QGroupBox(int columns, Orientation o, QWidget *parent = 0,
    const char *name = 0);
QGroupBox(int columns, Orientation o, const QString &title,
    QWidget *parent = 0, const char *name = 0);
```

Methods

```
void addSpace(int);
int alignment() const;
int columns() const;
Orientation orientation() const;
virtual void setAlignment(int);
virtual void setColumnLayout(int columns, Orientation o);
void setColumns(int);
void setOrientation(Orientation);
virtual void setTitle(const QString &);
QString title() const;
```

The following example uses a QGroupBox widget for its top level window. It has no contents, but it is given a title string, as shown in Figure 18-3.

```
/* showgroupbox.cpp */
#include <qapplication.h>
#include <qgroupbox.h>

int main(int argc,char **argv)
{
```

```
        QApplication app(argc,argv);
        QGroupBox *groupbox = new QGroupBox();
        groupbox->setTitle("Group Title");
        groupbox->show();
        app.setMainWidget(groupbox);
        return(app.exec());
    }
```

Figure 18-3: A QGroupBox as a top-level widget

QHBox

The QHBox widget is a simple container that organizes widgets side by side.

File

```
#include <qhbox.h>
```

Base Classes

```
QFrame QObject QPaintDevice QWidget Qt
```

Inherited By

```
KCharSelect KURLRequester QVBox
```

Constructors

```
QHBox(QWidget *parent = 0, const char *name = 0, WFlags f = 0,
    bool allowLines = TRUE);
```

Methods

```
void setSpacing(int);
bool setStretchFactor(QWidget *, int stretch);
QSize sizeHint() const;
```

The following example uses a QHBox as the top-level widget. It has four QLabel widgets as its child widgets. As shown in Figure 18-4, each label is displayed side by side, with a 5-pixel-wide space between them.

```
/* showhbox.cpp */
#include <qapplication.h>
#include <qhbox.h>
#include <qlabel.h>

int main(int argc,char **argv)
```

```
{
    QApplication app(argc,argv);
    QHBox *hbox = new QHBox();
    new QLabel("First",hbox);
    new QLabel("Second",hbox);
    new QLabel("Third",hbox);
    new QLabel("Fourth",hbox);
    hbox->setSpacing(5);
    hbox->show();
    app.setMainWidget(hbox);
    return(app.exec());
}
```

Figure 18-4: Labels displayed by a QHBox

QHButtonGroup

The QHButtonGroup is a container widget that organizes a collection of buttons in a horizontal row.

File

```
#include <qhbuttongroup.h>
```

Base Classes

```
QButtonGroup QFrame QGroupBox QObject QPaintDevice QWidget
    Qt
```

Constructors

```
QHButtonGroup(QWidget *parent = 0, const char *name = 0);
QHButtonGroup(const QString &title, QWidget *parent = 0,
    const char *name = 0);
```

Cross-Reference You can find example programs that use QHButtonGroup in Chapter 7.

QHeader

The QHeader widget is a container that controls the size and position of a number of column headings.

File

```
#include <qheader.h>
```

Base Classes

```
QObject QPaintDevice QWidget Qt
```

Constructors

```
QHeader(QWidget *parent = 0, const char *name = 0);
QHeader(int, QWidget *parent = 0, const char *name = 0);
```

Methods

```
int addLabel(const QString &, int size = - 1);
int addLabel(const QIconSet &, const QString &,
    int size = - 1);
int cellAt(int) const;
int cellPos(int) const;
int cellSize(int) const;
int count() const;
QIconSet *iconSet(int section) const;
bool isClickEnabled(int section = - 1) const;
bool isMovingEnabled() const;
bool isResizeEnabled(int section = - 1) const;
QString label(int section) const;
int mapToActual(int) const;
int mapToIndex(int section) const;
int mapToLogical(int) const;
int mapToSection(int index) const;
virtual void moveCell(int, int);
void moveSection(int section, int toIndex);
int offset() const;
Orientation orientation() const;
void removeLabel(int section);
void resizeSection(int section, int s);
int sectionAt(int pos) const;
int sectionPos(int section) const;
int sectionSize(int section) const;
virtual void setCellSize(int, int);
virtual void setClickEnabled(bool, int section = - 1);
virtual void setLabel(int, const QString &, int size = - 1);
virtual void setLabel(int, const QIconSet &, const QString &,
    int size = - 1);
virtual void setMovingEnabled(bool);
virtual void setOrientation(Orientation);
virtual void setResizeEnabled(bool, int section = - 1);
void setSortIndicator(int section, bool increasing = TRUE);
virtual void setTracking(bool enable);
QSize sizeHint() const;
QSizePolicy sizePolicy() const;
bool tracking() const;
```

Slots

```
virtual void setOffset(int pos);
```

Signals

```
void clicked(int section);
void indexChange(int section, int fromIndex, int toIndex);
void moved(int, int);
void pressed(int section);
```

```
void released(int section);
void sectionClicked(int);
void sizeChange(int section, int oldSize, int newSize);
```

The following example creates a QHeader with four columns, with text of differing lengths. The size of each column head can be adjusted by using the mouse. The headings all maintain the width assigned to them, even if some of the text is obscured. As shown in Figure 18-5, the header may extend beyond the right end of the window, and one header label may be sized to overlap another. Column headings can also be expanded beyond the size required to display the text. A group of signals issued by the QHeader widget can be used to maintain the size and status of the columns beneath the headings.

```
/* showheader.cpp */
#include <qapplication.h>
#include <qheader.h>

int main(int argc,char **argv)
{
    QApplication app(argc,argv);
    QHeader *header = new QHeader();
    header->addLabel("Column One");
    header->addLabel("Two");
    header->addLabel("Three");
    header->addLabel("Fourth Column");
    header->show();
    app.setMainWidget(header);
    return(app.exec());
}
```

Figure 18-5: A QHeader widget containing four column headings

QHGroupBox

The QHGroupBox is a container widget that organizes a collection of widgets in a horizontal row.

File
```
#include <qhgroupbox.h>
```

Base Classes
```
QFrame QGroupBox QObject QPaintDevice QWidget Qt
```

Constructors
```
QHGroupBox(QWidget *parent = 0, const char *name = 0);
QHGroupBox(const QString &title, QWidget *parent = 0,
    const char *name = 0);
```

The following example contains four labels inside a QHGroupBox widget. As shown in Figure 18-6, the QHGroupBox widget inherits from QFrame, so it displays a border around the contained widgets, and can optionally display a title.

```cpp
/* showhgroupbox.cpp */
#include <qapplication.h>
#include <qhgroupbox.h>
#include <qlabel.h>

int main(int argc,char **argv)
{
    QApplication app(argc,argv);
    QHGroupBox *hgroupbox = new QHGroupBox();
    new QLabel("First",hgroupbox);
    new QLabel("Second",hgroupbox);
    new QLabel("Third",hgroupbox);
    new QLabel("Fourth",hgroupbox);
    hgroupbox->setTitle("Group Box Title");
    hgroupbox->show();
    app.setMainWidget(hgroupbox);
    return(app.exec());
}
```

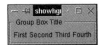

Figure 18-6: Four buttons contained by a QHGroupBox

QIconView

The QIconView widget displays a collection of icons and enables the user to make a selection.

File
```
#include <qiconview.h>
```

Base Classes
QFrame QObject QPaintDevice QScrollView QWidget Qt

Inherited By
KFileIconView KIconCanvas KIconView

Constructors
```
QIconView(QWidget *parent = 0, const char *name = 0,
    WFlags f = 0);
```

Methods
```
Arrangement arrangement() const;
bool autoArrange() const;
virtual void clear();
```

```
virtual void clearSelection();
uint count() const;
QIconViewItem *currentItem() const;
void ensureItemVisible(QIconViewItem *item);
bool eventFilter(QObject *o, QEvent *);
QIconViewItem *findFirstVisibleItem(const QRect &r) const;
QIconViewItem *findItem(const QPoint &pos) const;
QIconViewItem *findItem(const QString &text) const;
QIconViewItem *findLastVisibleItem(const QRect &r) const;
QIconViewItem *firstItem() const;
int gridX() const;
int gridY() const;
int index(const QIconViewItem *item) const;
virtual void insertItem(QIconViewItem *item,
    QIconViewItem *after = OL);
virtual void invertSelection();
QBrush itemTextBackground() const;
ItemTextPos itemTextPos() const;
bool itemsMovable() const;
QIconViewItem *lastItem() const;
int maxItemTextLength() const;
int maxItemWidth() const;
QSize minimumSizeHint() const;
virtual void repaintItem(QIconViewItem *item);
ResizeMode resizeMode() const;
virtual void selectAll(bool select);
SelectionMode selectionMode() const;
virtual void setArrangement(Arrangement am);
virtual void setAutoArrange(bool b);
virtual void setCurrentItem(QIconViewItem *item);
virtual void setFont(const QFont &);
virtual void setGridX(int rx);
virtual void setGridY(int ry);
virtual void setItemTextBackground(const QBrush &b);
virtual void setItemTextPos(ItemTextPos pos);
virtual void setItemsMovable(bool b);
virtual void setMaxItemTextLength(int w);
virtual void setMaxItemWidth(int w);
virtual void setPalette(const QPalette &);
virtual void setResizeMode(ResizeMode am);
virtual void setSelected(QIconViewItem *item, bool s,
    bool cb = FALSE);
virtual void setSelectionMode(SelectionMode m);
virtual void setShowToolTips(bool b);
void setSorting(bool sort, bool ascending = TRUE);
virtual void setSpacing(int sp);
virtual void setWordWrapIconText(bool b);
virtual void showEvent(QShowEvent *);
bool showToolTips() const;
QSize sizeHint() const;
QSizePolicy sizePolicy() const;
virtual void sort(bool ascending = TRUE);
bool sortDirection() const;
bool sorting() const;
```

```
int spacing() const;
virtual void takeItem(QIconViewItem *item);
bool wordWrapIconText() const;
```

Slots

```
virtual void arrangeItemsInGrid(const QSize &grid,
    bool update = TRUE);
virtual void arrangeItemsInGrid(bool update = TRUE);
virtual void setContentsPos(int x, int y);
virtual void updateContents();
```

Signals

```
void clicked(QIconViewItem *);
void clicked(QIconViewItem *, const QPoint &);
void currentChanged(QIconViewItem *item);
void doubleClicked(QIconViewItem *item);
void dropped(QDropEvent *e,
    const QValueList < QIconDragItem > &lst);
void itemRenamed(QIconViewItem *item, const QString &);
void itemRenamed(QIconViewItem *item);
void mouseButtonClicked(int button, QIconViewItem *item,
    const QPoint &pos);
void mouseButtonPressed(int button, QIconViewItem *item,
    const QPoint &pos);
void moved();
void onItem(QIconViewItem *item);
void onViewport();
void pressed(QIconViewItem *);
void pressed(QIconViewItem *, const QPoint &);
void returnPressed(QIconViewItem *item);
void rightButtonClicked(QIconViewItem *item, const QPoint
&pos);
void rightButtonPressed(QIconViewItem *item, const QPoint
&pos);
void selectionChanged();
void selectionChanged(QIconViewItem *item);
```

Enums

```
enum SelectionMode { Single=0, Multi, Extended, NoSelection };
enum Arrangement { LeftToRight=0, TopToBottom };
enum ResizeMode { Fixed=0, Adjust };
enum ItemTextPos { Bottom=0, Right };
```

The following example displays the five icons shown in Figure 18-7. The first icon has no pixmap and no text, so it uses the default pixmap and has no label. The next two icons also use the default pixmap, but they both have text for labels. The last two icons have both pixmaps and labels, and the icon labeled "Flag" has been selected by the mouse.

```
/* showiconview.cpp */
#include <qapplication.h>
#include <qiconview.h>

int main(int argc,char **argv)
```

```
{
    QIconViewItem *item;
    QApplication app(argc,argv);
    QIconView *iconview = new QIconView();
    item = new QIconViewItem(iconview);
    item = new QIconViewItem(iconview,"Icon Label");
    item = new QIconViewItem(iconview,"Icon With\nLong Label");
    QPixmap flag("flag.png");
    item = new QIconViewItem(iconview,"Flag",flag);
    QPixmap idea("idea.png");
    item = new QIconViewItem(iconview,"Idea",idea);
    iconview->show();
    app.setMainWidget(iconview);
    return(app.exec());
}
```

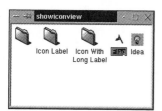

Figure 18-7: A QIconView widget displaying five icons

QInputDialog

The QInputDialog widget is a collection of static methods, each of which pops up a dialog that prompts the user for input.

File

```
#include <qinputdialog.h>
```

Base Classes

```
QDialog QObject QPaintDevice QWidget Qt
```

Methods

```
static double getDouble(const QString &caption,
    const QString &label, double num = 0,
    double from = - 2147483647, double to = 2147483647,
    int step = 1, bool *ok = 0, QWidget *parent = 0,
    const char *name = 0);
static int getInteger(const QString &caption,
    const QString &label, int num = 0, int from = - 2147483647,
    int to = 2147483647, int step = 1, bool *ok = 0,
    QWidget *parent = 0, const char *name = 0);
static QString getItem(const QString &caption,
    const QString &label, const QStringList &list,
    int current = 0, bool editable = TRUE, bool *ok = 0,
    QWidget *parent = 0, const char *name = 0);
```

```
static QString getText(const QString &caption,
    const QString &label, const QString &text = QString::null,
    bool *ok = 0, QWidget *parent = 0, const char *name = 0);
```

The following example prompts the user for a `double` value from 1.0 to 10.0. If the user selects the OK button, the Boolean value `OK` will be set to `true`; otherwise, it will be set to `false`. As shown in Figure 18-8, the arguments passed to `getDouble()` also set the caption at the top of the window and display a prompt immediately above the text window.

```
/* showcolordialog.cpp */
#include <qapplication.h>
#include <qinputdialog.h>
#include <iostream.h>

int main(int argc,char **argv)
{
    bool OK;
    QApplication app(argc,argv);
    double value = QInputDialog::getDouble(
        "A Double Value",
        "Enter a number from 1.0 to 10.0",
        8.902,
        1.0,10.0,
        1,&OK);
    if(OK)
        cout << "The value is: " << value <<  endl;
    else
        cout << "No data entered." << endl;
    return(app.exec());
}
```

Figure 18-8: A QInputDialog dialog prompting for a double value

QLCDNumber

The `QLCDNumber` widget displays a number using a font that looks like the digits of an LCD display.

File

```
#include <qlcdnumber.h>
```

Base Classes
```
QFrame QObject QPaintDevice QWidget Qt
```

Constructors
```
QLCDNumber(QWidget *parent = 0, const char *name = 0);
QLCDNumber(uint numDigits, QWidget *parent = 0,
    const char *name = 0);
```

Methods
```
bool checkOverflow(double num) const;
bool checkOverflow(int num) const;
int intValue() const;
Mode mode() const;
int numDigits() const;
SegmentStyle segmentStyle() const;
virtual void setMode(Mode);
virtual void setNumDigits(int nDigits);
virtual void setSegmentStyle(SegmentStyle);
QSize sizeHint() const;
QSizePolicy sizePolicy() const;
bool smallDecimalPoint() const;
double value() const;
```

Slots
```
void display(int num);
void display(double num);
void display(const QString &str);
virtual void setBinMode();
virtual void setDecMode();
virtual void setHexMode();
virtual void setOctMode();
virtual void setSmallDecimalPoint(bool);
```

Signals
```
void overflow();
```

Enums
```
enum Mode { Hex, HEX=Hex, Dec, DEC=Dec, Oct, OCT=Oct, Bin,
    BIN=Bin };
enum SegmentStyle { Outline, Filled, Flat };
```

You can find an example of the `QLCDNumber` widget in Chapter 3.

QLabel

The `QLabel` widget displays unadorned text in any font.

File
```
#include <qlabel.h>
```

Base Classes

```
QFrame QObject QPaintDevice QWidget Qt
```

Inherited By

```
KDockWindow KImageTrackLabel KStatusBarLabel KURLLabel
```

Constructors

```
QLabel(QWidget *parent, const char *name = 0, WFlags f = 0);
QLabel(const QString &text, QWidget *parent,
    const char *name = 0, WFlags f = 0);
QLabel(QWidget *buddy, const QString &, QWidget *parent,
    const char *name = 0, WFlags f = 0);
```

Methods

```
int alignment() const;
bool autoResize() const;
QWidget *buddy() const;
int heightForWidth(int) const;
int indent() const;
QSize minimumSizeHint() const;
QMovie *movie() const;
QPixmap *pixmap() const;
virtual void setAlignment(int);
void setAutoMask(bool);
virtual void setAutoResize(bool);
virtual void setBuddy(QWidget *);
void setIndent(int);
void setTextFormat(TextFormat);
QSize sizeHint() const;
QSizePolicy sizePolicy() const;
QString text() const;
TextFormat textFormat() const;
```

Slots

```
void clear();
virtual void setMovie(const QMovie &);
virtual void setNum(int);
virtual void setNum(double);
virtual void setPixmap(const QPixmap &);
virtual void setText(const QString &);
```

Cross-Reference Beginning with Chapter 2, there are many of examples of QLabel throughout the book.

QLineEdit

A QLineEdit widget is a simple one-line text editor used primarily for data entry.

File

```
#include <qlineedit.h>
```

Base Classes

    QObject QPaintDevice QWidget Qt

Inherited By

    KAccelInput KDateInternalYearSelector KLineEdit
        KPasswordEdit KRestrictedLine

Constructors

    QLineEdit(QWidget *parent, const char *name = 0);
    QLineEdit(const QString &, QWidget *parent,
        const char *name = 0);

Methods

    int alignment() const;
    void backspace();
    void copy() const;
    void cursorLeft(bool mark, int steps = 1);
    int cursorPosition() const;
    void cursorRight(bool mark, int steps = 1);
    void cursorWordBackward(bool mark);
    void cursorWordForward(bool mark);
    void cut();
    void del();
    QString displayText() const;
    EchoMode echoMode() const;
    bool edited() const;
    void end(bool mark);
    bool frame() const;
    bool hasMarkedText() const;
    void home(bool mark);
    bool isReadOnly() const;
    QString markedText() const;
    int maxLength() const;
    QSize minimumSizeHint() const;
    void paste();
    void setAlignment(int flag);
    virtual void setCursorPosition(int);
    virtual void setEchoMode(EchoMode);
    void setEdited(bool);
    virtual void setEnabled(bool);
    virtual void setFont(const QFont &);
    virtual void setFrame(bool);
    virtual void setMaxLength(int);
    virtual void setPalette(const QPalette &);
    void setReadOnly(bool);
    virtual void setSelection(int, int);
    virtual void setValidator(const QValidator *);
    QSize sizeHint() const;
    QSizePolicy sizePolicy() const;
    QString text() const;
    bool validateAndSet(const QString &, int, int, int);
    const QValidator *validator() const;

Slots

```
void clear();
void clearValidator();
void deselect();
void insert(const QString &);
void selectAll();
virtual void setText(const QString &);
```

Signals

```
void returnPressed();
void textChanged(const QString &);
```

Enums

```
enum EchoMode { Normal, NoEcho, Password };
```

There are examples of using the QLineEdit widget in Chapter 4.

QListBox

The QListBox widget displays a list of items that are selectable by the mouse.

File

```
#include <qlistbox.h>
```

Base Classes

```
QFrame QObject QPaintDevice QScrollView QWidget Qt
```

Inherited By

```
KListBox KSplitList
```

Constructors

```
QListBox(QWidget *parent = 0, const char *name = 0,
    WFlags f = 0);
```

Methods

```
bool autoBottomScrollBar() const;
bool autoScroll() const;
bool autoScrollBar() const;
bool autoUpdate() const;
bool bottomScrollBar() const;
int cellHeight(int i) const;
int cellHeight() const;
int cellWidth() const;
int cellWidth(int i) const;
void centerCurrentItem();
void changeItem(const QListBoxItem *, int index);
void changeItem(const QString &text, int index);
void changeItem(const QPixmap &pixmap, int index);
void changeItem(const QPixmap &pixmap, const QString &text,
    int index);
void clear();
```

```
LayoutMode columnMode() const;
uint count() const;
int currentItem() const;
QString currentText() const;
bool dragSelect() const;
QListBoxItem *findItem(const QString &text) const;
QListBoxItem *firstItem() const;
void inSort(const QListBoxItem *);
void inSort(const QString &text);
int index(const QListBoxItem *) const;
void insertItem(const QListBoxItem *, int index = - 1);
void insertItem(const QListBoxItem *,
    const QListBoxItem *after);
void insertItem(const QString &text, int index = - 1);
void insertItem(const QPixmap &pixmap, int index = - 1);
void insertItem(const QPixmap &pixmap, const QString &text,
    int index = - 1);
void insertStrList(const QStrList *, int index = - 1);
void insertStrList(const QStrList &, int index = - 1);
void insertStrList(const char **, int numStrings = - 1,
    int index = - 1);
void insertStringList(const QStringList &, int index = - 1);
bool isMultiSelection() const;
bool isSelected(int) const;
bool isSelected(const QListBoxItem *) const;
QListBoxItem *item(int index) const;
QListBoxItem *itemAt(QPoint) const;
int itemHeight(int index = 0) const;
QRect itemRect(QListBoxItem *item) const;
bool itemVisible(int index);
bool itemVisible(const QListBoxItem *);
long maxItemWidth() const;
QSize minimumSizeHint() const;
int numCols() const;
int numColumns() const;
int numItemsVisible() const;
int numRows() const;
const QPixmap *pixmap(int index) const;
void removeItem(int index);
LayoutMode rowMode() const;
bool scrollBar() const;
SelectionMode selectionMode() const;
void setAutoBottomScrollBar(bool enable);
void setAutoScroll(bool);
void setAutoScrollBar(bool enable);
void setAutoUpdate(bool);
virtual void setBottomItem(int index);
void setBottomScrollBar(bool enable);
virtual void setColumnMode(LayoutMode);
virtual void setColumnMode(int);
virtual void setCurrentItem(int index);
virtual void setCurrentItem(QListBoxItem *);
void setDragSelect(bool);
void setFixedVisibleLines(int lines);
```

```
virtual void setFont(const QFont &);
void setMultiSelection(bool multi);
virtual void setRowMode(LayoutMode);
virtual void setRowMode(int);
void setScrollBar(bool enable);
virtual void setSelected(QListBoxItem *, bool);
void setSelected(int, bool);
virtual void setSelectionMode(SelectionMode);
void setSmoothScrolling(bool);
virtual void setTopItem(int index);
virtual void setVariableHeight(bool);
virtual void setVariableWidth(bool);
QSize sizeHint() const;
bool smoothScrolling() const;
void sort(bool ascending = TRUE);
void takeItem(const QListBoxItem *);
QString text(int index) const;
int topItem() const;
void triggerUpdate(bool doLayout);
bool variableHeight() const;
bool variableWidth() const;
void viewportPaintEvent(QPaintEvent *);
```

Slots

```
virtual void clearSelection();
virtual void ensureCurrentVisible();
void invertSelection();
void selectAll(bool select);
```

Signals

```
void clicked(QListBoxItem *);
void clicked(QListBoxItem *, const QPoint &);
void currentChanged(QListBoxItem *);
void doubleClicked(QListBoxItem *);
void highlighted(int index);
void highlighted(const QString &);
void highlighted(QListBoxItem *);
void mouseButtonClicked(int, QListBoxItem *, const QPoint &);
void mouseButtonPressed(int, QListBoxItem *, const QPoint &);
void onItem(QListBoxItem *item);
void onViewport();
void pressed(QListBoxItem *);
void pressed(QListBoxItem *, const QPoint &);
void returnPressed(QListBoxItem *);
void rightButtonClicked(QListBoxItem *, const QPoint &);
void rightButtonPressed(QListBoxItem *, const QPoint &);
void selected(int index);
void selected(const QString &);
void selected(QListBoxItem *);
void selectionChanged();
void selectionChanged(QListBoxItem *);
```

Enums

```
enum SelectionMode { Single, Multi, Extended, NoSelection };
```

```
enum LayoutMode { FixedNumber, FitToWidth,
    FitToHeight=FitToWidth, Variable };
```

Cross-Reference There are examples of the QListBox widget in Chapters 3 and 8.

QListView

The QListView widget displays nested lists of items in the form of a tree, and allows for browsing through the resulting tree with the mouse.

File

```
#include <qlistview.h>
```

Base Classes

```
QFrame QObject QPaintDevice QScrollView QWidget Qt
```

Inherited By

```
KApplicationTree KFileDetailView KListView
```

Constructors

```
QListView(QWidget *parent = 0, const char *name = 0);
```

Methods

```
virtual int addColumn(const QString &label, int size = - 1);
virtual int addColumn(const QIconSet &iconset,
    const QString &label, int size = - 1);
bool allColumnsShowFocus() const;
int childCount() const;
virtual void clear();
virtual void clearSelection();
int columnAlignment(int) const;
QString columnText(int column) const;
int columnWidth(int column) const;
WidthMode columnWidthMode(int column) const;
int columns() const;
QListViewItem *currentItem() const;
void ensureItemVisible(const QListViewItem *);
bool eventFilter(QObject *o, QEvent *);
QListViewItem *firstChild() const;
QHeader *header() const;
virtual void insertItem(QListViewItem *);
bool isMultiSelection() const;
bool isOpen(const QListViewItem *) const;
bool isSelected(const QListViewItem *) const;
QListViewItem *itemAt(const QPoint &screenPos) const;
int itemMargin() const;
int itemPos(const QListViewItem *);
QRect itemRect(const QListViewItem *) const;
QSize minimumSizeHint() const;
void removeColumn(int index);
```

```
virtual void removeItem(QListViewItem *);
void repaintItem(const QListViewItem *) const;
bool rootIsDecorated() const;
QListViewItem *selectedItem() const;
SelectionMode selectionMode() const;
virtual void setAllColumnsShowFocus(bool);
virtual void setColumnAlignment(int, int);
virtual void setColumnText(int column, const QString &label);
virtual void setColumnText(int column, const QIconSet &iconset,
    const QString &label);
virtual void setColumnWidth(int column, int width);
virtual void setColumnWidthMode(int column, WidthMode);
virtual void setCurrentItem(QListViewItem *);
virtual void setFont(const QFont &);
virtual void setItemMargin(int);
virtual void setMultiSelection(bool enable);
virtual void setOpen(QListViewItem *, bool);
virtual void setPalette(const QPalette &);
virtual void setRootIsDecorated(bool);
virtual void setSelected(QListViewItem *, bool);
void setSelectionMode(SelectionMode mode);
void setShowSortIndicator(bool show);
virtual void setSorting(int column, bool increasing = TRUE);
virtual void setTreeStepSize(int);
void show();
bool showSortIndicator() const;
QSize sizeHint() const;
void sort();
virtual void takeItem(QListViewItem *);
int treeStepSize() const;
```

Slots

```
void invertSelection();
void selectAll(bool select);
void setContentsPos(int x, int y);
void triggerUpdate();
```

Signals

```
void clicked(QListViewItem *);
void clicked(QListViewItem *, const QPoint &, int);
void collapsed(QListViewItem *item);
void currentChanged(QListViewItem *);
void doubleClicked(QListViewItem *);
void expanded(QListViewItem *item);
void mouseButtonClicked(int, QListViewItem *, const QPoint &,
    int);
void mouseButtonPressed(int, QListViewItem *, const QPoint &,
    int);
void onItem(QListViewItem *item);
void onViewport();
void pressed(QListViewItem *);
```

```
void pressed(QListViewItem *, const QPoint &, int);
void returnPressed(QListViewItem *);
void rightButtonClicked(QListViewItem *, const QPoint &, int);
void rightButtonPressed(QListViewItem *, const QPoint &, int);
void selectionChanged();
void selectionChanged(QListViewItem *);
```

Enums

```
enum WidthMode { Manual, Maximum };
enum SelectionMode { Single, Multi, Extended, NoSelection };
```

The tree, or trees, displayed by the QListView widget are multilevel, and its sub-trees can be opened and closed with the mouse. The trees can be several layers deep, and a node of a tree can be one of a number of widget types. By creating different columns, there can be a number of trees. Scrollbars will appear on the bottom and right as necessary, and, if multiple columns are used, each tree can be resized by changing the size of the column headers.

The following example creates a single tree, with each leaf node represented by a check box. Each internal tree node (one that is capable of controlling child nodes) is a QListViewItem object. The QValueList template is used to create a list containing a collection of QListViewItem objects. The append() method of the QValueList is used to insert each of the QListViewItem objects. The inner loop creates five QCheckListItem objects, each of which encloses a QCheckBox for each of the parent tree nodes. Figure 18-9 shows the resulting tree: Two of the parent nodes are open, one of the members of the first parent is currently selected, and three of the check boxes have been selected by the mouse.

```
/* showlistiew.cpp */
#include <qapplication.h>
#include <qlistview.h>

int main(int argc,char **argv)
{
    QApplication app(argc,argv);

    QListView *listview = new QListView(0);
    listview->show();
    listview->addColumn("Column Heading");
    listview->setRootIsDecorated(TRUE);

    QValueList<QListViewItem *> valuelist;
    for(int i=1; i<6; i++) {
        QListViewItem *viewitem = new QListViewItem(listview,
                QString("Parent %1").arg(i));
        valuelist.append(viewitem);
        for(int j=1; j<6; j++) {
            new QCheckListItem(viewitem,
                QString("Child %1 of Parent %2").arg(j).arg(i),
```

```
                              QCheckListItem::CheckBox);
                }
        }

        listview->show();
        app.setMainWidget(listview);
        return(app.exec());
}
```

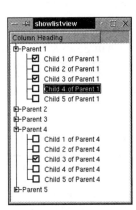

Figure 18-9: A QListView with five parent nodes

QMainWindow

The QMainWindow is typically used as a top-level window that supplies things the main window of an application requires. It provides a menu bar, toolbars, and a status bar.

File

```
#include <qmainwindow.h>
```

Base Classes

```
QObject QPaintDevice QWidget Qt
```

Constructors

```
QMainWindow(QWidget *parent = 0, const char *name = 0,
    WFlags f = WType_TopLevel);
```

Methods

```
void addToolBar(QToolBar *, ToolBarDock = Top,
    bool newLine = FALSE);
void addToolBar(QToolBar *, const QString &label,
    ToolBarDock = Top, bool newLine = FALSE);
QWidget *centralWidget() const;
bool eventFilter(QObject *, QEvent *);
bool getLocation(QToolBar *tb, ToolBarDock &dock, int &index,
    bool &nl, int &extraOffset) const;
bool isDockEnabled(ToolBarDock dock) const;
```

```
bool isDockEnabled(QToolBar *tb, ToolBarDock dock) const;
bool isDockMenuEnabled() const;
void lineUpToolBars(bool keepNewLines = FALSE);
QMenuBar *menuBar() const;
QSize minimumSizeHint() const;
void moveToolBar(QToolBar *, ToolBarDock = Top);
void moveToolBar(QToolBar *, ToolBarDock, bool nl, int index,
    int extraOffset = - 1);
bool opaqueMoving() const;
void removeToolBar(QToolBar *);
bool rightJustification() const;
virtual void setCentralWidget(QWidget *);
virtual void setDockEnabled(ToolBarDock dock, bool enable);
void setDockEnabled(QToolBar *tb, ToolBarDock dock,
    bool enable);
void show();
QSize sizeHint() const;
QStatusBar *statusBar() const;
QList<QToolBar> toolBars(ToolBarDock dock) const;
bool toolBarsMovable() const;
QToolTipGroup *toolTipGroup() const;
bool usesBigPixmaps() const;
bool usesTextLabel() const;
```

Slots

```
void setDockMenuEnabled(bool);
void setOpaqueMoving(bool);
virtual void setRightJustification(bool);
void setToolBarsMovable(bool);
virtual void setUsesBigPixmaps(bool);
void setUsesTextLabel(bool);
void whatsThis();
```

Signals

```
void endMovingToolBar(QToolBar *);
void pixmapSizeChanged(bool);
void startMovingToolBar(QToolBar *);
void toolBarPositionChanged(QToolBar *);
void usesTextLabelChanged(bool);
```

Enums

```
enum ToolBarDock { Unmanaged, TornOff, Top, Bottom, Right,
    Left, Minimized };
```

The following example shows how to set up a QMainWindow widget as the top-level window of your application. The QMainWindow widget acts as a container for other components (which can be accessed through the methods of QMainWindow). These components include QMenuBar, QStatusBar, QToolTipGroup, and a list of QToolBar objects. It also contains a QWidget at its center, which is intended to become the main display window of your application.

```
/* showmainwindow.cpp */
#include <qapplication.h>
#include <qmainwindow.h>
```

```
int main(int argc,char **argv)
{
    QApplication app(argc,argv);
    QMainWindow *mainwindow = new QMainWindow();
    mainwindow->show();
    app.setMainWidget(mainwindow);
    return(app.exec());
}
```

QMenuBar

A QMenuBar is a horizontal bar that is capable of managing the relationships among a group of pop-up menus.

File

```
#include <qmenubar.h>
```

Base Classes

```
QFrame QMenuData QObject QPaintDevice QWidget Qt
```

Inherited By

```
KMenuBar
```

Constructors

```
QMenuBar(QWidget *parent = 0, const char *name = 0);
```

Methods

```
bool customWhatsThis() const;
bool eventFilter(QObject *, QEvent *);
int heightForWidth(int) const;
void hide();
bool isDefaultUp() const;
QSize minimumSize() const;
QSize minimumSizeHint() const;
Separator separator() const;
void setDefaultUp(bool);
virtual void setSeparator(Separator when);
void show();
QSize sizeHint() const;
void updateItem(int id);
```

Signals

```
void activated(int itemId);
void highlighted(int itemId);
```

Enums

```
enum Separator { Never=0, InWindowsStyle=1 };
```

The following example shows a QMenuBar that contains two pop-up menus. Each pop-up menu contains a single menu item. Figure 18-10 shows the menu bar with the second pop-up menu activated.

```
/* showmenubar.cpp */
#include <qapplication.h>
#include <qmenubar.h>

int main(int argc,char **argv)
{
    QApplication app(argc,argv);
    QMenuBar *menubar = new QMenuBar();
    menubar->setSeparator(QMenuBar::InWindowsStyle);
    QPopupMenu* filePopup = new QPopupMenu();
    filePopup->insertItem("&Quit",&app,SLOT(quit()));
    menubar->insertItem("&File",filePopup);
    QPopupMenu* editPopup = new QPopupMenu();
    editPopup->insertItem("&Paste");
    menubar->insertItem("E&dit",editPopup);
    menubar->show();
    app.setMainWidget(menubar);
    return(app.exec());
}
```

Figure 18-10: A QMenuBar with two pop-up menus

QMessageBox

A QMessageBox is a dialog that pops up to display information to the user and waits for a response. It has a number of configurations, including various icons and optional buttons.

File

```
#include <qmessagebox.h>
```

Base Classes

```
QDialog QObject QPaintDevice QWidget Qt
```

Constructors

```
QMessageBox(QWidget *parent = 0, const char *name = 0);
QMessageBox(const QString &caption, const QString &text,
    Icon icon, int button0, int button1, int button2,
    QWidget *parent = 0, const char *name = 0,
    bool modal = TRUE, WFlags f = WStyle_DialogBorder);
```

Methods

```
static void about(QWidget *parent, const QString &caption,
    const QString &text);
static void aboutQt(QWidget *parent,
    const QString &caption = QString::null);
void adjustSize();
```

```
QString buttonText(int button) const;
static int critical(QWidget *parent, const QString &caption,
    const QString &text, int button0, int button1,
    int button2 = 0);
static int critical(QWidget *parent, const QString &caption,
    const QString &text,
    const QString &button0Text = QString::null,
    const QString &button1Text = QString::null,
    const QString &button2Text = QString::null,
    int defaultButtonNumber = 0, int escapeButtonNumber = - 1);
Icon icon() const;
const QPixmap *iconPixmap() const;
static int information(QWidget *parent, const QString &caption,
    const QString &text, int button0, int button1 = 0,
    int button2 = 0);
static int information(QWidget *parent, const QString &caption,
    const QString &text,
    const QString &button0Text = QString::null,
    const QString &button1Text = QString::null,
    const QString &button2Text = QString::null,
    int defaultButtonNumber = 0, int escapeButtonNumber = - 1);
static int message(const QString &caption, const QString &text,
    const QString &buttonText = QString::null,
    QWidget *parent = 0, const char *name = 0);
static bool query(const QString &caption, const QString &text,
    const QString &yesButtonText = QString::null,
    const QString &noButtonText = QString::null,
    QWidget *parent = 0, const char *name = 0);
void setButtonText(int button, const QString &);
void setIcon(Icon);
void setIcon(const QPixmap &);
void setIconPixmap(const QPixmap &);
void setText(const QString &);
void setTextFormat(TextFormat);
static QPixmap standardIcon(Icon icon, GUIStyle style);
QString text() const;
TextFormat textFormat() const;
static int warning(QWidget *parent, const QString &caption,
    const QString &text, int button0, int button1,
    int button2 = 0);
static int warning(QWidget *parent, const QString &caption,
    const QString &text,
    const QString &button0Text = QString::null,
    const QString &button1Text = QString::null,
    const QString &button2Text = QString::null,
    int defaultButtonNumber = 0, int escapeButtonNumber = - 1);
```

Enums

```
enum Icon { NoIcon=0, Information=1, Warning=2, Critical=3 };
enum (anon) { Ok=1, Cancel=2, Yes=3, No=4, Abort=5, Retry=6,
    Ignore=7, ButtonMask=0x07, Default=0x100, Escape=0x200,
    FlagMask=0x300 };
```

The following example uses one of the static methods to pop up a preconfigured QMessageBox. Figure 18-11 shows the message box as it appears with the *information* icon.

```
/* showmessgebox.cpp */
#include <qapplication.h>
#include <qmessagebox.h>

int main(int argc,char **argv)
{
    QApplication app(argc,argv);
    QMessageBox::information(0,
        "The Caption of an Informaton Box",
        "This is a QMessageBox that is configured\n"
        "to display information to the user and\n"
        "wait for a response.");
    return(app.exec());
}
```

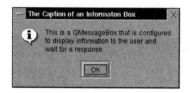

Figure 18-11: A QMessageBox using the information icon

QMultiLineEdit

The QMultiLineEdit widget is a text editor that can be used to enable the user to input text and make modifications to existing text.

File
```
#include <qmultilineedit.h>
```

Base Classes
```
QFrame QObject QPaintDevice QTableView QWidget Qt
```

Inherited By
```
KEdit
```

Constructors
```
QMultiLineEdit(QWidget *parent = 0, const char *name = 0);
```

Methods
```
int alignment() const;
bool atBeginning() const;
bool atEnd() const;
bool autoUpdate() const;
void cursorPosition(int *line, int *col) const;
void cursorWordBackward(bool mark);
```

```
void cursorWordForward(bool mark);
static int defaultTabStop();
EchoMode echoMode() const;
bool edited() const;
void getCursorPosition(int *line, int *col) const;
int hMargin() const;
virtual void insertAt(const QString &s, int line, int col,
    bool mark = FALSE);
virtual void insertLine(const QString &s, int line = - 1);
bool isOverwriteMode() const;
bool isReadOnly() const;
bool isUndoEnabled() const;
int length() const;
int maxLength() const;
int maxLineLength() const;
int maxLineWidth() const;
int maxLines() const;
QSize minimumSizeHint() const;
int numLines() const;
virtual void removeLine(int line);
void setAlignment(int flags);
virtual void setAutoUpdate(bool);
virtual void setCursorPosition(int line, int col,
    bool mark = FALSE);
static void setDefaultTabStop(int ex);
virtual void setEchoMode(EchoMode);
void setEdited(bool);
virtual void setFixedVisibleLines(int lines);
virtual void setFont(const QFont &font);
virtual void setHMargin(int);
void setMaxLength(int);
virtual void setMaxLineLength(int);
virtual void setMaxLines(int);
virtual void setSelection(int row_from, int col_from,
    int row_to, int col_t);
void setUndoDepth(int);
void setUndoEnabled(bool);
virtual void setValidator(const QValidator *);
void setWordWrap(WordWrap mode);
void setWrapColumnOrWidth(int);
void setWrapPolicy(WrapPolicy policy);
QSize sizeHint() const;
QSizePolicy sizePolicy() const;
QString text() const;
QString textLine(int line) const;
int undoDepth() const;
const QValidator *validator() const;
WordWrap wordWrap() const;
int wrapColumnOrWidth() const;
WrapPolicy wrapPolicy() const;
```

Slots

```
void append(const QString &);
void clear();
```

```
void copy() const;
void copyText() const;
void cut();
void deselect();
void insert(const QString &);
void paste();
void redo();
void selectAll();
virtual void setOverwriteMode(bool);
virtual void setReadOnly(bool);
virtual void setText(const QString &);
void undo();
```

Signals

```
void redoAvailable(bool);
void returnPressed();
void textChanged();
void undoAvailable(bool);
```

Enums

```
enum EchoMode { Normal, NoEcho, Password };
enum WordWrap { NoWrap, WidgetWidth, FixedPixelWidth,
    FixedColumnWidth };
enum WrapPolicy { AtWhiteSpace, Anywhere };
```

Chapter 8 contains examples of using a `QMultiLineEdit` widget.

QPopupMenu

The `QPopupMenu` widget is a menu that pops up. It normally appears as a member of a menu bar or a parent pop-up menu.

File

```
#include <qpopupmenu.h>
```

Base Classes

```
QFrame QMenuData QObject QPaintDevice QWidget Qt
```

Inherited By

```
KAccelMenu KPopupMenu KPopupMenu
```

Constructors

```
QPopupMenu(QWidget *parent = 0, const char *name = 0);
```

Methods

```
bool customWhatsThis() const;
int exec();
int exec(const QPoint &pos, int indexAtPoint = 0);
void hide();
int idAt(int index) const;
int idAt(const QPoint &pos) const;
```

```
int insertTearOffHandle(int id = - 1, int index = - 1);
bool isCheckable() const;
void popup(const QPoint &pos, int indexAtPoint = 0);
virtual void setActiveItem(int);
virtual void setCheckable(bool);
void setFont(const QFont &);
void show();
QSize sizeHint() const;
void updateItem(int id);
```

Signals

```
void aboutToShow();
void activated(int itemId);
void activatedRedirect(int itemId);
void highlighted(int itemId);
void highlightedRedirect(int itemId);
```

 Cross-Reference You can find a number of examples of QPopupMenu in Chapter 6.

QPrintDialog

The QprintDialog widget is an interface that enables a user to configure and control printing by an application.

File

```
#include <qprintdialog.h>
```

Base Classes

```
QDialog QObject QPaintDevice QWidget Qt
```

Constructors

```
QPrintDialog(QPrinter *, QWidget *parent = 0,
    const char *name = 0);
```

Methods

```
void addButton(QPushButton *but);
static bool getPrinterSetup(QPrinter *);
QPrinter *printer() const;
void setPrinter(QPrinter *, bool = FALSE);
```

The following example of QPrintDialog uses a QPrinter object to pop up the dialog window shown in Figure 18-12.

```
/* showprintdialog.cpp */
#include <qapplication.h>
#include <qprintdialog.h>
#include <qprinter.h>
#include <iostream.h>

int main(int argc,char **argv)
```

```
{
    QApplication app(argc,argv);
    QPrinter *printer = new QPrinter();
    bool OK = QPrintDialog::getPrinterSetup(printer);
    if(OK)
        cout << "Printer configuration set." << endl;
    else
        cout << "Printer configuration not set." << endl;
    return(app.exec());
}
```

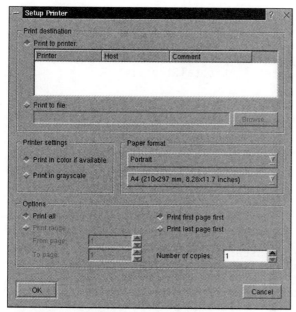

Figure 18-12: A QPrintDialog window

QProgressBar

The QProgressBar is a horizontal progress bar.

File

```
#include <qprogressbar.h>
```

Base Classes

```
QFrame QObject QPaintDevice QWidget Qt
```

Constructors

```
QProgressBar(QWidget *parent = 0, const char *name = 0,
    WFlags f = 0);
QProgressBar(int totalSteps, QWidget *parent = 0,
```

```
                    const char *name = 0, WFlags f = 0);
```

Methods

```
bool centerIndicator() const;
bool indicatorFollowsStyle() const;
QSize minimumSizeHint() const;
int progress() const;
void setCenterIndicator(bool on);
void setIndicatorFollowsStyle(bool);
void show();
QSize sizeHint() const;
QSizePolicy sizePolicy() const;
int totalSteps() const;
```

Slots

```
void reset();
virtual void setProgress(int progress);
virtual void setTotalSteps(int totalSteps);
```

The following example creates the progress bar shown in Figure 18-13, which has a total of 200 steps, with 122 of them complete. That is equivalent to a completion of 61 percent.

```cpp
/* showprogressbar.cpp */
#include <qapplication.h>
#include <qprogressbar.h>

int main(int argc,char **argv)
{
    QApplication app(argc,argv);
    QProgressBar *progressbar = new QProgressBar();
    progressbar->setTotalSteps(200);
    progressbar->setProgress(122);
    progressbar->show();
    app.setMainWidget(progressbar);
    return(app.exec());
}
```

Figure 18-13: A QProgressBar showing a completion percentage

QProgressDialog

The QProgressBar is a horizontal progress bar with a Cancel button. Note that this is a widget, not a pop-up window that inherits from QDialog.

File

```
#include <qprogressdialog.h>
```

Base Classes

```
QObject QPaintDevice QSemiModal QWidget Qt
```

Constructors

```
QProgressDialog(QWidget *parent = 0, const char *name = 0,
    bool modal = FALSE, WFlags f = 0);
QProgressDialog(const QString &labelText,
    const QString &cancelButtonText, int totalSteps,
    QWidget *parent = 0, const char *name = 0,
    bool modal = FALSE, WFlags f = 0);
```

Methods

```
bool autoClose() const;
bool autoReset() const;
QString labelText() const;
int minimumDuration() const;
int progress() const;
void setAutoClose(bool b);
void setAutoReset(bool b);
void setBar(QProgressBar *);
void setCancelButton(QPushButton *);
void setLabel(QLabel *);
QSize sizeHint() const;
int totalSteps() const;
bool wasCancelled() const;
```

Slots

```
void cancel();
void reset();
void setCancelButtonText(const QString &);
void setLabelText(const QString &);
void setMinimumDuration(int ms);
void setProgress(int progress);
void setTotalSteps(int totalSteps);
```

Signals

```
void cancelled();
```

The following example creates the progress bar shown in Figure 18-14, which also has a total of 200 steps, with 122 (or 61 percent) of them complete. The Cancel button issues the `cancelled()` signal and closes the window.

```
/* showprogressdialog.cpp */
#include <qapplication.h>
#include <qprogressdialog.h>

int main(int argc,char **argv)
{
    QApplication app(argc,argv);
    QProgressDialog *progressdialog = new QProgressDialog();
    progressdialog->setTotalSteps(200);
    progressdialog->setProgress(122);
    progressdialog->show();
```

```
        app.setMainWidget(progressdialog);
        return(app.exec());
}
```

Figure 18-14: A QProgressDialog showing the progress and a Cancel button

QPushButton

A QPushButton is a widget with a beveled edge that responds to the mouse by changing its appearance.

File

```
#include <qpushbutton.h>
```

Base Classes

```
QButton QObject QPaintDevice QWidget Qt
```

Inherited By

```
KColorButton KDialogBaseButton KDockButton_Private
    KIconButton KKeyButton
```

Constructors

```
QPushButton(QWidget *parent, const char *name = 0);
QPushButton(const QString &text, QWidget *parent,
    const char *name = 0);
QPushButton(const QIconSet &icon, const QString &text,
    QWidget *parent, const char *name = 0);
```

Methods

```
bool autoDefault() const;
QIconSet *iconSet() const;
bool isDefault() const;
bool isMenuButton() const;
void move(int x, int y);
void move(const QPoint &p);
QPopupMenu *popup() const;
void resize(int w, int h);
void resize(const QSize &);
virtual void setAutoDefault(bool autoDef);
virtual void setDefault(bool def);
virtual void setGeometry(int x, int y, int w, int h);
virtual void setGeometry(const QRect &);
void setIconSet(const QIconSet &);
virtual void setIsMenuButton(bool);
void setPopup(QPopupMenu *popup);
```

```
virtual void setToggleButton(bool);
QSize sizeHint() const;
QSizePolicy sizePolicy() const;
```

Slots
```
virtual void setOn(bool);
void toggle();
```

There are many examples of the QPushButton throughout the book.

QRadioButton

A QRadioButton is a button that can be toggled on or off by the mouse. When included in a group with other radio buttons, only one of them can be toggled on at any one time.

File
```
#include <qradiobutton.h>
```
Base Classes
```
QButton QObject QPaintDevice QWidget Qt
```
Constructors
```
QRadioButton(QWidget *parent, const char *name = 0);
QRadioButton(const QString &text, QWidget *parent,
    const char *name = 0);
```
Methods
```
bool isChecked() const;
virtual void setChecked(bool check);
QSize sizeHint() const;
QSizePolicy sizePolicy() const;
```

Cross-Reference   There are a number of examples of the QRadioButton in Chapter 7.

QScrollBar

The QScrollBar widget can be configured as either a vertical or horizontal scrollbar.

File
```
#include <qscrollbar.h>
```
Base Classes
```
QObject QPaintDevice QRangeControl QWidget Qt
```
Constructors
```
QScrollBar(QWidget *parent, const char *name = 0);
```

```
QScrollBar(Orientation, QWidget *parent, const char *name = 0);
QScrollBar(int minValue, int maxValue, int LineStep,
     int PageStep, int value, Orientation, QWidget *parent,
     const char *name = 0);
```

Methods

```
bool draggingSlider() const;
int lineStep() const;
int maxValue() const;
int minValue() const;
Orientation orientation() const;
int pageStep() const;
void setLineStep(int);
void setMaxValue(int);
void setMinValue(int);
virtual void setOrientation(Orientation);
void setPageStep(int);
virtual void setPalette(const QPalette &);
virtual void setTracking(bool enable);
void setValue(int);
QSize sizeHint() const;
QSizePolicy sizePolicy() const;
bool tracking() const;
int value() const;
```

Signals

```
void nextLine();
void nextPage();
void prevLine();
void prevPage();
void sliderMoved(int value);
void sliderPressed();
void sliderReleased();
void valueChanged(int value);
```

Unlike most widgets, every constructor of a QScrollBar widget requires a parent
widget. The following example creates a pair of QScrollBar objects. One is oriented horizontally and the other vertically. As shown in Figure 18-15, the geometry
of the parent widget and the two scrollbars are fixed so that the scrollbars appear
in the normal position at the bottom and on the right of the window.

```
/* showscrollbar.cpp */
#include <qapplication.h>
#include <qscrollbar.h>

int main(int argc,char **argv)
{
    QApplication app(argc,argv);
    QWidget *widget = new QWidget();
    QScrollBar *vscrollbar =
            new QScrollBar(Qt::Vertical,widget);
    vscrollbar->setGeometry(200,0,30,200);
    QScrollBar *hscrollbar =
```

```
                        new QScrollBar(Qt::Horizontal,widget);
        hscrollbar->setGeometry(0,200,200,30);
        widget->setFixedSize(230,230);
        widget->show();
        app.setMainWidget(widget);
        return(app.exec());
    }
```

Figure 18-15: One horizontal and one vertical QScrollBar

QScrollView

The QScrollView widget is a container widget that holds a single child widget and is capable of displaying a portion of it. It supplies scrollbars, as necessary, to allow the mouse to select which portion of the contained widget is visible.

File

```
#include <qscrollview.h>
```

Base Classes

```
QFrame QObject QPaintDevice QWidget Qt
```

Inherited By

```
KApplicationTree KFileDetailView KFileIconView KHTMLView
    KIconCanvas KIconView KListBox KListView KSplitList
    KTextBrowser QCanvasView QIconView QListBox QListView
    QTextBrowser QTextView
```

Constructors

```
QScrollView(QWidget *parent = 0, const char *name = 0,
    WFlags f = 0);
```

Methods

```
virtual void addChild(QWidget *child, int x = 0, int y = 0);
bool childIsVisible(QWidget *child);
int childX(QWidget *child);
int childY(QWidget *child);
QWidget *clipper() const;
int contentsHeight() const;
```

```
void contentsToViewport(int x, int y, int &vx, int &vy);
QPoint contentsToViewport(const QPoint &);
int contentsWidth() const;
int contentsX() const;
int contentsY() const;
QWidget *cornerWidget() const;
bool dragAutoScroll() const;
void enableClipper(bool y);
ScrollBarMode hScrollBarMode() const;
QScrollBar *horizontalScrollBar() const;
QSize minimumSizeHint() const;
virtual void moveChild(QWidget *child, int x, int y);
void removeChild(QWidget *child);
void removeChild(QObject *child);
void repaintContents(int x, int y, int w, int h,
    bool erase = TRUE);
void repaintContents(const QRect &r, bool erase = TRUE);
void resize(int w, int h);
void resize(const QSize &);
ResizePolicy resizePolicy() const;
virtual void setCornerWidget(QWidget *);
void setDragAutoScroll(bool b);
virtual void setHScrollBarMode(ScrollBarMode);
virtual void setResizePolicy(ResizePolicy);
virtual void setVScrollBarMode(ScrollBarMode);
void show();
void showChild(QWidget *child, bool yes = TRUE);
QSize sizeHint() const;
QSizePolicy sizePolicy() const;
void updateContents(int x, int y, int w, int h);
void updateContents(const QRect &r);
ScrollBarMode vScrollBarMode() const;
QScrollBar *verticalScrollBar() const;
QWidget *viewport() const;
QSize viewportSize(int, int) const;
void viewportToContents(int vx, int vy, int &x, int &y);
QPoint viewportToContents(const QPoint &);
int visibleHeight() const;
int visibleWidth() const;
```

Slots

```
void center(int x, int y);
void center(int x, int y, float xmargin, float ymargin);
void ensureVisible(int x, int y);
void ensureVisible(int x, int y, int xmargin, int ymargin);
virtual void resizeContents(int w, int h);
void scrollBy(int dx, int dy);
virtual void setContentsPos(int x, int y);
void setEnabled(bool enable);
void updateScrollBars();
```

Signals

```
void contentsMoving(int x, int y);
```

Enums

```
enum ResizePolicy { Default, Manual, AutoOne };
enum ScrollBarMode { Auto, AlwaysOff, AlwaysOn };
```

The following example inserts a QLCDNumber widget into a QScrollView widget. Figure 18-16 shows how a portion of the contained widget appears, with the scroll-bars that can be used to control which portion of the QLCDNumber widget is visible.

```cpp
/* showscrollview.cpp */
#include <qapplication.h>
#include <qscrollview.h>
#include <qlcdnumber.h>

int main(int argc,char **argv)
{
    QApplication app(argc,argv);
    QScrollView *scrollview = new QScrollView();
    QLCDNumber *number = new QLCDNumber();
    number->setNumDigits(8);
    number->display(982.89021);
    number->setMinimumSize(600,400);
    scrollview->addChild(number);
    scrollview->show();
    app.setMainWidget(scrollview);
    return(app.exec());
}
```

Figure 18-16: A QScrollView widget displaying a portion of its child widget

QSemiModal

A QSemiModal widget adds exclusivity to QWidget by prohibiting mouse access to any other window in the same application.

File
```
#include <qsemimodal.h>
```
Base Classes
```
QObject QPaintDevice QWidget Qt
```
Inherited By
```
QProgressDialog
```

Constructors
```
QSemiModal(QWidget *parent = 0, const char *name = 0,
    bool modal = FALSE, WFlags f = 0);
```

Methods
```
void move(int x, int y);
void move(const QPoint &p);
void resize(int w, int h);
void resize(const QSize &);
virtual void setGeometry(int x, int y, int w, int h);
virtual void setGeometry(const QRect &);
void show();
```

A QSemiModal widget is simply a QWidget with the one added feature: If the third argument on the constructor is TRUE, no other window in this application will respond to the mouse or keyboard. The following example demonstrates that QSemiModal can be used just like any other widget; and, as shown in Figure 18-17, it is capable of containing other widgets. Also, it is often important for modal widgets to provide the user with some means of escape, which in this example is the Exit button.

```
/* showsemimodal.cpp */
#include <qapplication.h>
#include <qpushbutton.h>
#include <qsemimodal.h>

int main(int argc,char **argv)
{
    QApplication app(argc,argv);
    QSemiModal *semimodal = new QSemiModal(0,"semimodal",TRUE);
    QPushButton *button = new QPushButton("Exit",semimodal);
    QObject::connect(button,
            SIGNAL(clicked()),&app,SLOT(quit()));
    semimodal->show();
    app.setMainWidget(semimodal);
    return(app.exec());
}
```

Figure 18-17: A QSemiModal widget containing a QPushButton

QSizeGrip

The QSizeGrip widget is a resizing handle designed for the lower-right corner of a window.

File
```
#include <qsizegrip.h>
```

Base Classes
```
QObject QPaintDevice QWidget Qt
```
Constructors
```
QSizeGrip(QWidget *parent, const char *name = 0);
```
Methods
```
QSize sizeHint() const;
QSizePolicy sizePolicy() const;
```

The following example demonstrates that a QSizeHandle can be added to any widget, and dragging it with the mouse will resize the containing widget. Figure 18-18 shows the normal position of the QResizeGrip widget in the lower-right corner.

```cpp
/* showsizegrip.cpp */
#include <qapplication.h>
#include <qsizegrip.h>

int main(int argc,char **argv)
{
    QApplication app(argc,argv);
    QWidget *widget = new QWidget();
    widget->setMinimumSize(200,150);
    QSizeGrip *sizegrip = new QSizeGrip(widget);
    sizegrip->setGeometry(170,120,30,30);
    widget->show();
    app.setMainWidget(widget);
    return(app.exec());
}
```

Figure 18-18: A QSIzeGrip in the lower right corner of a window

QSlider

A QSlider widget displays a track and a movable thumb that can be used with the mouse to adjust a value between two extremes.

File
```
#include <qslider.h>
```
Base Classes
```
QObject QPaintDevice QRangeControl QWidget Qt
```

Constructors

```
QSlider(QWidget *parent, const char *name = 0);
QSlider(Orientation, QWidget *parent, const char *name = 0);
QSlider(int minValue, int maxValue, int pageStep, int value,
    Orientation, QWidget *parent, const char *name = 0);
```

Methods

```
int lineStep() const;
int maxValue() const;
int minValue() const;
QSize minimumSizeHint() const;
Orientation orientation() const;
int pageStep() const;
void setLineStep(int);
void setMaxValue(int);
void setMinValue(int);
virtual void setOrientation(Orientation);
void setPageStep(int);
virtual void setPalette(const QPalette &);
virtual void setTickInterval(int);
virtual void setTickmarks(TickSetting);
virtual void setTracking(bool enable);
QSize sizeHint() const;
QSizePolicy sizePolicy() const;
QRect sliderRect() const;
int tickInterval() const;
TickSetting tickmarks() const;
bool tracking() const;
int value() const;
```

Slots

```
void addStep();
virtual void setValue(int);
void subtractStep();
```

Signals

```
void sliderMoved(int value);
void sliderPressed();
void sliderReleased();
void valueChanged(int value);
```

Enums

```
enum TickSetting { NoMarks=0, Above=1, Left=Above, Below=2,
    Right=Below, Both=3 };
```

The following example, shown in Figure 18-19, displays one vertical and one horizontal slider, with optional tick marks on both.

```
/* showslider.cpp */
#include <qapplication.h>
#include <qslider.h>

int main(int argc,char **argv)
{
```

```
QApplication app(argc,argv);
QWidget *widget = new QWidget();
QSlider *vslider =
        new QSlider(Qt::Vertical,widget);
vslider->setTickmarks(QSlider::Left);
vslider->setGeometry(200,0,30,200);
QSlider *hslider =
        new QSlider(Qt::Horizontal,widget);
hslider->setTickmarks(QSlider::Above);
hslider->setGeometry(0,200,200,30);
widget->setFixedSize(230,230);
widget->show();
app.setMainWidget(widget);
return(app.exec());
}
```

Figure 18-19: One horizontal and one vertical QSLider

QSpinBox

The QSpinBox widget displays a text window with a current value or setting, along with a pair of buttons that enables the user to switch from one value or setting to the next.

File

```
#include <qspinbox.h>
```

Base Classes

```
QFrame QObject QPaintDevice QRangeControl QWidget Qt
```

Inherited By

```
KIntSpinBox
```

Constructors

```
QSpinBox(QWidget *parent = 0, const char *name = 0);
QSpinBox(int minValue, int maxValue, int step = 1,
    QWidget *parent = 0, const char *name = 0);
```

Methods

```
ButtonSymbols buttonSymbols() const;
virtual QString cleanText() const;
int lineStep() const;
int maxValue() const;
int minValue() const;
virtual QString prefix() const;
void setButtonSymbols(ButtonSymbols);
void setLineStep(int);
void setMaxValue(int);
void setMinValue(int);
virtual void setSpecialValueText(const QString &text);
virtual void setValidator(const QValidator *v);
virtual void setWrapping(bool on);
QSize sizeHint() const;
QSizePolicy sizePolicy() const;
QString specialValueText() const;
virtual QString suffix() const;
QString text() const;
const QValidator *validator() const;
int value() const;
bool wrapping() const;
```

Slots

```
virtual void setEnabled(bool);
virtual void setPrefix(const QString &text);
virtual void setSuffix(const QString &text);
virtual void setValue(int value);
virtual void stepDown();
virtual void stepUp();
```

Signals

```
void valueChanged(int value);
void valueChanged(const QString &valueText);
```

Enums

```
enum ButtonSymbols { UpDownArrows, PlusMinus };
```

The following example creates the spin box shown in Figure 18-20. The numeric values can range from 10 to 100, and selecting one of the arrow buttons will adjust the value by 10. It is possible to customize the displayed value with prefixes and suffixes, or the displayed string can be replaced completely with a call to `setSpecialValueText()`.

```
/* showspinbox.cpp */
#include <qapplication.h>
#include <qspinbox.h>

int main(int argc,char **argv)
{
    QApplication app(argc,argv);
```

```
        QSpinBox *spinbox = new QSpinBox(10,100,5);
        spinbox->show();
        app.setMainWidget(spinbox);
        return(app.exec());
    }
```

Figure 18-20: A QSpinBox used to select an integer value

QSplitter

The QSplitter widget contains a pair of windows with on-demand scrollbars, and enables the relative size of each to be adjusted with the mouse.

File

```
#include <qsplitter.h>
```

Base Classes

```
QFrame QObject QPaintDevice QWidget Qt
```

Inherited By

```
KCombiView KFilePreview
```

Constructors

```
QSplitter(QWidget *parent = 0, const char *name = 0);
QSplitter(Orientation, QWidget *parent = 0,
    const char *name = 0);
```

Methods

```
QSize minimumSizeHint() const;
void moveToFirst(QWidget *);
void moveToLast(QWidget *);
bool opaqueResize() const;
Orientation orientation() const;
void refresh();
virtual void setOpaqueResize(bool = TRUE);
virtual void setOrientation(Orientation);
virtual void setResizeMode(QWidget *w, ResizeMode);
void setSizes(QValueList < int >);
QSize sizeHint() const;
QSizePolicy sizePolicy() const;
QValueList<int> sizes() const;
```

Enums

```
enum ResizeMode { Stretch, KeepSize, FollowSizeHint };
```

Cross-Reference You can find examples of QSplitter in Chapters 7 and 8.

QStatusBar

The `QStatusBar` widget displays a line of text that can be dynamically set and cleared. It also contains a `QSizeGrip` widget used to resize itself and its parent window.

File

```
#include <qstatusbar.h>
```

Base Classes

```
QObject QPaintDevice QWidget Qt
```

Inherited By

```
KStatusBar
```

Constructors

```
QStatusBar(QWidget *parent = 0, const char *name = 0);
```

Methods

```
void addWidget(QWidget *, int stretch = 0, bool = FALSE);
bool isSizeGripEnabled() const;
void removeWidget(QWidget *);
void setSizeGripEnabled(bool);
```

Slots

```
void clear();
void message(const QString &);
void message(const QString &, int);
```

The following example displays the window containing the `QStatusBar` widget shown in Figure 18-21. A widget of this sort is normally included at the bottom of a window.

```cpp
/* showstatusbar.cpp */
#include <qapplication.h>
#include <qstatusbar.h>

int main(int argc,char **argv)
{
    QApplication app(argc,argv);
    QStatusBar *statusbar = new QStatusBar();
    statusbar->setSizeGripEnabled(TRUE);
    statusbar->message("The QSatusBar widget");
    statusbar->show();
    app.setMainWidget(statusbar);
    return(app.exec());
}
```

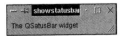

Figure 18-21: A QStatusBar widget with the QSizeGrip widget enabled

QTabBar

The `QTabBar` widget displays a row of tabs that can be individually selected with the mouse.

File

```
#include <qtabbar.h>
```

Base Classes

```
QObject QPaintDevice QWidget Qt
```

Constructors

```
QTabBar(QWidget *parent = 0, const char *name = 0);
```

Methods

```
virtual int addTab(QTab *);
int currentTab() const;
virtual int insertTab(QTab *, int index = - 1);
bool isTabEnabled(int) const;
int keyboardFocusTab() const;
virtual void layoutTabs();
virtual void removeTab(QTab *);
virtual void setShape(Shape);
virtual void setTabEnabled(int, bool);
Shape shape() const;
void show();
QSize sizeHint() const;
QSizePolicy sizePolicy() const;
QTab *tab(int);
```

Slots

```
virtual void setCurrentTab(int);
virtual void setCurrentTab(QTab *);
```

Signals

```
void selected(int);
```

Enums

```
enum Shape { RoundedAbove, RoundedBelow, TriangularAbove,
        TriangularBelow };
```

The following example creates the `QTabBar` with four tabs, as shown in Figure 18-22. At the right end of the bar is a spin button that appears whenever the parent window is not wide enough to contain all the tabs. The call to the `addTab()` method returns an integer ID number that is used to issue the `selected()` signal whenever the tab is selected.

```
/* showtabbar.cpp */
#include <qapplication.h>
#include <qtabbar.h>

int main(int argc,char **argv)
```

```
{
    QApplication app(argc,argv);
    QTabBar *tabbar = new QTabBar();
    tabbar->addTab(new QTab("First"));
    tabbar->addTab(new QTab("Second"));
    tabbar->addTab(new QTab("Third"));
    tabbar->addTab(new QTab("Fourth"));
    tabbar->show();
    app.setMainWidget(tabbar);
    return(app.exec());
}
```

Figure 18-22: A QTabBar with four tabs and a horizontal spin button

QTabDialog

The QTabDialog widget is the container that stacks the contained widgets and allows for the selection of the current by using the tabs at the top.

File

```
#include <qtabdialog.h>
```

Base Classes

```
QDialog QObject QPaintDevice QWidget Qt
```

Constructors

```
QTabDialog(QWidget *parent = 0, const char *name = 0,
    bool modal = FALSE, WFlags f = 0);
```

Methods

```
void addTab(QWidget *, const QString &);
void addTab(QWidget *child, const QIconSet &iconset,
    const QString &label);
void addTab(QWidget *, QTab *);
void changeTab(QWidget *, const QString &);
void changeTab(QWidget *child, const QIconSet &iconset,
    const QString &label);
QWidget *currentPage() const;
bool hasApplyButton() const;
bool hasCancelButton() const;
bool hasDefaultButton() const;
bool hasHelpButton() const;
bool hasOkButton() const;
void insertTab(QWidget *, const QString &, int index = - 1);
void insertTab(QWidget *child, const QIconSet &iconset,
    const QString &label, int index = - 1);
void insertTab(QWidget *, QTab *, int index = - 1);
```

```
bool isTabEnabled(QWidget *) const;
bool isTabEnabled(const char *) const;
void removePage(QWidget *);
void setApplyButton(const QString &text);
void setApplyButton();
void setCancelButton(const QString &text);
void setCancelButton();
void setDefaultButton(const QString &text);
void setDefaultButton();
void setFont(const QFont &font);
void setHelpButton(const QString &text);
void setHelpButton();
void setOKButton(const QString &text = QString::null);
void setOkButton(const QString &text);
void setOkButton();
void setTabEnabled(QWidget *, bool);
void setTabEnabled(const char *, bool);
void show();
void showPage(QWidget *);
QString tabLabel(QWidget *);
```

Signals

```
void aboutToShow();
void applyButtonPressed();
void cancelButtonPressed();
void defaultButtonPressed();
void helpButtonPressed();
void selected(const QString &);
```

Cross-Reference See Chapter 5 for an example of the `QTabDialog` widget.

QTabWidget

A `QTabWidget` displays a row of tabs that can be individually selected with the mouse.

File

```
#include <qtabwidget.h>
```

Base Classes

```
QObject QPaintDevice QWidget Qt
```

Constructors

```
QTabWidget(QWidget *parent, const char *name, WFlags f);
QTabWidget(QWidget *parent = 0, const char *name = 0);
```

Methods

```
void addTab(QWidget *, const QString &);
void addTab(QWidget *child, const QIconSet &iconset,
    const QString &label);
```

```
void addTab(QWidget *, QTab *);
void changeTab(QWidget *, const QString &);
void changeTab(QWidget *child, const QIconSet &iconset,
    const QString &label);
QWidget *currentPage() const;
void insertTab(QWidget *, const QString &, int index = - 1);
void insertTab(QWidget *child, const QIconSet &iconset,
    const QString &label, int index = - 1);
void insertTab(QWidget *, QTab *, int index = - 1);
bool isTabEnabled(QWidget *) const;
int margin() const;
QSize minimumSizeHint() const;
void removePage(QWidget *);
void setMargin(int);
void setTabEnabled(QWidget *, bool);
void setTabPosition(TabPosition);
void showPage(QWidget *);
QSize sizeHint() const;
QString tabLabel(QWidget *);
TabPosition tabPosition() const;
```

Signals

```
void selected(const QString &);
```

Enums

```
enum TabPosition { Top, Bottom };
```

The following example creates a QTabWidget container with four widgets, as shown
in Figure 18-23. At the right end of the bar is a spin button that appears whenever
the parent window is not wide enough to contain all the tabs.

```
/* showtabwidget.cpp */
#include <qapplication.h>
#include <qtabwidget.h>
#include <qlabel.h>

int main(int argc,char **argv)
{
    QLabel *label;
    QApplication app(argc,argv);
    QTabWidget *tabwidget = new QTabWidget();
    label = new QLabel("The First Widget Label",tabwidget);
    tabwidget->addTab(label,"First");
    label = new QLabel("The Second Widget Label",tabwidget);
    tabwidget->addTab(label,"Second");
    label = new QLabel("The Third Widget Label",tabwidget);
    tabwidget->addTab(label,"Third");
    label = new QLabel("The Fourth Widget Label",tabwidget);
    tabwidget->addTab(label,"Fourth");
    tabwidget->show();
    app.setMainWidget(tabwidget);
    return(app.exec());
}
```

Figure 18-23: A QTabWidget with four tabs and a horizontal spin button

QTextBrowser

A QTextBrowser widget displays text in a window and provides a set of positioning methods. The basic text display is inherited from QTextView. Highlighted sections can be extracted.

File

```
#include <qtextbrowser.h>
```

Base Classes

```
QFrame QObject QPaintDevice QScrollView QTextView QWidget Qt
```

Inherited By

```
KTextBrowser
```

Constructors

```
QTextBrowser(QWidget *parent = 0, const char *name = 0);
```

Methods

```
void scrollToAnchor(const QString &name);
virtual void setSource(const QString &name);
void setText(const QString &contents,
    const QString &context = QString::null);
QString source() const;
```

Slots

```
virtual void backward();
virtual void forward();
virtual void home();
```

Signals

```
void backwardAvailable(bool);
void forwardAvailable(bool);
void highlighted(const QString &);
void textChanged();
```

The following example displays some lines of text, as shown in Figure 18-24.

```
/* showtextbrowser.cpp */
#include <qapplication.h>
#include <qtextbrowser.h>

char text[] =
    "This is the text being displayed\n"
    "by the text browser. Both vertical\n"
    "and horizontal scroll bars will\n"
    "appear as necessary.";
```

```
int main(int argc,char **argv)
{
    QApplication app(argc,argv);
    QTextBrowser *textbrowser = new QTextBrowser();
    textbrowser->show();
    textbrowser->setText(QString(text));
    app.setMainWidget(textbrowser);
    return(app.exec());
}
```

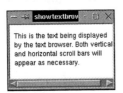

Figure 18-24: A QTextBrowser widget displaying text

QTextView

A QTextView **widget displays text in a window.**

File

```
#include <qtextview.h>
```

Base Classes

```
QFrame QObject QPaintDevice QScrollView QWidget Qt
```

Inherited By

```
KTextBrowser QTextBrowser
```

Constructors

```
QTextView(QWidget *parent = 0, const char *name = 0);
QTextView(const QString &text,
    const QString &context = QString::null,
    QWidget *parent = 0, const char *name = 0);
```

Methods

```
void append(const QString &text);
virtual QString context() const;
QString documentTitle() const;
bool hasSelectedText() const;
int heightForWidth(int w) const;
const QColor & linkColor() const;
bool linkUnderline() const;
QMimeSourceFactory *mimeSourceFactory() const;
const QBrush & paper();
const QBrush & paper() const;
```

```
const QColorGroup & paperColorGroup() const;
QString selectedText() const;
void setLinkColor(const QColor &);
void setLinkUnderline(bool);
void setMimeSourceFactory(QMimeSourceFactory *factory);
void setPaper(const QBrush &pap);
void setPaperColorGroup(const QColorGroup &colgrp);
void setStyleSheet(QStyleSheet *styleSheet);
virtual void setText(const QString &text,
    const QString &context);
void setText(const QString &text);
void setTextFormat(TextFormat);
QStyleSheet *styleSheet() const;
virtual QString text() const;
TextFormat textFormat() const;
```

Slots

```
void copy();
void selectAll();
```

The following example displays a block of text, as shown in Figure 18-25.

```
/* showtextview.cpp */
#include <qapplication.h>
#include <qtextview.h>

char text[] =
    "This is the text being displayed\n"
    "by the text view. Both vertical\n"
    "and horizontal scroll bars will\n"
    "appear as necessary.";

int main(int argc,char **argv)
{
    QApplication app(argc,argv);
    QTextView *textview = new QTextView(text);
    textview->show();
    app.setMainWidget(textview);
    return(app.exec());
}
```

Figure 18-25: A QTextView widget displaying text

QToolBar

The QToolBar widget is a panel that contains controls. A toolbar control can be any widget, but is most commonly a small button with an icon instead of text.

File

```
#include <qtoolbar.h>
```

Base Classes

```
QObject QPaintDevice QWidget Qt
```

Constructors

```
QToolBar(const QString &label, QMainWindow *,
    QMainWindow::ToolBarDock = QMainWindow::Top,
    bool newLine = FALSE, const char *name = 0);
QToolBar(const QString &label, QMainWindow *, QWidget *,
    bool newLine = FALSE, const char *name = 0, WFlags f = 0);
QToolBar(QMainWindow *parent = 0, const char *name = 0);
```

Methods

```
void addSeparator();
void clear();
bool event(QEvent *e);
bool eventFilter(QObject *, QEvent *);
void hide();
bool isHorizontalStretchable() const;
bool isVerticalStretchable() const;
QString label() const;
QMainWindow *mainWindow();
QSize minimumSize() const;
QSize minimumSizeHint() const;
Orientation orientation() const;
void setHorizontalStretchable(bool b);
virtual void setLabel(const QString &);
virtual void setOrientation(Orientation);
virtual void setStretchableWidget(QWidget *);
void setVerticalStretchable(bool b);
void show();
```

Signals

```
void orientationChanged(Orientation);
```

The following example creates a QToolBar and attaches it to a QMainWindow widget. Figure 18-26 shows the toolbar at the top, but the QMainWindow widget allows the toolbar to be docked on any of the four sides. This toolbar is populated by a normal QPushButton widget and three QToolButton widgets. One of the QTool Button widgets displays an arrow, while the other two display pixmaps. They were omitted to keep this example simple, but the buttons would normally be assigned slot methods that would be called when a button is activated.

```
/* showtoolbar.cpp */
#include <qapplication.h>
```

```cpp
#include <qmainwindow.h>
#include <qtoolbar.h>
#include <qtoolbutton.h>
#include <qpushbutton.h>

int main(int argc,char **argv)
{
    QApplication app(argc,argv);
    QMainWindow *mainwindow = new QMainWindow();
    QToolBar *toolbar = new QToolBar("Bar",mainwindow);
    new QPushButton("Button",toolbar);
    QPixmap idea("idea.png");
    new QToolButton(idea,"Idea","Group",0,0,toolbar);
    QPixmap flag("flag.png");
    new QToolButton(flag,"Flag","Group",0,0,toolbar);
    new QToolButton(Qt::UpArrow,toolbar);
    mainwindow->show();
    app.setMainWidget(mainwindow);
    return(app.exec());
}
```

Figure 18-26: A QToolBar with four buttons

QToolButton

A QToolButton widget is a special button designed to be included as a member of a toolbar. It can be displayed as text, a pixmap, or both.

File

```cpp
#include <qtoolbutton.h>
```

Base Classes

QButton QObject QPaintDevice QWidget Qt

Constructors

```cpp
QToolButton(QWidget *parent, const char *name = 0);
QToolButton(const QPixmap &pm, const QString &textLabel,
    const QString &grouptext, QObject *receiver,
    const char *slot, QToolBar *parent, const char *name = 0);
QToolButton(const QIconSet &s, const QString &textLabel,
    const QString &grouptext, QObject *receiver,
    const char *slot, QToolBar *parent, const char *name = 0);
QToolButton(ArrowType type, QWidget *parent,
    const char *name = 0);
```

Methods

```
bool autoRaise() const;
QIconSet iconSet(bool on = FALSE) const;
QIconSet offIconSet() const;
QIconSet onIconSet() const;
QPopupMenu *popup() const;
int popupDelay() const;
void setAutoRaise(bool enable);
virtual void setIconSet(const QIconSet &, bool on = FALSE);
void setOffIconSet(const QIconSet &);
void setOnIconSet(const QIconSet &);
void setPopup(QPopupMenu *popup);
void setPopupDelay(int delay);
QSize sizeHint() const;
QSizePolicy sizePolicy() const;
QString textLabel() const;
bool usesBigPixmap() const;
bool usesTextLabel() const;
```

Slots

```
virtual void setOn(bool enable);
virtual void setTextLabel(const QString &, bool);
void setTextLabel(const QString &);
virtual void setToggleButton(bool enable);
virtual void setUsesBigPixmap(bool enable);
virtual void setUsesTextLabel(bool enable);
void toggle();
```

For an example of a QToolButton, see the entry for QToolBar in this chapter.

QVBox

A QVBox is a simple container that organizes its child widgets one above the other.

File

```
#include <qvbox.h>
```

Base Classes

```
QFrame QHBox QObject QPaintDevice QWidget Qt
```

Inherited By

```
KCharSelect
```

Constructors

```
QVBox(QWidget *parent = 0, const char *name = 0, WFlags f = 0,
    bool allowLines = TRUE);
```

The following example uses a QVBox as the top-level widget. It has four QLabel widgets as its child widgets. As shown in Figure 18-27, each label is displayed one above the other, with a 5-pixel-wide space between them.

```
/* showvbox.cpp */
#include <qapplication.h>
#include <qvbox.h>
#include <qlabel.h>

int main(int argc,char **argv)
{
    QApplication app(argc,argv);
    QVBox *vbox = new QVBox();
    new QLabel("First",vbox);
    new QLabel("Second",vbox);
    new QLabel("Third",vbox);
    new QLabel("Fourth",vbox);
    vbox->setSpacing(5);
    vbox->show();
    app.setMainWidget(vbox);
    return(app.exec());
}
```

Figure 18-27: Labels displayed by a QVBox

QVButtonGroup

The QVButtonGroup is a container widget that organizes a collection of buttons in a vertical column.

File

```
#include <qvbuttongroup.h>
```

Base Classes

```
QButtonGroup QFrame QGroupBox QObject QPaintDevice QWidget
    Qt
```

Constructors

```
QVButtonGroup(QWidget *parent = 0, const char *name = 0);
QVButtonGroup(const QString &title, QWidget *parent = 0,
    const char *name = 0);
```

You can find an example of QVButtonGroup in Chapter 7.

QVGroupBox

The QVGroupBox is a container widget that organizes a collection of widgets in a vertical column.

File

```
#include <qvgroupbox.h>
```

Base Classes

```
QFrame QGroupBox QObject QPaintDevice QWidget Qt
```

Constructors

```
QVGroupBox(QWidget *parent = 0, const char *name = 0);
QVGroupBox(const QString &title, QWidget *parent = 0,
    const char *name = 0);
```

The following example contains four labels inside a QVGroupBox widget. As shown in Figure 18-28, the QVGroupBox widget inherits from QFrame, so it displays a border around the contained widgets, and can optionally display a title.

```
/* showvgroupbox.cpp */
#include <qapplication.h>
#include <qvgroupbox.h>
#include <qlabel.h>

int main(int argc,char **argv)
{
    QApplication app(argc,argv);
    QVGroupBox *vgroupbox = new QVGroupBox();
    new QLabel("First",vgroupbox);
    new QLabel("Second",vgroupbox);
    new QLabel("Third",vgroupbox);
    new QLabel("Fourth",vgroupbox);
    vgroupbox->setTitle("Group Box Title");
    vgroupbox->show();
    app.setMainWidget(vgroupbox);
    return(app.exec());
}
```

Figure 18-28: Four buttons contained by a QVGroupBox

QWidget

The QWidget class is the base class of all user interface classes.

File

```
#include <qwidget.h>
```

Base Classes

```
QObject QPaintDevice Qt
```

Inherited By

Every widget in Qt and KDE use `QWidget` as a base class.

Constructors

```
QWidget(QWidget *parent = 0, const char *name = 0,
    WFlags f = 0);
```

Methods

```
bool acceptDrops() const;
virtual void adjustSize();
bool autoMask() const;
const QColor & backgroundColor() const;
BackgroundMode backgroundMode() const;
BackgroundOrigin backgroundOrigin() const;
const QPixmap *backgroundPixmap() const;
QSize baseSize() const;
QString caption() const;
QRect childrenRect() const;
QRegion childrenRegion() const;
void clearMask();
virtual bool close(bool alsoDelete);
const QColorGroup & colorGroup() const;
const QCursor & cursor() const;
virtual bool customWhatsThis() const;
void drawText(int x, int y, const QString &);
void drawText(const QPoint &, const QString &);
void erase();
void erase(int x, int y, int w, int h);
void erase(const QRect &);
void erase(const QRegion &);
static QWidget *find(WId);
FocusPolicy focusPolicy() const;
QWidget *focusProxy() const;
QWidget *focusWidget() const;
QFont font() const;
QFontInfo fontInfo() const;
QFontMetrics fontMetrics() const;
PropagationMode fontPropagation() const;
const QColor & foregroundColor() const;
QRect frameGeometry() const;
QSize frameSize() const;
const QRect & geometry() const;
void grabKeyboard();
void grabMouse();
void grabMouse(const QCursor &);
bool hasFocus() const;
bool hasMouseTracking() const;
int height() const;
virtual int heightForWidth(int) const;
const QPixmap *icon() const;
QString iconText() const;
bool isActiveWindow() const;
bool isDesktop() const;
```

```
bool isEnabled() const;
bool isEnabledTo(QWidget *) const;
bool isEnabledToTLW() const;
bool isFocusEnabled() const;
bool isMinimized() const;
bool isModal() const;
bool isPopup() const;
bool isTopLevel() const;
bool isUpdatesEnabled() const;
bool isVisible() const;
bool isVisibleTo(QWidget *) const;
bool isVisibleToTLW() const;
static QWidget *keyboardGrabber();
QLayout *layout() const;
QPoint mapFromGlobal(const QPoint &) const;
QPoint mapFromParent(const QPoint &) const;
QPoint mapToGlobal(const QPoint &) const;
QPoint mapToParent(const QPoint &) const;
int maximumHeight() const;
QSize maximumSize() const;
int maximumWidth() const;
QRect microFocusHint() const;
int minimumHeight() const;
QSize minimumSize() const;
virtual QSize minimumSizeHint() const;
int minimumWidth() const;
static QWidget *mouseGrabber();
const QPalette & palette() const;
PropagationMode palettePropagation() const;
QWidget *parentWidget() const;
QPoint pos() const;
void recreate(QWidget *parent, WFlags f, const QPoint &p,
    bool showIt = FALSE);
QRect rect() const;
void releaseKeyboard();
void releaseMouse();
virtual void reparent(QWidget *parent, WFlags, const QPoint &,
    bool showIt = FALSE);
void reparent(QWidget *parent, const QPoint &,
    bool showIt = FALSE);
void scroll(int dx, int dy);
void scroll(int dx, int dy, const QRect &);
virtual void setAcceptDrops(bool on);
virtual void setActiveWindow();
virtual void setAutoMask(bool);
virtual void setBackgroundColor(const QColor &);
virtual void setBackgroundMode(BackgroundMode);
void setBackgroundOrigin(BackgroundOrigin);
virtual void setBackgroundPixmap(const QPixmap &);
void setBaseSize(const QSize &);
void setBaseSize(int basew, int baseh);
virtual void setCursor(const QCursor &);
void setFixedHeight(int h);
void setFixedSize(const QSize &);
```

```
void setFixedSize(int w, int h);
void setFixedWidth(int w);
virtual void setFocusPolicy(FocusPolicy);
virtual void setFocusProxy(QWidget *);
virtual void setFont(const QFont &);
void setFont(const QFont &, bool iReallyMeanIt);
virtual void setFontPropagation(PropagationMode);
virtual void setMask(const QBitmap &);
virtual void setMask(const QRegion &);
void setMaximumHeight(int maxh);
void setMaximumSize(const QSize &);
virtual void setMaximumSize(int maxw, int maxh);
void setMaximumWidth(int maxw);
void setMinimumHeight(int minh);
void setMinimumSize(const QSize &);
virtual void setMinimumSize(int minw, int minh);
void setMinimumWidth(int minw);
void setName(const char *name);
virtual void setPalette(const QPalette &);
void setPalette(const QPalette &, bool iReallyMeanIt);
virtual void setPalettePropagation(PropagationMode);
void setSizeIncrement(const QSize &);
virtual void setSizeIncrement(int w, int h);
void setStyle(QStyle *);
static void setTabOrder(QWidget *, QWidget *);
QSize size() const;
virtual QSize sizeHint() const;
QSize sizeIncrement() const;
virtual QSizePolicy sizePolicy() const;
QStyle & style() const;
bool testWFlags(WFlags n) const;
bool testWState(uint n) const;
QWidget *topLevelWidget() const;
virtual void unsetCursor();
void unsetFont();
void unsetPalette();
void updateGeometry();
QRect visibleRect() const;
int width() const;
WId winId() const;
static QWidgetMapper *wmapper();
int x() const;
int y() const;
```

Slots

```
void clearFocus();
bool close();
void constPolish() const;
virtual void hide();
void iconify();
void lower();
virtual void move(int x, int y);
void move(const QPoint &);
virtual void polish();
```

```
void raise();
void repaint();
void repaint(bool erase);
void repaint(int x, int y, int w, int h, bool erase = TRUE);
void repaint(const QRect &, bool erase = TRUE);
void repaint(const QRegion &, bool erase = TRUE);
virtual void resize(int w, int h);
void resize(const QSize &);
virtual void setCaption(const QString &);
virtual void setEnabled(bool);
virtual void setFocus();
virtual void setGeometry(int x, int y, int w, int h);
virtual void setGeometry(const QRect &);
virtual void setIcon(const QPixmap &);
virtual void setIconText(const QString &);
virtual void setMouseTracking(bool enable);
virtual void setUpdatesEnabled(bool enable);
virtual void show();
void showFullScreen();
virtual void showMaximized();
virtual void showMinimized();
virtual void showNormal();
void update();
void update(int x, int y, int w, int h);
void update(const QRect &);
```

Enums

```
enum BackgroundMode { FixedColor, FixedPixmap, NoBackground,
      PaletteForeground, PaletteButton, PaletteLight,
      PaletteMidlight, PaletteDark, PaletteMid, PaletteText,
      PaletteBrightText, PaletteBase, PaletteBackground,
      PaletteShadow, PaletteHighlight, PaletteHighlightedText
};
enum PropagationMode { NoChildren, AllChildren, SameFont,
      SamePalette=SameFont };
enum FocusPolicy { NoFocus=0, TabFocus=0x1, ClickFocus=0x2,
      StrongFocus=0x3, WheelFocus=0x7 };
enum BackgroundOrigin { WidgetOrigin, ParentOrigin };
```

Throughout the book, you can find a number of examples using QWidget, both as a standalone widget and as a base class.

QWidgetStack

The QWidgetStack widget is a container that displays only one widget at a time.

File

```
#include <qwidgetstack.h>
```

Base Classes

```
QFrame QObject QPaintDevice QWidget Qt
```

Constructors

```
QWidgetStack(QWidget *parent = 0, const char *name = 0);
```

Methods

```
void addWidget(QWidget *, int);
int id(QWidget *) const;
QSize minimumSizeHint() const;
void removeWidget(QWidget *);
void setFrameRect(const QRect &);
void show();
QSize sizeHint() const;
QWidget *visibleWidget() const;
QWidget *widget(int) const;
```

Slots

```
void raiseWidget(int);
void raiseWidget(QWidget *);
```

Signals

```
void aboutToShow(int);
void aboutToShow(QWidget *);
```

The following example creates and adds three QPushButton widgets to a
QWidgetStack. As shown in Figure 18-29, the only widget displayed is the one
that had its ID number used in a call to raiseWidget().

```
/* showwidgetstack.cpp */
#include <qapplication.h>
#include <qwidgetstack.h>
#include <qpushbutton.h>

int main(int argc,char **argv)
{
    QPushButton *button;
    QApplication app(argc,argv);
    QWidgetStack *widgetstack = new QWidgetStack();
    button = new QPushButton("First Button",widgetstack);
    widgetstack->addWidget(button,1);
    button = new QPushButton("Second Button",widgetstack);
    widgetstack->addWidget(button,2);
    button = new QPushButton("Third Button",widgetstack);
    widgetstack->addWidget(button,3);
    widgetstack->raiseWidget(2);
    widgetstack->show();
    app.setMainWidget(widgetstack);
    return(app.exec());
}
```

 Figure 18-29: A QWidgetStack widget displaying one of its widgets

QWizard

The QWizard widget can be used to create a dialog that guides the user through a sequence of steps. Each step consists of a single window. The QWizard widget provides the paging mechanism and the control buttons.

File

```
#include <qwizard.h>
```

Base Classes

```
QDialog QObject QPaintDevice QWidget Qt
```

Inherited By

```
KWizard
```

Constructors

```
QWizard(QWidget *parent = 0, const char *name = 0,
    bool modal = FALSE, WFlags f = 0);
```

Methods

```
virtual void addPage(QWidget *, const QString &);
virtual bool appropriate(QWidget *) const;
QPushButton *backButton() const;
QPushButton *cancelButton() const;
QWidget *currentPage() const;
bool eventFilter(QObject *, QEvent *);
QPushButton *finishButton() const;
QPushButton *helpButton() const;
QPushButton *nextButton() const;
QWidget *page(int pos) const;
int pageCount() const;
virtual void removePage(QWidget *);
virtual void setAppropriate(QWidget *, bool);
void setFont(const QFont &font);
void show();
virtual void showPage(QWidget *);
QString title(QWidget *) const;
```

Slots

```
virtual void setBackEnabled(QWidget *, bool);
virtual void setFinish(QWidget *, bool);
virtual void setFinishEnabled(QWidget *, bool);
virtual void setHelpEnabled(QWidget *, bool);
virtual void setNextEnabled(QWidget *, bool);
```

Signals

```
void helpClicked();
```

The following example displays the empty QWizard widget shown in Figure 18-30.

```
/* showwizard.cpp */
#include <qapplication.h>
#include <qwizard.h>

int main(int argc,char **argv)
{
    QPushButton *button;
    QApplication app(argc,argv);
    QWizard *wizard = new QWizard();
    wizard->show();
    app.setMainWidget(wizard);
    return(app.exec());
}
```

Figure 18-30: The QWizard widget

Summary

This chapter provided an alphabetical listing of every Qt widget. Each widget was listed along with the following:

✦ The constructor, or constructors, that can be used to create instances of the widget

✦ The name of the header file in which the widget is defined

✦ All of the superclasses from which the widget inherits capabilities

✦ All of the subclasses that derive the capabilities of the widget

✦ The slots and signals that are used to connect an event in one widget to a method call in another

✦ The public methods available to your application

The next chapter lists the KDE widgets. A KDE widget is any KDE class that inherits from QWidget.

✦   ✦   ✦

The Widgets of KDE

In This Chapter

Determining
the footprint
of the constructors
for each widget

Determining the
header file required
for each widget

Determining the
superclasses and
subclasses of
each widget

Determining the slots
and signals available
in each widget

Determining all
of the public
methods available
in each widget

Getting started with
a small sample for
the widget

This chapter consists of an alphabetical listing of all the widgets. A widget is a class that contains a displayable window. In KDE, all classes that have a displayable window inherit the window capabilities from the QWidget class. Furthermore, many of the widgets are dialogs — that is, they inherit from QDialog which, in turn, inherits from QWidget. The only difference is that a widget must have a parent and be displayed inside another window, and a dialog has its own top-level window.

Each widget is listed with the name of its header file, the names of all the superclasses, the names of all the KDE and Qt subclasses, the public methods, slots, signals, and the enumerated types.

There are examples of all the widgets except for some of the base and helper classes. The example code provided for each widget creates a displayable form of the widget. Some of the widgets are assigned as the top-level widget and displayed as the main window. Some special purpose widgets, however, are included in a specific environment. In many cases, the widgets are more complicated than can be demonstrated in a simple example, so there are references to locations elsewhere in this book where the widget is used in an example.

KAboutContainer

The KAboutContainer is a skeleton widget that allows you to construct your own About box.

File
    #include <kaboutdialog.h>
Base Classes
    QFrame QObject QPaintDevice QWidget Qt

Constructors

```
KAboutContainer(QWidget *parent = 0, const char *name = 0,
    int margin = 0, int spacing = 0,
    int childAlignment = AlignCenter,
    int innerAlignment = AlignCenter);
```

Methods

```
void addImage(const QString &fileName,
    int alignment = AlignLeft);
void addPerson(const QString &name, const QString &email,
    const QString &url, const QString &task,
    bool showHeader = false, bool showframe = false,
    bool showBold = false);
void addTitle(const QString &title, int alignment = AlignLeft,
    bool showframe = false, bool showBold = false);
void addWidget(QWidget *widget);
virtual QSize minimumSizeHint(void) const;
virtual QSize sizeHint(void) const;
```

Signals

```
void mailClick(const QString &name, const QString &address);
void urlClick(const QString &url);
```

The KAboutContainer widget displays nothing in its window by default, but provides a collection of methods that allows your application to add as many elements as you would like to it. The following example creates the window shown in Figure 19-1 by adding a block of centered text and the information about an individual.

```
/* showaboutcontainer.cpp */
#include <kapp.h>
#include <kaboutdialog.h>

int main(int argc,char **argv)
{
    KApplication app(argc,argv,"aboutcontainer");
    KAboutContainer *aboutcontainer = new KAboutContainer();
    aboutcontainer->addTitle(
        "A title is a line (or block)\n"
        "of text that is stored in the window.\n",
        Qt::AlignCenter);
    aboutcontainer->addPerson("Phillip Space",
        "phil@nobody.com","http://www.belugalake.com",
        "Responsible for coloring pixels");
    aboutcontainer->show();
    app.setMainWidget(aboutcontainer);
    return(app.exec());
}
```

Figure 19-1: A KAboutContainer widget displaying two items

KAboutContainerBase

The KAboutContainerBase widget is capable of positioning and displaying one or more KAboutContainer widgets.

File
```
#include <kaboutdialog.h>
```

Base Classes
```
QObject QPaintDevice QWidget Qt
```

Constructors
```
KAboutContainerBase(int layoutType, QWidget *parent = 0,
    char *name = 0);
```

Methods
```
KAboutContainer *addContainer(int childAlignment,
    int innerAlignment);
KAboutContainer *addContainerPage(const QString &title,
    int childAlignment = AlignCenter,
    int innerAlignment = AlignCenter);
QFrame *addEmptyPage(const QString &title);
QFrame *addTextPage(const QString &title, const QString &text,
    bool richText = false, int numLines = 10);
void setImage(const QString &fileName);
void setImageBackgroundColor(const QColor &color);
void setImageFrame(bool state);
void setProduct(const QString &appName, const QString &version,
    const QString &author, const QString &year);
void setTitle(const QString &title);
virtual void show(void);
virtual QSize sizeHint(void) const;
```

Slots
```
virtual void slotMailClick(const QString &name,
    const QString &address);
virtual void slotMouseTrack(int mode, const QMouseEvent *e);
virtual void slotUrlClick(const QString &url);
```

Signals

```
void mailClick(const QString &name, const QString &address);
void mouseTrack(int mode, const QMouseEvent *e);
void urlClick(const QString &url);
```

Enums

```
enum LayoutType { AbtPlain=0x0001, AbtTabbed=0x0002,
    AbtTitle=0x0004, AbtImageLeft=0x0008,
    AbtImageRight=0x0010, AbtImageOnly=0x0020,
    AbtProduct=0x0040,
    AbtKDEStandard=AbtTabbed|AbtTitle|AbtImageLeft,
    AbtAppStandard=AbtTabbed|AbtTitle|AbtProduct,
    AbtImageAndTitle=AbtPlain|AbtTitle|AbtImageOnly };
```

Cross-Reference   There are examples of using the KAboutContainerBase widget (inside a KAboutDialog) in Chapter 5.

KAboutContributor

The KAboutContributor widget uses a standard format to present the name and other information about an individual contributor for display inside an About box.

File

```
#include <kaboutdialog.h>
```

Base Classes

```
QFrame QObject QPaintDevice QWidget Qt
```

Constructors

```
KAboutContributor(QWidget *parent = 0, const char *name = 0,
    const QString &username = QString::null,
    const QString &email = QString::null,
    const QString &url = QString::null,
    const QString &work = QString::null,
    bool showHeader = false, bool showFrame = true,
    bool showBold = false);
```

Methods

```
QString getEmail(void);
QString getName(void);
QString getURL(void);
QString getWork(void);
void setEmail(const QString &text,
    const QString &header = QString::null, bool update = true);
void setName(const QString &text,
    const QString &header = QString::null, bool update = true);
void setURL(const QString &text,
```

```
        const QString &header = QString::null, bool update = true);
    void setWork(const QString &text,
        const QString &header = QString::null, bool update = true);
    virtual QSize sizeHint(void) const;
```

Signals

```
    void openURL(const QString &url);
    void sendEmail(const QString &name, const QString &email);
```

The following example creates and displays the KAboutContributor widget shown in Figure 19-2:

```
/* showaboutcontributor.cpp */
#include <kapp.h>
#include <kaboutdialog.h>

int main(int argc,char **argv)
{
    KApplication app(argc,argv,"aboutcontributor");
    KAboutContributor *aboutcontributor =
        new KAboutContributor(0,0,
        "Phillip Space",
        "phil@nobody.com","http://www.belugalake.com",
        "Responsible for coloring pixels");
    aboutcontributor->show();
    app.setMainWidget(aboutcontributor);
    return(app.exec());
}
```

Figure 19-2: A KAboutContributor widget displays information about a single individual.

KAboutDialog

The KAboutDialog widget is a pop-up dialog that displays information about the application.

File

```
    #include <kaboutdialog.h>
```

Base Classes

```
    KDialog KDialogBase QDialog QObject QPaintDevice QWidget Qt
```

Inherited By

```
    KAboutKDE
```

Constructors

```
KAboutDialog(QWidget *parent = 0, const char *name = 0,
    bool modal = true);
KAboutDialog(int dialogLayout, const QString &caption,
    int buttonMask, ButtonCode defaultButton,
    QWidget *parent = 0, const char *name = 0,
    bool modal = false, bool separator = false,
    const QString &user1 = QString::null,
    const QString &user2 = QString::null,
    const QString &user3 = QString::null);
```

Methods

```
KAboutContainer *addContainer(int childAlignment,
    int innerAlignment);
KAboutContainer *addContainerPage(const QString &title,
    int childAlignment = AlignCenter,
    int innerAlignment = AlignCenter);
void addContributor(const QString &name, const QString &email,
    const QString &url, const QString &work);
QFrame *addPage(const QString &title);
QFrame *addTextPage(const QString &title, const QString &text,
    bool richText = false, int numLines = 10);
void adjust();
static void imageURL(QWidget *parent, const QString &caption,
    const QString &path, const QColor &imageColor,
    const QString &url);
void setAuthor(const QString &name, const QString &email,
    const QString &url, const QString &work);
void setImage(const QString &fileName);
void setImageBackgroundColor(const QColor &color);
void setImageFrame(bool state);
void setLogo(const QPixmap &);
void setMaintainer(const QString &name, const QString &email,
    const QString &url, const QString &work);
void setProduct(const QString &appName, const QString &version,
    const QString &author, const QString &year);
void setTitle(const QString &title);
void setVersion(const QString &name);
virtual void show(void);
virtual void show(QWidget *centerParent);
```

Signals

```
void openURL(const QString &url);
void sendEmail(const QString &name, const QString &email);
```

Enums

```
enum LayoutType { AbtPlain=0x0001, AbtTabbed=0x0002,
    AbtTitle=0x0004, AbtImageLeft=0x0008,
    AbtImageRight=0x0010, AbtImageOnly=0x0020,
    AbtProduct=0x0040,
    AbtKDEStandard=AbtTabbed|AbtTitle|AbtImageLeft,
    AbtAppStandard=AbtTabbed|AbtTitle|AbtProduct,
    AbtImageAndTitle=AbtPlain|AbtTitle|AbtImageOnly };
```

You can find examples of `KAboutDialog` in Chapter 5.

KAboutKDE

The `KAboutKDE` dialog is based on the `KAboutDialog`, and is configured to display in the standard KDE format.

File
```
#include <kaboutkde.h>
```
Base Classes
```
KAboutDialog KDialog KDialogBase QDialog QObject
    QPaintDevice QWidget Qt
```
Constructors
```
KAboutKDE(QWidget *parent = 0, const char *name = 0,
    bool modal = true);
```

Examples showing the KDE standard form of the `KAboutDialog` can be found in Chapter 5.

KAboutWidget

The `KAboutWidget` uses one of several formats to display information about an application. It provides a collection of methods that can be used to insert information to be displayed. This is the main widget of `KAboutDialog`.

File
```
#include <kaboutdialog.h>
```
Base Classes
```
QObject QPaintDevice QWidget Qt
```
Constructors
```
KAboutWidget(QWidget *parent = 0, const char *name = 0);
```
Methods
```
void addContributor(const QString &name, const QString &email,
    const QString &url, const QString &work);
void adjust();
void setAuthor(const QString &name, const QString &email,
    const QString &url, const QString &work);
void setLogo(const QPixmap &);
void setMaintainer(const QString &name, const QString &email,
    const QString &url, const QString &work);
void setVersion(const QString &name);
```

Signals

```
void openURL(const QString &url);
void sendEmail(const QString &name, const QString &email);
```

Cross-Reference Chapter 5 provides examples of using KAboutWidget **as the main widget of** KAboutDialog.

KAccelMenu

The KAccelMenu **widget is a helper class for simplifying the use of** KAccel **and** KKeyDialog.

File

```
#include <kaccelmenu.h>
```

Base Classes

```
QFrame QMenuData QObject QPaintDevice QPopupMenu QWidget Qt
```

Constructors

```
KAccelMenu(KAccel *k, QWidget *parent = 0,
    const char *name = 0);
```

Methods

```
int insItem(const QPixmap &pixmap, const char *text,
    const char *action, const QObject *receiver,
    const char *member, const char *accel = 0);
int insItem(const char *text, const char *action,
    const QObject *receiver, const char *member,
    const char *accel = 0);
int insItem(const QPixmap &pixmap, const char *text,
    const char *action, const QObject *receiver,
    const char *member, KStdAccel::StdAccel accel);
int insItem(const char *text, const char *action,
    const QObject *receiver, const char *member,
    KStdAccel::StdAccel accel);
```

KAnimWidget

The KAnimWidget **produces animation by displaying individual pixmaps in a sequence.**

File

```
#include <kanimwidget.h>
```

Base Classes
```
QFrame QObject QPaintDevice QWidget Qt
```
Constructors
```
KAnimWidget(const QStringList &icons, int size = 0,
    QWidget *parent = 0L, const char *name = 0L);
KAnimWidget(QWidget *parent = 0L, const char *name = 0L);
```
Methods
```
void setIcons(const QStringList &icons);
void setSize(int size);
void start();
void stop();
```
Signals
```
void clicked();
```

The following example displays the window shown in Figure 19-3 by loading the pixmaps named flag1.png through flag4.png and displaying them as an animated sequence of frames, one after the other. It will look for the icon files in the share/icons/small directories and in the pics directory for the application. This example will look for the files in ~/.kde/animwidget/pics.

```
/* showanimwidget.cpp */
#include <kapp.h>
#include <kanimwidget.h>
#include <qstringlist.h>

int main(int argc,char **argv)
{
    KApplication app(argc,argv,"animwidget");
    QStringList icons;
    QWidget *widget = new QWidget();
    icons.append("flag1");
    icons.append("flag2");
    icons.append("flag3");
    icons.append("flag4");
    KAnimWidget *kanimwidget = new KAnimWidget(icons,0,widget);
    kanimwidget->start();
    widget->show();
    app.setMainWidget(widget);
    return(app.exec());
}
```

Figure 19-3: One frame of an animated sequence controlled by a KAnimWidget

KAuthIcon

The KAuthIcon widget is the base class of widgets designed to indicate whether a user has (or is denied) the capability to perform some action.

File
```
#include <kauthicon.h>
```
Base Classes
```
QObject QPaintDevice QWidget Qt
```
Inherited By
```
KRootPermsIcon KWritePermsIcon
```
Constructors
```
KAuthIcon(QWidget *parent = 0, const char *name = 0);
```
Methods
```
virtual QSize sizeHint() const;
virtual bool status() const = 0;
```
Slots
```
virtual void updateStatus() = 0;
```
Signals
```
void authChanged(bool authorized);
```

KBugReport

The KBugReport is the base class for dialogs that accept bug reports from the user. You should not need to create one of these because KHelpMenu creates a KBugReport dialog for you.

File
```
#include <kbugreport.h>
```
Base Classes
```
KDialog KDialogBase QDialog QObject QPaintDevice QWidget Qt
```
Constructors
```
KBugReport(QWidget *parent = OL, bool modal = true,
    const KAboutData *aboutData = OL);
```

KButtonBox

The KButtonBox is a container holding a group of buttons organized either vertically or horizontally.

File

```
#include <kbuttonbox.h>
```

Base Classes

```
QObject QPaintDevice QWidget Qt
```

Constructors

```
KButtonBox(QWidget *parent, int _orientation = HORIZONTAL,
    int border = 0, int _autoborder = 6);
```

Methods

```
QPushButton *addButton(const QString &text,
    bool noexpand = FALSE);
void addStretch(int scale = 1);
void layout();
virtual void resizeEvent(QResizeEvent *);
virtual QSize sizeHint() const;
```

Enums

```
enum (anon) { VERTICAL=1, HORIZONTAL=2 };
```

Cross-Reference You can find examples of KButtonBox in Chapter 7.

KCharSelect

The KCharSelect widget enables the user to select a font, and then select a single character from the font.

File

```
#include <kcharselect.h>
```

Base Classes

```
QFrame QHBox QObject QPaintDevice QVBox QWidget Qt
```

Constructors

```
KCharSelect(QWidget *parent, const char *name,
    const QString &font = QString::null, const QChar &chr = ,
    int tableNum = 0);
```

Methods

```
virtual QChar chr();
virtual void enableFontCombo(bool e);
virtual void enableTableSpinBox(bool e);
virtual QString font();
virtual bool isFontComboEnabled();
virtual bool isTableSpinBoxEnabled();
virtual void setChar(const QChar &chr);
```

```
virtual void setFont(const QString &font);
virtual void setTableNum(int tableNum);
virtual QSize sizeHint() const;
virtual int tableNum();
```

Signals

```
void activated(const QChar &c);
void activated();
void focusItemChanged();
void focusItemChanged(const QChar &c);
void fontChanged(const QString &_font);
void highlighted(const QChar &c);
void highlighted();
```

The following example displays the KCharSelect window shown in Figure 19-4:

```cpp
/* showcharselect.cpp */
#include <kapp.h>
#include <kcharselect.h>
#include <qstring.h>

int main(int argc,char **argv)
{
    KApplication app(argc,argv,"showcharselect");
    QWidget *widget = new QWidget();
    KCharSelect *kcharselect =
            new KCharSelect(widget,"charselect");
    kcharselect->resize(kcharselect->sizeHint());
    widget->resize(kcharselect->sizeHint());
    widget->show();
    app.setMainWidget(widget);
    return(app.exec());
}
```

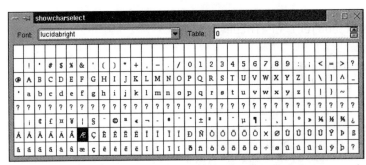

Figure 19-4: A KCharSelect widget with both a font and character selected

KCharSelectTable

The `KCharSelectTable` widget is the character-display portion of the `KCharSelect` widget.

File

```
#include <kcharselect.h>
```

Base Classes

```
QFrame QObject QPaintDevice QTableView QWidget Qt
```

Constructors

```
KCharSelectTable(QWidget *parent, const char *name,
    const QString &_font, const QChar &_chr, int _tableNum);
```

Methods

```
virtual QChar chr();
virtual void setChar(const QChar &_chr);
virtual void setFont(const QString &_font);
virtual void setTableNum(int _tableNum);
virtual QSize sizeHint() const;
```

Signals

```
void activated(const QChar &c);
void activated();
void focusItemChanged();
void focusItemChanged(const QChar &c);
void highlighted(const QChar &c);
void highlighted();
void tableDown();
void tableUp();
```

For an example, see `KCharSelect`.

KCModule

The `KCModule` widget is the base class of all of the control modules. The resulting widget appears as one of the `kcontrol` windows, and can be used to adjust configuration settings.

File

```
#include <kcmodule.h>
```

Base Classes

```
QObject QPaintDevice QWidget Qt
```

Constructors
```
KCModule(QWidget *parent = 0, const char *name = 0) : QWidget
    ( parent , name ) , _btn ( Help | Default | Reset |
    Cancel | Apply | Ok );
```

Methods
```
int buttons();
virtual void defaults();
static void init();
virtual void load();
virtual QString quickHelp();
virtual void save();
virtual void sysdefaults();
```

Signals
```
void changed(bool state);
```

Enums
```
enum Button { Help=1, Default=2, Reset=4, Cancel=8, Apply=16,
    Ok=32, SysDefault=64 };
```

KColorButton

The KColorButton widget is a pushbutton filled with a color instead of text;
when selected, it pops up a dialog that enables the user to select another color.

File
```
#include <kcolorbtn.h>
```

Base Classes
```
QButton QObject QPaintDevice QPushButton QWidget Qt
```

Constructors
```
KColorButton(QWidget *parent, const char *name = OL);
KColorButton(const QColor &c, QWidget *parent,
    const char *name = OL);
```

Methods
```
const QColor color() const;
void setColor(const QColor &c);
```

Signals
```
void changed(const QColor &newColor);
```

The following example creates a KColorButton using red. As shown in Figure 19-5,
selecting the button causes the dialog to appear. The user can then select another
color, which will both change the color of the KColorButton and emit the changed()
signal.

```
/* showcolorbutton.cpp */
#include <kapp.h>
#include <kcolorbtn.h>
#include <qcolor.h>

int main(int argc,char **argv)
{
    KApplication app(argc,argv,"showcolorbutton");
    KColorButton *colorbutton =
            new KColorButton(0,"colorbutton");
    colorbutton->setColor(QColor("red"));
    colorbutton->resize(colorbutton->sizeHint());
    colorbutton->show();
    app.setMainWidget(colorbutton);
    return(app.exec());
}
```

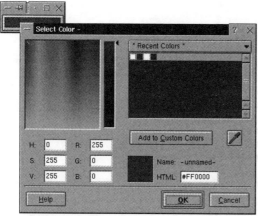

Figure 19-5: The KColorButton pops up a dialog for color selection.

KColorCells

The KColorCells widget displays a collection of colors and enables the user to select one of them.File

```
#include <kcolordlg.h>
```

Base Classes

```
QFrame QObject QPaintDevice QTableView QWidget Qt
```

Constructors

```
KColorCells(QWidget *parent, int rows, int cols);
```

Methods

```
QColor color(int indx);
int getSelected();
int numCells();
void setAcceptDrags(bool _acceptDrags);
void setColor(int colNum, const QColor &col);
void setShading(bool _shade);
```

Signals

```
void colorSelected(int col);
```

The following example displays the list of color cells shown in Figure 19-6:

```
/* showcolorcells.cpp */
#include <kapp.h>
#include <kcolordlg.h>

int main(int argc,char **argv)
{
    KApplication app(argc,argv,"showcolorcells");
    KColorCells *colorcells =
            new KColorCells(0,1,5);
    colorcells->setColor(0,QColor("magenta"));
    colorcells->setColor(1,QColor("red"));
    colorcells->setColor(2,QColor("blue"));
    colorcells->setColor(3,QColor("green"));
    colorcells->setColor(4,QColor("cyan"));
    colorcells->show();
    app.setMainWidget(colorcells);
    return(app.exec());
}
```

Figure 19-6: A KColorCells widget displaying
a row of five colors

KColorCombo

The KColorCombo widget displays a pull-down list of colors for selection with
the mouse.

File

```
#include <kcolordlg.h>
```

Base Classes

```
QComboBox QObject QPaintDevice QWidget Qt
```

Constructors

```
KColorCombo(QWidget *parent, const char *name = OL);
```

Methods

```
void setColor(const QColor &col);
```

Slots

```
void slotActivated(int index);
void slotHighlighted(int index);
```

Signals

```
void activated(const QColor &col);
void highlighted(const QColor &col);
```

The following example displays a KColorCombo widget. Figure 19-7 shows the KColorCombo widget after it has been pulled down and a color selection made.

```
/* showcolorcombo.cpp */
#include <kapp.h>
#include <kcolordlg.h>

int main(int argc,char **argv)
{
    KApplication app(argc,argv,"showcolorcombo");
    KColorCombo *colorcombo = new KColorCombo(0,"colorcombo");
    colorcombo->show();
    app.setMainWidget(colorcombo);
    return(app.exec());
}
```

Figure 19-7: A KColorCombo widget enables color selection from a list.

KColorDialog

The KColorDialog is a color selection dialog with several features, including custom colors.

File
```
#include <kcolordlg.h>
```

Base Classes
```
KDialog KDialogBase QDialog QObject QPaintDevice QWidget Qt
```

Constructors
```
KColorDialog(QWidget *parent = OL, const char *name = OL,
    bool modal = FALSE);
```

Methods
```
QColor color();
static int getColor(QColor &theColor, QWidget *parent = OL);
static QColor grabColor(const QPoint &p);
```

Slots
```
void setColor(const QColor &col);
```

Signals
```
void colorSelected(const QColor &col);
```

Cross-Reference You can find an example of the KColorDialog widget in Chapter 11.

KColorPatch

The KColorPatch widget displays a rectangular region of color and responds to being selected with the mouse.

File
```
#include <kcolordlg.h>
```

Base Classes
```
QFrame QObject QPaintDevice QWidget Qt
```

Constructors
```
KColorPatch(QWidget *parent);
```

Methods
```
void setColor(const QColor &col);
```

Signals

```
void colorChanged(const QColor &);
```

The following example uses a KColorPatch widget as the top-level window to display a region of color, as shown in Figure 19-8.

```cpp
/* showcolorpatch.cpp */
#include <kapp.h>
#include <kcolordlg.h>

int main(int argc,char **argv)
{
    KApplication app(argc,argv,"showcolorpatch");
    KColorPatch *colorpatch = new KColorPatch(0);
    colorpatch->setColor(QColor("blue"));
    colorpatch->show();
    app.setMainWidget(colorpatch);
    return(app.exec());
}
```

Figure 19-8: A KColorPatch displaying a region of color

KComboBox

The KComboBox widget is a button that allows the user to make a selection from a list. It always displays the current selection at its top.

File

```
#include <kcombobox.h>
```

Base Classes

```
KCompletionBase QComboBox QObject QPaintDevice QWidget Qt
```

Inherited By

```
KFileComboBox KFileFilter KURLComboBox
```

Constructors

```
KComboBox(QWidget *parent = 0, const char *name = 0);
KComboBox(bool rw, QWidget *parent = 0, const char *name = 0);
```

Methods

```
bool autoCompletion() const;
int cursorPosition() const;
```

```
bool isContextMenuEnabled() const;
bool isEditable() const;
virtual void setAutoCompletion(bool autocomplete);
virtual void setEnableContextMenu(bool showMenu);
```

Slots

```
void rotateText(KeyBindingType);
```

Signals

```
void completion(const QString &);
void nextMatch(KeyBindingType);
void previousMatch(KeyBindingType);
void returnPressed();
void returnPressed(const QString &);
void rotateDown(KeyBindingType);
void rotateUp(KeyBindingType);
```

The following example creates a KComboBox with four selections. Figure 19-9 shows the widget after the mouse has been used to pop up the list, and with the third selection as the default.

```
/* showcombobox.cpp */
#include <kapp.h>
#include <kcombobox.h>

const char *list[] = {
    "First Selection",
    "Second Selection",
    "Third Selection",
    "Fourth Selection"
};

int main(int argc,char **argv)
{
    KApplication app(argc,argv,"showcombobox");
    KComboBox *combobox = new KComboBox();
    combobox->insertStrList(list,4);
    combobox->show();
    app.setMainWidget(combobox);
    return(app.exec());
}
```

Figure 19-9: A KComboBox with the third list member selected

KContainerLayout

The KContainerLayout widget is a layout manager that can be configured to manage widget positions and sizes in a number of ways.

File

```
#include <kcontainer.h>
```

Base Classes

```
QFrame QObject QPaintDevice QWidget Qt
```

Constructors

```
KContainerLayout(QWidget *parent - 0, const char *name = 0,
    int orientation = KContainerLayout::Horizontal,
    bool homogeneos = FALSE, int spacing = 5, WFlags f = 0,
    bool allowLines = TRUE);
KContainerLayoutItem(QWidget *w, bool e = FALSE,
    bool f = FALSE, int p = 0);
```

Methods

```
const int endOffset() const;
const bool expand() const;
const bool fill() const;
int getNumberOfWidgets() const;
const bool homogeneos() const;
const int orientation() const;
int packEnd(QWidget *w, bool e = FALSE, bool f = FALSE,
    int p = 1);
int packStart(QWidget *w, bool e = FALSE, bool f = FALSE,
    int p = 1);
const int padding() const;
void setEndOffset(int i);
void setExpand(bool b);
void setFill(bool b);
void setHomogeneos(bool b);
void setOrientation(int i);
void setPadding(int i);
void setSpacing(int i);
void setStartOffset(int i);
void sizeToFit();
const int spacing() const;
const int startOffset() const;
QWidget *widget();
```

Enums

```
enum (anon) { Horizontal=0, Vertical };
```

Cross-Reference   Example programs that use KContainerLayout can be found in Chapters 3 and 6.

KDatePicker

The KDatePicker presents a calendar to the user and enables a date to be selected with the mouse.

File
```
#include <kdatepik.h>
```

Base Classes
```
QFrame QObject QPaintDevice QWidget Qt
```

Constructors
```
KDatePicker(QWidget *parent = 0, QDate = QDate::currentDate ()
    , const char * name = 0 );
```

Methods
```
const QDate & getDate();
bool setDate(const QDate &);
void setEnabled(bool);
void setFontSize(int);
QSize sizeHint() const;
```

Signals
```
void dateChanged(QDate);
void dateEntered(QDate);
void dateSelected(QDate);
void tableClicked();
```

The following example displays a KDatePicker widget as the top-level window. As shown in Figure 19-10, the left and right arrows at the top allow the mouse to be used to change the month and year. A date is selected from the calendar. If the KDatePicker window is resized, each part of the calendar and its controls are also resized, so all of the parts maintain their aspects.

```cpp
/* showdatepicker.cpp */
#include <kapp.h>
#include <kdatepik.h>

int main(int argc,char **argv)
{
    KApplication app(argc,argv,"showdatepicker");
    KDatePicker *datepicker = new KDatePicker();
    datepicker->resize(datepicker->sizeHint());
    datepicker->show();
```

```
        app.setMainWidget(datepicker);
        return(app.exec());
}
```

Figure 19-10: A KDatePicker widget

KDateTable

A KDateTable displays a single month and enables the user to select a day with
the mouse.

File
```
#include <kdatetbl.h>
```

Base Classes
```
QFrame QObject QPaintDevice QTableView QWidget Qt
```

Constructors
```
KDateTable(QWidget *parent = 0,
    QDate date = QDate::currentDate () , const char * name =
    0 , WFlags f = 0 );
```

Methods
```
const QDate & getDate();
bool setDate(const QDate &);
void setFontSize(int size);
QSize sizeHint() const;
```

Signals
```
void dateChanged(QDate);
void tableClicked();
```

The KDateTable widget is not a standalone date selector, but is meant to be a component in another widget, such as the KDatePicker. For one thing, the name of the
month is not displayed, as you can see in Figure 19-11.

```
/* showdatetable.cpp */
#include <kapp.h>
#include <kdatetbl.h>
```

```
int main(int argc,char **argv)
{
    KApplication app(argc,argv,"showdatetable");
    KDateTable *datetable = new KDateTable();
    datetable->show();
    app.setMainWidget(datetable);
    return(app.exec());
}
```

Figure 19-11: A KDateTable widget

KDialog

The KDialog widget is a base class for modeless KDE widgets. It extends QDialog to include a set of standard KDE methods for dialogs. It is the base class on which KDialogBase is built.

File
```
#include <kdialog.h>
```

Base Classes
```
QDialog QObject QPaintDevice QWidget Qt
```

Inherited By
```
KAboutDialog KAboutKDE KBugReport KColorDialog KCookieWin
    KDialogBase KEdFind KEdGotoLine KEdReplace KEditToolbar
    KFileDialog KFileDialogConfigureDlg KFontDialog
    KIconDialog KKeyDialog KLineEditDlg KPasswordDialog
    KTextPrintDialog KURLRequesterDlg KabAPI
```

Constructors
```
KDialog(QWidget *parent = 0, const char *name = 0,
    bool modal = false, WFlags f = 0);
```

Methods
```
static int marginHint();
static void resizeLayout(QWidget *widget, int margin,
    int spacing);
static void resizeLayout(QLayoutItem *lay, int margin,
```

```
      int spacing);
   static int spacingHint();
```

Slots

```
   virtual void setCaption(const QString &caption);
   virtual void setPlainCaption(const QString &caption);
```

Signals

```
   void layoutHintChanged();
```

KDialogBase

The KDialogBase is the base class for building dialogs in KDE. Among other things, it contains the standard set of KDE buttons for dialogs.

File

```
   #include <kdialogbase.h>
```

Base Classes

```
   KDialog QDialog QObject QPaintDevice QWidget Qt
```

Inherited By

```
   KAboutDialog KAboutKDE KBugReport KColorDialog KCookieWin
      KEdFind KEdGotoLine KEdReplace KEditToolbar KFileDialog
      KFileDialogConfigureDlg KFontDialog KIconDialog
      KKeyDialog KLineEditDlg KPasswordDialog KTextPrintDialog
      KURLRequesterDlg KabAPI
```

Constructors

```
   KDialogBase(QWidget *parent = 0, const char *name = 0,
      bool modal = true, const QString &caption = QString::null,
      int buttonMask = Ok | Apply | Cancel,
      ButtonCode defaultButton = Ok, bool separator = false,
      const QString &user1 = QString::null,
      const QString &user2 = QString::null,
      const QString &user3 = QString::null);
   KDialogBase(int dialogFace, const QString &caption,
      int buttonMask, ButtonCode defaultButton,
      QWidget *parent = 0, const char *name = 0,
      bool modal = true, bool separator = false,
      const QString &user1 = QString::null,
      const QString &user2 = QString::null,
      const QString &user3 = QString::null);
   KDialogBase(const QString &caption,
      int buttonMask = Yes | No | Cancel,
      ButtonCode defaultButton = Yes,
      ButtonCode escapeButton = Cancel, QWidget *parent = 0,
      const char *name = 0, bool modal = true,
```

```
        bool separator = false, QString yes = QString::null,
        QString no = QString::null, QString cancel =
    QString::null);
```

Methods

```
    QPushButton *actionButton(ButtonCode id);
    int activePageIndex() const;
    QGrid *addGridPage(int n, QGrid::Direction dir,
        const QString &itemName,
        const QString &header = QString::null,
        const QPixmap &pixmap = QPixmap () );
    QHBox *addHBoxPage(const QString &itemName,
        const QString &header = QString::null,
        const QPixmap &pixmap = QPixmap () );
    QFrame *addPage(const QString &item,
        const QString &header = QString::null,
        const QPixmap &pixmap = QPixmap () );
    QVBox *addVBoxPage(const QString &itemName,
        const QString &header = QString::null,
        const QPixmap &pixmap = QPixmap () );
    virtual void adjustSize();
    QSize calculateSize(int w, int h);
    void delayedDestruct();
    void disableResize();
    void enableButtonSeparator(bool state);
    static const QPixmap *getBackgroundTile();
    void getBorderWidths(int &ulx, int &uly, int &lrx, int &lry)
        const;
    QRect getContentsRect();
    QWidget *getMainWidget();
    static bool haveBackgroundTile();
    QString helpLinkText();
    void incInitialSize(const QSize &s, bool noResize = false);
    QGrid *makeGridMainWidget(int n, QGrid::Direction dir);
    QHBox *makeHBoxMainWidget();
    QFrame *makeMainWidget();
    QVBox *makeVBoxMainWidget();
    int pageIndex(QWidget *widget) const;
    QFrame *plainPage();
    static void setBackgroundTile(const QPixmap *pix);
    void setButtonApplyText(const QString &text = QString::null,
        const QString &tooltip = QString::null,
        const QString &quickhelp = QString::null);
    void setButtonCancelText(const QString &text = QString::null,
        const QString &tooltip = QString::null,
        const QString &quickhelp = QString::null);
    void setButtonOKText(const QString &text = QString::null,
        const QString &tooltip = QString::null,
        const QString &quickhelp = QString::null);
    void setButtonText(ButtonCode id, const QString &text);
    void setButtonTip(ButtonCode id, const QString &text);
    void setButtonWhatsThis(ButtonCode id, const QString &text);
```

```
    void setIconListAllVisible(bool state);
    void setInitialSize(const QSize &s, bool noResize = false);
    void setMainWidget(QWidget *widget);
    void setTreeListAutoResize(bool state);
    void showButton(ButtonCode id, bool state);
    void showButtonApply(bool state);
    void showButtonCancel(bool state);
    void showButtonOK(bool state);
    bool showPage(int index);
    void showTile(bool state);
```

Slots

```
    void enableButton(ButtonCode id, bool state);
    void enableButtonApply(bool state);
    void enableButtonCancel(bool state);
    void enableButtonOK(bool state);
    void enableLinkedHelp(bool state);
    void helpClickedSlot(const QString &);
    void setHelp(const QString &path, const QString &topic);
    void setHelpLinkText(const QString &text);
    void updateBackground();
```

Signals

```
    void apply();
    void applyClicked();
    void backgroundChanged();
    void cancelClicked();
    void closeClicked();
    void defaultClicked();
    void helpClicked();
    void hidden();
    void noClicked();
    void okClicked();
    void tryClicked();
    void user1Clicked();
    void user2Clicked();
    void user3Clicked();
    void yesClicked();
```

Enums

```
    enum ButtonCode { Help=0x00000001, Default=0x00000002,
        Ok=0x00000004, Apply=0x00000008, Try=0x00000010,
        Cancel=0x00000020, Close=0x00000040, User1=0x00000080,
        User2=0x00000100, User3=0x00000200, No=0x00000080,
        Yes=0x00000100, Stretch=0x80000000 };
    enum ActionButtonStyle { ActionStyle0=0, ActionStyle1,
        ActionStyle2, ActionStyle3, ActionStyle4,
        ActionStyleMAX };
    enum DialogType { TreeList=KJanusWidget::TreeList,
        Tabbed=KJanusWidget::Tabbed, Plain=KJanusWidget::Plain,
        Swallow=KJanusWidget::Swallow,
        IconList=KJanusWidget::IconList };
```

There are several examples of using KDialogBase to build dialogs in Chapter 4.

KDialogBaseButton

The KDialogBaseButton is used internally by KDialogBase to add the unique button ID numbers that are used in the callback methods.

File
```
#include <kdialogbase.h>
```

Base Classes
```
QButton QObject QPaintDevice QPushButton QWidget Qt
```

Constructors
```
KDialogBaseButton(const QString &text, int key,
    QWidget *parent = 0, const char *name = 0);
```

Methods
```
inline int id();
```

There are several examples of using KDialogBase to build dialogs in Chapter 4.

KDirectionButton

The KDirectionButton is a QButton widget that is displayed as an up, down, left, or right arrow.

File
```
#include <kdbtn.h>
```

Base Classes
```
QButton QObject QPaintDevice QWidget Qt
```

Inherited By
```
KTabButton
```

Constructors
```
KDirectionButton(QWidget *parent = 0, const char *name = 0);
KDirectionButton(ArrowType d, QWidget *parent = 0,
    const char *name = 0);
```

Methods
```
ArrowType direction();
void setDirection(ArrowType d);
```

The following example displays the right pointing arrow shown in Figure 19-12. The arrow direction names are UpArrow, DownArrow, LeftArrow, and RightArrow.

```
/* showdirectionbutton.cpp */
#include <kapp.h>
#include <kdbtn.h>

int main(int argc,char **argv)
{
    KApplication app(argc,argv,"showdirectionbutton");
    KDirectionButton *directionbutton =
            new KDirectionButton(Qt::RightArrow);
    directionbutton->show();
    app.setMainWidget(directionbutton);
    return(app.exec());
}
```

Figure 19-12: A KDirectionButton widget with a right-pointing arrow

KDockMainWindow

The KDockMainWindow is a special version of KTMainWindow that allows KDockWidgets to be docked along its edges.

File
```
#include <kdockwidget.h>
```

Base Classes
```
KTMainWindow KXMLGUIBuilder KXMLGUIClient QObject
    QPaintDevice QWidget Qt
```

Constructors
```
KDockMainWindow(const char *name = OL);
```

Methods
```
void activateDock();
KDockWidget *createDockWidget(const QString &name,
    const QPixmap &pixmap, QWidget *parent = OL);
QPopupMenu *dockHideShowMenu();
KDockWidget *getMainDockWidget();
void makeDockInvisible(KDockWidget *dock);
void makeDockVisible(KDockWidget *dock);
void makeWidgetDockVisible(QWidget *widget);
```

```
KDockManager *manager();
void readDockConfig(KConfig *c = OL,
    QString group = QString::null);
void setMainDockWidget(KDockWidget *);
void setView(QWidget *);
void writeDockConfig(KConfig *c = OL,
    QString group = QString::null);
```

The following example uses a KDockMainWindow as the top-level widget shown in Figure 19-13:

```
/* showdockmainwindow.cpp */
#include <kapp.h>
#include <kdockwidget.h>

int main(int argc,char **argv)
{
    KApplication app(argc,argv,"showdatetable");
    KDockMainWindow *dockmainwindow = new KDockMainWindow();
    dockmainwindow->setBackgroundColor(QColor("blue"));
    dockmainwindow->show();
    app.setMainWidget(dockmainwindow);
    return(app.exec());
}
```

Figure 19-13: A KDockMainWindow widget used as a top-level window

For an example of adding dockable widgets, see KDockWidget.

KDockWidget

A KDockWidget is a special container widget that can hold any widget that you would like to be one of the dockable widgets in a KDockMainWindow widget.

File
```
#include <kdockwidget.h>
```
Base Classes
```
QObject QPaintDevice QWidget Qt
```

Constructors

```
KDockWidget(KDockManager *dockManager, const char *name,
    const QPixmap &pixmap, QWidget *parent = OL);
```

Methods

```
KDockManager *dockManager();
int dockSite();
int enableDocking();
virtual bool event(QEvent *);
QWidget *getWidget();
bool isDockBackPossible();
void makeDockVisible();
KDockWidget *manualDock(KDockWidget *target,
    DockPosition dockPos, int spliPos = 50,
    QPoint pos = QPoint ( 0 ) , bool check = false );
bool mayBeHide();
bool mayBeShow();
void setDockSite(int pos);
void setEnableDocking(int pos);
void setHeader(KDockWidgetAbstractHeader *ah);
void setToolTipString(const QString &ttStr);
void setWidget(QWidget *w);
virtual void show();
const QString & toolTipString();
```

Slots

```
void changeHideShowState();
void dockBack();
void undock();
```

Signals

```
void docking(KDockWidget *dw, KDockWidget::DockPosition dp);
void headerCloseButtonClicked();
void headerDockbackButtonClicked();
void iMBeingClosed();
void setDockDefaultPos();
```

Enums

```
enum DockPosition { DockNone=0, DockTop=0x0001,
    DockLeft=0x0002, DockRight=0x0004, DockBottom=0x0008,
    DockCenter=0x0010, DockDesktop=0x0020,
    DockCorner=DockTop|DockLeft|DockRight|DockBottom,
    DockFullSite=DockCorner|DockCenter,
    DockFullDocking=DockFullSite|DockDesktop };
```

The following example uses three KDockWidget widgets to add three widgets to a KDockMainWindow. As shown in Figure 19-14, the widgets are displayed in a paneled window. The entire window can be configured using a mouse. Also, in addition to the bars between the widgets that can be used to expand and contract the window sizes, there is a control bar (which is also dockable) that can be used to enable or disable the appearance of each docked widgets. The call to setMainDockWidget() specifies the widget that is to appear in the space left by the widgets docked on the edges — in this example, it is the area in the upper-right corner.

```
/* showdockwidget.cpp */
#include <kapp.h>
#include <kdockwidget.h>

int main(int argc,char **argv)
{
    KApplication app(argc,argv,"showdatetable");
    KDockMainWindow *dockmainwindow = new KDockMainWindow();

    QPixmap pixmap("idea.png");

    KDockWidget *mainDock =
        dockmainwindow->createDockWidget("Main Dock",pixmap);
    QWidget *actualMain = new QWidget(mainDock);
    actualMain->setBackgroundColor(QColor("green"));
    actualMain->setMinimumSize(200,200);
    dockmainwindow->setView(mainDock);
    dockmainwindow->setMainDockWidget(mainDock);

    KDockWidget *leftDock =
        dockmainwindow->createDockWidget("Left Dock",pixmap);
    QWidget *actualLeft = new QWidget(leftDock);
    actualLeft->setBackgroundColor(QColor("blue"));
    actualLeft->setMinimumSize(200,200);
    leftDock->manualDock(mainDock,
        KDockWidget::DockLeft,20);

    KDockWidget *bottomDock =
        dockmainwindow->createDockWidget("Bottom Dock",pixmap);
    QWidget *actualBottom = new QWidget(bottomDock);
    actualBottom->setBackgroundColor(QColor("red"));
    actualBottom->setMinimumSize(200,200);
    bottomDock->manualDock(mainDock,
        KDockWidget::DockBottom,20);

    dockmainwindow->activateDock();
    app.setMainWidget(dockmainwindow);
    return(app.exec());
}
```

Figure 19-14: KDockWidgets used to dock three widgets in a KDockMainWindow

KDoubleNumInput

The `KDoubleNumInput` widget is designed to input and verify user input of floating point numbers.

File

```
#include <knuminput.h>
```

Base Classes

```
KNumInput QObject QPaintDevice QWidget Qt
```

Constructors

```
KDoubleNumInput(double value, QWidget *parent = 0,
    const char *name = 0);
KDoubleNumInput(KNumInput *below, double value,
    QWidget *parent = 0, const char *name = 0);
```

Methods

```
virtual QSize minimumSizeHint() const;
void setFormat(const char *format);
virtual void setLabel(QString label,
    int a = AlignLeft | AlignTop);
void setRange(double lower, double upper, double step = 1,
    bool slider = true);
void setSpecialValueText(const QString &text);
double value() const;
```

Slots

```
void setPrefix(QString prefix);
void setSuffix(QString suffix);
void setValue(double);
```

Signals

```
void valueChanged(double);
```

As shown in Figure 19-15, the input window can be accompanied by a slider that can be used to select the value. If a step value is specified but the slider is not selected, a spin button will be used instead.

```
/* showdoublenuminput.cpp */
#include <kapp.h>
#include <knuminput.h>

int main(int argc,char **argv)
{
    KApplication app(argc,argv,"showdoublenuminput");
    KDoubleNumInput *doublenuminput = new KDoubleNumInput(980);
    doublenuminput->setRange(100.0,1000.0,10,true);
    doublenuminput->show();
    app.setMainWidget(doublenuminput);
    return(app.exec());
}
```

Figure 19-15: A KDoubleNumInput widget with a slider

KDualColorButton

The KDualColorButton widget displays a pair of overlapping buttons, each in a different color, and responds to the mouse by reporting the color when the user selects a button.

File
```
#include <kdualcolorbtn.h>
```

Base Classes
```
QObject QPaintDevice QWidget Qt
```

Constructors
```
KDualColorButton(QWidget *parent = 0, const char *name = 0);
KDualColorButton(const QColor &fgColor, const QColor &bgColor,
    QWidget *parent = 0, const char *name = 0);
```

Methods
```
QColor background();
DualColor current();
QColor currentColor();
QColor foreground();
virtual QSize sizeHint() const;
```

Slots
```
void slotSetBackground(const QColor &c);
void slotSetCurrent(KDualColorButton::DualColor s);
void slotSetCurrentColor(const QColor &c);
void slotSetForeground(const QColor &c);
```

Signals
```
void bgChanged(const QColor &c);
void currentChanged(KDualColorButton::DualColor s);
void fgChanged(const QColor &c);
```

Enums
```
enum DualColor { Foreground, Background };
```

The following example presents the pair of color buttons depicted in Figure 19-16. A double-click on one of the buttons will bring up a color dialog window that enables the user to change the color.

```
/* showdualcolorbutton.cpp */
#include <kapp.h>
#include <kdualcolorbtn.h>
```

```
int main(int argc,char **argv)
{
    KApplication app(argc,argv,"showdualcolorbutton");
    KDualColorButton *dualcolorbutton = new KDualColorButton(
        QColor("red"),QColor("green"));
    dualcolorbutton->show();
    app.setMainWidget(dualcolorbutton);
    return(app.exec());
}
```

 Figure 19-16: A KDualColorButton widget enables the selection of one of two colors.

KEdFind

The KEdFind is a dialog that will accept a string, along with a couple of parameters, that can be used to start a search through the text.

File
```
#include <keditcl.h>
```

Base Classes
```
KDialog KDialogBase QDialog QObject QPaintDevice QWidget Qt
```

Constructors
```
KEdFind(QWidget *parent = 0, const char *name = 0,
    bool modal = true);
```

Methods
```
bool case_sensitive();
QString getText();
bool get_direction();
void setText(QString string);
```

Signals
```
void done();
void search();
```

The following example displays the KEdFind dialog shown in Figure 19-17:

```
/* showedfind.cpp */
#include <kapp.h>
#include <keditcl.h>

int main(int argc,char **argv)
{
```

```
        KApplication app(argc,argv,"showedfind");
        KEdFind *edfind = new KEdFind();
        edfind->setText("The search string");
        edfind->show();
        return(app.exec());
    }
```

Figure 19-17: The KEdFind dialog prompts for the necessary information to do a string search.

KEdGotoLine

The KEdGotoLine widget is a text display or text editor's request for a line number.

File

```
#include <keditcl.h>
```

Base Classes

```
KDialog KDialogBase QDialog QObject QPaintDevice QWidget Qt
```

Constructors

```
KEdGotoLine(QWidget *parent = 0, const char *name = 0,
    bool modal = true);
```

Methods

```
int getLineNumber();
```

Slots

```
void selected(int);
```

The following example displays the KEdGotoLine dialog shown in Figure 19-18:

```
/* showedgotoline.cpp */
#include <kapp.h>
#include <keditcl.h>

int main(int argc,char **argv)
{
    KApplication app(argc,argv,"showedgotoline");
    KEdGotoLine *edgotoline = new KEdGotoLine();
    edgotoline->show();
    return(app.exec());
}
```

Figure 19-18: The KEdGotoLine dialog prompts for a line number in the text.

KEdit

The KEdit widget is a simple text editor.

File

```
#include <keditcl.h>
```

Base Classes

```
QFrame QMultiLineEdit QObject QPaintDevice QTableView
    QWidget Qt
```

Constructors

```
KEdit(QWidget *_parent = NULL, const char *name = NULL);
```

Methods

```
void cleanWhiteSpace();
int currentColumn();
int currentLine();
void doGotoLine();
void insertText(QTextStream *);
void installRBPopup(QPopupMenu *);
bool isModified();
QString markedText();
bool repeatSearch();
void replace();
void saveText(QTextStream *);
void search();
void selectFont();
void setModified(bool = true);
void spellcheck_start();
void spellcheck_stop();
```

Slots

```
void computePosition();
void corrected(QString originalword, QString newword,
    unsigned pos);
void misspelling(QString word, QStringList *, unsigned pos);
void repaintAll();
void replace_all_slot();
void replace_search_slot();
void replace_slot();
void replacedone_slot();
```

```
    void search_slot();
    void searchdone_slot();
```

Signals
```
    void CursorPositionChanged();
    void gotUrlDrop(QDropEvent *e);
    void toggle_overwrite_signal();
```

Enums
```
    enum (anon) { NONE, FORWARD, BACKWARD };
```

The following example displays the edit window shown in Figure 19-19:

```
/* showedit.cpp */
#include <kapp.h>
#include <keditcl.h>

int main(int argc,char **argv)
{
    KApplication app(argc,argv,"showedit");
    KEdit *edit = new KEdit();
    edit->show();
    app.setMainWidget(edit);
    return(app.exec());
}
```

Figure 19-19: The KEdit widget is a fundamental text editor.

KEdReplace

The KEdReplace widget is the search-and-replace dialog of a text editor.

File
```
    #include <keditcl.h>
```

Base Classes
```
    KDialog KDialogBase QDialog QObject QPaintDevice QWidget Qt
```

Constructors
```
    KEdReplace(QWidget *parent = 0, const char *name = 0,
        bool modal = true);
```

Methods

```
bool case_sensitive();
QString getReplaceText();
QString getText();
bool get_direction();
void setText(QString);
```

Signals

```
void done();
void find();
void replace();
void replaceAll();
```

The following example displays the KEdReplace dialog shown in Figure 19-20:

```
/* showedreplace.cpp */
#include <kapp.h>
#include <keditcl.h>

int main(int argc,char **argv)
{
    KApplication app(argc,argv,"showedreplace");
    KEdReplace *edreplace = new KEdReplace();
    edreplace->show();
    return(app.exec());
}
```

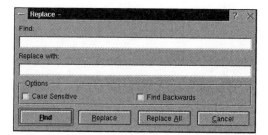

Figure 19-20: The KEdReplace dialog prompts for search-and-replace strings.

KFileDialog

The KFileDialog widget is a dialog used to browse and select files.

File

```
#include <kfiledialog.h>
```

Base Classes

```
KDialog KDialogBase QDialog QObject QPaintDevice QWidget Qt
```

Constructors

```
KFileDialog(const QString &urlName, const QString &filter,
    QWidget *parent, const char *name, bool modal);
```

Methods

```
KURL baseURL() const;
QString currentFilter() const;
static QString getExistingDirectory(
    const QString &url = QString::null, QWidget *parent = 0,
    const QString &caption = QString::null);
static QString getOpenFileName(
    const QString &dir = QString::null,
    const QString &filter = QString::null, QWidget *parent = 0,
    const QString &caption = QString::null);
static QStringList getOpenFileNames(
    const QString &dir = QString::null,
    const QString &filter = QString::null, QWidget *parent = 0,
    const QString &caption = QString::null);
static KURL getOpenURL(const QString &url = QString::null,
    const QString &filter = QString::null, QWidget *parent = 0,
    const QString &caption = QString::null);
List getOpenURLs(const QString &url = QString::null,
    const QString &filter = QString::null, QWidget *parent = 0,
    const QString &caption = QString::null);
static QString getSaveFileName(
    const QString &dir = QString::null,
    const QString &filter = QString::null, QWidget *parent = 0,
    const QString &caption = QString::null);
static KURL getSaveURL(const QString &url = QString::null,
    const QString &filter = QString::null, QWidget *parent = 0,
    const QString &caption = QString::null);
Mode mode() const;
QString selectedFile() const;
QStringList selectedFiles() const;
KURL selectedURL() const;
List selectedURLs() const;
void setFilter(const QString &filter);
void setLocationLabel(const QString &text);
void setMode(KFile::Mode m);
void setPreviewWidget(const QWidget *w);
void setSelection(const QString &name);
void setURL(const KURL &url, bool clearforward = true);
virtual void show();
KToolBar *toolBar() const;
```

Signals

```
void fileHighlighted(const QString &);
void fileSelected(const QString &);
void filterChanged(const QString &filter);
void historyUpdate(bool, bool);
```

The following example displays the file dialog window shown in Figure 19-21. The first argument to the constructor is the name of the directory in which the file search is to begin. If a NULL directory is specified, as in this example, the current working directory will be used until a file has been chosen; from then on, the last directory in which a file has been chosen will be used at startup. The second argument is the filter that determines which files are to be included in the list. Directories are always included, but files are included only if their names match the currently selected regular expression filter.

```cpp
/* showfiledialog.cpp */
#include <kapp.h>
#include <kfiledialog.h>

int main(int argc,char **argv)
{
    KApplication app(argc,argv,"showfiledialog");
    QString filter(
        "*.cpp|C++ Source Files\n"
        "*.h|C and C++ Header Files\n"
        "*.awk\n"
        "*.o|Object files\n"
        "*|All Files");
    KFileDialog *filedialog = new KFileDialog(0,filter,
        0,"filedialog",FALSE);
    filedialog->show();
    return(app.exec());
}
```

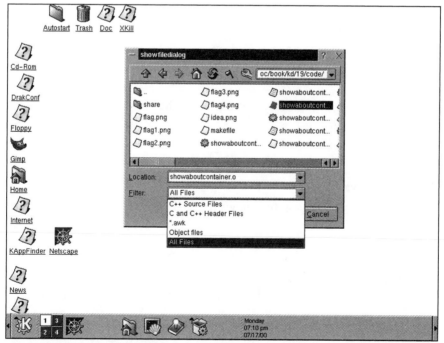

Figure 19-21: The KFileDialog widget displaying a list of files and the available filters

KFontChooser

The `KFontChooser` is a widget that enables the user to interactively select a font.

File
```
#include <kfontdialog.h>
```

Base Classes
```
QObject QPaintDevice QWidget Qt
```

Constructors
```
KFontChooser(QWidget *parent = OL, const char *name = OL,
    bool onlyFixed = false,
    const QStringList &fontList = QStringList () , bool
    makeFrame = true , int visibleListSize = 8 );
```

Methods
```
void enableColumn(int column, bool state);
QFont font();
static void getFontList(QStringList &list, const char
*pattern);
static QString getXLFD(const QFont &theFont);
QString sampleText();
void setFont(const QFont &font, bool onlyFixed = false);
void setSampleText(const QString &text);
virtual QSize sizeHint(void) const;
```

Signals
```
void fontSelected(const QFont &font);
```

Enums
```
enum FontColumn { FamilyList=0x01, StyleList=0x02,
    SizeList=0x04 };
```

Cross-Reference You can find an example that uses the `KFontChooser` in Chapter 5.

KFontDialog

The `KFontDialog` is a dialog that allows the user to interactively select a font.

File
```
#include <kfontdialog.h>
```

Base Classes
```
KDialog KDialogBase QDialog QObject QPaintDevice QWidget Qt
```

Constructors

```
KFontDialog(QWidget *parent = OL, const char *name = 0,
    bool modal = false, bool onlyFixed = false,
    const QStringList &fontlist = QStringList () , bool
    makeFrame = true );
```

Methods

```
QFont font();
static int getFont(QFont &theFont, bool onlyFixed = false,
    QWidget *parent = OL, bool makeFrame = true);
static int getFontAndText(QFont &theFont, QString &theString,
    bool onlyFixed = false, QWidget *parent = OL,
    bool makeFrame = true);
void setFont(const QFont &font, bool onlyFixed = false);
```

Signals

```
void fontSelected(const QFont &font);
```

Cross-Reference Examples that use KFontDialog can be found in Chapter 10.

KFormulaEdit

This KFormulaEdit widget can be used to display and edit formulas.

File

```
#include <kformulaedit.h>
```

Base Classes

```
QObject QPaintDevice QWidget Qt
```

Constructors

```
KFormulaEdit(QWidget *parent = 0, const char *name = 0,
    WFlags f = 0, bool restricted = false);
```

Methods

```
void enableSizeHintSignal(bool b);
KFormula *getFormula() const;
void redraw(int all = 1);
void setExtraChars(QString c);
void setText(QString text);
void setUglyForm(QString ugly);
virtual QSize sizeHint() const;
virtual QSizePolicy sizePolicy() const;
QString text() const;
QString uglyForm() const;
```

Slots

```
void insertChar(int c);
```

Signals

```
void formulaChanged(const QString &);
void sizeHint(QSize);
```

The following example uses the KFormulaEdit widget to display the formula shown in Figure 19-22. The formula was formatted from a C-type expression (the "ugly" form) by the fromUgly method of KFormula. The formula can be edited — setting the restricted flag to TRUE on the constructor limits the editing to only expressions that can be evaluated.

```
/* showformulaedit.cpp */
#include <kapp.h>
#include <kformulaedit.h>

int main(int argc,char **argv)
{
    KApplication app(argc,argv,"showformulaedit");
    KFormulaEdit *formulaedit = new KFormulaEdit(0,0,0,TRUE);
    QString fn = KFormula::fromUgly("44.2 - k*(99.2 + 544)");
    formulaedit->setText(fn);
    formulaedit->show();
    app.setMainWidget(formulaedit);
    return(app.exec());
}
```

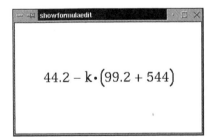

Figure 19-22: A KFormulaEdit widget displaying a formula

KFormulaToolBar

The KFormulaToolBar is a toolbar widget that provides special formatting and character input to the KFormulaEdit widget.

File

```
#include <kformulatoolbar.h>
```

Base Classes
```
KToolBar QFrame QObject QPaintDevice QWidget Qt
```
Constructors
```
KFormulaToolBar(QWidget *parent = OL, const char *name = OL,
    int _item_size = - 1);
```
Methods
```
void connectToFormula(KFormulaEdit *formula);
```

The following example displays the KFormulaToolBar shown in Figure 19-23:

```
/* showformulatoolbar.cpp */
#include <kapp.h>
#include <kformulatoolbar.h>

int main(int argc,char **argv)
{
    KApplication app(argc,argv,"showformulatoolbar");
    KFormulaToolBar *formulatoolbar = new KFormulaToolBar();
    formulatoolbar->show();
    app.setMainWidget(formulatoolbar);
    return(app.exec());
}
```

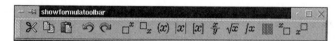

Figure 19-23: A KFormulaToolbar widget

KGradientSelector

The KGradientSelector widget displays levels of gradients between two colors.
It enables the mouse to be used to select a color between the extremes.

File
```
#include <kselect.h>
```
Base Classes
```
KSelector QObject QPaintDevice QRangeControl QWidget Qt
```
Constructors
```
KGradientSelector(Orientation o, QWidget *parent = OL,
    const char *name = OL);
```

Methods

```
void setColors(const QColor &col1, const QColor &col2);
void setText(const QString &t1, const QString &t2);
```

The following example shows the colors of the gradients between red and white, as shown in Figure 19-24. It also displays two lines of text to demonstrate the contrast between the two extremes. At the bottom of the figure is the pointer inherited from QRangeControl that marks the point of the current selection.

```
/* showgradientselector.cpp */
#include <kapp.h>
#include <kselect.h>

int main(int argc,char **argv)
{
    KApplication app(argc,argv,"showgradientselector");
    KGradientSelector *gradientselector =
            new KGradientSelector(KSelector::Horizontal);
    gradientselector->setColors(QColor("red"),QColor("white"));
    gradientselector->setText("White on Red","Red on White");
    gradientselector->show();
    app.setMainWidget(gradientselector);
    return(app.exec());
}
```

Figure 19-24: A KGradientSelector widget showing both color gradient and text

KHSSelector

The KHSSelector widget enables the user to make a color selection by choosing a hue and/or saturation with the mouse.

File
```
#include <kcolordlg.h>
```
Base Classes
```
KXYSelector QObject QPaintDevice QWidget Qt
```
Constructors
```
KHSSelector(QWidget *parent);
```

The following example displays the multicolored window shown in Figure 19-25. The color selection is made with the mouse by positioning the indicator inherited from KXYSelector.

```
/* showhsselector.cpp */
#include <kapp.h>
#include <kcolordlg.h>

int main(int argc,char **argv)
{
    KApplication app(argc,argv,"showhsselector");
    KHSSelector *hsselector = new KHSSelector(0);
    hsselector->show();
    app.setMainWidget(hsselector);
    return(app.exec());
}
```

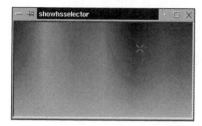

Figure 19-25: A KHSSelector widget showing the currently selected color point

KHTMLView

The KHTMLView widget can be used to display a Web page.

File
```
#include <khtmlview.h>
```

Base Classes
```
QFrame QObject QPaintDevice QScrollView QWidget Qt
```

Constructors
```
KHTMLView(KHTMLPart *part, QWidget *parent,
    const char *name = 0);
```

Methods
```
bool dndEnabled() const;
int frameWidth() const;
bool gotoNextLink();
bool gotoPrevLink();
bool hasSelection() const;
void layout(bool force = false);
int marginHeight();
int marginWidth() const;
KHTMLPart *part() const;
```

```
void print();
QString selectedText() const;
void setDNDEnabled(bool b);
void setMarginHeight(int y);
void setMarginWidth(int x);
void setURLCursor(const QCursor &c);
void toggleActLink(bool);
const QCursor & urlCursor() const;
static const QList<KHTMLView> *viewList();
```

Signals

```
void selectionChanged();
```

The following example uses a KHTMLView object to display the Web page shown in Figure 19-26. It does this by creating a KURL object that is a wrapper for a URL. In this example, the URL is on the local disk, but it could be anywhere on the Internet. The KURL object is used by a KHTMLPart object to open the actual Web page. Instead of using a standalone constructor, the view() method of the KHTMLPart object is called on to return a KHTMLView object, which is already set to display the page. The size of the KHTMLView is set and, when the widget is displayed, the page itself is displayed.

```
/* showhtmlview.cpp */
#include <kapp.h>
#include <iostream.h>
#include <kurl.h>
#include <khtml_part.h>
#include <khtmlview.h>

int main(int argc,char **argv)
{
    KApplication app(argc,argv,"showhtmlview");
    KURL kurl = "file:/home/testpage.html";
    KHTMLPart *part = new KHTMLPart();
    if(!part->openURL(kurl))
        cout << "The URL failed to open" << endl;
    KHTMLView *htmlview = part->view();
    htmlview->resize(400,200);
    htmlview->show();
    app.setMainWidget(htmlview);
    return(app.exec());
}
```

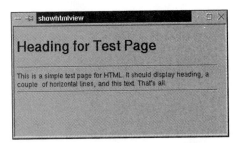

Figure 19-26: A KHTMLVIew widget from a KHTMLPart object displays a Web page.

KIconButton

The KIconButton is a button widget that pops up a KIconDialog window and then displays the selected icon.

File

```
#include <kicondialog.h>
```

Base Classes

```
QButton QObject QPaintDevice QPushButton QWidget Qt
```

Constructors

```
KIconButton(QWidget *parent = OL, const char *name = OL);
KIconButton(KIconLoader *loader, QWidget *parent,
    const char *name = OL);
```

Methods

```
const QString icon();
void setIcon(QString icon);
void setIconType(int group, int context, bool user = false);
```

Signals

```
void iconChanged(QString icon);
```

The following example displays a KIconButton containing an icon. This example specifies a starting icon by calling setIcon(), as shown in Figure 19-27. If no icon were specified, the button would initially be blank, and remain that way until an icon were chosen from the KIconDialog.

```
/* showiconbutton.cpp */
#include <kapp.h>
#include <kicondialog.h>

int main(int argc,char **argv)
{
    KApplication app(argc,argv,"showiconbutton");
    KIconButton *iconbutton = new KIconButton();
    iconbutton->setIcon("go");
    iconbutton->show();
    app.setMainWidget(iconbutton);
    return(app.exec());
}
```

Figure 19-27: A KIconButton displaying the currently selected icon

KIconDialog

The `KIconDialog` widget is a dialog that can be used to make icon selections.

File
```
#include <kicondialog.h>
```

Base Classes
```
KDialog KDialogBase QDialog QObject QPaintDevice QWidget Qt
```

Constructors
```
KIconDialog(QWidget *parent = OL, const char *name = OL);
KIconDialog(KIconLoader *loader, QWidget *parent = 0,
    const char *name = 0);
```

Methods
```
QString selectIcon(int group = KIcon::Desktop,
    int context = KIcon::Application, bool user = false);
```

The following example displays a `KIconDialog` window. The one shown in Figure 19-28 is displaying the icons of the system applications.

```cpp
/* showicondialog.cpp */
#include <kapp.h>
#include <kicondialog.h>

int main(int argc,char **argv)
{
    KApplication app(argc,argv,"showicondialog");
    KIconDialog *icondialog = new KIconDialog();
    icondialog->show();
    return(app.exec());
}
```

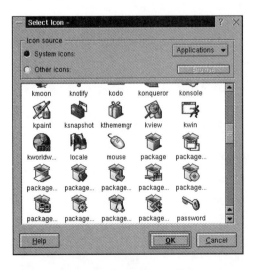

Figure 19-28: A KIconDialog displaying the system application icons

KIconView

The `KIconView` widget displays a collection of icons from which the user can make a selection. This widget extends `QIconView` to use the standard KDE settings for handling mouse buttons and making selections.

File

```
#include <kiconview.h>
```

Base Classes

```
QFrame QIconView QObject QPaintDevice QScrollView QWidget Qt
```

Inherited By

```
KFileIconView KIconCanvas
```

Constructors

```
KIconView(QWidget *parent = 0, const char *name = 0,
    WFlags f = 0);
```

Signals

```
void doubleClicked(QIconViewItem *item, const QPoint &pos);
void executed(QIconViewItem *item);
void executed(QIconViewItem *item, const QPoint &pos);
```

The following example displays the five icons shown in Figure 19-29. The first icon has no pixmap and no text, so it uses the default pixmap and has no label. The next two icons also use the default pixmap, but they both have text for labels. The last two icons have both pixmaps and labels, and the icon labeled "Flag" has been selected by the mouse.

```
/* showiconview.cpp */
#include <kapp.h>
#include <kiconview.h>

int main(int argc,char **argv)
{
    QIconViewItem *item;
    KApplication app(argc,argv,"showiconview");
    KIconView *iconview = new KIconView();
    item = new QIconViewItem(iconview);
    item = new QIconViewItem(iconview,"Icon Label");
    item = new QIconViewItem(iconview,"Icon With\nLong Label");
    QPixmap flag("flag.png");
    item = new QIconViewItem(iconview,"Flag",flag);
    QPixmap idea("idea.png");
    item = new QIconViewItem(iconview,"Idea",idea);
    iconview->show();
    app.setMainWidget(iconview);
    return(app.exec());
}
```

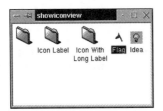

Figure 19-29: A KIconView widget displaying five icons

KImageTrackLabel

The KImageTrackLabel widget extends the QLabel to add the capability to track and monitor mouse activities.

File
```
#include <kaboutdialog.h>
```

Base Classes
```
QFrame QLabel QObject QPaintDevice QWidget Qt
```

Constructors
```
KImageTrackLabel(QWidget *parent, const char *name = 0,
    WFlags f = 0);
```

Signals
```
void mouseTrack(int mode, const QMouseEvent *e);
```

Enums
```
enum MouseMode { MousePress=1, MouseRelease, MouseDoubleClick,
    MouseMove };
```

The following example displays a KImageTrackLabel widget as the simple text widget shown in Figure 19-30. If a slot were attached to the mouseTrack() slot, every mouse action would be reported.

```cpp
/* showimagetracklabel.cpp */
#include <kapp.h>
#include <kaboutdialog.h>

int main(int argc,char **argv)
{
    KApplication app(argc,argv,"showimagetracklabel");
    KImageTrackLabel *imagetracklabel =
                new KImageTrackLabel(0);
    imagetracklabel->setText("Mouse Tracking Label");
    imagetracklabel->show();
    app.setMainWidget(imagetracklabel);
    return(app.exec());
}
```

Figure 19-30: A KImageTrackLabel is a label that tracks the mouse.

KIntNumInput

The KIntNumInput widget is designed to accept and verify user input of integer values.

File

```
#include <knuminput.h>
```

Base Classes

```
KNumInput QObject QPaintDevice QWidget Qt
```

Constructors

```
KIntNumInput(int value, QWidget *parent = 0, int base = 10,
    const char *name = 0);
KIntNumInput(KNumInput *below, int value, QWidget *parent = 0,
    int base = 10, const char *name = 0);
```

Methods

```
virtual QSize minimumSizeHint() const;
virtual void setLabel(QString label,
    int a = AlignLeft | AlignTop);
void setRange(int lower, int upper, int step = 1,
    bool slider = true);
void setSpecialValueText(const QString &text);
int value() const;
```

Slots

```
void setEditFocus(bool mark = true);
void setPrefix(QString prefix);
void setSuffix(QString suffix);
void setValue(int);
```

Signals

```
void valueChanged(int);
```

As shown in Figure 19-31, the input window can be accompanied by both a slider and a spin button, which can both be used to select the value. Also, the value can be typed directly into the data window.

```
/* showintnuminput.cpp */
#include <kapp.h>
#include <knuminput.h>

int main(int argc,char **argv)
{
```

```
KApplication app(argc,argv,"showintnuminput");
KIntNumInput *intnuminput = new KIntNumInput(980);
intnuminput->setRange(100,1000,10,true);
intnuminput->show();
app.setMainWidget(intnuminput);
return(app.exec());
}
```

Figure 19-31: A KIntNumInput widget with both a spin button and a slider

KIntSpinBox

The KIntSpinBox widget is designed to accept and verify user input of integer values.

File
```
#include <knuminput.h>
```

Base Classes
```
QFrame QObject QPaintDevice QRangeControl QSpinBox QWidget
    Qt
```

Constructors
```
KIntSpinBox(int lower, int upper, int step, int value,
    int base = 10, QWidget *parent = 0, const char *name = 0);
```

Methods
```
void setEditFocus(bool mark);
```

The following example creates the KIntSpinBox shown in Figure 19-32. The value can be set by either using the spin box to change the number by the step value or by typing the value directly into the data window.

```
/* showintspinbox.cpp */
#include <kapp.h>
#include <knuminput.h>

int main(int argc,char **argv)
{
    KApplication app(argc,argv,"showintspinbox");
    KIntSpinBox *intspinbox = new KIntSpinBox(100,1000,10,980);
    intspinbox->show();
    app.setMainWidget(intspinbox);
    return(app.exec());
}
```

Figure 19-32: A KIntSpinBox widget with its spin button

KKeyButton

The KKeyButton widget is a QButton that looks likea keyboard button.

File
```
#include <kkeydialog.h>
```
Base Classes
```
QButton QObject QPaintDevice QPushButton QWidget Qt
```
Constructors
```
KKeyButton(const char *name = 0, QWidget *parent = 0);
```
Methods
```
void setEdit(bool edit);
void setText(const QString &text);
```

The following example program uses a KKeyButton widget as its top-level widget
and is shown in Figure 19-33:

```
/* showkeybutton.cpp */
#include <kapp.h>
#include <kkeydialog.h>

int main(int argc,char **argv)
{
    KApplication app(argc,argv,"showkeybutton");
    KKeyButton *keybutton = new KKeyButton();
    keybutton->setText("Key Button");
    keybutton->show();
    app.setMainWidget(keybutton);
    return(app.exec());
}
```

Figure 19-33: A KKeyButton widget is a raised button.

KLed

The KLed widget is displayed as an LED that can be used as an indicator in different
shapes and colors.

File
```
#include <kled.h>
```
Base Classes
```
QObject QPaintDevice QWidget Qt
```

Constructors

```
KLed(const QColor &col = Qt::green, QWidget *parent = 0,
    const char *name = 0);
KLed(const QColor &col, KLed::State st, KLed::Look look,
    KLed::Shape shape, QWidget *parent = 0,
    const char *name = 0);
```

Methods

```
const QColor color() const;
int getDarkFactor() const;
Look look() const;
void setColor(const QColor &color);
void setDarkFactor(int darkfactor);
void setLook(Look look);
void setShape(Shape s);
void setState(State state);
State state() const;
void toggleState();
```

Slots

```
void off();
void on();
void toggle();
```

Enums

```
enum State { Off, On, NoOfStates };
enum Shape { NoShape, Rectangular, Circular,
    NoOfShapes=Circular };
enum Look { NoLook, Flat, Raised, Sunken, NoOfLooks=Sunken };
```

The following KLed example is shown in Figure 19-34. It is a round indicator that looks raised and as if it were turned on. It is in the default color, which is green.

```
/* showled.cpp */
#include <kapp.h>
#include <kled.h>

int main(int argc,char **argv)
{
    KApplication app(argc,argv,"showled");
    KLed *led = new KLed();
    led->setLook(KLed::Raised);
    led->setShape(KLed::Circular);
    led->setState(KLed::On);
    led->resize(10,10);
    led->show();
    app.setMainWidget(led);
    return(app.exec());
}
```

Figure 19-34: A round, raised KLed widget

KLineEdit

The KLineEdit widget is a single-line text editor.

File

```
#include <klineedit.h>
```

Base Classes

```
KCompletionBase QLineEdit QObject QPaintDevice QWidget Qt
```

Inherited By

```
KRestrictedLine
```

Constructors

```
KLineEdit(const QString &string, QWidget *parent,
    const char *name = 0);
KLineEdit(QWidget *parent = 0, const char *name = 0);
```

Methods

```
void cursorAtEnd();
bool isContextMenuEnabled() const;
virtual void setCompletionMode(
    KGlobalSettings::Completion mode);
virtual void setEnableContextMenu(bool showMenu);
```

Slots

```
void rotateText(KeyBindingType);
```

Signals

```
void completion(const QString &);
void nextMatch(KeyBindingType);
void previousMatch(KeyBindingType);
void returnPressed(const QString &);
```

The following example creates and displays the KLineEdit window shown in
Figure 19-35. The KLineEdit widget is based on the QlineEdit widget. The features
KLineEdit adds include optional text completion and configurable key bindings./*
showlineedit.cpp */

```
#include <kapp.h>
#include <klineedit.h>

int main(int argc,char **argv)
{
    KApplication app(argc,argv,"showlineedit");
    KLineEdit *lineedit = new KLineEdit();
    lineedit->show();
    app.setMainWidget(lineedit);
    return(app.exec());
}
```

Figure 19-35: The KLineEdit widget inherits from QlineEdit.

Cross-Reference See Chapter 4 for examples of the `QLineEdit` widget.

KLineEditDlg

The `KLineEditDlg` is a dialog that contains a `QLineEdit` widget for editing a single line of text.

File
```
#include <klineeditdlg.h>
```

Base Classes
```
KDialog KDialogBase QDialog QObject QPaintDevice QWidget Qt
```

Constructors
```
KLineEditDlg(const QString &_text, const QString &_value,
    QWidget *parent);
```

Methods
```
static QString getText(const QString &_text,
    const QString &_value, bool *ok, QWidget *parent);
QString text();
```

Slots
```
void slotClear();
```

The following example displays a `KLineEditDlg` window with a caption string and default text, as shown in Figure 19-36:

```
/* showlineeditdlg.cpp */
#include <kapp.h>
#include <klineeditdlg.h>

int main(int argc,char **argv)
{
    bool OK;
    QString str;
    KApplication app(argc,argv,"showlineeditdlg");
    str = KLineEditDlg::getText(
        "The caption",
        "The editable text",
        &OK,
        0);
    if(OK) {
        // The OK button was selected
```

```
        } else {
            // The CANCEL button was selected
        }
        return(app.exec());
}
```

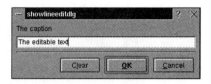

Figure 19-36: The KLineEditDlg dialog contains a QLineEdit widget.

KListBox

The KListBox widget displays a list of items that the user can select with the mouse. This widget extends QListBox to use the standard KDE settings for handling mouse buttons and making selections.

File

```
#include <klistbox.h>
```

Base Classes

```
QFrame QListBox QObject QPaintDevice QScrollView QWidget Qt
```

Inherited By

```
KSplitList
```

Constructors

```
KListBox(QWidget *parent = 0, const char *name = 0,
    WFlags f = 0);
```

Signals

```
void doubleClicked(QListBoxItem *item, const QPoint &pos);
void executed(QListBoxItem *item);
void executed(QListBoxItem *item, const QPoint &pos);
```

The following example displays the KListBox window shown in Figure 19-37:

```
/* showlistbox.cpp */
#include <kapp.h>
#include <klistbox.h>

int main(int argc,char **argv)
{
    KApplication app(argc,argv,"showlistbox");
    KListBox *listbox = new KListBox();
    for(int i=0; i<20; i++) {
        QString str;
```

```
            str.sprintf("Selection %d\n",i);
            listbox->insertItem(str);
        }
        listbox->setMinimumWidth(120);
        listbox->show();
        app.setMainWidget(listbox);
        return(app.exec());
    }
```

Figure 19-37: The KListBox widget displaying a currently selected item

KListView

The KListView widget displays nested lists of items, in the form of a tree, which the user can browse through with the mouse. This widget extends QListView to use the standard KDE settings for handling mouse buttons and making selections.

File

    #include <klistview.h>

Base Classes

    QFrame QListView QObject QPaintDevice QScrollView QWidget Qt

Inherited By

    KApplicationTree KFileDetailView

Constructors

    KListView(QWidget *parent = 0, const char *name = 0);

Methods

    virtual bool isExecuteArea(const QPoint &point);

Signals

    void doubleClicked(QListViewItem *item, const QPoint &pos,
        int c);
    void executed(QListViewItem *item);
    void executed(QListViewItem *item, const QPoint &pos, int c);

This class is a simple extension of QListView and works much the same way.

Cross-Reference You can see an example that uses QListView in Chapter 18.

KMenuBar

A KMenuBar is a horizontal bar that is capable of managing the relationship among a group of pop-up menus. This widget extends QMenuBar to use the standard KDE settings for handling mouse buttons and making selections.

File

    #include <kmenubar.h>

Base Classes

    QFrame QMenuBar QMenuData QObject QPaintDevice QWidget Qt

Constructors

    KMenuBar(QWidget *parent = 0, const char *name = 0);

The following example shows a KMenuBar that contains two pop-up menus. Each pop-up menu contains a single menu item. Figure 19-38 shows the menu bar with the second pop-up menu activated.

```
/* showmenubar.cpp */
#include <kapp.h>
#include <kmenubar.h>
#include <kpopupmenu.h>

int main(int argc,char **argv)
{
    KApplication app(argc,argv,"showmenubar");

    KMenuBar *menubar = new KMenuBar();
    menubar->setSeparator(KMenuBar::InWindowsStyle);
    KPopupMenu* filePopup = new KPopupMenu();
    filePopup->insertItem("&Quit",&app,SLOT(quit()));
    menubar->insertItem("&File",filePopup);
    KPopupMenu* editPopup = new KPopupMenu();
    editPopup->insertItem("&Paste");
    menubar->insertItem("E&dit",editPopup);
    menubar->show();
    app.setMainWidget(menubar);
    return(app.exec());
}
```

Figure 19-38: The KMenuBar showing a pop-up menu

KNumInput

The KNumInput widget is a base class that can be used to implement a numeric input widget.

File
```
#include <knuminput.h>
```
Base Classes
```
QObject QPaintDevice QWidget Qt
```
Inherited By
```
KDoubleNumInput KIntNumInput
```
Constructors
```
KNumInput(QWidget *parent = 0, const char *name = 0);
KNumInput(KNumInput *below, QWidget *parent = 0,
    const char *name = 0);
```
Methods
```
virtual void setLabel(QString label,
    int a = AlignLeft | AlignTop);
void setSteps(int minor, int major);
virtual QSize sizeHint() const;
QSizePolicy sizePolicy() const;
```

KPaletteTable

The KPaletteTable widget enables the user to select a color.

File
```
#include <kcolordlg.h>
```
Base Classes
```
QObject QPaintDevice QWidget Qt
```
Constructors
```
KPaletteTable(QWidget *parent, int minWidth = 210,
    int cols = 16);
```
Methods
```
void addToCustomColors(const QColor &);
void addToRecentColors(const QColor &);
QString palette();
```
Slots
```
void setPalette(const QString &paletteName);
```
Signals
```
void colorSelected(const QColor &, const QString &);
```

The following example displays a KPaletteTable widget. As shown in Figure 19-39, there is more than one way to select a color. On the left of the figure, the KPalette Table widget presents a rectangular selection of colors, while the KPaletteTable widget on the right presents a list of colors by their names.

```cpp
/* showpalettetable.cpp */
#include <kapp.h>
#include <kcolordlg.h>

int main(int argc,char **argv)
{
    KApplication app(argc,argv,"showpalettetable");
    KPaletteTable *palettetable = new KPaletteTable(0);
    palettetable->show();
    app.setMainWidget(palettetable);
    return(app.exec());
}
```

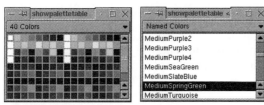

Figure 19-39: A pair of KPaletteTable widgets showing two ways to select a color

KPanelApplet

The KPanelApplet is a base class that can be used to create KDE applets.

File
```cpp
#include <kpanelapplet.h>
```
Base Classes
```cpp
QObject QPaintDevice QWidget Qt
```
Constructors
```cpp
KPanelApplet(QWidget *parent = 0, const char *name = 0);
```
Methods
```cpp
virtual void about();
int actions();
bool flags();
virtual int heightForWidth(int width);
virtual void help();
void init(int &argc, char **argv);
Orientation orientation() const;
```

```
Position position() const;
virtual void preferences();
bool process(const QCString &fun, const QByteArray &data,
    QCString &replyType, QByteArray &replyData);
virtual void removedFromPanel();
void setActions(int a);
void setFlags(int f);
void updateLayout();
virtual int widthForHeight(int height);
```

Enums

```
enum Actions { About=1, Help=2, Preferences=4 };
enum Flags { Stretch=1, TopLevel=2 };
enum Position { Left=0, Right, Top, Bottom };
```

Cross-Reference

There is an example of using the KPanelApplet class to create an applet in Chapter 15.

KPasswordDialog

The KPasswordDialog widget can be used for entry of a password or for the verification process of establishing a new password.

File

```
#include <kpassdlg.h>
```

Base Classes

```
KDialog KDialogBase QDialog QObject QPaintDevice QWidget Qt
```

Constructors

```
KPasswordDialog(int type, QString prompt,
    bool enableKeep = false, int extraBttn = 0);
```

Methods

```
void addLine(QString key, QString value);
static void disableCoreDumps();
static int getNewPassword(QCString &password, QString prompt);
static int getPassword(QCString &password, QString prompt,
    int *keep = 0L);
bool keep() const;
const char *password() const;
void setPrompt(QString prompt);
```

Enums

```
enum Types { Password, NewPassword };
```

The following example demonstrates how the KPasswordDialog widget can be used to request a password from the user. As shown in Figure 19-40, the entered string appears as a row of asterisks. If the method getNewPassword() is used instead of getPassword(), the password must be entered twice for verification.

```
/* showpassworddialog.cpp */
#include <kapp.h>
#include <kpassdlg.h>

int main(int argc,char **argv)
{
    int code;
    QCString password;
    QString prompt = "Enter your password";
    KApplication app(argc,argv,"showpassworddialog");
    code = KPasswordDialog::getPassword(password,prompt);
    if(code == QDialog::Accepted) {
        // A password was entered
    } else if(code == QDialog::Rejected) {
        // A password was not entered
    }
    return(app.exec());
}
```

Figure 19-40: A KPasswordDialog widget with an obscured password entered

KPasswordEdit

The KPasswordEdit widget is a single-line editor that obscures the text so it can be used as a password.

File
    #include <kpassdlg.h>

Base Classes
    QLineEdit QObject QPaintDevice QWidget Qt

Constructors
    KPasswordEdit(QWidget *parent = 0, const char *name = 0);

Methods
    void erase();
    const char *password();

Enums
    enum EchoModes { OneStar, ThreeStars, NoEcho };

The following example displays the KPasswordEdit widget shown in Figure 19-41:

```
/* showpasswordedit.cpp */
#include <kapp.h>
#include <kpassdlg.h>

int main(int argc,char **argv)
{
    KApplication app(argc,argv,"showpasswordedit");
    KPasswordEdit *passwordedit = new KPasswordEdit();
    passwordedit->show();
    app.setMainWidget(passwordedit);
    return(app.exec());
}
```

Figure 19-41: A KPasswordEdit widget with obscured text entered

KPopupMenu

The KPopupMenu widget is used in combination with a KMenuBar and other KPopupMenu objects to create the KDE standard menu forms. This widget extends QPopupMenu to use the standard KDE settings for handling mouse buttons and making selections.

File

```
#include <kpopmenu.h>
```

Base Classes

```
QFrame QMenuData QObject QPaintDevice QPopupMenu QWidget Qt
```

Constructors

```
KPopupMenu(QWidget *parent = 0, const char *name = 0);
KPopupMenu(const QString &title, QWidget *parent = 0,
    const char *name = 0);
```

Methods

```
void changeTitle(int id, const QString &text);
void changeTitle(int id, const QPixmap &icon,
    const QString &text);
int insertTitle(const QString &text, int id = - 1,
    int index = - 1);
int insertTitle(const QPixmap &icon, const QString &text,
    int id = - 1, int index = - 1);
void setTitle(const QString &title);
QString title(int id = - 1);
QPixmap titlePixmap(int id);
```

Cross-Reference　For an example of using a KPopupMenu with a KMenuBar, see the KMenuBar entry in this chapter. You can find examples of using a QPopupMenu in Chapter 6.

KProgress

The KProgress widget is a progress bar that can be oriented horizontally or vertically.

File

```
#include <kprogress.h>
```

Base Classes

```
QFrame QObject QPaintDevice QRangeControl QWidget Qt
```

Constructors

```
KProgress(QWidget *parent = 0, const char *name = 0);
KProgress(Orientation, QWidget *parent = 0,
    const char *name = 0);
KProgress(int minValue, int maxValue, int value, Orientation,
    QWidget *parent = 0, const char *name = 0);
```

Methods

```
const QColor & barColor() const;
const QPixmap *barPixmap() const;
BarStyle barStyle() const;
QString format() const;
Orientation orientation() const;
void setBarColor(const QColor &);
void setBarPixmap(const QPixmap &);
void setBarStyle(BarStyle style);
void setFormat(const QString &format);
void setOrientation(Orientation);
void setTextEnabled(bool);
virtual QSize sizeHint() const;
virtual QSizePolicy sizePolicy() const;
bool textEnabled() const;
```

Slots

```
void advance(int prog);
void setValue(int);
```

Signals

```
void percentageChanged(int);
```

Enums

```
enum Orientation { Horizontal, Vertical };
enum BarStyle { Solid, Blocked };
```

The following example displays the horizontal KProgress widget shown in Figure 19-42. A number of methods can be used to change the appearance and style of the progress bar.

```
/* showprogress.cpp */
#include <kapp.h>
#include <kprogress.h>

int main(int argc,char **argv)
{
    KApplication app(argc,argv,"showprogress");
    KProgress *progress = new KProgress(0,500,350,
        KProgress::Horizontal);
    progress->show();
    app.setMainWidget(progress);
    return(app.exec());
}
```

Figure 19-42: A KProgress widget showing a percentage of completion

KRestrictedLine

The KRestrictedLine widget accepts a single line of text as input, and limits the input to only a set of specified characters.

File
```
#include <krestrictedline.h>
```

Base Classes
```
KCompletionBase KLineEdit QLineEdit QObject QPaintDevice
    QWidget Qt
```

Constructors
```
KRestrictedLine(QWidget *parent = 0, const char *name = 0,
    const QString &valid = QString::null);
```

Methods
```
void setValidChars(const QString &valid);
```

Signals
```
void invalidChar(int);
```

The following example displays the KRestrictedLine widget shown in Figure 19-43. The call to setValidChars() limits the input to uppercase and lowercase vowels, and the uppercase letter *Y*. Any other character entered will not be accepted, and will result in the invalidChar() signal.

```
/* showrestrictedline.cpp */
#include <kapp.h>
#include <krestrictedline.h>

int main(int argc,char **argv)
{
    KApplication app(argc,argv,"showrestrictedline");
    KRestrictedLine *restrictedline = new KRestrictedLine();
    restrictedline->setValidChars("aeiouAEIOUY");
    restrictedline->show();
    app.setMainWidget(restrictedline);
    return(app.exec());
}
```

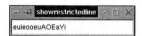

Figure 19-43: A KRestricedLine widget showing some of the allowed characters

KRootPermsIcon

The KRootPermissions widget displays an icon to indicate whether the current user has root permissions.

File
    #include <kauthicon.h>

Base Classes
    KAuthIcon QObject QPaintDevice QWidget Qt

Constructors
    KRootPermsIcon(QWidget *parent = 0, const char *name = 0);

Methods
    bool status() const;

Slots
    void updateStatus();

The following example uses a KRootPermsIcon widget as its top-level window and will display one of the two icons shown in Figure 19-44, depending on whether the user has root permissions.

```
/* showrootpermsicon.cpp */
#include <kapp.h>
#include <kauthicon.h>

int main(int argc,char **argv)
{
    KApplication app(argc,argv,"showrootpermsicon");
    KRootPermsIcon *rootpermsicon = new KRootPermsIcon();
    rootpermsicon->show();
    app.setMainWidget(rootpermsicon);
    return(app.exec());
}
```

Figure 19-44: The two forms of the KRootPermsIcon widget display

KRuler

The KRuler widget displays a vertical or horizontal window that is marked and labeled like a ruler.

File

#include <kruler.h>

Base Classes

QFrame QObject QPaintDevice QWidget Qt

Constructors

```
KRuler(KRuler::direction dir, QWidget *parent = 0,
    const char *name = 0, WFlags f = 0, bool allowLines =
TRUE);
KRuler(KRuler::direction dir, int widgetWidth,
    QWidget *parent = 0, const char *name = 0, WFlags f = 0,
    bool allowLines = TRUE);
```

Methods

```
inline int getBigMarkDistance() const;
int getEndOffset() const;
int getLength() const;
bool getLengthFix() const;
inline int getLittleMarkDistance() const;
inline int getMaxValue() const;
inline int getMediumMarkDistance() const;
metric_style getMetricRulerStyle() const;
inline int getMinValue() const;
inline int getOffset() const;
paint_style getPaintRulerStyle() const;
```

```
inline double getPixelPerMark() const;
bool getShowBigMarks() const;
bool getShowEndMarks() const;
bool getShowLittleMarks() const;
bool getShowMediumMarks() const;
bool getShowPointer() const;
bool getShowTinyMarks() const;
paint_style getTickStyle() const;
inline int getTinyMarkDistance() const;
inline int getValue() const;
void setBigMarkDistance(int);
void setEndLabel(const QString &);
void setLength(int);
void setLengthFix(bool fix);
void setLittleMarkDistance(int);
void setMaxValue(int);
void setMediumMarkDistance(int);
void setMinValue(int);
void setOffset(int offset);
void setPixelPerMark(double);
void setRange(int min, int max);
void setRulerStyle(KRuler::metric_style);
void setRulerStyle(KRuler::paint_style);
void setTickStyle(KRuler::paint_style);
void setTinyMarkDistance(int);
void setValue(int);
void setValuePerBigMark(int);
void setValuePerLittleMark(int);
void setValuePerMediumMark(int);
void showBigMarkLabel(bool);
void showBigMarks(bool);
void showEndLabel(bool);
void showEndMarks(bool);
void showLittleMarkLabel(bool);
void showLittleMarks(bool);
void showMediumMarkLabel(bool);
void showMediumMarks(bool);
void showPointer(bool);
void showTinyMarks(bool);
void slidedown(int count = 1);
void slideup(int count = 1);
```

Slots

```
void slotEndOffset(int);
void slotNewOffset(int);
void slotNewValue(int);
```

Enums

```
enum direction { horizontal, vertical };
enum metric_style { custom=0, pixel, inch, millimetres,
      centimetres, metres };
enum paint_style { flat, raised, sunken };
```

The following example program displays the KRuler shown in Figure 19-45:

```
/* showruler.cpp */
#include <kapp.h>
#include <kruler.h>

int main(int argc,char **argv)
{
    KApplication app(argc,argv,"showruler");
    KRuler *ruler = new KRuler(KRuler::horizontal);
    ruler->setRulerStyle(KRuler::pixel);
    ruler->setLength(1000);
    ruler->setValue(750);
    ruler->showBigMarks(TRUE);
    ruler->showTinyMarks(FALSE);
    ruler->showMediumMarks(FALSE);
    ruler->showLittleMarks(FALSE);
    ruler->showEndMarks(FALSE);
    ruler->showEndLabel(FALSE);
    ruler->show();
    app.setMainWidget(ruler);
    return(app.exec());
}
```

Figure 19-45: A simple KRuler

KSelector

The KSelector widget is a base class that can be used to create a widget for selecting a horizontal or vertical position within a window.

File
```
#include <kselect.h>
```
Base Classes
```
QObject QPaintDevice QRangeControl QWidget Qt
```
Inherited By
```
KGradientSelector KValueSelector
```
Constructors
```
KSelector(Orientation o, QWidget *parent = 0L,
    const char *name = 0L);
```

Methods

```
QRect contentsRect();
bool indent() const;
Orientation orientation() const;
void setIndent(bool i);
```

Signals

```
void valueChanged(int value);
```

Enums

```
enum Orientation { Horizontal, Vertical };
```

The following example displays a horizontal KSelector widget, as shown in Figure 19-46. The indicator in the bottom border of the window can be moved by the mouse, causing the valueChanged() signal to be emitted.

```
/* showselector.cpp */
#include <kapp.h>
#include <kselect.h>

int main(int argc,char **argv)
{
    KApplication app(argc,argv,"showselector");
    KSelector *selector = new KSelector(KSelector::Horizontal);
    selector->show();
    app.setMainWidget(selector);
    return(app.exec());
}
```

Figure 19-46: A horizontal KSelector widget showing the selection indicator at the bottom

KSeparator

The KSeparator widget is the standard KDE separator widget. It is used in menus and other windows to create logical groupings.

File

```
#include <kseparator.h>
```

Base Classes

```
QFrame QObject QPaintDevice QWidget Qt
```

Constructors

```
KSeparator(QWidget *parent = 0, const char *name = 0,
    WFlags f = 0);
KSeparator(int orientation, QWidget *parent = 0,
    const char *name = 0, WFlags f = 0);
```

Methods

```
int orientation() const;
void setOrientation(int);
virtual QSize sizeHint() const;
```

The following example displays the horizontal KSeparator widget shown in Figure 19-47:

```
/* showseparator.cpp */
#include <kapp.h>
#include <kseparator.h>

int main(int argc,char **argv)
{
    KApplication app(argc,argv,"showseparator");
    KSeparator *separator = new KSeparator(Qt::Horizontal);
    separator->show();
    app.setMainWidget(separator);
    return(app.exec());
}
```

Figure 19-47: A horizontal KSeparator widget

KSpellConfig

The KSpellConfig widget serves as a dialog that configures the operation of the spell checker for the user.

File

```
#include <ksconfig.h>
```

Base Classes

```
QObject QPaintDevice QWidget Qt
```

Constructors

```
KSpellConfig(QWidget *parent = 0, const char *name = 0,
    KSpellConfig *spellConfig = 0, bool addHelpButton = true);
KSpellConfig(const KSpellConfig &);
```

Methods

```
int client() const;
bool dictFromList() const;
const QString dictionary() const;
int encoding() const;
QStringList ignoreList() const;
bool noRootAffix() const;
bool runTogether() const;
void setClient(int client);
void setDictFromList(bool dfl);
void setDictionary(const QString qs);
void setEncoding(int enctype);
void setIgnoreList(QStringList _ignorelist);
void setNoRootAffix(bool);
void setRunTogether(bool);
bool writeGlobalSettings();
```

Slots

```
void activateHelp(void);
```

The following example displays, as the top-level window, the KSpellConfig window shown in Figure 19-48:

```
/* showspellconfig.cpp */
#include <kapp.h>
#include <ksconfig.h>

int main(int argc,char **argv)
{
    KApplication app(argc,argv,"showspellconfig");
    KSpellConfig *spellconfig = new KSpellConfig();
    spellconfig->show();
    app.setMainWidget(spellconfig);
    return(app.exec());
}
```

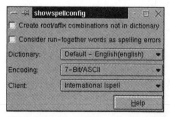

Figure 19-48: The KSpellConfig widget

KSpellDlg

The KSpellDlg widget displays a misspelled word and a list of suggestions for corrections, and responds to buttons specifying the action to be taken.

File

```
#include <kspelldlg.h>
```

Base Classes

```
QObject QPaintDevice QWidget Qt
```

Constructors

```
KSpellDlg(QWidget *parent, const char *name,
    bool _progressbar = FALSE, bool _modal = FALSE);
```

Methods

```
void init(const QString &_word, QStringList *_sugg);
inline QString replacement();
void standby();
```

Slots

```
void slotProgress(unsigned int p);
```

Signals

```
void command(int);
```

The following example of KSpellDlg initializes the display with the misspelled word and list of suggestions, as shown in Figure 19-49. The init() method inserts the data and enables all the buttons, and the standby() method disables the buttons.

```
/* showspelldlg.cpp */
#include <kapp.h>
#include <kspelldlg.h>

int main(int argc,char **argv)
{
    KApplication app(argc,argv,"showspelldlg");
    QString word = "tehn";
    QStringList *suggestion = new QStringList();
    suggestion->append("the");
    suggestion->append("then");
    suggestion->append("ten");
    KSpellDlg *spelldlg = new KSpellDlg(0,"spelldlg");
    spelldlg->init(word,suggestion);
    spelldlg->show();
    app.setMainWidget(spelldlg);
    return(app.exec());
}
```

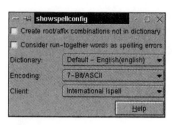

Figure 19-49: The KSpellDlg widget

KSplitList

The KSplitList widget is a KListBox that uses a signal to report its current width. This enables each item to adjust itself to fit, such as for a multicolumn format (a split list).

File
```
#include <kkeydialog.h>
```

Base Classes
```
KListBox QFrame QListBox QObject QPaintDevice QScrollView
    QWidget Qt
```

Constructors
```
KSplitList(QWidget *parent = 0, const char *name = 0);
```

Methods
```
int getId(int index);
void setVisibleItems(int numItem);
```

Signals
```
void newWidth(int newWidth);
```

The following example displays the KSplitList widget shown in Figure 19-50:

```
/* showsplitlist.cpp */
#include <kapp.h>
#include <kkeydialog.h>

int main(int argc,char **argv)
{
    KApplication app(argc,argv,"showsplitlist");
    KSplitList *splitlist = new KSplitList();
    for(int i=0; i<20; i++) {
        QString str;
        str.sprintf("Selection %d\n",i);
        splitlist->insertItem(str);
    }
```

```
      splitlist->show();
      app.setMainWidget(splitlist);
      return(app.exec());
}
```

Figure 19-50: The KSplitList widget

KStatusBar

The KStatusBar widget is included as part of the display of KTMainWindow. It can be used to display status as text, graphics, or a custom widget.

File

```
#include <kstatusbar.h>
```

Base Classes

```
QObject QPaintDevice QStatusBar QWidget Qt
```

Constructors

```
KStatusBar(QWidget *parent = 0L, const char *name = 0L);
```

Methods

```
void changeItem(const QString &text, int id);
inline void insertFixedItem(const QString &text, int ID,
    bool permanent = false);
void insertItem(const QString &text, int ID, int stretch = 0,
    bool permanent = false);
void removeItem(int id);
void setItemAlignment(int id, int align);
void setItemFixed(int id, int width = - 1);
```

Signals

```
void pressed(int);
void released(int);
```

Enums

```
enum BarStatus { Toggle, Show, Hide };
```

Chapter 6 includes examples that use KStatusBar.

KStatusBarLabel

The KStatusBarLabel is a special mouse-sensitive label designed for use inside the KStatusBar widget.

File

```
#include <kstatusbar.h>
```

Base Classes

```
QFrame QLabel QObject QPaintDevice QWidget Qt
```

Constructors

```
KStatusBarLabel(const QString &text, int _id,
    KStatusBar *parent = OL, const char *name = OL);
```

Signals

```
void itemPressed(int id);
void itemReleased(int id);
```

The following example creates and displays the KStatusBarLabel widget shown in Figure 19-51. The constructor includes not only the label text, but also the ID number provided with the signals.

```
/* showstatusbarlabel.cpp */
#include <kapp.h>
#include <kstatusbar.h>

int main(int argc,char **argv)
{
    KApplication app(argc,argv,"showstatusbarlabel");
    KStatusBarLabel *statusbarlabel =
            new KStatusBarLabel("Label text",4);
    statusbarlabel->show();
    app.setMainWidget(statusbarlabel);
    return(app.exec());
}
```

Figure 19-51: The KStatusBarLabel widget is a QLabel that is sensitive to the mouse.

KTextBrowser

The KTextBrowser widget is a text browser that has the added capability to recognize and respond to URL and e-mail links.

File
```
#include <ktextbrowser.h>
```

Base Classes
```
QFrame QObject QPaintDevice QScrollView QTextBrowser
    QTextView QWidget Qt
```

Constructors
```
KTextBrowser(QWidget *parent = 0, const char *name = 0,
    bool notifyClick = false);
```

Methods
```
void setNotifyClick(bool notifyClick);
```

Signals
```
void mailClick(const QString &name, const QString &address);
void urlClick(const QString &url);
```

The following example displays the text shown in Figure 19-52. The URL and e-mail response can be activated and deactivated by calling setNotifyClick().

```
/* showtextbrowser.cpp */
#include <kapp.h>
#include <ktextbrowser.h>

char text[] =
    "This is the text being displayed\n"
    "by the text browser. Both vertical\n"
    "and horizontal scroll bars will\n"
    "appear as necessary.";

int main(int argc,char **argv)
{
    KApplication app(argc,argv,"showtextbrowser");
    KTextBrowser *textbrowser = new KTextBrowser();
    textbrowser->show();
    textbrowser->setText(QString(text));
    app.setMainWidget(textbrowser);
    return(app.exec());
}
```

Figure 19-52: The KTextBrowswer widget displays text.

KTextPrintDialog

The KTextPrintDialog is a user interface that can be used to modify the contents of a KTextPrintConfig object.

File

```
#include <ktextprint.h>
```

Base Classes

```
KDialog KDialogBase QDialog QObject QPaintDevice QWidget Qt
```

Constructors

```
KTextPrintDialog(QWidget *parent, KTextPrintConfig &);
```

Methods

```
ColorMode colorMode();
void getData(KTextPrintConfig &);
Orientation orientation();
void setData(KTextPrintConfig &);
```

Slots

```
void setDest(int);
```

The following example of KTextPrintDialog displays the contents of the default KTextPrintDialog object, as shown in Figure 19-53:

```
/* showtextprintdialog.cpp */
#include <kapp.h>
#include <ktextprint.h>

int main(int argc,char **argv)
{
    KApplication app(argc,argv,"showtextprintdialog");
    KTextPrintConfig textprintconfig;
    KTextPrintDialog *textprintdialog =
        new KTextPrintDialog(0,textprintconfig);
    textprintdialog->show();
    return(app.exec());
}
```

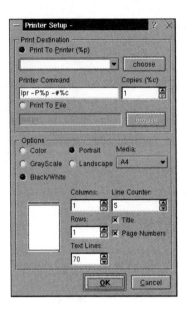

Figure 19-53: The default printer settings shown in a KTextPrintDialog window

KTMainWindow

The `KTMainWindow` widget is the standard KDE top-level window.

File
```
#include <ktmainwindow.h>
```

Base Classes
```
KXMLGUIBuilder KXMLGUIClient QObject QPaintDevice QWidget Qt
```

Inherited By
```
KDockMainWindow
```

Constructors
```
KTMainWindow(const char *name = 0L,
    WFlags f = WDestructiveClose);
```

Methods
```
int addToolBar(KToolBar *toolbar, int index = - 1);
static bool canBeRestored(int number);
static const QString classNameOfToplevel(int number);
virtual void createGUI(
    const QString &xmlfile = QString::null);
void enableStatusBar(
    KStatusBar::BarStatus stat = KStatusBar::Toggle);
void enableToolBar(
```

```
        KToolBar::BarStatus stat = KToolBar::Toggle, int id = 0);
    virtual KXMLGUIFactory *guiFactory();
    bool hasMenuBar();
    bool hasStatusBar();
    bool hasToolBar(int ID = 0);
    QPopupMenu *helpMenu(
        const QString &aboutAppText = QString::null,
        bool showWhatsThis = true);
    QWidget *indicator();
    QRect mainViewGeometry() const;
    KMenuBar *menuBar();
    bool restore(int number);
    void setEnableToolBar(
        KToolBar::BarStatus stat = KToolBar::Toggle,
        const QString &name = mainToolBar);
    void setFrameBorderWidth(int);
    void setIndicatorWidget(QWidget *indicator);
    void setMaximumToolBarWraps(unsigned int wraps);
    void setMenu(KMenuBar *menuBar);
    void setStatusBar(KStatusBar *statusBar);
    void setView(QWidget *view, bool show_frame = TRUE);
    virtual void show();
    QSize sizeHint() const;
    KStatusBar *statusBar();
    KToolBar *toolBar(int ID = 0);
    KToolBar *toolBar(const QString &name);
    QWidget *view() const;
```

Slots

```
    void appHelpActivated(void);
    virtual void setCaption(const QString &caption);
    virtual void setPlainCaption(const QString &caption);
```

Cross-Reference

You can find examples of the KTMainWindow **widget in Chapter 6.**

KToolBar

The KtoolBar widget is a toolbar that can contain several different kinds of tool widgets, and can be dragged and docked in several locations.

File

```
#include <ktoolbar.h>
```

Base Classes

```
QFrame QObject QPaintDevice QWidget Qt
```

Inherited By

```
KFormulaToolBar
```

Constructors

```
KToolBar(QWidget *parent = 0L, const char *name = 0L,
    bool _honor_mode = false);
```

Methods

```
void addConnection(int id, const char *signal,
    const QObject *receiver, const char *slot);
void alignItemRight(int id, bool right = true);
KAnimWidget *animatedWidget(int id);
BarPosition barPos() const;
void changeComboItem(int id, const QString &text,
    int index = - 1);
void clear();
void clearCombo(int id);
bool contextMenuEnabled() const;
int count();
bool enable(BarStatus stat);
void enableFloating(bool arrrrrgh);
void enableMoving(bool flag = true);
bool fullSize() const;
KToolBarButton *getButton(int id);
QComboBox *getCombo(int id);
QString getComboItem(int id, int index = - 1);
KLineEdit *getLined(int id);
QString getLinedText(int id);
QWidget *getWidget(int id);
virtual int heightForWidth(int width) const;
void hideItem(int id);
int iconSize() const;
IconText iconText() const;
int insertAnimatedWidget(int id, QObject *receiver,
    const char *slot, const QStringList &icons,
    int index = - 1);
int insertButton(const QString &icon, int id,
    bool enabled = true, const QString &text = QString::null,
    int index = - 1);
int insertButton(const QString &icon, int id,
    const char *signal, const QObject *receiver,
    const char *slot, bool enabled = true,
    const QString &text = QString::null, int index = - 1);
int insertButton(const QPixmap &pixmap, int id,
    bool enabled = true, const QString &text = QString::null,
    int index = - 1);
int insertButton(const QPixmap &pixmap, int id,
    const char *signal, const QObject *receiver,
    const char *slot, bool enabled = true,
    const QString &text = QString::null, int index = - 1);
int insertButton(const QPixmap &pixmap, int id,
```

```
            QPopupMenu *popup, bool enabled, const QString &_text,
            int index = - 1);
    int insertCombo(QStrList *list, int id, bool writable,
            const char *signal, const QObject *receiver,
            const char *slot, bool enabled = true,
            const QString &tooltiptext = QString::null, int size = 70,
            int index = - 1,
            QComboBox::Policy policy = QComboBox::AtBottom);
    int insertCombo(const QStringList &list, int id, bool writable,
            const char *signal, const QObject *receiver,
            const char *slot, bool enabled = true,
            const QString &tooltiptext = QString::null, int size = 70,
            int index = - 1,
            QComboBox::Policy policy = QComboBox::AtBottom);
    int insertCombo(const QString &text, int id, bool writable,
            const char *signal, QObject *recevier, const char *slot,
            bool enabled = true,
            const QString &tooltiptext = QString::null, int size = 70,
            int index = - 1,
            QComboBox::Policy policy = QComboBox::AtBottom);
    void insertComboItem(int id, const QString &text, int index);
    void insertComboList(int id, QStrList *list, int index);
    void insertComboList(int id, const QStringList &list,
            int index);
    int insertLineSeparator(int index = - 1);
    int insertLined(const QString &text, int ID,
            const char *signal, const QObject *receiver,
            const char *slot, bool enabled = true,
            const QString &toolTipText = QString::null, int size = 70,
            int index = - 1);
    int insertSeparator(int index = - 1);
    int insertWidget(int id, int width, QWidget *_widget,
            int index = - 1);
    bool isButtonOn(int id);
    int maxHeight();
    int maxWidth();
    virtual QSize maximumSizeHint() const;
    virtual QSize minimumSizeHint() const;
    void removeComboItem(int id, int index);
    void removeItem(int id);
    void saveState();
    void setAutoRepeat(int id, bool flag = true);
    void setBarPos(BarPosition bpos);
    void setButton(int id, bool flag);
    void setButtonIcon(int id, const QString &_icon);
    void setButtonPixmap(int id, const QPixmap &_pixmap);
    void setCurrentComboItem(int id, int index);
    void setDelayedPopup(int id, QPopupMenu *_popup,
        bool toggle = false);
    void setEnableContextMenu(bool enable = true);
    void setFlat(bool flag);
```

```
void setFullSize(bool flag = true);
void setIconSize(int size);
void setIconSize(int size, bool update);
void setIconText(IconText it);
void setIconText(IconText it, bool update);
void setItemAutoSized(int id, bool yes = true);
void setItemEnabled(int id, bool enabled);
void setItemNoStyle(int id, bool no_style = true);
void setLinedText(int id, const QString &text);
void setMaxHeight(int h);
void setMaxWidth(int dw);
void setTitle(const QString &_title);
void setToggle(int id, bool flag = true);
void setXML(const QString &xmlfile, const QDomDocument &xml);
void showItem(int id);
virtual QSize sizeHint() const;
virtual QSizePolicy sizePolicy() const;
void toggleButton(int id);
void updateRects(bool resize = false);
virtual int widthForHeight(int height) const;
```

Signals

```
void clicked(int id);
void doubleClicked(int id);
void highlighted(int id, bool isHighlighted);
void highlighted(int id);
void modechange();
void moved(BarPosition);
void pressed(int);
void released(int);
void toggled(int);
```

Enums

```
enum IconText { IconOnly=0, IconTextRight, TextOnly,
     IconTextBottom };
enum BarStatus { Toggle, Show, Hide };
enum BarPosition { Top=0, Left, Right, Bottom, Floating,
     Flat };
```

 Cross-Reference   There are several examples of the KToolBar **widget in Chapter 6.**

KToolBarButton

The KToolBarButton widget is used internally by the KToolBar widget to display buttons that respond to the mouse.

The KToolBarButton is constructed by calling one of the insertButton() methods of KToolBar. Using the ID number, a call to the KToolBar method getButton() can be used to retrieve a pointer to the button, making the methods listed here available.

File
```
#include <ktoolbarbutton.h>
```

Base Classes
```
QButton QObject QPaintDevice QWidget Qt
```

Constructors
```
KToolBarButton(const QString &icon, int id, QWidget *parent,
    const char *name = OL, const QString &txt = QString::null);
KToolBarButton(const QPixmap &pixmap, int id, QWidget *parent,
    const char *name = OL, const QString &txt = QString::null);
KToolBarButton(QWidget *parent = OL, const char *name = OL);
```

Methods
```
void on(bool flag = true);
QPopupMenu *popup();
virtual void setDefaultIcon(const QString &icon);
virtual void setDefaultPixmap(const QPixmap &pixmap);
void setDelayedPopup(QPopupMenu *p, bool toggle = false);
virtual void setDisabledIcon(const QString &icon);
virtual void setDisabledPixmap(const QPixmap &pixmap);
void setEnabled(bool enable = true);
virtual void setIcon(const QString &icon);
virtual void setIcon(const QString &icon, bool generate);
void setNoStyle(bool no_style = true);
virtual void setPixmap(const QPixmap &pixmap);
virtual void setPixmap(const QPixmap &pixmap, bool generate);
void setPopup(QPopupMenu *p);
void setRadio(bool f = true);
virtual void setText(const QString &text);
void setToggle(bool toggle = true);
void toggle();
```

Slots
```
void modeChange();
```

Signals
```
void clicked(int);
void doubleClicked(int);
void highlighted(int, bool);
void pressed(int);
void released(int);
void toggled(int);
```

Cross-Reference Chapter 6 includes examples of creating KToolBarButton widgets inside a KToolBar.

KWizard

The KWizard widget can be used to create a dialog that guides the user through a sequence of steps. Each step consists of a single window. The KWizard widget provides the paging mechanism and the control buttons. This widget extends QWizard to include a set of standard KDE methods for dialogs. It is the base class on which KDialogBase is built.

File
```
#include <kwizard.h>
```

Base Classes
```
QDialog QObject QPaintDevice QWidget QWizard Qt
```

Constructors
```
KWizard(QWidget *parent = 0, const char *name = 0,
    bool modal = false, WFlags f = 0);
```

The following example displays the empty KWizard widget shown in Figure 19-54:

```
/* showwizard.cpp */
#include <kapp.h>
#include <kwizard.h>

int main(int argc,char **argv)
{
    QApplication app(argc,argv);
    KWizard *wizard = new KWizard();
    wizard->show();
    app.setMainWidget(wizard);
    return(app.exec());
}
```

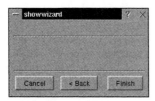

Figure 19-54: The KWizard widget

KXYSelector

The KXYSelector widget is a base class that can be used in place of QWidget, and it adds the capability of using the mouse to select a point on the face of the widget.

File

```
#include <kselect.h>
```

Base Classes

```
QObject QPaintDevice QWidget Qt
```

Inherited By

```
KHSSelector
```

Constructors

```
KXYSelector(QWidget *parent = OL, const char *name = OL);
```

Methods

```
QRect contentsRect();
void setRange(int _minX, int _minY, int _maxX, int _maxY);
void setValues(int _xPos, int _yPos);
int xValue();
int yValue();
```

Signals

```
void valueChanged(int _x, int _y);
```

The following example of the KXZWidget displays the cross hairs position indicator shown in Figure 19-55:

```
/* showxyselector.cpp */
#include <kapp.h>
#include <kselect.h>

int main(int argc,char **argv)
{
    QApplication app(argc,argv);
    KXYSelector *xyselector = new KXYSelector();
    xyselector->show();
    app.setMainWidget(xyselector);
    return(app.exec());
}
```

Figure 19-55: The KXYSelector widget with its cross hairs position indicator

Summary

This chapter provided an alphabetical listing of each KDE widget. Each widget was listed along with the following:

✦ The constructor, or constructors, that can be used to create instances of the widget

✦ The name of the header file in which the widget is defined

✦ All of the superclasses from which the widget inherits its capabilities

✦ All of the subclasses that derive the capabilities of the widget

✦ The slots and signals that are used to connect an event in one widget to a method call in another

✦ The public methods available to your application

This chapter and the previous one include many examples of programs that run in the KDE environment. While there are many differences between these programs and those written for other systems, there are also many similarities. The next chapter contains a point-by-point comparison of the basic structure of a simple KDE program and the same program written for Windows.

✦　　✦　　✦

Comparative Anatomy of Windowing Programs

If you are familiar with programming using the Win32 API, this chapter can help you understand the structure of a KDE/Qt application. At the lowest levels, the two programming models are very similar. They both operate using a main loop that waits for events to arrive; and when an event does arrive, a function is called to notify the application.

To make the comparison as simple as possible, this chapter implements the same short program for both Win32 and KDE.

The comparison in this chapter has nothing to do with which windowing system is "better." Moreover, no attempt is made to use any kind of standard optimal programming techniques. These two programs are contrived to be as much alike as possible, so a person who understands one of them can easily understand the structure of the other.

A Win32 Program

The following example is a Windows program that fills a window with concentric boxes. Whenever the window resizes, the boxes also resize to fit it. The resulting window looks like the one shown in Figure 20-1.

BoxBox

```
 1 /* boxbox.c  (win32) */
 2 #include <windows.h>
 3
 4 #define STEP 3
 5
 6 static char name[] = "BoxBox";
 7 static int xBox1;
 8 static int yBox1;
 9 static int xBox2;
10 static int yBox2;
11
12 LRESULT CALLBACK callback(HWND,UINT,WPARAM,LPARAM);
13
14 int WINAPI WinMain(HINSTANCE instance,
15         HINSTANCE prev,PSTR commandLine,int showCommand)
16 {
17     HWND window;
18     MSG message;
19     WNDCLASSEX winclass;
20
21     winclass.cbSize = sizeof (winclass);
22     winclass.style = CS_HREDRAW | CS_VREDRAW;
23     winclass.lpfnWndProc = callback;
24     winclass.cbClsExtra = 0;
25     winclass.cbWndExtra = 0;
26     winclass.hInstance = instance;
27     winclass.hIcon = LoadIcon(NULL,IDI_APPLICATION);
28     winclass.hCursor = LoadCursor(NULL,IDC_ARROW);
29     winclass.lpszMenuName = NULL;
30     winclass.lpszClassName = name;
31     winclass.hIconSm = LoadIcon(NULL,IDI_APPLICATION);
32     winclass.hbrBackground =
33             (HBRUSH)GetStockObject(WHITE_BRUSH);
34
35     RegisterClassEx(&winclass);
36     window = CreateWindow (name,"Boxes in Boxes",
37             WS_OVERLAPPEDWINDOW,
38             CW_USEDEFAULT,CW_USEDEFAULT,
39             CW_USEDEFAULT,CW_USEDEFAULT,
40             NULL,NULL,instance,NULL);
41     ShowWindow(window,showCommand);
42     UpdateWindow (window);
43
44     while(GetMessage(&message,NULL,0,0)) {
45         TranslateMessage(&message);
46         DispatchMessage(&message);
47     }
48     return(message.wParam);
49 }
50
51 LRESULT CALLBACK callback(HWND window,UINT messageType,
52         WPARAM wParam,LPARAM lParam)
```

```
53 {
54     int x1;
55     int y1;
56     int x2;
57     int y2;
58     HDC hdc;
59     PAINTSTRUCT ps;
60
61     switch (messageType) {
62     case WM_SIZE:
63         xBox1 = 10;
64         yBox1 = 10;
65         xBox2 = LOWORD(lParam) - 10;
66         yBox2 = HIWORD(lParam) - 10;
67         return(0);
68     case WM_PAINT:
69         hdc = BeginPaint(window,&ps);
70         SetViewportOrgEx(hdc,0,0,NULL);
71         x1 = xBox1;
72         x2 = xBox2;
73         y1 = yBox1;
74         y2 = yBox2;
75         while((x1 < x2) && (y1 < y2)) {
76             MoveToEx(hdc,x1,y1,NULL);
77             LineTo(hdc,x2,y1);
78             LineTo(hdc,x2,y2);
79             LineTo(hdc,x1,y2);
80             LineTo(hdc,x1,y1);
81             x1 += STEP;
82             y1 += STEP;
83             x2 -= STEP;
84             y2 -= STEP;
85         }
86         EndPaint(window,&ps);
87         return(0);
88     case WM_DESTROY:
89         PostQuitMessage(0);
90         return(0);
91     }
92     return(DefWindowProc(window,messageType,
93             wParam,lParam));
94 }
```

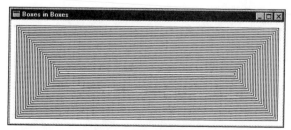

Figure 20-1: A Win32 main window

The program has only two functions. The function `WinMain()`, beginning on line 14, is the original one called by the operating system to start the program. The function `callback()`, on line 51, is called by the operating system whenever an event arrives.

A KDE Program

The following example is a KDE program that fills a window with concentric boxes. If the size of the window changes, the size of the boxes also changes. The window looks like the one shown in Figure 20-2. The example is in two files: a header file that defines the BoxBox widget, and a C++ source file that contains a mainline for the program as well as the bodies of the methods of the BoxBox class.

BoxBox Header

```
1 /* boxbox.h (KDE) */
2 #ifndef BOXBOX_H
3 #define BOXBOX_H
4
5 #include <qwidget.h>
6
7 class BoxBox: public QWidget
8 {
9 public:
10     BoxBox(QWidget *parent=0,const char *name=0);
11 private:
12     int xBox1;
13     int yBox1;
14     int xBox2;
15     int yBox2;
16 protected:
17     virtual void paintEvent(QPaintEvent *);
18     virtual void resizeEvent(QResizeEvent *);
19 };
20
21 #endif
```

BoxBox

```
1 /* boxbox.cpp (KDE) */
2 #include <kapp.h>
3 #include <qpainter.h>
4 #include "boxbox.h"
5
6 #define STEP 3
7
8 int main(int argc,char **argv)
9 {
10     KApplication app(argc,argv,"boxbox");
11     BoxBox boxbox;
```

```
12        boxbox.show();
13        app.setMainWidget(&boxbox);
14        return(app.exec());
15 }
16 BoxBox::BoxBox(QWidget *parent,const
17         char *name) : QWidget(parent,name)
18 {
19        resize(400,200);
20 }
21 void BoxBox::paintEvent(QPaintEvent *)
22 {
23        QPainter p;
24
25        int x1 = xBox1;
26        int y1 = yBox1;
27        int x2 = xBox2;
28        int y2 = yBox2;
29
30        p.begin(this);
31        while((x1 < x2) && (y1 < y2)) {
32            p.moveTo(x1,y1);
33            p.lineTo(x2,y1);
34            p.lineTo(x2,y2);
35            p.lineTo(x1,y2);
36            p.lineTo(x1,y1);
37            x1 += STEP;
38            y1 += STEP;
39            x2 -= STEP;
40            y2 -= STEP;
41        }
42        p.end();
43 }
44 void BoxBox::resizeEvent(QResizeEvent *e)
45 {
46        QSize size = e->size();
47        xBox1 = 10;
48        yBox1 = 10;
49        xBox2 = size.width() - 10;
50        yBox2 = size.height() - 10;
51 }
```

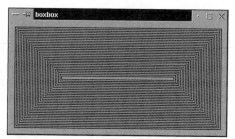

Figure 20-2: A KDE top-level window

This program has a `main()` function that is used to initialize the KDE environment, create the widget to be displayed, set up the widget as the top-level window, and go into an execution loop. Besides the constructor, there are two methods, each of which executes on the arrival of a specific event.

A Point-by-Point Win32 and KDE Comparison

This section describes the similarities and differences between the KDE and Win32 programs by detailing some specifics. As you will see, the difference lies in the details, not in the underlying technology.

Initialization

Line 10 of the KDE program constructs a `KApplication` object, which also initializes the GUI interface and other parts of the underlying graphics software. There is no counterpart to this function in the Win32 program because the Win32 API is part of the operating system and is already initialized. However, KDE is not a part of the operating system, so it is necessary to initialize windowing software.

This construction of the `KApplication` object assigns the program its name, which, by default, is used as a title that appears at the top of the window. The parallel action in the Win32 version is the call to `CreateWindow()` on line 36.

The Main Window

Line 11 of the KDE program creates a `BoxBox` object, which is to be the top-level window of the application. Lines 21 through 33 of the Win32 version define the main window, and the call to `RegisterClassEx()` on line 35 registers it with the operating system. As you can see, a lot more setup is required to create a Win32 top-level window than a KDE top-level window. This is because all of the settings must be specified up front for Win32; whereas KDE uses a standard set of defaults for everything and has functions available so your program can change things after the window is built.

Responding to Events

Both the KDE and Win32 programs are event-driven. In other words, once both programs are initialized and their windows are displayed, KDE and Win32 wait until an event (mouse, keyboard, or whatever) occurs. When an event does occur, a function is called to pass the information from the system to the application. Both of the programs need to respond to two specific events: when the size of the window changes, and when all or part of the window has been exposed and should be drawn.

On line 21, the KDE program overrides the inherited `QWidget` virtual method `paintEvent()` that is to be called whenever the window needs to be drawn.

This function draws the set of nested boxes using the size and location values that were retrieved from the latest call to resizeEvent(). The Win32 program achieves the same thing with the case statement on line 68.

On line 44, the KDE program overrides the inherited QWidget virtual method resizeEvent() that is to be called whenever the window first appears, and whenever it changes size. The same thing is achieved in the callback() function of the Win32 program with the case statement on line 62. In both cases, the new size information is stored in the local variables named xBox1, yBox1, xBox2, and yBox2.

> **Note** These two methods of handling events are more alike than they are different. A KDE application specifies a different callback method for each event. In the Win32 program, the single callback function can be used as a dispatcher that contains separate case statements for each event—thus calling a separate function for each event.

The Main Loop

The KDE program calls exec() on line 14. This function does not return until it is time for the program to exit. It has the job of waiting for events and then causing the appropriate method (or methods) to be called. The main loop of the Win32 program is on lines 44 through 47. The function GetMessage() waits until it receives an event, and then it returns. The call to TranslateMessage() translates keyboard codes into characters, and DispatchMessage() forwards the event to the correct window.

Program Shutdown

When shutting down the Win32 program, the callback function is called with a WM_DESTROY message. A call to PostQuitMessage() is made on line 89, which places a quit message in the input queue; when it is read, the program terminates. This gives you the opportunity to clean things up before shutting down, or (by failure to post the quit message) refuse to quit.

The KDE application shutdown is built into the environment that is set up during the initialization process of the KApplication object. Closing the top-level window closes the application. Also, exiting the application will close the top-level window. The title bar at the top of the window is connected to the shutdown process so that the mouse can be used to close the window.

Global Data

Because the Win32 program is written in C, it requires the use of global storage to hold values that will remain between calls to the callback function. Of course, the Win32 version could be written in C++ and objects could be devised that would encapsulate the global data, but that approach is not a part of the API itself. In this example, global data is stored in the variables xBox1, yBox1, xBox2, and yBox2 on lines 7 through 10.

KDE, being written in C++, has the capability of storing data inside each individual class. In this example, the corners of the outermost rectangle are stored in xBox1, yBox1, xBox2, and yBox2, defined in lines 12 through 15 of the header file.

A GNOME Program

Just for the sake of further comparison, the following example is a GNOME/GTK+ program that also fills a window with concentric boxes. As with the previous examples, if the size of the window changes, the size of the boxes also changes. The window looks like the one shown in Figure 20-3.

```
 1  /** boxbox.c (Gnome) **/
 2  #include <gnome.h>
 3
 4  gint eventDelete(GtkWidget *widget,
 5          GdkEvent *event,gpointer data);
 6  gint eventDestroy(GtkWidget *widget,
 7          GdkEvent *event,gpointer data);
 8  gboolean eventExpose(GtkWidget *widget,
 9          GdkEvent *event,gpointer data);
10  gint eventConfigure(GtkWidget *widget,
11          GdkEventConfigure *event,gpointer data);
12
13  #define STEP 3
14
15  static char name[] = "BoxBox";
16  static int xBox1;
17  static int yBox1;
18  static int xBox2;
19  static int yBox2;
20
21  int main(int argc,char *argv[])
22  {
23      GtkWidget *app;
24      GtkWidget *area;
25
26      gnome_init(name,"1.0",argc,argv);
27      app = gnome_app_new(name,"Boxes in Boxes");
28      gtk_signal_connect(GTK_OBJECT(app),"delete_event",
29              GTK_SIGNAL_FUNC(eventDelete),NULL);
30      gtk_signal_connect(GTK_OBJECT(app),"destroy",
31              GTK_SIGNAL_FUNC(eventDestroy),NULL);
32
33      area = gtk_drawing_area_new();
34      gnome_app_set_contents(GNOME_APP(app),area);
35
36      gtk_signal_connect(GTK_OBJECT(area),"expose_event",
37              GTK_SIGNAL_FUNC(eventExpose),NULL);
38      gtk_signal_connect(GTK_OBJECT(area),"configure_event",
39              GTK_SIGNAL_FUNC(eventConfigure),NULL);
```

```
40
41      gtk_widget_show_all(app);
42      gtk_main();
43      exit(0);
44  }
45  gboolean eventExpose(GtkWidget *widget,
46          GdkEvent *event,gpointer data) {
47      int x1;
48      int y1;
49      int x2;
50      int y2;
51
52      x1 = xBox1;
53      y1 = yBox1;
54      x2 = xBox2;
55      y2 = yBox2;
56      while((x1 < x2) && (y1 < y2)) {
57          gdk_draw_line(widget->window,
58                  widget->style->black_gc,
59                  x1,y1,x2,y1);
60          gdk_draw_line(widget->window,
61                  widget->style->black_gc,
62                  x2,y1,x2,y2);
63          gdk_draw_line(widget->window,
64                  widget->style->black_gc,
65                  x2,y2,x1,y2);
66          gdk_draw_line(widget->window,
67                  widget->style->black_gc,
68                  x1,y2,x1,y1);
69          x1 += STEP;
70          y1 += STEP;
71          x2 -= STEP;
72          y2 -= STEP;
73      }
74      return(TRUE);
75  }
76  gint eventConfigure(GtkWidget *widget,
77          GdkEventConfigure *event,gpointer data)
78  {
79      xBox1 = 10;
80      yBox1 = 10;
81      xBox2 = event->width - 10;
82      yBox2 = event->height - 10;
83      return(TRUE);
84  }
85  gint eventDelete(GtkWidget *widget,
86          GdkEvent *event,gpointer data) {
87      return(FALSE);
88  }
89  gint eventDestroy(GtkWidget *widget,
90          GdkEvent *event,gpointer data) {
91      gtk_main_quit();
92      return(0);
93  }
```

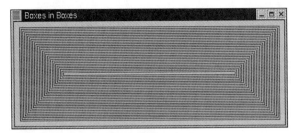

Figure 20-3: A GNOME main window

This program has a `main()` function that is used to initialize GNOME, create the window to be displayed, specify the callbacks, and go into an execution loop. There are four other functions, each of which executes on the arrival of a specific event.

As you can see, a bit more effort is required here to get things set up to respond to events. The calls to `gtk_signal_connect()` on lines 36 and 38 are required in order for the program to receive the events that set the size of the window and draw it. It is also necessary to set up callbacks to respond to the mouse so that the application can be halted by the user — this is done with the calls to `gtk_signal_connect()` on lines 28 and 30.

Summary

The underlying architecture of a Win32 application and a KDE application is the same. Both are based on events. A GNOME application also has similar features.

The comparison in this chapter showed the following:

✦ Win32, KDE, and GNOME all use the concept of an infinite loop waiting for the arrival of events.

✦ They all require about the same amount of code, but one may require more detail in a particular area that another.

✦ All three applications share the concept of a top-level window as the main display, and all top-level windows are capable of receiving events.

✦ They all supply a method for guaranteeing that an application closes down cleanly.

This chapter concludes the third, and final, part of the book. The appendixes that follow serve two purposes. Appendixes A and B explain where and how to load and install the software. Appendixes C through G are some cross-reference listings that can be quite handy when programming KDE/Qt.

✦   ✦   ✦

What's on the CD-ROM?

This appendix provides you with information on the contents of the CD-ROM that accompanies this book.

There are four utility programs included on this CD:

- ✦ autoconf 2.13
- ✦ automake 1.4
- ✦ gcc 2.95.2
- ✦ bzip 1.0.1 source and bzip 1.0.0 binary

The source code of KDE 2.0 is on the CD, which includes:

- ✦ KDE Software Development environment
- ✦ KDE's GUI Desktop
- ✦ Konquerer web browser
- ✦ KOffice
- ✦ A number of games and utilities

Also included are the source code examples from the book, and an electronic, searchable version of the book that can be viewed with Adobe Acrobat Reader.

System Requirements

To install this software, you will need a Linux system with a CD-ROM drive and at least 30 megabytes of free disk space (depending on your installation choices).

Installing the Utilities from the CD

To use any of the files on the CD, it is necessary for it to be mounted. It is normally mounted on the /mnt/cdrom directory. Depending on your version of Linux, the mounting occurs automatically when you insert the CD, or you may need to use the mount command.

To install autoconf from the CD to your hard drive, follow these steps:

1. You only need to install autoconf if you do not have a current version already installed. The version on the CD is 2.13. To test whether your version is current, enter this command:

   autoconf --version

2. Change to the directory named /usr/local.

3. Enter the following command, which will create the directory /usr/local/autoconf-2.13, and fill it with the source files:

   tar xvzf /mnt/cdrom/utilities/autoconf-2.13.tar.gz

4. Change to the new directory and read the file named INSTALL for detailed installation instructions.

To install automake from the CD to your hard drive, follow these steps:

1. You only need to install automake if you do not have a current version already installed. The version on the CD is 1.4. To test whether your version is current, enter this command:

   automake --version

2. Change to the directory named /usr/local.

3. Enter the following command, which will create the directory /usr/local/automake-1.4, and fill it with the source files:

   tar xvzf /mnt/cdrom/utilities/automake-1.4.tar.gz

4. Change to the new directory and read the file named INSTALL for detailed installation instructions.

To install the gcc from the CD to your hard drive, follow these steps:

1. You only need to install gcc if you do not have a current version already installed. The version on the CD is 2.95.2. To test whether your version is current, enter the following command:

   gcc --version

2. Change to the directory named /usr/local.

3. Enter the following command, which will create the directory /usr/local/ gcc-2.95.2, and fill it with the source files:

```
tar xvzf /mnt/cdrom/utilities/gcc-2.95.2.tar.gz
```

4. Change to the new directory and either read either the file named install/ INDEX or use your Web browser on install/index.html for detailed installation instructions.

To install the bunzip2 from the CD to your hard drive, follow these steps:

1. There is no need to install bunzip2 on your system if one is already there. To determine the installed version, enter the following command:

```
bunzip2 --version
```

2. Change to the directory named /usr/local.

3. Enter the following command, which will create the directory /usr/local/ bzip2-1.0.1, and fill it with the source files:

```
tar xvzf /mnt/cdrom/utilities/bzip2-1.0.1.tar.gz
```

4. Change to the new directory and read the file named README for detailed installation instructions.

Installing KDE 2 from the CD

To install the KDE2 from the CD to your hard drive, follow these steps:

1. Create a new directory to hold the KDE installation. For example, it could be /usr/local/kde2, /opt/kde2, /usr/local/kde, or another location if you prefer.

2. In the new directory, enter this sequence of commands to create the qt directory and compile the qt libraries:

```
tar xvzf /mnt/cdrom/kde/qt-x11-2.2.1.tar
cd qt-2.2.1
exort QTDIR=$PWD
./configure -sm -gif -system-jpeg -no-opengl
make
```

3. Set the KDEDIR environment variable to the installation directory you created in step 1 with a command like this:

```
export KDEDIR=/opt/kde2
```

4. Compile the kdesupport package with these commands:

```
cp /mnt/cdrom/kde/kdesupport-2.0.tar.bz2 .
bunzip2 kdesupport-2.0.tar.bz2
```

```
tar xvf kdsupport-2.0.tar
cd kdesupport-2.0
./configure
make all
make install
```

5. In the same way, compile the kdelibs package with these commands:

```
cp /mnt/cdrom/kde/kdelibs-2.0.tar.bz2 .
bunzip2 kdelibs-2.0.tar.bz2
tar xvf kdlibs-2.0.tar
cd kdelibs-2.0
./configure
make all
make install
```

6. Finally, using the same sequence of commands as in the previous steps, compile all the rest of the packages in the /mnt/cdrom/kde directory. These may be compiled in any order. (Note: The packages named kde-i18n- are for internationalization and do not need to be included.) The generalized form of the command sequence looks like the following:

```
cp /mnt/cdrom/kde/<package>.tar.bz2 .
bunzip2 <package>.tar.bz2
tar xvf <package>.tar
cd <package>
./configure
make all
make install
```

Installing the Adobe Acrobat Reader from the CD

Included in the Acrobat tar file is a file named INSTGUID.TXT, which contains detailed information on the installation process. To get to this file, you will need to extract all of the files, which you can do with the following command:

```
tar xvzf linux-ar-405.tar.gz
```

This will create a subdirectory named ILINXR.install containing a set of installation files. Follow the instructions in the INSTGUID.TXT installation guide to install the reader.

To get versions of the Acrobat Reader for other flavors of UNIX, or to check for version upgrades, go to http://www.adobe.com/products/acrobat.

What's on the CD

The CD-ROM contains source code examples, applications, and an electronic version of the book. Following is a summary of the contents of the CD-ROM, arranged by category.

Source Code

Every program in any listing in the book is on the CD in the directory named `examples`. In the `kde` directory you will find the complete source of KDE and all of its standard utilities and programs. The `utilities` directory contains the source of some utilities that are necessary for compiling KDE and KDE applications.

Electronic version of KDE/Qt Programming Bible

The complete (and searchable) text of this book is on the CD-ROM in Adobe's Portable Document Format (PDF), readable with the Adobe Acrobat Reader (also included). For more information on Adobe Acrobat Reader, go to `www.adobe.com`.

Troubleshooting

If you have difficulty installing or using the CD-ROM programs, try the following solutions:

✦ **Read the README and other text files.** There is a lot of documentation that comes with each of the parts of KDE, and with the utilities. You may have to look through a few of them to find one that addresses your particular question.

✦ **Visit the appropriate Web site for the latest information.** Software is constantly being updated and existing problems are being overcome. The Web site not only contains the latest version of the software, it will also have the latest version of the documentation. Also, there is usually a FAQ that is updated whenever a new problem is discovered.

If you still have trouble with the CD, please call the IDG Books Worldwide Customer Service phone number: (800) 762-2974. Outside the United States, call (317) 572-3993. IDG Books will provide technical support only for installation and other general quality control items; for technical support on the applications themselves, consult the program's vendor or author.

✦   ✦   ✦

Setting Up for Software Development

You need to install a number of software components before you can write a KDE/Qt application. If you have a relatively recent Linux CD, you certainly have a lot of what you need — and you may have it all.

This appendix can serve as a sort of checklist to make sure you have everything you need. However, keep in mind that — like everything else in the world of open source — things are subject to change, including the names and URLs of items listed here. Furthermore, a newer version of something may operate differently and have slightly different requirements than those outlined in this appendix.

Linux

If you do not have Linux, you probably will purchase a CD. A commercial CD has the advantages of containing most of the items you need, being easier to install than a downloaded version, and providing telephone support to get you started.

If, however, you want to get a copy of Linux over the Internet, be careful which version you choose. Mainly, you don't want to get an experimental version. A Linux version number indicates whether it is a stable or developmental version. Unless you are working on the Linux kernel itself, use a stable version. If the second digit following the version number is even (2.0, 2.2, and so on), it is a stable version. There may be a third number in the version number (like 2.2.8) that indicates bug fixes. To get the latest version of the kernel, get the highest even-numbered version.

Table B-1 lists some of the more popular Linux distributions. Any one of them can run KDE successfully and can be used as a KDE development platform. This list is certainly not complete—there are a number of other excellent distributors of Linux, with more appearing every day.

Table B-1 Some of the More Common Linux Distributions	
Distribution	**URL**
Caldera	`http://www.caldera.com`
Corel	`http://linux.corel.com`
Debian	`http://www.debian.org/`
LinuxPro	`http://www.wgs.com`
Mandrake	`http://www.mandrake.com`
Red Hat	`http://www.redhat.com`
Slackware	`http://www.slackware.com`
StormLinux	`http://stormlinux.com`
SuSE	`http://www.suse.com`
TurboLinux	`http://www.turbolinux.com`

gcc (egcs)

This is the C compiler that you need to compile your programs. In April 1999, because of future plans, the Free Software Foundation appointed the *egcs Steering Committee* to maintain gcc. At that time, the name was changed from gcc to egcs. However, the executable of the program is still named gcc because it has to work with all of the existing make files.

There certainly will be a version of the gcc compiler included in your Linux distribution. But new features are added from time to time, so you need to make sure you have a version that is as current as your KDE software. You can get the latest version from a number of locations on the Internet. Following is the home page of the compiler:

```
http://www.gnu.ai.mit.edu/software/gcc/gcc.html
```

XFree86

This is the low-level windowing software used by Qt. All Linux distributions include this software, and install it during normal installation. This is very stable software, but there are occasional releases (as of this writing, the latest version is X11R6.4). If you find that you need to get a new version (or need to find out more information about it), the XFree86 home page is as follows:

```
http://www.xfree86.org
```

autoconf and automake

If you compile the GNOME distribution source code, you need these utility programs. These utilities are used to automatically create the make files and then compile the programs. If you have some difficulty with the compilation process, you should make sure you have the latest versions. If they are not available in your Linux distribution, you can download them from the following:

```
ftp://ftp.gnu.org/pub/gnu/automake/
ftp://ftp.gnu.org/pub/gnu/autoconf/
```

You can use these utility programs to compile your own programs. In fact, if you intend to write a large application, it is a good idea.

KDE and Qt

Conveniently, whenever you get a copy of KDE, a matching version of Qt comes with it. Because both KDE and Qt are constantly changing, it is important to use the version of Qt that is supplied along with KDE to guarantee compatibility.

To locate a place to download the software, go to the following Web site:

```
http://www.kde.org/mirrors.html
```

This site provides a list of mirror sites that maintain versions of the software. Some of them only provide the stable (released) versions, while others will also provide the unstable (developmental) versions. You need to decide whether you would prefer to use a released version of KDE, or if you would like to go for the latest developmental version. Deciding which to choose really depends on what you are trying to do.

If you choose to go with a stable version, you will need to choose one of the mirror sites, follow the instructions in the README files, and choose the directories that are right for your version of Linux. Quite a few different packaging options are available for KDE. There are RPM files for Red Hat, DEB files for Debian, and tar files for general installation. Just find the one that matches your system and follow the instructions.

Obtaining and Installing the Latest Version

If you want to get the latest version of the software and keep it updated, you can download all of the source code in such a way that you can continuously download upgrades that only include the things that have changed since the last time you downloaded. Once you have implemented the procedure described in this appendix, the process of updating your version of the source is automatic and simple.

CVS Software

CVS (Concurrent Version System) is a source code control system that keeps track of changes to the source files of programs. All of KDE and Qt are managed by CVS.

You need to have the utility named `cvs` installed on your system. It is probably already there, or on your CD, but if not, you can get a copy of it from the following:

```
http://www.cvshome.org/
```

If you are going to be doing software development, the CVS software is worth getting to know. This is especially true if more than one person is going to be modifying the software because CVS can be used to check source code modules in and out, preventing problems caused by having multiple versions of the same source code.

Creating a CVS Configuration File

Before you run CVS, a couple of things need to be preset. In your home directory, create a text file named `.cvsrc` with the following content:

```
cvs -z4 -q
diff -u3 -p
update -dP
checkout -P
```

Make sure you get the cases right for the letter *p* on the option settings. On the `diff` line it is lowercase, and on both the `update` and `checkout` lines, it is uppercase.

Setting the CVSROOT Environment Variable

You need to set an environment variable that tells CVS where to find the source on the remote site. Enter the following:

```
export CVSROOT=:pserver:anonymous@anoncvs.kde.org:/home/kde
```

Logging in to the Remote CVS Server

Create the directory that you want to be the parent directory of your source tree. Each portion of KDE that you check out will create a subdirectory, so change to the new directory and enter the following command:

```
cvs login
```

You may be prompted for a password; if you are, just press Return or Enter. It could take some time for the server to respond, so you may have to wait a couple of minutes.

Downloading a Copy of the Source Files

You can choose which parts you download and which parts you don't, but you need to enter a separate command for each. The following list of commands (which can be edited into a script and executed all at once) will download all of the source. You may not want it all, so you can omit some of these commands.

```
cvs checkout kde-qt-addon
cvs checkout qt-copy
cvs checkout kdelibs
cvs checkout kde-i18n
cvs checkout kdeadmin
cvs checkout kdebase
cvs checkout kdegames
cvs checkout kdegraphics
cvs checkout kdemultimedia
cvs checkout kdenetwork
cvs checkout kdesdk
cvs checkout kdesupport
cvs checkout kdetoys
cvs checkout kdeutils
cvs checkout kdevelop
cvs checkout kdoc
cvs checkout kfte
cvs checkout klyx
cvs checkout kmusic
cvs checkout koffice
cvs checkout korganizer
cvs checkout ksite
cvs checkout kdepim
```

Keeping Up with Changes

You can grab a new copy of the source code whenever you want by downloading only the source that has changed since your last download. You do everything the same as you did for the original download, except use `update` instead of `checkout` on the `cvs` command line. For example, to download the latest version of the `qt-copy` directory, enter the following command:

```
cvs update qt-copy
```

If you want to stay updated with the latest versions of everything, use the same script you used with `checkout`, but change all the commands to `update` instead. You can run the script again and again to stay current.

Compiling the Code

Each of the directories of source code will need to be compiled separately. The first one to compile is the `qt-copy` directory, because almost all of the other directories depend on it being there. Change to the `qt-copy` directory and enter the following four commands:

```
make -f Makefile.cvs
./configure -sm -gif -system-libpng -system-jpeg
make
make install
```

Then, in each of the other directories, use these four commands:

```
make -f Makefile.cvs
./configure
make
make install
```

There are some interdependencies among the libraries produced by the different directories. Some directories have to be compiled before others will compile successfully. Once you have `qt-copy` compiled, the next ones should be `kde-qt-addon`, `kdebase`, and `kdelibs`.

You may find that you have to switch back and forth among the directories before you get a clean compile on all of them. The first two of the four commands only need to be entered once. If you have to restart a directory, start with the third command.

✦   ✦   ✦

Methods

This appendix contains an alphabetical list of all the pub-
lic methods in all the KDE and Qt widgets. Because slots
are actually methods that can be called directly, they are also
included. Signals, on the other hand, are not callable, so they
are not in the list.

You can use this list to determine whether a certain method is
available somewhere in the heritage of a widget you are using.
It often happens that you can remember the name of a method
(or the approximate name of a method) but can't recall exactly
where it is located. If you come across some code that is using
an otherwise unknown method, you can use this list as a reference to determine where the code is located in the heritage.
Also, if the same method appears in more than one class in the
inheritance of a widget, you can determine (by looking in this
list and examining the order of inheritance) which method is
actually being called.

The list contains some of the nonwidget classes, but only the
ones that are used as a base class for at least one widget.
Private and protected methods are not included.

KDE/Qt Public Methods

```
abort()   QPrinter
aborted()   QPrinter
about()   QMessageBox KPanelApplet
aboutApplication()   KHelpMenu
aboutData()   KInstance
aboutKDE()   KHelpMenu
aboutQt()   QMessageBox
accel()   KAction QButton QMenuData
accelCount()   KWCommand
accelString()   KWCommand
accept()   QWheelEvent QKeyEvent QCloseEvent
        QDropEvent
        QDragMoveEvent
acceptAction()   QDropEvent
acceptDrop()   QIconViewItem
acceptDrops()   QWidget
acceptSlave()   KLauncher
```

```
accum()  QGLFormat
ackRead()  KProcIO
action()  QDropEvent KActionCollection KXMLGUIClient
actionButton()  KDialogBase
actionCollection()  KXMLGUIClient KEditToolbarWidget
         KDirOperator
actions()  KActionCollection KPanelApplet
activate()  QLayout KAction KDockManager KDockSplitter
activateDir()  KFileViewSignaler
activateDock()  KDockMainWindow
activateFile()  KFileViewSignaler
activateHelp()  KSpellConfig
activateMenu()  KFileViewSignaler
active()  QCanvasItem
activeModalWidget()  QApplication
activePageIndex()  KDialogBase
activePopupWidget()  QApplication
activeTabLine()  KThemeBase
activeTextColor()  KApplication
activeTitleColor()  KApplication
activeWindow()  QApplication QWorkspace
add()  QToolTip QWhatsThis QLayout KFileBookmarkManager
         KabAPI
addAccel()  KWCommand
addAnimation()  QCanvas
addBottomMenuBar()  KTMLayout
addBottomToolBar()  KTMLayout
addButton()  KToolBarRadioGroup QPrintDialog KButtonBox
addChild()  QScrollView
addCmdLineOptions()  KApplication KUniqueApplication
addColSpacing()  QGridLayout
addColumn()  QListView
addCommand()  KWCommandGroup
addConnection()  KToolBar
addContainer()  KAboutDialog KAboutContainerBase
addContainerPage()  KAboutDialog KAboutContainerBase
addContributor()  KAboutDialog KAboutWidget
addCookies()  KCookieServer
addDefaultURL()  KURLComboBox
addDesktopGroup()  KApplicationTree
addDir()  KDirWatch
addEmptyPage()  KAboutContainerBase
addFactory()  KSycoca
addFlatBar()  KTMLayout
addGridPage()  KDialogBase
addGroup()  KWCommandDispatcher
addHBoxPage()  KDialogBase
addHotSpot()  KToolBoxManager
addImage()  KAboutContainer
addIndicatorWidget()  KTMLayout
addItem()  QLayout QGridLayout QBoxLayout KTMLayout QCanvas
         KCompletion
addItemList()  KFileView
addItemToChunk()  QCanvas
```

```
addItemToChunkContaining()   QCanvas
addKipcEventMask()   KApplication
addLabel()   QHeader
addLayout()   QGridLayout QBoxLayout
addLeftToolBar()   KTMLayout
addLine()   KPasswordDialog QRangeControl
addMainItem()   KTMLayout
addMultiCell()   QGridLayout
addMultiCellWidget()   QGridLayout
addOperation()   QNetworkProtocol
addPage()   KPropertiesDialog QWizard KDialogBase KAboutDialog
         QRangeControl
addPath()   QUrl
addPerson()   KAboutContainer
addPersonal()   KSpell
addressbook()   KabAPI
addRightToolBar()   KTMLayout
addRowSpacing()   QGridLayout
addSeparator()   QToolBar
addSpace()   QGroupBox
addSpacing()   QBoxLayout
addStatusBar()   KTMLayout
addStep()   QSlider
addStretch()   QBoxLayout KButtonBox
addStrut()   QBoxLayout
addTab()   QTabDialog QTabBar QTabWidget KTabCtl
addTextPage()   KAboutDialog KAboutContainerBase
addTitle()   KAboutContainer
addToCustomColors()   KPaletteTable
addToolBar()   KTMainWindow QMainWindow
addTopMenuBar()   KTMLayout
addTopToolBar()   KTMLayout
addToRecentColors()   KPaletteTable
addURL()   KRecentFilesAction
addVBoxPage()   KDialogBase
addView()   QCanvas
addWidget()   KAboutContainer QGridLayout QBoxLayout
         QStatusBar QWidgetStack
adjust()   KAboutDialog KAboutWidget
adjustSize()   QWidget QMessageBox KDialogBase
advance()   QCanvasItem QCanvas KProgress
advice()   KCookieWin
alignItemRight()   KToolBar
alignment()   QStyleSheetItem QLayoutItem QLineEdit QGroupBox
         QLabel QMultiLineEdit
allColumnsShowFocus()   QListView
allDefault()   KKeyChooser
allItems()   QCanvas
allMatches()   KCompletion
allocateJavaServer()   KJavaAppletServer
allocCell()   QPixmap
allowedInContext()   QStyleSheetItem
allowsErrorInteraction()   QSessionManager
allowsInteraction()   QSessionManager
```

```
allWidgets()  QApplication
alpha()  QGLFormat
angleLength()  QCanvasEllipse
angleStart()  QCanvasEllipse
animateClick()  QButton
animated()  QCanvasItem
animatedWidget()  KToolBar
answerRect()  QDragMoveEvent
append()  QIconDrag QTextView QMultiLineEdit
appHelpActivated()  KHelpMenu KTMainWindow
appletClass()  KJavaApplet KJavaAppletWidget
appletId()  KJavaApplet
appletName()  KJavaApplet KJavaAppletWidget
applyChanges()  KPropsPage KFilePropsPage
         KFilePermissionsPropsPage KExecPropsPage
         KURLPropsPage KApplicationPropsPage KBindingPropsPage
         KDevicePropsPage
applyConfigFile()  KThemeBase
appropriate()  QWizard
areaPoints()  QCanvasPolygonalItem QCanvasRectangle
         QCanvasPolygon QCanvasEllipse
areaPointsAdvanced()  QCanvasPolygonalItem
arg()  QNetworkOperation QNPInstance
argc()  QApplication KApplication QNPInstance
argn()  QNPInstance
args()  KProcess
argv()  QApplication QNPInstance
arrangeItemsInGrid()  QIconView
arrangement()  QIconView
arrowType()  KThemeBase
ascii()  QKeyEvent
atBeginning()  QMultiLineEdit
atEnd()  QMultiLineEdit
autoAdd()  QLayout
autoArrange()  QIconView
autoBottomScrollBar()  QListBox
autoClose()  QProgressDialog
autoCompletion()  QComboBox KComboBox
autoDefault()  QPushButton
autoDelete()  QNetworkProtocol KRun
autoMask()  QWidget
autoRaise()  QToolButton
autoRepeat()  QButton
autoReset()  QProgressDialog
autoResize()  QButton QComboBox QLabel
autoScroll()  QListBox
autoScrollBar()  QListBox
autoUpdate()  KFileReader QListBox QMultiLineEdit
back()  KDirOperator
backButton()  QWizard
background()  KDualColorButton
backgroundColor()  QWidget QPainter QCanvas
backgroundMode()  QWidget QPainter
backgroundOrigin()  QWidget
```

```
backgroundPixmap()  QWidget QCanvas
backspace()  QLineEdit
backward()  QTextBrowser
barColor()  KProgress
barPixmap()  KProgress
barPos()  KToolBar
barStyle()  KProgress
base()  KIntValidator
baseSize()  QWidget
baseURL()  KJavaApplet KFileDialog KJavaAppletWidget
beep()  QApplication
begin()  QPainter
bevelContrast()  KThemeBase
blockSignals()  QObject
border()  KThemePixmap
borderPixmap()  KThemeBase
borderWidth()  KThemeBase
bottom()  QIntValidator QDoubleValidator KIntValidator
        KFloatValidator KWriteView
bottom_end()  KWriteView
bottomOfView()  KWriteView
bottomScrollBar()  QListBox
bound()  QRangeControl
boundingRect()  QPainter QCanvasItem QCanvasSprite
        QCanvasPolygonalItem QCanvasText
boundingRectAdvanced()  QCanvasItem
brush()  QPainter QCanvasPolygonalItem
brushOrigin()  QPainter
buddy()  QLabel
build()  Kded
builderInstance()  KXMLGUIBuilder
button()  QMouseEvent KURLRequester
buttonRect()  QPlatinumStyle KDEStyle KThemeStyle KStepStyle
buttons()  KCModule
buttonSymbols()  QSpinBox
buttonText()  QMessageBox
buttonXShift()  KThemeBase
buttonYShift()  KThemeBase
calculateSize()  KDialogBase
canBeRestored()  KTMainWindow
cancel()  QSessionManager QProgressDialog
cancelButton()  QWizard
canDecode()  QUriDrag QColorDrag KColorDrag QTextDrag
        QImageDrag QIconDrag
canDisplay()  KPropertiesDialog
canvas()  QCanvasItem QCanvasView
capStyle()  QPen
caption()  QWidget KApplication
cascade()  QWorkspace
case_sensitive()  KEdFind KEdReplace
cdUp()  QUrlOperator QUrl KDirOperator
cellAt()  QHeader
cellBrush()  QWellArray
cellContent()  QWellArray
```

cellGeometry() QGridLayout
cellHeight() QListBox
cellPos() QHeader
cellSize() QHeader
cellWidth() QListBox
center() QScrollView
centerCurrentItem() QListBox
centerIndicator() QProgressBar
centralWidget() QMainWindow
changeComboItem() KToolBar
changeHideShowState() KDockWidget
changeInterval() QTimer
changeItem() KSelectAction QComboBox KStatusBar QMenuData
        QListBox
changeMenuAccel() KAccel
changeSize() QSpacerItem
changeTab() QTabDialog QTabWidget
changeTitle() KPopupMenu
charsets() KInstance
check() KSpell
checkAvailable() KRootPixmap
checkColorTable() KPixmap
checkCookies() KCookieServer
checkFileChanged() QConfigDB
checkList() KSpell
CheckLockFile() QConfigDB
checkOverflow() QLCDNumber
checkRecoverFile() KApplication
checkWord() KSpell
child() QObject QChildEvent
childClients() KXMLGUIClient
childCount() QListViewItem QListView
childIsVisible() QScrollView
children() QObject
childrenRect() QWidget
childrenRegion() QWidget
childX() QScrollView
childY() QScrollView
chr() KCharSelect KCharSelectTable
chunkSize() QCanvas
className() QObject
classNameOfToplevel() KTMainWindow
CleanLockFiles() QConfigDB
cleanText() QSpinBox
cleanup() QPainter KDialogBaseTile
cleanUp() KSpell
cleanWhiteSpace() KEdit
clear() QAccel KAccel QClipboard QTranslator KCompletion
        KGlobalAccel KSelectAction KPanelMenu QComboBox
        QLineEdit KAccelInput QStatusBar QToolBar QConfigDB
        QLabel QMenuData QIconView KFileView KCombiView
        KFilePreview QListView QListBox QMultiLineEdit
        KToolBar
clearArguments() KProcess

```
clearCombo()   KToolBar
clearEdit()   QComboBox
clearFocus()   QWidget
clearItem()   KAccel
clearMask()   QWidget
clearOperationQueue()   QNetworkProtocol
clearSelection()   QIconView KFileIconView KFileView
        KCombiView KFilePreview KFileDetailView QListView
        QListBox
clearURLList()   KRecentFilesAction
clearValidator()   QComboBox QLineEdit
clearView()   KFileIconView KFileView KCombiView KFilePreview
        KFileDetailView
client()   QIOWatch QTimeWatch KSpellConfig
clientBuilder()   KXMLGUIClient
clipboard()   QApplication
clipper()   QScrollView
clipRegion()   QPainter
close()   QWidget KDirOperator QPopupFrame
close_xim()   QApplication
closeAllWindows()   QApplication
closeStderr()   KProcess
closeStdin()   KProcess
closeStdout()   KProcess
closingDown()   QApplication
codeBase()   KJavaApplet KJavaAppletWidget
collidesWith()   QCanvasItem QCanvasSprite
        QCanvasPolygonalItem QCanvasRectangle QCanvasEllipse
        QCanvasText
collisions()   QCanvasItem QCanvas
color()   QBrush QPen QStyleSheetItem QCanvasText KColorDialog
        KColorButton KLed KColorCells
colorGroup()   QWidget KThemeBase
colorMode()   QPrinter QApplication KTextPrintDialog
colorSpec()   QApplication
colspan()   QTextTableCell
colStretch()   QGridLayout
column()   QTextTableCell
columnAlignment()   QListView
columnMode()   QListBox
columns()   QGroupBox QListView
columnText()   QListView
columnWidth()   QListView
columnWidthMode()   QListView
comboButtonFocusRect()   QCommonStyle QMotifStyle
        QWindowsStyle QPlatinumStyle KDEStyle KStepStyle
comboButtonRect()   QCommonStyle QMotifStyle QWindowsStyle
        QPlatinumStyle KDEStyle KStepStyle
comboWidth()   KSelectAction
commitData()   QApplication KApplication
compare()   QIconViewItem
completionMode()   KCompletion KCompletionBase
completionObject()   KCompletionBase KDirOperator
component()   KAction
```

```
computePosition()  KEdit
config()  KInstance
configGlobal()  KAccel
configGroup()  KAccel KGlobalAccel
configModule()  KURIFilterPlugin
configName()  KURIFilterPlugin
configurable()  KAccel
configureKeys()  KKeyDialog
connect()  QObject
connectHighlight()  KActionCollection
connectItem()  QAccel KAccel KGlobalAccel QMenuData
connectToFormula()  KFormulaToolBar
constPolish()  QWidget
container()  KAction
containerCount()  KAction
containerStates()  KXMLGUIClient
containerTags()  KXMLGUIBuilder
contains()  QIconViewItem QTranslator KDirWatch
contentsHeight()  QScrollView
contentsRect()  QFrame KSelector KXYSelector
contentsToViewport()  QScrollView
contentsWidth()  QScrollView
contentsX()  KWriteView QScrollView
contentsY()  KWriteView QScrollView
context()  QGLWidget QTextView
contextHelpActivated()  KHelpMenu
contextId()  KJavaAppletContext
contextMenuEnabled()  KToolBar
contexts()  QStyleSheetItem
contrast()  KApplication
convertFromImage()  QPixmap KPixmap
convertFromPlainText()  QStyleSheet
convertToImage()  QPixmap
cookiesPending()  KCookieServer
copy()  QUrlOperator QLineEdit QTextView QMultiLineEdit
copyText()  QMultiLineEdit
cornerWidget()  QScrollView
corrected()  KEdit
count()  QKeyEvent QAccel KAccel KGlobalAccel
           KActionCollection KFileReader QComboBox QHeader
           QButtonGroup QMenuData QIconView KFileView QListBox
           KToolBar
create()  KLibFactory KJavaApplet KJavaAppletContext
           QGLContext KJavaAppletWidget
create_xim()  QApplication
createApplet()  KJavaAppletServer
createContainer()  KXMLGUIBuilder
createContext()  KJavaAppletServer
createCustomElement()  KXMLGUIBuilder
createDockWidget()  KDockMainWindow
createGUI()  KTMainWindow
createHeuristicMask()  QPixmap
createSection()  QConfigDB
creator()  QPrinter
```

```
critical()  QMessageBox
ctime()  KDirWatch
current()  QListBoxItem KDualColorButton
currentColor()  KDualColorButton
currentColumn()  KEdit
currentContents()  KFileReader
currentContext()  QGLContext
currentDesktop()  KWinModule
currentDir()  KPropertiesDialog
currentFilter()  KFileDialog KFileFilter
currentItem()  KSelectAction KListAction QComboBox QIconView
        QListView QListBox
currentKey()  KAccel KGlobalAccel
currentLine()  KEdit
currentPage()  QTabDialog QWizard QTabWidget
currentTab()  QTabBar KDockTabBar
currentText()  KSelectAction KListAction QComboBox QListBox
cursor()  QWidget
cursorAtEnd()  KLineEdit
cursorDown()  KWriteView
cursorFlashTime()  QApplication
cursorLeft()  QLineEdit KWriteView
cursorPageDown()  KWriteView
cursorPageUp()  KWriteView
cursorPosition()  KComboBox QLineEdit QMultiLineEdit
cursorRight()  QLineEdit KWriteView
cursorUp()  KWriteView
cursorWordBackward()  QLineEdit QMultiLineEdit
cursorWordForward()  QLineEdit QMultiLineEdit
customColor()  QColorDialog
customCount()  QColorDialog
customTags()  KXMLGUIBuilder
customWhatsThis()  QWidget QMenuBar QPopupMenu
cut()  QLineEdit QMultiLineEdit
data()  QDropEvent QCustomEvent QPicture QClipboard
date()  KDateValidator
dcopClient()  KApplication KUniqueApplication
deactivate()  KDockSplitter
decimals()  QDoubleValidator
decode()  QUriDrag QColorDrag KColorDrag QTextDrag QImageDrag
        QUrl
decodeLocalFiles()  QUriDrag
decodeToUnicodeUris()  QUriDrag
decoWidth()  KThemeBase
defaultBorder()  QLayout
defaultCodec()  QApplication
defaultDepth()  QPixmap
defaultFormat()  QGLFormat
defaultFrameWidth()  QCommonStyle QCDEStyle KDEStyle
        KThemeStyle
defaultKey()  KAccel KGlobalAccel
defaultName()  KPropertiesDialog
defaultOptimization()  QPixmap
defaultOverlayFormat()  QGLFormat
```

```
dockWindows()  KWinModule
docName()  QPrinter
document()  KXMLGUIClient
documentTitle()  QTextView
doCursorCommand()  KWriteView
doEditCommand()  KWriteView
doGotoLine()  KEdit
doMove()  KToolBoxManager
doResize()  KToolBoxManager
doubleBuffer()  QGLWidget QGLFormat
doubleClickInterval()  QApplication
doXResize()  KToolBoxManager
doYResize()  KToolBoxManager
drag()  QDragObject
dragAccepted()  QDragResponseEvent
dragAutoScroll()  QScrollView
dragCopy()  QDragObject
dragEnabled()  QIconViewItem
draggingSlider()  QScrollBar
dragMove()  QDragObject
dragSelect()  QListBox
draw()  QCanvasItem QTextTableCell
drawArc()  QPainter
drawArea()  QCanvas
drawArrow()  QMotifStyle QCDEStyle QWindowsStyle KDEStyle
        KThemeStyle KStepStyle
drawBaseButton()  KThemeStyle
drawBaseMask()  KThemeStyle
drawBevelButton()  QMotifStyle QWindowsStyle QPlatinumStyle
        KDEStyle KThemeStyle KStepStyle
drawButton()  QMotifStyle QWindowsStyle QPlatinumStyle
        KDEStyle KThemeStyle KStepStyle
drawButtonMask()  KDEStyle KThemeStyle
drawCheckMark()  QMotifStyle QWindowsStyle QPlatinumStyle
        KThemeStyle
drawChord()  QPainter
drawComboButton()  QCommonStyle QMotifStyle QWindowsStyle
        QPlatinumStyle KDEStyle KThemeStyle KStepStyle
drawComboButtonMask()  QCommonStyle KDEStyle KThemeStyle
drawEllipse()  QPainter
drawExclusiveIndicator()  QMotifStyle QCDEStyle QWindowsStyle
        QPlatinumStyle KDEStyle KThemeStyle KStepStyle
drawExclusiveIndicatorMask()  QMotifStyle QWindowsStyle
        KDEStyle KThemeStyle KStepStyle
drawFocusRect()  QMotifStyle QWindowsStyle KDEStyle
        KThemeStyle KStepStyle
drawImage()  QPainter
drawIndicator()  QMotifStyle QCDEStyle QWindowsStyle
        QPlatinumStyle KDEStyle KThemeStyle KStepStyle
drawIndicatorMask()  QPlatinumStyle KDEStyle KThemeStyle
        KStepStyle
drawKBarHandle()  KStyle KDEStyle KThemeStyle KStepStyle
drawKickerAppletHandle()  KStyle KDEStyle
drawKickerHandle()  KStyle
```

```
embedClientIntoWindow()  QXEmbed
embeddedWinId()  QXEmbed
emitAccelString()  KWCommand
emitSignals()  KCompletionBase
empty()  QConfigDB
enable()  KToolBar
enableButton()  KDialogBase
enableButtonApply()  KDialogBase
enableButtonCancel()  KDialogBase
enableButtonOK()  KDialogBase
enableButtonSeparator()  KDialogBase
enableClipper()  QScrollView
enableColumn()  KFontChooser
enabled()  QToolTip QCanvasItem QToolTipGroup
enableDocking()  KDockWidget
enableFloating()  KToolBar
enableFontCombo()  KCharSelect
enableLinkedHelp()  KDialogBase
enableMoving()  KToolBar
enableRead()  KSocket
enableReadSignals()  KProcIO
enableSignals()  KCompletionBase
enableSizeHintSignal()  KFormulaEdit
enableSounds()  KCompletion
enableStatusBar()  KTMainWindow
enableStyles()  KApplication
enableTableSpinBox()  KCharSelect
enableToolBar()  KTMainWindow
enableWrite()  KSocket
encode()  QUrl
encodedData()  QDropEvent QMimeSource QStoredDrag QTextDrag
        QImageDrag QIconDrag
encodedPathAndQuery()  QUrl
encoding()  KSpellConfig
end()  QPainter QLineEdit KWriteView
endOffset()  KContainerLayout
ensureCurrentVisible()  QListBox
ensureItemVisible()  QIconView KFileIconView KFileView
        KCombiView KFilePreview KFileDetailView QListView
ensureVisible()  QScrollView
enter_loop()  QApplication
enterInstance()  QNPWidget
enterWhatsThisMode()  QWhatsThis
entryMap()  KConfigBase KConfig
erase()  QWidget KPasswordEdit
erased()  QPaintEvent
eraseRect()  QPainter
error()  QStyleSheet
errorCode()  QNetworkOperation
event()  QObject KNotifyClient QToolBar KDockWidget
        KDockSplitter
eventFilter()  QObject KDEStyle KStepStyle KDockManager
        QFileDialog QWizard QComboBox QMainWindow QToolBar
        KDockTabCtl KDockSplitter QXEmbed QMenuBar QIconView
```

```
fontItalic()   QStyleSheetItem
fontMetrics()   QWidget QPainter QApplication
fontPropagation()   QWidget
fontSize()   QStyleSheetItem KFontSizeAction
fontUnderline()   QStyleSheetItem
fontWeight()   QStyleSheetItem
foreground()   KDualColorButton
foregroundColor()   QWidget
format()   QDropEvent QMimeSource QStoredDrag QTextDrag
        QImageDrag QIconDrag KProgress QGLWidget QGLContext
forward()   KDirOperator QTextBrowser
foundMimeType()   KHTMLRun
fputs()   KProcIO
frame()   QCanvasSprite QLineEdit
frameCount()   QCanvasSprite
frameGeometry()   QWidget
frameRect()   QFrame
frameShadow()   QFrame
frameShape()   QFrame
frameSize()   QWidget
frameStyle()   QFrame
frameWidth()   QFrame KThemeBase KHTMLView
free()   QNetworkOperation
freeCell()   QPixmap
freeJavaServer()   KJavaAppletServer
freeze()   QLayout
fromPage()   QPrinter
fullPage()   QPrinter
fullSize()   KToolBar
fullSpan()   QCustomMenuItem
geometry()   QWidget QLayout QLayoutItem QSpacerItem
        QWidgetItem QTextTableCell
get()   QUrlOperator KDialogBaseTile QConfigDB
get_direction()   KEdFind KEdReplace
getAnother()   KDockSplitter
getBackgroundTile()   KDialogBase
getBigMarkDistance()   KRuler
getBookmark()   KFileBookmarkManager
getBorderWidths()   KDialogBase
getButton()   KToolBar
getButtonShift()   QCommonStyle QWindowsStyle QPlatinumStyle
        KThemeStyle
getColor()   QColorDialog KColorDialog
getCombo()   KToolBar
getComboItem()   KToolBar
getConfigState()   KConfigBase
getContentsRect()   KDialogBase
getCurrent()   KIconCanvas
getCursorPosition()   QMultiLineEdit
getDarkFactor()   KLed
getData()   KTextPrintConfig KWCommand KWCommandGroup
        KWCommandDispatcher KTextPrintDialog
getDate()   KDateTable KDatePicker
getDefaultContext()   KJavaAppletContext
```

```
getPid()  KProcess
getPixelPerMark()  KRuler
getPresentation()  KNotifyClient
getPrevPage()  KDockTabCtl
getPrinterSetup()  QPrintDialog
getReplaceText()  KEdReplace
getResult()  KDateInternalMonthPicker
getRgba()  QColorDialog
getRoot()  KFileBookmarkManager
getSaveFileName()  QFileDialog KFileDialog
getSaveURL()  KFileDialog
getSBExtent()  KThemeBase
getSelected()  KColorCells
getShowBigMarks()  KRuler
getShowEndMarks()  KRuler
getShowLittleMarks()  KRuler
getShowMediumMarks()  KRuler
getShowPointer()  KRuler
getShowTinyMarks()  KRuler
getTabPos()  KDockTabCtl
getText()  QInputDialog KEdFind KEdReplace KLineEditDlg
getTickStyle()  KRuler
getTinyMarkDistance()  KRuler
getToolButtonID()  KAction
getURL()  QNPInstance KURLRequesterDlg KAboutContributor
getURLNotify()  QNPInstance
getValue()  KRuler
getWidget()  KDockWidget KToolBar
getWork()  KAboutContributor
getXLFD()  KFontChooser
getYear()  KDateInternalYearSelector
globalPos()  QMouseEvent QWheelEvent
globalX()  QMouseEvent QWheelEvent
globalY()  QMouseEvent QWheelEvent
gotFocus()  QFocusEvent
gotoNextLink()  KHTMLView
gotoPrevLink()  KHTMLView
grabColor()  KColorDialog
grabKey()  KGlobalAccel
grabKeyboard()  QWidget
grabMouse()  QWidget
grabWidget()  QPixmap
grabWindow()  QPixmap
gradientHint()  KThemeBase
gridX()  QIconView
gridY()  QIconView
group()  QToolTip KConfigBase KAction QButton
groupList()  KConfigBase KConfig
groups()  KActionCollection
guiFactory()  KTMainWindow
GUIStyle()  QStyle
handle()  QPainter QPaintDevice QSessionManager
handleSignals()  KCompletionBase
hasActionGroup()  KDesktopFile
```

hasApplicationType()   KDesktopFile
hasApplyButton()   QTabDialog
hasCancelButton()   QTabDialog
hasClipping()   QPainter
hasDefaultButton()   QTabDialog
hasDeviceType()   KDesktopFile
hasError()   KRun
hasFinished()   KRun
hasFocus()   QWidget
hasGlobalMouseTracking()   QApplication
hasGroup()   KConfigBase KConfig
hasHeightForWidth()   QLayoutItem QWidgetItem QTextTableCell
        QGridLayout QBoxLayout
hasHelpButton()   QTabDialog
hasHost()   QUrl
hasIconSet()   KAction
hasKey()   KConfigBase KConfig
hasLinkType()   KDesktopFile
hasMarkedText()   QLineEdit
hasMenuBar()   KTMainWindow
hasMimeTypeType()   KDesktopFile
hasMouseTracking()   QWidget
hasMultipleMatches()   KCompletion
hasOkButton()   QTabDialog
hasOnlyLocalFileSystem()   QNetworkProtocol
hasOpenGL()   QGLFormat
hasOpenGLOverlays()   QGLFormat
hasOverlay()   QGLFormat
hasPassword()   QUrl
hasPath()   QUrl
hasRef()   QUrl
hasSelectedText()   QTextView
hasSelection()   KHTMLView
hasStatusBar()   KTMainWindow
hasToolBar()   KTMainWindow
hasUser()   QUrl
hasViewXForm()   QPainter
hasWId()   KWinModule
hasWorldXForm()   QPainter
haveBackgroundTile()   KDialogBase
hbm()   QPixmap
header()   QListView
height()   QWidget QPixmap QIconViewItem QListViewItem
        QCanvasRectangle QCanvasEllipse QCanvas QListBoxItem
        QListBoxText QListBoxPixmap KToolBoxManager
heightDlg()   KSpell
heightForWidth()   QWidget QLayoutItem QWidgetItem
        QTextTableCell QGridLayout QBoxLayout KPanelApplet
        QLabel QMenuBar QTextView KToolBar
help()   KPanelApplet
helpButton()   QWizard
helpClickedSlot()   KDialogBase
helpLinkText()   KDialogBase
helpMenu()   KTMainWindow

```
hide()   QWidget QToolTip QCanvasItem KSpell QDialog QToolBar
         QMenuBar QPopupMenu
hideItem()   KToolBar
hideModeChanger()   KCompletionBase
highlightFile()   KFileViewSignaler
highlightingEnabled()   KActionCollection
highlightWidth()   KThemeBase
highPriority()   QObject
hMargin()   QMultiLineEdit
home()   QLineEdit KDirOperator KWriteView QTextBrowser
homogeneos()   KContainerLayout
horizontalPixmap()   KThemeCache
horizontalScrollBar()   QScrollView
host()   QUrl
hScrollBarMode()   QScrollView
icon()   QWidget KApplication QMessageBox KIconButton
         KPopupTitle
iconify()   QWidget
iconLoader()   KInstance
iconName()   KAction
iconPixmap()   QMessageBox
iconProvider()   QFileDialog
iconSet()   KAction QPushButton QToolButton QHeader QMenuData
iconSize()   KFileIconView KToolBar
iconText()   QWidget KToolBar
iconView()   QIconViewItem
id()   KWCommand KDialogBaseButton KDockTabCtl QButtonGroup
       QWidgetStack
idAt()   QMenuData QPopupMenu
idleTimeout()   KLauncher
ignore()   QWheelEvent QKeyEvent QCloseEvent QDropEvent
         QDragMoveEvent KSpell
ignoreList()   KSpellConfig
ignoreWhatsThis()   QAccel
image()   QClipboard
imageFormat()   QPixmap
imageURL()   KAboutDialog
inactiveTabLine()   KThemeBase
inactiveTextColor()   KApplication
inactiveTitleColor()   KApplication
incInitialSize()   KDialogBase
indent()   KSelector QLabel
index()   QIconViewItem QIconView QListBox
indexOf()   QMenuData
indicator()   KTMainWindow
indicatorFollowsStyle()   QProgressBar
indicatorSize()   QMotifStyle QWindowsStyle QPlatinumStyle
         KDEStyle KThemeStyle KStepStyle
info()   QUrlOperator
information()   QMessageBox
inherits()   QObject
init()   KabAPI KCModule KPanelApplet KSpellDlg
initialize()   QPainter QXEmbed
initSockaddr()   KSocket
```

```
insert()  QStyleSheet QTranslator KActionMenu
        KActionCollection KContextMenuManager KThemeCache
        QLineEdit QButtonGroup QMultiLineEdit
insertAnimatedWidget()  KToolBar
insertAt()  QMultiLineEdit
insertButton()  KToolBar
insertChar()  KFormulaEdit
insertChild()  QObject
insertChildClient()  KXMLGUIClient
insertCombo()  KToolBar
insertComboItem()  KToolBar
insertComboList()  KToolBar
inserted()  QChildEvent
insertFixedItem()  KStatusBar
insertionPolicy()  QComboBox
insertItem()  QListViewItem QAccel KAccel KGlobalAccel
        KPanelMenu QComboBox KStatusBar QMenuData QIconView
        KFileIconView KFileView KCombiView KFilePreview
        KFileDetailView QListView QListBox
insertLayout()  QBoxLayout
insertLine()  QMultiLineEdit
insertLined()  KToolBar
insertLineSeparator()  KToolBar
insertMenu()  KPanelMenu
insertPage()  KDockTabCtl
insertSeparator()  QMenuData KToolBar
insertSorted()  KFileView KCombiView
insertSpacing()  QBoxLayout
insertStdItem()  KAccel
insertStretch()  QBoxLayout
insertStringList()  QComboBox QListBox
insertStrList()  QComboBox QListBox
insertTab()  QTabDialog QTabBar QTabWidget KDockTabBar
insertTearOffHandle()  QPopupMenu
insertText()  KEdit
insertTitle()  KPopupMenu
insertWidget()  QBoxLayout KToolBar
insItem()  KAccelMenu
inSort()  QListBox
installEventFilter()  QObject
installRBPopup()  KEdit
installTranslator()  QApplication
installX11EventFilter()  KApplication
instance()  KActionCollection KXMLGUIClient QNPWidget
instanceName()  KInstance
intermediateBuffer()  KSpell
intersects()  QIconViewItem
intValue()  QLCDNumber
invalidate()  QLayout QLayoutItem QGridLayout QBoxLayout
invalidateHeight()  QListViewItem KJanusWidget
invertSelection()  QIconView KFileView QListView QListBox
invokeBrowser()  KApplication
invokeHTMLHelp()  KApplication
invokeMailer()  KApplication
```

```
inWhatsThisMode()  QWhatsThis
ipv4_addr()  KSocket KServerSocket
is3DFocus()  KThemeBase
isA()  QObject
isAccepted()  QWheelEvent QKeyEvent QCloseEvent QDropEvent
isActionAccepted()  QDropEvent
isActive()  QPainter QTimer
isActiveWindow()  QWidget QXtWidget
isAnchor()  QStyleSheetItem
isAutoRepeat()  QKeyEvent
isAvailable()  KSharedPixmap
isBuilding()  KSycoca
isButtonOn()  KToolBar
isCheckable()  QPopupMenu
isChecked()  KToggleAction QCheckBox QRadioButton
isClickEnabled()  QHeader
isColor()  KThemeBase
isCompletionObjectAutoDeleted()  KCompletionBase
isContentsPreviewEnabled()  QFileDialog
isContextMenuEnabled()  KComboBox KLineEdit
isCreated()  KJavaApplet
isDefault()  QPushButton
isDefaultUp()  QMenuBar
isDesktop()  QWidget
isDesktopFile()  KDesktopFile KPropsPage
isDir()  QUrlOperator
isDirty()  KConfigBase KPropsPage
isDockBackPossible()  KDockWidget
isDockEnabled()  QMainWindow
isDockMenuEnabled()  QMainWindow
isDollarExpansion()  KConfigBase
isDown()  QButton
isEditable()  KSelectAction KComboBox
isEmpty()  QLayout QLayoutItem QSpacerItem QWidgetItem
        QTextTableCell
isEnabled()  QWidget QAccel KAccel QSocketNotifier
        KGlobalAccel KAction
isEnabledTo()  QWidget
isEnabledToTLW()  QWidget
isExclusive()  QButtonGroup
isExclusiveToggle()  QButton
isExecuteArea()  KListView
isExpandable()  QListViewItem
isExtDev()  QPaintDevice
isFocusEnabled()  QWidget
isFontComboEnabled()  KCharSelect
isGlobal()  KNotify
isHorizontalStretchable()  QToolBar
isInfoPreviewEnabled()  QFileDialog
isItemChecked()  QMenuData
isItemEnabled()  QAccel KAccel KGlobalAccel QMenuData
isLocalFile()  QUrl
IsLocked()  QConfigDB
isMenuButton()  QPushButton
```

isMinimized() QWidget
isModal() QWidget
isModeChangerVisible() KCompletionBase
isModified() KEdit
isMovingEnabled() QHeader
isMultiCellPixmap() QPixmap
isMultiSelection() QListView QListBox
isNull() QPixmap QPicture
isOK() KJavaProcess
isOld() KThemePixmap
isOn() QCheckListItem QButton
isOpen() QListViewItem QListView
isOverwriteMode() QMultiLineEdit
isPageEnabled() KDockTabCtl
isPhase2() QSessionManager
isPixmap() KThemeBase
isPlugged() KAction
isPopup() QWidget
isQBitmap() QPixmap
isRadioButtonExclusive() QButtonGroup
isReadable() KFileReader
isReadOnly() KConfigBase QLineEdit QMultiLineEdit
isRelativeUrl() QUrl
isResizeEnabled() QHeader
isRestored() KApplication
isReversed() KFileView
isRO() QConfigDB
isRoot() KFileReader KDirOperator
isRunning() KURLCompletion KProcess KJavaProcess
isSelectable() QIconViewItem QListViewItem QListBoxItem
isSelected() QIconViewItem QListViewItem KDirOperator
        KFileIconView KFileView KCombiView KFilePreview
        KFileDetailView QListView QListBox
isSeparator() QCustomMenuItem
isSessionRestored() QApplication
isSharing() QGLWidget QGLContext
isShowTabIcon() KDockTabBar KDockTabCtl
isSizeGripEnabled() QStatusBar
isSorted() KCompletion
isSoundsEnabled() KCompletion
isTabEnabled() QTabDialog QTabBar QTabWidget KDockTabBar
        KTabCtl
isTableSpinBoxEnabled() KCharSelect
isToggleButton() QButton
isTopLevel() QWidget QLayout
isUndoEnabled() QMultiLineEdit
isUpdatesEnabled() QWidget
isValid() QUrl QGLWidget QGLContext
isVerticalStretchable() QToolBar
isVisible() QWidget
isVisibleTo() QWidget
isVisibleToTLW() QWidget
isWidgetType() QObject
item() QStyleSheet KPropertiesDialog QListBox

```
itemAbove()   QListViewItem
itemAt()   QListView QListBox
itemBelow()   QListViewItem
itemHeight()   QListBox
itemMargin()   QListView
itemParameter()   QMenuData
itemPos()   QListViewItem QListView
itemRect()   QListView QListBox
items()   KCompletion KDirLister KSelectAction
        KPropertiesDialog KFileView
itemsMovable()   QIconView
itemTextBackground()   QIconView
itemTextPos()   QIconView
itemVisible()   QListBox
iterator()   QLayout QLayoutItem QGridLayout QBoxLayout
        KTMLayout
jarFile()   KJavaApplet KJavaAppletWidget
job()   KDirLister
joinStyle()   QPen
kApplication()   KApplication
kdeFonts()   KApplication
keep()   KPasswordDialog
key()   QKeyEvent QIconViewItem QListViewItem QAccel
keyboardFocusTab()   QTabBar
keyboardGrabber()   QWidget
keyDict()   KAccel KGlobalAccel KActionCollection
keyToString()   QAccel KAccel
kfsstnd_prefixes()   KSycoca
kill()   KProcess
killTimer()   QObject
killTimers()   QObject
ksConfig()   KSpell
kstyle()   KApplication
kurl()   KPropertiesDialog
label()   QHeader QToolBar
labelText()   QProgressDialog
lastItem()   QIconView
lastMatch()   KCompletion
lastPosition()   KSpell
launcher()   KApplication
layout()   QWidget QLayout QLayoutItem KButtonBox KHTMLView
layoutTabs()   QTabBar
leaveInstance()   QNPWidget
leaveWhatsThisMode()   QWhatsThis
length()   QMultiLineEdit
library()   KLibLoader
lineEdit()   QComboBox KURLRequester
lineShapesOk()   QFrame
lineStep()   QScrollBar QRangeControl QSlider QSpinBox
lineTo()   QPainter
lineUpToolBars()   QMainWindow
lineWidth()   QFrame
linkColor()   QTextView
linkUnderline()   QTextView
```

```
listBox()   QListBoxItem QComboBox
listChildren()   QUrlOperator
listContents()   KFileReader
listStyle()   QStyleSheetItem
listSync()   KKeyChooser
listView()   QListViewItem
load()   QPixmap QPicture KPixmap QTranslator QConfigDB
        KCModule
loadConfig()   KDockWidgetAbstractHeader KDockWidgetHeader
loadEntries()   KRecentFilesAction
loadFiles()   KIconCanvas
loadFromData()   QPixmap
loadFromShared()   KSharedPixmap
locale()   KConfigBase
localFileToUri()   QUriDrag
lock()   QConfigDB
logicalFontSize()   QStyleSheetItem
logicalFontSizeStep()   QStyleSheetItem
look()   KLed
loopLevel()   QApplication
lostFocus()   QFocusEvent
lower()   QWidget
macEventFilter()   QApplication
macProcessEvent()   QApplication
mainViewGeometry()   KTMainWindow
mainWidget()   QLayout QApplication
mainWindow()   QToolBar
makeCompletion()   KCompletion KURLCompletion KShellCompletion
        KDirOperator
makeCurrent()   QGLWidget QGLContext
makeDirCompletion()   KDirOperator
makeDockInvisible()   KDockMainWindow
makeDockVisible()   KDockMainWindow KDockWidget
makeDrag()   KColorDrag
makeGridMainWidget()   KDialogBase
makeHBoxMainWidget()   KDialogBase
makeMainWidget()   KDialogBase
makeOverlayCurrent()   QGLWidget
makeStdCaption()   KApplication
makeVBoxMainWidget()   KDialogBase
makeWidgetDockVisible()   KDockManager KDockMainWindow
manager()   KDockMainWindow
manualDock()   KDockWidget
map()   QSignalMapper
mapFromGlobal()   QWidget
mapFromParent()   QWidget
mapToActual()   QHeader
mapToGlobal()   QWidget
mapToIndex()   QHeader
mapToLogical()   QHeader
mapToParent()   QWidget
mapToSection()   QHeader
margin()   QFrame QStyleSheetItem QLayout QTabWidget
marginHeight()   KHTMLView
```

```
marginHint()  KDialog
margins()  QPrinter
marginWidth()  KHTMLView
markedText()  QLineEdit KEdit
mask()  QPixmap
match()  KFileReader
matchesFilter()  KDirLister
maxCount()  QComboBox
maxHeight()  KToolBar
maximumHeight()  QWidget
maximumSize()  QWidget QLayout QLayoutItem QSpacerItem
        QWidgetItem QTextTableCell QGridLayout QBoxLayout
maximumSizeHint()  KToolBar
maximumSliderDragDistance()  QCommonStyle QWindowsStyle
        QPlatinumStyle
maximumWidth()  QWidget
maxItems()  KRecentFilesAction KURLComboBox
maxItemTextLength()  QIconView
maxItemWidth()  QIconView QListBox
maxLength()  QLineEdit QMultiLineEdit
maxLineLength()  QMultiLineEdit
maxLines()  QMultiLineEdit
maxLineWidth()  QMultiLineEdit
maxPage()  QPrinter
maxValue()  QScrollBar QRangeControl QSlider QSpinBox
maxWidth()  KToolBar
mayBeHide()  KDockWidget
mayBeShow()  KDockWidget
menu()  KHelpMenu
menuBar()  QLayout KTMainWindow QMainWindow
message()  QMessageBox QStatusBar
metaObject()  QObject
microFocusHint()  QWidget
midLineWidth()  QFrame
mightBeRichText()  QStyleSheet
mimeSourceFactory()  QTextView
miniIcon()  KApplication
minimumDuration()  QProgressDialog
minimumHeight()  QWidget
minimumSize()  QWidget QLayout QLayoutItem QSpacerItem
        QWidgetItem QTextTableCell QGridLayout QBoxLayout
        KTMLayout QToolBar QMenuBar
minimumSizeHint()  KAboutContainer QWidget QLineEdit
        QMainWindow QSlider QTabWidget QToolBar KIntNumInput
        KDoubleNumInput QXEmbed QLabel QMenuBar QProgressBar
        QScrollView QIconView QSplitter QListView QListBox
        QMultiLineEdit QWidgetStack KToolBar
minimumWidth()  QWidget
minPage()  QPrinter
minValue()  QScrollBar QRangeControl QSlider QSpinBox
misspelling()  KEdit
mkdir()  QUrlOperator KDirOperator
modalCheck()  KSpell
mode()  QNPInstance KURLCompletion QFileDialog KFileDialog
```

```
              KDirOperator QLCDNumber
modeChange()  KToolBarButton
mouseGrabber()  QWidget
mouseX()  KToolBoxManager
mouseY()  KToolBoxManager
move()  QWidget QIconViewItem QCanvasItem QCanvasSprite
              QDialog QSemiModal QPushButton
moveBy()  QIconViewItem QCanvasItem QCanvasPolygon
              QCanvasText
moveCell()  QHeader
moveChild()  QScrollView
moveDlg()  KSpell
moveDown()  KFileBookmarkManager
moveFocus()  QButtonGroup
moveSection()  QHeader
moveTo()  QPainter
moveToFirst()  QSplitter
moveToLast()  QSplitter
moveToolBar()  QMainWindow
moveUp()  KFileBookmarkManager
movie()  QLabel
multiCellBitmap()  QPixmap
multiCellHandle()  QPixmap
multiCellOffset()  QPixmap
name()  QObject QStyleSheetItem KLibrary KURIFilterPlugin
              KWCommand KWCommandGroup
nameFilter()  QUrlOperator
needUpdate()  Kded
newIconLoader()  KInstance
newInstance()  KUniqueApplication KCookieServer
newPage()  QPrinter
newStream()  QNPInstance
newStreamCreated()  QNPInstance
newWindow()  QNPInstance
next()  QListBoxItem
nextButton()  QWizard
nextItem()  QIconViewItem
nextMatch()  KCompletion
nextSibling()  QListViewItem
normalExit()  KProcess
noRootAffix()  KSpellConfig
notify()  QApplication QIOWatch QTimeWatch
notifyURL()  QNPInstance
numberOfColumns()  QStyleSheetItem
numCells()  KColorCells
numCols()  QGridLayout QListBox QWellArray
numColumns()  QListBox
numCopies()  QPrinter
numDigits()  QLCDNumber
numDirs()  KDirOperator KFileView
numFiles()  KDirOperator KFileView
numItemsVisible()  QListBox
numLines()  QMultiLineEdit
numRows()  QGridLayout QListBox QWellArray
```

```
object()  QGuardedPtrPrivate
objectTrees()  QObject
off()  KLed
offIconSet()  QToolButton
offset()  QHeader
offsetX()  QCanvasPixmap
offsetY()  QCanvasPixmap
oldPos()  QMoveEvent
oldSize()  QResizeEvent
on()  KToolBarButton KLed
onIconSet()  QToolButton
opaqueMoving()  QMainWindow
opaqueResize()  QSplitter
openURL()  KDirLister
operation()  QNetworkOperation
operationInProgress()  QNetworkProtocol
optimization()  QPixmap
orientation()  QPrinter KTextPrintDialog QHeader QScrollBar
        QSlider KProgress KSelector QToolBar KPanelApplet
        QGroupBox QSplitter KContainerLayout KSeparator
outputFileName()  QPrinter
outputToFile()  QPrinter
overlayContext()  QGLWidget
overlayTransparentColor()  QGLContext
overrideCursor()  QApplication
packEnd()  KContainerLayout
packStart()  KContainerLayout
padding()  KContainerLayout
page()  QWizard KDockTabCtl
pageCaption()  KDockTabCtl
pageCount()  QWizard KDockTabCtl
pageDown()  KWriteView
pageIndex()  KDialogBase
pageOrder()  QPrinter
pageSize()  QPrinter
pageStep()  QScrollBar QRangeControl QSlider
pageUp()  KWriteView
paint()  QCustomMenuItem
paintBranches()  QListViewItem
paintCell()  QListViewItem QCheckListItem
paintFocus()  QListViewItem QCheckListItem
paintingActive()  QPaintDevice
palette()  QWidget QToolTip QApplication KPaletteTable
palettePropagation()  QWidget
paper()  QTextView
paperColorGroup()  QTextView
parameter()  KJavaApplet KJavaAppletWidget
parent()  QObject QListViewItem
parentClient()  KXMLGUIClient
parentCollection()  KAction
parentWidget()  QWidget QToolTip
part()  KHTMLView
password()  QUrl KPasswordDialog KPasswordEdit
paste()  QLineEdit QMultiLineEdit
```

```
path()   QUrl
pen()   QPainter QCanvasPolygonalItem
pixBorderWidth()   KThemeBase
pixmap()   QBrush QDragObject QIconViewItem QListViewItem
         QFileIconProvider QClipboard KAction QListBoxItem
         QListBoxPixmap KThemeCache QButton QComboBox QLabel
         KURLLabel QMenuData QListBox
pixmapBrush()   KThemeBase
pixmapHotSpot()   QDragObject
pixmapRect()   QIconViewItem
plainPage()   KDialogBase
plainText()   KAction
plane()   QGLFormat
play()   QPicture KAudioPlayer
plug()   KAction KToggleAction KSelectAction KFontAction
         KActionMenu KActionSeparator
plugAccel()   KAction
plugActionList()   KXMLGUIClient
points()   QCanvasPolygon
polish()   QWidget QApplication QMotifStyle KDEStyle
         KThemeStyle KStepStyle
polishPopupMenu()   QMotifStyle QWindowsStyle QPlatinumStyle
         KDEStyle
popup()   KActionMenu QPushButton QToolButton KToolBarButton
         QPopupMenu
popupDelay()   QToolButton
popupMenu()   KSelectAction KActionMenu
popupMenuItemHeight()   QMotifStyle QWindowsStyle
         QPlatinumStyle KDEStyle KThemeStyle
popupSubmenuIndicatorWidth()   QCommonStyle
port()   QUrl KServerSocket
pos()   QWidget QMouseEvent QWheelEvent QMoveEvent QDropEvent
         QPainter QIconViewItem
position()   KPanelApplet
postApplyChanges()   KFilePropsPage
postEvent()   QApplication
postURL()   QNPInstance
preferences()   KPanelApplet
prefix()   QSpinBox
prev()   QListBoxItem
previewMode()   QFileDialog
previousMatch()   KCompletion
prevItem()   QIconViewItem
print()   QNPInstance KTextPrintConfig KHTMLView
printer()   QPrintDialog
printerName()   QPrinter
printerSelectionOption()   QPrinter
printFullPage()   QNPInstance
printProgram()   QPrinter
priority()   KURIFilterPlugin
process()   KUniqueApplication KCookieServer KSycoca
         KBuildSycoca KPanelMenu KPanelApplet
processClientCmdline()   QXEmbed
processEvents()   QApplication
```

```
processOneEvent()  QApplication
progress()  QProgressDialog QProgressBar
propagateSessionManager()  KApplication
property()  QObject
protocol()  QUrl
protocolDetail()  QNetworkOperation
provides()  QDropEvent QMimeSource
put()  QUrlOperator
qglClearColor()  QGLWidget
qglColor()  QGLWidget
QString()  QUrl
query()  QUrl KTrader QMessageBox
queryList()  QObject
quickHelp()  KCModule
quit()  QApplication KJavaAppletServer
raise()  QWidget
raiseWidget()  QWidgetStack
random()  KApplication
randomString()  KApplication
rasterOp()  QPainter
rawArg()  QNetworkOperation
read()  KFileBookmarkManager
readActions()  KDesktopFile
readBoolEntry()  KConfigBase
readColorEntry()  KConfigBase
readComment()  KDesktopFile
readConfig()  KDockManager KTextPrintConfig KWCommand
        KWCommandGroup KWCommandDispatcher KDirOperator
readDateTimeEntry()  KConfigBase
readDockConfig()  KDockMainWindow
readDoubleNumEntry()  KConfigBase
readEntry()  KConfigBase
readFontEntry()  KConfigBase
readIcon()  KDesktopFile
readIntListEntry()  KConfigBase
readListEntry()  KConfigBase
readln()  KProcIO
readLongNumEntry()  KConfigBase
readName()  KDesktopFile
readNumEntry()  KConfigBase
readPath()  KDesktopFile
readPointEntry()  KConfigBase
readPropertyEntry()  KConfigBase
readRectEntry()  KConfigBase
readSettings()  KAccel KGlobalAccel
readSizeEntry()  KConfigBase
readType()  KDesktopFile
readUnsignedLongNumEntry()  KConfigBase
readUnsignedNumEntry()  KConfigBase
readURL()  KDesktopFile
realize()  QTextTableCell
reason()  QFocusEvent
recreate()  QWidget KBuildSycoca Kded
rect()  QWidget QPaintEvent QPixmap QIconViewItem
```

```
                QCanvasRectangle
redirect()  QPainter
redo()  QMultiLineEdit
redraw()  KFormulaEdit
ref()  QUrl
refresh()  QSplitter
region()  QPaintEvent
registerNetworkProtocol()  QNetworkProtocol
release()  QSessionManager
releaseKeyboard()  QWidget
releaseMouse()  QWidget
reloadXML()  KXMLGUIClient
remove()  QToolTip QWhatsThis QTranslator QUrlOperator
        KActionMenu KActionCollection KFileBookmarkManager
        KabAPI QButtonGroup
removeAnimation()  QCanvas
removeButton()  KToolBarRadioGroup
removeChild()  QObject QScrollView
removeChildClient()  KXMLGUIClient
removeColumn()  QListView
removeComboItem()  KToolBar
removeContainer()  KXMLGUIBuilder
removeCustomElement()  KXMLGUIBuilder
removed()  QChildEvent
removeDeletedMenu()  KAccel
removedFromPanel()  KPanelApplet
removeDir()  KDirWatch
removeEventFilter()  QObject
removeHotSpot()  KToolBoxManager
removeItem()  QListViewItem QAccel KAccel QCanvas KCompletion
        KGlobalAccel QComboBox KStatusBar QMenuData QListView
        QListBox KToolBar
removeItemAt()  QMenuData
removeItemFromChunk()  QCanvas
removeItemFromChunkContaining()  QCanvas
removeKipcEventMask()  KApplication
removeLabel()  QHeader
removeLine()  QMultiLineEdit
removeMappings()  QSignalMapper
removePage()  QTabDialog QWizard QTabWidget KDockTabCtl
removePostedEvents()  QApplication
removeTab()  QTabBar KDockTabBar
removeToolBar()  QMainWindow
removeTranslator()  QApplication
removeURL()  KRecentFilesAction KURLComboBox
removeView()  QCanvas
removeWidget()  QStatusBar QWidgetStack
rename()  QIconViewItem QUrlOperator KFileBookmarkManager
        KPropertiesDialog
renameEnabled()  QIconViewItem
renderPixmap()  QGLWidget
repaint()  QWidget QIconViewItem QListViewItem KRootPixmap
        QTableView
repaintAll()  KEdit
```

```
repaintContents()  QScrollView
repaintItem()  QIconView QListView
repairEventFilter()  QAccel
reparent()  QWidget
reparseConfiguration()  KConfigBase KConfig
repeatSearch()  KEdit
replace()  KEdit
replace_all_slot()  KEdit
replace_search_slot()  KEdit
replace_slot()  KEdit
replacedone_slot()  KEdit
replaceEnv()  KURLCompletion
replaceHome()  KURLCompletion
replacement()  KSpellDlg
reportBug()  KHelpMenu
representative()  KAction
requestPhase2()  QSessionManager
requestShutDown()  KApplication
reread()  KFileBookmarkManager
rereadDir()  QFileDialog KDirOperator
reset()  QProgressDialog QGLContext QProgressBar
resetAll()  KProcIO
resetReason()  QFocusEvent
resetXForm()  QPainter
resize()  QWidget QPixmap QCanvas KToolBoxManager QDialog
        QSemiModal QPushButton KJavaAppletWidget QScrollView
resizeContents()  QScrollView
resizeEvent()  KButtonBox QPopupFrame
resizeLayout()  KDialog
resizeMode()  QLayout QIconView
resizePolicy()  QScrollView
resizeSection()  QHeader
resortDir()  QFileDialog
resource()  KDesktopFile
restartCommand()  QSessionManager
restartDirScan()  KDirWatch
restartHint()  QSessionManager
restore()  QPainter KTMainWindow
restoreOverrideCursor()  QApplication
restoreWorldMatrix()  QPainter
result()  QDialog
resume()  KProcess
retune()  QCanvas
rgba()  QGLFormat
richText()  QTextTableCell
rightJustification()  QMainWindow
rollback()  KConfigBase KConfig
rootIsDecorated()  QListView
rootItem()  KDirLister
rotate()  QPainter
rotateText()  KComboBox KLineEdit
roundButton()  KThemeBase
roundComboBox()  KThemeBase
roundSlider()  KThemeBase
```

```
selectedText()   QTextView KHTMLView
selectedURL()   KFileDialog KURLRequesterDlg
selectedURLs()   KFileDialog
selectFont()   KEdit
selectIcon()   KIconDialog
selectionMode()   QIconView KFileView QListView QListBox
self()   KLibLoader KDirWatch KSycoca KTrader
selfMask()   QPixmap
selfNesting()   QStyleSheetItem
send()   KNotifyClient KJavaProcess
sendEvent()   QApplication
sendPostedEvents()   QApplication
separator()   QMenuBar
separatorPos()   KDockSplitter
serialNumber()   QPixmap
service()   KOpenWithDlg
sessionConfig()   KApplication
sessionId()   QApplication QSessionManager
set()   KDialogBaseTile
setAccel()   KAction QButton QMenuData
setAcceptDrags()   KColorCells
setAcceptDrops()   QWidget
setAccum()   QGLFormat
setAction()   QDropEvent
setActionGroup()   KDesktopFile
setActions()   KPanelApplet
setActive()   QCanvasItem
setActiveItem()   QPopupMenu
setActiveWindow()   QWidget QXtWidget
setAdvancePeriod()   QCanvas
setAlignment()   QStyleSheetItem QLayoutItem QLineEdit
        QGroupBox QLabel QMultiLineEdit
setAllChanged()   QCanvas
setAllColumnsShowFocus()   QListView
setAlpha()   QGLFormat
setAltPixmap()   KURLLabel
setAnchor()   QStyleSheetItem
setAngles()   QCanvasEllipse
setAnimated()   QCanvasItem
setAppletClass()   KJavaApplet KJavaAppletWidget
setAppletId()   KJavaApplet
setAppletName()   KJavaApplet KJavaAppletWidget
setApplyButton()   QTabDialog
setAppropriate()   QWizard
setArg()   QNetworkOperation
setArrangement()   QIconView
setAuthor()   KAboutDialog KAboutWidget
setAutoAdd()   QLayout
setAutoArrange()   QIconView
setAutoBottomScrollBar()   QListBox
setAutoClose()   QProgressDialog
setAutoCompletion()   QComboBox KComboBox
setAutoDefault()   QPushButton
setAutoDelete()   QNetworkProtocol KRun KSpell
```

```
setAutoDeleteCompletionObject()   KCompletionBase
setAutoMask()   QWidget QLabel
setAutoRaise()   QToolButton
setAutoRepeat()   QButton KToolBar
setAutoReset()   QProgressDialog
setAutoResize()   QButton QComboBox QLabel
setAutoScroll()   QListBox
setAutoScrollBar()   QListBox
setAutoUpdate()   KFileReader KFileIconView KFileDetailView
        QListBox QMultiLineEdit
setBackEnabled()   QWizard
setBackgroundColor()   QWidget QPainter QCanvas QComboBox
        KURLLabel QTableView
setBackgroundMode()   QWidget QPainter
setBackgroundOrigin()   QWidget
setBackgroundPixmap()   QWidget QCanvas
setBackgroundTile()   KDialogBase
setBar()   QProgressDialog
setBarColor()   KProgress
setBarPixmap()   KProgress
setBarPos()   KToolBar
setBarStyle()   KProgress
setBase()   KIntValidator
setBaseSize()   QWidget
setBaseURL()   KJavaApplet KJavaAppletWidget
setBigMarkDistance()   KRuler
setBinMode()   QLCDNumber
setBorder()   KThemePixmap KTabCtl
setBottom()   QIntValidator QDoubleValidator
setBottomItem()   QListBox
setBottomScrollBar()   QListBox
setBrush()   QPainter QCanvasPolygonalItem
setBrushOrigin()   QPainter
setBuddy()   QLabel
setBuilderInstance()   KXMLGUIBuilder
setButton()   QButtonGroup KToolBar
setButtonApplyText()   KDialogBase
setButtonCancelText()   KDialogBase
setButtonIcon()   KToolBar
setButtonOKText()   KDialogBase
setButtonPixmap()   KToolBar
setButtonSymbols()   QSpinBox
setButtonText()   QMessageBox KDialogBase
setButtonTip()   KDialogBase
setButtonWhatsThis()   KDialogBase
setCancelButton()   QTabDialog QProgressDialog
setCancelButtonText()   QProgressDialog
setCanvas()   QCanvasItem QCanvasView
setCapStyle()   QPen
setCaption()   QWidget KTMainWindow KDialog
setCellBrush()   QWellArray
setCellSize()   QHeader QWellArray
setCenterIndicator()   QProgressBar
setCentralWidget()   QMainWindow
```

```
setChanged()  QCanvas
setChangedChunk()  QCanvas
setChangedChunkContaining()  QCanvas
setChar()  KCharSelect KCharSelectTable
setCheckable()  QPopupMenu
setChecked()  KToggleAction QCheckBox QRadioButton
setClassArgs()  KJavaProcess
setClickEnabled()  QHeader
setClient()  KSpellConfig
setClientBuilder()  KXMLGUIClient
setClipping()  QPainter
setClipRect()  QPainter
setClipRegion()  QPainter
setCodeBase()  KJavaApplet KJavaAppletWidget
setColor()  QBrush QColorDrag KColorDrag QPen QStyleSheetItem
        QCanvasText KColorDialog KColorButton KColorCombo
        KLed KColorCells KColorPatch
setColorMode()  QPrinter QApplication
setColors()  KGradientSelector
setColorSpec()  QApplication
setCols()  KTextPrintPreview
setColStretch()  QGridLayout
setColumnAlignment()  QListView
setColumnLayout()  QGroupBox
setColumnMode()  QListBox
setColumns()  QGroupBox
setColumnText()  QListView
setColumnWidth()  QListView
setColumnWidthMode()  QListView
setComboWidth()  KSelectAction
setCompletion()  KFileComboBox
setCompletionMode()  KCompletion KCompletionBase KLineEdit
setCompletionObject()  KCompletionBase
setComponent()  KAction
setConfigGlobal()  KAccel
setConfigGroup()  KAccel KGlobalAccel
setContainerStates()  KXMLGUIClient
setContentsPos()  QScrollView QIconView QListView
setContentsPreview()  QFileDialog
setContentsPreviewEnabled()  QFileDialog
setContext()  QGLWidget
setContextId()  KJavaAppletContext
setContexts()  QStyleSheetItem
setCornerWidget()  QScrollView
setCreator()  QPrinter
setCurrentComboItem()  KToolBar
setCurrentItem()  KSelectAction KListAction QComboBox
        KDirOperator QIconView KFileView QListView QListBox
setCurrentTab()  QTabBar KDockTabBar
setCursor()  QWidget
setCursorFlashTime()  QApplication
setCursorPosition()  QLineEdit QMultiLineEdit
setCustomColor()  QColorDialog
setDarkFactor()  KLed
```

```
setData()   QCustomEvent QPicture QClipboard KTextPrintConfig
        KWCommand KWCommandGroup KWCommandDispatcher
        KTextPrintDialog
setDate()   KDateTable KDatePicker
setDecimals()   QDoubleValidator
setDecMode()   QLCDNumber
setDefault()   QPushButton
setDefaultButton()   QTabDialog
setDefaultCodec()   QApplication
setDefaultFormat()   QGLFormat
setDefaultIcon()   KToolBarButton
setDefaultOptimization()   QPixmap
setDefaultOverlayFormat()   QGLFormat
setDefaultPixmap()   KToolBarButton
setDefaults()   KURLComboBox
setDefaultSheet()   QStyleSheet
setDefaultTabStop()   QMultiLineEdit
setDefaultUp()   QMenuBar
setDelay()   QToolTipGroup
setDelayedPopup()   KToolBarButton KToolBar
setDepth()   QGLFormat
setDescription()   KAccel
setDesktopGroup()   KConfigBase
setDesktopSettingsAware()   QApplication
setDest()   KTextPrintDialog
setDictFromList()   KSpellConfig
setDictionary()   KSpellConfig
setDimension()   QWellArray
setDir()   KURLCompletion QFileDialog
setDirection()   QBoxLayout KDirectionButton
setDirectRendering()   QGLFormat
setDirOnlyMode()   KDirLister
setDirty()   KPropsPage
setDisabledIcon()   KToolBarButton
setDisabledPixmap()   KToolBarButton
setDiscardCommand()   QSessionManager
setDisplayMode()   QStyleSheetItem
setDNDEnabled()   KHTMLView
setDockEnabled()   QMainWindow
setDockMenuEnabled()   QMainWindow
setDockSite()   KDockWidget
setDocName()   QPrinter
setDollarExpansion()   KConfigBase
setDoubleBuffer()   QGLFormat
setDoubleBuffering()   QCanvas
setDoubleClickInterval()   QApplication
setDown()   QButton
setDragAutoScroll()   QScrollView
setDragEnabled()   QIconViewItem
setDragSelect()   QListBox
setDropEnabled()   QIconViewItem
setDuplicatesEnabled()   QComboBox
setEchoMode()   QLineEdit QMultiLineEdit
setEdit()   KKeyButton
```

```
setEditable()  KSelectAction
setEdited()  QLineEdit QMultiLineEdit
setEditFocus()  KIntSpinBox KIntNumInput
setEditText()  QComboBox
setEmail()  KAboutContributor
setEnableContextMenu()  KComboBox KLineEdit KToolBar
setEnabled()  QWidget QToolTip QCanvasItem QAccel KAccel
        QSocketNotifier QToolTipGroup KGlobalAccel KAction
        KActionMenu KWCommandDispatcher KToolBarButton
        QComboBox QLineEdit QSpinBox KDockTabCtl QScrollView
        KDatePicker
setEnableDocking()  KDockWidget
setEnableToolBar()  KTMainWindow
setEncodedData()  QStoredDrag
setEncodedPathAndQuery()  QUrl
setEncoding()  KSpellConfig
setEndLabel()  KRuler
setEndOffset()  KContainerLayout
setErrorCode()  QNetworkOperation
setExclusive()  QButtonGroup
setExclusiveGroup()  KToggleAction
setExecutable()  KProcess
setExpand()  KContainerLayout
setExpandable()  QListViewItem
setExtraArgs()  KJavaProcess
setExtraChars()  KFormulaEdit
setFactory()  KXMLGUIClient
setFadeEffect()  KRootPixmap
setFileDirty()  KDirWatch
setFileName()  QUrl QConfigDB KWritePermsIcon
setFilenames()  QUriDrag
setFill()  KContainerLayout
setFilter()  QFileDialog KFileDialog KFileFilter
setFilters()  QFileDialog
setFinish()  QWizard
setFinishEnabled()  QWizard
setFixedHeight()  QWidget
setFixedSize()  QWidget
setFixedVisibleLines()  QListBox QMultiLineEdit
setFixedWidth()  QWidget
setFlags()  KPanelApplet
setFlat()  KToolBar
setFloat()  KURLLabel
setFocus()  QWidget
setFocusPolicy()  QWidget
setFocusProxy()  QWidget
setFont()  QWidget QPainter QCustomMenuItem QToolTip
        QCanvasText QApplication KFontAction QTabDialog
        QWizard KFontDialog QComboBox QLineEdit KDockTabBar
        KFontChooser KTabCtl KCharSelect KURLLabel QPopupMenu
        QIconView QListView QListBox QMultiLineEdit
        KCharSelectTable
setFontFamily()  QStyleSheetItem
setFontItalic()  QStyleSheetItem
```

```
setImage()   QImageDrag QClipboard KAboutDialog
        KAboutContainerBase
setImageBackgroundColor()   KAboutDialog KAboutContainerBase
setImageFrame()   KAboutDialog KAboutContainerBase
setIndent()   KSelector QLabel
setIndicatorFollowsStyle()   QProgressBar
setIndicatorWidget()   KTMainWindow
setInfoPreview()   QFileDialog
setInfoPreviewEnabled()   QFileDialog
setInitialSize()   KDialogBase
setInsertionPolicy()   QComboBox
setInstance()   KActionCollection
setIsMenuButton()   QPushButton
setItemAlignment()   KStatusBar
setItemAutoSized()   KToolBar
setItemChecked()   QMenuData
setItemEnabled()   QAccel KAccel KGlobalAccel QMenuData
        KToolBar
setItemFixed()   KStatusBar
setItemMargin()   QListView
setItemNoStyle()   KToolBar
setItemParameter()   QMenuData
setItems()   KCompletion KSelectAction
setItemsMovable()   QIconView
setItemTextBackground()   QIconView
setItemTextPos()   QIconView
setJARFile()   KJavaApplet KJavaAppletWidget
setJoinStyle()   QPen
setJVMPath()   KJavaProcess
setJVMVersion()   KJavaProcess
setKey()   QIconViewItem
setKeyBinding()   KCompletionBase
setKeyDict()   KAccel KGlobalAccel KActionCollection
setLabel()   QProgressDialog QHeader QToolBar KNumInput
        KIntNumInput KDoubleNumInput
setLabelText()   QProgressDialog
setLength()   KRuler
setLengthFix()   KRuler
setLinedText()   KToolBar
setLineStep()   QScrollBar QSlider QSpinBox
setLineWidth()   QFrame
setLinkColor()   QTextView
setLinkUnderline()   QTextView
setListBox()   QComboBox
setListStyle()   QStyleSheetItem
setLittleMarkDistance()   KRuler
setLocationLabel()   KFileDialog
setLogicalFontSize()   QStyleSheetItem
setLogicalFontSizeStep()   QStyleSheetItem
setLogo()   KAboutDialog KAboutWidget
setLook()   KLed
setMainClass()   KJavaProcess
setMainDockWidget()   KDockMainWindow
setMaintainer()   KAboutDialog KAboutWidget
```

setMainWidget() QApplication KDialogBase QPopupFrame
setMapping() QSignalMapper
setMargin() QFrame QStyleSheetItem QLayout QTabWidget
setMarginHeight() KHTMLView
setMarginWidth() KHTMLView
setMask() QWidget QPixmap
setMaxCount() QComboBox
setMaxHeight() KToolBar
setMaximumHeight() QWidget
setMaximumSize() QWidget
setMaximumToolBarWraps() KTMainWindow
setMaximumWidth() QWidget
setMaximumWraps() KTMLayout
setMaxItems() KRecentFilesAction KURLComboBox
setMaxItemTextLength() QIconView
setMaxItemWidth() QIconView
setMaxLength() QLineEdit QMultiLineEdit
setMaxLineLength() QMultiLineEdit
setMaxLines() QMultiLineEdit
setMaxValue() QScrollBar QSlider QSpinBox KRuler
setMaxWidth() KToolBar
setMediumMarkDistance() KRuler
setMenu() KTMainWindow
setMenuBar() QLayout
setMidLineWidth() QFrame
setMimeSourceFactory() QTextView
setMinimumDuration() QProgressDialog
setMinimumHeight() QWidget
setMinimumSize() QWidget
setMinimumWidth() QWidget
setMinMax() QPrinter
setMinValue() QScrollBar QSlider QSpinBox KRuler
setMode() KURLCompletion QFileDialog KFileDialog
        KDirOperator QLCDNumber
setModified() KEdit
setMouseTracking() QWidget
setMovie() QLabel KURLLabel
setMovingEnabled() QHeader
setMultiSelection() QListView QListBox
setName() QWidget QObject KAboutContributor
setNameFilter() QUrlOperator KDirLister KFileReader
        KDirOperator
setNextEnabled() QWizard
setNoChange() QCheckBox
setNoRootAffix() KSpellConfig
setNoStyle() KToolBarButton
setNotifyClick() KTextBrowser
setNum() QLabel
setNumberOfColumns() QStyleSheetItem
setNumCopies() QPrinter
setNumDigits() QLCDNumber
setOctMode() QLCDNumber
setOffIconSet() QToolButton
setOffset() QCanvasPixmap QHeader KRuler

```
setOKButton()   QTabDialog
setOkButton()   QTabDialog
setOn()   QCheckListItem QPushButton QToolButton
setOnIconSet()   QToolButton
setOpaqueMoving()   QMainWindow
setOpaqueResize()   QSplitter
setOpen()   QListViewItem QListView
setOperator()   KFileView
setOptimization()   QPixmap
setOption()   QGLFormat
setOrient()   KTextPrintPreview
setOrientation()   QPrinter QHeader QScrollBar QSlider
        KProgress QToolBar QGroupBox QSplitter
        KContainerLayout KSeparator
setOrigin()   QGridLayout
setOutputFileName()   QPrinter
setOutputToFile()   QPrinter
setOverlay()   QGLFormat
setOverrideCursor()   QApplication
setOverwriteMode()   QMultiLineEdit
setPadding()   KContainerLayout
setPageCaption()   KDockTabCtl
setPageEnabled()   KDockTabCtl
setPageNumbers()   KTextPrintPreview
setPageOrder()   QPrinter
setPageSize()   QPrinter
setPageStep()   QScrollBar QSlider
setPalette()   QWidget QToolTip QApplication QComboBox
        QLineEdit QScrollBar QSlider KPaletteTable QIconView
        QListView QTableView
setPalettePropagation()   QWidget
setPaper()   QTextView
setPaperColorGroup()   QTextView
setParameter()   KJavaApplet KJavaAppletContext
        KJavaAppletServer KJavaAppletWidget
setPassword()   QUrl
setPath()   QUrlOperator QUrl
setPen()   QPainter QCanvasPolygonalItem QCanvasLine
setPixelPerMark()   KRuler
setPixmap()   QBrush QDragObject QIconViewItem QListViewItem
        QClipboard QButton KToolBarButton KDockTabBar
        KDockTabCtl QLabel KURLLabel
setPlainCaption()   KTMainWindow KDialog
setPlane()   QGLFormat
setPoint()   QDropEvent
setPoints()   QCanvasPolygon QCanvasLine
setPopup()   QPushButton QToolButton KToolBarButton
setPopupDelay()   QToolButton
setPort()   QUrl
setPrefix()   QSpinBox KIntNumInput KDoubleNumInput
setPreviewMode()   QFileDialog
setPreviewWidget()   KFileDialog KDirOperator KFilePreview
setPrinter()   QPrintDialog
setPrinterName()   QPrinter
```

```
setSender()   QSenderObject
setSeparator()   QMenuBar
setSeparatorPos()   KDockSplitter
setSequence()   QCanvasSprite
setShading()   KColorCells
setShape()   QTabBar KLed KTabCtl
setShortText()   KAction
setShowAll()   KJanusWidget
setShowHiddenFiles()   KFileReader QFileDialog KDirOperator
setShowingDotFiles()   KDirLister
setShowLocalProtocol()   KURLRequester
setShowSortIndicator()   QListView
setShowToolTips()   QIconView
setSize()   QCanvasRectangle QCanvasEllipse KJavaApplet
        KAnimWidget
setSizeGripEnabled()   QStatusBar
setSizeIncrement()   QWidget
setSizeLimit()   QComboBox
setSizes()   QSplitter
setSmallDecimalPoint()   QLCDNumber
setSmoothScrolling()   QListBox
setSorted()   KCompletion
setSortIndicator()   QHeader
setSorting()   KDirOperator QIconView KFileView KCombiView
        KFileDetailView QListView
setSortMode()   KFileView
setSource()   QTextBrowser
setSpacing()   QLayout QGrid QHBox QIconView KContainerLayout
setSpecialValueText()   QSpinBox KIntNumInput KDoubleNumInput
setStartDragDistance()   QApplication
setStartDragTime()   QApplication
setStartOffset()   KContainerLayout
setState()   QNetworkOperation KLed
setStatusBar()   KTMainWindow
setStencil()   QGLFormat
setSteps()   QRangeControl KNumInput
setStereo()   QGLFormat
setStretchableWidget()   QToolBar
setStretchFactor()   QBoxLayout QHBox
setStyle()   QWidget QBrush QPen QApplication
setStyleSheet()   QTextView
setSubtype()   QTextDrag
setSuffix()   QSpinBox KIntNumInput KDoubleNumInput
setSystemProperty()   KJavaProcess
setTabArray()   QPainter
setTabCaption()   KDockTabBar
setTabEnabled()   QTabDialog QTabBar QTabWidget KDockTabBar
        KTabCtl
setTabFont()   KDockTabCtl KTabCtl
setTableNum()   KCharSelect KCharSelectTable
setTabOrder()   QWidget
setTabPos()   KDockTabBar KDockTabCtl
setTabPosition()   QTabWidget
setTabStops()   QPainter
```

```
setTabTextColor()  KDockTabCtl
setTarget()  QDragObject
setText()  QTextDrag QIconViewItem QListViewItem QCanvasText
        QClipboard KAction QMessageBox KEdFind KEdReplace
        QButton KKeyButton KToolBarButton QLineEdit
        KGradientSelector KFormulaEdit QLabel KURLLabel
        QTextView QTextBrowser QMultiLineEdit
setTextAlignment()  KURLLabel
setTextColor()  KDockTabBar
setTextEnabled()  KProgress
setTextFlags()  QCanvasText
setTextFormat()  QMessageBox QLabel QTextView
setTextLabel()  QToolButton
setTickInterval()  QSlider
setTickmarks()  QSlider
setTickStyle()  KRuler
setTile()  QCanvas
setTinyMarkDistance()  KRuler
setTipText()  KURLLabel
setTitle()  KFileBookmarkManager KAboutDialog
        KAboutContainerBase KPopupTitle KTextPrintPreview
        QGroupBox KPopupMenu KToolBar
setToggle()  KToolBarButton KToolBar
setToggleButton()  QPushButton QToolButton
setToolBarsMovable()  QMainWindow
setToolTip()  KAction KDockTabBar KDockTabCtl
setToolTipString()  KDockWidget
setTop()  QIntValidator QDoubleValidator
setTopItem()  QListBox
setTopLevel()  KDockWidgetAbstractHeader KDockWidgetHeader
setTopWidget()  KApplication
setTotalSteps()  QProgressDialog QProgressBar
setTracking()  QHeader QScrollBar QSlider
setTransparentMode()  KURLLabel
setTreeListAutoResize()  KDialogBase
setTreeStepSize()  QListView
setTristate()  QCheckBox
setUglyForm()  KFormulaEdit
setUnderline()  KURLLabel
setUndoDepth()  QMultiLineEdit
setUndoEnabled()  QMultiLineEdit
setUnicodeUris()  QUriDrag
setup()  QPrinter QListViewItem QCheckListItem
setUpdatePeriod()  QCanvas
setUpdatesEnabled()  QWidget
setUris()  QUriDrag
setUrl()  QNetworkProtocol
setURL()  KFileReader
setUrl()  QFileDialog
setURL()  KFileDialog KURLComboBox KDirOperator KURLRequester
        KURLLabel KAboutContributor
setURLCursor()  KHTMLView
setURLs()  KURLComboBox
setUseCursor()  KURLLabel
```

```
setUseHighlightColors()  QMotifStyle
setUser()  QUrl
setUsesBigPixmap()  QToolButton
setUsesBigPixmaps()  QMainWindow
setUsesTextLabel()  QToolButton QMainWindow
setUseTips()  KURLLabel
setValidator()  QComboBox QLineEdit QSpinBox QMultiLineEdit
setValidChars()  KRestrictedLine
setValue()  QScrollBar QRangeControl QSlider QSpinBox
           KProgress KIntNumInput KDoubleNumInput KRuler
setValuePerBigMark()  KRuler
setValuePerLittleMark()  KRuler
setValuePerMediumMark()  KRuler
setValues()  KXYSelector
setVariableHeight()  QListBox
setVariableWidth()  QListBox
setVelocity()  QCanvasItem
setVersion()  KAboutDialog KAboutWidget
setVerticalStretchable()  QToolBar
setView()  KTMainWindow KDockMainWindow KDirOperator
setViewMode()  QFileDialog KFileView
setViewName()  KFileView
setViewport()  QPainter
setViewXForm()  QPainter
setVisible()  QCanvasItem
setVisibleItems()  KSplitList
setVisiblePage()  KDockTabCtl
setVScrollBarMode()  QScrollView
setWhatsThis()  QAccel KAction QMenuData
setWheelScrollLines()  QApplication
setWhiteSpaceMode()  QStyleSheetItem
setWidget()  KDockWidget
setWidth()  QPen KSplitListItem
setWindow()  QPainter QNPWidget
setWinStyleHighlightColor()  QApplication
setWordWrap()  QMultiLineEdit
setWordWrapIconText()  QIconView
setWork()  KAboutContributor
setWorldMatrix()  QPainter
setWorldXForm()  QPainter
setWrapColumnOrWidth()  QMultiLineEdit
setWrapping()  QSpinBox
setWrapPolicy()  QMultiLineEdit
setX()  QCanvasItem
setXML()  KToolBar
setXVelocity()  QCanvasItem
setY()  QCanvasItem
setYear()  KDateInternalYearSelector
setYVelocity()  QCanvasItem
setZ()  QCanvasItem
shade()  KThemeBase
shape()  QTabBar
shear()  QPainter
shortcutKey()  QAccel
```

```
shortText()  KAction
show()  QWidget QCanvasItem KJavaApplet KJavaAppletContext
         KTMainWindow QDialog QTabDialog QWizard KAboutDialog
         KFileDialog QSemiModal QMainWindow QTabBar QToolBar
         KAboutContainerBase KDockTabBar KDockTabCtl
         KDockWidget KTabCtl KJavaAppletWidget QMenuBar
         QPopupMenu QProgressBar QScrollView QListView
         QTableView QWidgetStack
showApplet()  KJavaAppletServer
showBigMarkLabel()  KRuler
showBigMarks()  KRuler
showButton()  KDialogBase
showButtonApply()  KDialogBase
showButtonCancel()  KDialogBase
showButtonOK()  KDialogBase
showChild()  QScrollView
showEndLabel()  KRuler
showEndMarks()  KRuler
showEvent()  QIconView
showFullScreen()  QWidget
showHiddenFiles()  KFileReader QFileDialog KDirOperator
showItem()  KToolBar
showLittleMarkLabel()  KRuler
showLittleMarks()  KRuler
showLocalProtocol()  KURLRequester
showMaximized()  QWidget
showMediumMarkLabel()  KRuler
showMediumMarks()  KRuler
showMinimized()  QWidget
showModeChanger()  KCompletionBase
showNormal()  QWidget
showOnButtonPress()  KContextMenuManager
showPage()  QTabDialog QWizard KDialogBase QTabWidget
showPointer()  KRuler
showSortIndicator()  QListView
showTabIcon()  KDockTabBar KDockTabCtl
showTile()  KDialogBase
showTinyMarks()  KRuler
showToolTips()  QIconView
shred()  KShred
signalsBlocked()  QObject
singleShot()  QTimer
size()  QWidget QResizeEvent QPixmap QPicture QIconViewItem
         QCanvasRectangle QCanvas KJavaApplet
sizeHint()  KAboutContainer QFrame QWidget QCustomMenuItem
         QLayoutItem QSpacerItem QWidgetItem QTextTableCell
         QGridLayout QBoxLayout KTMLayout KTMainWindow
         QProgressDialog QSizeGrip QCheckBox QPushButton
         QRadioButton QToolButton QComboBox QLineEdit QHeader
         QMainWindow QScrollBar QSlider QSpinBox KProgress
         QTabBar QTabWidget QWorkspace KAboutContainerBase
         KAuthIcon KButtonBox KDualColorButton KFontChooser
         KNumInput KPopupTitle KTabCtl QXEmbed KFormulaEdit
         QGrid QHBox KCharSelect QLabel KURLLabel QLCDNumber
```

```
                QMenuBar QPopupMenu QProgressBar QScrollView
                QIconView QSplitter QListView QListBox QMultiLineEdit
                QWellArray KCharSelectTable KDateInternalMonthPicker
                KDateTable QWidgetStack KAboutContributor KDatePicker
                KSeparator KToolBar
sizeIncrement()   QWidget
sizeLimit()   QComboBox
sizePolicy()   QFrame QWidget QSizeGrip QCheckBox QPushButton
                QRadioButton QToolButton QComboBox QLineEdit QHeader
                QScrollBar QSlider QSpinBox KProgress QTabBar
                QWorkspace KNumInput QXEmbed KFormulaEdit QLabel
                QLCDNumber QProgressBar QScrollView QIconView
                QSplitter QMultiLineEdit KToolBar
sizes()   QSplitter
sizeToFit()   KContainerLayout
slidedown()   KRuler
sliderButtonLength()   KThemeBase
sliderLength()   QMotifStyle QWindowsStyle QPlatinumStyle
                KDEStyle KThemeStyle KStepStyle
sliderRect()   QSlider
slideup()   KRuler
slotAccept()   KServerSocket
slotActivated()   KColorCombo
slotAddExtension()   KApplicationPropsPage
slotApply()   KPropertiesDialog
slotAppRegistered()   KLauncher
slotBrowseExec()   KExecPropsPage
slotCancel()   KPropertiesDialog
slotClear()   KLineEditDlg KOpenWithDlg
slotDelExtension()   KApplicationPropsPage
slotDequeue()   KLauncher
slotDoHousekeeping()   KProcessController
slotEndOffset()   KRuler
slotHighlighted()   KOpenWithDlg KColorCombo
slotItemHighlighted()   KApplicationTree
slotKInitData()   KLauncher
slotMailClick()   KAboutContainerBase
slotMakeCompletion()   KCompletion
slotMouseTrack()   KAboutContainerBase
slotNewOffset()   KRuler
slotNewValue()   KRuler
slotNextMatch()   KCompletion
slotOK()   KOpenWithDlg
slotPreviousMatch()   KCompletion
slotProgress()   KSpellDlg
slotRead()   KSocket
slotSave()   KCookieServer
slotSelected()   KOpenWithDlg
slotSelectionChanged()   KApplicationTree
slotSetBackground()   KDualColorButton
slotSetCurrent()   KDualColorButton
slotSetCurrentColor()   KDualColorButton
slotSetForeground()   KDualColorButton
slotSlaveGone()   KLauncher
```

```
stopDirScan()  KDirWatch
stopJava()  KJavaProcess
stopScan()  KDirWatch
storeContainerStateBuffer()  KXMLGUIClient
storeFileAge()  QConfigDB
streamAsFile()  QNPInstance
streamDestroyed()  QNPInstance
stretch()  QTextTableCell
stringToKey()  QAccel KAccel
style()  QWidget QBrush QPen QApplication
styleSheet()  QStyleSheetItem QTextView
subtractLine()  QRangeControl
subtractPage()  QRangeControl
subtractStep()  QSlider
suffix()  QSpinBox
suggestions()  KSpell
superClasses()  QObject
supportedOperations()  QNetworkProtocol QLocalFs
supports()  KFilePropsPage KFilePermissionsPropsPage
        KExecPropsPage KURLPropsPage KApplicationPropsPage
        KBindingPropsPage KDevicePropsPage
supportsMargin()  QLayout
suspend()  KProcess
swapBuffers()  QGLWidget QGLContext
symbol()  KLibrary
sync()  KConfigBase KSimpleConfig
syncX()  QApplication
sysdefaults()  KCModule
tab()  QTabBar
tabArray()  QPainter
tabbarMetrics()  QCommonStyle QMotifStyle QWindowsStyle
        KThemeStyle
tabCaption()  KDockTabBar
tabFont()  KDockTabCtl
tabLabel()  QTabDialog QTabWidget
table()  QTextTableCell
tableNum()  KCharSelect
tabName()  KPropsPage
tabPosition()  QTabWidget
tabStops()  QPainter
tabTextColor()  KDockTabCtl
tag()  QStyleSheet
take()  KActionCollection
takeContainerStateBuffer()  KXMLGUIClient
takeItem()  QListViewItem QIconView QListView QListBox
target()  QDragObject
tempSaveName()  KApplication
testOption()  QGLFormat
testWFlags()  QWidget
testWState()  QWidget
text()  QKeyEvent QIconViewItem QListViewItem QCheckListItem
        QWhatsThis QCanvasText QClipboard KAction
        QListBoxItem QMessageBox KLineEditDlg KOpenWithDlg
        QButton QComboBox QLineEdit QSpinBox KFormulaEdit
```

```
                QLabel KURLLabel QMenuData QListBox QTextView
            QMultiLineEdit
textColor()  KDockTabBar
textEnabled()  KProgress
textFlags()  QCanvasText
textFor()  QWhatsThis
textFormat()  QMessageBox QLabel QTextView
textLabel()  QToolButton
textLine()  QMultiLineEdit
textRect()  QIconViewItem
tickInterval()  QSlider
tickmarks()  QSlider
tile()  QCanvas QWorkspace
tileHeight()  QCanvas
tilesHorizontally()  QCanvas
tilesVertically()  QCanvas
tileWidth()  QCanvas
timerId()  QTimerEvent
title()  QWizard KPopupTitle QGroupBox KPopupMenu
titlePixmap()  KPopupMenu
toggle()  QButton QPushButton QToolButton KToolBarButton KLed
toggleActLink()  KHTMLView
toggleButton()  KToolBar
toggleState()  KLed
toggleType()  QButton
toolBar()  KTMainWindow KFileDialog
toolBars()  QMainWindow
toolBarsMovable()  QMainWindow
toolTip()  KAction
toolTipGroup()  QMainWindow
toolTipString()  KDockWidget
top()  QIntValidator QDoubleValidator KIntValidator
        KFloatValidator KWriteView
top_home()  KWriteView
toPage()  QPrinter
topItem()  QListBox
topLevelWidget()  QWidget
topLevelWidgets()  QApplication
topOfView()  KWriteView
toString()  QUrl
totalHeight()  QListViewItem
totalHeightForWidth()  QLayout
totalMaximumSize()  QLayout
totalMinimumSize()  QLayout
totalSizeHint()  QLayout
totalSteps()  QProgressDialog QProgressBar
tr()  QObject
tracking()  QHeader QScrollBar QSlider
translate()  QPainter QApplication
treeStepSize()  QListView
triggerUpdate()  QListView QListBox
trueMatrix()  QPixmap
tryExec()  KDesktopFile
type()  QEvent QCheckListItem QSocketNotifier QIOWatch
```

```
uglyForm()  KFormulaEdit
uncached()  KThemeBase
undo()  QMultiLineEdit
undock()  KDockWidget
undoDepth()  QMultiLineEdit
ungrabKey()  KGlobalAccel
unicodeUriToUri()  QUriDrag
unloadLibrary()  KLibLoader
unlock()  QConfigDB
unplug()  KAction KActionMenu KActionSeparator
unplugAccel()  KAction
unplugActionList()  KXMLGUIClient
unPolish()  KDEStyle KThemeStyle KStepStyle
unsetCursor()  QWidget
unsetFont()  QWidget
unsetPalette()  QWidget
unsetWindow()  QNPWidget
unsqueeze()  QTranslator
update()  QWidget QCanvas KAction
updateAccelList()  KWKeyConfigTab
updateAccessed()  KThemePixmap
updateBackground()  KDialogBase
updateContents()  QScrollView QIconView
updateDirectory()  KDirLister
updateGeometry()  QWidget
updateGL()  QGLWidget
updateItem()  KAccel QMenuBar QMenuData QPopupMenu
updateLayout()  KPanelApplet
updateMinimumHeight()  KJanusWidget
updateName()  KDockSplitter
updateOverlayGL()  QGLWidget
updateRects()  KToolBar
updateScrollBars()  QScrollView
updateStatus()  KAuthIcon KRootPermsIcon KWritePermsIcon
updateUrl()  KPropertiesDialog
updateView()  KFileIconView KFileView KCombiView KFilePreview
        KFileDetailView
uriToLocalFile()  QUriDrag
uriToUnicodeUri()  QUriDrag
url()  QNetworkProtocol KDirLister QFileDialog KDirOperator
        KURLRequester KURLLabel
urlCursor()  KHTMLView
urls()  KURLComboBox
useGlobalKeyBindings()  KCompletionBase
useHighlightColors()  QMotifStyle
user()  QUrl
userAgent()  QNPInstance
userEvent()  KNotifyClient
usesBigPixmap()  QToolButton
usesBigPixmaps()  QMainWindow
usesTextLabel()  QToolButton QMainWindow
validate()  QValidator QIntValidator QDoubleValidator
        KDateValidator KIntValidator KFloatValidator
validateAndSet()  QLineEdit
```

```
winStyleHighlightColor()  QApplication
winVersion()  QApplication
wmapper()  QWidget
wordLeft()  KWriteView
wordRight()  KWriteView
wordWrap()  QMultiLineEdit
wordWrapIconText()  QIconView
worldMatrix()  QPainter
wrapColumnOrWidth()  QMultiLineEdit
wrapping()  QSpinBox
wrapPolicy()  QMultiLineEdit
write()  QNPInstance KFileBookmarkManager
writeConfig()  KDockManager KTextPrintConfig KWCommand
        KWCommandGroup KWCommandDispatcher
writeDockConfig()  KDockMainWindow
writeEntry()  KConfigBase
writeGlobalSettings()  KSpellConfig
writeReady()  QNPInstance
writeSettings()  KAccel KGlobalAccel
writeStdin()  KProcess KProcIO
x()  QWidget QMouseEvent QWheelEvent QIconViewItem
        QCanvasItem KToolBoxManager
x11AppCells()  QPaintDevice
x11AppColormap()  QPaintDevice
x11AppDefaultColormap()  QPaintDevice
x11AppDefaultVisual()  QPaintDevice
x11AppDepth()  QPaintDevice
x11AppDisplay()  QPaintDevice
x11AppDpiX()  QPaintDevice
x11AppDpiY()  QPaintDevice
x11AppScreen()  QPaintDevice
x11AppVisual()  QPaintDevice
x11Cells()  QPaintDevice
x11ClientMessage()  QApplication
x11Colormap()  QPaintDevice
x11DefaultColormap()  QPaintDevice
x11DefaultVisual()  QPaintDevice
x11Depth()  QPaintDevice
x11Display()  QPaintDevice
x11EventFilter()  QApplication KGlobalAccel
x11ProcessEvent()  QApplication
x11Screen()  QPaintDevice
x11SetAppDpiX()  QPaintDevice
x11SetAppDpiY()  QPaintDevice
x11Visual()  QPaintDevice
xForm()  QPainter QPixmap QBitmap
xFormDev()  QPainter
xioErrhandler()  KApplication
xmlFile()  KXMLGUIClient
xtWidget()  QXtWidget
xValue()  KXYSelector
```

```
xVelocity()  QCanvasItem
y()  QWidget QMouseEvent QWheelEvent QIconViewItem
     QCanvasItem KToolBoxManager
yearEnteredSlot()  KDateInternalYearSelector
yValue()  KXYSelector
yVelocity()  QCanvasItem
z()  QCanvasItem
```

✦   ✦   ✦

Returned By

Objects are normally constructed by directly calling the constructor for the class, but objects can also be produced by calling either a static method of some class or a method of an object.

There are different reasons for returning objects from a method call. It is common to return an object just to contain a collection of returned values. Sometimes the returned value is an object that is being used internally by the object producing it, and sometimes the method acts as a kind of factory that creates an object using information that has been stored in the parent object.

This appendix lists all of the methods that return objects, with three exceptions. The methods that return `QString`, `QCString`, and `QSize` objects are not included in this list; there are several hundred methods that return each of these objects, making such a listing virtually useless.

Methods that Return Objects

```
KAboutContainer
    KAboutContainerBase::addContainer()
    KAboutContainerBase::addContainerPage()
    KAboutDialog::addContainer()
    KAboutDialog::addContainerPage()

KAboutData
    KInstance::aboutData()

KAction
    KActionCollection::action()
    KActionCollection::take()
    KStdAction::aboutApp()
    KStdAction::aboutKDE()
    KStdAction::action()
    KStdAction::actualSize()
    KStdAction::addBookmark()
    KStdAction::back()
    KStdAction::close()
    KStdAction::configureToolbars()
```

```
KStdAction::copy()
KStdAction::cut()
KStdAction::editBookmarks()
KStdAction::find()
KStdAction::findNext()
KStdAction::findPrev()
KStdAction::firstPage()
KStdAction::fitToHeight()
KStdAction::fitToPage()
KStdAction::fitToWidth()
KStdAction::forward()
KStdAction::goTo()
KStdAction::gotoLine()
KStdAction::gotoPage()
KStdAction::help()
KStdAction::helpContents()
KStdAction::home()
KStdAction::keyBindings()
KStdAction::lastPage()
KStdAction::mail()
KStdAction::next()
KStdAction::open()
KStdAction::openNew()
KStdAction::paste()
KStdAction::preferences()
KStdAction::print()
KStdAction::printPreview()
KStdAction::prior()
KStdAction::quit()
KStdAction::redisplay()
KStdAction::redo()
KStdAction::replace()
KStdAction::reportBug()
KStdAction::revert()
KStdAction::save()
KStdAction::saveAs()
KStdAction::saveOptions()
KStdAction::selectAll()
KStdAction::spelling()
KStdAction::undo()
KStdAction::up()
KStdAction::whatsThis()
KStdAction::zoom()
KStdAction::zoomIn()
KStdAction::zoomOut()
KXMLGUIClient::action()

KActionCollection
    KAction::parentCollection()
    KEditToolbarWidget::actionCollection()
    KXMLGUIClient::actionCollection()
    KDirOperator::actionCollection()
```

KAnimWidget
    KToolBar::animatedWidget()

KApplication
    KApplication::kApplication()

KCModule
    KURIFilterPlugin::configModule()

KCharsets
    KGlobal::charsets()
    KInstance::charsets()

KCmdLineArgs
    KCmdLineArgs::parsedArgs()

KColorDrag
    KColorDrag::makeDrag()

KCompTreeNode
    KCompTreeNode::childAt()
    KCompTreeNode::find()
    KCompTreeNode::firstChild()
    KCompTreeNode::insert()
    KCompTreeNode::lastChild()

KCompletion
    KCompletionBase::completionObject()
    KDirOperator::completionObject()
    KDirOperator::dirCompletionObject()

KConfig
    KApplication::sessionConfig()
    KGlobal::config()
    KInstance::config()

KConfigBase
    KConfigGroupSaver::config()

KCookieList
    KCookieJar::getCookieList()

KDialogBase
    KPropertiesDialog::dialog()

KDirWatch
    KDirWatch::self()

KDockManager
    KDockWidget::dockManager()
    KDockMainWindow::manager()

KDockWidget
    KDockWidgetAbstractHeaderDrag::dockWidget()
    KDockWidget::manualDock()
    KDockManager::findWidgetParentDock()
    KDockManager::getDockWidgetFromName()
    KDockMainWindow::createDockWidget()
    KDockMainWindow::getMainDockWidget()

KFileBookmark
    KFileBookmarkManager::getBookmark()
    KFileBookmarkManager::getRoot()

KFileDialog
    KURLRequester::fileDialog()

KFileItem
    KDirLister::find()
    KDirLister::rootItem()
    KPropertiesDialog::item()

KFileManager
    KFileManager::getFileManager()

KFileReader
    KDirOperator::fileReader()

KFileView
    KDirOperator::view()

KFileViewItem
    KFileListViewItem::fileInfo()
    KFileIconViewItem::fileInfo()
    KFileView::firstItem()
    KFileViewItemList::findByName()
    KFileViewItem::next()

KFileViewItemList
    KDirOperator::selectedItems()
    KFileReader::currentContents()
    KFileView::items()
    KFileView::selectedItems()

KFormula
    KFormulaEdit::getFormula()

KHTMLPart
    KHTMLPart::parentPart()
    KHTMLView::part()

KHTMLPartBrowserExtension
    KHTMLPart::browserExtension()

```
KHTMLSettings
    KHTMLFactory::defaultHTMLSettings()

KHTMLView
    KHTMLPart::view()

KIcon
    KIconTheme::iconPath()

KIconLoader
    KGlobal::iconLoader()
    KInstance::iconLoader()

KIconTheme
    KIconLoader::theme()

KInstance
    KGlobal::instance()
    KActionCollection::instance()
    KXMLGUIBuilder::builderInstance()
    KXMLGUIClient::instance()
    KHTMLFactory::instance()
    KWriteFactory::instance()

KJSProxy
    KHTMLPart::jScript()

KJavaAppletContext
    KJavaAppletContext::getDefaultContext()

KJavaAppletServer
    KJavaAppletServer::allocateJavaServer()

KLibFactory
    KLibrary::factory()
    KLibLoader::factory()

KLibLoader
    KLibLoader::self()

KLibrary
    KLibLoader::library()

KLineEdit
    KToolBar::getLined()
    KURLRequester::lineEdit()

KLocale
    KGlobal::locale()

KMenuBar
    KTMainWindow::menuBar()
```

```
KMimeMagic
    KMimeMagic::self()

KMimeMagicResult
    KMimeMagic::findBufferFileType()
    KMimeMagic::findBufferType()
    KMimeMagic::findFileType()

KOpenWithHandler
    KOpenWithHandler::getOpenWithHandler()

KPanelMenu
    KPanelMenu::insertMenu()

KPixmap
    KPixmapEffect::blend()
    KPixmapEffect::channelIntensity()
    KPixmapEffect::contrast()
    KPixmapEffect::createTiled()
    KPixmapEffect::desaturate()
    KPixmapEffect::dither()
    KPixmapEffect::fade()
    KPixmapEffect::gradient()
    KPixmapEffect::hash()
    KPixmapEffect::intensity()
    KPixmapEffect::pattern()
    KPixmapEffect::toGray()
    KPixmapEffect::unbalancedGradient()

KProtocolManager
    KProtocolManager::self()

KRecentFilesAction
    KStdAction::openRecent()

KServiceGroup
    KBuildServiceGroupFactory::addNewEntry()
    KBuildServiceGroupFactory::createEntry()

KServiceType
    KBuildServiceTypeFactory::findServiceTypeByName()

KServiceTypeProfile
    KServiceTypeProfile::serviceTypeProfile()

KSpellConfig
    KSpell::ksConfig()
    KWrite::ksConfig()

KStandardDirs
    KGlobal::dirs()
    KInstance::dirs()
```

KStatusBar
    KTMainWindow::statusBar()

KStyle
    KApplication::kstyle()

KSycoca
    KSycoca::self()

KSycocaEntry
    KBuildServiceFactory::createEntry()
    KBuildServiceTypeFactory::createEntry()
    KBuildImageIOFactory::createEntry()
    KSycocaFactory::createEntry()

KSycocaResourceList
    KSycocaFactory::resourceList()

KTarDirectory
    KTarBase::directory()

KTarEntry
    KTarDirectory::entry()

KThemePixmap
    KThemeCache::horizontalPixmap()
    KThemeCache::pixmap()
    KThemeCache::verticalPixmap()
    KThemeBase::borderPixmap()
    KThemeBase::scalePixmap()
    KThemeBase::uncached()

KToggleAction
    KStdAction::showMenubar()
    KStdAction::showStatusbar()
    KStdAction::showToolbar()

KToolBar
    KTMainWindow::toolBar()
    KFileDialog::toolBar()

KToolBarButton
    KToolBar::getButton()

KTrader
    KTrader::self()

KURIFilter
    KURIFilter::self()

KURL
    KCmdLineArgs::makeURL()
    KCmdLineArgs::url()

```
            KDirLister::url()
            KFileItem::url()
            KURIFilterData::uri()
            KURIFilter::filteredURI()
            KDirOperator::url()
            KFileDialog::baseURL()
            KFileDialog::getOpenURL()
            KFileDialog::getSaveURL()
            KFileDialog::selectedURL()
            KPropertiesDialog::currentDir()
            KPropertiesDialog::kurl()
            KURLRequesterDlg::getURL()
            KURLRequesterDlg::selectedURL()
            KHTMLPart::baseURL()
            KHTMLPart::completeURL()

KWCommand
        KWCommandGroup::addCommand()

KWCommandData
        KWCommandGroupData::command()
        KWCommandGroupData::containsAccel()

KWCommandGroup
        KWCommandDispatcher::addGroup()

KWCommandGroupData
        KWKeyData::group()

KWCursor
        KWBookmark::cursor()

KWLineAttribute
        KWLineAttributeList::first()
        KWLineAttributeList::next()

KWriteDoc
        KWrite::doc()

KWriteView
        KWrite::view()

KWriteWidget
        KWrite::widget()

KXMLGUIBuilder
        KXMLGUIClient::clientBuilder()

KXMLGUIClient
        KXMLGUIClient::parentClient()
```

```
KXMLGUIFactory
    KTMainWindow::guiFactory()
    KXMLGUIClient::factory()

KeyValueMap
    QConfigDB::get()

QBaseBucket
    QBaseBucket::getNext()

QBitArray
    QBitArray::~()
    QBitArray::copy()

QBitmap
    QBitmap::xForm()
    QCursor::bitmap()
    QCursor::mask()
    QPixmap::createHeuristicMask()
    QPixmap::mask()
    QVariant::asBitmap()
    QVariant::toBitmap()

QBrush
    QPainter::brush()
    QColorGroup::brush()
    QPalette::brush()
    QVariant::asBrush()
    QVariant::toBrush()
    QIconView::itemTextBackground()
    QTextView::paper()
    QWellArray::cellBrush()
    QCanvasPolygonalItem::brush()
    KThemeBase::pixmapBrush()

QButton
    QButtonGroup::find()
    QButtonGroup::selected()

QButtonGroup
    QButton::group()

QCanvas
    QCanvasItem::canvas()
    QCanvasView::canvas()

QCanvasItemList
    QCanvasItem::collisions()
    QCanvas::allItems()
    QCanvas::collisions()
```

QCanvasPixmap
    QCanvasPixmapArray::image()

QChar
    QChar::lower()
    QChar::mirroredChar()
    QChar::upper()
    QString::at()
    KCharsets::fromEntity()
    KCharSelectTable::chr()
    KCharSelect::chr()

QClipboard
    QApplication::clipboard()

QColor
    QColorDialog::getColor()
    QApplication::winStyleHighlightColor()
    QBrush::color()
    QColor::dark()
    QColor::light()
    QMovie::backgroundColor()
    QPainter::backgroundColor()
    QColorGroup::background()
    QColorGroup::base()
    QColorGroup::brightText()
    QColorGroup::button()
    QColorGroup::buttonText()
    QColorGroup::color()
    QColorGroup::dark()
    QColorGroup::foreground()
    QColorGroup::highlight()
    QColorGroup::highlightedText()
    QColorGroup::light()
    QColorGroup::mid()
    QColorGroup::midlight()
    QColorGroup::shadow()
    QColorGroup::text()
    QPalette::color()
    QPen::color()
    QTextCharFormat::color()
    QStyleSheetItem::color()
    QVariant::asColor()
    QVariant::toColor()
    QWidget::backgroundColor()
    QWidget::foregroundColor()
    QTextView::linkColor()
    QGLContext::overlayTransparentColor()
    QCanvas::backgroundColor()
    QCanvasText::color()
    KApplication::activeTextColor()
    KApplication::activeTitleColor()
    KApplication::inactiveTextColor()

```
            KApplication::inactiveTitleColor()
            KColorGroup::background()
            KColorGroup::base()
            KColorGroup::dark()
            KColorGroup::foreground()
            KColorGroup::light()
            KColorGroup::mid()
            KColorGroup::text()
            KConfigBase::readColorEntry()
            KGlobalSettings::toolBarHighlightColor()
            KPalette::color()
            KRootProp::readColorEntry()
            KColorButton::color()
            KColorCells::color()
            KColorDialog::color()
            KColorDialog::grabColor()
            KDockTabBar::textColor()
            KDockTabCtl::tabTextColor()
            KDualColorButton::background()
            KDualColorButton::currentColor()
            KDualColorButton::foreground()
            KLed::color()
            KProgress::barColor()
            KFormula::getBackColor()
            KFormula::getForeColor()
            KHTMLSettings::bgColor()
            KHTMLSettings::linkColor()
            KHTMLSettings::textColor()
            KHTMLSettings::vLinkColor()
            KWriteDoc::colors()

QColorGroup
        QPalette::active()
        QPalette::disabled()
        QPalette::inactive()
        QPalette::normal()
        QVariant::asColorGroup()
        QVariant::toColorGroup()
        QWidget::colorGroup()
        QTextView::paperColorGroup()
        KThemeBase::colorGroup()

QComboBox
        KToolBar::getCombo()

QCursor
        QApplication::overrideCursor()
        QVariant::asCursor()
        QVariant::toCursor()
        QWidget::cursor()
        KCursor::arrowCursor()
        KCursor::blankCursor()
        KCursor::crossCursor()
```

```
        KCursor::handCursor()
        KCursor::ibeamCursor()
        KCursor::sizeAllCursor()
        KCursor::sizeBDiagCursor()
        KCursor::sizeFDiagCursor()
        KCursor::sizeHorCursor()
        KCursor::sizeVerCursor()
        KCursor::upArrowCursor()
        KCursor::waitCursor()
        KHTMLPart::urlCursor()
        KHTMLView::urlCursor()

QCustomMenuItem
        QMenuItem::custom()

QDataStream
        QDataStream::readBytes()
        QDataStream::readRawBytes()
        QDataStream::writeBytes()
        QDataStream::writeRawBytes()
        QGDict::read()
        QGDict::write()
        QGList::read()
        QGList::write()
        QGVector::read()
        QGVector::write()
        KSaveFile::dataStream()
        KTempFile::dataStream()
        KSycoca::findEntry()
        KSycoca::findFactory()

QDate
        QDate::addDays()
        QDateTime::date()
        KLocale::readDate()
        KDatePicker::getDate()
        KDateTable::getDate()

QDateTime
        QUrlInfo::lastModified()
        QUrlInfo::lastRead()
        QDateTime::addDays()
        QDateTime::addSecs()
        QDateTime::currentDateTime()
        QFileInfo::lastModified()
        QFileInfo::lastRead()
        KConfigBase::readDateTimeEntry()
        KTarEntry::datetime()

QDir
        QFileDialog::dir()
        QDir::current()
```

```
        QDir::home()
        QDir::root()
        QFileInfo::dir()

QDomAttr
        QDomNode::toAttr()
        QDomDocument::createAttribute()
        QDomElement::attributeNode()
        QDomElement::removeAttributeNode()
        QDomElement::setAttributeNode()

QDomCDATASection
        QDomNode::toCDATASection()
        QDomDocument::createCDATASection()

QDomCharacterData
        QDomNode::toCharacterData()

QDomComment
        QDomDocument::createComment()

QDomDocument
        QDomNode::ownerDocument()
        QDomNode::toDocument()
        KXMLGUIClient::document()

QDomDocumentFragment
        QDomNode::toDocumentFragment()
        QDomDocument::createDocumentFragment()

QDomDocumentType
        QDomNode::toDocumentType()
        QDomDocument::doctype()

QDomElement
        QDomNode::toElement()
        QDomDocument::createElement()
        QDomDocument::documentElement()

QDomEntity
        QDomNode::toEntity()

QDomEntityReference
        QDomNode::toEntityReference()
        QDomDocument::createEntityReference()

QDomImplementation
        QDomDocument::implementation()

QDomMimeSourceFactory
        QDomDocument::mimeSourceFactory()
        QDomMimeSourceFactory::defaultDomFactory()
```

```
QDomNamedNodeMap
    QDomNode::attributes()
    QDomDocumentType::entities()
    QDomDocumentType::notations()
    QDomElement::attributes()

QDomNode
    QDomNode::appendChild()
    QDomNode::cloneNode()
    QDomNode::firstChild()
    QDomNode::insertAfter()
    QDomNode::insertBefore()
    QDomNode::lastChild()
    QDomNode::namedItem()
    QDomNode::nextSibling()
    QDomNode::parentNode()
    QDomNode::previousSibling()
    QDomNode::removeChild()
    QDomNode::replaceChild()
    QDomNodeList::item()
    QDomNamedNodeMap::item()
    QDomNamedNodeMap::namedItem()
    QDomNamedNodeMap::removeNamedItem()
    QDomNamedNodeMap::setNamedItem()

QDomNodeList
    QDomNode::childNodes()
    QDomDocument::elementsByTagName()

QDomNotation
    QDomNode::toNotation()

QDomProcessingInstruction
    QDomNode::toProcessingInstruction()
    QDomDocument::createProcessingInstruction()

QDomText
    QDomNode::toText()
    QDomDocument::createTextNode()
    QDomText::splitText()

QFile
    KSaveFile::file()
    KTempFile::file()

QFileIconProvider
    QFileDialog::iconProvider()

QFont
    QFontDialog::getFont()
    QApplication::font()
    QFontDatabase::font()
    QFont::defaultFont()
```

```
        QFontInfo::font()
        QPainter::font()
        QTextCharFormat::font()
        QVariant::asFont()
        QVariant::toFont()
        QWidget::font()
        QToolTip::font()
        QCanvasText::font()
        QDomElement::toFont()
        KCharsets::fontForChar()
        KConfigBase::readFontEntry()
        KGlobal::fixedFont()
        KGlobal::generalFont()
        KGlobal::menuFont()
        KGlobal::toolBarFont()
        KRootProp::readFontEntry()
        KDockTabCtl::tabFont()
        KFontChooser::font()
        KFontDialog::font()
        KFormula::getFont()

QFontInfo
        QPainter::fontInfo()
        QWidget::fontInfo()

QFontMetrics
        QApplication::fontMetrics()
        QPainter::fontMetrics()
        QWidget::fontMetrics()

QFrame
        KAboutContainerBase::addEmptyPage()
        KAboutContainerBase::addTextPage()
        KAboutDialog::addPage()
        KAboutDialog::addTextPage()
        KDialogBase::addPage()
        KDialogBase::makeMainWidget()
        KDialogBase::plainPage()

QGLContext
        QGLContext::currentContext()
        QGLWidget::context()
        QGLWidget::overlayContext()

QGLFormat
        QGLFormat::defaultFormat()
        QGLFormat::defaultOverlayFormat()
        QGLContext::format()
        QGLWidget::format()

QGrid
        KDialogBase::addGridPage()
        KDialogBase::makeGridMainWidget()
```

```
QHBox
    KDialogBase::addHBoxPage()
    KDialogBase::makeHBoxMainWidget()

QHeader
    QListView::header()

QIODevice
    QImageIO::ioDevice()
    QPNGImageWriter::device()
    QDataStream::device()
    QTextStream::device()

QIconSet
    QVariant::asIconSet()
    QVariant::toIconSet()
    QHeader::iconSet()
    QMenuItem::iconSet()
    QMenuData::iconSet()
    QPushButton::iconSet()
    QTab::iconSet()
    QToolButton::iconSet()
    QToolButton::offIconSet()
    QToolButton::onIconSet()
    KAction::iconSet()

QIconView
    QIconViewItem::iconView()

QIconViewItem
    QIconViewItem::nextItem()
    QIconViewItem::prevItem()
    QIconView::currentItem()
    QIconView::findFirstVisibleItem()
    QIconView::findItem()
    QIconView::findLastVisibleItem()
    QIconView::firstItem()
    QIconView::lastItem()

QImage
    QImageDecoder::image()
    QClipboard::image()
    QImage::convertBitOrder()
    QImage::convertDepth()
    QImage::convertDepthWithPalette()
    QImage::copy()
    QImage::createAlphaMask()
    QImage::createHeuristicMask()
    QImage::mirror()
    QImage::smoothScale()
    QImage::swapRGB()
    QImageIO::image()
```

```
            QPixmap::convertToImage()
            QVariant::asImage()
            QVariant::toImage()
            KIconEffect::apply()
            KIconEffect::doublePixels()
            KImageEffect::blend()
            KImageEffect::channelIntensity()
            KImageEffect::contrast()
            KImageEffect::desaturate()
            KImageEffect::dither()
            KImageEffect::fade()
            KImageEffect::flatten()
            KImageEffect::gradient()
            KImageEffect::hash()
            KImageEffect::intensity()
            KImageEffect::modulate()
            KImageEffect::toGray()
            KImageEffect::unbalancedGradient()
            KPixmapIO::convertToImage()
            KPixmapIO::getImage()

QImageFormat
        QImageFormatType::decoderFor()

QImageFormatType
        QImageDecoder::format()

QJpUnicodeConv
        QJpUnicodeConv::newConverter()

QLayout
        QLayoutItem::layout()
        QLayout::layout()
        QWidget::layout()

QLayoutItem
        QGLayoutIterator::current()
        QGLayoutIterator::next()
        QGLayoutIterator::takeCurrent()
        KTMLayoutIterator::current()
        KTMLayoutIterator::next()
        KTMLayoutIterator::takeCurrent()

QLayoutIterator
        QLayoutItem::iterator()
        QLayout::iterator()
        QGridLayout::iterator()
        QBoxLayout::iterator()
        KTMLayout::iterator()

QLineEdit
        QComboBox::lineEdit()
```

```
QListBox
    QComboBox::listBox()
    QListBoxItem::listBox()

QListBoxItem
    QListBox::findItem()
    QListBox::firstItem()
    QListBox::item()
    QListBox::itemAt()
    QListBoxItem::next()
    QListBoxItem::prev()

QListView
    QListViewItem::listView()

QListViewItem
    QListViewItem::firstChild()
    QListViewItem::itemAbove()
    QListViewItem::itemBelow()
    QListViewItem::nextSibling()
    QListViewItem::parent()
    QListView::currentItem()
    QListView::firstChild()
    QListView::itemAt()
    QListView::selectedItem()
    QListViewItemIterator::current()

QMainWindow
    QToolBar::mainWindow()

QMenuBar
    QLayout::menuBar()
    QMainWindow::menuBar()

QMenuItem
    QMenuData::findItem()

QMetaObject
    QMetaObject::new_metaobject()
    QMetaObject::superClass()
    QObject::metaObject()

QMetaProperty
    QMetaObject::new_metaproperty()
    QMetaObject::property()

QMimeSource
    QClipboard::data()
    QMimeSourceFactory::data()

QMimeSourceFactory
    QMimeSourceFactory::defaultFactory()
    QTextView::mimeSourceFactory()
```

```
QMovie
    QLabel::movie()

QNPInstance
    QNPStream::instance()
    QNPWidget::instance()
    QNPlugin::newInstance()

QNPStream
    QNPInstance::newStream()

QNPWidget
    QNPInstance::newWindow()
    QNPInstance::widget()

QNPlugin
    QNPlugin::actual()
    QNPlugin::create()

QNetworkOperation
    QNetworkProtocol::operationInProgress()
    QUrlOperator::get()
    QUrlOperator::listChildren()
    QUrlOperator::mkdir()
    QUrlOperator::put()
    QUrlOperator::remove()
    QUrlOperator::rename()

QNetworkProtocol
    QNetworkProtocolFactoryBase::createObject()
    QNetworkProtocolFactory::createObject()
    QNetworkProtocol::getNetworkProtocol()

QObject
    QConnection::object()
    QChildEvent::child()
    QGuardedPtrPrivate::object()
    QObject::child()
    QObject::parent()
    KLibFactory::create()
    KAction::component()

QObjectList
    QObject::children()
    QObject::objectTrees()
    QObject::queryList()

QPaintDevice
    QPainter::device()
    QGLContext::device()

QPalette
    QApplication::palette()
    QPalette::copy()
```

```
            QVariant::asPalette()
            QVariant::toPalette()
            QWidget::palette()
            QToolTip::palette()

        QPen
            QPainter::pen()
            QCanvasPolygonalItem::pen()
            QDomElement::toPen()

        QPixmap
            QFileIconProvider::pixmap()
            QMessageBox::iconPixmap()
            QMessageBox::standardIcon()
            QBrush::pixmap()
            QClipboard::pixmap()
            QDragObject::pixmap()
            QIconSet::pixmap()
            QMovie::framePixmap()
            QPixmapCache::find()
            QPixmap::grabWidget()
            QPixmap::grabWindow()
            QPixmap::xForm()
            QVariant::asPixmap()
            QVariant::toPixmap()
            QWidget::backgroundPixmap()
            QWidget::icon()
            QButton::pixmap()
            QComboBox::pixmap()
            QIconViewItem::pixmap()
            QLabel::pixmap()
            QListBox::pixmap()
            QListBoxItem::pixmap()
            QListBoxPixmap::pixmap()
            QListViewItem::pixmap()
            QMenuItem::pixmap()
            QMenuData::pixmap()
            QGLWidget::renderPixmap()
            QCanvas::backgroundPixmap()
            QDomMimeSourceFactory::pixmap()
            KApplication::icon()
            KApplication::miniIcon()
            KIconEffect::apply()
            KIconLoader::loadIcon()
            KWM::icon()
            KWM::miniIcon()
            KFileItem::pixmap()
            KMimeType::pixmap()
            KMimeType::pixmapForURL()
            KService::pixmap()
            KAction::pixmap()
            KDialogBaseTile::get()
            KDialogBase::getBackgroundTile()
            KPixmapIO::convertToPixmap()
```

```
            KPopupTitle::icon()
            KPopupMenu::titlePixmap()
            KPopupTitle::icon()
            KPopupMenu::titlePixmap()
            KProgress::barPixmap()
            KThemePixmap::border()
            KURLLabel::pixmap()
            KFileViewItem::pixmap()

QPoint
            QCursor::hotSpot()
            QCursor::pos()
            QDragObject::pixmapHotSpot()
            QMouseEvent::globalPos()
            QMouseEvent::pos()
            QWheelEvent::globalPos()
            QWheelEvent::pos()
            QMoveEvent::oldPos()
            QMoveEvent::pos()
            QDropEvent::pos()
            QImage::offset()
            QPainter::brushOrigin()
            QPainter::pos()
            QPainter::xForm()
            QPainter::xFormDev()
            QPoint::*()
            QRect::bottomLeft()
            QRect::bottomRight()
            QRect::center()
            QRect::topLeft()
            QRect::topRight()
            QVariant::asPoint()
            QVariant::toPoint()
            QWidget::mapFromGlobal()
            QWidget::mapFromParent()
            QWidget::mapToGlobal()
            QWidget::mapToParent()
            QWidget::pos()
            QWMatrix::map()
            QIconViewItem::pos()
            QScrollView::contentsToViewport()
            QScrollView::viewportToContents()
            QDomElement::toPoint()
            KConfigBase::readPointEntry()

QPointArray
            QPainter::xForm()
            QPainter::xFormDev()
            QVariant::asPointArray()
            QVariant::toPointArray()
            QWMatrix::map()
            QCanvasPolygonalItem::areaPoints()
            QCanvasPolygonalItem::areaPointsAdvanced()
            QCanvasRectangle::areaPoints()
```

```
            QCanvasPolygon::areaPoints()
            QCanvasPolygon::points()
            QCanvasEllipse::areaPoints()

    QPopupMenu
            QMenuItem::popup()
            QPushButton::popup()
            QToolButton::popup()
            KSelectAction::popupMenu()
            KActionMenu::popupMenu()
            KDockManager::dockHideShowMenu()
            KDockMainWindow::dockHideShowMenu()
            KHelpMenu::menu()
            KTMainWindow::helpMenu()
            KToolBarButton::popup()

    QPrinter
            QPrintDialog::printer()

    QPushButton
            QWizard::backButton()
            QWizard::cancelButton()
            QWizard::finishButton()
            QWizard::helpButton()
            QWizard::nextButton()
            KButtonBox::addButton()
            KDialogBase::actionButton()

    QRect
            QLayoutItem::geometry()
            QSpacerItem::geometry()
            QWidgetItem::geometry()
            QLayout::geometry()
            QPaintEvent::rect()
            QDragMoveEvent::answerRect()
            QFontMetrics::boundingRect()
            QImage::rect()
            QGridLayout::cellGeometry()
            QMovie::getValidRect()
            QPainter::boundingRect()
            QPainter::viewport()
            QPainter::window()
            QPainter::xForm()
            QPainter::xFormDev()
            QPixmap::rect()
            QRect::&()
            QRect::intersect()
            QRect::normalize()
            QRect::unite()
            QRegion::boundingRect()
            QRichTextFormatter::lineGeometry()
            QTextTableCell::geometry()
            QRichTextIterator::lineGeometry()
            QVariant::asRect()
```

```
QVariant::toRect()
QWidget::childrenRect()
QWidget::frameGeometry()
QWidget::geometry()
QWidget::microFocusHint()
QWidget::rect()
QWidget::visibleRect()
QWMatrix::map()
QFrame::contentsRect()
QFrame::frameRect()
QCommonStyle::comboButtonFocusRect()
QCommonStyle::comboButtonRect()
QIconViewItem::pixmapRect()
QIconViewItem::rect()
QIconViewItem::textRect()
QListBox::itemRect()
QListView::itemRect()
QMotifStyle::comboButtonFocusRect()
QMotifStyle::comboButtonRect()
QPlatinumStyle::buttonRect()
QPlatinumStyle::comboButtonFocusRect()
QPlatinumStyle::comboButtonRect()
QSlider::sliderRect()
QTab::rect()
QWindowsStyle::comboButtonFocusRect()
QWindowsStyle::comboButtonRect()
QCanvasItem::boundingRect()
QCanvasItem::boundingRectAdvanced()
QCanvasSprite::boundingRect()
QCanvasPolygonalItem::boundingRect()
QCanvasRectangle::rect()
QCanvasText::boundingRect()
QDomElement::toRect()
KConfigBase::readRectEntry()
KDEStyle::buttonRect()
KDEStyle::comboButtonFocusRect()
KDEStyle::comboButtonRect()
KWin::clientArea()
KWin::edgeClientArea()
KWM::geometry()
KWM::geometryRestore()
KWM::iconGeometry()
KWM::setProperties()
KWM::windowRegion()
KDialogBase::getContentsRect()
KXYSelector::contentsRect()
KSelector::contentsRect()
KThemeStyle::buttonRect()
KTMainWindow::mainViewGeometry()
KFormula::getCursorPos()
KStepStyle::buttonRect()
KStepStyle::comboButtonFocusRect()
KStepStyle::comboButtonRect()
KStepStyle::buttonRect()
```

```
        KStepStyle::comboButtonFocusRect()
        KStepStyle::comboButtonRect()

    QRegion
        QPaintEvent::region()
        QPainter::clipRegion()
        QRegion::&()
        QRegion::eor()
        QRegion::intersect()
        QRegion::subtract()
        QRegion::unite()
        QVariant::asRegion()
        QVariant::toRegion()
        QWidget::childrenRegion()

    QRichText
        QTextTableCell::richText()

    QScrollBar
        QScrollView::horizontalScrollBar()
        QScrollView::verticalScrollBar()

    QSignal
        QMenuItem::signal()

    QSizePolicy
        QSizeGrip::sizePolicy()
        QWidget::sizePolicy()
        QFrame::sizePolicy()
        QCheckBox::sizePolicy()
        QComboBox::sizePolicy()
        QHeader::sizePolicy()
        QIconView::sizePolicy()
        QLabel::sizePolicy()
        QLCDNumber::sizePolicy()
        QLineEdit::sizePolicy()
        QMultiLineEdit::sizePolicy()
        QProgressBar::sizePolicy()
        QPushButton::sizePolicy()
        QRadioButton::sizePolicy()
        QScrollBar::sizePolicy()
        QScrollView::sizePolicy()
        QSlider::sizePolicy()
        QSpinBox::sizePolicy()
        QSplitter::sizePolicy()
        QTabBar::sizePolicy()
        QToolButton::sizePolicy()
        QWorkspace::sizePolicy()
        KNumInput::sizePolicy()
        KProgress::sizePolicy()
        KToolBar::sizePolicy()
        QXEmbed::sizePolicy()
        KFormulaEdit::sizePolicy()
```

QSpacerItem
    QLayoutItem::spacerItem()
    QSpacerItem::spacerItem()

QStatusBar
    QMainWindow::statusBar()

QStrList
    QImageDecoder::inputFormats()
    QImage::inputFormats()
    QImage::outputFormats()
    QImageIO::inputFormats()
    QImageIO::outputFormats()
    QMetaProperty::enumKeys()
    QMetaProperty::valueToKeys()
    QMetaObject::propertyNames()
    QMetaObject::signalNames()
    QMetaObject::slotNames()
    QDir::encodedEntryList()
    KProcess::args()

QStringList
    QFileDialog::getOpenFileNames()
    QFileDialog::selectedFiles()
    QFontDatabase::charSets()
    QFontDatabase::families()
    QFontDatabase::styles()
    QFont::substitutions()
    QImage::inputFormatList()
    QImage::outputFormatList()
    QImage::textKeys()
    QImage::textLanguages()
    QMimeSourceFactory::filePath()
    QObject::superClasses()
    QSessionManager::discardCommand()
    QSessionManager::restartCommand()
    QVariant::asStringList()
    QVariant::toStringList()
    QDir::entryList()
    QStringList::fromStrList()
    QStringList::grep()
    QStringList::split()
    KCharsets::availableCharsetNames()
    KCompletion::allMatches()
    KCompletion::items()
    KConfig::groupList()
    KConfigBase::groupList()
    KConfigBase::readListEntry()
    KDesktopFile::readActions()
    KIconLoader::loadAnimated()
    KIconLoader::queryIcons()
    KIconTheme::inherits()
    KIconTheme::list()
    KIconTheme::queryIcons()

```
            KLocale::languageList()
            KPalette::getPaletteList()
            KProtocolManager::listing()
            KProtocolManager::protocols()
            KRootProp::listEntries()
            KStandardDirs::allTypes()
            KStandardDirs::findAllResources()
            KStandardDirs::findDirs()
            KStandardDirs::resourceDirs()
            KStringHandler::capwords()
            KStringHandler::reverse()
            KStringHandler::split()
            KCookieJar::getDomainList()
            KImageIO::mimeTypes()
            KImageIO::types()
            KMimeType::patterns()
            KMimeType::propertyNames()
            KService::libraryDependencies()
            KService::propertyNames()
            KService::serviceTypes()
            KServiceType::propertyDefNames()
            KServiceType::propertyNames()
            KTarDirectory::entries()
            KSelectAction::items()
            KActionCollection::groups()
            KXMLGUIBuilder::containerTags()
            KXMLGUIBuilder::customTags()
            KFileDialog::getOpenFileNames()
            KFileDialog::selectedFiles()
            KURLComboBox::urls()
            KHTMLPart::frameNames()
            KHTMLPartBrowserHostExtension::frameNames()
            KSpellConfig::ignoreList()
            KSpell::suggestions()

    QStyle
        QApplication::style()
        QWidget::style()

    QStyleSheet
        QStyleSheetItem::styleSheet()
        QStyleSheet::defaultSheet()
        QTextView::styleSheet()

    QStyleSheetItem
        QStyleSheet::item()

    QTab
        QTabBar::tab()

    QTextCharFormat
        QTextCharFormat::formatWithoutCustom()
        QTextCharFormat::makeTextFormat()
        QTextFormatCollection::registerFormat()
```

```
        QTextRichString::formatAt()
        QRichTextFormatter::format()
        QRichTextIterator::format()

    QTextCodec
        QApplication::defaultCodec()
        QTextCodec::codecForContent()
        QTextCodec::codecForIndex()
        QTextCodec::codecForLocale()
        QTextCodec::codecForMib()
        QTextCodec::codecForName()
        QTextCodec::loadCharmap()
        QTextCodec::loadCharmapFile()

    QTextCustomItem
        QTextCharFormat::customItem()
        QTextRichString::customItemAt()
        QStyleSheet::tag()

    QTextDecoder
        QBig5Codec::makeDecoder()
        QEucJpCodec::makeDecoder()
        QEucKrCodec::makeDecoder()
        QGbkCodec::makeDecoder()
        QJisCodec::makeDecoder()
        QSjisCodec::makeDecoder()
        QTextCodec::makeDecoder()
        QUtf8Codec::makeDecoder()
        QUtf16Codec::makeDecoder()

    QTextEncoder
        QTextCodec::makeEncoder()
        QUtf16Codec::makeEncoder()

    QTextFlow
        QTextParagraph::flow()

    QTextParagraph
        QTextParagraph::lastChild()
        QTextParagraph::nextInDocument()
        QTextParagraph::prevInDocument()
        QRichTextIterator::outmostParagraph()
        QRichText::getParBefore()

    QTextStream
        QTextStream::readRawBytes()
        QTextStream::writeRawBytes()
        KSaveFile::textStream()
        KTempFile::textStream()

    QTime
        QTime::addMSecs()
        QTime::addSecs()
        QDateTime::time()
```

QToolButton
    QWhatsThis::whatsThisButton()
    KURLRequester::button()

QToolTipGroup
    QMainWindow::toolTipGroup()
    QToolTip::group()

QUrl
    QFileDialog::url()

QUrlInfo
    QUrlOperator::info()

QUrlOperator
    QNetworkProtocol::url()

QVBox
    KDialogBase::addVBoxPage()
    KDialogBase::makeVBoxMainWidget()

QValidator
    QComboBox::validator()
    QLineEdit::validator()
    QMultiLineEdit::validator()
    QSpinBox::validator()

QVariant
    QObject::property()
    QVariant::asMap()
    QVariant::mapBegin()
    QVariant::mapEnd()
    QVariant::mapFind()
    QVariant::toMap()
    KConfigBase::readPropertyEntry()
    KMimeType::property()
    KService::property()
    KServiceType::property()

QWMatrix
    QPainter::worldMatrix()
    QPixmap::trueMatrix()
    QWMatrix::invert()
    QWMatrix::rotate()
    QWMatrix::scale()
    QWMatrix::shear()
    QWMatrix::translate()

QWidget
    QTabDialog::currentPage()
    QWizard::currentPage()
    QWizard::page()
    QLayoutItem::widget()
    QWidgetItem::widget()

```
QLayout::mainWidget()
QApplication::activeModalWidget()
QApplication::activePopupWidget()
QApplication::activeWindow()
QApplication::desktop()
QApplication::focusWidget()
QApplication::mainWidget()
QApplication::widgetAt()
QDragObject::source()
QDragObject::target()
QDropEvent::source()
QFocusData::focusWidget()
QFocusData::home()
QFocusData::next()
QFocusData::prev()
QWidget::find()
QWidget::focusProxy()
QWidget::focusWidget()
QWidget::keyboardGrabber()
QWidget::mouseGrabber()
QWidget::parentWidget()
QWidget::topLevelWidget()
QLabel::buddy()
QMainWindow::centralWidget()
QMenuItem::widget()
QScrollView::clipper()
QScrollView::cornerWidget()
QScrollView::viewport()
QTabWidget::currentPage()
QToolTip::parentWidget()
QWidgetStack::visibleWidget()
QWidgetStack::widget()
QWorkspace::activeWindow()
KAction::container()
KAction::representative()
KContainerLayout::widget()
KDialogBase::getMainWidget()
KDockTabCtl::getFirstPage()
KDockTabCtl::getLastPage()
KDockTabCtl::getNextPage()
KDockTabCtl::getPrevPage()
KDockTabCtl::page()
KDockTabCtl::visiblePage()
KDockWidget::getWidget()
KDockSplitter::getAnother()
KDockSplitter::getFirst()
KDockSplitter::getLast()
KTMainWindow::indicator()
KTMainWindow::view()
KToolBar::getWidget()
KXMLGUIFactory::container()
KXMLGUIBuilder::createContainer()
KCombiView::widget()
KFileDetailView::widget()
```

```
        KFileIconView::widget()
        KFilePreview::widget()
        KFileView::widget()

QWidgetList
        QApplication::allWidgets()
        QApplication::topLevelWidgets()
        QWorkspace::windowList()

QWindowsMime
        QWindowsMime::convertor()

QtTriple
        QRichTextFormatter::position()
        QRichTextIterator::position()
```

◆   ◆   ◆

Enumerated Types

Enumerated types are named constants inside classes. They are usually used to specify the value of optional configuration settings for an object.

This appendix lists the enumerated types alphabetically by their names. There are a few anonymous enumerated types, and these are listed first. There are also several of the enumerated types that have the same name but are found in different classes. To use one of these, you must refer to it by its fully qualified name. For example, there are five enumerated types named `Orientation`. To refer to an `Orientation` value in the `KSelector` class, you would code it as follows:

```
KSelector::Vertical
```

To refer to an `Orientation` value of the `QPrinter` class, you would code it this way:

```
QPrinter::Portrait;
```

Because defining a named set of enumerations is also defining a type, these type names can be used to specify argument types passed to methods. This way, the compiler effectively has the capability to verify that a valid value is being passed to a method; because if the value is of the correct enumerated type, it must be one of the known values. There are a few anonymous enumerations, and they are listed first.

KDE/Qt Enumerated Types

```
(anonymous)
    KApplication::(anon) { SETTINGS_MOUSE,
SETTINGS_COMPLETION,
        SETTINGS_PATHS, SETTINGS_POPUPMENU };
    KButtonBox::(anon) { VERTICAL=1,
HORIZONTAL=2 };
```

```
KContainerLayout::(anon) { Horizontal=0, Vertical };
KEdit::(anon) { NONE, FORWARD, BACKWARD };
KFileBookmark::(anon) { URL, Folder };
KKeyChooser::(anon) { NoKey=1, DefaultKey, CustomKey };
KMessageBox::(anon) { Ok=1, Cancel=2, Yes=3, No=4,
   Continue=5 };
KNotifyClient::(anon) { Default=-1, None=0, Sound=1,
   Messagebox=2, Logfile=4, Stderr=8 };
KWActionGroup::(anon) { ugNone, ugPaste, ugDelBlock,
   ugIndent, ugUnindent, ugReplace, ugSpell, ugInsChar,
   ugDelChar, ugInsLine, ugDelLine };
KWM::(anon) { noDecoration=0, normalDecoration=1,
   tinyDecoration=2, noFocus=256, standaloneMenuBar=512,
   desktopIcon=1024, staysOnTop=2048 };
KWM::(anon) { horizontal=1, vertical=2, fullscreen=3 };
QLayout::(anon) { unlimited=QWIDGETSIZE_MAX };
QMessageBox::(anon) { Ok=1, Cancel=2, Yes=3, No=4, Abort=5,
   Retry=6, Ignore=7, ButtonMask=0x07, Default=0x100,
   Escape=0x200, FlagMask=0x300 };
QPaintDeviceMetrics::(anon) { PdmWidth=1, PdmHeight,
   PdmWidthMM, PdmHeightMM, PdmNumColors, PdmDepth, PdmDpiX,
   PdmDpiY };
QTextStream::(anon) { skipws=0x0001, left=0x0002,
   right=0x0004, internal=0x0008, bin=0x0010, oct=0x0020,
   dec=0x0040, hex=0x0080, showbase=0x0100,
   showpoint=0x0200, uppercase=0x0400, showpos=0x0800,
   scientific=0x1000, fixed=0x2000 };

Action
   KWAction::Action { replace, wordWrap, wordUnWrap, newLine,
      delLine, insLine, killLine };
   QDropEvent::Action { Copy, Link, Move, Private,
      UserAction=100 };

ActionButtonStyle
   KDialogBase::ActionButtonStyle { ActionStyle0=0,
      ActionStyle1, ActionStyle2, ActionStyle3, ActionStyle4,
      ActionStyleMAX };

Actions
   KPanelApplet::Actions { About=1, Help=2, Preferences=4 };

AdditionalStyleValues
   QStyleSheetItem::AdditionalStyleValues { Undefined=-1 };

AlignmentFlags
   Qt::AlignmentFlags { AlignLeft=0x0001, AlignRight=0x0002,
      AlignHCenter=0x0004, AlignTop=0x0008, AlignBottom=0x0010,
      AlignVCenter=0x0020,
      AlignCenter=AlignVCenter|AlignHCenter, SingleLine=0x0040,
      DontClip=0x0080, ExpandTabs=0x0100, ShowPrefix=0x0200,
      WordBreak=0x0400, DontPrint=0x1000 };
```

AnchorEdge
    KWin::AnchorEdge { Top, Bottom, Left, Right };

Arrangement
    QIconView::Arrangement { LeftToRight=0, TopToBottom };

ArrowStyle
    KThemeBase::ArrowStyle { MotifArrow, LargeArrow,
      SmallArrow };

ArrowType
    Qt::ArrowType { UpArrow, DownArrow, LeftArrow, RightArrow
      };

BackgroundMode
    QWidget::BackgroundMode { FixedColor, FixedPixmap,
      NoBackground, PaletteForeground, PaletteButton,
      PaletteLight, PaletteMidlight, PaletteDark, PaletteMid,
      PaletteText, PaletteBrightText, PaletteBase,
      PaletteBackground, PaletteShadow, PaletteHighlight,
      PaletteHighlightedText };

BackgroundOrigin
    QWidget::BackgroundOrigin { WidgetOrigin, ParentOrigin };

BarPosition
    KToolBar::BarPosition { Top=0, Left, Right, Bottom,
      Floating, Flat };

BarStatus
    KStatusBar::BarStatus { Toggle, Show, Hide };
    KToolBar::BarStatus { Toggle, Show, Hide };

BarStyle
    KProgress::BarStyle { Solid, Blocked };

BGMode
    Qt::BGMode { TransparentMode, OpaqueMode };

BorderType
    KThemePixmap::BorderType { Top=0, Bottom, Left, Right,
      TopLeft, TopRight, BottomLeft, BottomRight };

BrushStyle
    Qt::BrushStyle { NoBrush, SolidPattern, Dense1Pattern,
      Dense2Pattern, Dense3Pattern, Dense4Pattern,
      Dense5Pattern, Dense6Pattern, Dense7Pattern, HorPattern,
      VerPattern, CrossPattern, BDiagPattern, FDiagPattern,
      DiagCrossPattern, CustomPattern=24 };

Button
    KCModule::Button { Help=1, Default=2, Reset=4, Cancel=8,
      Apply=16, Ok=32, SysDefault=64 };

ButtonCode
    KDialogBase::ButtonCode { Help=0x00000001,
        Default=0x00000002, Ok=0x00000004, Apply=0x00000008,
        Try=0x00000010, Cancel=0x00000020, Close=0x00000040,
        User1=0x00000080, User2=0x00000100, User3=0x00000200,
        No=0x00000080, Yes=0x00000100, Stretch=0x80000000 };

ButtonState
    Qt::ButtonState { NoButton=0x00, LeftButton=0x01,
        RightButton=0x02, MidButton=0x04, MouseButtonMask=0x07,
        ShiftButton=0x08, ControlButton=0x10, AltButton=0x20,
        KeyButtonMask=0x38 };

ButtonSymbols
    QSpinBox::ButtonSymbols { UpDownArrows, PlusMinus };

ByteOrder
    QDataStream::ByteOrder { BigEndian, LittleEndian };

CaptionLayout
    KApplication::CaptionLayout { CaptionAppLast=1,
        CaptionAppFirst, CaptionNoApp };

Category
    QChar::Category { NoCategory, Mark_NonSpacing,
        Mark_SpacingCombining, Mark_Enclosing,
        Number_DecimalDigit, Number_Letter, Number_Other,
        Separator_Space, Separator_Line, Separator_Paragraph,
        Other_Control, Other_Format, Other_Surrogate,
        Other_PrivateUse, Other_NotAssigned, Letter_Uppercase,
        Letter_Lowercase, Letter_Titlecase, Letter_Modifier,
        Letter_Other, Punctuation_Connector, Punctuation_Dask,
        Punctuation_Open, Punctuation_Close,
        Punctuation_InitialQuote, Punctuation_FinalQuote,
        Punctuation_Other, Symbol_Math, Symbol_Currency,
        Symbol_Modifier, Symbol_Other };

CharSet
    QFont::CharSet { ISO_8859_1, Latin1=ISO_8859_1, AnyCharSet,
        ISO_8859_2, Latin2=ISO_8859_2, ISO_8859_3,
        Latin3=ISO_8859_3, ISO_8859_4, Latin4=ISO_8859_4,
        ISO_8859_5, ISO_8859_6, ISO_8859_7, ISO_8859_8,
        ISO_8859_9, Latin5=ISO_8859_9, ISO_8859_10,
        Latin6=ISO_8859_10, ISO_8859_11, ISO_8859_12,
        ISO_8859_13, Latin7=ISO_8859_13, ISO_8859_14,
        Latin8=ISO_8859_14, ISO_8859_15, Latin9=ISO_8859_15,
        KOI8R, Set_Ja, Set_1=Set_Ja, Set_Ko, Set_Th_TH, Set_Zh,
        Set_Zh_TW, Set_N=Set_Zh_TW, Unicode, Set_GBK, Set_Big5 };

Clear
    QTextCustomItem::Clear { ClearNone, ClearLeft, ClearRight,
        ClearBoth };

ColorGroup
    QPalette::ColorGroup { Normal, Disabled, Active, Inactive,
        NColorGroups };

ColorMode
    KPixmap::ColorMode { Auto, Color, Mono, LowColor, WebColor
        };
    KTextPrint::ColorMode { Color, GrayScal, BlackWhite };
    QApplication::ColorMode { NormalColors, CustomColors };
    QPixmap::ColorMode { Auto, Color, Mono };
    QPrinter::ColorMode { GrayScale, Color };

ColorRole
    QColorGroup::ColorRole { Foreground, Button, Light,
        Midlight, Dark, Mid, Text, BrightText, ButtonText, Base,
        Background, Shadow, Highlight, HighlightedText,
        NColorRoles };

ColorSpec
    QApplication::ColorSpec { NormalColor=0, CustomColor=1,
        ManyColor=2 };

Communication
    KProcess::Communication { NoCommunication=0, Stdin=1,
        Stdout=2, Stderr=4, AllOutput=6, All=7, NoRead };

Completion
    KGlobalSettings::Completion { CompletionNone=1,
        CompletionAuto, CompletionMan, CompletionShell };

ConfigState
    KConfigBase::ConfigState { NoAccess, ReadOnly, ReadWrite };

ConnectionState
    QNetworkProtocol::ConnectionState { ConHostFound,
        ConConnected, ConClosed };

ConstructorFlags
    KWrite::ConstructorFlags { kBrowser=1, kHandleOwnDND=2 };

Context
    KIcon::Context { Any, Action, Application, Device,
        FileSystem, MimeType };

Corner
    QGridLayout::Corner { TopLeft, TopRight, BottomLeft,
        BottomRight };

DCOPServiceType_t
    KService::DCOPServiceType_t { DCOP_None=0, DCOP_Unique,
        DCOP_Multi };

Decomposition
    QChar::Decomposition { Single, Canonical, Font, NoBreak,
        Initial, Medial, Final, Isolated, Circle, Super, Sub,
        Vertical, Wide, Narrow, Small, Square, Compat, Fraction
        };

DialogCode
    QDialog::DialogCode { Rejected, Accepted };

DialogType
    KDialogBase::DialogType { ,
        TreeList=KJanusWidget::TreeList,
        Tabbed=KJanusWidget::Tabbed, Plain=KJanusWidget::Plain,
        Swallow=KJanusWidget::Swallow,
        IconList=KJanusWidget::IconList };

direction
    KRuler::direction { horizontal, vertical };

Direction
    QBoxLayout::Direction { LeftToRight, RightToLeft,
        TopToBottom, BottomToTop, Down=TopToBottom,
        Up=BottomToTop };
    QChar::Direction { DirL, DirR, DirEN, DirES, DirET, DirAN,
        DirCS, DirB, DirS, DirWS, DirON, DirLRE, DirLRO, DirAL,
        DirRLE, DirRLO, DirPDF, DirNSM, DirBN };
    QGrid::Direction { Horizontal, Vertical };

DisplayMode
    QStyleSheetItem::DisplayMode { DisplayBlock, DisplayInline,
        DisplayListItem, DisplayNone };

DisposalMethod
    QPNGImageWriter::DisposalMethod { Unspecified, NoDisposal,
        RestoreBackground, RestoreImage };

DockPosition
    KDockWidget::DockPosition { DockNone=0, DockTop=0x0001,
        DockLeft=0x0002, DockRight=0x0004, DockBottom=0x0008,
        DockCenter=0x0010, DockDesktop=0x0020,
        DockCorner=DockTop|DockLeft|DockRight|DockBottom,
        DockFullSite=DockCorner|DockCenter,
        DockFullDocking=DockFullSite|DockDesktop };

DragMode
    QDragObject::DragMode { DragDefault, DragCopy, DragMove,
        DragCopyOrMove };

DualColor
    KDualColorButton::DualColor { Foreground, Background };

EchoMode
    QLineEdit::EchoMode { Normal, NoEcho, Password };
    QMultiLineEdit::EchoMode { Normal, NoEcho, Password };

EchoModes
    KPasswordEdit::EchoModes { OneStar, ThreeStars, NoEcho };

Editable
    KPalette::Editable { Yes, No, Ask };

Effects
    KIconEffect::Effects { NoEffect, ToGray, Colorize, ToGamma,
      DeSaturate, LastEffect };

Encoding
    QTextStream::Encoding { Locale, Latin1, Unicode,
      UnicodeNetworkOrder, UnicodeReverse, RawUnicode };

Endian
    QImage::Endian { IgnoreEndian, BigEndian, LittleEndian };

Error
    QNetworkProtocol::Error { NoError=0, ErrValid,
      ErrUnknownProtocol, ErrUnsupported, ErrParse,
      ErrLoginIncorrect, ErrHostNotFound, ErrListChlidren,
      ErrMkdir, ErrRemove, ErrRename, ErrGet, ErrPut,
      ErrFileNotExisting, ErrPermissionDenied };

ExpandData
    QSizePolicy::ExpandData { NoDirection=0, Horizontal=1,
      Vertical=2, BothDirections=Horizontal|Vertical };

fileResult
    KWrite::fileResult { OK, CANCEL, RETRY, ERROR };

FileView
    KFile::FileView { Default=0, Simple=1, Detail=2,
      SeparateDirs=4, PreviewContents=8, PreviewInfo=16 };

FilterSpec
    QDir::FilterSpec { Dirs=0x001, Files=0x002, Drives=0x004,
      NoSymLinks=0x008, All=0x007, TypeMask=0x00F,
      Readable=0x010, Writable=0x020, Executable=0x040,
      RWEMask=0x070, Modified=0x080, Hidden=0x100,
      System=0x200, AccessMask=0x3F0, DefaultFilter=-1 };

FixedType
    KCharsets::FixedType { FixedUnknown, Fixed, Proportional };

Flags
    KPanelApplet::Flags { Stretch=1, TopLevel=2 };

```
QMetaProperty::Flags { UnresolvedEnum=0x00000001,
   UnresolvedSet=0x00000002, UnresolvedEnumOrSet=0x00000004,
   UnresolvedStored=0x00000008,
   UnresolvedDesignable=0x00000010,
   NotDesignable=0x00000020, NotStored=0x00000040 };
```

FocusPolicy
```
   QWidget::FocusPolicy { NoFocus=0, TabFocus=0x1,
      ClickFocus=0x2, StrongFocus=0x3, WheelFocus=0x7 };
```

FontColumn
```
   KFontChooser::FontColumn { FamilyList=0x01, StyleList=0x02,
      SizeList=0x04 };
```

FormatOption
```
   QGL::FormatOption { DoubleBuffer=0x0001,
      DepthBuffer=0x0002, Rgba=0x0004, AlphaChannel=0x0008,
      AccumBuffer=0x0010, StencilBuffer=0x0020,
      StereoBuffers=0x0040, DirectRendering=0x0080,
      HasOverlay=0x0100, SingleBuffer=DoubleBuffer<<16,
      NoDepthBuffer=DepthBuffer<<16, ColorIndex=Rgba<<16,
      NoAlphaChannel=AlphaChannel<<16,
      NoAccumBuffer=AccumBuffer<<16,
      NoStencilBuffer=StencilBuffer<<16,
      NoStereoBuffers=StereoBuffers<<16,
      IndirectRendering=DirectRendering<<16,
      NoOverlay=HasOverlay<<16 };
```

Gradient
```
   KThemeBase::Gradient { GrNone, GrHorizontal, GrVertical,
      GrDiagonal, GrPyramid, GrRectangle, GrElliptic,
      GrReverseBevel };
```

GradientMode
```
   KPixmap::GradientMode { Horizontal, Vertical, Diagonal,
      CrossDiagonal };
```

GradientType
```
   KImageEffect::GradientType { VerticalGradient,
      HorizontalGradient, DiagonalGradient,
      CrossDiagonalGradient, PyramidGradient,
      RectangleGradient, PipeCrossGradient, EllipticGradient };
   KPixmapEffect::GradientType { VerticalGradient,
      HorizontalGradient, DiagonalGradient,
      CrossDiagonalGradient, PyramidGradient,
      RectangleGradient, PipeCrossGradient, EllipticGradient };
```

Group
```
   KIcon::Group { NoGroup=-1, Desktop=0, Toolbar, MainToolbar,
      Small, LastGroup, User };
```

GUIStyle
```
   Qt::GUIStyle { MacStyle, WindowsStyle, Win3Style, PMStyle,
      MotifStyle };
```

Icon
    QMessageBox::Icon { NoIcon=0, Information=1, Warning=2,
        Critical=3 };

IconText
    KToolBar::IconText { IconOnly=0, IconTextRight, TextOnly,
        IconTextBottom };

ImageConversionFlags
    Qt::ImageConversionFlags { ColorMode_Mask=0x00000003,
        AutoColor=0x00000000, ColorOnly=0x00000003,
        MonoOnly=0x00000002, AlphaDither_Mask=0x0000000c,
        ThresholdAlphaDither=0x00000000,
        OrderedAlphaDither=0x00000004,
        DiffuseAlphaDither=0x00000008, NoAlpha=0x0000000c,
        Dither_Mask=0x00000030, DiffuseDither=0x00000000,
        OrderedDither=0x00000010, ThresholdDither=0x00000020,
        DitherMode_Mask=0x000000c0, AutoDither=0x00000000,
        PreferDither=0x00000040, AvoidDither=0x00000080 };

InstanceMode
    QNPInstance::InstanceMode { Embed=1, Full=2, Background=3
        };

ItemTextPos
    QIconView::ItemTextPos { Bottom=0, Right };

ItemType
    KToolBarItem::ItemType { Lined=0, Button, Combo, Frame,
        Toggle, AnyWidget, Separator };

Joining
    QChar::Joining { OtherJoining, Dual, Right, Center };

Key
    Qt::Key { Key_Escape=0x1000, Key_Tab=0x1001,
        Key_Backtab=0x1002, Key_BackTab=Key_Backtab,
        Key_Backspace=0x1003, Key_BackSpace=Key_Backspace,
        Key_Return=0x1004, Key_Enter=0x1005, Key_Insert=0x1006,
        Key_Delete=0x1007, Key_Pause=0x1008, Key_Print=0x1009,
        Key_SysReq=0x100a, Key_Home=0x1010, Key_End=0x1011,
        Key_Left=0x1012, Key_Up=0x1013, Key_Right=0x1014,
        Key_Down=0x1015, Key_Prior=0x1016, Key_PageUp=Key_Prior,
        Key_Next=0x1017, Key_PageDown=Key_Next, Key_Shift=0x1020,
        Key_Control=0x1021, Key_Meta=0x1022, Key_Alt=0x1023,
        Key_CapsLock=0x1024, Key_NumLock=0x1025,
        Key_ScrollLock=0x1026, Key_F1=0x1030, Key_F2=0x1031,
        Key_F3=0x1032, Key_F4=0x1033, Key_F5=0x1034,
        Key_F6=0x1035, Key_F7=0x1036, Key_F8=0x1037,
        Key_F9=0x1038, Key_F10=0x1039, Key_F11=0x103a,
        Key_F12=0x103b, Key_F13=0x103c, Key_F14=0x103d,
        Key_F15=0x103e, Key_F16=0x103f, Key_F17=0x1040,
        Key_F18=0x1041, Key_F19=0x1042, Key_F20=0x1043,
        Key_F21=0x1044, Key_F22=0x1045, Key_F23=0x1046,

```
Key_F24=0x1047, Key_F25=0x1048, Key_F26=0x1049,
Key_F27=0x104a, Key_F28=0x104b, Key_F29=0x104c,
Key_F30=0x104d, Key_F31=0x104e, Key_F32=0x104f,
Key_F33=0x1050, Key_F34=0x1051, Key_F35=0x1052,
Key_Super_L=0x1053, Key_Super_R=0x1054, Key_Menu=0x1055,
Key_Hyper_L=0x1056, Key_Hyper_R=0x1057, Key_Space=0x20,
Key_Any=Key_Space, Key_Exclam=0x21, Key_QuoteDbl=0x22,
Key_NumberSign=0x23, Key_Dollar=0x24, Key_Percent=0x25,
Key_Ampersand=0x26, Key_Apostrophe=0x27,
Key_ParenLeft=0x28, Key_ParenRight=0x29,
Key_Asterisk=0x2a, Key_Plus=0x2b, Key_Comma=0x2c,
Key_Minus=0x2d, Key_Period=0x2e, Key_Slash=0x2f,
Key_0=0x30, Key_1=0x31, Key_2=0x32, Key_3=0x33,
Key_4=0x34, Key_5=0x35, Key_6=0x36, Key_7=0x37,
Key_8=0x38, Key_9=0x39, Key_Colon=0x3a,
Key_Semicolon=0x3b, Key_Less=0x3c, Key_Equal=0x3d,
Key_Greater=0x3e, Key_Question=0x3f, Key_At=0x40,
Key_A=0x41, Key_B=0x42, Key_C=0x43, Key_D=0x44,
Key_E=0x45, Key_F=0x46, Key_G=0x47, Key_H=0x48,
Key_I=0x49, Key_J=0x4a, Key_K=0x4b, Key_L=0x4c,
Key_M=0x4d, Key_N=0x4e, Key_O=0x4f, Key_P=0x50,
Key_Q=0x51, Key_R=0x52, Key_S=0x53, Key_T=0x54,
Key_U=0x55, Key_V=0x56, Key_W=0x57, Key_X=0x58,
Key_Y=0x59, Key_Z=0x5a, Key_BracketLeft=0x5b,
Key_Backslash=0x5c, Key_BracketRight=0x5d,
Key_AsciiCircum=0x5e, Key_Underscore=0x5f,
Key_QuoteLeft=0x60, Key_BraceLeft=0x7b, Key_Bar=0x7c,
Key_BraceRight=0x7d, Key_AsciiTilde=0x7e,
Key_nobreakspace=0x0a0, Key_exclamdown=0x0a1,
Key_cent=0x0a2, Key_sterling=0x0a3, Key_currency=0x0a4,
Key_yen=0x0a5, Key_brokenbar=0x0a6, Key_section=0x0a7,
Key_diaeresis=0x0a8, Key_copyright=0x0a9,
Key_ordfeminine=0x0aa, Key_guillemotleft=0x0ab,
Key_notsign=0x0ac, Key_hyphen=0x0ad,
Key_registered=0x0ae, Key_macron=0x0af, Key_degree=0x0b0,
Key_plusminus=0x0b1, Key_twosuperior=0x0b2,
Key_threesuperior=0x0b3, Key_acute=0x0b4, Key_mu=0x0b5,
Key_paragraph=0x0b6, Key_periodcentered=0x0b7,
Key_cedilla=0x0b8, Key_onesuperior=0x0b9,
Key_masculine=0x0ba, Key_guillemotright=0x0bb,
Key_onequarter=0x0bc, Key_onehalf=0x0bd,
Key_threequarters=0x0be, Key_questiondown=0x0bf,
Key_Agrave=0x0c0, Key_Aacute=0x0c1,
Key_Acircumflex=0x0c2, Key_Atilde=0x0c3,
Key_Adiaeresis=0x0c4, Key_Aring=0x0c5, Key_AE=0x0c6,
Key_Ccedilla=0x0c7, Key_Egrave=0x0c8, Key_Eacute=0x0c9,
Key_Ecircumflex=0x0ca, Key_Ediaeresis=0x0cb,
Key_Igrave=0x0cc, Key_Iacute=0x0cd,
Key_Icircumflex=0x0ce, Key_Idiaeresis=0x0cf,
Key_ETH=0x0d0, Key_Ntilde=0x0d1, Key_Ograve=0x0d2,
Key_Oacute=0x0d3, Key_Ocircumflex=0x0d4,
Key_Otilde=0x0d5, Key_Odiaeresis=0x0d6,
Key_multiply=0x0d7, Key_Ooblique=0x0d8, Key_Ugrave=0x0d9,
```

```
        Key_Uacute=0x0da, Key_Ucircumflex=0x0db,
        Key_Udiaeresis=0x0dc, Key_Yacute=0x0dd, Key_THORN=0x0de,
        Key_ssharp=0x0df, Key_agrave=0x0e0, Key_aacute=0x0e1,
        Key_acircumflex=0x0e2, Key_atilde=0x0e3,
        Key_adiaeresis=0x0e4, Key_aring=0x0e5, Key_ae=0x0e6,
        Key_ccedilla=0x0e7, Key_egrave=0x0e8, Key_eacute=0x0e9,
        Key_ecircumflex=0x0ea, Key_ediaeresis=0x0eb,
        Key_igrave=0x0ec, Key_iacute=0x0ed,
        Key_icircumflex=0x0ee, Key_idiaeresis=0x0ef,
        Key_eth=0x0f0, Key_ntilde=0x0f1, Key_ograve=0x0f2,
        Key_oacute=0x0f3, Key_ocircumflex=0x0f4,
        Key_otilde=0x0f5, Key_odiaeresis=0x0f6,
        Key_division=0x0f7, Key_oslash=0x0f8, Key_ugrave=0x0f9,
        Key_uacute=0x0fa, Key_ucircumflex=0x0fb,
        Key_udiaeresis=0x0fc, Key_yacute=0x0fd, Key_thorn=0x0fe,
        Key_ydiaeresis=0x0ff, Key_unknown=0xffff };

KeyBindingType
    KCompletionBase::KeyBindingType { TextCompletion,
        PrevCompletionMatch, NextCompletionMatch, RotateUp,
        RotateDown };

KToolBarPos
    KStyle::KToolBarPos { Top=0, Left, Right, Bottom, Floating,
        Flat };

KToolButtonType
    KStyle::KToolButtonType { Icon=0, IconTextRight, Text,
        IconTextBottom };

LayoutMode
    QListBox::LayoutMode { FixedNumber, FitToWidth,
        FitToHeight=FitToWidth, Variable };

LayoutType
    KAboutContainerBase::LayoutType { AbtPlain=0x0001,
        AbtTabbed=0x0002, AbtTitle=0x0004, AbtImageLeft=0x0008,
        AbtImageRight=0x0010, AbtImageOnly=0x0020,
        AbtProduct=0x0040,
        AbtKDEStandard=AbtTabbed|AbtTitle|AbtImageLeft,
        AbtAppStandard=AbtTabbed|AbtTitle|AbtProduct,
        AbtImageAndTitle=AbtPlain|AbtTitle|AbtImageOnly };
    KAboutDialog::LayoutType { AbtPlain=0x0001,
        AbtTabbed=0x0002, AbtTitle=0x0004, AbtImageLeft=0x0008,
        AbtImageRight=0x0010, AbtImageOnly=0x0020,
        AbtProduct=0x0040,
        AbtKDEStandard=AbtTabbed|AbtTitle|AbtImageLeft,
        AbtAppStandard=AbtTabbed|AbtTitle|AbtProduct,
        AbtImageAndTitle=AbtPlain|AbtTitle|AbtImageOnly };

LicenseKey
    KAboutData::LicenseKey { License_GPL=1, License_LGPL=2,
        License_BSD=3, License_Artistic=4 };
```

Lighting
    KImageEffect::Lighting { NorthLite, NWLite, WestLite,
        SWLite, SouthLite, SELite, EastLite, NELite };
    KPixmapEffect::Lighting { NorthLite, NWLite, WestLite,
        SWLite, SouthLite, SELite, EastLite, NELite };

ListStyle
    QStyleSheetItem::ListStyle { ListDisc, ListCircle,
        ListSquare, ListDecimal, ListLowerAlpha, ListUpperAlpha
            };

Look
    KLed::Look { NoLook, Flat, Raised, Sunken,
        NoOfLooks=Sunken };

Margin
    QStyleSheetItem::Margin { MarginLeft, MarginRight,
        MarginTop, MarginBottom, MarginAll, MarginVertical,
        MarginHorizontal };

MatchType
    KIcon::MatchType { MatchExact, MatchBest };

Media
    KTextPrintConfig::Media { A4, B5, Letter, Legal, Executive,
        A0, A1, A2, A3, A5, A6, A7, A8, A9, B0, B1, B10, B2, B3,
        B4, B6, B7, B8, B9, C5E, Comm10E, DLE, Folio, Ledger,
        Tabloid, NPageSize };

MenuId
    KHelpMenu::MenuId { menuHelpContents=0, menuWhatsThis=1,
        menuAboutApp=2, menuAboutKDE=3, menuReportBug=4 };

Message
    KIPC::Message { PaletteChanged=0, FontChanged,
        StyleChanged, BackgroundChanged, SettingsChanged,
        IconChanged, UserMessage=32 };

metric_style
    KRuler::metric_style { custom=0, pixel, inch, millimetres,
        centimetres, metres };

Mode
    KFile::Mode { File=1, Directory=2, Files=4, ExistingOnly=8,
        LocalOnly=16 };
    KImageIO::Mode { Reading, Writing };
    KURLComboBox::Mode { Files=-1, Directories=1, Both=0 };
    KURLCompletion::Mode { ExeCompletion=1, FileCompletion };
    QFileDialog::Mode { AnyFile, ExistingFile, Directory,
        ExistingFiles };
    QIconSet::Mode { Normal, Disabled, Active };
    QLCDNumber::Mode { Hex, HEX=Hex, Dec, DEC=Dec, Oct,
        OCT=Oct, Bin, BIN=Bin };

```
Modifier
    Qt::Modifier { SHIFT=0x00200000, CTRL=0x00400000,
      ALT=0x00800000, MODIFIER_MASK=0x00e00000,
      UNICODE_ACCEL=0x10000000, ASCII_ACCEL=UNICODE_ACCEL };

ModulationType
    KImageEffect::ModulationType { Intensity, Saturation,
      HueShift, Contrast };

MouseMode
    KImageTrackLabel::MouseMode { MousePress=1, MouseRelease,
      MouseDoubleClick, MouseMove };

NodeType
    QDomNode::NodeType { BaseNode=0, ElementNode=1,
      AttributeNode=2, TextNode=3, CDATASectionNode=4,
      EntityReferenceNode=5, EntityNode=6,
      ProcessingInstructionNode=7, CommentNode=8,
      DocumentNode=9, DocumentTypeNode=10,
      DocumentFragmentNode=11, NotationNode=12,
      CharacterDataNode=13 };

Operation
    QNetworkProtocol::Operation { OpListChildren=1, OpMkdir=2,
      OpRemove=4, OpRename=8, OpGet=32, OpPut=64 };

Optimization
    QPixmap::Optimization { DefaultOptim, NoOptim,
      MemoryOptim=NoOptim, NormalOptim, BestOptim };

Orientation
    KProgress::Orientation { Horizontal, Vertical };
    KSelector::Orientation { Horizontal, Vertical };
    KTextPrint::Orientation { Portrait, Landscape };
    QPrinter::Orientation { Portrait, Landscape };
    Qt::Orientation { Horizontal, Vertical };

PageOrder
    QPrinter::PageOrder { FirstPageFirst, LastPageFirst };

PageSize
    QPrinter::PageSize { A4, B5, Letter, Legal, Executive, A0,
      A1, A2, A3, A5, A6, A7, A8, A9, B0, B1, B10, B2, B3, B4,
      B6, B7, B8, B9, C5E, Comm10E, DLE, Folio, Ledger,
      Tabloid, NPageSize };

paint_style
    KRuler::paint_style { flat, raised, sunken };

PaintDeviceFlags
    QInternal::PaintDeviceFlags { UndefinedDevice=0x00,
      Widget=0x01, Pixmap=0x02, Printer=0x03, Picture=0x04,
      System=0x05, DeviceTypeMask=0x0f, ExternalDevice=0x10 };
```

PaintUnit
    Qt::PaintUnit { PixelUnit, LoMetricUnit, HiMetricUnit,
      LoEnglishUnit, HiEnglishUnit, TwipsUnit };

PDevCmd
    QPaintDevice::PDevCmd { PdcNOP=0, PdcDrawPoint=1,
      PdcDrawFirst=PdcDrawPoint, PdcMoveTo=2, PdcLineTo=3,
      PdcDrawLine=4, PdcDrawRect=5, PdcDrawRoundRect=6,
      PdcDrawEllipse=7, PdcDrawArc=8, PdcDrawPie=9,
      PdcDrawChord=10, PdcDrawLineSegments=11,
      PdcDrawPolyline=12, PdcDrawPolygon=13,
      PdcDrawQuadBezier=14, PdcDrawText=15,
      PdcDrawTextFormatted=16, PdcDrawPixmap=17,
      PdcDrawImage=18, PdcDrawText2=19,
      PdcDrawText2Formatted=20,
      PdcDrawLast=PdcDrawText2Formatted, PdcBegin=30,
      PdcEnd=31, PdcSave=32, PdcRestore=33, PdcSetdev=34,
      PdcSetBkColor=40, PdcSetBkMode=41, PdcSetROP=42,
      PdcSetBrushOrigin=43, PdcSetFont=45, PdcSetPen=46,
      PdcSetBrush=47, PdcSetTabStops=48, PdcSetTabArray=49,
      PdcSetUnit=50, PdcSetVXform=51, PdcSetWindow=52,
      PdcSetViewport=53, PdcSetWXform=54, PdcSetWMatrix=55,
      PdcSaveWMatrix=56, PdcRestoreWMatrix=57, PdcSetClip=60,
      PdcSetClipRegion=61, PdcReservedStart=0,
      PdcReservedStop=199 };

PenCapStyle
    Qt::PenCapStyle { FlatCap=0x00, SquareCap=0x10,
      RoundCap=0x20, MPenCapStyle=0x30 };

PenJoinStyle
    Qt::PenJoinStyle { MiterJoin=0x00, BevelJoin=0x40,
      RoundJoin=0x80, MPenJoinStyle=0xc0 };

PenStyle
    Qt::PenStyle { NoPen, SolidLine, DashLine, DotLine,
      DashDotLine, DashDotDotLine, MPenStyle=0x0f };

PermissionSpec
    QFileInfo::PermissionSpec { ReadUser=0400, WriteUser=0200,
      ExeUser=0100, ReadGroup=0040, WriteGroup=0020,
      ExeGroup=0010, ReadOther=0004, WriteOther=0002,
      ExeOther=0001 };

Placement
    QTextCustomItem::Placement { PlaceInline=0, PlaceLeft,
      PlaceRight };

Policy
    QComboBox::Policy { NoInsertion, AtTop, AtCurrent,
      AtBottom, AfterCurrent, BeforeCurrent };

Position
    KPanelApplet::Position { Left=0, Right, Top, Bottom };

PreviewMode
    QFileDialog::PreviewMode { NoPreview, Contents, Info };

PropagationMode
    QWidget::PropagationMode { NoChildren, AllChildren,
      SameFont, SamePalette=SameFont };

RasterOp
    Qt::RasterOp { CopyROP, OrROP, XorROP, NotAndROP,
      EraseROP=NotAndROP, NotCopyROP, NotOrROP, NotXorROP,
      AndROP, NotEraseROP=AndROP, NotROP, ClearROP, SetROP,
      NopROP, AndNotROP, OrNotROP, NandROP, NorROP,
      LastROP=NorROP };

Reason
    QFocusEvent::Reason { Mouse, Tab, ActiveWindow, Popup,
      Shortcut, Other };
    QNPInstance::Reason { ReasonDone=0, ReasonBreak=1,
      ReasonError=2, ReasonUnknown=-1 };

RegionType
    QRegion::RegionType { Rectangle, Ellipse };

ResizeMode
    QIconView::ResizeMode { Fixed=0, Adjust };
    QLayout::ResizeMode { FreeResize, Minimum, Fixed };
    QSplitter::ResizeMode { Stretch, KeepSize, FollowSizeHint
      };

ResizePolicy
    QScrollView::ResizePolicy { Default, Manual, AutoOne };

RestartHint
    QSessionManager::RestartHint { RestartIfRunning,
      RestartAnyway, RestartImmediately, RestartNever };

RGBComponent
    KImageEffect::RGBComponent { Red, Green, Blue, Gray, All };
    KPixmapEffect::RGBComponent { Red, Green, Blue };

RunMode
    KProcess::RunMode { DontCare, NotifyOnExit, Block };

SaveMode
    QTranslator::SaveMode { Everything, Stripped };

SButton
    KThemeBase::SButton { SBBottomLeft, SBBottomRight,
      SBOpposite };

ScaleHint
    KThemeBase::ScaleHint { FullScale, HorizontalScale,
    VerticalScale, TileScale };
    KThemeCache::ScaleHint { FullScale, HorizontalScale,
    VerticalScale };

ScrollBarMode
    QScrollView::ScrollBarMode { Auto, AlwaysOff, AlwaysOn };

SegmentStyle
    QLCDNumber::SegmentStyle { Outline, Filled, Flat };

SelectionMode
    KFile::SelectionMode { Single=1, Multi=2, Extended=4,
    NoSelection=8 };
    QIconView::SelectionMode { Single=0, Multi, Extended,
    NoSelection };
    QListBox::SelectionMode { Single, Multi, Extended,
    NoSelection };
    QListView::SelectionMode { Single, Multi, Extended,
    NoSelection };

Separator
    QMenuBar::Separator { Never=0, InWindowsStyle=1 };

ShadeStyle
    KThemeBase::ShadeStyle { Motif, Windows, Next };

Shadow
    QFrame::Shadow { Plain=0x0010, Raised=0x0020,
    Sunken=0x0030, MShadow=0x00f0 };

Shape
    KLed::Shape { NoShape, Rectangular, Circular,
    NoOfShapes=Circular };
    QFrame::Shape { NoFrame=0, Box=0x0001, Panel=0x0002,
    WinPanel=0x0003, HLine=0x0004, VLine=0x0005,
    StyledPanel=0x0006, PopupPanel=0x0007, MShape=0x000f };
    QTabBar::Shape { RoundedAbove, RoundedBelow,
    TriangularAbove, TriangularBelow };

ShmPolicies
    KPixmapIO::ShmPolicies { ShmDontKeep, ShmKeepAndGrow };

SignPosition
    KLocale::SignPosition { ParensAround=0,
    BeforeQuantityMoney=1, AfterQuantityMoney=2,
    BeforeMoney=3, AfterMoney=4 };

Size
    QIconSet::Size { Automatic, Small, Large };

SizeType
    QSizePolicy::SizeType { Fixed=0, Minimum=MayGrow,
      Maximum=MayShrink, Preferred=MayGrow|MayShrink,
      MinimumExpanding=Minimum|ExpMask,
      Expanding=MinimumExpanding|MayShrink };

SlantType
    KCharsets::SlantType { SlantUnknown, Normal, Italic };

SortMode
    KFile::SortMode { Increasing, Decreasing };

SortSpec
    QDir::SortSpec { Name=0x00, Time=0x01, Size=0x02,
      Unsorted=0x03, SortByMask=0x03, DirsFirst=0x04,
      Reversed=0x08, IgnoreCase=0x10, DefaultSort=-1 };

Spec
    QColor::Spec { Rgb, Hsv };

Specification
    QMetaProperty::Specification { Unspecified, Class,
      Reference, Pointer, ConstCharStar };

spellStatus
    KSpell::spellStatus { Starting=0, Running, Cleaning,
      Finished, Error, Crashed };

State
    KLed::State { Off, On, NoOfStates };
    QNetworkProtocol::State { StWaiting=0, StInProgress,
      StDone, StFailed, StStopped };
    QValidator::State { Invalid, Intermediate,
      Valid=Intermediate, Acceptable };

States
    KIcon::States { DefaultState, ActiveState, DisabledState,
      LastState };

Status
    QMovie::Status { SourceEmpty=-2, UnrecognizedFormat=-1,
      Paused=1, EndOfFrame=2, EndOfLoop=3, EndOfMovie=4,
      SpeedChanged=5 };

status_t
    KLaunchRequest::status_t { Init=0, Launching, Running,
      Error };

StdAccel
    KStdAccel::StdAccel { Open=0, New, Close, Save, Print,
      Quit, Cut, Copy, Paste, Undo, Redo, Find, Replace,

```
                    Insert, Home, End, Prior, Next, Help, FindNext, FindPrev,
                    ZoomIn, ZoomOut, AddBookmark, TextCompletion,
                    PrevCompletion, NextCompletion, RotateUp, RotateDown,
                    PopupMenuContext, WhatThis, Reload, NB_STD_ACCELS };
```

StdAction
```
        KStdAction::StdAction { New=1, Open, OpenRecent, Save,
            SaveAs, Revert, Close, Print, PrintPreview, Mail, Quit,
            Undo, Redo, Cut, Copy, Paste, SelectAll, Find, FindNext,
            FindPrev, Replace, ActualSize, FitToPage, FitToWidth,
            FitToHeight, ZoomIn, ZoomOut, Zoom, Redisplay, Up, Back,
            Forward, Home, Prior, Next, Goto, GotoPage, GotoLine,
            FirstPage, LastPage, AddBookmark, EditBookmarks,
            Spelling, ShowMenubar, ShowToolbar, ShowStatusbar,
            SaveOptions, KeyBindings, Preferences, ConfigureToolbars,
            Help, HelpContents, WhatsThis, ReportBug, AboutApp,
            AboutKDE, NULL1, NULL2, NULL3, NULL4, NULL5, NULL6,
            NULL7, NULL8, NULL9, NULL10, NULL11, NULL12, NULL13,
            NULL14, NULL15, NULL16, NULL17, NULL18, NULL19, NULL20 };
```

StdSizes
```
        KIcon::StdSizes { SizeSmall=16, SizeMedium=32,
            SizeLarge=48 };
```

StreamMode
```
        QNPInstance::StreamMode { Normal=1, Seek=2, AsFile=3,
            AsFileOnly=4 };
```

StyleHint
```
        QFont::StyleHint { Helvetica, Times, Courier, OldEnglish,
            System, AnyStyle, SansSerif=Helvetica, Serif=Times,
            TypeWriter=Courier, Decorative=OldEnglish };
```

TabPos
```
        KDockTabBar::TabPos { TAB_TOP, TAB_RIGHT };
```

TabPosition
```
        QTabWidget::TabPosition { Top, Bottom };
```

TextFormat
```
        Qt::TextFormat { PlainText, RichText, AutoText };
```

TickSetting
```
        QSlider::TickSetting { NoMarks=0, Above=1, Left=Above,
            Below=2, Right=Below, Both=3 };
```

ToggleState
```
        QButton::ToggleState { Off, NoChange, On };
```

ToggleType
```
        QButton::ToggleType { SingleShot, Toggle, Tristate };
```

```
ToolBarDock
    QMainWindow::ToolBarDock { Unmanaged, TornOff, Top, Bottom,
    Right, Left, Minimized };

Type
    KProtocolManager::Type { T_STREAM, T_FILESYSTEM, T_NONE,
    T_ERROR };
    QCheckListItem::Type { RadioButton, CheckBox, Controller };
    QEvent::Type { None=0, Timer=1, MouseButtonPress=2,
    MouseButtonRelease=3, MouseButtonDblClick=4, MouseMove=5,
    KeyPress=6, KeyRelease=7, FocusIn=8, FocusOut=9,
    Enter=10, Leave=11, Paint=12, Move=13, Resize=14,
    Create=15, Destroy=16, Show=17, Hide=18, Close=19,
    Quit=20, Reparent=21, ShowMaximized=21, ShowMinimized=22,
    ShowNormal=23, WindowActivate=24, WindowDeactivate=25,
    ShowToParent=26, HideToParent=27, Accel=30, Wheel=31,
    AccelAvailable=32, CaptionChange=33, IconChange=34,
    ParentFontChange=35, ApplicationFontChange=36,
    ParentPaletteChange=37, ApplicationPaletteChange=38,
    Clipboard=40, SockAct=50, DragEnter=60, DragMove=61,
    DragLeave=62, Drop=63, DragResponse=64, ChildInserted=70,
    ChildRemoved=71, LayoutHint=72, ActivateControl=80,
    DeactivateControl=81, Configure=82, ConfigureLayout=83,
    User=1000 };
    QSocketNotifier::Type { Read, Write, Exception };
    QVariant::Type { Invalid, Map, List, String, StringList,
    Font, Pixmap, Brush, Rect, Size, Color, Palette,
    ColorGroup, IconSet, Point, Image, Int, UInt, Bool,
    Double, CString, PointArray, Region, Bitmap, Cursor };
    QXMLSimpleParser::Type { Element, Attlist, Entity,
    Notation };

Types
    KIcon::Types { Fixed, Scalable };
    KPasswordDialog::Types { Password, NewPassword };

UndoFlags
    KWrite::UndoFlags { kUndoPossible=1, kRedoPossible=2 };

URITypes
    KURIFilterData::URITypes { NET_PROTOCOL=0, LOCAL_FILE,
    LOCAL_DIR, EXECUTABLE, HELP, SHELL, BLOCKED, ERROR,
    UNKNOWN };

ViewMode
    KFileView::ViewMode { Files=1, Directories=2,
    All=Files|Directories };
    QFileDialog::ViewMode { Detail, List };

Weight
    QFont::Weight { Light=25, Normal=50, DemiBold=63, Bold=75,
    Black=87 };
```

```
WeightType
    KCharsets::WeightType { WeightUnknown, Medium, Bold };

WhiteSpaceMode
    QStyleSheetItem::WhiteSpaceMode { WhiteSpaceNormal,
      WhiteSpacePre, WhiteSpaceNoWrap };

WidgetFlags
    Qt::WidgetFlags { WType_TopLevel=0x00000001,
      WType_Modal=0x00000002, WType_Popup=0x00000004,
      WType_Desktop=0x00000008, WType_Mask=0x0000000f,
      WStyle_Customize=0x00000010,
      WStyle_NormalBorder=0x00000020,
      WStyle_DialogBorder=0x00000040,
      WStyle_NoBorder=0x00000000, WStyle_Title=0x00000080,
      WStyle_SysMenu=0x00000100, WStyle_Minimize=0x00000200,
      WStyle_Maximize=0x00000400,
      WStyle_MinMax=WStyle_Minimize|WStyle_Maximize,
      WStyle_Tool=0x00000800, WStyle_StaysOnTop=0x00001000,
      WStyle_Dialog=0x00002000, WStyle_ContextHelp=0x00004000,
      WStyle_NoBorderEx=0x00008000, WStyle_Mask=0x0000fff0,
      WDestructiveClose=0x00010000, WPaintDesktop=0x00020000,
      WPaintUnclipped=0x00040000, WPaintClever=0x00080000,
      WResizeNoErase=0x00100000, WMouseNoMask=0x00200000,
      WNorthWestGravity=0x00400000, WRepaintNoErase=0x00800000,
      WX11BypassWM=0x01000000 };

WidgetState
    Qt::WidgetState { WState_Created=0x00000001,
      WState_Disabled=0x00000002, WState_Visible=0x00000004,
      WState_ForceHide=0x00000008, WState_OwnCursor=0x00000010,
      WState_MouseTracking=0x00000020,
      WState_CompressKeys=0x00000040,
      WState_BlockUpdates=0x00000080,
      WState_InPaintEvent=0x00000100,
      WState_Reparented=0x00000200,
      WState_ConfigPending=0x00000400,
      WState_Resized=0x00000800, WState_AutoMask=0x00001000,
      WState_Polished=0x00002000, WState_DND=0x00004000,
      WState_Modal=0x00008000, WState_Reserved1=0x00010000,
      WState_Reserved2=0x00020000, WState_Reserved3=0x00040000,
      WState_Reserved4=0x00080000,
      WState_TranslateBackground=0x00100000,
      WState_ForceDisabled=0x00200000,
      WState_Exposed=0x00400000 };

WidgetType
    KThemeBase::WidgetType { PushButton=0, ComboBox,
      HScrollBarSlider, VScrollBarSlider, Bevel, ToolButton,
      ScrollButton, HScrollDeco, VScrollDeco, ComboDeco,
      MenuItem, InactiveTab, ArrowUp, ArrowDown, ArrowLeft,
```

ArrowRight, PushButtonDown, ComboBoxDown,
HScrollBarSliderDown, VScrollBarSliderDown, BevelDown,
ToolButtonDown, ScrollButtonDown, HScrollDecoDown,
VScrollDecoDown, ComboDecoDown, MenuItemDown, ActiveTab,
SunkenArrowUp, SunkenArrowDown, SunkenArrowLeft,
SunkenArrowRight, HScrollGroove, VScrollGroove, Slider,
SliderGroove, IndicatorOn, IndicatorOff, ExIndicatorOn,
ExIndicatorOff, HBarHandle, VBarHandle, ToolBar,
Splitter, CheckMark, MenuBar, DisArrowUp, DisArrowDown,
DisArrowLeft, DisArrowRight, ProgressBar, ProgressBg,
MenuBarItem, Background };

WidthMode
    QListView::WidthMode { Manual, Maximum };

WindowState
    KWin::WindowState { WithdrawnState=0, NormalState=1,
    IconicState=3 };

WindowsVersion
    Qt::WindowsVersion { WV_32s=0x0001, WV_95=0x0002,
    WV_98=0x0003, WV_DOS_based=0x000f, WV_NT=0x0010,
    WV_2000=0x0020, WV_NT_based=0x00f0 };

WordWrap
    QMultiLineEdit::WordWrap { NoWrap, WidgetWidth,
    FixedPixelWidth, FixedColumnWidth };

WrapPolicy
    QMultiLineEdit::WrapPolicy { AtWhiteSpace, Anywhere };

✦　　✦　　✦

Signals

An event can be broadcast from an object by the object emitting a signal. Any object wishing to receive the signal needs to establish a connection through a slot. In the simplest cases, the signals carry no information — the very fact that the signal was issued is information enough. In other cases, argument values included with the signal.

This appendix lists the signals in alphabetical order. Each entry includes the parameter list and the list of classes that are capable of emitting a signal of that name and that footprint.

KDE/Qt Signals

```
aboutToQuit() QApplication
aboutToShow() QTabDialog QPopupMenu
aboutToShow(int) QWidgetStack
aboutToShow(QWidget *) KDockTabCtl
QWidgetStack
accepted(KSocket *) KServerSocket
actionHighlighted(KAction *) KActionCollection
activated() KGlobalAccel KAction KCharSelect
KCharSelectTable
activated(int) QAccel QSocketNotifier
KSelectAction KPanelMenu
        KWCommand KWCommandGroup QComboBox
QMenuBar QPopupMenu
activated(QChar &) KCharSelect
KCharSelectTable
activated(QColor &) KColorCombo
activated(QString &) KSelectAction QComboBox
activatedMenu(KFileViewItem *)
KFileViewSignaler
activatedRedirect(int) QPopupMenu
appearanceChanged() KApplication
applied() KPropertiesDialog
apply() KDialogBase
applyButtonPressed() QTabDialog
applyClicked() KDialogBase
authChanged(bool) KAuthIcon
backgroundChanged() KDialogBase
backgroundChanged(int) KApplication
backwardAvailable(bool) QTextBrowser
```

```
bgChanged(QColor &) KDualColorButton
cancelButtonPressed() QTabDialog
cancelClicked() KDialogBase
canceled() KDirLister KPropertiesDialog
cancelled() QProgressDialog
change() KDockManager
changed() KFileBookmarkManager KPropsPage KAccelInput
changed(bool) KCModule
changed(QConfigDB *) QConfigDB
changed(QString &) KWCommand KColorButton
clear() KDirLister
clicked() QButton KAnimWidget KToolBar
clicked(int) KToolBarButton QHeader QButtonGroup
clicked(QIconViewItem *) QIconView QListView
clicked(QIconViewItem *, const QPoint &) QIconView
clicked(QListBoxItem *) QListBox
clicked(QListBoxItem *, const QPoint &) QListBox
clicked(QListViewItem *, const QPoint &, int) QListView
closeClicked() KDialogBase
closeEvent(KSocket *) KSocket
closeMe(int) KDateInternalYearSelector
         KDateInternalMonthPicker
collapsed(QListViewItem *) QListView
colorChanged(QColor &) KColorPatch
colorSelected(int) KColorCells
colorSelected(QColor &) KColorDialog
colorSelected(QColor &, QString &) KPaletteTable
command(int) KSpellDlg
completed() KDirLister
completion(QString &) KComboBox KLineEdit KDirOperator
connectionStateChanged(int, QString &) QNetworkProtocol
         QUrlOperator
contents(KFileViewItemList &, bool) KFileReader
contentsMoving(int, int) QScrollView
corrected(QString, QString, unsigned) KSpell
createdDirectory(QUrlInfo &, QNetworkOperation *)
         QNetworkProtocol QUrlOperator
currentChanged(KDualColorButton::DualColor) KDualColorButton
currentChanged(QIconViewItem *) QIconView QListView
currentChanged(QListBoxItem *) QListBox
CursorPositionChanged() KEdit
data(QByteArray &, QNetworkOperation *) QNetworkProtocol
         QUrlOperator
databaseChanged() KSycoca
dataChanged() QClipboard
dataTransferProgress(int, int, QNetworkOperation *)
         QNetworkProtocol QUrlOperator
dateChanged(QDate) KDateTable KDatePicker
dateEntered(QDate) KDatePicker
dateSelected(QDate) KDatePicker
death() KSpell
defaultButtonPressed() QTabDialog
defaultClicked() KDialogBase
deleted(QString &) KDirWatch
```

```
deleteItem(KFileItem *) KDirLister
desktopChange(int) KWinModule
desktopNameChange(int, QString) KWinModule
desktopNumberChange(int) KWinModule
destroyed() QObject
dialog3() KSpell
dirActivated(KFileViewItem *) KFileViewSignaler KDirOperator
dirDeleted() KFileReader
dirEntered(QString &) QFileDialog
dirEntry(KFileViewItem *) KFileReader
dirty(QString &) KDirWatch
docking(KDockWidget *, KDockWidget::DockPosition dp)
        KDockWidget
dockWindowAdd(WId) KWinModule
dockWindowRemove(WId) KWinModule
done() KEdFind KEdReplace
done(bool) KSpell KSharedPixmap
done(QString &) KSpell
doPrint(KTextPrint &) KTextPrintConfig
doubleClicked(int) KToolBar KToolBarButton
doubleClicked(QIconViewItem *) QIconView
doubleClicked(QIconViewItem *, QPoint &) KIconView
doubleClicked(QListBoxItem *) QListBox
doubleClicked(QListBoxItem *, QPoint &) KListBox
doubleClicked(QListViewItem *) QListView
doubleClicked(QListViewItem *, QPoint &, int) KListView
dropEventPass(QDropEvent *) KWriteView
dropped(QDropEvent *, QValueList < QIconDragItem > &)
        QIconView
embeddedWindowDestroyed() QXEmbed
enabled(bool) KAction
enableOk(bool) KEditToolbarWidget
endMovingToolBar(QToolBar *) QMainWindow
enteredURL() KURLLabel
enteredURL(QString &) KURLLabel
error() KRun
error(int, QString &) KFileReader
executed(QIconViewItem *) KIconView
executed(QIconViewItem *, QPoint &) KIconView
executed(QListBoxItem *) KListBox
executed(QListBoxItem *, QPoint &) KListBox
executed(QListViewItem *) KListView
executed(QListViewItem *, QPoint &, int) KListView
expanded(QListViewItem *) QListView
ez() KSpell
eza() KSpell
fgChanged(QColor &) KDualColorButton
fileChanged() QConfigDB
fileDirty(QString &) KDirWatch
fileHighlighted(KFileViewItem *) KDirOperator
        KFileViewSignaler
fileHighlighted(QString &) QFileDialog KFileDialog
fileSelected(KFileViewItem *) KDirOperator KFileViewSignaler
fileSelected(QString &) QFileDialog KFileDialog
```

```
filterChanged() KFileFilter KFileReader
filterChanged(QString &) KFileDialog
find() KEdReplace
finished() KRun KIconCanvas
finished(QNetworkOperation *) QNetworkProtocol QUrlOperator
finishedLoading() KDirOperator
focusItemChanged() KCharSelect KCharSelectTable
focusItemChanged(QChar &) KCharSelect KCharSelectTable
fontChanged(QString &) KCharSelect
fontHighlighted(QFont &) QFontDialog
fontSelected(QFont &) QFontDialog KFontDialog KFontChooser
fontSizeChanged(int) KFontSizeAction
formulaChanged(QString &) KFormulaEdit
forwardAvailable(bool) QTextBrowser
gotUrlDrop(QDropEvent *) KEdit
guiThreadAwake() QApplication
headerCloseButtonClicked() KDockWidget
headerDockbackButtonClicked() KDockWidget
helpButtonPressed() QTabDialog
helpClicked() QWizard KDialogBase
hidden() KDialogBase
highlighted() KCharSelect KCharSelectTable
highlighted(int) KToolBar QComboBox QListBox QMenuBar
          QPopupMenu
highlighted(int, bool) KToolBar KToolBarButton
highlighted(QChar &) KCharSelect KCharSelectTable
highlighted(QColor &) KColorCombo
highlighted(QListBoxItem *) QListBox
highlighted(QString &) QComboBox QListBox QTextBrowser
highlighted(QString &, QString &) KApplicationTree
highlightedRedirect(int) QPopupMenu
historyUpdate(bool, bool) KFileDialog
iconChanged(int) KApplication
iconChanged(QString icon) KIconButton
iMBeingClosed() KDockWidget
indexChange(int, int, int) QHeader
inserted(KAction *) KActionCollection
invalidChar(int) KRestrictedLine
itemChanged(QNetworkOperation *) QNetworkProtocol QUrlOperator
itemPressed(int) KStatusBarLabel
itemReleased(int) KStatusBarLabel
itemRenamed(QIconViewItem *) QIconView
itemRenamed(QIconViewItem *, QString &) QIconView
itemsDeleted(KFileViewItemList &) KFileReader
kdisplayFontChanged() KApplication
kdisplayPaletteChanged() KApplication
kdisplayStyleChanged() KApplication
keyChange() KKeyChooser
keycodeChanged() KAccel
kipcMessage(int, int) KApplication
lastWindowClosed() QApplication
layoutHintChanged() KDialog
leftClickedURL() KURLLabel
leftClickedURL(QString &) KURLLabel
```

```
leftURL() KURLLabel
leftURL(QString &) KURLLabel
mailClick(QString &, QString &) KAboutContainer
        KAboutContainerBase KTextBrowser
mapped(int) QSignalMapper
mapped(QString &) QSignalMapper
match(QString &) KCompletion
matches(QStringList &) KCompletion
middleClickedURL() KURLLabel
middleClickedURL(QString &) KURLLabel
misspelling(QString originalword, QStringList *, unsigned pos)
        KSpell
modechange() KToolBar
mouseButtonClicked(int, QListBoxItem *, QPoint &) QListBox
mouseButtonPressed(int, QIconViewItem *, QPoint &) QIconView
mouseButtonPressed(int, QListViewItem *, QPoint &, int)
        QListView
mouseTrack(int, QMouseEvent *) KAboutContainerBase
        KImageTrackLabel
moved() QIconView
moved(BarPosition) KToolBar
moved(int, int) QHeader
multipleMatches() KCompletion
nameChanged(QString) KIconCanvas
newChild(QUrlInfo &, QNetworkOperation *) QNetworkProtocol
newItems(FileItemList &) KDirLister
newWidth(int) KSplitList
nextLine() QScrollBar
nextMatch(KeyBindingType) KComboBox KLineEdit
nextPage() QScrollBar
noClicked() KDialogBase
objectCreated(QObject *) KLibFactory
okClicked() KDialogBase
onHotSpot(int) KToolBoxManager
onItem(QIconViewItem *) QIconView
onItem(QListBoxItem *) QListBox
onItem(QListViewItem *) QListView
onViewport() QIconView QListView QListBox
openURL(QString &) KAboutDialog KAboutWidget KAboutContributor
orientationChanged(Orientation) QToolBar
overflow() QLCDNumber
pageSelected(QWidget *) KDockTabCtl
percentageChanged(int) KProgress
pixmapChanged() KDialogBaseTile
pixmapSizeChanged(bool) QMainWindow
posChanged(int, int) KToolBoxManager
pressed() QButton
pressed(int) KStatusBar KToolBar KToolBarButton QButtonGroup
        QHeader
pressed(QIconViewItem *) QIconView
pressed(QIconViewItem *, QPoint &) QIconView
pressed(QListBoxItem *) QListBox
pressed(QListBoxItem *, QPoint &) QListBox
pressed(QListViewItem *) QListView
```

```
pressed(QListViewItem *, QPoint &, int) QListView
previousMatch(KeyBindingType) KComboBox KLineEdit
prevLine() QScrollBar
prevPage() QScrollBar
processedSize(unsigned long bytes) KShred
processExited(KProcess *) KProcess
progress(int) KIconCanvas
progress(unsigned int) KSpell
propertiesClosed() KPropertiesDialog
readEvent(KSocket *) KSocket
readReady(KProcIO *) KProcIO
ready(KSpell *) KSpell
received(QString &) KJavaProcess
receivedStderr(KProcess *, char *, int) KProcess
receivedStdout(int, int &) KProcess
receivedStdout(KProcess *, char *, int) KProcess
redirection(KURL &) KDirLister
redoAvailable(bool) QMultiLineEdit
released() QButton
released(int) KStatusBar KToolBar KToolBarButton
        QButtonGroup QHeader
removed(KAction *) KActionCollection
removed(QNetworkOperation *) QNetworkProtocol QUrlOperator
removeTip() QToolTipGroup
replace() KEdReplace
replaceAll() KEdReplace
replaceDock(KDockWidget *, KDockWidget *) KDockManager
resized() QCanvas
returnPressed() KComboBox QLineEdit KURLRequester
        QMultiLineEdit
returnPressed(QIconViewItem *) QIconView
returnPressed(QListBoxItem *) QListBox
returnPressed(QListViewItem *) QListView
returnPressed(QString &) KComboBox KLineEdit KURLRequester
rightButtonClicked(QIconViewItem *, QPoint &) QIconView
rightButtonClicked(QListBoxItem *, QPoint &) QListBox
rightButtonPress(int, QPoint) KDockTabBar
rightButtonPressed(QIconViewItem *, QPoint &) QIconView
rightButtonPressed(QListViewItem *, QPoint &, int) QListView
rightClickedURL() KURLLabel
rightClickedURL(QString &) KURLLabel
rotateDown(KeyBindingType) KComboBox
rotateUp(KeyBindingType) KComboBox
saveYourself() KApplication
search() KEdFind
sectionClicked(int) QHeader
selected(int) QListBox QTabBar
selected(int, int) QWellArray
selected(QListBoxItem *) QListBox
selected(QString &) QListBox QTabDialog QTabWidget
selected(QString &, QString &) KApplicationTree
selectionChanged() KHTMLView QIconView QListBox QListView
selectionChanged(QIconViewItem *) QIconView
selectionChanged(QListBoxItem *) QListBox
```

```
selectionChanged(QListViewItem *) QListView
sendEmail(QString &, QString &) KAboutDialog KAboutWidget
        KAboutContributor
setDockDefaultPos() KDockWidget
setDockDefaultPos(KDockWidget *) KDockManager
setStatus(QString &) KabAPI
settingsChanged(int) KApplication
showAboutApplication() KHelpMenu
showPreview(KURL &) KFilePreview
showTip(QString &) QToolTipGroup
shutDown() KApplication
sizeChange(int, int, int) QHeader
sizeChanged(int, int) KToolBoxManager
sizeHint(QSize) KFormulaEdit
sliderMoved(int) QScrollBar QSlider
sliderPressed() QScrollBar QSlider
sliderReleased() QScrollBar QSlider
stackingOrderChanged() KWinModule
start(QNetworkOperation *) QNetworkProtocol QUrlOperator
started(QString &) KDirLister
startedNextCopy(QList < QNetworkOperation > &) QUrlOperator
startLoading(int) KIconCanvas
startMovingToolBar(QToolBar *) QMainWindow
stateChanged(int) QButton
tableClicked() KDateTable KDatePicker
tableDown() KCharSelectTable
tableUp() KCharSelectTable
tabSelected(int) KDockTabBar KTabCtl
tabShowPopup(int, QPoint) KDockTabCtl
textChanged() QTextBrowser QMultiLineEdit
textChanged(QString &) QComboBox QLineEdit KURLRequester
timeout() QTimer
toggled(bool) KToggleAction QButton
toggled(int) KToolBarButton KToolBar
toggle_overwrite_signal() KEdit
toolBarPositionChanged(QToolBar *) QMainWindow
tryClicked() KDialogBase
undoAvailable(bool) QMultiLineEdit
updateInformation(int, int) KDirOperator
urlActivated(KURL &) KURLComboBox
urlChanged(QString &) KFileReader
urlClick(QString &) KAboutContainer KAboutContainerBase
        KTextBrowser
urlEntered(KURL &) KDirOperator
urlSelected(KURL &) KRecentFilesAction
user1Clicked() KDialogBase
user2Clicked() KDialogBase
user3Clicked() KDialogBase
usesTextLabelChanged(bool) QMainWindow
valid(bool) KAccelInput
valueChanged(double) KDoubleNumInput
valueChanged(int) KIntNumInput KSelector QScrollBar
        QSlider QSpinBox
valueChanged(int, int) KXYSelector
```

```
valueChanged(QString &) QSpinBox
windowActivate(WId) KWinModule
windowActivated(QWidget *) QWorkspace
windowAdd(WId) KWinModule
windowChange(WId) KWinModule
windowRemove(WId) KWinModule
workspaceAreaChanged() KWinModule
writeEvent(KSocket *) KSocket
wroteStdin(KProcess *) KProcess
yesClicked() KDialogBase
```

✦   ✦   ✦

Slots

Slots are used as receivers of information emitted by signals. Many of the slots have parameters defined, and the footprint of a slot's parameters must match that of the signal it is designed to receive.

This appendix contains an alphabetical listing of the slots that are defined in the KDE and Qt classes. A slot is also a method and can be called directly, but these methods are really designed to be called indirectly by the application emitting a signal.

KDE/Qt Slots

```
aboutApplication() KHelpMenu
aboutKDE() KHelpMenu
acceptSlave(KSocket *) KLauncher
activateHelp(void) KSpellConfig
addItem(const QString &) KCompletion
addStep() QSlider
advance() QCanvas
advance(int prog) KProgress
allDefault() KKeyChooser
animateClick() QButton
append(const QString &) QMultiLineEdit
appHelpActivated() KHelpMenu KTMainWindow
arrangeItemsInGrid(const QSize &grid, bool
        update = TRUE)
         QIconView
arrangeItemsInGrid(bool update = TRUE)
         QIconView
back() KDirOperator
backward() QTextBrowser
build() Kded
cancel() QProgressDialog
cascade() QWorkspace
cdUp() KDirOperator
center(int x, int y) QScrollView
center(int x, int y, float xmargin, float
     ymargin) QScrollView
changeHideShowState() KDockWidget
checkFileChanged() QConfigDB
cleanup() KDialogBaseTile
clear() KCompletion QLineEdit QStatusBar
        QLabel
         QMultiLineEdit
clearEdit() QComboBox
```

clearFocus() QWidget
clearSelection() QListBox
clearValidator() QComboBox QLineEdit
close() QWidget
close(int r) QPopupFrame
closeAllWindows() QApplication
computePosition() KEdit
constPolish() QWidget
contextHelpActivated() KHelpMenu
copy() QTextView QMultiLineEdit
copyText() QMultiLineEdit
corrected(QString originalword, QString newword, unsigned pos)
        KEdit
cut() QMultiLineEdit
deselect() QLineEdit QMultiLineEdit
display(int num) QLCDNumber
display(double num) QLCDNumber
display(const QString &str) QLCDNumber
dockBack() KDockWidget
enableButton(ButtonCode id, bool state) KDialogBase
enableButtonApply(bool state) KDialogBase
enableButtonCancel(bool state) KDialogBase
enableButtonOK(bool state) KDialogBase
enableLinkedHelp(bool state) KDialogBase
ensureCurrentVisible() QListBox
ensureVisible(int x, int y) QScrollView
ensureVisible(int x, int y, int xmargin, int ymargin)
        QScrollView
forward() KDirOperator QTextBrowser
hasMultipleMatches() KCompletion
helpClickedSlot(const QString &) KDialogBase
hide() QWidget
home() KDirOperator QTextBrowser
iconify() QWidget
idleTimeout() KLauncher
insert(const QString &) QLineEdit QMultiLineEdit
insertChar(int c) KFormulaEdit
invertSelection() QListView QListBox
listSync() KKeyChooser
lower() QWidget
makeCompletion(const QString &) KDirOperator
makeDirCompletion(const QString &) KDirOperator
map() QSignalMapper
message(const QString &) QStatusBar
message(const QString &, int) QStatusBar
misspelling(QString word, QStringList *, unsigned pos) KEdit
mkdir() KDirOperator
modeChange() KToolBarButton
move(int x, int y) QWidget
move(const QPoint &) QWidget
needUpdate() Kded
notify(int socket) QIOWatch
notify() QTimeWatch
off() KLed

```
on() KLed
paste() QMultiLineEdit
play() KAudioPlayer
polish() QWidget
quit() QApplication
raise() QWidget
raiseWidget(int) QWidgetStack
raiseWidget(QWidget *) QWidgetStack
recreate() Kded
redo() QMultiLineEdit
removeItem(const QString &) KCompletion
repaint() QWidget
repaint(bool erase) QWidget
repaint(int x, int y, int w, int h, bool erase = TRUE) QWidget
repaint(const QRect &, bool erase = TRUE) QWidget
repaint(const QRegion &, bool erase = TRUE) QWidget
repaint() KRootPixmap
repaintAll() KEdit
replace_all_slot() KEdit
replace_search_slot() KEdit
replace_slot() KEdit
replacedone_slot() KEdit
reportBug() KHelpMenu
rereadDir() KDirOperator
reset() QProgressDialog QProgressBar
resize(int w, int h) QWidget
resize(const QSize &) QWidget
resizeContents(int w, int h) QScrollView
rotateText(KeyBindingType) KComboBox KLineEdit
saveConfiguration() KFileDialogConfigure
scrollBy(int dx, int dy) QScrollView
search_slot() KEdit
searchdone_slot() KEdit
selectAll() QLineEdit
selectAll(bool select) QListView QListBox
selectAll() QTextView QMultiLineEdit
selected(int) KEdGotoLine
send() KNotifyClient
setAltPixmap(const QPixmap &pixmap) KURLLabel
setBackEnabled(QWidget *, bool) QWizard
setBackgroundColor(const QColor &bgcolor) KURLLabel
setBackgroundColor(const QString &bgcolor) KURLLabel
setBinMode() QLCDNumber
setCancelButtonText(const QString &) QProgressDialog
setCaption(const QString &) QWidget
setCaption(const QString &caption) KTMainWindow KDialog
setColor(const QColor &col) KColorDialog
setCols(int) KTextPrintPreview
setContentsPos(int x, int y) QScrollView QIconView QListView
setCurrentTab(int) QTabBar
setCurrentTab(QTab *) QTabBar
setDecMode() QLCDNumber
setDelay(bool) QToolTipGroup
setDest(int) KTextPrintDialog
```

```
setDir(const QString &) QFileDialog
setDirty() KPropsPage
setDockMenuEnabled(bool) QMainWindow
setEditFocus(bool mark = true) KIntNumInput
setEditText(const QString &) QComboBox
setEnabled(bool) QWidget QToolTipGroup KAction QSpinBox
        KDockTabCtl QScrollView
setFilter(const QString &) QFileDialog
setFilters(const QString &) QFileDialog
setFilters(const char **) QFileDialog
setFilters(const QStringList &) QFileDialog
setFinish(QWidget *, bool) QWizard
setFinishEnabled(QWidget *, bool) QWizard
setFloat(bool do_float = true) KURLLabel
setFocus() QWidget
setFont(const QFont &font) KURLLabel
setGeometry(int x, int y, int w, int h) QWidget
setGeometry(const QRect &) QWidget
setGlow(bool glow = true) KURLLabel
setHelp(const QString &path, const QString &topic) KDialogBase
setHelpEnabled(QWidget *, bool) QWizard
setHelpLinkText(const QString &text) KDialogBase
setHexMode() QLCDNumber
setHighlightedColor(const QColor &highcolor) KURLLabel
setHighlightedColor(const QString &highcolor) KURLLabel
setIcon(const QPixmap &) QWidget
setIconText(const QString &) QWidget
setItems(const QStringList &) KCompletion
setLabelText(const QString &) QProgressDialog
setMinimumDuration(int ms) QProgressDialog
setMouseTracking(bool enable) QWidget
setMovie(const QMovie &) QLabel
setMovie(const QMovie &movie) KURLLabel
setNextEnabled(QWidget *, bool) QWizard
setNum(int) QLabel
setNum(double) QLabel
setOctMode() QLCDNumber
setOffset(int pos) QHeader
setOn(bool) QPushButton
setOn(bool enable) QToolButton
setOpaqueMoving(bool) QMainWindow
setOrient(int) KTextPrintPreview
setOverwriteMode(bool) QMultiLineEdit
setPageNumbers(bool) KTextPrintPreview
setPalette(const QString &paletteName) KPaletteTable
setPixmap(const QPixmap &) QLabel KURLLabel
setPlainCaption(const QString &caption) KTMainWindow KDialog
setPrefix(const QString &text) QSpinBox
setPrefix(QString prefix) KIntNumInput KDoubleNumInput
setProgress(int progress) QProgressDialog QProgressBar
setReadOnly(bool) QMultiLineEdit
setRightJustification(bool) QMainWindow
setRows(int) KTextPrintPreview
setSelectedColor(const QColor &selcolor) KURLLabel
```

```
setSelectedColor(const QString &selcolor) KURLLabel
setSmallDecimalPoint(bool) QLCDNumber
setSuffix(const QString &text) QSpinBox
setSuffix(QString suffix) KIntNumInput KDoubleNumInput
setText(const QString &) QLineEdit QLabel QMultiLineEdit
setText(const QString &text) KURLLabel
setTextAlignment(TextAlignment align) KURLLabel
setTextLabel(const QString &, bool) QToolButton
setTextLabel(const QString &) QToolButton
setTipText(const QString &tip) KURLLabel
setTitle(bool) KTextPrintPreview
setToggleButton(bool enable) QToolButton
setToolBarsMovable(bool) QMainWindow
setTotalSteps(int totalSteps) QProgressDialog QProgressBar
setUnderline(bool underline = true) KURLLabel
setUpdatesEnabled(bool enable) QWidget
setUrl(const QUrlOperator &url) QFileDialog
setURL(const QString &url) KURLLabel
setUseCursor(bool use_cursor, const QCursor *cursor = 0)
        KURLLabel
setUsesBigPixmap(bool enable) QToolButton
setUsesBigPixmaps(bool) QMainWindow
setUsesTextLabel(bool) QToolButton QMainWindow
setUseTips(bool tips = true) KURLLabel
setValue(int) QSlider QSpinBox KProgress KIntNumInput
setValue(double) KDoubleNumInput
setVisiblePage(int id) KDockTabCtl
setWidth(int newWidth) KSplitListItem
show() QWidget
showFullScreen() QWidget
showMaximized() QWidget
showMinimized() QWidget
showNormal() QWidget
slotAccept(int) KServerSocket
slotActivated(int index) KColorCombo
slotAddExtension() KApplicationPropsPage
slotApply() KPropertiesDialog
slotAppRegistered(const QCString &appId) KLauncher
slotBrowseExec() KExecPropsPage
slotCancel() KPropertiesDialog
slotClear() KLineEditDlg KOpenWithDlg
slotDelExtension() KApplicationPropsPage
slotDequeue() KLauncher
slotDoHousekeeping(int socket) KProcessController
slotEndOffset(int) KRuler
slotHighlighted(const QString &_name, const QString &_exec)
        KOpenWithDlg
slotHighlighted(int index) KColorCombo
slotItemHighlighted(QListViewItem *i) KApplicationTree
slotKInitData(int) KLauncher
slotMailClick(const QString &name, const QString &address)
        KAboutContainerBase
slotMakeCompletion(const QString &string) KCompletion
slotMouseTrack(int mode, const QMouseEvent *e)
```

```
            KAboutContainerBase
slotNewOffset(int) KRuler
slotNewValue(int) KRuler
slotNextMatch() KCompletion
slotOK() KOpenWithDlg
slotPreviousMatch() KCompletion
slotProgress(unsigned int p) KSpellDlg
slotRead(int) KSocket
slotSave() KCookieServer
slotSelected(const QString &_name, const QString &_exec)
         KOpenWithDlg
slotSelectionChanged(QListViewItem *i) KApplicationTree
slotSetBackground(const QColor &c) KDualColorButton
slotSetCurrent(KDualColorButton::DualColor s) KDualColorButton
slotSetCurrentColor(const QColor &c) KDualColorButton
slotSetForeground(const QColor &c) KDualColorButton
slotSlaveGone() KLauncher
slotToggled(int) KToolBarRadioGroup
slotUrlClick(const QString &url) KAboutContainerBase
slotWrite(int) KSocket
stepDown() QSpinBox
stepUp() QSpinBox
stop() KToolBoxManager
subtractStep() QSlider
tile() QWorkspace
toggle() QButton QPushButton QToolButton KLed
triggerUpdate() QListView
undo() QMultiLineEdit
undock() KDockWidget
update() QWidget
update(int x, int y, int w, int h) QWidget
update(const QRect &) QWidget
update() QCanvas
updateBackground() KDialogBase
updateContents() QIconView
updateGL() QGLWidget
updateOverlayGL() QGLWidget
updateScrollBars() QScrollView
updateStatus() KAuthIcon KRootPermsIcon KWritePermsIcon
whatsThis() QMainWindow
yearEnteredSlot() KDateInternalYearSelector
```

✦   ✦   ✦

Index

Continued

Continued

Continued

Notes

Notes

IDG Books Worldwide, Inc.
End-User License Agreement

READ THIS. You should carefully read these terms and conditions before opening the software packet(s) included with this book ("Book"). This is a license agreement ("Agreement") between you and IDG Books Worldwide, Inc. ("IDGB"). By opening the accompanying software packet(s), you acknowledge that you have read and accept the following terms and conditions. If you do not agree and do not want to be bound by such terms and conditions, promptly return the Book and the unopened software packet(s) to the place you obtained them for a full refund.

1. **License Grant.** IDGB grants to you (either an individual or entity) a nonexclusive license to use one copy of the enclosed software program(s) (collectively, the "Software") solely for your own personal or business purposes on a single computer (whether a standard computer or a workstation component of a multiuser network). The Software is in use on a computer when it is loaded into temporary memory (RAM) or installed into permanent memory (hard disk, CD-ROM, or other storage device). IDGB reserves all rights not expressly granted herein.

2. **Ownership.** IDGB is the owner of all right, title, and interest, including copyright, in and to the compilation of the Software recorded on the disk(s) or CD-ROM ("Software Media"). Copyright to the individual programs recorded on the Software Media is owned by the author or other authorized copyright owner of each program. Ownership of the Software and all proprietary rights relating thereto remain with IDGB and its licensers.

3. **Restrictions On Use and Transfer.**

    (a) You may only (i) make one copy of the Software for backup or archival purposes, or (ii) transfer the Software to a single hard disk, provided that you keep the original for backup or archival purposes. You may not (i) rent or lease the Software, (ii) copy or reproduce the Software through a LAN or other network system or through any computer subscriber system or bulletin-board system, or (iii) modify, adapt, or create derivative works based on the Software.

    (b) You may not reverse engineer, decompile, or disassemble the Software. You may transfer the Software and user documentation on a permanent basis, provided that the transferee agrees to accept the terms and conditions of this Agreement and you retain no copies. If the Software is an update or has been updated, any transfer must include the most recent update and all prior versions.

4. **Restrictions on Use of Individual Programs.** You must follow the individual requirements and restrictions detailed for each individual program in Appendix A of this Book. These limitations are also contained in the individual

license agreements recorded on the Software Media. These limitations may include a requirement that after using the program for a specified period of time, the user must pay a registration fee or discontinue use. By opening the Software packet(s), you will be agreeing to abide by the licenses and restrictions for these individual programs that are detailed in Appendix A and on the Software Media. None of the material on this Software Media or listed in this Book may ever be redistributed, in original or modified form, for commercial purposes.

5. Limited Warranty.

   (a) IDGB warrants that the Software and Software Media are free from defects in materials and workmanship under normal use for a period of sixty (60) days from the date of purchase of this Book. If IDGB receives notification within the warranty period of defects in materials or workmanship, IDGB will replace the defective Software Media.

   (b) IDGB AND THE AUTHOR OF THE BOOK DISCLAIM ALL OTHER WARRANTIES, EXPRESS OR IMPLIED, INCLUDING WITHOUT LIMITATION IMPLIED WARRANTIES OF MERCHANTABILITY AND FITNESS FOR A PARTICULAR PURPOSE, WITH RESPECT TO THE SOFTWARE, THE PROGRAMS, THE SOURCE CODE CONTAINED THEREIN, AND/OR THE TECHNIQUES DESCRIBED IN THIS BOOK. IDGB DOES NOT WARRANT THAT THE FUNCTIONS CONTAINED IN THE SOFTWARE WILL MEET YOUR REQUIREMENTS OR THAT THE OPERATION OF THE SOFTWARE WILL BE ERROR FREE.

   (c) This limited warranty gives you specific legal rights, and you may have other rights that vary from jurisdiction to jurisdiction.

6. Remedies.

   (a) IDGB's entire liability and your exclusive remedy for defects in materials and workmanship shall be limited to replacement of the Software Media, which may be returned to IDGB with a copy of your receipt at the following address: Software Media Fulfillment Department, Attn.: *KDE 2/Qt Programming Bible*, IDG Books Worldwide, Inc., 10475 Crosspoint Blvd., Indianapolis, IN 46256, or call 1-800-762-2974. Please allow three to four weeks for delivery. This Limited Warranty is void if failure of the Software Media has resulted from accident, abuse, or misapplication. Any replacement Software Media will be warranted for the remainder of the original warranty period or thirty (30) days, whichever is longer.

   (b) In no event shall IDGB or the author be liable for any damages whatsoever (including without limitation damages for loss of business profits, business interruption, loss of business information, or any other pecuniary loss) arising from the use of or inability to use the Book or the Software, even if IDGB has been advised of the possibility of such damages.

(c) Because some jurisdictions do not allow the exclusion or limitation of liability for consequential or incidental damages, the above limitation or exclusion may not apply to you.

7. **U.S. Government Restricted Rights.** Use, duplication, or disclosure of the Software for or on behalf of the United States of America, its agencies and/or instrumentalities (the "U.S. Government") is subject to restrictions as stated in paragraph (c)(1)(ii) of the Rights in Technical Data and Computer Software clause of DFARS 252.227-7013, or subparagraphs (c) (1) and (2) of the Commercial Computer Software — Restricted Rights clause at FAR 52.227-19, and in similar clauses in the NASA FAR supplement, as applicable.

8. **General.** This Agreement constitutes the entire understanding of the parties and revokes and supersedes all prior agreements, oral or written, between them and may not be modified or amended except in a writing signed by both parties hereto that specifically refers to this Agreement. This Agreement shall take precedence over any other documents that may be in conflict herewith. If any one or more provisions contained in this Agreement are held by any court or tribunal to be invalid, illegal, or otherwise unenforceable, each and every other provision shall remain in full force and effect.

GNU General Public License

Version 2, June 1991

Copyright © 1989, 1991 Free Software Foundation, Inc.
59 Temple Place, Suite 330, Boston, MA 02111-1307, USA

Preamble

The licenses for most software are designed to take away your freedom to share and change it. By contrast, the GNU General Public License is intended to guarantee your freedom to share and change free software—to make sure the software is free for all its users. This General Public License applies to most of the Free Software Foundation's software and to any other program whose authors commit to using it. (Some other Free Software Foundation software is covered by the GNU Library General Public License instead.) You can apply it to your programs, too.

When we speak of free software, we are referring to freedom, not price. Our General Public Licenses are designed to make sure that you have the freedom to distribute copies of free software (and charge for this service if you wish), that you receive source code or can get it if you want it, that you can change the software or use pieces of it in new free programs; and that you know you can do these things.

To protect your rights, we need to make restrictions that forbid anyone to deny you these rights or to ask you to surrender the rights. These restrictions translate to certain responsibilities for you if you distribute copies of the software, or if you modify it.

For example, if you distribute copies of such a program, whether gratis or for a fee, you must give the recipients all the rights that you have. You must make sure that they, too, receive or can get the source code. And you must show them these terms so they know their rights.

We protect your rights with two steps: (1) copyright the software, and (2) offer you this license which gives you legal permission to copy, distribute and/or modify the software.

Also, for each author's protection and ours, we want to make certain that everyone understands that there is no warranty for this free software. If the software is modified by someone else and passed on, we want its recipients to know that what they have is not the original, so that any problems introduced by others will not reflect on the original authors' reputations.

Finally, any free program is threatened constantly by software patents. We wish to avoid the danger that redistributors of a free program will individually obtain patent licenses, in effect making the program proprietary. To prevent this, we have made it clear that any patent must be licensed for everyone's free use or not licensed at all.

The precise terms and conditions for copying, distribution and modification follow.

TERMS AND CONDITIONS FOR COPYING, DISTRIBUTION, AND MODIFICATION

0. This License applies to any program or other work which contains a notice placed by the copyright holder saying it may be distributed under the terms of this General Public License. The "Program", below, refers to any such program or work, and a "work based on the Program" means either the Program or any derivative work under copyright law: that is to say, a work containing the Program or a portion of it, either verbatim or with modifications and/or translated into another language. (Hereinafter, translation is included without limitation in the term "modification".) Each licensee is addressed as "you".

Activities other than copying, distribution and modification are not covered by this License; they are outside its scope. The act of running the Program is not restricted, and the output from the Program is covered only if its contents constitute a work based on the Program (independent of having been made by running the Program). Whether that is true depends on what the Program does.

1. You may copy and distribute verbatim copies of the Program's source code as you receive it, in any medium, provided that you conspicuously and appropriately publish on each copy an appropriate copyright notice and disclaimer of warranty; keep intact all the notices that refer to this License and to the absence of any warranty; and give any other recipients of the Program a copy of this License along with the Program.

You may charge a fee for the physical act of transferring a copy, and you may at your option offer warranty protection in exchange for a fee.

2. You may modify your copy or copies of the Program or any portion of it, thus forming a work based on the Program, and copy and distribute such modifications or work under the terms of Section 1 above, provided that you also meet all of these conditions:

a) You must cause the modified files to carry prominent notices stating that you changed the files and the date of any change.

b) You must cause any work that you distribute or publish, that in whole or in part contains or is derived from the Program or any part thereof, to be licensed as a whole at no charge to all third parties under the terms of this License.

c) If the modified program normally reads commands interactively when run, you must cause it, when started running for such interactive use in the most ordinary way, to print or display an announcement including an appropriate copyright notice and a notice that there is no warranty (or else, saying that you provide a warranty) and that users may redistribute the program under these conditions, and telling the user how to view a copy of this License. (Exception: if the Program itself is interactive but does not normally print such an announcement, your work based on the Program is not required to print an announcement.)

These requirements apply to the modified work as a whole. If identifiable sections of that work are not derived from the Program, and can be reasonably considered independent and separate works in themselves, then this License, and its terms, do not apply to those sections when you distribute them as separate works. But when you distribute the same sections as part of a whole which is a work based on the Program, the distribution of the whole must be on the terms of this License, whose permissions for other licensees extend to the entire whole, and thus to each and every part regardless of who wrote it.

Thus, it is not the intent of this section to claim rights or contest your rights to work written entirely by you; rather, the intent is to exercise the right to control the distribution of derivative or collective works based on the Program.

In addition, mere aggregation of another work not based on the Program with the Program (or with a work based on the Program) on a volume of a storage or distribution medium does not bring the other work under the scope of this License.

3. You may copy and distribute the Program (or a work based on it, under Section 2) in object code or executable form under the terms of Sections 1 and 2 above provided that you also do one of the following:

a) Accompany it with the complete corresponding machine-readable source code, which must be distributed under the terms of Sections 1 and 2 above on a medium customarily used for software interchange; or,

b) Accompany it with a written offer, valid for at least three years, to give any third party, for a charge no more than your cost of physically performing source distribution, a complete machine-readable copy of the corresponding source code, to be distributed under the terms of Sections 1 and 2 above on a medium customarily used for software interchange; or,

c) Accompany it with the information you received as to the offer to distribute corresponding source code. (This alternative is allowed only for noncommercial distribution and only if you received the program in object code or executable form with such an offer, in accord with Subsection b above.)

The source code for a work means the preferred form of the work for making modifications to it. For an executable work, complete source code means all the source code for all modules it contains, plus any associated interface definition files, plus the scripts used to control compilation and installation of the executable. However, as a special exception, the source code distributed need not include anything that is normally distributed (in either source or binary form) with the major components (compiler, kernel, and so on) of the operating system on which the executable runs, unless that component itself accompanies the executable.

If distribution of executable or object code is made by offering access to copy from a designated place, then offering equivalent access to copy the source code from the same place counts as distribution of the source code, even though third parties are not compelled to copy the source along with the object code.

4. You may not copy, modify, sublicense, or distribute the Program except as expressly provided under this License. Any attempt otherwise to copy, modify, sublicense or distribute the Program is void, and will automatically terminate your rights under this License. However, parties who have received copies, or rights, from you under this License will not have their licenses terminated so long as such parties remain in full compliance.

5. You are not required to accept this License, since you have not signed it. However, nothing else grants you permission to modify or distribute the Program or its derivative works. These actions are prohibited by law if you do not accept this License. Therefore, by modifying or distributing the Program (or any work based on the Program), you indicate your acceptance of this License to do so, and all its terms and conditions for copying, distributing or modifying the Program or works based on it.

6. Each time you redistribute the Program (or any work based on the Program), the recipient automatically receives a license from the original licensor to copy, distribute or modify the Program subject to these terms and conditions. You may not impose any further restrictions on the recipients' exercise of the rights granted herein. You are not responsible for enforcing compliance by third parties to this License.

7. If, as a consequence of a court judgment or allegation of patent infringement or for any other reason (not limited to patent issues), conditions are imposed on you (whether by court order, agreement or otherwise) that contradict the conditions of this License, they do not excuse you from the conditions of this License. If you cannot distribute so as to satisfy simultaneously your obligations under this License and any other pertinent obligations, then as a consequence you may not distribute the Program at all. For example, if a patent license would not permit royalty-free redistribution of the Program by all those who receive copies directly or indirectly through you, then the only way you could satisfy both it and this License would be to refrain entirely from distribution of the Program.

If any portion of this section is held invalid or unenforceable under any particular circumstance, the balance of the section is intended to apply and the section as a whole is intended to apply in other circumstances.

It is not the purpose of this section to induce you to infringe any patents or other property right claims or to contest validity of any such claims; this section has the sole purpose of protecting the integrity of the free software distribution system, which is implemented by public license practices. Many people have made generous contributions to the wide range of software distributed through that system in reliance on consistent application of that system; it is up to the author/donor to decide if he or she is willing to distribute software through any other system and a licensee cannot impose that choice.

This section is intended to make thoroughly clear what is believed to be a consequence of the rest of this License.

8. If the distribution and/or use of the Program is restricted in certain countries either by patents or by copyrighted interfaces, the original copyright holder who places the Program under this License may add an explicit geographical distribution limitation excluding those countries, so that distribution is permitted only in or among countries not thus excluded. In such case, this License incorporates the limitation as if written in the body of this License.

9. The Free Software Foundation may publish revised and/or new versions of the General Public License from time to time. Such new versions will be similar in spirit to the present version, but may differ in detail to address new problems or concerns.

Each version is given a distinguishing version number. If the Program specifies a version number of this License which applies to it and "any later version", you have the option of following the terms and conditions either of that version or of any later version published by the Free Software Foundation. If the Program does not specify a version number of this License, you may choose any version ever published by the Free Software Foundation.

10. If you wish to incorporate parts of the Program into other free programs whose distribution conditions are different, write to the author to ask for permission. For software which is copyrighted by the Free Software Foundation, write to the Free Software Foundation; we sometimes make exceptions for this. Our decision will be guided by the two goals of preserving the free status of all derivatives of our free software and of promoting the sharing and reuse of software generally.

NO WARRANTY

11. BECAUSE THE PROGRAM IS LICENSED FREE OF CHARGE, THERE IS NO WARRANTY FOR THE PROGRAM, TO THE EXTENT PERMITTED BY APPLICABLE LAW. EXCEPT WHEN OTHERWISE STATED IN WRITING THE COPYRIGHT HOLDERS AND/OR OTHER PARTIES PROVIDE THE PROGRAM "AS IS" WITHOUT WARRANTY OF ANY KIND, EITHER EXPRESSED OR IMPLIED, INCLUDING,

BUT NOT LIMITED TO, THE IMPLIED WARRANTIES OF MERCHANTABILITY AND FITNESS FOR A PARTICULAR PURPOSE. THE ENTIRE RISK AS TO THE QUALITY AND PERFORMANCE OF THE PROGRAM IS WITH YOU. SHOULD THE PROGRAM PROVE DEFECTIVE, YOU ASSUME THE COST OF ALL NECESSARY SERVICING, REPAIR OR CORRECTION.

12. IN NO EVENT UNLESS REQUIRED BY APPLICABLE LAW OR AGREED TO IN WRITING WILL ANY COPYRIGHT HOLDER, OR ANY OTHER PARTY WHO MAY MODIFY AND/OR REDISTRIBUTE THE PROGRAM AS PERMITTED ABOVE, BE LIABLE TO YOU FOR DAMAGES, INCLUDING ANY GENERAL, SPECIAL, INCIDENTAL OR CONSEQUENTIAL DAMAGES ARISING OUT OF THE USE OR INABILITY TO USE THE PROGRAM (INCLUDING BUT NOT LIMITED TO LOSS OF DATA OR DATA BEING RENDERED INACCURATE OR LOSSES SUSTAINED BY YOU OR THIRD PARTIES OR A FAILURE OF THE PROGRAM TO OPERATE WITH ANY OTHER PROGRAMS), EVEN IF SUCH HOLDER OR OTHER PARTY HAS BEEN ADVISED OF THE POSSIBILITY OF SUCH DAMAGES.

*****End Of Terms And Conditions*****